D1566577

THE GROWTH OF
PHILOSOPHIC RADICALISM

THE GROWTH OF
PHILOSOPHIC RADICALISM

BY
ELIE HALÉVY
TRANSLATED BY MARY MORRIS

WITH A PREFACE BY
JOHN PLAMENATZ
CHICHELE PROFESSOR OF SOCIAL AND POLITICAL THEORY
IN THE UNIVERSITY OF OXFORD

PART I
THE YOUTH OF BENTHAM
(1776-1789)

PART II
THE EVOLUTION OF
THE UTILITARIAN DOCTRINE
FROM 1789 TO 1815

PART III
PHILOSOPHIC RADICALISM

Augustus M. Kelley Publishers
305 Allwood Road, Clifton, N.J. 07012

Reprinted 1972 *by*
Augustus M. Kelley Publishers
REPRINTS OF ECONOMIC CLASSICS
Clifton New Jersey 07012

ISBN 0–678–08005–4
LCN 72–85214

AUGUSTUS M. KELLEY · PUBLISHERS
CLIFTON 1972

NOTE

The original French edition is in three volumes and is here translated in full. In order to make it possible to produce the English edition in one volume, part of Appendix I and the whole of Appendices II, III and IV have been omitted from the translation. The notes have been considerably shortened and are here printed at the foot of each page for easy reference, instead of at the end of each volume as in the original French.

PREFACE

JOHN PLAMENATZ

Towards the end of his penultimate chapter Halévy says that ' the morality of the Utilitarians is their economic psychology put into the imperative.' His book is an account of how they came by the psychology, how they erected upon it a theory of prudential morality, and how they used their psychology and their moral theory to explain social and political institutions and to justify the reforms they proposed. The book is both historical and analytical; it traces the influence of one thinker upon another and distinguishes carefully between their doctrines. It is comprehensive, learned and discriminating. I can think of only one other history of social and political ideas that combines these qualities to the same degree: J. W. Allen's *Political Thought in the Sixteenth Century*.

The Growth of Philosophic Radicalism is not an easy book to read. It is so full of matter, so full of ideas, even though carefully and lucidly presented, that it calls for a considerable and sustained effort from the reader. It is easy to get lost in the details of the book, not because they do not form part of a carefully arranged whole, but because they demand close attention. Passing from one topic to another, the reader is apt to lose sight of the general argument. It is a book to be read twice, for it is on a second reading that the parts are seen to fall into their places in the whole.

Halévy's theme is not Utilitarianism in all its forms but what he calls philosophic radicalism: that is to say, Utilitarian principles used to assess critically the established order and to advocate large schemes of reform. He is concerned primarily with Bentham and James Mill, and secondarily with the classical economists. The economists were, most of them, a good deal less radical than Bentham and the elder Mill, but they were ' philosophical ' and ' practical ' in much the same way. They too rested their theories on broad assumptions

vii

about human needs and motives, and they too were keen to influence policy. Their explanations of economic behaviour were similar to Bentham's and Mill's explanations of human behaviour in general, and both Bentham and Mill wrote about economics. That Utilitarianism, as a moral and political theory, has much in common with classical economics is obvious, and was noticed long before Halévy wrote his book; but he has explained the connection in greater detail and more carefully than anyone else. Utilitarianism is indeed an ' economic theory of morals '; or at least this label serves as well as any to mark it off from other moral theories. And it is most conspicuously ' economic ' in the form given to it by Bentham and James Mill, by the radical as distinct from the conservative Utilitarians.

Hume, the most conservative of the major Utilitarian thinkers, had explained how such an idea as justice arises among men and serves to control their behaviour. His explanation was psychological and sociological, and also utilitarian; he tried to show how, given their situation and their needs, men acquire this idea, and how it is the interest of each of them that it should be generally accepted. Morality is the keeping of rules to which men attach a special importance because experience teaches them that the rules are in the interest of them all. What makes the rules moral, according to Hume, is that people respond to the breach or the observance of them in certain ways; they disapprove, and so discourage, breaches, and they approve, and so encourage, observances. Thus, though the morality of a rule does not consist in its utility, in the ways that people feel about it and use it, nevertheless, they come to feel in these ways because the rule is useful.

This account of morality, though it treats moral rules as if they were at bottom solutions to practical problems, though it has something in common with classical economics, is not yet ' an economic psychology put into the imperative '. To be sure, it represents moral rules as being, as it were, the best terms that the individual can get from his fellows. Given his enduring needs and his situation, the rules formulate what he can reasonably require of others and concede to them. These terms or rules are not imposed on him by God, nor does he discover them by intuition; they are related to his needs and situation, to what is enduring about them and common to him and others. He cannot satisfy his needs except in collaboration and competition with others, and the basic rules of this collaboration and competition acquire the status of moral rules.

These rules, as Hume sees them, man-made though they are and serving purely human needs and purposes, are an enduring store of wisdom to be taken on trust. They are lessons of experience learnt once and for all. Everyone must, of course, be trained to observe them, but most people come to accept them without enquiring how they arise and what makes them useful, though they have, no doubt, some sense of their utility. A social and political order is maintained, not because most people understand how its rules and conventions are generally useful, but because they in fact are so. The mere subject is not, and ought not to be, critical of the established order; in his own and the general interest he should take it on trust. And even the ruler does well to respect tradition; the chances are that he will best promote the general interest by doing so. Society provides ready-made solutions for recurrent problems, or ready-made procedures and principles for the solution of problems, and the ruler, as well as the subject, does well to rely heavily on what society provides without enquiring too much whether he can improve on it.

But the philosophic radicals refused to take established rules and institutions on trust. While they accepted Hume's account of the origins and functions of social rules, they took notice of the fact that rules can outlast their usefulness and can in the course of time operate in ways that give to some groups advantages not to be justified on the ground that they are ultimately in the general interest. These privileged groups are keen to preserve their privileges, and can rely on the inertia, the respect for tradition, of the unprivileged. The radicals looked for a criterion they could use to assess the utility of established institutions and practices, and Bentham took over from Beccaria a formula that came originally from Francis Hutcheson's *Inquiry concerning Moral Good and Evil*, the greatest happiness principle. He not only took over this formula but put forward rules for measuring, as he thought in terms of happiness, the consequences of actions and policies. He aimed, as Hume had not done, at being scientific, at formulating precise standards that everyone who understood them would accept for deciding what should be done. These are the standards that Halévy refers to when he speaks of an ' economic psychology put into the imperative '.

Critics of Bentham sometimes accuse him of attempting what Hume said cannot be done, of deriving moral rules from statements of fact. But this is not what Halévy has in mind when he speaks of an economic psychology put into the imperative. Bentham does sometimes speak as if it followed from men's having certain characteristics that they ought to behave in certain ways, and so uses arguments that Hume would have condemned as improper; but at other times he speaks rather as if men, because they have these characteristics, can be relied upon to accept certain rules when they see clearly the consequences of doing so. Man is, he thinks, so made that he seeks to *maximise* his own happiness, and can therefore be relied upon to accept rules and practices which are in the long-term interest of all *maximisers* of happiness, if it is proved to him that they are so. Society is well ordered when its rules and practices are such as to enable its members to maximise their happiness most efficiently; just as, in the eyes of the classical economists, the economy is well ordered when it is such that everyone has incentives to put the resources at his disposal to the most productive use.

The radical Utilitarians were both egalitarians and liberals, though Halévy looks upon them as much more the first than the second. Certainly, their basic formula, *the greatest happiness of the greatest number*, is at a first glance more obviously egalitarian than liberal; it requires the spreading of happiness as widely as it can be spread and says nothing of liberty. But there is another principle, almost as much to the fore in the arguments of Bentham and James Mill as the greatest happiness principle, asserting that every man is to be reckoned the best judge of his own interest. This is not to say that he is always a good judge of it, but rather that nobody has as powerful motives as he has for becoming a good judge of it. In the long run it is more in the general interest to educate everyone to be as good a judge as he can be of his own interest than to relegate the business of promoting the general interest to an irresponsible and uncriticised minority. This business is, of course, always the business of a minority, but they are likely to do it best when they are open to criticism for what they do by citizens (and organised groups of citizens) with a lively and articulate sense of their own interests. Bentham advocated freedom of discussion and association even before he became a convert to democracy. There was never a time when he did not set great store by independence of mind and a critical attitude to authority.

It may be that Halévy, when he said that the radical Utilitarians cared less for freedom than for equality, meant that they cared for freedom, not for its own sake, but as a means to the more efficient pursuit of happiness. If it could be shown that happiness could be more effectively promoted by restricting freedom than by enlarging it, they would be bound by their own principles to favour restricting it. Freedom is not, for them, a part of the supreme end of policy in the way that equality is; it is not implicit in what Halévy calls ' the sacred formula '.

Yet Bentham, who seems to Halévy more egalitarian than liberal, has also been criticised for putting forward a principle which obliges him to prefer happiness to equality, when the two conflict. Where the choice is between a larger sum of happiness unequally divided and a smaller sum divided more equally, the Utilitarian, if he is consistent, must choose the larger sum. Equality is, for him, just as much as a means as liberty is, and he can favour it only to the extent that it promotes the supreme end of action and policy, which is to maximise happiness.

Certainly, the greatest happiness principle can be so interpreted as to make both equality and liberty means to something more desirable than they are. But this interpretation, though it is in keeping with that principle as Bentham quite often formulates it, goes against the spirit of his philosophy. He was, I venture to suggest, as much a liberal as an egalitarian; though the case for equality as well as for freedom has been better put than he put it. Just as he assumed that every man is to be reckoned the best judge of his own interest, so too he assumed that any man's capacity for happiness is to be reckoned as great as any other's. This is not to say that in fact no man's capacity for happiness is greater than another's, or that everyone is in fact the best judge of his own interest; it is to say only that social rules, since they apply either to everyone or to broad categories of persons, ought in practice to rest on these assumptions, for they apply either to everyone in the community or to broad categories of persons.

It is difficult to see, given Bentham's account of human nature, why anyone should wish to promote the greatest happiness. However little anyone cares for justice for its own sake, however much he is out to maximise his own happiness, it is justice and not ' the greatest happiness of the greatest number ' that is his enduring interest. He wants in his dealings with others the best terms he can get for himself, and since everyone else wants this also, the terms most generally acceptable are those that are in everyone's interest. This is what really follows from the psychology of Bentham and James Mill and from Hume's account of the origins of justice, which they accepted without seeing its implications clearly: this and not the greatest happiness principle. Even if happiness could be measured as Bentham (though with some reservations) thought it could, the greatest happiness principle would be irrelevant. Given that everyone is, or aspires to be, a rational ' maximiser ' of his own happiness, what really matters to him is that he should be not less well placed than others are to pursue his happiness, and not that the sum of happiness in general should be as great as possible. So, in a way, Halévy is right; the theory of morals of the Utilitarians, their ' economic psychology put into the imperative ', has a strong egalitarian bias. But it has it, I suggest, in spite of the greatest happiness principle rather than on account of it.

So, too, and for a not dissimilar reason, their moral theory has a strong liberal bias. It explains justice and other moral principles as serving the interests of beings who are enterprising and rational pursuers of happiness. The better they are aware of their interests and the keener and more intelligent their pursuit of happiness, the more they care about justice and other principles, and the more concerned they are that established institutions and practices should conform to them. The good citizen, as Bentham conceives of him, is alert and critical as well as prudent; he does not, to be sure, resist authority except in extreme cases when ' the probable mischiefs of obedience ' are greater than ' the probable mischiefs of resistance ', but his motto, so we are told, is ' to censure freely ' as much as ' to obey punctually '.

Freedom has had champions more perceptive and discriminating than Bentham and James Mill. One such champion was John Stuart Mill, who was also a philosophical radical; but the best of his writings on freedom come after the period covered by Halévy's book. His idea of freedom, though it coincides to some extent with his father's and Bentham's, takes him into regions, psychological and social, unknown to (or at least neglected by) them. Freedom, as he conceives of it, has little to do with the rational pursuit of happiness. If we compare his liberalism with theirs, we see how much more sophisticated it is; and yet they too, in their simpler and cruder ways, were genuine liberals.

The philosophic radicals, though they looked radical enough to the Whigs and Tories of their time, to us seem moderate. We think of them as doctrinaires rather than as extremists; they disliked violence, and the reforms they proposed were modest, if we compare them with what is happening in many parts of the world today. No doubt, if we take all the reforms they advocated and helped to bring about over a period of years, we can see that they contributed greatly to change the England of their day. Yet they always, in pressing for any particular reform, took account of the circumstances, including the attitudes, arguments, and interests of those who opposed the reform. This moderation, this concern to give due weight to all relevant claims and expectations, was a part of their philosophy. They put a high value on what they called security, and they took pride in their prudence. Everyone, as they saw it, wants security, wants a stable social order; for unless he has it, he cannot predict the future and therefore cannot pursue happiness rationally, cannot be a good judge of his own interest. This is so, even if he wants to change the social order radically, for what he wants is a new stable order in place of the old one. The more he insists on changing the established order without taking account of the needs and expectations of those who must suffer by the change, the less stable the new social order is likely to be. The radicalism of the philosophic radicals was, as Halévy makes clear, nearly always a prudent radicalism.

Their opponents were often less offended by the changes they wanted to make than by the reasons they gave for making them. It was above all intellectually that they were radicals; their most disturbing and ' outrageous ' attacks were levelled, not so much at established institutions, as at the arguments used to support them. In this respect, the philosophic radicals were not unworthy disciples of Hume, the great destroyer in the realm of ideas who was socially and politically a conservative. They, of course, were not conservatives; they were reformers, and their philosophy served to justify their reforms. It was, as they saw it, pre-eminently a practical philosophy, one to be used to guide action, and especially policy. Nevertheless, they too, like Hume, were much more subverters of established beliefs than of established practices; though their subversion was less discreet.

No radicals have been less demagogues than Bentham and his disciples. Despite the egalitarian bias of their philosophy, they never tried to win the support of the masses and despised such popular leaders as William Cobbett and ' Orator ' Hunt. They were intellectuals who addressed their arguments to other intellectuals or to the small circles, official and social, of the well-informed, who make policy or are in touch with those who make it. They were not, at least not consciously, élitists, but they did take it for granted that social and political questions are discussed intelligently and realistically only by a minority. They continued to take this for granted even after they took up the cause of parliamentary reform. Even the more radical of them, who wanted the vote given (eventually) not just to all men but to women also, and who advocated universal and compulsory education, assumed that the leaders in society would be recruited chiefly from the propertied and most highly educated classes. Bentham and James Mill both expected that an extension of the franchise to much more than the middle class would serve only to strengthen that class politically, for the middle class, so it seemed to them, were the natural leaders of the classes below them, having many interests in common with them and being better placed to promote those interests rationally and effectively. Democracy is to be desired, not so much because it converts all classes into good citizens, able to take an active and intelligent part in discussing or making policy, but because it provides the few whose social opportunities (and abilities) make leaders of them with strong incentives for taking account of the interests of all classes. The political ideal of Bentham and James Mill was an ' aristocracy ' of the able and the enterprising, kept mentally alert by freedom of discussion and public-spirited by responsibility to the people generally.

Halévy, an historian of ideas rather than a philosopher, was concerned above all to distinguish carefully between the arguments of the Utilitarians, to show how they were related to the controversies of their age, and to see what practical conclusions were drawn from them. He was not concerned to assess Utilitarianism as a type of ethical theory, to consider its strong and its weak points as an explanation of moral discourse and its social functions. But since his book appeared, there has been, especially in the English-speaking countries (the countries in which theories of a Utilitarian type have flourished most), a good deal of speculation about ethics generally and Utilitarianism in particular. There has also been speculation about the social studies and the methods they use. In the light of discussions that have gone on in recent years, it is perhaps easier than it was in Halévy's time to assess the originality and the limitations of the Utilitarians as moral and social theorists.

Three claims, I think, can be made for them: they were among the first to put forward elaborate and coherent explanations of the social origins and functions of morality, they took an interest in the language of morals and tried to explain what is peculiar to it, and they made use of methods which since their time have come to be more and more widely used to explain how men behave or to provide them with guides to action. They constructed, on the basis of a small number of fairly simple assumptions about men's wants and preferences and the conditions in which they have to satisfy them, elaborate explanations of what men do or what they would be well advised to do. They applied, outside the sphere of economics, a type of explanation much used by economists in their day and since; though it was not from the economists but from Hobbes that they took the method.

It was Hume, rather than Bentham and James Mill, who put forward fresh and ingenious ideas about the social functions and the language of morals, but they did take up some of his suggestions and tried to be more precise and systematic than he had been. They were not as lucid and rigorous as they wished to be, and were sometimes in their attempts to go beyond Hume more confused than he was. They both spoke at times of moral terms as if their function were rather to control behaviour than to describe it, and yet they also offered definitions of them that make them merely descriptive. For example, in the *Fragment on Mackintosh*, his longest essay on morals, James Mill explains that moral terms are marks of approval and disapproval serving to encourage some kinds of behaviour and to deter from others, and yet also says that the morality of an action consists in its conduciveness to pleasure. He vacillates between two different accounts of what men do when they pass moral judgements without seeing that they are different. As much, I think, can be said of Bentham; and yet he, even more than the elder Mill, was a pioneer in speculating about the persuasive uses of language, and more especially of moral and political terms. Thus, though Bentham and Mill failed to learn one of the most important of the lessons given to the social theorist by their master Hume, that to explain the social functions of morality is not to explain what men do when they pass moral judgements, they took a keen and a philosophical interest in the use of words. They saw that if they were to achieve their two ambitions (to explain clearly and correctly how men behave and to help them to act rationally to achieve the happiness they desire) they must construct a moral and a political vocabulary better suited to these purposes than the one in current use. Bentham in particular sought to improve the language of morals and politics, to make it more useful.

Social ' scientists ' today no longer speak, as Bentham and his disciples did, of ' maximising happiness ', but they still speak of ' maximising '. That is to say, they still, in trying to explain certain kinds or certain spheres of human action, assume that men are out to get as much as they can of something measurable; and they still, when they recommend one policy rather than another, often do so on the ground that it produces more of something generally desired or generally agreed to be desirable. Their methods and arguments are similar in type to those of Bentham, though what they seek to measure is not happiness as he conceived of it. They have more sophisticated ideas than he had about measurement, and are much readier than he was to admit that there are limits to what can be measured. There are not many social theorists today who believe, as the early Utilitarians seem to have done (though they too occasionally had doubts), that one moral code or form of government or even economy is to be preferred to another on the ground that it satisfies human wants more fully. But when, taking for granted a wider social and political context, they consider some narrower sphere of activity or advocate one policy in preference to others, they often put forward as an explanation of it or argument for it that it does or would satisfy people's wants more fully or at a smaller cost. Social theorists are by no means agreed about the limits within which explanations and arguments of a utilitarian type can properly be used, and have not even (to my knowledge) gone into the question at all thoroughly. Nobody seems to have made up his mind just where the limits are to be drawn, though many agree that they must be drawn much more narrowly than Bentham drew them. Nevertheless, explanations and arguments of a type that Bentham was the first to use with considerable rigour and in a variety of spheres are still widely used today.

Halévy says nothing in his book about the limits of Utilitarianism; he does not enquire what can properly be explained or justified by such methods as Bentham and his disciples used, whether in the form they used them or modified and improved. His business with them is historian's and not philosopher's business; he wants to explain what they tried to do and not what can properly be done by their methods. Yet his survey of their arguments, because it is lucid, comprehensive and fair, does bring home two points to the reader with a taste for philosophy: that those among the principles put forward by Bentham and his disciples that really can be used to guide action are much more useful to makers of public policy than to the private individual, and that the force of their arguments does not depend on the greatest happiness principle. The first of these points was clear to Halévy himself but the second, I suspect, was not. At least, it is not a conclusion that he draws or even hints at in his book, though anyone reading it could find in it evidence in plenty to support the conclusion.

Bentham, of course, believed that his principles could be applied to all spheres of human action. And yet he was himself much more concerned to apply them to legal and political procedures and to matters of public policy than to other spheres. The maker of policy, especially when he takes the social system as a whole for granted or wants to change only a small part of it, deals with categories of persons whose common interests (given the stability of the system) can quite often be defined more or less precisely. These persons, or some of them, are perhaps organised to define and to push their common interests, or there is wide agreement as to what these interests are. The maker of policy can then try, given the resources at his disposal, to make them go as far as he can in promoting the interests of the people for whom he is responsible; he can consider alternative policies and choose one in preference to the others on the ground that it is likely to contribute more to advancing the known interests of these people. He can as he comes to his decision act very much in the spirit of Bentham's philosophy. The more sophisticated the community in which he acts, the more groups there are inside it organised to make precise demands on makers of policy, and the more information at his disposal, the more he can act in this spirit.

No doubt, the maker of public policy (or the maker of policy in private organisations, whose situation is in many respects like that of the public official) does not aim at ' maximising ' happiness; he aims at something else which he may or may not believe increases the happiness of the people for whom he is responsible. Whether or not he believes it, the calculations he makes and the considerations he takes into account are much the same. So, too, with Bentham and his disciples. They proposed a variety of reforms, and took great trouble to make it clear what they wanted to achieve and how (in their opinion) it could be achieved. Bentham in particular displayed rare ingenuity in defining the ends of policy and the best means to them. But these ends were not happiness but other things which he believed (without troubling to prove it) make for happiness. For example, he wanted to prevent as much crime as possible at the least cost in terms of punishment, and was resourceful and ingenious in suggesting how this could be done. He excelled at defining principles that could be used as guides in making policy; but these principles of his (though he thought otherwise) have nothing to do with promoting the greatest happiness of the greatest number, conceived as a sum of pleasures.

The philosphic radicals were at once abstract theorists and practical reformers, and Halévy brings out admirably the relations between their theories and the reforms they advocated. He does it as it must be done to be done well, comprehensively and in detail. It has long been fashionable to point to the defects of the early Utilitarians and their intellectual cousins, the classical economists, to their excessive confidence and to their narrow vision; but what school of thinkers have brought greater intelligence to bear on the problems of their country?

1971

CONTENTS

INTRODUCTION

WHAT ideas are aroused in the mind of a student or teacher of philosophy, by the name of the Utilitarian doctrine? He would recall the rules of Bentham's moral arithmetic and the title of an essay by Stuart Mill. He is aware that there is a fairly close connection between the morals of utility and the psychology of the association of ideas, and that, generally speaking, the Utilitarians were associationists. But is he aware that the moral arithmetic aims much less at founding a moral theory than at founding a science of law, at providing a mathematical basis for the theory of legal punishment? Is he aware, other than vaguely, that orthodox political economy, the tradition of Adam Smith, Malthus and Ricardo, formed a part of the doctrine? Is he aware, further, that at the time when Utilitarianism was an organised philosophy and not merely a current opinion, to be a Utilitarian it was necessary to be a Radical (hence the name Philosophical Radicals), and that the supporters of the Utilitarian morality were at the same time the theorists of representative democracy and universal suffrage? But can anyone who is not aware of this really claim to be acquainted with the Utilitarian doctrine or even with the principle of Utility itself? For a proposition is set up as a principle precisely because of its logical fecundity, that is, by the number of consequences which follow from it. Properly to understand the principle of Utility, it is necessary to understand all its consequences, and all its juristic, economic and political applications. Our aim is to make the knowledge of the Utilitarian morality more exact by making it more complete. Our study is of Utilitarianism as a whole.

Now what method should be chosen in order to study the doctrine at once in its unity and in all its complexity? Would it be possible, in order to simplify the statement of it, to suppose Philosophical Radicalism already fully established and to analyse the sum of the opinions, both philosophical and social, theoretical and practical, which might be held by such a man as Stuart Mill about the year

1832 ? This method has serious disadvantages. According to whether the statement of the doctrine showed up its unity or its contradictions, we should be suspected in the first case of having made use of arbitrary and artificial processes in reconstituting it, or, in the second case, of having purposely emphasised the contradictions in order to simplify the task of criticism. It is undoubtedly better to let the facts speak for themselves, to show after what varied fortunes so many different theories came one after the other to form an integral part of Utilitarianism, to study the actual development of the fundamental concepts, to tell the story of the growth of Philosophical Radicalism. In this way the subject of our study assumes a new amplitude, by reason of the importance of the Utilitarian doctrine in the history of the public mind in England. For England, like France, had its century of liberalism : and to the century of the French Revolution corresponded, on the other side of the Channel, the century of the Industrial Revolution : to the juristic and spiritualistic philosophy of the Rights of Man corresponded the Utilitarian philosophy of the identity of interests. The interests of all individuals are identical. Every individual is the best judge of his own interests. Therefore it is necessary to break down all artificial barriers which traditional institutions set up between individuals, and all the social restraints based on the supposed necessity of protecting individuals against each other and against themselves. It is a philosophy of emancipation, very different in its inspiration and principles, but akin in many of its applications, to the sentimental philosophy of J.-J. Rousseau. The philosophy of the Rights of Man eventually led, on the Continent, to the Revolution of 1848 ; in England at the same time the philosophy of the identity of interests resulted in the triumph of the free-trade doctrine of the Manchester School. From this point of view we are studying the historical and logical origins of Philosophical Radicalism, in somewhat the same way as we might study the formation of the principles of 1789 ; and consequently our study is a chapter in the philosophy of history as well as a chapter in the history of philosophy.

But are we perhaps extending too widely the limits of our subject ? We do not think so. We believe that there is a historical circumstance which gives our study as defined a character as is possible. In Jeremy Bentham, Philosophical Radicalism had its great man ; and the period of his philosophical and literary career may be held to be, in the history of Philosophical Radicalism, the period of the formation of the doctrine.—1776 was the year of the American Revolution, which prepared the way for the European revolutions ; it was the year in which Adam Smith published his *Wealth of Nations* ; in which Major Cartwright drew up for the first time in England the future Radical and Chartist programme of annual parliaments and universal suffrage ; but it was also the year in which Bentham, who was then twenty-eight years old, published his first work, the *Fragment on Government.*—

1832 was the year of the reform which, for the first time in England, granted the benefit of the vote to the industrial districts, and, to a certain extent, to the working classes, and gave to Radical opinion the chance of expressing itself and of exerting an influence on the legislation of the nation ; but it was also the year in which Jeremy Bentham died, at the age of eighty-four, venerated by a group of disciples as a patriarch, a spiritual leader, almost a god, with James Mill as his Saint Paul. Moreover, it was to the theoretic and practical reform of law that Bentham gave his attention from the beginning ; it was here that he was really an inventor. If the reformers of the economic and political régime, and of philosophy itself, ended by looking upon Bentham as the founder of a school, it was not because Bentham had been on all these points the principal or the only author of the new doctrines—he invented neither the law of Malthus nor the psychology of Hartley ; and while he established the Utilitarian theory of political Radicalism he did not invent its programme. Many men and many circumstances contributed to the formation of Philosophical Radicalism. Who were these men ? What were these circumstances ? How did it come about that, about the year 1832, a large number of individuals—among the most intelligent and the most energetic of their generation—were led to profess common opinions and a collective doctrine ? And what was the precise part played by Bentham in the formation of the Benthamite School ? Is this way the historical problem which we are attempting to solve assumes a definite form.

PART I
(1776-1789)

THE YOUTH OF BENTHAM

FOREWORD

ON the one hand the development of the physical sciences, the discovery of Newton's principle which made it possible to found on a single law a complete science of nature, and the conception of the hope of discovering an analogous principle capable of serving for the establishment of a synthetic science of the phenomena of moral and social life ; on the other hand a profound crisis in society, a crisis which was itself due in part to the development of science and to the progress of its practical applications, a crisis which called for transformations of the judicial, economic, and political régimes and gave rise to schemes for reform and to reformers without number, a crisis, finally, which demanded a single principle capable of uniting into a single theoretic whole so many scattered notions :—these are the general causes of the formation of Philosophical Radicalism. They had been at work since the eighteenth century ; but the Utilitarian doctrine had not as yet assumed its definitive shape. Bentham, who was already the author of a complete code, a *View of a Complete Body of Legislation*, did not become famous as a reformer of the science of law till the early years of the following century. Twenty-five years of crisis come between the two extreme periods of his life : the one previous to 1789 when, still unknown, he was a philosopher of the eighteenth century, in the style of Voltaire, Hume, Helvetius and Beccaria ; the other subsequent to 1815, when he was the theorist of a party of democratic agitation organised according to the methods peculiar to the nineteenth century.

It is therefore necessary in order to describe the formation of Philosophical Radicalism first to explain the original state through which the Utilitarian doctrine passed in the eighteenth century. How did it come about that Bentham was destined by his own genius, and by circumstances more or less special, eventually to be the head of the school ? The circumstances which explain this fact are complex and various ; and the progress of the doctrine did not come about in all points with the same speed or according to the same law.

3

By the beginning of 1789 the Utilitarian doctrine, as regards judicial matters, may be held to have been established in every particular ; but the English were proud of the comparative excellence of their judicial institutions, and felt no need of reforming them : thus Bentham, the disciple of the Frenchman Helvetius and the Italian Beccaria, the admirer of Frederick and Catherine, wrote in French a book which appeared on the Continent and was arranged and edited by a Swiss. The doctrine was ahead of the age. About the same time the Utilitarian political economy, with the exception of the additions that Malthus and Ricardo later made to the doctrine of Adam Smith, may equally be held to have been fully formed, with its theory of value and its thesis of commercial and industrial Liberalism. Bentham adopted the already popular ideas of Adam Smith. The *Inquiry into the Nature and Causes of the Wealth of Nations* was contemporaneous with the American Revolution and the collapse of the mercantile system : it is a faithful expression of the spirit of the age. In politics, finally, the Utilitarians were sceptics and authoritarians, indifferent to the means which governments might employ to destroy prejudices and bring about reforms. Yet this was the time when the future Radical programme was being worked out in the midst of revolutions and disturbances. In politics, the Utilitarian doctrine was behind the age.

CHAPTER I

ORIGINS AND PRINCIPLES

J EREMY BENTHAM was born in 1748, and the smallest events of his childhood show that the period was one of transition and of stress. His father had been a Jacobite, but had ultimately rallied to the Hanoverian dynasty.[1] The women of his family were pious and superstitious, and he grew up in an atmosphere of ghost stories, and was tormented by diabolical visions.[2] His father, however, had provided him with a French tutor who made him read *Candide* at the age of ten.[3] The loose morality of the time and the weakening of religious faith, at any rate among the enlightened classes, were universally admitted and deplored.[4] But this break-up of existing moral standards was really only hiding the birth of a new world. A new era was beginning for western society. In France, the ' century of Louis XIV ' was coming to an end, the period which had opened with Descartes' ' Discourse on Method ' and closed with the book by Voltaire which has named and immortalised it, the classical century, the century of law and order ; while the century of the Revolution was signalled by the *Esprit des Lois* and by the first writings of Rousseau, the Romantic century, the century of an emancipation at once religious, intellectual and moral. In England Hume was publishing his *Inquiry into the Human Understanding*, and Hartley his *Observations on Man*. This was the beginning of the Utilitarian century, the century of the Industrial Revolution, of the economists and of the great inventors. The crisis had been brewing for fifty years : two names contemporaneous with the Revolution of 1688 symbolise the new era :—' Locke and Newton ',

[1] Bentham, *Works*, Bowring's edition, vol. x. p. 2.
[2] Bowring, vol. x. pp. 13, 19, 21.
[3] Bowring, vol. x. p. 11.
[4] On the critical nature of this period of history see especially Hartley's *Observations on Man*, Conclusion.

5

names which have become proverbially associated both in England and on the Continent.

It is the universality of law which alone makes it intelligible. To say of any relation that it is necessary is to say not that it is intelligible but that it is constant. For me to be able to exert an influence on external nature it is not necessary for me to understand the relations of phenomena to each other as intelligible relations ; but merely that these relations should be constant and that by producing a first phenomenon I can be sure to cause the appearance of a second phenomenon, which I desire to produce. No man needs knowledge in excess of his power. This is the Newtonian conception of the laws of nature : it agrees with the new scientific conception, which is defined as being no longer contemplative and theoretical, but active and practical, as aiming at securing our domination over external nature through the knowledge of natural laws.

Further, it is possible to conduct one's study of man as an individual and as a social being in the same way that the physicist studies other matters, and here again to apply the Newtonian method with a view to determining the smallest possible number of general simple laws which, once discovered, will enable all the detail of phenomena to be explained by a synthetic and deductive method. It follows that it is possible to construct a practical science on the basis of this knowledge, and to extend our power to the same extent as we extend our faculty of foresight. The name of Locke is popularly taken to stand for that preoccupation with social affairs which had already been in Hobbes' mind when he attempted to determine, by means of observation, the necessary end of our actions and the order of sequence of our thoughts so as to be able to base on them a rational political theory.[1] Given a science of the mind and a science of society which exhibit the qualities both of the experimental and of the exact sciences analogous to the physics of Newton, should it not be possible to found on these new disciplines a moral and legal theory which would be scientific—the achievement of the universal practical science ? Such is the problem which exercised thinking people in England throughout Bentham's century. What is known as Utilitarianism, or Philosophical Radicalism, can be defined as nothing but an attempt to apply the principles of Newton to the affairs of politics and of morals.

In this moral Newtonianism the principle of the association of ideas and the principle of utility take the place of the principle of universal attraction. Now although Locke is universally recognised as the forerunner of the new spirit, there is in his writings no trace

---

[1] Hobbes, before Newton, had already used the metaphor of gravity to define moral determinism.

either of a methodical development of a Utilitarian morality [1] or of a universal application of the principle of association ; [2] in 1730, however, there appeared at the head of a new edition of a philosophical work, *A Dissertation concerning the Principle and Criterion of Virtue and the Origin of the Passions*,[3] whose author, Gay, who, moreover, claimed to be a disciple of Locke, can be considered as the true founder of the new philosophy, the Utilitarian morality and the psychology of association. It is true that there is still a theological element in Gay's philosophy, for he appeals in his moral theory to the idea of everlasting rewards and penalties, but if we set aside this element which is foreign to the spirit of the doctrine, and which in a sense cancels itself out, Gay's philosophy can be summed up as follows. All men seek pleasure and avoid pain ; to seek pleasure is at once the necessary and the normal law of all human action, and those actions are obligatory which lead to happiness. Now although it may easily be admitted that all men agree on the end to be sought, it is clear that they cease to agree with regard to the means to be adopted in order to attain this necessary end. This is because everyone does not connect happiness with the same ideas, or, in other words, because the associations of ideas vary from individual to individual ; and these individual variations are themselves submitted to a law which the moralist must know if he wishes to lead men to happiness. Nothing seems at first sight clearer and easier to understand than this attempt to found a Utilitarian morality on the psychology of association. It will only be necessary, however, to follow up the development of the two new principles from their appearance in Gay's treatise till the time when Bentham founds on them his whole social doctrine, and their true obscurity and complexity will then become quite evident.

Consider first the principle of association. The recognised founder of the doctrine of association was David Hartley, whose *Observations on Man, his Frame, his Duty, and his Expectations* [4] appeared in 1749. In certain ways, perhaps, he did not definitely prepare the way for the Utilitarian doctrine in so far as it was destined to make possible the formation of autonomous moral sciences. He did, in fact, make morals and politics dependent on the religious idea ; and it must be borne in mind that his aim was to show in the mechanism of the laws of nature the justification of Christian

---

[1] See, however, *Essay concerning Human Understanding*, bk. i, ch. 3, § 6.

[2] It was only in 1695 that Locke announced to Molyneux in a private letter certain additions ' relative to the connection of ideas which had not yet been considered. . . .'

[3] *An Essay on the Origin of Evil*, by Dr. William King. The name of Gay does not appear in the title.

[4] Hartley is also the author of a pamphlet entitled *Conjecturae quaedam de sensu, motu et idearum generatione* (1746).

optimism. In any case he wished to found a ' psychology ' (a word
which does not, I believe, occur in the writings of any of his English
predecessors), a theory of human and animal intelligence, a branch of
' natural philosophy ', a science which, when once the ' general
laws ' which govern ' phenomena ' have been discovered by means
of ' analysis ', will be of a deductive or ' synthetic ' character.¹ In
this way Hartley openly introduced Newton's method and terminology into psychology.² He reduced the explanation of the facts to
the simplest possible terms, and brought all associations under the
single heading of association through contiguity. He combined his
psychological theory with a physiological theory,³ whose central
idea was likewise borrowed from Newton, and in which ' vibrations
in miniature ' or ' vibratiuncules ' took the place of the Cartesian
' traces '. Are we not entitled to hold that these physiological and
medical preoccupations may have helped to produce in Hartley his
belief in determinism and his disposition to account scientifically
for the mechanism of mental phenomena ? In the year 1774
Priestley, the disciple of Locke, Gay and Hume, read Dr. Reid's
Inquiry into the Human Mind, and was distressed to see that the
attempt of his masters to found a positive science of the phenomena
of the human mind was in danger of coming to nothing ; he wrote
a whole book to refute Reid, Oswald and Beattie ; ⁴ and further
announced his intention of obtaining permission from Hartley's son
to re-edit the *Observations on Man*. Hartley himself had admitted
that the psychological and physiological parts of his book were not
indissolubly connected. In 1775 Priestley published *Hartley's
Theory of the Human Mind, on the Principle of the Association of
Ideas*, an abridged edition of the *Observations* in which he omits
everything to do with the doctrine of vibrations, in order, he tells us,
to simplify the doctrine and make the ' doctrine of association . . .
the only *postulatum*, or thing *taken for granted*, in this work '.⁵
This publication rapidly attained popularity, and definitely established Hartley's reputation. Bentham refers to it in a note in his
Introduction to the Principles of Morals and Legislation, in which
he is explaining the influence of habit through the operation of the
principle of the association of ideas ; and in a later passage he admits
that it was from Hartley that he learnt to treat happiness as a sum of
simple pleasures, united by association.⁶ The success of the book
proves that the English public endorsed the verdict of Priestley.

¹ *Observations on Man*, part 1, ch. 3, prop. lxxxviii.
² *On Man*, part 1, ch. 1.   ³ *Ibid.*
⁴ *An Examination of Dr. Reid's Inquiry into the Human Mind on the Principles
of Common Sense, Dr. Beattie's Essay on the Nature and Immutability of Truth,
and Doctor Oswald's Appeal to Common Sense in behalf of Religion*, by Joseph
Priestley.
⁵ *Hartley's Theory of the Human Mind*, Preface.
⁶ Bowring, vol. i. p. 57. Bowring, vol. v. p. 286.

ORIGINS AND PRINCIPLES

9

'Something was done in this field of knowledge by Descartes, very much by Mr. Locke, but most of all by Dr. Hartley, who has thrown more useful light upon the theory of the mind than Newton did upon the theory of the natural world '.[1]

Now Hume in his *Treatise of Human Nature*, which had appeared in 1738, and later in his *Inquiry into the Human Understanding*, had preceded Hartley in the attempt to interpret all the phenomena of mental life on the basis of the principle of the association of ideas ; and Hume was a far deeper thinker than Hartley. In spite of this, or perhaps even because of it, there is in his philosophy a fundamental ambiguity which will always cause adherents of the doctrine of association to hesitate to accept him as their master.

Hume, it is true, presented his *Treatise* as ' an attempt to introduce the Experimental Method of Reasoning into Moral Subjects '. He hoped to do for moral philosophy what Newton had done for natural philosophy, and he thought he had discovered in the principle of association ' a kind of attraction, which in the mental world will be found to have as extraordinary effects as in the natural, and to show itself in as many and as various forms '.[2] Psychological phenomena mutually attract one another ; they are, Hume explicitly declares, in a causal relation to each other : ' The constant conjunction of our resembling perceptions, is a convincing proof, that the one are the causes of the other '.[3] For the construction of a moral science presupposes moral determinism ; and is it not the chief use of history ' only to discover the constant and universal principles of human nature, by showing men in all varieties of circumstances and situations and furnishing material from which we may form our observations and become acquainted with the regular springs of human action and behaviour ' ?[4]

Moreover, does not every kind of social action presuppose the possibility of constructing a social science ? All laws founded on rewards and punishments assume that hope and fear exert a regular and uniform influence capable of producing good actions and preventing bad ones. ' So great is the force of laws, and of particular forms of government, and so little dependence have they on the humours and tempers of men, that consequences almost as general and certain may sometimes be deduced from them, as any which the mathematical sciences afford us '.[5]

Was there ever a thinker who showed more confidence in human reason, or scholar who believed more firmly that theoretic science could be transformed into practical science ?

But side by side with this tendency towards systematisation there is present in Hume a contradictory tendency. There certainly are

[1] *Remarks on Reid, Beattie and Oswald*, p. 2.
[2] *Treatise*, bk. i. part i. sect. iv.   [3] *Ibid.* bk. i. part i. sect. i.
[4] *Inquiry*, sect. viii. p. i.   [5] *Essays*, vol. i. p. 99.

laws, or, to keep Hume's terminology, ' principles '[1] which unite images one to another, notably the principles of association by likeness and by contiguity. Their action, however, is neither infallible nor exclusive. They are ' general ' principles which form ' weak ' connections between ideas and leave room for uncertainty in the sequence of psychological phenomena. Ideas are not inseparably connected, and Hume never tires of insisting on ' the liberty of the imagination to transpose and change its ideas '.[2] It is only in appearance that the connection between effects and their causes, which is the basis of universal determinism, seems to be more rigid than the associations of contiguous or similar images. Hume analyses the association of cause and effect and finds in it nothing but a complication of the associations of similarity and contiguity ; therefore the association of cause and effect is like them indeterminable. The order of nature is a product of the imagination, reason a wonderful and unintelligible instinct which, were it not for the effect of habit, would be a perpetual source of astonishment.[3] In this case would not the result of philosophical reflection be to destroy natural beliefs and to paralyse instinct ? By no means ; rather does the last stage of the argument consist in understanding that scepticism can be thought, not lived ; and that reason is insignificant as compared with the instinct by which we live. If, then, the sceptical doubt which attacks the reason and the senses is an incurable disease, it can nevertheless be diminished by slackening the effort of reflection, since it is of reflection that it is born : ' carelessness and inattention alone can afford us any remedy (for scepticism) : for this reason I rely entirely upon them '.[4] Corresponding expressions are to be found in Montaigne. In fact, though he is more of a dialectician and analyst and less of a man of learning, Hume is in many respects the English Montaigne. To him associationism is a philosophy against the philosophers, a series of reasonings turned against reasoning itself, in a word, an irrationalism.

There was then undoubtedly a dualism in Hume's method. From one point of view his method was a rationalistic one. He sought to determine in the moral sphere causes and laws analogous to the principle of universal attraction. He founded those moral sciences which a whole school of thought later set about arranging in a synthetic and deductive form. He was the author of the associationist dogmatism and also of the economic doctrine of his compatriot, friend and disciple, Adam Smith. But, from another point of view, he is universally regarded as a sceptic, who sought to banish the idea of necessity from the world, and who, far from working to create

[1] Note this obscure use of the word ' principle ', which was used to satiety by the Benthamite School.
[2] *Treatise*, bk. i. part i. sect. iii.   [3] *Ibid*. bk. i. part iii. sect. xvi.
[4] *Ibid*. bk. i. part iv. sect. ii.

new sciences, came to destroy the scientific and rational appearance of those disciplines that had already been set up. Besides, Hume's criticism does not tend, in any way, to paralyse or suspend action. In the last resort it is rather reflection which Hume condemns, precisely because it paralyses the power of action. The persistence of life, despite the contradictions of reason, proves empirically that optimism is not tied to rationalism, and that it is a good thing to trust to instinct, to give oneself up to Nature, without being duped by any logical illusion, without confusing nature with providence, or instinct with reason. Hume's philosophy is naturalism rather than scepticism, and it is for this reason that a school of doctrinaires will always regard him with mistrust. It is true that Bentham considered him one of his masters ; but the considered view of Priestley, as expressed in the Treatise which in 1774 he devoted to the refutation of the philosophy of common sense, was that Hume, by affecting scepticism, had compromised the sound doctrine of Locke and Hartley.[1] Fifty years later, James Mill, the acknowledged disciple of Bentham, while he allowed Hume the honour of having made a ' great discovery ', deplores the fact that after a number of ' brilliant developments ' ' he was misled by the pursuit of a few surprising and paradoxical results '.[2] The conflict between the two tendencies, the one rationalistic, the other naturalistic, is none the less real in the associationist logic itself : we shall see it recurring again and again in the great movement of ideas which we are about to examine.

But the philosophers who belonged to this movement were primarily practical reformers. They sought in the principle of the association of ideas a basis on which to form a social science, at once theoretical and capable of being transformed into an art. When Gay, in his dissertation, proposed to extend the principle of association so as to explain all psychological phenomena, it was in order to form a moral philosophy based on what he might even then have called the principle of utility. In fact, however, this name occurs for the first time in Hume ; and it was to Hume that Bentham, in his first work, The Fragment on Government, which appeared in 1776, gave credit for the discovery of the principle.[3] Now Hume can justly be considered a forerunner of the Utilitarian morality, but he must not be held to be the founder of doctrinal Utilitarianism more than of doctrinal Associationism.

In one way, indeed, the actual science of morality did not mean the

---

[1] In his reaction against Hume's scepticism, Priestley even goes as far as materialism.

[2] In the article ' Education ' in the fifth supplement to the Encyclopædia Britannica.

[3] Bowring, vol. i. p. 242 ; and p. 268, note.

same to Hume as it subsequently meant to the Utilitarian moralists. It is true that he proceeded along Newtonian lines ; he definitely intended to apply the experimental method in the analysis of the notion of personal merit. If he can establish between the distinction of good and evil and some other definite psychological distinction a relation of co-existence of such a kind that the two distinctions vary together in the same proportion and under the influence of the same causes, he will then, he thinks, be able to conclude that the two distinctions are identical. The general law will enable the phenomena to be accounted for even when they seem different or indeed contradictory.[1] The Rhine flows northwards, the Rhone southwards, yet both have their source in the same mountain and are drawn in opposite directions by the same principle of gravity. The parallel of the principle of universal attraction in the sphere of morality is the principle of utility. In fact we say of an action that it is morally praiseworthy according to the extent to which it seems to conform to the interests of society. But precisely because he claims to adopt a purely experimental method, Hume does not think that it is the task of the moralist to issue commands. He seeks *that which is* ; it is by a strange *petitio principii* that most moralists, having proceeded along the same lines, become all at once engaged in defining *that which ought to be*.[2] Now if this involves a *petitio principii*, the objection applies to Bentham, since his dominating idea is just this—that he has discovered in the principle of utility a practical commandment as well as a scientific law, a proposition which teaches us at one and the same time what is and what ought to be.[3] According to Hume, reason is essentially inactive ; its sole purpose being to compare ideas, it is powerless to distinguish between the good and the evil in action. Moral judgment is not based on an idea but on an impression—on a ' feeling ' ; the task of the moralist is to analyse this feeling, to define what moral feeling actually is.[4] While it is true that Bentham does not use the words reason and feeling in quite the same sense as Hume, it is characteristic that in his *Introduction to the Principles of Morals and Legislation* he explicitly proposes to withdraw morality from the control of feeling and to subject it to the rule of reason.[5]

But from another point of view it is interesting to notice that in Hume's writings, just because of the complex nature of his thought and his mistrust of simple solutions, there is present the germ of the various interpretations of the principle of utility which might be, and indeed subsequently were, put forward. The view that pleasure is the end of human action agrees with the general thesis upheld by

[1] *Inquiry concerning the Principles of Morals*, sect. i.
[2] *Treatise*, bk. iii. part i.
[3] MSS. Univ. Coll. No. 10, Bentham to Dumont, Sept. 6th, 1822.
[4] *Treatise*, bk. iii. part i. sect. ii.   [5] Bowring, vol. i. p. v.

Hume. ' Ask a man, *why he uses exercise* ; he will answer, *because he desires to keep his health*. If you then inquire, *why he desires health*, he will readily reply, *because sickness is painful*. If you push your inquiries further and desire a reason, *why he hates pain*, it is impossible he can ever give any. This is an ultimate end, and is never referred to by any other object.' [1] But that which is pleasant to me is not necessarily pleasant to my neighbour, nor is what is painful to me, painful to him. If my pleasure is the natural object of my desire, and my pain the natural object of my aversion, how is it conceivable that the moral sense which inspires me to pursue the general utility and not my private interest, should be a constituent part of my nature ? There are three possible answers to this question, all of which are to be found in Hume ; they form three logically distinct and perhaps contradictory doctrines ; nevertheless there is not one of them which is not present, more or less explicitly, in every Utilitarian doctrine.

In the first place, it may be admitted that the identification of personal and general interest is spontaneously performed within each individual conscience by means of the feeling of sympathy which interests us directly in the happiness of our neighbour ; this may be called the principle of the fusion of interests. Since the principle of sympathy can thus be regarded as a special form of the principle of utility, the eighteenth-century moralists who are responsible for the ' moral sense ' theory may in many cases be already considered ' Utilitarians '—a view of them which is confirmed by an examination of their works. This is the meaning of the observations of John Brown in his essay, published in 1751, in which he discussed Lord Shaftesbury's treatise.[2] According to Brown's judicious observations, Shaftesbury, by a curious linguistic survival, continued to employ an idealistic language to express ideas of utility which the Platonists had not foreseen. The evolution is more marked with Hutcheson, Professor of Moral Philosophy at Glasgow, the forerunner of Hume and the master of Adam Smith. It is even plausible to conjecture that it was through him that Hume and Adam Smith were brought into direct relations with each other.[3] He anticipated Hume in demanding that the Newtonian method should be introduced into morals,[4] and Bentham in defining those actions ·as the most perfectly virtuous which ' appear to have the most universal unlimited Tendency to the greatest and most extensive Happiness '.[5]

Already he made use of the formula afterwards made classical by Bentham—' The *moral Evil*, or *Vice*,' of a given action, ' is as the

[1] *Inquiry*, Appendix I.
[2] *Essays on the Characteristics of the Earl of Shaftesbury*, by John Brown (Essay II).
[3] Rae, *Life of Adam Smith*, p. 15 ; W. R. Scott, *Francis Hutcheson*, pp. 120-1.
[4] See Preface to 1755 ed. of *System of Moral Philosophy*.
[5] *Inquiry concerning Moral Good and Evil*, sect. iii. § 8.

Degree of Misery, and *Number* of Sufferers ; so that, *that Action* is *best*, which accomplishes the *Greatest Happiness* for the *Greatest Number* '.[1] And there is a chapter in his *Moral Philosophy* which includes some elements of what, in Bentham's school, came to be known as moral arithmetic.[2] Hume, lastly, regarded the egoistic system as a product of that exaggerated need for theoretical simplification which ends by complicating explanations, and which stands condemned by the experimental method even more in morals than in physics.[3] He denied the possibility of establishing a contradiction between egoistic and social feeling : these feelings are not more mutually opposed than are egoism and ambition, egoism and vindictiveness, egoism and vanity ; on the contrary, are not social feelings necessary to give content to the empty form of our egoism ? Once admit the principle of utility, and the principle of sympathy seems to follow as a necessary consequence of it ; for it is only through sympathy that the happiness of a stranger can affect us. We shall see in what follows that in spite of all its efforts the Utilitarian morality is never able completely to rid itself of the principle of the sympathetic fusion of interests. Bentham includes in his *Introduction* the pleasures of sympathy, which he also calls benevolence or good-will, and admits that sympathy as well as interest may bind individuals to one another.[4]

But a very different tendency is revealed in the development of moral philosophy in England, prior to Bentham. The idea that egoism is, if not the exclusive, at least the predominating inclination of human nature was gaining ground with the moralists of the eighteenth century. Hume admitted that the maxim may be false *in fact*, but he strongly insisted on the idea that it is true *in politics*. For on the one hand, while isolated individuals are sometimes influenced by the feeling of honour, it ceases to influence them once they are considered as members of a party : for is not a man sure of the approval of his party in everything which ministers to the common interest ? Further, since every assembly adopts its decisions by a majority of votes, it is only necessary that the egoistic motive should influence a majority (and this will always be the case) for the whole assembly to be seduced by this particular interest and to act as if it contained no single member who concerned himself with the prosperity and the liberty of the public.[5] But is it not the predominating preoccupation of all the Utilitarian moralists to make politics an experimental and objective science ? This explains the fact that Bentham was inclined to admit, like Hume and with

[1] *Inquiry concerning Moral Good and Evil*, sect. iii. § 8.
[2] *Moral Philosophy*, bk. ii. ch. vii.
[3] *Inquiry concerning the Principles of Morals*, Appendix II. ' Of Self-love.'
[4] Bowring, vol. i. pp. 18, 52-3, 69, 143.
[5] *Essays*, part i.   Essay VI. ' Of the Independency of Parliament.'

fewer reservations, that egoism has, if not an exclusive, at least a predominating influence on human actions : he narrows it down still further by declaring that ' of all passions, that is the most given to calculation, from the excesses of which, by reason of its strength, constancy, and universality, society has most to apprehend ' ; the passion, that is, which ' corresponds to the motive of pecuniary interest '.[1] The aim of Bentham, as of all Utilitarian philosophers, was to establish morals as an exact science. He therefore sought to isolate in the human soul that feeling which seems to be the most easily measurable. Now the feeling of sympathy seems to fulfil this condition less than any other. How can it be said without absurdity that the feeling of sympathy varies with the number of its objects according to a law ? Egoistic feelings, on the other hand, are better qualified than any others to admit an objective equivalent. The fear of a pain can with some accuracy be estimated and compared with other fears when the sufferings in question are really egoistic ; in the case, for instance, of the fear of a definite fine : this is why the idea of applying the principle of utility to the theory of penal law seems to have been the first to occur to Bentham. A hope can with some accuracy be estimated and compared with other hopes when the pleasures hoped for are of an egoistic nature ; in the case, for instance, of the hope of receiving a definite number of coins of equal value : this is why political economy, the ' dogmatics of egoism ', is perhaps the most famous of the applications of the principle of utility.

But even granting the predominance of egoistic motives, there are two distinct ways in which the principle of utility can be, and in fact has been, interpreted. These interpretations, in addition to the thesis of the fusion of interests, give birth to two new theses.

In the first place it is possible to use the following line of argument : since it is recognised that the predominating motives in human nature are egoistic, and further that the human species lives and survives, it must be admitted that the various egoisms harmonise of their own accord and automatically bring about the good of the species. Bentham went even further and argued from the persistence of the human species that egoistic motives must predominate : could humanity survive for a single moment if each individual were engaged in promoting the interest of his neighbour at the expense of his own ?[2] This thesis was eminently paradoxical ; yet it was destined to become famous : it may be called the thesis of the natural identity of interests.

Mandeville, in his *Fable of the Bees*, which appeared in 1723, had developed the theory that the vices of individuals are to the advantage of the public : *private vices, public benefits*. He had prided himself

---

[1] Bowring, vol. i. pp. 90-91.
[2] Bowring, vol. i. p. 339.

on pointing out ' that neither the friendly qualities and kind affections that are natural to man nor the real *virtues* he is capable of acquiring by reason and self-denial are the foundation of society ; but that what we call *Evil* in this world, *moral* as well as natural, is the grand principle that makes us sociable creatures '.[1] But what is it that Mandeville calls evil or vice ? Is it egoism ? If egoism is useful to the public, and if further it be agreed to call virtuous such qualities in individuals as are useful to the public, why persist in calling egoism a vice ? [2] This is the criticism which was brought against Mandeville by all the moralists connected with the Utilitarian tradition, from Hume and Brown down to Godwin and Malthus.[3] If Mandeville had started by reconsidering the current terminology, which was founded on the notions of an erroneous and confused morality, he would have discovered the thesis of the identity of interests and would have worked to advance moral science instead of acting the *littérateur* and maker of paradoxes. For political economy, ever since Adam Smith, has rested entirely on the thesis of the natural identity of interests. By the mechanism of exchange and the division of labour individuals, without desiring or knowing it, and while pursuing each his own interest, are working for the direct realisation of the general interest. It is possible that Adam Smith, who founds his moral theory on the principle of sympathy, would have been prepared to admit that the thesis of the natural identity of interests, though true in political economy, was false in morals. It is easy to understand, however, how tempting it was to the theorists of the egoistic system to appropriate a thesis which seemed to justify their doctrine.

Further, the thesis which asserts a direct harmonisation of the various egoisms may reasonably be held to be paradoxical ; and without giving up the thesis of the natural identity of interests, it is possible to compromise on the more moderate doctrine, developed by Hartley, which maintains that the identification of interests is brought about in a way which, though it is no doubt necessary, is only progressive and gradual. Hartley's chief preoccupation was to demonstrate that the mechanism of association coincided with the Christian optimism which bases itself on considerations of finality.[4] He began by establishing, in pure Benthamite language, that all those pleasures which to us appear irreducible and specifically different, in reality differ only in respect of the extent to which they are complicated, and are all collections of simple elements, associated

[1] *Fable of the Bees*, part i. ' A Search into the Nature of Society,' *sub finem.*
[2] Bowring, vol. v. p. 68.
[3] Hume, *Essay XXIV.* ' Of Refinement in the Arts.' Godwin, *Political Justice*, 2nd ed. bk. viii. ch. vii. ; Malthus, *Principles of Population*, App. 9th ed. p. 492.
[4] As early as 1735 Hartley had written two treatises entitled *The Progress of Happiness deduced from Reason.*

in diverse ways.[1] He then considered himself able, by the mere mechanism of association, to account for the formation of all feelings, sympathetic as well as egoistic, and to prove, besides, that the quantity of pleasure tends to outweigh the quantity of pain in accordance with a mathematical progression. ' Thus association would convert a state, in which pleasure and pain were both conceived by turns, into one in which pure pleasure alone would be perceived ; at least, would cause the beings who were under its influence to an indefinite degree, to approach to this last state nearer than by any definite difference.' [2] Hartley tells us in so many words that this is the promise of paradise regained : ' Association tends to make us all ultimately similar ; so that if one be happy, all must '.[3] Priestley borrowed the theory from Hartley and freed it from the theological elements which had complicated it with him.[4] It developed into the theory of indefinite progress, and as such we shall see what became of it.

But there is yet another argument which can be used : while still admitting that individuals are chiefly or even exclusively egoistic, it is yet possible to deny that their egoisms will ever harmonise either immediately or even ultimately. It is therefore argued that in the interest of individuals the interest of the individual must be identified with the general interest, and that it is the business of the legislator to bring about this identification. This may be called the principle of the artificial identification of interests. Hume approved the maxim of political writers according to which *every man should*, on principle, *be held a knave*, and, once this principle had been laid down, concluded that the art of politics consists in governing individuals through their own interests, in creating artifices of such a kind that in spite of their avarice and their ambition they shall co-operate for the public good. If politics are not carried on in this way, it is vain to boast of possess- ing the advantages of a good constitution ; for it will in the end be found that a man's sole guarantee of his liberty and property consists in the good-will of his rulers, which amounts to saying that he has no guarantee at all.[5]—Now this is the form in which Bentham first adopted the principle of utility. It is true that he occasionally applied, by accident, the principle of the fusion of interests. It is true that in political economy he adopted, with the ideas of Adam Smith, the principle of the natural identity of interests. But the primitive and original form in which in his doctrine the principle of utility is invested is the principle of the artificial identification of interests. Bentham appealed to the legislator to solve, by means

---

[1] See *On Man*, part i. sect. ii. prop. xiv. cor. 10.
[2] *On Man*, part i. ch. i. sect. ii. cor. 9.
[3] *Ibid*. cor. 12.
[4] See the opening part of the *Essay on the First Principles of Government*.
[5] *Essay* VI. ' Of the Independency of Parliament.'

of a well-regulated application of punishments, the great problem of morals, to identify the interest of the individual with the interest of the community—his first great work was an ' introduction to the principles ' not only ' of morals ', but also, and above all, ' of legislation '.

This was the method which had lately been pursued by the French philosopher, Helvetius, in his famous book *De l'Esprit*. And however much this book may be forgotten to-day, it is impossible to exaggerate the extent of its influence throughout Europe at the time of its appearance.[1] This influence was particularly deep and lasting in England, and among the first to submit to it was Bentham ; for Helvetius gave himself out to be a disciple of Hume, and the English public now encountered in the writings of the French philosopher the ideas of their own national philosophers, arrayed to some extent in foreign dress.[2] Besides, the time was past when Voltaire and Montesquieu went to England to learn philosophy and politics. The contrary was now the case : the English ' freethinkers ' having become discredited in their own country, had formed a school in France, and to France the English went to repair the broken tradition. It was at this time that it became customary for young men of good family to complete their education by travelling in France. Jeremy Bentham's father was only a wealthy bourgeois, but he knew and loved French, and wrote his diary in a strange sort of French, mixed up with English words and anglicisms. He entrusted his son, who at the age of six already knew Latin and Greek, to a French tutor ; and under his direction Jeremy quickly passed from Perrault's *Contes* to those of Voltaire, and, if we are to believe his assertions, already discovered, in a passage from *Télémaque*, the first glimmerings of the principle of utility.[3] Then in 1755 Bentham went to Westminster School, and in 1760 to Oxford (he was then only twelve years old, and was exempted from taking the oath on account of his youth) ; bachelor of arts in 1763, he was inscribed as a student at Lincoln's Inn, and then returned to Oxford to hear the lectures of the famous professor of law, Blackstone. But he does not seem to have been influenced, unless it be by repulsion, either by the surroundings in which he grew up, or by the teachers to whom he listened. At this time the only influences which affected him profoundly were French. In 1770 he made the journey to Paris ;[4] and a little later began to correspond with his brother in French.[5] He read Voltaire, one of whose *Contes* ('Le Taureau Blanc') he translated into English ; Montesquieu, whom he did not much appreciate ;[6]

---

[1] Morellet, *Mémoires*. vol. i. p. 68.   [2] Bowring, vol. x. p. 56, etc.
[3] Bowring, vol. x. p. 10.
[4] See Add. MSS. Brit. Mus. 33,537, ff. 229-233.   [5] *Ibid*. ff. 361-2.
[6] See, *e.g.*, MSS. Univ. Coll. No. 100, a fragment entitled *Histoire du progrès de l'esprit humain dans la carrière de la législation*.

Maupertuis, from whom he borrowed some of the formulae of his
' moral calculus ' ; Chastellux, whose treatise *De la Félicité Publique*
(On Public Happiness) he liked and with whom he got into touch.[1]
Finally, it was in 1769 that he read Helvetius and discovered his
vocation. He had been tormented in his childhood by the problem
of the meaning of the word *genius*. In Helvetius he found its
etymological meaning : *genius* comes from *gigno* and means *invention*.
Which, then, was his genius ? And, further, which was the most
useful of all the kinds of genius ? Helvetius gave him the answer :
the genius of legislation. But did he possess the genius of legislation ? ' With a trembling voice ' he told himself ' yes '.[2] His
ambition he acknowledged some years later, in the first lines of one
of his manuscript works : ' What Bacon was to the physical world,
Helvetius was to the moral. The moral world has therefore had its
Bacon ; but its Newton is yet to come '.[3]

Helvetius, following Hume's example, wished to ' treat morals
like any other science and to make an experimental morality like an
experimental physics '.[4] The principle he assigned to morals is
' the interest of the public, that is to say of the greatest number ',
and he made justice consist in ' performing actions useful to the
greatest number '.[5] The fundamental thesis of his book is that
interest alone can dispense the praise and blame attached to actions
and to ideas. Take first the case of ideas. Why do we set up a
hierarchy among the sciences ? It is not because of their intrinsic
characteristics, of the greater or less extent of their complexity or
difficulty. The science of chess is perhaps as complicated as
abstract mathematics, but it is less useful and consequently less
esteemed : it is in proportion to their usefulness that we esteem
the various types of knowledge.[6] This is a principle which Bentham
later took up again and applied, in his *Chrestomathia*, to an attempt
to classify the sciences. Take the case of actions. ' If the physical
universe is subject to the laws of motion, the moral universe is no
less subject to the laws of interest ' ; and if personal interest is the
one universal measure of the merit of men's actions, then probity
in the case of an individual is, by definition, nothing but ' the habit
of such actions as are personally useful to that individual '.[7] In the
case of an individual, perhaps ; but is it true in the case of society ?
There is always the same problem to be met, and Helvetius
answered it by adopting the principle of the artificial identification
of interests.

He refuted the theory of climates which Montesquieu had developed
in his *Esprit des Lois*.[8] In place of Montesquieu's physical and

[1] Add. MSS. Brit. Mus. 33,538, ff. 203-4.
[2] Bowring, vol. x. p. 27. [3] MSS. Univ. Coll. No. 32.
[4] *De l'Esprit*, Preface. [5] *Ibid*. discours ii. ch. xxiii. xxiv.
[6] *Ibid*. dis. ii. ch. i. [7] *Ibid*. dis. ii. ch. ii.
[8] *Ibid*. dis. iii. ch. xxvii.

almost geographical determinism, Helvetius set up a moral determinism. Man is less the product of geographical than of social circumstances—of education in the widest sense of the word. ' It is in moral causes alone ', he tells us, ' that the true cause of the inequality of minds must be sought '.[1] The conclusion from this theory is that man, thanks to the knowledge he acquires of the laws of human nature, is endowed with an unlimited power to change or to reform mankind. This is the theory adopted, at the end of the nineteenth century, by educationalists such as James Mill, the disciple of Bentham, or Robert Owen, the disciple of Godwin : by education individuals are taught to identify their interest with the general interest. Now Bentham and Godwin were both disciples of Helvetius. Admitted that all the inequalities between individuals arise from moral causes, the inequality between the sexes must originate in a like manner. It is due to causes which are social and modifiable, not physiological and immutable.[2] Helvetius was a feminist ; and it was Mary Wollstonecraft, the wife of Godwin, who later, in the year 1792, founded English feminism with her *Vindication of the Rights of Women* ; and in the years immediately preceding 1832, the majority of the Utilitarian Radicals, with Bentham at their head, were likewise feminists. It is clear whose was the influence which inspired Bentham with the hope of making morals into an exact science, when it is remembered that Helvetius declared that there exists a pedagogic art, an art of inspiring and of ruling the passions, whose principles are ' as certain as the principles of geometry '.[3]

Helvetius further claimed that the word ' education ' should be understood in the widest sense : ' everyone, if I may say so, has for teachers *both the form of government under which he lives*, and his friends and his mistresses, and the people about him, and the books he reads, and, finally, chance, that is to say an infinite number of events whose connection and causes we are unable, through ignorance, to perceive '.[4] The legislator is therefore a pedagogue, a moralist ; morality and legislation are ' one and the same science '.[5] It is by means of good laws alone that virtuous men can be made ; the whole art of the legislator consists in forcing men, through their feeling of self-love, to be always just to one another.[6] The whole study of the moralists consists in determining the use that should be made of rewards and penalties and the help that can be drawn from them in binding together the personal and the general interest. Helvetius saw in this union ' the chief task that morality should set itself ' ;[7] and, in still more precise terms, he outlined, as follows, the

---

[1] *De l'Esprit*, dis. iii. ch. xxvii.
[2] *Ibid*. dis. ii. ch. xx.　　　　　　[3] *Ibid*. dis. iii. ch. xxv.
[4] *Ibid*. dis. iii. ch. i.　　　　　　[5] *Ibid*. dis. ii. ch. xxiv.
[6] *Ibid*. dis. ii. ch. xxiv.　　　　　[7] *Ibid*. dis. ii. ch. xxii.

very programme which Bentham soon afterwards attempted to carry out : ' The excellence of laws depends on the uniformity of the views of the legislator, and on the interdependence of the laws themselves. But in order to establish this interdependence, it must be possible *to reduce all the laws to some simple principle*, such as *the principle of the utility of the public*, that is to say, of the greatest number of men subject to the same form of government ; a principle whose full extent and fruitfulness are known to no one ; *a principle which embraces the whole of morals and of legislation* '.[1]

Before it spread in England, the doctrine of Helvetius had spread in Italy, where Beccaria, in a well-known book, tried systematically to apply the principles of Helvetius' philosophy to the content of the penal law.[2] The *Dei delitti e delle pene* appeared in 1764 ; Morellet's French translation in 1766 ; the first English translation in 1767. Bentham was the disciple of Beccaria as well as of Helvetius. On the one hand, he carried the application of the principle of utility to the solution of juridical problems further than it had been taken by Beccaria. He planned and began to draw up a Universal Code, and drew up an entire Penal Code ; and he had intended to call his *Introduction*, ' Introduction to a Penal Code ',[3] until he finally adopted a title which was obviously borrowed from Helvetius. On the other hand he made use of various observations, scattered throughout Beccaria's little treatise, to endow the Utilitarian philosophy with a mathematical precision ; and he found there, rather more explicitly than in Helvetius, his formula of ' the greatest happiness of the greatest number ', *la massima felicità divisa nel maggior numero*.[4] In the analysis, instituted by Beccaria, of the elements which make up the gravity of a pain,—intensity and duration, proximity and certainty,—he perceived the first elements of his moral calculus.[5] ' Oh, my master ', he exclaimed, ' first evangelist of Reason, you who have raised your Italy so far above England, and I would add above France, were it not that Helvetius, without writing on the subject of laws, had already assisted you and had provided you with your fundamental ideas ; you who speak reason about laws, when in France there was spoken only jargon : a jargon, however, which was reason itself as compared with the English jargon ; you who have made so many useful excursions into the path of utility, what is there left for us to do ?—Never to turn aside from that path '.[6] No thinker has ever shown less anxiety than Bentham to hide what he owes to his predecessors, to his contemporaries and to his century.

---

[1] *De l'Esprit*, dis. ii. ch. xvii.
[2] See Beccaria's letter to Morellet, May 1766.
[3] Bowring, x. p. 194.   [4] *Dei delitti e delle pene*. Introd.
[5] MSS. Univ. Coll. No. 27 ; *Introduction to Morals and Legislation*, p. 109.
[6] *Ibid*. No. 32, fragment entitled *Introduction, Principes Projets Matière*.

Finally, at the very time when Bentham was looking for inspiration to France and to Italy, the Utilitarian morality, long since prepared, and set forth in ever more perfect form by such thinkers as Gay, Hutcheson, Hume and Brown, continued to develop in England around Bentham. The fundamental ideas on which his philosophy was later to be based were already the current ideas of the contemporaries of his youth ; and it is a curious thing that at about this time the Utilitarian doctrine found in England almost its final expression in the works of two popular writers, both clerics, the Dissenter Priestley and the Anglican Paley.

Priestley, in an essay published in 1768, on *The First Principles of Government, and on the Nature of Political, Civil, and Religious Liberty*, proposed to adopt, as ' grand criterium ' to settle all the questions of politics, ' the good and the happiness of the members, that is to say of the majority of the members of a State '. He marvelled that the idea had until then escaped the notice of so many writers ; ' for this one general idea, suitably followed up, throws the greatest possible light on the whole system of politics and of morals ' and he even added ' of theology ' : [1] for one cannot conceive of God as preoccupied otherwise than with the happiness of His creatures. But this strange thinker, this professed heretic, determinist and materialist, who denied the divinity of Christ and was nevertheless a Christian minister, and moreover a prolific historian, a political agitator and a great chemist,—' Proteus-Priestley ',[2] as he was called,—lacked the steadfastness of purpose necessary to undertake, in solitude and meditation, the systematic application of the principle which he had, or thought he had discovered. Was it indeed from him that Bentham borrowed the formula of ' the greatest happiness of the greatest number ' ? [3] Bentham somewhere affirms that it is so ; [4] but elsewhere he says that he found it in Beccaria. He could have found it in Helvetius. It was natural that a current idea should on all sides rather tend to find expression in the same formulae.

Paley, who may likewise have borrowed from Priestley the main idea of his book, applied in the year 1785 in his *Principles of Moral and Political Philosophy* the principle of utility to the problems of morals and of theology. Happiness he defined as a sum of pleasures, which differ only in their duration and intensity, or, more exactly, as the excess of a sum of pleasures over a sum of pains.[5] He held that moral actions differ from immoral actions by their tendency, and that the criterium of law is utility.[6] The problem of understanding how public and private interest come to be bound together he solved,

---

[1] 1st ed. 1768 ; 2nd ed. 1771.   [2] *Pursuits of Literature*, p. 10.
[3] *An Essay*, etc., sect. ii. ' Political Liberty.'
[4] *Deontology* (French translation), p. 355.
[5] *Moral and Political Philosophy*, bk. i. ch. vi.   [6] *Ibid.* bk. ii. ch. vi.

as Gay had done, by having recourse to a God who rewards and avenges.[1] This work rapidly became the classical manual of morals at Cambridge University, where Paley lectured for seven consecutive years. Here for some time past Locke's philosophy had been taught,[2] but it was henceforth to be replaced by ' Locke and Paley '. Paley remained for half a century the acknowledged representative of the Utilitarian morality. The ' Paleyans ' came to be denounced long before the ' Benthamites '.[3] Even as late as 1828 Austin, the disciple of Bentham, evidently drew inspiration in the philosophical part of his law lectures from Paley's *Principles* rather than from Bentham's *Introduction*. Later still, Coleridge included in the selfsame reproof those whom he ironically called ' the sages of the nation '—not Bentham and Malthus, but Paley and Malthus.[4]

Bentham's friends were concerned at the success of the new book ; they lost patience with Bentham's extraordinary laziness in getting his manuscripts printed and producing the printed proofs of his works. Since 1772 he had been engaged on a great work which was to reform the science of law.[5] In 1775 he thought he had advanced a long way with the *Plan for a Digest*, or, in other words, of an integral Code ; and that he had almost finished a *Commentary on the Commentaries*, in which he refuted the whole system of the great English lawyer, Blackstone. Nevertheless, in 1776, he confined himself to detaching a few pages from this last work, and publishing the *Fragment on Government*, in which he discussed the principles of constitutional law in Blackstone.[6] Yet he never stopped writing, and was then at work on the *Critical Elements of Jurisprudence*, which was already well advanced in 1776.[7] This was the time when prison reform was the topic of discussion in London : in a *View of the Hard Labour Bill*, he contented himself with publishing, in 1778, a very specialised application of the fundamental principles of his theory of punishment to the organisation of the penitentiary régime. For the *Société Économique* of Berne [8] had just offered, for the year 1779, a prize to the author of the best proposal for reform of the criminal laws, and Bentham thought of competing. In point of fact he was too late ; [9] and he embarked, in London, in the year 1780, on the printing of the *Penal Code*, which he had just written. But once again it came to nothing ; [10] he wearied of the delays in printing and turned his attention elsewhere. He had always been keenly interested in the problems of chemistry : [11] in his corre-

[1] *Moral and Political Philosophy*, bk. i. ch. vii.
[2] See Leslie Stephen, *English Thought in the Eighteenth Century*.
[3] See, *e.g.*, Brown, *Philosophy of the Human Mind*, pp. 501, 534.
[4] *Literary Remains of S. T. Coleridge*, p. 328.
[5] Add. MSS. Brit. Mus. 33,537, f. 242, to his father, Oct. 14, 1772.
[6] *Ibid*. ff. 316-7, to his brother.
[7] *Ibid*. 33,538, f. 67, verso.   [8] *Ibid*. ff. 141-2.
[9] *Ibid*. ff. 313-4.   [10] *Ibid*. 33,539, f. 25.   [11] *Ibid*. 33,537, ff. 204-5.

spondence with his brother Samuel he devoted more space to them
than to the problems of law or politics ; and it was as a student
of chemistry, not as a social reformer, that he made the acquaintance
of Priestley in 1775 ; [1] in 1783 he published a translation of a
German work on applied chemistry.[2] Nevertheless, he was still
working, either in his barrister's chambers at Lincoln's Inn, or at
Bowood Castle with his patron, Lord Shelburne, at his great work
on jurisprudence. At this time he had in mind ' a general view of
a body of legislation ' ; he examined to the bottom questions of
principle, and drew up a treatise on ' indirect legislation ' and
another on ' the transplanting of laws '.[3] He was looking for a way
of spreading his ideas on the Continent, and in 1785 he joined his
brother Samuel, who had secured a position of some standing in
Russia. He took an interest in economic questions, and published
a *Defence of Usury*, which enjoyed a great success. Once again
he turned his attention to the reform of the penitentiary régime, and
in collaboration with his brother outlined the plan of the *Panopticon*,
the model prison, to secure the adoption of which he was to devote
more than twenty years of fruitless effort. But there was still no
sign of his great theoretical work. In vain his friend George Wilson
warned him of the publication of Paley's book : many of Paley's
ideas on punishment were identical with those which Wilson had
always held to be among Bentham's most important discoveries.
Bentham answered jestingly that it was the fault of Wilson and his
criticisms that he had refrained from publishing the work. Wilson
protested : ' The cause lies in your constitution. With one-tenth
part of your genius, and a common degree of steadiness, both Sam
and you would long since have risen to great eminence. But your
history, since I have known you, has been to be always running from
a good scheme to a better. In the meantime, life passes away and
nothing is completed '. In 1788 Wilson renewed the attack : who
could be sure that Paley had not plagiarised Bentham ? Had not
some copies gone astray—those in particular which Bentham had
entrusted to Lord Ashburton in 1781 ? [4] In fact, in spite of the
immediate success secured by Paley's book, and in spite of the fact
that Bentham was so lazy and indifferent, and allowed himself to
be outstripped, already it seems possible to guess at the profound
reasons for which Bentham and not Paley was called upon to become
the head of the Utilitarian school.

Paley was a clergyman : hence the theological basis which he
gave to the Utilitarian morality. Now the theological character

---

[1] Add. MSS, Brit. Mus. 33,537, f. 327 and f. 362.
[2] *An Essay on the Usefulness of Chemistry and its Application to the Various
Occasions of Life.*
[3] MSS. Univ. Coll. Nos. 87 and 88.
[4] Bowring, vol. x. pp. 163 *et seq.*

of his Utilitarianism, though it may have made his teaching in an official university more acceptable, prevented his ever becoming what Bentham wished to be : he lacked the intransigeance of the revolutionary and of the doctrinaire. When, in 1772, Cambridge University was agitated by the question of subscription, of compulsory adherence to the thirty-nine fundamental articles of the Anglican Church, and a petition was being signed to secure the suppression of this formal requirement, Paley, in spite of his sympathy for the liberal party, evaded it, humorously alleging that he had not the wherewithal to afford to keep a conscience.[1] Bentham took questions of conscience more seriously : he never forgot, all his life, the horror with which he had seen five Methodist students expelled for heresy during his time at Oxford—nor the horror with which he found himself obliged publicly to adhere, without faith, to the Thirty-nine Articles : he compared the agonies he suffered on that day to those of Jesus on the cross.[2] Paley might well, in his criticism of the theory of the ' moral sense ', express in terms very akin to those used by Bentham his fear ' that a system of morality, founded on instincts, will find reasons and excuses for established opinions and practices ' ;[3] he was himself a conservative whose system contained within it an almost complete justification of established institutions, judicial no less than religious and political. Bentham, who had gone to the bar at the wish of an ambitious father, only pleaded there once or twice ; already this disciple of Helvetius and Beccaria revolted against making money at the trade of interpreting a vicious law, at the expense of the public.[4] Had he ' drowned ' himself in his career, he would soon have had neither the talent nor the inclination necessary for undertaking his great work. ' In the track I am in ', he wrote to his father in 1772, ' I march up with alacrity and hope : in any other I should crawl on with despondency and reluctance. . . . Forgive me, Sir, if I declare simply, and once for all, that till this great business is disposed of, I feel myself unable of any other '.[5] Already he dreamed of founding a school, of giving instructions to disciples who should publish and spread abroad his writings ; already he found at Lincoln's Inn, in Lind [6] and in Wilson,[7] zealous friends ready to work under his orders and to make his ideas public. Having left the schools and deserted the bar, he felt free at last, free to carry on that tireless war against abuses which was to occupy his whole life.

Wholly preoccupied with practice, he was not worried by meta-

---

[1] *Memoirs of William Paley*, by George Wilson Meadley (1810 ed.), p. 89.
[2] *Not Paul But Jesus*, Introd.
[3] *Moral and Political Philosophy*, bk. i. ch. v.
[4] Bowring, vol. v. p. 349.
[5] MSS. Brit. Mus. 33,537, ff. 242-3.   [6] See below, ch. iii. 2.
[7] MSS. Brit. Mus. 33,538, f. 222.

physical questions.[1] The problem of the reality of the external
world concerned him but little. ' Let it be true that the bread
(which is set before me) . . . does not exist. If I make no practical
inference from this fine philosophy, I am never the better for it.
If I make any from it, I starve '.[2] Neither was he much concerned
by the problems of free-will. The Scottish philosopher, Gregory,
through the medium of Wilson, asked him his opinion on a
work in which he had recently discussed the question : Bentham
shirked the question, alleging that he lacked time, and added con-
fidentially in his reply to Wilson that he did not care a straw for
liberty and necessity : how could a man with an active profession
trouble himself with such purely speculative questions ?[3] Perhaps
even, as Dumont surmises,[4] it is in this indifference that the real
cause of his laziness in publishing his work must be sought. To him
the whole value of the *Introduction* depended on its being the preface
to an immense work, wholly practical and legislative—the reform of
the entire system of law : what concern had he with a discussion
of principles for its own sake ? He had already drawn up in their
entirety and confided to Dumont for publication in France the
manuscripts of ' A General View of a Complete Body of Legislation ',
when finally, after the repeated entreaties of his friends, the *Introduction to the Principles* appeared in 1789.

The *Introduction* opens with a proposition, copied almost word for
word from Helvetius :[5] ' Nature has placed mankind under the
governance of two sovereign masters, *pain* and *pleasure*. It is for
them alone to point out what we ought to do, as well as to determine
what we shall do. On the one hand the standard of right and wrong,
on the other the chain of causes and effects, are fastened to their
throne. . . . The *principle of utility* recognises this subjection, and
assumes it for the foundation of that system, the object of which
is to rear the fabric of felicity by the hands of reason and of law. . . .
By the principle of utility is meant that principle which approves or
disapproves of every action whatsoever, according to the tendency
which it appears to have to augment or diminish the happiness of the
party whose interest is in question : or, what is the same thing in
other words, to promote or to oppose that happiness. I say of
every action whatsoever ; and therefore not only of every action of
a private individual, but of every measure of government.' There
are two points to remember in this definition since they gave to
Bentham's work its true character.

In the first place, Bentham distinguished as little as possible

---

[1] Yet he considers himself a metaphysician . . . but by metaphysic he seems to
mean general logic.

[2] MSS. Univ. Coll. No. 69.

[3] Bowring, x. 216.

[4] Dumont, *Discours Préliminaire*, pp. x-xi.

[5] Bowring, i. p. 1.

between the problem of morals and the problem of legislation. ' By the hands of reason ', he wrote, ' *and of law* ', and again, ' every action of a private individual ' and ' *every measure of government* '. Morals and legislation have the same principle, the same method. Morals, in the wide sense, can be defined as ' the art of directing men's actions to the production of the greatest possible quantity of happiness, on the part of those whose interest is in view '.[1] Either the man whose actions I intend to direct is myself, in which case morals is the *art of governing myself* or *private morals* : or else the men whose actions I intend to direct are men other than myself. In this case, if they are not adults, the art of governing them is called *education*, which is either *private* or *public* : if they are adults, the art of directing their actions so as to produce the greatest happiness of the greatest number appertains to *legislation*, if the acts of the government are of a permanent kind, or to *administration*, if they are of a temporary kind dictated by circumstances.—Thus Bentham certainly appears to make legislation a special branch of morals ; but it is easy to see in what sense he understands morals and why it is legitimate to say that he confuses the notions of morals and legislation. He is the disciple of Helvetius, although good sense causes him to modify a paradoxical doctrine ; morals, for him, are of a commanding, governmental nature ; or again, if you like, he accepts the principle of utility in the specific form of the artificial identification of interests. The science of human nature allows human nature to be overcome in the interest of mankind, just as, in the interest of mankind, the science of physical nature allows physical nature to be overcome. Further he writes, in language directly inspired by Helvetius, that ' the business of government is to promote the happiness of the society, by punishing and rewarding '.[2] And again he speaks of the magistrate as ' operating in the character of a tutor upon all the members of the state, by the direction he gives to their hopes and to their fears. Indeed, under a solicitous and attentive government, the ordinary preceptor, nay even the parent himself, is but a deputy, as it were, to the magistrate : whose controlling influence, different in this respect from that of the ordinary preceptor, dwells with a man to his life's end '.[3]

Secondly, the end which Bentham had in view was to found, for the first time, the art of morals and legislation on an objective science of behaviour. The principle of utility differs from the other moral precepts which have been successively put forward, in that it is the expression not of a subjective preference of the moralist, but of an objective law of human nature. It is not susceptible of *direct* proof, since that which is used to prove everything cannot itself be proved. But it is an empirical fact that there is not, nor has there

---

[1] Bowring, vol. i. p. 142.   [2] Bowring, vol. i. p. 35.
[3] Bowring, vol. i. p. 30.

ever been, a living human creature so stupid and so perverse as not to have referred to it in many, if not in most, of the decisions of life. It is a principle which men habitually adopt and apply without giving it a thought. Hence the principle is susceptible of at least *indirect* proof. It can be proved that ' when a man attempts to combat the principle of utility, it is with reasons drawn, without his being aware of it, from that very principle itself. His arguments, if they prove anything, prove not that the principle is *wrong*, but that, according to the applications he supposes to be made of it, it is *misapplied* '.[1] But the principle of utility approves or disapproves of actions according as they tend to augment or to diminish the happiness of the individuals under consideration. Consequently, to say that all men refer unconsciously to the principle of utility is to say that all men consider happiness as a quantity, pleasures and pains as values which are arithmetically calculable, and the ends of human action as a possible object of science. Now this, which Bentham postulates, certainly lacks the self-evidence of an axiom. According to him, to state a moral principle other than the principle of utility is to reveal its contradictory character and thus to refute it. The truth is that the refutation of a moral principle contrary to the principle of utility consists, in Bentham's philosophy, simply in proving that it cannot serve as the basis of a social science.

Take first the principle of asceticism, which, Bentham tells us, ' like the principle of utility, approves or disapproves of any action, according to the tendency which it appears to have to augment or diminish the happiness of the party whose interest is in question ; but in an inversive manner : approving of actions in so far as they tend to diminish his happiness ; disapproving of them in so far as they tend to augment it '.[2] The morals of self-sacrifice are perhaps born of the observation that it is well to sacrifice immediate pleasure to future pleasure : thus pleasure still remains the end of action. It might also be based on the fact that the interest of individuals must be sacrificed to the public interest ; but what, Bentham asks, is the public interest if not the sum of individual interests ? The principle of asceticism cannot serve as a basis for the science of government ; it is not susceptible of universalisation : ' Whatever merit a man may have thought there would be in making himself miserable, no such notion seems ever to have occurred to any of them, that it may be a merit, much less a duty, to make others miserable : although it should seem, that if a certain quantity of misery were a thing so desirable, it would not matter much whether it were brought by each man upon himself, or by one man upon another '.[3]

Another principle adverse to the principle of utility is that which

[1] Bowring, vol. i. pp. 2-3.   [2] Bowring, vol. i. p. 4.
[3] Bowring, vol. i. p. 5.

Bentham calls the principle of sympathy and antipathy, or elsewhere the capricious or arbitrary principle. Under this head Bentham groups all principles, except the principle of asceticism, which philosophers have successively put forward as the foundation of morality. Here there are two alternatives :—Either these different principles are reducible to the principle of utility—in this case *reason*, for example, would signify the obligation to aim at the greatest happiness of the greatest number, *law*, that which conforms to utility, and *natural laws*, the prescriptions or ' dictates ' of utility : but if this is the case, what is the use of these roundabout or metaphorical expressions ?[1] Or else, the principle of sympathy and antipathy, in all its forms, is a nominal and not a real principle : it does not so much constitute a positive principle as signify the complete absence of principle. ' What one expects to find in a principle is something that points out some external consideration, as a means of warranting and guiding the internal sentiments of approbation and disapprobation : this expectation is but ill fulfilled by a proposition, which does neither more nor less than hold up each of those sentiments as a ground and standard for itself.'[2] If each individual tries to impose on others his instinctive and un-reasoning preferences the arbitrary principle is a *despotic* principle ; but there is no room, in science, for authoritarianism, for what Bentham, alluding to the αὐτὸς ἔφα of the Pythagoreans, calls ' ipsedixitism '. If the individuals agree to have each his own criterium, his own manner of judging and feeling in morality, the arbitrary principle is an *anarchic* principle, but there is no place, in science, for subjectivism, for what Bentham calls ' sentimentalism '.[3]

In short, it is only the principle of utility, to the exclusion of the ascetic and sentimental principles, which can act as a criterium in morals and in legislation and be the basis of a social science. ' Arithmetic and medicine—these are the branches of art and science to which, in so far as the maximum of happiness is the object of his endeavours, the legislator must look for his means of operation :— the pains or losses of pleasure produced by a maleficent act correspond to the symptoms produced by a disease ',[4] and it is, in fact, from the analogy of these two sciences that Bentham draws his inspiration. In laying down the rules of his moral arithmetic,[5] he is trying to construct a kind of mathematical morality analogous to mathematical physics. In seeking the principle of a natural classification of motives and of crimes, he proceeds as does the doctor who is classifying diseases ; or again, to keep within the same class of science, he proceeds like the botanist who is classifying kinds and species, or

---

[1] See MSS. Univ. Coll. No. 69.   [2] Bowring, vol. i. p. 8.
[3] Bowring, vol. i. p. 3.   [4] Bowring, vol. iii. p. 224.
[5] This expression, which has become classical, does not occur in the *Introduction* but in Dumont's *Traités de Législation*.

like the chemist who wishes to provide a language for the new science, to create a scientific nomenclature. Were not botany and chemistry Bentham's favourite sciences ?

How can the calculus be applied to the affairs of morals ? The *ends* which the legislator has in view are pleasure and absence of pain : he must know therefore their *value*.[1] The *instruments* which he has to employ to realise these ends are also pleasures and pains ; the four *sanctions* enumerated by Bentham, the political, the moral, the religious and the physical, are all reducible to the last,[2] and all consist in the hope of certain pleasures and the fear of certain pains ; and the value of these, from this point of view also, should be known to the legislator. Hence the science of legislation presupposes as its first condition, the possibility of a quantitative comparison of pleasures. All the English moralists, from Hobbes to Bentham, played their part in elaborating the rules of this calculus : Bentham worked out the collective result. For a person, considered by himself, the value of a pleasure or a pain, considered by itself, will be greater or less according to the following circumstances : 1st, its *intensity*, 2nd. its *duration*, 3rd. its *certainty* or *uncertainty*, 4th. its *propinquity* or *distance*. These, according to Bentham, are the four *elements*, or elsewhere the four *dimensions*, of pleasure or of pain. But the value of a pleasure or of a pain, considered in relation to pleasures and pains which may follow or accompany it, varies according to two other circumstances : its *fecundity*, the chance it has of being followed by sensations of the *same* kind ; its *purity*, the chance it has of not being followed by sensations of the *opposite* kind. To these six elements a seventh must be added, if one has in view no longer a person considered in himself, but a given *number* of persons. This is the *extent* of a pleasure, that is to say ' the number of persons to whom it *extends*, or (in other words) who are affected by it '. Thanks to our knowledge of these elements, the formula of the greatest happiness of the greatest number acquires a scientific meaning. Bentham tried to define, to the smallest details, the rules of his moral arithmetic. All the numbers with which it deals are not of the same kind. The intensity of a pleasure has a minimum : the smallest degree of pleasure which is distinguishable from a state of insensibility. The duration of pleasure has a minimum : the smallest extent of duration which is perceptible to consciousness. From their minimum taken as unity, the intensity and duration of a pleasure are amounts capable of unlimited growth. The propinquity of a pleasure has as its maximum the actual realisation of that pleasure. The probability of a pleasure has as its maximum the absolute certainty belonging to a pleasure actually experienced. From this maximum taken as unity the proximity and certainty of a pleasure are amounts capable of un-

[1] Bowring, vol. i. pp. 15-17.   [2] Bowring, vol. i. pp. 14-15.

limited diminution. Degrees of intensity and duration must therefore be expressed by whole numbers, and degrees of propinquity and certainty by fractions. Further, the operations of moral arithmetic are not all of the same kind. Pleasures of different values are *added*, but the value of a given pleasure is *multiplied* by the number of individuals who feel it ; and the elements which make up the value of a pleasure are *multiplied* by each other—the numbers which express the intensity by those which express the duration, the numbers which express the amount by those which express the propinquity or probability. No doubt Bentham did not expect that this method of calculation could be applied, without modification, to all judgments of moral approbation and disapprobation, and to all legislative acts. It can, however, always be kept in mind ; and the more we conform to it, the more we shall be inclined to attribute to morals the character of an exact science.[1]

The theory of the calculus of pleasures and pains rests on the hypothesis that all pleasures and all pains are comparable in respect of quantity. Now in the case of the extensive quantity the objects in question must be homogeneous if they are to be comparable. Bentham admits, however, that pleasures, and likewise pains, are heterogeneous, and fall into distinct classes ; and he is led in consequence to think of the science of legislation as a science of classification, not of calculation. Having represented ' what belongs to all sorts of pleasures and pains alike ', he goes on ' to exhibit, each by itself, the several sorts of pains and pleasures '.[2] He distinguishes fourteen simple pleasures and twelve simple pains, and further insists on the distinction, among these feelings of pleasure and pain, between those which presuppose a pleasure or a pain, experienced by another person, and which can be called *extra-regarding*, and those which presuppose nothing of the kind and which can be called *self-regarding*. Here, then, is verified, in an unexpected way, a dominant idea of the new morality, the thesis of the predominance of egoism : for, if the four classes made up by the pleasures and pains of benevolence and malevolence be excepted, all the feelings of pleasures enumerated by Bentham are self-regarding feelings.[3]

Now what is the principle on which this classification is founded ? It might appear, at first sight, to be classification by causes ; but Bentham himself does not allow this interpretation. ' What determines a lot of pleasure, for example, to be regarded as one complex pleasure, rather than as divers simple ones, is the nature of the exciting cause. Whatever pleasures are excited all at once by the action of the same cause, are apt to be looked upon as constituting all together but one pleasure.'[4] Thus the identity of the cause may indeed constitute the *unity* of the complex phenomenon, but

[1] Bowring, vol. i. p. 16.　　[2] Bowring, vol. i. p. 17 *sqq.*
[3] Bowring, vol. i. pp. 20-21.　　[4] Bowring, vol. i. p. 17.

not its *simplicity*. Does the simplicity of a phenomenon consist, then, in its being irreducible by analysis ? ' Pains and pleasures ', Bentham tells us, ' may be called by one general word, interesting perceptions. Interesting perceptions are either simple or complex. The simple ones are those which cannot any one of them be resolved into more : complex are those which are resolvable into diverse simple ones.' [1] But if there exists a number, great or small, of simple kinds of sensations which are irreducible to each other, what becomes of the possibility of a calculus of the phenomena of sensibility, of a quantitative comparison of pleasures and pains ? I know, I am able to foretell that a man will prefer one hour of work to two hours of work, two shillings of wages to one shilling of wages ; but I do not know, except through observation and in a particular case, I cannot foretell in general whether a man will prefer to satisfy his hunger, his need for exercise, or his need for self-devotion. The science of nature implies the possibility of reducing the heterogeneous to the homogeneous, or at least of bringing heterogeneous phenomena under a common mode of representation by the homogeneous. Must we not admit that in Bentham the taste for classification has got the better of the analytical spirit ?—Actually, this taste for classification is due, in Bentham, to a most serious and scientific preoccupation, which is, let us repeat it, to put an end to the era of subjectivism in morals and to found an objective morality.

For him who accepts the principle of utility, the value of an act consists in the pleasures and pains which result from it. No doubt, in estimating an action it is not unimportant to know whether or not it was intentional, but this is only in so far as the intention implies that the agent was aware of the consequences of the act, and justifies the fear, on the part of the public, of a repetition of the act.[2] There is, on the other hand, a common view that leads one to believe that the intention borrows its moral character not from the consequences of the intentional act, but from the motives which inspired it. Now the motive is always a pleasure or a pain, a pleasure which one expects to see continued or produced by the act in question, a pain which one expects to see stopped or prevented. And pleasure, in itself, is a good, it is indeed the absolute good : pain, in itself, is an evil, it is indeed the absolute evil. It must therefore be maintained, contrary to the common view, *that there does not exist a kind of motive which is in itself bad.*[3] But if this proposition is true, the scientific study of motives becomes a delicate matter : since in order to study them we are obliged to make use of words, and current language is ill constructed and uses, to designate motives, words to which, as Hartley had already observed,[4] a favourable or unfavourable meaning

---

[1] Bowring, vol. i. p. 17.
[2] Bowring, vol. i. p. 40 *sqq.*   [3] Bowring, vol. i. p. 46 *sqq.*
[4] *On Man*, part i. ch. iii. sect. i. prop. lxxx. cor. 5.

is attached. ' Confining himself to the language most in use, a man can scarce avoid running, in appearance, into perpetual contradictions. His propositions will appear, on the one hand, repugnant to truth ; and on the other hand, adverse to utility. As paradoxes, they will excite contempt : as mischievous paradoxes, indignation '.[1] Mandeville's great mistake was that he tried to express new moral ideas in an ancient language.[2] The remedy lies in setting aside the old terminology, and reforming the language of morals ; and since the fundamental error which vitiates the language is its sentimentalism, which attributes a good or evil valuation to motives in themselves, motives should no longer be designated by *sentimental* or *passionate* terms, but instead by terms which are *neutral* and do not connote praise or blame ; and they should be known only as classified according to their consequences—as social (these being further distinguished into purely social and semi-social), unsocial, and personal, motives. In this way it will be possible to talk of morals no longer in the manner of a *littérateur* or a satirist, but as a scientist, that is impartially and objectively.

The *Introduction to the Principles of Morals and Legislation* now appears to us as the consummation of a long intellectual process whose stages we have tried very briefly to mark. Which, among the ideas to which Bentham gives expression and which have become popularised under his name, can he himself be held to have originated ? This is an awkward question to answer. Bentham did not invent the moral arithmetic, the elements of which are to be found in Maupertuis, in Beccaria, in Hartley, and even in Hobbes. He did not invent the principle of utility, the formula of which is to be found in Hume. He did not invent the formula of ' the greatest happiness of the greatest number ' which occurs in Hutcheson, in Beccaria, and in Priestley. It really matters little in what particular thinker, and at what actual date, he discovered the principles of his philosophy ; the simplest and the truest thing to say is that he borrowed them from the current language of contemporary thought. The especial quality of the writers of the Utilitarian school, and of Bentham in particular, is that they were not so much great inventors as great arrangers of ideas : and it was due to this genius for logical arrangement that, by reducing to formulae the current philosophy of their country and of their century, they succeeded in forming a school which could unite in the profession of a common doctrine.

We can go further and ask whether Bentham did not found his doctrine on elementary principles, whose real obscurity and complexity, as now revealed to us by the study of their historical development, he failed to understand. Did he see that the principle of the association of ideas and the principle of utility itself permit of diverse

[2] Bowring, vol. i. p. 49.   [2] *Ibid.*

and perhaps contradictory interpretations ? He does not seem to have done so ; for the whole force of his criticism is concentrated not on the principles of metaphysics but on established institutions, as a source of corruption and oppression. He liked to think that he had discovered in the principle of utility a simple positive principle on which all men would be able to agree so as to reform society on a systematic plan ; and this belief, when once formed, strengthened in him his taste for theoretic simplification joined with a passion for practical reform. Thus it helped the future success of his school and made him of all individual persons the most representative of a century which aimed at making science at once simpler and more useful. In order to make intelligible the bearing, at once speculative and practical, of his work, Bentham multiplied his analogies and metaphors. A second Lavoisier, he sought to give to morals a scientific nomenclature.[1] A second Aristotle, he sought to establish that logic of the will which exists by the same right as the logic of the understanding.[2] Or again, cursorily comparing the new moral science with medicine and with mechanics, he sought to found a psychological dynamics on a scientific pathology.[3] This amounts to achieving the task pursued in common, since the beginning of the century, by all English moralists and psychologists—the founding of a scientific morality on a scientific psychology.

[1] Bowring, vol. iii. p. 273.   [2] Bowring, vol. i. p. iv.
[3] Bowring, vol. i. p. 205.

CHAPTER II

BENTHAM'S PHILOSOPHY OF LAW

IT was to the reform of the science of law that Bentham devoted his life. In his *Introduction to the Principles of Morals and Legislation* he based a theory of punishment and a classification of crimes on the mental and moral pathology which has been outlined in the preceding pages. But already, before the publication of the *Introduction*, he had worked out a complete theory of law, which was not published until many years later, at the beginning of the nineteenth century, when it became known to the public through the *Traités de Législation Civile et Pénale* and the *Théorie des Peines et des Récompenses*.

At the time when Bentham was first beginning to think and to write, an attempt had just been made to systematise English law : [1] Blackstone, the famous author of the *Commentaries on the Laws of England*, had been Bentham's tutor at Oxford in the years 1763 and 1764. Bentham, however, boasted that even then he was not taken in by Blackstone's formulae.[2] Even though both took up a systematic point of view, they did not both adopt the same method in forming their juridical theory.[3] Blackstone adopted the method of *exposition*, and taught law as it was ; Bentham the method of *censure*, teaching law ' as it should be '.[4] Blackstone's is perhaps the best method that has so far been discovered of arranging juridical matter, but it is none the less a ' technical ' method ; that is to say, it is founded on a knowledge of the traditional rules of the legal profession,[5] as opposed to the ' natural ' method which is founded on a knowledge of the general laws of human nature. The science of law as set forth by Blackstone is not a science of reasoning but a science of learning, or,

---

[1] Blackstone, i. Comm. 4.   [2] Bowring, vol. i. p. 249 ; vol. x. p. 45.
[3] Bentham claimed to be the ' anti-Blackstone ' from the time when he wrote the *Fragment on Government* until four years before his death when he was still engaged in refuting Blackstone.
[4] Bowring, vol. i. p. 229.   [5] *Ibid.* p. 237.

to quote Beccaria, ' a domestic tradition '.[1]   If it rests on principles
at all, it can only be on principles which are merely nominal and
fictitious, invented to square with given consequences, or even such
that they can only be adapted to those pretended consequences by a
series of legal fictions.   A disciple of Helvetius, be his name Beccaria
or Bentham, devoted to logical exactitude, desirous of the general
good, and hostile to all class interests, was sure to recognise that the
interests of the judicial as of all other bodies, are sinister and contrary to the interests of the public, and to aim, in the sphere of law,
at substituting for technical fictions the reality of the principle
of utility, that is, the greatest happiness of the greatest number.

In the *Traités de Législation* of 1802, a distinction is drawn between substantive and adjective law.[2]   Adjective law comprises the
whole body of laws of procedure, which define the way in which laws,
once set up, must be applied by the courts without differentiation
between the interests of the judge and those of the public.   But in
the *Introduction to the Principles of Morals and Legislation*, Bentham
does not allude to this fundamental distinction.   At this time he had
only considered reform of procedure by the way, and he was thinking
of the theory of substantive law only when he proposed to divide up
all law into civil, penal and constitutional.   Besides, he had not so far
dealt systematically with constitutional law.[3]   At this time it was
civil and penal law that he was especially studying.   Bentham distinguishes between *purely imperative* law, stated, for example, in the
following way : ' Stealing is forbidden ', and *punitive* law, stated thus :
' Whoever steals will be condemned to be hung '.   Civil law is
made up of the definition of rights (or, what comes to the same
thing, of *obligations*, since the two terms are not only reciprocal but
inseparable) ;   penal law of the definition of those acts by which
rights are violated, that is, of crimes (or, what comes to the same
thing, of *punishments*, which are their reciprocals).[4]   The State, considered as exercising judicial functions, creates obligations and
suppresses failure to meet these obligations by punishments.   Now
the very fact that crimes are committed proves that neither the
principle of the fusion of interests nor that of the natural identity of
interests holds good in these matters ;   the first, because every time
a crime is committed hostile feelings prevail over feelings of sympathy,
the second, because the individual finds that his interest, or at least
what seems to be his interest, lies in betraying the interest of his
neighbour.   The problem for the statesman is to define obligations
and punishments in such a way that private interest shall be brought
by artificial means to coincide with the public interest : ' Law alone
has accomplished what all the natural feelings were not able to do.'[5]

[1] *Dei delitti e delle pene*, § IV.   [2] Bowring, vol. iii. p. 158.
[3] Bowring, vol. i. p. 153.   [4] Bowring, vol. i. p. 151.
[5] Bowring, vol. i. p. 307.

I. CIVIL LAW

The aim of civil law is to define rights. But rights always involve obligations. If I secure a right to the services of another man, an obligation is thereby imposed on him to render me those services. If I acquire the right to use and dispose of a horse, then other men incur the obligation of refraining from using it. Now obligation can be considered in two different ways according to whether the point of view adopted is professional, the standpoint adopted by members of the legal profession, or ' natural ', the standpoint adopted by Utilitarian philosophers.

In the first case, that is from the formal or ' technical ' point of view, the essence of obligation is respect for juridical formality. I have sworn according to prescribed forms that I will act in a given way at a given date in the future. Hence I am bound to act in that way. I am so bound because an oath is of its nature binding, because the juridical formality must be observed. From this point of view the conception of obligation is an original and ultimate conception ; and *obligation is a good* since obligation is by definition conformity to legal order.

The Utilitarian point of view is opposed to this. Law necessarily restricts liberty in proportion to the obligations it creates. It is only at the expense of liberty that it is possible to create rights and to protect person and property and even liberty itself. But every restriction of liberty involves to a greater or a less extent a natural feeling of pain. Hence to impose an obligation is to inflict a pain or to take away a pleasure. Now pain is an evil, pleasure a good. Therefore *all obligation is an evil.* If an obligation is to be justified, it cannot contain in itself the principle of its own justification, as the pseudo-philosophy of the professional jurists would have it do ; it can only be justified on the ground that it is a necessary evil, endowed with a relative utility.

From this point of view, every obligation which is imposed upon me must be expressed as a *service* which I do to another : it is the service which justifies and, at the same time, limits the obligation. Further, it should be noted that although obligations presuppose services, services do not necessarily presuppose obligations. Services can be rendered freely. History shows that they existed before laws were set up ; and before the existence of governments they formed the only social link between man and man. Parents supported their children before the law made it their duty to do so. To-day, too, there are many services which are rendered freely—services of good-will, of convention and of common interest ; and however many new obligations may be created by law, on many points sociability will always have to supplement the impotence of the law.

The notion of services is therefore earlier than the notion of obligations ; and, in the province of civil law, the original notion, from the point of view of the upholder of the principle of general utility, is that of service and not of obligation.[1]

This involved a revolution in juridical terminology, the final conclusions from which do not yet appear to have been drawn in the *Traités de Législation*. Here Bentham distinguished between rights over things—Robinson Crusoe lived for many years without exercising power over any person, he could not have lived without exercising power over things—and rights over services, that is to say rights to the various ways in which one man can be useful to another, either in securing him some good or in keeping him from some evil. But is not this verbal distinction open to the same objection as the distinction between *jura personarum* and *jura rerum*, a distinction classical in Roman law and retained by Blackstone ? *Jura rerum* means ' rights over things ', and that in itself is enough to invalidate the whole classification ; since the heading ' rights over persons ' embraces rights over things almost as much as rights over persons—for instance, the rights of the husband over the goods of his wife, and of the son over the goods of his father, and so on.[2] Must we not go further and maintain, as James Mill,[3] Bentham's disciple, subsequently maintained, that rights are powers, more or less extensive, guaranteed by the government to an individual enabling him to make use of a person or a thing for the satisfaction of his desires. But since satisfying a man's desire is doing him a *service*, cannot the term ' service ' be applied equally well to people and to things ? It has been used in a restricted sense by both the Roman and the English jurists. Should it not now be used to signify the sum of those means of satisfying our desires which we are authorised, by virtue of rights, to take whether from persons or from things ? Now the revolution which has taken place is a revolution not only in words but in things. The examination of Bentham's classification of obligation reveals the profound opposition between the two theories —what we have called the professional or ' technical ' theory on the one hand, and the ' natural ' theory on the other.

According to Bentham,[4] the means of acquiring rights over services or, in other words, the causes which determine the legislator to create obligations, can be referred to three heads. The first of these is the existence of a *superior need*, that is to say a ' *need of receiving the service, superior to the inconvenience of rendering it* '. The duties of a father to his children may be burdensome for him, but this evil is nothing in comparison with the evil which would result from their neglect. The duty of defending the state may be still more burdensome ; but if the state were not defended, it would not exist.

---

[1] Bowring, vol. iii. p. 179.   [2] Bowring, vol. iii. p. 184.
[3] *See* James Mill, *Jurisprudence*, III.   [4] Bowring, vol. i. p. 339.

The second of these causes is the existence of a *former service*, that is to say of a ' *service rendered, in consideration of which there is required of him who has received the benefit, an indemnity, an equivalent, in favour of him who has supported the burthen* '. This is the basis of the rights of parents over children when in the order of nature the strength of riper years succeeds the helplessness of childhood ; it is the basis also of the right of wives that their marriage shall continue after age has withered the beauty which was the first cause of the love they inspired. Or, finally, to take more specific instances, supposing that a surgeon has rendered aid to a sick man who had lost consciousness and was unable to ask it, or that a depositary has employed his labour or has made pecuniary sacrifices to preserve the deposit without being required to do so ; in the one case the sick man is legally indebted to the surgeon, in the other the deposer to the depositary. Repayment of past services is the means of creating future services.—There remains the third cause ; the existence of some pact, convention or contract, that is to say of ' *the making of a promise between two or more persons, upon the understanding that it is regarded as legally binding* '. Now it is easy to see that the order in which these three sources of obligation have been enumerated here is exactly the reverse of the order in which an acceptance of the professional or technical conception of obligation would require them to be placed.

In fact, from this point of view, the typical and perfect form of obligation is that which arises from the contract. This is the most *formal* of all types of obligation : the two parties have been brought together and have agreed, in an act in proper form, on all the conditions to which they promise to conform in the future. The agreement must be respected because the formalities were observed at the outset.—But what can be said of the case where the obligation is founded on a ' former service ' ? The jurist who considers the existence of a preceding contract as the really legitimate source of obligation will evade the difficulty by a fiction, and will say that there is here an obligation *quasi ex contractu*, and that everything has taken place as if there had been a contract. In other words, where the Utilitarian language is simple and direct the traditional philosophy of law is forced to resort to fictions and roundabout expressions.—Finally, all juridical systems, of whatever kind, are forced to allow certain cases where obligation rests, purely and simply, on a ' superior need '. Even the jurists who hold that the pact makes law of itself, and that the contract is sacred because it is a contract, are forced to recognise that a contract can be broken for the sake of public utility or in a case of *force majeure*. But by this admission they refute their theory. If, in fact, the contract ought to be broken purely and simply because it is better from the point of view of general utility that it should not be observed, this must mean that it is the principle of utility and not the principle of contract which is sovereign in the sphere of legislation. Instead of treating the case of ' superior

need ' as an exception to the general rule, it is better to treat it on
the contrary as the typical and primitive case of obligation. In the
cases where the contract is annulled, the jurists generally get out of
the difficulty by maintaining that the bargain was null in itself—
another useless fiction.[1] No bargain is null in itself or valid in
itself. In every case it is the law which gives or denies it validity.
But the law needs reasons whether to allow or to disallow it. An
equivocal origin must not be admitted in jurisprudence any more
than in physics. Now the relevance of the pact is that it proves
the interest of the contracting parties. It is the ground of utility
which gives the pact its strength, and it is on this ground alone that
the cases in which it should be kept and those in which it should be
annulled can be distinguished.

Bentham enumerates nine cases in which, in his opinion, the law
ought not to sanction exchanges, and in which the interests of the
parties should be regulated as if the bargain did not exist.[2] Let
us take the first of these cases, that of ' undue concealment ', where
the object acquired turns out to be of an inferior value to that which
has served as the motive of its acquisition ; as, for instance, when I
have bought a horse and discover later that some defect in it which is
not easily noticeable but which lowers its value was concealed from
me at the moment of the purchase. In a case like this, and admitting
certain specified conditions, the contract of exchange should be
annulled. Moreover, it is not so easy as might appear to estimate
utility and to calculate profit and loss ; for since, in this transaction,
one of the parties has gained as much as the other has lost, why
could not the gain and the loss be treated as equivalent ? The
reason is to be found in a principle of mental pathology fundamental
to Bentham, according to which ' the *advantage of gaining* cannot be
compared with the *evil of losing* '.[3] This proposition is itself deduced
from two others. On the one hand every man naturally expects to
preserve what he has ; the feeling of expectation is natural to man
and is founded on the ordinary course of events, since, taking the
whole sum of men, acquired wealth is not only preserved but even
increased. All loss is therefore unexpected, and gives rise to
deception, which is a pain—the pain of frustrated expectation. On
the other hand the deduction (or addition) of a portion of wealth
will produce in the sum of happiness of each individual a deduction
(or an addition) more or less great according to the proportion between
the portion deducted or added and the remaining or original portion.
This causes the inequality in the situation of the loser and of the
winner. At the gaming-table, for example, in spite of the fact
that the chances in money are even, the chances in happiness are
always unfavourable. If I possess a thousand pounds and play
with five hundred, either I win and my fortune is increased by a
third, or I lose, and it is diminished by a half. If, possessing a

[1] Bowring, vol. i. p. 333.   [2] Bowring, vol. i. p. 331.   [3] *Ibid.*

thousand pounds, I play with a thousand, either I win, and at most my happiness is doubled with the doubling of my fortune, or I lose, and my happiness is destroyed.[1] Such are the considerations, drawn from the principle of utility, on which the legislator should take his stand in pronouncing invalid contracts of exchange in certain cases when they occasion more disadvantages than profits.

This does not, however, amount to saying that contracts ought to be annulled in *all* cases in which they ultimately prove disadvantageous, nor must they be annulled in cases where the unfavourable events are only accidental and subsequent to the conclusion of the bargain. To make invalid must be the exception, and to ratify the rule. Once more, this is not because the pact makes law, but because it is useful as a general rule that conventions should be respected. Every time an individual who possesses something relinquishes it in another's interest, or, finding himself capable of rendering a service, renders it to another man, he is renouncing a pleasure or accepting a pain ; but this is a thing that he cannot do without motive. Now *motive* means *pleasure* : the *pleasure of friendship* or of benevolence if he gives the thing for nothing ; the *pleasure of gain* if he makes it a means of exchange ; *the good of security* if he has given it to save himself from some evil ; the *pleasure of reputation* if he hopes by giving it to gain the good opinion of his fellows. The sum of enjoyments is therefore necessarily increased for both the parties concerned in the transaction. The total advantage of advantageous exchanges is more than the equivalent of the total disadvantage of unfavourable bargains. The gains of commerce are greater than its losses, since the world is richer now than it was in its uncivilised state. To sum up, *every alienation implies advantage*, and it is on the strength of this consideration of utility that alienations must as a general rule be upheld.[2] Further, it is not enough that conventions should be sanctioned by the law, they must also be interpreted. In all countries the law has provided, and has done right to provide, for the shortsightedness of individuals by doing for them what they would have done for themselves if their imagination had been able to anticipate the course of events. With regard to the obligations which a contract, once signed, legally imposes on the contracting parties, a distinction must be made [3] between the *original* obligations, that is to say, obligations which are expressly mentioned in the contract, and *adjectitious* obligations which the contracting parties neglected to mention in the original contract but which the law considers should be added to the original obligations.

It is here that the lawyers find it convenient to resort to the fiction of quasi-contracts. ' Where there has been no convention, there they suppose that there have been one, two, a thousand ; they have

[1] Bowring, vol. i. p. 304.　　　　　　[2] Bowring, vol. i. p. 330.
[3] Bowring, vol. iii. pp. 190-1.

the effrontery or the folly to ascribe wishes to you which they avow you never had : and this is what is called *reasoning* among them.' In plain language it is, according to Bentham, on the consideration of their utility, that is, of their tendency to produce the greatest happiness of the greatest number, that these adjectitious obligations must be determined. Bentham's analyses always follow the same order ; they pass from the abstract to the concrete, from the fictitious to the real. ' The word obligation may be employed in an abstract sense : it may, for the convenience of discourse, be spoken of as a fictitious entity ; but it ought to be possible to decipher such language into the language of pure and simple truth—into that of fact. To understand abstract terms, is to know how to translate figurative language into language without figure.' [1] In this Bentham is acting as the faithful disciple of Hume. Hume had refuted the theory which maintained that a feeling of obligation was necessarily attached to the notion of promise. He had tried to prove that promises are human inventions, founded on considerations of necessity and social utility, and that their apparently obligatory nature is due to man's natural egoism, reinforced by the feeling for the general interest and by the ' artifices of the politicians ' ; and that the mystery of the promise or contract is comparable, in the last resort, to the mysteries of trans-substantiation and of holy orders, ' where a certain form of words, along with a certain intention, changes entirely the nature of an external object, and even of a human creature '.[2] Bentham would not have been unwilling to compare the fictions of the legal profession to the absurd mysteries invented by the priests. Hume's psychology refers the abstract idea, which is the type of all the fictitious entities [3] of which Bentham speaks, to the sensible impressions of which it is the copy. In his philosophy of law Bentham, like Hume before him, refers the idea of obligation to the services which justify it, to the pleasures and pains which make up its whole reality.

In short, it is in the compensation of the evil of obligation by the good of service that there appears the calculus, the operation of moral arithmetic, which forms the essence of civil law. A bad law is a law which imposes an obligation without rendering any service. Now what will be the practical application of this arithmetic of pleasures and pains ? The definition of the right of property may be taken to constitute the chief object of civil law : what is justice but the respect for the right of property once that right has been defined ? What is then the definition of the right of property which follows logically from the principle of utility ? It is strange to remark what uncertainty there is on this point in the Utilitarian

---

[1] Bowring, vol. iii. p. 181. [2] *Treatise*, bk. iii. part ii. sect. v.
[3] Bentham borrowed this expression from d'Alembert. See *Introduction to Principles of Morals and Legislation*, Preface, p. 109.

doctrine of the eighteenth century as expounded by the forerunners
of Bentham and even by Bentham himself.

Locke had tried to found the right of property directly on the
notion of utility. According to him natural reason ' tells us that
men, being once born, have a right to their preservation, and
consequently to meat and drink and such other things as Nature
affords for their subsistence ', and again : ' God, who hath given the
world to men in common, hath also given them reason to make use
of it to the best advantage of life and convenience '.[1] But do we
possess a measure of the utility of things ? And, first of all, what
is the utility in question ? Is it the apparent utility whose definition
we should find in the expression of the desires of each individual ?
But is it certain that desire is the measure of need ? Do we not
desire unlimited possessions ? and does not the pleasure of possessing
without enjoying in itself constitute a joy which must be taken into
consideration like any other, from the point of view of the principle
of utility ? Or is the utility in question the real absolute utility,
conceived as independent of individual and momentary preferences ?
How can this be measured ? Is it possible, perhaps, to look for an
objective measure of the utility resulting from the possession of an
object not in the verbal expression of a desire, but in the amount of
labour which a given individual is prepared to provide in order to
gain possession of it ? In this way, by starting from the notion
of utility, one would be led to found the right of property on the
notion of labour. This, again, is what Locke does. ' Though ',
he says, ' the earth and all inferior creatures be common to all men,
yet every man has a " property " in his own " person ". This
nobody has any right to but himself. The " labour " of his body
and the " work " of his hands, we may say, are properly his. Whatsoever, then, he removes out of the state that Nature hath provided
and left it in, he hath mixed his labour with it, and joined to it
something that is his own, and thereby makes it his property . . . this
law of reason makes the deer that Indian's who hath killed it '.[2]
Nevertheless, though we have tried to show by what logical stages it
would be possible to pass from the one to the other, these two notions
of property remain distinct. The desire to possess may drive us to
work and to produce beyond our needs : ' if gathering the acorns or
other fruits of the earth, makes a right to them, then any one may
engross as much as he will '. Locke admits the contradiction and
specifies that ' the same law of Nature that does by this means give
us property, does also bound that property too. " God has given
us all things richly " is the voice of reason confirmed by inspiration. But how far has he given it us ? " To enjoy." As much as
any one can make use of, to any advantage, of life before it spoils,
so much he may by his labour fix a property in. Whatever is beyond

[1] Locke, *Of Government*, bk. ii. ch. v. §§ 25, 26.
[2] Locke, *Of Government*, bk. ii. ch. v. §§ 27, 30.

this is more than his share, and belongs to others.   Nothing was made
by God for man to spoil or destroy '.[1]
Now nature does not of itself regulate the amount of labour provided
in proportion to the utility of the object.   According to Locke, this
result is attained in a primitive society where the products of labour
decay quickly and where therefore the producer cannot preserve
them in a lasting way ; but this ceases to be the case with the invention of money, a conventional sign of value which can be accumulated
indefinitely and kept for ever.   Locke might have added that
neither does society regulate property in proportion to the amount
of labour ; for the individual who has laboured is free to transfer
the property earned by his labour to an individual who has not
laboured.   Locke's theory, then, whether he founds the right of
property on utility or whether he founds it on labour, is doubly
revolutionary.   Priestley, a disciple of Locke, founded ' the very
idea of property, or right of any kind . . . on a regard for the general
good of the society, under whose protection it is enjoyed ; and
nothing is properly a *man's own*, but what general rules, which have
for their object the good of the whole, give to him '.   And he drew
the conclusion that in all cases in which owners of property abuse
their rights, ' that awful and ultimate tribunal, in which every
citizen hath an equal voice, may demand the resignation of them '.[2]
Again, Adam Smith also was inspired by Locke in his economic
theory, and founded value on labour, a theory which all the Utilitarian
political economists borrowed from him.   Consequently, Adam
Smith could not do otherwise than point out the gulf which divides
society as it is, with its capitalists and landed proprietors, from a
society in which each man receives the product of his own labour.
We shall see too how, at the time of the French Revolution, William
Godwin appropriated Adam Smith's observations, and, with the
principle of utility as his basis, formulated for the first time in the
modern world, a doctrine which was at once communistic and
anarchistic.
But, from another point of view, Hume, in his *Treatise*, took up
quite a different attitude.   He distinguished three kinds of goods :
the goods of the spirit, the goods of the body, and finally external
goods—those which we acquire by our labour or by fortune.   Now,
the goods of this third category are exposed to the violence of the
rest of mankind, and, moreover, they do not exist in sufficient
quantities to supply the desires and the needs of all.[3]   It is therefore
necessary to lay down ' general rules ' for the defence of property ;
but these rules ' are not derived from any utility or advantage, which
either the *particular* person or the public may reap from his enjoyment of any *particular* goods, beyond what would result from the

[1] Locke, *Of Government*, bk. ii. ch. v. § 31.
[2] Priestley, *Essay on . . . Government*, sect. ii. p. 41 (1771 ed.).
[3] *Treatise*, bk. iii. part ii. sect. ii.

possession of them by any other person '. Since for one thing, the same commodity might at the same moment be equally useful to several people. Then again, the determination of the utility of a thing is subject to too many controversies, and men, in judging it, are too biased and too full of passions for it to be possible to base on this determination any fixed and general rule. On the day when men shall be willing to agree together to set up a rule of justice, ' it must immediately occur to them, as the most natural expedient, that everyone continue to enjoy what he is at present master of, and that property or constant possession be conjoin'd to the immediate possession '. [1] Such is the effect of habit, that it is difficult for us to live without possessing those things which we have long possessed, and easy to live without those things which we have never enjoyed. Hume therefore founded the right of property directly on a consideration neither of utility nor of labour (for it is only the power of the association of ideas which joins the idea of the labourer to the idea of the land on which he labours) but simply on habit and on established associations. *Occupation* is a title to property, and no doubt there is a general ground of utility in favour of this : men are unwilling to leave property in suspense even for the shortest time, or, to open the least door to violence and disorder. But above all there is a definite reason drawn from the association of ideas : ' the first possession always engages the attention most ; and did we neglect it, there would be no colour of reason for assigning property to any succeeding possession '. [2] The same applies and with even more force to *prescription*. [3] The same again applies in the case in which we acquire objects as property by *accession* ; we are the proprietors of the fruits of our garden, and of the dung of our flock by virtue of the normal operation of the laws of association : ' where objects are connected together in the imagination, they are apt to be put on the same footing, and are commonly suppos'd to be endow'd with the same qualities '. [4] *Succession*, finally, is a legitimate title to property : by the influence of the *relation* between them, or of the association of ideas, are we not naturally led to turn our attention to the son after the father's death, and to attribute to him a title to the possessions of his father ? [5]

In the Benthamite philosophy of civil law, the conservative and the revolutionary tendencies both appear in turn, although the first constantly and to a great extent predominates over the second. Bentham attributed [6] four aims to civil law : subsistence, abundance, security and equality. The law can do nothing directly to produce subsistence and abundance. For abundance, which presupposes subsistence, is brought about gradually through the operation of the same causes which produce subsistence ; but, as regards subsistence, need and the satisfaction of need are punishment and reward enough

---

[1] *Treatise*, bk. iii. part ii. sect. iii.   [2] *Ibid.*   [3] *Ibid.*   [4] *Ibid.*
[5] *Ibid.*   [6] Bowring, vol. i. pp. 302-3.

to exempt the legislator from intervening : if no direct laws to promote subsistence had been made, it can be imagined that no one would have neglected it. There remains the second pair of aims—security and equality. It is by the analysis of the right of property undertaken by Bentham that we are enabled to determine how far these two ends can be pursued concurrently, and how far the one ought to be sacrificed to the other.

Man differs from the beasts in that he does not live in the present only ; he lives in the future also and counts on the future. Security is a good in that it justifies that feeling of safety which makes it possible for man to make a general scheme of conduct, to bind together the various successive moments of his existence so as to make of them a single life. Any menace to this feeling of *expectation* produces a pain, the pain of *disappointment* or of *frustrated expectation* ; a pain of which the Utilitarian principle prescribes the avoidance, and one whose gravity is proportional to the actual intensity of the feeling of expectation. The principle which enjoins the avoidance of the pain of frustrated expectation (or *disappointment preventing principle*) is, according to Bentham, second in importance only to the principle of utility from which it is derived ; it is the precise form of the principle of security and is the very foundation of property.[1] Property is the justified expectation of drawing certain advantages from the thing which you think you possess ; it is not a physical reality but a belief set up as a certainty. This expectation is created by the law : in the state of nature, the number of cases in which a man can count upon the secure enjoyment of the goods of which he has gained possession by his own hand is very small indeed. It is an expectation which the law must guard against destroying once it has been created. In consulting this grand principle of security, what ought the legislator to direct, Bentham asks, with regard to the mass of property which exists ? ' He ought to maintain the distribution which is actually established. This, under the name of justice, is with reason regarded as his first duty : it is a general and simple rule applicable to all states, adapted to all plans, even those which are most opposed to each other '.[2]

In founding the right of property on the principle of security Bentham was in his thought and expression a true disciple of Hume. Vice and virtue, said Hume, do not exist in external objects, in relations, or in facts : ' vice and virtue, therefore, may be compar'd to sounds, colours, heat and cold, which, according to modern philosophy, are not qualities in objects, but perceptions in the mind '.[3] Justice is but the legal consecration accorded to habits, which had arisen from the previous operation of the association of ideas. Bentham says likewise that ' There is no form, or colour, or visible

[1] Bowring, vol. i. pp. 307-9   [2] *Ibid.* p. 311.
[3] Hume, *Treatise*, bk. iii. part i. sect. i.

trace, by which it is possible to express the relation which constitutes property. It belongs not to physics, but to metaphysics : it is altogether a creature of the mind.'[1] The act of wearing a garment, or of eating a piece of food, can be accurately defined in so far as it is a material act, but it does not constitute what is called the proprietorship of the garment or of the food ; what does constitute it is a feeling of expectation, partly confirmed, and to a great extent artificially created, by the law. As regards the different titles to property, Bentham enumerates them in the same order in which Hume had enumerated them—an order which is moreover classical and common to Hutcheson and to Hume. Bentham refused to call them ' titles ', a name which was too abstract and too juridical for his taste, preferring the expression ' investitive ' or ' collative events '—an expression which brings the mind back to the physical reality to which is attached the feeling of expectation and with which the idea of property is associated.[2] In Bentham, *actual possession* corresponds to *occupation*, *ancient bona-fide possession* to *prescription* (yet Bentham considers that ancient bona-fide possession, *notwithstanding opposite title*, corresponds more exactly to prescription), and to *accession* correspond those other investitive events which he is careful to enumerate in detail.[3] These different ' collations ' of property are useful, Bentham tells us, to the extent to which they encourage labour, and consequently, with the increase of social wealth, the increase of the chances of happiness for humanity ; they are useful, above all, in that they satisfy the feeling of expectation. The feeling of expectation had already been considered by Hume as the principal ingredient in the complex notion of justice. ' This experience,' says Hume, ' assures us still more, that the sense of interest has become common to all our fellows, and gives us a confidence of the future regularity of their conduct : And 'tis only on the expectation of this, that our moderation and abstinence are founded ' ; and he adds that ' justice establishes itself by a kind of convention or agreement ; that is, by a sense of interest, suppos'd to be common to all, and where every single act is performed in expectation that others are to perform the like '.[4] ' The views of jurists,' says Bentham, ' must have been extremely confused, since they have paid no particular attention to a sentiment so fundamental in human life: the word expectation is scarcely to be found in their vocabulary ; an argument can scarcely be found in their works, founded upon this principle. They have followed it, without doubt, in many instances, but it has been from instinct, and not from reason. If they had known its extreme importance, they would not have omitted to name it ; to point it out instead of leaving it in the crowd.'[5] We can now understand the nature of the revolution which Bentham proposed to effect : he wished to translate the

---

[1] Bowring, vol. i. p. 308.   [2] *Ibid*. vol. iii. p. 189.   [3] *Ibid*. vol. i. p. 326.
[4] Hume, *Treatise*, bk. iii. part ii. sect. ii.   [5] Bowring, vol. i. p. 308.

technical abstractions of the legal terminology into the realistic language of the new English psychology.

What then becomes of Bentham's view according to which the principle of utility is distinguishable from all ' arbitrary ' principles, in that it is a principle not of conservation but of reform ? If we start from the principle of utility, and proceed by the mediation of the principle of security (or, which comes to the same thing, of the *disappointment preventing principle*), shall we not be led to justify, without exception and without criticism, all inveterate habits, all established beliefs, in a word, all juridical prejudices ? ' There is nothing more diversified than the condition of property in America, England, Hungary, Russia : in the first country the cultivator is proprietor ; in the second he is farmer ; in the third he is attached to the soil ; in the fourth he is a slave. Still the supreme principle of security directs the preservation of all these distributions, how different soever their natures, and though they do not produce the same amount of happiness.'[1] And Bentham, taking his stand on this essentially conservative definition of property and justice, condemned, as Hobbes had done, that classical education which accustoms us to respect in the history of antiquity ' public acts of injustice, atrocious in themselves, (abolition of debts and divisions of lands) always coloured under specious names, always accompanied by a pompous eulogium respecting the Roman virtues '[2]

We have seen, however, that among the four goods of civil society Bentham includes the good of equality together with the good of security ; moreover, what he means by the word equality, taken in its strict sense, is neither political nor civil equality, but equality ' taken as relative to the distribution of property '. The law should never create an inequality : for, in a society constituted to secure the greatest happiness of the greatest number, there is no reason why the law should seek to give more to one individual than to another ; and, besides, the advantage gained on the one side by the favoured party would not compensate for the loss sustained by all those who are not favoured in the same way. But in a society in which wealth is already unevenly distributed there is a contradiction between what is prescribed by the principles of security and of equality respectively. What are the reasons which justify, in Bentham's view, the tendency towards the equalisation of fortunes ? What are they worth when set against the reasons drawn from the conservative principle of expectation, and how can the two be reconciled ?

The good of equality could not be founded for Bentham, as it would for a spiritualistic philosopher, on such an assertion, for instance, as that of the indivisibility of the human person. It must be deduced from the principle of utility, if that principle is indeed the sole principle of morals. Bentham has attempted this deduction

[1] Bowring, vol. i. p. 311.   [2] *Ibid.* p. 318.

by means of a series of propositions which he calls axioms of mental pathology.[1] Among these, the two following, which are independent of each other and on which all the others depend, may be considered fundamental. First axiom : each portion of wealth is connected with a corresponding portion of happiness. Second axiom : the excess of happiness on the part of the most wealthy will not be so great as the excess of his wealth. Further Bentham recognises the approximate and almost conventional nature of the first proposition, and calls common experience to witness in justification of the second. Possibly, however, a third proposition, which Bentham also presents as an axiom will make it possible at the same time to express the first axiom in a more precise form, and also to reduce the second axiom to the first. Bentham does in fact tell us that ' the loss of a portion of wealth will produce a loss of happiness to each individual, more or less great, according to the proportion between the portion he loses and the portion he retains '. Now what Bentham asserts in this proposition of a negative increase of the quantity of wealth is equally true of a positive increase. In that case we are able to say not only that for each particle of wealth there is a corresponding particle of happiness, but also that the increase of happiness corresponds, in a fixed relation, to the increase of wealth. The increase will be less great than the increase of wealth because it will be equal not to the absolute amount of the increase, but to the relation of this quantity and the quantity of wealth already acquired, a proportion which is ever diminishing : this verifies the second axiom.[2] Further, below a certain level, the proportion grows (either positively or negatively) faster than the law would demand ; it grows beyond all limits. If, in taking three-fourths of my fortune, you trench upon my physical wants, and in taking only the half, you leave these wants untouched, the loss of happiness will not simply be the half, but the double, the quadruple, the tenfold of what it is in the other case : ' one knows not ', says Bentham, ' where to stop '.

It is easy to see, by discussing methodically all the possible cases, that consequences favourable to the equalitarian thesis follow from these two axioms. First let us examine the case of the effect of a portion of wealth which has always been in the hands of the interested parties. In this case, the greater the disproportion between the two masses of wealth, the less probable is it that there will be an equally great disproportion between the two corresponding masses of happiness, and, conversely, the more nearly equal the actual proportion, the greater will be the total mass of happiness. Now take the case of the effect produced by a mass of wealth coming for the first time into the hands of a new possessor. In this case, among co-partakers of equal fortunes, the more the distribution of a portion of wealth leaves this equality undisturbed, the greater will be the total mass of happiness ; and, among co-partakers with unequal

[1] Bowring, vol. i. p. 304.   [2] Bowring, vol. iii. pp. 228-9.

fortunes, the more the distribution helps to lessen their inequality and bring them nearer to one another, the greater will be the total mass of happiness.   Thirdly, let us consider the effect produced by a mass of wealth which is leaving the hands of the interested parties. In this case, in the case of equal fortunes, the greater the number of people between whom a given loss will be divided, the less considerable will be the resulting diminution in the total mass of happiness ; and, in the case of unequal fortunes, the diminution of happiness caused by a diminution of wealth will be smaller in proportion to the extent to which the distribution of the loss is such as to bring the parties as near as possible to equality.   Finally, let us determine the effect produced by a particle of wealth which, in order to pass into the hands of one man as a gain, must be sustained as loss by another.   In this case, as between competitors with equal fortunes, what is gained by one must be lost by the other, but the evil of the loss will always outweigh the advantage of the gain ; in the case of unequal fortunes, if, on the one hand, the loser is the less rich, the evil of the loss will be aggravated by the inequality ; [1] if, on the other hand, the loser is the richer of the two, the evil effected by the menace to security will be partly compensated for by the good, which is in proportion to the amount of progress made towards equality.[2]   This last instance shows that the good of equality has to be weighed against the good of security ; and further that the good of security always remains ' pre-eminent ' in relation to the good of equality. For clearly, there can be security without equality, but without security it is impossible to see how equality, even if once established, could persist for a single moment.   How can these two goods be reconciled ?   Bentham, who is very circumspect and very conservative in these matters, confines himself to suggesting two methods.

The one, which is wholly negative, consists in suppressing the obstacles which an ill-formed legislation has put in the way of the free circulation of wealth, and, consequently, of its gradual levelling.[3] English law, in particular, puts restraints on the power of alienating land by the juridical stratagem of entail.   These wholly negative checks should be suppressed.   For the man who seeks to transfer landed property proves thereby that he is unwilling to keep it, that he cannot improve it, and that he may possibly be obliged to let it deteriorate in order to satisfy a present want.   The man who wishes to buy proves on the contrary, by this readiness, that he certainly does not intend to let it deteriorate, and perhaps even that he means to increase its value.

The other method, which is positive, solves, so Bentham maintains, the problem of distributing wealth more evenly without disappointing any expectation.   The only mediator between the

---

[1] Cf. Hume, *An Inquiry concerning the Principles of Morals*, sect. iii. part ii.
[2] Bowring, vol. iii. p. 230.   [3] Bowring, vol. i. p. 333.

opposing interests of equality and security is time. ' Would you follow the counsels of equality without contravening those of security, wait for the natural period which puts an end to hopes and fears—the period of death.' Then, indeed, for a moment, the property has no proprietor, and the legislator can dispose of it without damaging the expectations of the original proprietor, who is no more, and without damaging, at least to the same extent, the expectations of the heirs and legatees, who have not yet become proprietors.[1] Hence the possibility of a series of legislative measures, which tend to equality without injuring security.

With regard to expropriation, Bentham maintains that there is one indispensable condition demanded by the principle of security without which all reform is a greater evil than those which it is intended to remedy,—the condition, that is, that *complete compensation be accorded to those whose salary is diminished or whose employments are suppressed.* It is to the advantage of society to grant this indemnification, for the evil to society of the compensation comes to an end with the death of the individuals to whom the indemnity is granted : ' the only benefit that can be legitimately derived from them (*i.e.* from the reforms in question) is limited to the conversion of perpetual into transitory charges '.[2] It is on the strength of the same principle that, in order to dissolve monastic orders and convents, it would have sufficed to prohibit these societies from receiving new members. They would have disappeared gradually and the individuals would have suffered no privation at all.[3]

But it is in the case of wills and successions that the method instituted by Bentham is especially applicable. The legislator must have three aims in view in dealing with the law of successions—to provide for the subsistence of the rising generation ; to prevent the pain of disappointment ; and to promote the equalisation of fortunes. With regard to wills, he will limit the freedom to bequeath in so far as this limitation will not prove an excessive encouragement to dissipation. As regards successions, he will institute equal division between children,[4] and, failing immediate ascendants and descendants and their direct descendants, he will turn over the goods to the public exchequer on the condition, required by the principle stated above, ' of distributing the interest as an annuity among all the relations in the ascending line, in whatever degree, in equal portions '. It might be objected to this legislative arrangement that ' the collateral relations who would be excluded . . . may be in want ', but Bentham's doctrine does not found the right of property directly on the principle of utility and on the consideration of needs, but on the principle of security and the consideration of expectations, and the collaterals concerned ' have for their natural resource the

[1] Bowring, vol. i. p. 312.   [2] *Ibid.* p. 320-1.   [3] *Ibid.* p. 320.
[4] Adam Smith advocated equal division in 1776 (*Wealth of Nations*, vol. i. pp. 386-7).

property of their respective ancestors ; and they cannot have fixed
their expectations or their plan of life upon this foundation·'.[1]

Thus the philosophy of utility, which claims to be a realistic
philosophy, is opposed, as far as civil law is concerned, to the contract
philosophy which seems to be sustained by vague notions and legal
fictions. Further, although it is to Helvetius and Beccaria that
Bentham owes, as we shall see, his theory of penal law, it is undeniably
to Hume that he owes the criticism of the notion of contract and
the theory of the right of property. Now we distinguished two
tendencies in Hume, the one towards naturalism, the other towards
rationalism ; clearly in this case the first predominates over the
second. Bentham affirms the ' pre-eminence ' of the good of
security over the good of equality. That security is a good has the
self-evidence of an axiom ; that equality is a good must be demonstrated mathematically, by deduction from other axioms. It is
even questionable whether in making *equality* one of the distinct
ends of civil law Bentham was not following a prejudice based on
external considerations. It is one of his theses that the sentimental
principle, though confused and vague, is not radically false like the
ascetic principle ; in its conclusions, when these have been sufficiently
analysed, it usually coincides with the principle of utility. Now
the notion of *equity* is a current notion in juridical philosophy : the
problem for the philosopher of utility is to discover logical detours,
capable of conferring on this vague notion the character of an exact
and rigorous mathematical truth ; and this is what Bentham did
in fact attempt. If the principle of security is for Bentham the
fundamental principle of civil law, his juridical philosophy would
seem to be in its essence a philosophy of tradition, empirical in
nature. There is no natural law true for all times and for all countries.
There are as many distinct laws as there are habits, that is, inveterate
associations of ideas, in every century and in every nation. How do
associations of ideas, which are fortuitous, contingent, and variable,
bring about an appearance of order ? This is the mystery of nature
before which Hume's naturalism invites us to bow down our reason.
But the new Utilitarian morality embraces, besides, a rationalistic
tendency, which was already noticeable in Hume, and was much
more definite in Helvetius and in Bentham. It is probable that the
tendency of the philosophy of civil law in Bentham towards equalitarianism is proportionate to the tendency of the rationalistic inspiration to predominate at times over the naturalistic inspiration.
    The rationalist believes in the all-powerfulness of science : was it not
this belief which was at this very time prompting the philosopher of
utility to work for the constitution of an exact science of morals and
of politics ?   Just as science guarantees to man the power to transform
physical nature at will and without limits, so also, if it be true to its

----

[1] Bowring, vol. i. p. 334.

word, it should guarantee him the possibility of transforming human nature without limits. Physiological and physical causes are negligible : education has the faculty of transforming the human character to an unlimited extent, of making all men intellectually equal, and therefore worthy of possessing equal wealth. This is the theory of Helvetius, Bentham's master. Hartley, too, for whom the law of indefinite progress was a strictly intellectual law, derived from the law of the association of ideas, affirmed the necessary tendency of the human race towards a final state in which all men would be at once perfectly happy and perfectly equal. Hartley also was a source of inspiration to Bentham.

Further, the rationalist is inclined to neglect the particular in order to confine himself to the consideration of the general. The existence of ' general facts ' provide him with a convenient means of distinguishing, in a roundabout way, the necessary from the accidental. Granted the existence of individuals, he finds it convenient to admit, first of all, that all individuals can be considered sensibly equal. In a ' general observation ' which precedes his ' propositions of pathology upon which the advantage of equality is founded ', Bentham admits that this is a convention and a postulate. After stating the ' axiom ' that ' each portion of wealth is connected with a corresponding portion of happiness ', he certainly adds that, to speak accurately, one should say ' has a certain *chance* of being so connected '. But unless we leave out of account ' the sensibility of the particular individual, and the exterior circumstances in which he may be placed ', any kind of general proposition is impossible. These two abstractions are sufficiently justified, Bentham tells us, if, on the one hand, they are nearer the truth than any others which could be substituted for them, and if, on the other hand, they form the least unsuitable basis for the legislator. Thus we seem to be rendering Bentham's thought exactly if we say that we must be equalitarians just in so far as we are desirous of setting up a science of morality as a rational science.

Had they ever been faced by a revolutionary crisis, the supporters of the principle of utility could not have avoided splitting into two extreme factions, some heading straight for equalitarian communism, and others becoming apologists of the hereditary and traditionalistic principle. As for the Utilitarian philosophy, properly so called, the philosophy which Bentham was already striving to found, and of which he was one day to be the recognised head, it already seems to tend towards holding a course equally removed from the two extremes. What were the reasons for this ? They were many, and were not yet all of them revealed to Bentham ; but the moderate equalitarianism, which was later to be the doctrine of the sect, already found a precise expression in the manuscripts from which Dumont extracted the *Traités*—' When security and equality are in opposition, there should be no hesitation : equality should give way. . . . The establishment of equality is a chimera : the only thing which can be done is to lessen inequality '.[1]

2. PENAL LAW

Penal law defines crimes, and lays down punishments in order to suppress them. Now the conception of punishment, like the conception of obligation, varies according to whether it is considered from the point of view of the principle of utility, or from the technical point of view of the legal profession.

The magistrate acquires the habit, derived from his profession, of administering a punishment for every crime with which he has to deal. He thus comes inseparably to associate the idea of punishment with the idea of crime ; he comes to believe that there is a natural connection between these two terms, and that crime of its very nature demands punishment—that the criminal *deserves* to be punished. What is true in civil law of the idea of obligation is true in penal law of the idea of desert : in the ' technical ' system it is taken to be a fundamental idea which cannot be explained by any simpler notion. From this point of view, punishment appears as a good, since it is the expression of the legal order.

This conception of punishment took shape in the classical philosophy of law. Montesquieu, though a liberal and a reformer, was a magistrate by profession, and in spite of everything was bound by the prejudices of the profession to which he belonged : he considered laws as ' necessary analogies from the *nature of things* ,' and thought it evident, on the strength of an analogy of equity, prior to all positive law, ' that an intelligent being who has done evil to another *deserves* to receive the same evil '. Consequently, in order to put an end to the rule of arbitration in matters concerning the law, he proposed to arrange for the punishment to be derived not ' from the caprice of the legislator but from the *nature of the thing* ', and required that a qualitative analogy be established between the crime and the punishment. For example, it is *natural* that crimes against the security of possessions should be punished by loss of possessions. Punishment, thus conceived, becomes a ' kind of retaliation '; it is ' drawn from the nature of the thing, derived from reason and from the sources of good and evil '.[2] Montesquieu hoped, by thus setting up a kind of objective connection between the nature of the crime and the nature of the punishment, to remove the determination of punishments from what he calls ' the caprice of the legislator '. Bentham, however, thought that Montesquieu's doctrine was also founded on what he called the ' arbitrary ' principle, the principle of sympathy and antipathy. Perhaps it may be the principle of sympathy that makes one speak of the crime as deserving

---

[1] Bowring, vol. i. p. 311. [2] Montesquieu, *Esprit des Lois*, liv. i. ch. i.

the punishment. The equation of these two terms satisfies some need of symmetry in us ; it springs from a kind of professional perversion both of ideas and sentiments. However, it is primarily the principle of antipathy which predominates here. ' It is the principle of antipathy which makes one speak of the crime as *deserving* a punishment ; it is the corresponding principle of sympathy which makes one speak of some action as *deserving* a reward ; this word *merit* can lead to nothing but passions and errors.' [1] Even in the eighteenth century, until about 1760, the greater part of Europe regarded the right to punish as founded on the exigencies of ' *la vindicte publique*' (public vengeance). ' Men punish because they hate ' ... wrote Bentham about the year 1773, ' crimes, they are told, they ought to hate. Crimes it is made a matter of merit for them to hate. . . . How then should they punish but *as* they hate ? . . . What standard clearer ? To know whether they hate in common —to know which of two crimes it is they hate most—what have they but to consult their feelings ? ' [2]

Actually, however, Bentham's aim in applying the principle of utility in the sphere of morals and legislation was to make the reign of reason prevail in these matters over that of instinct and feeling. From the point of view of the professional magistrate punishment, since it satisfies the love of symmetry and the instinct for vengeance, is a good, and is defined as the expression of the legal order. But from the point of view of utility all punishment is an evil since it consists in the infliction of a pain, and pain is an evil. As far as its intrinsic nature goes, punishment is indistinguishable from crime ; it is a kind of counter-crime, committed with the authority of the law. What then is the difference between them ? Is it that ' the crime, for the profit of one man, produces a universal evil ; the punishment, by the suffering of one man, produces a general good '? Rights are violated by acts, and the law has two objects in view with regard to these acts : to repair the evil of the act once it has occurred, and to prevent its recurrence in the future. In the first case, the legal remedy is called a remedy of satisfaction : in the second, two kinds of method can again be adopted ; first to wait until the act is on the point of being committed, and then to intervene, or secondly, to create such motives as will hinder the desire to commit it. The first kind of remedy, which can only be employed in a small number of cases, comprises all preventive and suppressive measures ; the second all penal remedies or punishments. ' According to the principle of utility, legal penalties are evils inflicted under legal forms on individuals proved guilty of some harmful act which is forbidden by law, and inflicted with a view to preventing the occurrence of similar acts ' : [3] or again, in order to introduce into the definition of punishment the notion of

[1] See Bowring, vol. i. pp. 383, 391.　　[2] Bowring, vol. x. p. 69.
[3] *Théorie des Peines*, p. 6 (see Bowring, vol. iii. p. 169).

service, whose domain Bentham extends to cover the whole domain of law, ' legal punishments are services imposed upon those who undergo them for the good of society : thus the punishment of a criminal is spoken of as a debt which he has paid '.[1] To avoid recurrence of the crime, punishment operates in two ways : in correcting the will, and in removing the power, to injure. It influences the will through fear, in reforming the criminal ; it removes the power by some physical act, in incapacitating the criminal.[2] The problem, in the infliction of punishments, can again be reduced to a particular case of the moral arithmetic : to regulate the evil of the punishment so that it does not exceed the good of the service.

It should be added, moreover, that the application of the principle of utility to penal law makes possible a justification in relation to the principle of vengeance. For ' every species of satisfaction, which naturally brings in its train a punishment to the offender, brings a pleasure of vengeance for the party injured '. Now the pleasure of revenge, considered in itself, is a good ; it is therefore an enjoyment which should be cultivated for the same reasons as all other enjoyments. To condemn the pleasures derived from the feeling of antipathy, to declare that ' the desire of vengeance is odious ; all satisfaction drawn from this source is vicious ; forgiveness of injuries is the noblest of virtues ', is to listen to the promptings of the sentimental principle and to speak oneself the language not of reason but of antipathy.[3] The motive of revenge is useful and even necessary to society. Except in those rare heroic cases in which the accuser follows up a crime through sheer love of the public good, the accuser acts on the selfish motive of pecuniary interest, or on the unsocial motive of malevolence : if therefore it is useful that crimes should be followed up at all, it is useful that it should happen in this way.[4] And if, nevertheless, the pleasure of revenge is not great enough to justify the punishment, this is not because it is evil in itself (all pleasure is a good) : it is because this pleasure is in no case equivalent to the punishment (that is, the pain) suffered by the criminal. For the evil of loss is greater than the good of gain—one might be tempted to see in this a fresh application of the principle of security.[5]

This definition of punishment is the fundamental idea, one might almost say the sole idea, from which is developed the entire Benthamite philosophy of penal law. Now it had already been popularised by Beccaria, whose *Dei delitti e delle pene*, which appeared in 1764, had, in 1766, been translated into French by l'Abbé Morellet, at the request of Malesherbes. It became an object of European study, and was soon afterwards translated into English.[6] Bentham had been influenced directly by the writings of Hume,

---

[1] Bowring, vol. iii. p. 179.   [2] Bowring, vol. i. p. 390.
[3] *Ibid*. pp. 371-382.   [4] *Ibid*. vol. i. p. 74.   [5] *Ibid*. vol. iv. pp. 225-6.
[6] Morellet's French translation went through seven editions in six months. The first English translation appeared in 1767.

but he had also come under the same influence indirectly, through the mediation of Helvetius. He had been influenced, directly and profoundly, by Helvetius; unconsciously and indirectly he was once more influenced by him through the channel of his Italian disciple, Beccaria. Like his predecessors, Helvetius and Hume, Beccaria adopted the Newtonian metaphor in order to apply it in the sphere of the mind. ' Such ', he wrote, ' is the wretched condition of the mind of man that he has an exact knowledge of the revolutions of the celestial bodies, although they are so far distant from him, while the notions of morals which are far nearer and far more important remain shrouded in the darkness of uncertainty. Eddying at will in the whirlpool of the passions they are at once established by ignorance and admitted by error '. This is because the very distance of the celestial bodies makes them appear simpler : ' moral principles lose their clearness through being too near our reach '.[1] But there is ' a secret force, like the force of gravity, which makes us always tend towards our well-being, and which grows weaker only by reason of the obstacles which are opposed to it. All men's actions are the result of this tendency, and chastisements, which I will call *political obstacles*, prevent the fatal effects of their collision but do not destroy its cause, which is inseparable from humanity. Like a cunning architect, the legislator is concerned at once to lessen the destructive forces of gravity and to collect together all those which can contribute to the solidity of the edifice '. ' Pleasure and pain ', wrote Beccaria, taking up one of the formulae of Helvetius, ' are the great motives of sensible beings ', and ' the divine Legislator has chosen punishments and rewards as the most powerful of the motives which govern men '.[2] Consequently it was on the two principles of the new philosophy— the principle of utility and the principle of the association of ideas— that Beccaria based his theory of punishment. ' The aim of punishment is neither to torment nor to afflict a sensible being, nor to prevent a crime which has already been committed from taking effect . . . the aim of chastisement is nothing but to prevent the criminal from injuring society any more, and to deter his fellow-citizens from attempting similar crimes.'[3] Now, punishment fulfils this task by reason of the principle of the association of ideas : ' it is proved that the union of ideas is the cement which binds together the whole edifice of the human understanding, and that without it pleasure and pain would be isolated feelings, having no effect on practice '.[4] Laws aim at uniting inseparably, in the minds of men, the two ideas of crime and chastisement, so that they should come, by insensible degrees, to consider punishment as a certain effect of wrong-doing '.

In what then does Bentham's originality in relation to Beccaria

[1] Peccaria, *Dei delitti e delle pene*, § ix.
[2] *Ibid.* § vi.   [3] *Ibid.* § xii.   [4] *Ibid.* § xix.

consist ? It consists in that superior faculty of logical arrangement which was destined one day, after many vicissitudes, to set him up as the head of a school. Beccaria laid down a principle and outlined a system, but neither in the rigorous definition of the principle, nor in the systematic development of its consequences, did he come near to Bentham.

According to Beccaria the basis of punishment is the principle of utility. Nevertheless, he sometimes admits into his exposition the principle of the ' *immutable analogies of things* ',[1] an indeterminate principle whose relation to the principle of utility is not always obvious. More frequently he falls into confusing, in appearance at least, the Utilitarian with the contractual principle. For instance, he condemns the death penalty by taking his stand at once on the principle of the social contract and on the principle of utility— principles which are therefore considered as distinct yet nevertheless equally legitimate. He tells us that the infliction of the death penalty is a violation of the social contract. For since the laws represent the general will, and are no more than the whole sum of the small portions of liberty surrendered by each person, how could it be supposed that the sacrifice of life itself might be included in the sacrifice of the smallest possible portion of liberty surrendered by each person ? On the other hand, he also considers the infliction of the death penalty neither necessary nor useful ; for punishments frighten less by their momentary severity than by their duration.[2] The same is true of Blackstone : is he drawing inspiration from Beccaria or from Hutcheson [3] when he tells us with great precision that the purpose of punishment is not to expiate a crime already committed but to prevent future crimes of the same kind ? [4] But having shown that the justification of punishment lies in utility, he returns, in his definition of the right to punish, to the theory of the social contract. It is on the strength of this contract that the right to punish crimes against the law of nature (*mala in se*) no less than crimes against social laws (*mala prohibita*) is delegated to the sovereign power.[5] Now, is it possible to conceive a coherent philosophy based on two notions which cannot be reduced the one to the other ? Or, if one of these two principles is to be conceived of as derived by analogy from the other, must not the principle of utility be allowed the priority, since law, according to Beccaria, is nothing but the manifestation of power which is most useful to the majority. It remained for Bentham, a better logician, to draw the distinction between the two principles, and in all cases to refer the question of law to the question of end or utility without roundabout or fictitious means. And above all it remained for him, once the principle was laid down, to derive from it not the material for a few

---

[1] *Dei delitti e delle pene*, § xxi.   [2] *Ibid.* §§ xxviii., xxix.
[3] *Philosophiae Moralis Institutio Compendiaria*, lib. iii. c. 8.
[4] *Commentaries*, IV. Comm. 11-12.   [5] *Ibid.* IV. Comm. 7-11.

detached observations, as Beccaria had done, but an attempt at a scientific and systematic theory of penal law. We have seen that Bentham considered that the science of morality founded on the principle of utility is at once a science of classification and a mathematical science. He applied his method to the material of penal law also : he wanted to found a natural classification of crimes and punishments, and to define mathematically the true proportion of punishment to crime.

Bentham considered that the entire task of the natural classification of crimes remained to be done ; for Beccaria had stated that were it necessary to examine and distinguish the different kinds of crime and the way in which they should be punished, ' their nature varies so greatly according to times and places that the detail would be both vast and wearisome '. Thus, he confines himself to pointing out what he calls ' general principles ' and drawing a hasty distinction between crimes which tend directly to the destruction of the society or of its representative (crimes of treason), those which hurt the individual security of citizens by attacking their lives, their goods, or their honour (these he also calls both ' crimes against the security of the individual citizen ' and ' attempts on the liberty and security of citizens '), and finally, actions contrary to those which the law lays down or prohibits in the interest of the public good.[1] This is an extremely vague classification, not founded on the principle of utility, since by virtue of this principle the last category would include all crimes without exception. But what is true of the classification suggested by Beccaria is even more true of the classifications which are taught in the schools. In some cases the classifications are such that there is no common characteristic corresponding to each of the classes which have been distinguished ; this, according to Bentham, is the case with the distinctions drawn by Roman law between *delicta privata et publica*, *publica ordinaria et publica extraordinaria*.[2] Now what would be the condition of any science, of botany, for instance, in which classes were distinguished in such a way that it was impossible to find common characteristics corresponding to them ? In other cases the distinctions established by processes of classification in common use are vague distinctions in which the separations between classes correspond to no defined reality. The division established by Roman law between *culpa lata*, *levis*, *levissima* is a distinction which resides not in the object of classification itself, but in the feeling which some person or other, and in particular a judge, is inclined to experience in regard to the object in question.[3] It is wholly handed over to the arbitrary estimation of the judge to determine into which of these three classes a given case must be placed. In a

---

[1] *Dei delitti e delle pene*, § viii.
[2] Bowring, vol. i. p. 139.   [3] *Ibid*. p. 45.

general way all technical classifications have the same fault of basing themselves not on the nature of the crime but on the nature of the punishment. The definition of *felonies* in English penal law is a typical instance : *felonies* are crimes which are punished by the death penalty, as opposed to *misdemeanours* and to *trespasses* which are punished by a lesser penalty. But how can we hope to found a theory of punishment on this classification of crimes when the classification assumes and takes for granted the established system, which is just what we propose critically to examine ? A revolution was called for in the language of penal law—difficult by reason of those class interests which are favoured by a technical terminology, yet necessary. Just as botany had had its Linnaeus, as chemistry had had its Lavoisier,[1] so the science of law needed a man to provide it with a nomenclature.

The procedure of classification to which Bentham tried to conform is the ' dichotomic procedure ',[2] called by him the ' exhaustive method '. This method consists in first defining the logical domain which one proposes to study, and then dividing this into two parts, and so on until the domain be used up or exhausted. Bentham admits, however, that it would be difficult to work out the dichotomic method rigorously. His business is, on the one hand, to secure a systematic enumeration of all the possible modifications of crime, whether or no they have names ; and, on the other hand, to find a place on the list for all names of crimes which are in common use. If we merely had in view the first of these aims it would suffice to conform purely and simply to nature, and follow the dichotomic procedure without modification : but by this means we should arrive at an entirely new and unintelligible juridical language, which would leave unexplained words in common use. As it is, it will be necessary, in using the dichotomic procedure, to be constantly preoccupied with looking up current expressions by the way, and even sometimes to renounce the pedantry involved in following the procedure rigorously.

In accordance with the principle of utility, every act which is or which may be detrimental to the community must be held to be a crime.[3] But the evil which it causes to the community can now, from a new point of view, be divided into distinct classes according to the individuals or groups of individuals who suffer it. Here the dichotomic method is applicable : the individuals who suffer the evil are either assignable, that is to say, are such that they can be designated by name or by some special circumstance, or, in every other case, unassignable. The assignable individuals who suffer the evil resulting from the action are either individuals other than the agent, or the agent himself. The unassignable individuals are either the totality of the individuals who make up the community, or a

---

[1] And its Bergman—see MSS. Univ. Coll. No. 33.
[2] Bowring, vol. i. pp. 96-7.   [3] Bowring, vol. i. 97.

subordinate group of that community.[1] Hence there are four classes of crime : *private* crimes, which affect one or more individuals other than the agent ; *semi-public*, which affect a group of unassignable individuals other than the agent ; *reflexive*, which affect the agent ; and *public*, which affect the whole community.

By applying the dichotomic method each class can in its turn be divided, with the exception of the fourth, with regard to which Bentham acknowledged himself unable rigorously to observe the rule he had laid down at the outset.[2] In the case of both private and reflexive crimes, the method to be adopted is the same. The happiness of an individual depends partly on his *person*, partly on the *exterior objects* that surround him. These exterior objects on which his happiness depends are either things which make up his *property*, or else persons from whom he expects services, either by reason of his legal condition, or simply because of those considerations of good-will, which make up *reputation*. Thus there will be crimes against the person, crimes against reputation, crimes against property, and crimes against condition.[3] The same division applies, in part at least, to semi-public crimes, provided only that a distinction is made between the cases in which the evil which results from these crimes is unintentional (crimes based on *some calamity*, as for example a flood, a contagious disease or a fire), and those in which it is intentional (crimes of *pure malice*), and that our attention is confined to the latter kind, which will also be found to be crimes against the person, against reputation, against property or against condition.[4]

The same method further makes possible a distinction in kind within each division of each class. Take the first division of the first class : private crimes, crimes against the person. The person is composed, or held to be composed, of body and soul. The acts which exert an injurious influence on the bodily part of the person do so either immediately, without affecting the will of the person, or mediately, and by means of this faculty. When the influence is exerted mediately, it is by means of a mental constraint, which is properly called *constraint* when it imposes on us a positive way of acting, *restraint* when it tends to prevent us acting in a given determinate way. Since the whole surface of the earth can be divided into two parts, one greater than the other, the restriction in the case in which the part of the earth to which access is forbidden to us is the larger of the two will be called *confinement*, in the opposite case, *banishment*. If the injurious actions are injurious directly, they are either mortal or not mortal. If not mortal, they are either reparable, in which case they are *simple corporal injuries*, or irreparable, in which case they are *irreparable* corporal injuries. If,

---

[1] Bentham may have been indebted for the principle of the division to the Instructions of the Empress Catherine, MSS. Univ. Coll. No. 32.

[2] He obtains eleven subdivisions (Bowring, i. 101).

[3] Bowring, vol. i. 99-100.   [4] *Ibid.*

on the other hand, the evil resulting from the action is suffered by
the spiritual part of the person, the pain suffered is a pain either of
apprehension, and the crime is called *menacement*—or of positive
suffering, when the crime is called *simple mental injury*. From
this there are nine kinds of crime against the person obtained by
dichotomy—simple corporal injuries ; irreparable corporal injuries ;
simple injurious restriction ; simple injurious compulsion ; illegitimate confinement ; illegitimate banishment ; illegitimate homicide ;
illegitimate menaces ; simple mental injuries.[1] We have now reached
the point at which the application of the dichotomic method brings
us back to the known forms of crime. At this point, the principles
having been laid down, there is nothing further to do except to
proceed to draw up a code, properly so called. Bentham also works
out the application of the method of classification by dichotomy
to the three other kinds included within the first class : there, once
again, he comes to a stop. A regular analysis could not be applied
either to reflexive crimes (since the preliminary question would arise
as to whether they were suitable matter for legislation), nor to
semi-public or public crimes, in view of the complication of local
circumstances.[2]

The classification of crimes, thus conceived, is a ' natural ' classification, since, being founded exclusively on the principle of utility,
it ignores the motives which could have inspired the acts called
criminal, and, in contrast to a ' sentimental ' classification, takes
account only of the consequences of the act once committed—
consequences which are injurious to the community in various
ways. It is also, to Bentham's mind, a ' natural ' classification in
opposition to a ' technical ' classification, because it ignores the
penalties with which, in a given time and country, the courts
habitually punish those acts which are judged criminal. In short,
it ignores local prejudices. In this the ' natural ' system of jurisprudence, as understood by Bentham, resembles ' natural law ' in
the classical sense of the term. Ancient law, whose arbitrary
generalisations Bentham refutes, distinguishes between *natural laws*,
which are eternal and universal, and *positive laws*, which vary with
time and place. But Bentham's analysis has the double merit
that it points out that this distinction is invalid (since all laws without
exception are, or ought to be, founded solely on a calculus of utility),
and yet also explains it and gives it a relative justification in a system
founded on the principle of utility. The analysis of crimes, Bentham
tells us, has been carried by him to the point at which the divisions
obtained would cease to hold good of all nations without exception.
And it is for this reason that he has pushed the analysis of the class
of private crimes further than that of the other classes. For the
first class of crimes is in a privileged position. Private crimes have
among others these characteristics : they are, and must be, every-

[1] Bowring, vol. i. 114-5.   [2] *Ibid.* 113-4.

where condemned by the censure of opinion in a more energetic fashion than are semi-public crimes, as such, and very much more so than are public crimes ; they are more constantly censured by opinion than are reflexive crimes (they would be universally censured were it not for the influence exerted by the two false principles of asceticism and antipathy) ; they are less apt than are semi-public and public crimes to be given definitions which vary with states and countries (in this they resemble reflexive crimes).[1] These three characteristics, and particularly the last, explain why these crimes have been considered by jurists to constitute so many infractions of a natural law, which they suppose to be endowed with an existence superior to the written laws of all countries and of all times. Bentham considers that this natural law is a fiction. Yet in his system it clearly corresponds to a reality.[2] Nothing is less like the empiricism of a historian, or of an ' antiquary ' like Montesquieu, than Bentham's doctrine. What Bentham is teaching, under new formulae, is still a law founded on knowledge of the universal nature of man (Bentham uses the word in this sense), a law that can be used for the jurisprudence of all nations, a law whose ' language will serve as a glossary by which all systems of positive law might be explained, while the matter serves as a standard by which they might be tried '.[3]

But the legislator only defines crimes in order to prevent them by punishments. It remains, therefore, after having defined and classified crimes, to define and classify punishments. Now in the Utilitarian philosophy the crime and the punishment, though differing in their effects, do not differ in their intrinsic nature : both punishments and crimes are equally evils inflicted by the free intervention of men's activities. It is to be expected, therefore, that the same division which applies to crimes will apply to punishments, and that the catalogue of punishments will be the same as the catalogue of crimes : an individual can only be effectively punished by being stricken in his person, his property, his reputation or his condition. The punishments which directly affect the person, in its active or in its passive faculties, make up the class of *corporal* punishments. Bentham subdivides these again ; and although, in Bentham, this new division is not at all points symmetrical with the subdivision of the kinds of crime against the person, it is none the less true both that the symmetry is easy to establish,[4] and also that Bentham, in order to set up his table of crimes against the person, has often simply taken the names of punishments and called them crimes by a simple transposition (illegitimate confinement ; illegitimate banishment). As regards the punishments which affect property, reputation or

---

[1] Bowring, vol. i. 139.
[2] *Traités*, Principes de Législation, ch. xiii.; Hildreth's trans. p. 67 (see Bowring, vol. i. 139).
[3] Bowring, vol. i. 139.   [4] See Bowring, vol. i. 395.

condition, they have the common characteristic of depriving the
individual of some advantage which he formerly enjoyed ; as
opposed to the class of corporal punishments, they can be considered
as forming the single class of privative punishments (the ' forfeitures '
of English law).

But this symmetry of crimes and punishments must not be taken
to imply (though the illusion would be a natural one) that on the
strength of a kind of law of retaliation each crime is to be considered
as having to submit to the punishment which is intrinsically analogous
to it. For one thing, this symmetry exists in fact only between
punishments in general and crimes of the first class ; and crimes
of the first class differ from crimes of all other classes precisely in
that they alone admit the possibility of applying the principle of
retaliation.[1] Must one then refrain from defining the punishments
which correspond to all the other crimes ? Further, the notion
of retaliation in no way satisfies the principle of utility. Men feel,
in general, that punishment and crime should be proportional.
But while the principle of retaliation, in order to satisfy a kind of
professional demand for symmetry, unreasonably demands that the
proportion between these two terms should be qualitative, the
principle of utility demands that it should be quantitative. The
evil of the penalty, recognised in advance by the possible delinquent,
must counterbalance the good for the criminal which results from
the crime, and consequently prevent the crime. Coming after
Montesquieu, who had at least the merit of calling attention to the
idea of proportionality in penal law,[2] Beccaria seems to have understood this : every punishment, he writes, ' must essentially be
public, prompt, necessary, proportional to the crime, the least of
the punishments which are possible under the given circumstances,
and dictated by the laws '.[3] But Bentham considers all the elements
enumerated by Beccaria as being merely so many elements of the
proportionality itself. What qualities must the punishment exhibit
in order that the proportionality of the punishment and the crime
may be established, and in order that a legislative arithmetic may
be possible ? What rules must preside over the establishment of this
proportionality ?

In the *Introduction to the Principles of Morals and Legislation*,
Bentham assigns eleven distinct qualities to legal punishments ;
but he himself admits that the eleven qualities are not of equal
importance. The object of one, the eleventh, the quality of
remissibility, is to palliate an accidental evil and remedy judicial
errors. Three are grouped together by Bentham as aiming at what
he holds to be three secondary ends of punishment : moral reformation, the incapacitation of the guilty party, and the compensation
of the injured party. There remain seven properties, which are

[1] Bowring, vol. i. 140.   [2] *Ibid.* 90.   [3] *Dei delitti e delle pene*, Conclusion.

to make punishment such that it will intimidate possible guilty persons, by *example*.[1] These can themselves be divided into three groups.

The object of four of them is to define the real value of the punishment.

First, since all punishment is an evil, the punishment must be reducible to what is strictly necessary ; it must exhibit what Bentham calls the property of *frugality* or *economy* : ' The perfection of frugality, in a mode of punishment, is where not only no superfluous pain is produced on the part of the person punished, but even that same operation by which he is subjected to pain, is made to answer the purpose of producing pleasure on the part of some other person ' ; pecuniary penalties, which merely consist in the obligation on the part of the guilty person to compensate the injured person, satisfy this condition. Secondly, in order that the gravity of the punishment may, in a general way, be determined quantitatively by the gravity of the crime, the punishment must be *divisible* ; it must be possible, whenever there is committed a graver crime, or an aggravation of the same crime, to make a proportionate increase in the punishment. This property is but an expression of what may be held to be the general postulate of the whole doctrine of utility, a postulate of which all the speculations of the school, whether in juridical, in economic, or even in constitutional matters, are no more than one long test. In accordance with this postulate, which is in a sense a double one, not only are pleasures and pains comparable as regards quantity, but it is also possible to find objective quantitative equivalents to pleasures and pains.

There is, however, a general difficulty in the application of the postulate in affairs of penal law, a difficulty bearing on the possibility of establishing a correspondence between the modification of the sensibility and its supposed objective equivalent, between punishment in the psychological and punishment in the legal sense of the word. On the one hand, is it true that a like punishment, in the objective sense of the word, always produces a like feeling of pain ? This is not true in the same degree of all punishments. The punishment of banishment causes the condemned man to suffer in proportion to the price he sets on living in the land from which he is banished ; one and the same pecuniary punishment is more or less grave according to the state of fortune of the man condemned. Consequently it is desirable that a given punishment should be not only divisible, but also, what is not the same thing, should be *equal to itself*.[2]—On the other hand, given a series of punishments differing in their nature, how is it possible to establish a correspondence between the series of legal penalties and the series of subjective feelings of pain which they will produce, feelings which differ in degree only, not in kind ? The legislator may propose increasing a

[1] Bowring, vol. i. 91 *sqq.*   [2] Bowring, vol. i. 403.

legal penalty by adding another penalty, or, above all, he may sometimes substitute one penalty for another in a case where the criminal
is unwilling or unable to submit to the first.   How can these be
compared with each other ?   There is here no money to perform,
even in a rough and ready way, the function of common denominator.
A fine, or a punishment by imprisonment, are essentially divisible,
being capable of any numerical degree.   But in order to compare
a sum of money with a sum of imprisonment resort must be had to
an artifice ; we must say, for example, ' that one day in prison shall
be counted to acquit a debt equal to the revenue of one day '.   The
two penalties are thus made *commensurable*.   Legal punishment
must have the property of commensurability, as well as those of
divisibility and equality, in order to make possible in these matters
an arithmetic of pleasures and pains.

The object of two other properties is to define what Bentham
calls the apparent value of the punishment.   For, according to
Bentham, the evil resulting from any act, whether crime or punishment, splits itself into two parts.[1]   The evil of the first kind is that
which is suffered by one or more assignable individuals, as a consequence of the act.   The evil of the second kind, namely the alarm
caused and the danger created, is that which, resulting from the
evil of the first kind, spreads either over the whole society, or to
some number of unassignable individuals.   But the proportion of
the evil of the second kind to the evil of the first kind varies according
to whether the act in question is a crime or a punishment.   Crime
produces an evil of the first kind and an evil of the second kind : it
inflicts suffering on an individual who was unable to avoid it, and
it spreads alarm and creates a danger.   Punishment produces an
evil of the first kind and, in the long run, a good of the second kind :
it inflicts suffering on an individual who has incurred it voluntarily,
but, in its after-effects, it reassures public opinion and removes a
danger.[2]   To speak more accurately, it is untrue to say that punishment produces a good of the second kind exclusively : in threatening
anyone who may be tempted to commit the act which the law treats
as a crime, it creates alarm and danger.   But it rests with the public
to annul the danger by refraining from committing the harmful
act.   As to the evil of the alarm, which is less than the evil of the
punishment (since the fear of an evil is a lesser evil than the evil
itself), this is an essential part of the punishment.   The *real* value
of the punishment is the whole evil of the punishment, everything
which is experienced when it is inflicted.   Its *apparent* value is the
probable evil which would present itself to the public imagination
from the mere description of the punishment, or from the sight of
its execution.   Now when a punishment is actually inflicted, the real
punishment represents the loss, while the apparent punishment

[1] For the whole theory see *Introduction*, ch. vii. § i. (Bowring, vol. i. 69 *sqq.*).
[2] Bowring, vol. i. 395.

represents the gain. Therefore the aim of penal law is to achieve, the production of an evil of the second kind without producing an evil of the first kind,—to inspire in possible criminals a feeling of alarm without it ever being necessary to resort to the infliction of the punishment itself.[1] Punishment has two properties which incline to this end, and which make it possible to avoid any increase in the real value of the punishment by means of increasing its apparent value. In order that the idea of punishment be strongly associated in men's minds with the idea of crime, punishment should be *exemplary*, that is to say, enveloped in a striking solemnity, and *characteristic*, or *analogous to the crime*, that is to say, there should be not only a quantitative proportionality but also a qualitative analogy between the crime and the punishment. As in civil law the idea of equity, so in penal law the idea of retaliation finds in the philosophy of utility a subordinate place and a relative justification dependent on the principle of utility.[2]

There remains a last characteristic which is distinct from all the others : that which Bentham calls the characteristic of *popularity*. On the strength of the principle of utility itself, the legislator, in his choice of punishments, must carefully avoid those which would offend established prejudices.[3] For the net advantage of a law is as it were its gross advantage less the allowance made for the discontent it causes and the inconvenience which this discontent may produce. But this last rule might run the risk of annulling all the others if once the sanction of law were given, in the name of the principle of utility itself, to prejudices which are often contrary to this principle. Bentham adds, in fact, that this quality must be taken to have only a provisional value. It presupposes, in the people, or in a part of the people, the existence of a prejudice which it is the business of the legislator to attempt to correct. It indicates slackness on the part of the legislator in permitting the people to struggle against their own interest for want of the instruction which ought to be and which could be given them.[4] Thus Bentham ends by insisting yet again on the universal character of the science of law, when once the people are enlightened on the principle of utility. It would be ridiculous to say that he did not recognise the modifications to the application of the principle that are necessitated by the diversity of national conditions ; for we see that he counts *popularity*, that is to say adaptation to local prejudices, among the fundamental characteristics of punishment, and, further, that he wrote the whole of a small *Essay on the Influence of Time and Place in Matters of Legislation*. But in this treatise itself, Bentham remains a disciple of Helvetius and is hostile to the fatalistic theory of climates. However

[1] Bowring, vol. i. 398-9.   [2] *Ibid.* 404.
[3] Bentham reduces this element to the consideration of the feeling of expectation (see Bowring, vol. i. 323).
[4] Bowring, vol. i. 95.

great may be the influence of physical conditions—climate, soil,
geographical conditions—alongside of moral conditions—government, religion, customs—history proves that there is no climate
and no soil whose resistance to the happiness of man cannot be
overcome ; and that wherever men can live they can be given a
government, a religion and customs which will make them happy.
Take the example of Peter the Great. ' What he has not done in
point of legislation, is not to be attributed to the effects of climate :
this did not set the bounds to his success ; he accomplished all
that he designed, and if his mind has been embued with a perfect
system of legislation, he would have found greater facility in its
establishment, than in establishing an imperfect one.' [1]
    It is possible then to establish a proportionality between punish-
ments and crimes : a moral arithmetic is possible in penal law. It
remains to lay down the elementary rules of this juridical arithmetic.
Bentham sets forth thirteen. But the sixth of these thirteen rules
is addressed to the judge rather than to the legislator : it demands,
in order ' that the quantity actually inflicted on each individual
offender may correspond to the quantity intended for similar
offenders in general ', that ' the several circumstances influencing
sensibility ought always to be taken into account '.[2] The thirteenth
rule is less an addition than a qualification of the preceding rules :
the mathematical spirit of proportion must not be adhered to to the
extent of making the laws subtle, complicated and obscure, since
there is a superior good—that of simplicity.[3] There remain eleven
fundamental rules for establishing the proportion between punishment and crime. They can be reduced to two fundamental rules,
the one fixing the inferior, and the other the superior limit beyond
which the punishment must never go. First fundamental rule : see
that the evil of the punishment exceeds the profit of the offence.
Otherwise there would be an advantage in committing the crime.
Second fundamental rule : while the evil of the punishment must
exceed the profit of the crime, it must exceed it by as little as possible.
For every punishment is an evil and must be inflicted just in so far
as it is necessary and no further. The first fundamental rule sums
up the first four rules of Bentham's table ; [4] the second fundamental
rule is the fifth of the table.[5]
    The six remaining rules explain the artifices by which it is possible
to keep punishment between the two limits. Now it is characteristic
that only one of these six rules tends to diminish the punishment :
in fixing the extent of the punishment attention must be paid to
those circumstances in which any kind of punishment whatsoever
would be too heavy.[6] The other five rules, on the other hand, tend
to increase the punishment.—The less certain the punishment, the
greater it must be made.[7]—The less near the punishment, the greater

[1] Bowring, vol. i. 178.   [2] Ibid. 88.   [3] Ibid. 89-90.   [4] Ibid. 87-88.
[5] Ibid. 88.   [6] Ibid. 89.   [7] Ibid. 8 sqq.

it must be made.[1]—When the act is of such a kind that it affords conclusive proof of a habit, the punishment must be great enough to exceed not only the gain of that individual crime, but the gain of all the similar crimes which may be supposed to have been committed by the same criminal and to have gone unpunished.[2]— Finally, when a punishment which is particularly adapted to attain its end by reason of its quality cannot exist in less than a certain quantity, it may sometimes be useful, in order to employ it, slightly to exceed the quantity which would be strictly necessary from other points of view : this is especially the case, Bentham tells us, when the penalty is intended to operate as a moral lesson.[3]

Here is a curious fact, which should be laid bare. In his anxiety to endow the science of legislation with the character of an exact and impassive science, Bentham regards what he calls the objections of ' humanity ' as being so many ' capricious ' objections, as far as the determination of punishments is concerned. ' Attend not to the sophistries of reason, which often deceive, but be governed by your hearts, which will always lead you to right. I reject, without hesitation, the punishment you propose : it violates natural feelings, it harrows up the susceptible mind, it is tyrannical and cruel.' This is the language of those who in the *Principles of Penal Law* are termed ' sentimental orators '.[4] Doubtless, all punishment is bad ; all punishment, consequently, must appear revolting to the feelings. Therefore, if the repugnance felt by a sensitive heart is a sufficient objection against a penal law, all penal law must be swept away. But, on the other hand, punishment is necessary : we must therefore repudiate the promptings of sentiment.

The first rule laid down by Bentham demands that ' the evil of the punishment exceed the profit of the offence '. Now, other things being equal, the strength of the temptation is in proportion to the profit from the crime ; but the quantity of the punishment must increase with the profit from the crime ; therefore, other things being equal, it should increase, Bentham tells us, with the strength of the temptation. This maxim appears harsh ; it shocks the sensibility. And, doubtless, allowance must be made for the element of temptation so as to lessen the punishment in so far as the stronger influence of a slight temptation indicates a worse disposition in the agent. But the exception must not be confused with the rule. To say that the proof of a depraved disposition is less conclusive is not to say that the depravity is less. For in spite of contrary indications it is always possible that the crime would have been committed even if the temptation had been less strong. The attenuating circumstance is only a matter of presumption ; the crime is a matter of certainty. Men are too much inclined to regard the strength of the

---

[1] Bowring, vol. i. 8 *sqq.*   [2] *Ibid.*   [3] *Ibid.*
[4] Bowring, vol. i. 412.

temptation as an excuse for the offender. This is due to the principle of sympathy and antipathy. ' A man who punishes because he hates, and only because he hates, such a man, when he does not find anything odious in the disposition, is not for punishing at all ; and when he does, he is not for carrying the punishment further than his hatred carries him. Hence the aversion we find so frequently expressed against the maxim, that the punishment must rise with the strength of the temptation ; a maxim, the contrary of which, as we shall see, would be as cruel to offenders themselves, as it would be subversive of the purposes of punishment.' [1] Innocent people would not be protected against crime, and further the evil of the punishments suffered by offenders would be absolutely without profit, if once it ceased to be proportioned to the demands of the principle of utility.

Beccaria makes the mildness of punishment an object of his studies : he is perhaps chiefly preoccupied with making punishments milder.[2] But Bentham does not approve the expression, for it lacks the neutrality, the objectivity which becomes the language of science. ' To call a *punishment mild*, is to associate contradictory ideas ; to call a *punishment economic*, is to use the language of calculation and of reason.' [3] The morality of utility is not a generous morality which distributes pleasure without measure, because pleasure is a good ; it is, to use Bentham's expression, an economic morality which only metes out charily immediate pleasure to individuals with a view to insuring to them the future possession of pleasure. ' The question is not whether a penal code is more or less severe : this is a bad way of looking at the subject. The whole question can be reduced to judging whether or no the severity of the code is necessary.' [4] In this matter it is interesting to point out the contrast afforded by his doctrine to the doctrine of Beccaria.

Before Bentham, Beccaria had set himself to estimate the value of the four elements in punishment : *intensity*, *proximity*, *certainty* and *duration*. These four elements, which became an integral part of the moral arithmetic created by Bentham, and with him passed into the sphere of moral philosophy, properly so called, were borrowed by him from the *Dei delitti e delle pene*.[5] Granted that intensity, proximity and certainty are integral elements of the value, or, what amounts to the same thing, of the gravity of a punishment, it is possible, in view of such and such subsidiary reasons, to diminish the importance of one element and increase that of another. The gravity of the punishment will remain unaltered granted that the increase on the one side compensates for the diminution on the other, as is necessary if the punishment is intended still to have the same

---

[1] Bowring, vol. i. 67-8.
[2] Beccaria, *Dei delitti e delle pene*, § xxvii.   [3] Bowring, vol. i. 398.
[4] *Traités*, Code Pénal, part iii. ch. 8 (see Bowring, vol. i. 399 *seq.*).
[5] MSS. University College, No. 27, *Preface to a Body of Law*.

efficacy. Beccaria seems to ignore this. He seems to be primarily concerned with the sentimental task of diminishing the severity, that is to say the *intensity*, and not to notice that he is constantly allowing the other quantitative elements of the punishment to be increased to an extent that in some cases even more than compensates for the decrease in the intensity of the punishments. From this arise many mistakes of calculation which Bentham obviously sets out to correct.

' The surest way to prevent crime,' wrote Beccaria, ' is not by the severity of the penalty but by the certainty of punishment. It is by the vigilance of the magistrate and by that inflexible severity which is a virtue in the judge only in proportion to the mildness of the legislation.' [1] From the same data Bentham argues differently. The advantage of the crime necessarily outweighs the evil of the punishment in respect of proximity and certainty ; therefore what the evil of the punishment lacks in proximity and certainty, must be made up by adding to its intensity, if it is to compensate the evil of the crime. Now, if Beccaria's reasoning is more ' humanitarian ' than Bentham's, it is certainly less rigorous from a logical point of view. Beccaria tells us that in the infliction of the punishment the evil of certainty must be increased so that the evil of intensity can be diminished ; and on the other hand the evil of proximity must be increased in order to diminish, at one blow, the evil of intensity and the evil of uncertainty. That is to say that uncertainty is held now to be an evil and now a good, according to the point of view which has to be adopted in order to justify the diminution of the intensity of the punishment. But the intensity of punishment is an evil on just the same ground as are its certainty and proximity ; it is only an illusion of language which makes us, to some extent, attribute to it a greater reality. ' The punishment is just and useful in proportion to its promptness and to the rapidity with which it follows the crime it is punishing ', wrote Beccaria. Just, ' because then the criminal does not have to suffer the cruel torments of uncertainty.' And useful, ' because the less the time that elapses between the action and the penalty it has deserved, the more will the two ideas of *crime* and *punishment* be ineffaceably united in the mind.' [2] The two epithets ' just ' and ' useful ' are badly chosen. For to Beccaria, ' just ' seems to mean ' mild ', productive of a smaller sum total of punishment ; ' useful ' means ' efficacious ', productive of a greater sum of punishment. Promptness in applying the penalty would thus have the contradictory result of at once lessening and increasing the punishment.

Duration is another element of the moral arithmetic. Beccaria considers it in his discussion of the death penalty. He condemns the death penalty in the first place because he considers it as the maximum

---

[1] *Dei delitti e delle pene*, § xxvii.
[2] *Ibid*, § xix.

of punishment, the loss of ' the greatest of goods ' : ' moments of unhappiness spread out over the whole course of a lifetime could be compared to the appalling moment of the ultimate penalty only ', he thinks, ' by the spectator who calculates its duration and its sum, and not by the guilty man whose present ills distract his mind from the thought of the evils of the future '.[1] But, immediately afterwards, he condemns it on the ground that ' punishments frighten mankind less by their momentary severity than by their duration '. Now if they frighten less, it is because they are less severe, because as a whole their value is less ; the death penalty is less severe than perpetual imprisonment.[2] A ' sentimental ' illusion has falsified Beccaria's calculations ; and owing to this mistake in calculation he increases penalties when meaning to lessen them. Bentham avoids making this error in logic. When he criticises the death penalty, it is not because it is very rigorous, but because, for instance, it is not equal, since the value of life is not the same for all individuals, and also because it cannot be remitted.[3] No doubt he seems to be guilty of the same fallacy as Beccaria in the passage where he discusses the penalty of imprisonment. ' By making the pain more severe, you will make it shorter ; the sum total will be less. Instead of weakening the painful sensations by diffusing them over a long period of mitigated imprisonment, you will increase their effect considerably, if you bring them together in the short space of a severe imprisonment. The same quantity of pain will therefore go farther this way than in any other.'[4] We must bear in mind also that punishment is costly in proportion to its duration not only for him who undergoes it but also for the society which inflicts it. But Bentham immediately adds a second reason, which is decisive for him : the infliction of 'a severer and shorter penal servitude does not produce what he calls evil of the third order, which is completely useless for the prevention of crime—that is to say, the evil of relaxing the faculties of the individual, suspending his industry, and allowing his business to pass into other hands. ' All these evils which . . . are too distant and contingent to contribute anything beforehand by the impression it is intended to produce, are saved by placing the magnitude of the punishment in intensity rather than in duration '.

Assuredly, Bentham cannot be separated from the time in which he lived. The contemporary of Beccaria and of Voltaire, he denounced the same abuses, and ended by joining in their demand for a general ' lightening ' of penalties. Perhaps nowhere else in Europe was the death penalty so freely used as in England. There were a hundred and sixty capital felonies in 1765,[5] and still more in 1786

---

[1] *Dei delitti e delle pene*, § xxviii.
[2] Voltaire made this objection in his *Prix de la Justice et de l'Humanité*, 1777.
[3] Bowring, vol. i. 444-5.   [4] *Ibid.* 420.
[5] Blackstone, IV. Comm. 18.

if we may believe Romilly.[1]   If we may credit Bentham, there were
a hundred executions for forgery between February 1800 and
April 1801.[2]   Even Blackstone, who was so conservative, was alarmed
at the condition in which he found the penal law of his country.[3]
Bentham of course was equally moved : having stated that, in the
infliction of penalties, ' the greatest danger would be to err on the
side of punishing *too little*, because the punishment would be
inefficacious ', he admitted that ' to err on the side of punishing *too
much* is on the contrary the natural bent of the mind of mankind
and of legislators, either through the antipathy which leads to an
excessive severity, or through lack of pity for men who are thought
to be dangerous and vile ' ; consequently, ' it is here that precautions
must be taken '.[4]   Yet what shocked Bentham most in English penal
law was perhaps less the extent to which it used the death penalty
than the inefficiency of a penal law which was so severe that people
did not even think of applying it : consequently, the infliction of
punishment instead of being defined by law on rational considerations,
was left to the arbitrary decision of the judge.   ' Since the kindness
of the national character was in contradiction to the laws, it was the
customs which triumphed and the laws which were evaded : men
multiplied the number of pardons, shut their eyes to crimes, and
made difficulties about bearing witness ; and the juries, in order to
avoid excessive severity, often became excessively indulgent.   From
this resulted a penal system which was incoherent and contradictory,
which was a mixture of violence and weakness, and depended on
the temper of a judge which varied from circuit to circuit, and was
sometimes sanguinary and sometimes of no effect.' [5]

A scientific theory of punishment defined as a useful and necessary
evil ; a scientific classification of crimes and punishments, founded
on the complete knowledge of the consequences of any given act—
whether they be useful or harmful to the community as a whole ;
an analysis of the characteristics which legal punishment should
possess in order to make it capable of a really scientific valuation
and hence of being proportioned to the crime in accordance with
the methodical rules enumerated by Bentham :—in this way there
develops a theory of penal law which no longer resorts, as the theory
of Montesquieu and the jurists had done, to the fictions of the
' nature of things ' and of legal retaliation.   The rules laid down by
Bentham are on the one hand absolutely universal : they are true
regardless of time and place.   On the other hand they are capable
of an absolutely rigid application to all particular cases which may
arise.   These were the problems in connection with penal law

---

[1] Romilly, *Observations on . . . Executive Justice.*
[2] Bowring, vol. x. 356.   [3] Blackstone, IV. Comm. 3, 4.
[4] Bowring, vol. i. 401.
[5] *Traités*, Code Pénal, part 3, ch. ix. (see Bowring, vol. i. 558-9).

which first attracted the attention of Bentham ; and it was the facility with which he thought he had been able to find a solution of a more or less mathematical nature for these problems in the principle of utility which led him to believe that the same principle would provide him with the solution of all moral and legislative problems. Here there is nothing or practically nothing of that dualism which complicates the interpretation of his philosophy of civil law, but rather a simple principle methodically followed up to its ultimate conclusions.[1]   This is because Bentham's philosophy of civil law was derived from Hume, while his philosophy of penal law on the other hand came from Helvetius : the naturalistic tendency fades away while the rationalism remains.

But, we may ask, might not this confidence in reason which inspired Helvetius and Bentham with the hope of founding a mathematically exact science of legal punishment, also inspire the hope that a day will come when all legal constraint, all attack on the liberty of individuals, will be superfluous, since men will have become reasonable through the progress of science ? This point of view was beginning to be current on all sides around Bentham towards the end of the eighteenth century ; and this expectation of an approaching era of absolute emancipation satisfied the demands of the prevailing sentimentalism, which regarded as odious all punishment and all constraint. But the philosophy of Bentham is neither liberalism nor sentimentalism. It is true that Bentham happens to find himself in agreement with the liberals when he protests against the oppression by an egoistic professional body, and with the sentimentalists when he denounces the excessive severity of punishments. But an agreement about principles must not be inferred from a partial agreement about conclusions. Bentham would not include liberty as one of the ends of civil law : he considered it only as a secondary form of security.[2]   It was not his view that liberty should really be the means employed to bring about the general interest. His philosophy is essentially a philosophy written for legislators and men engaged in government, that is to say for men whose profession it is to restrict liberty. Further he mistrusted sensibility and opposed reason to sentiment : he had already so coloured the philosophy of reform in England as to distinguish it for all time from the humanitarian philosophy which prevailed in the country of Rousseau, and even in that of Beccaria. The disciple of Helvetius, he regarded man as an animal, capable of pleasure and pain, and the legislator as a wise man who knows the laws obeyed by human sensibility ; he did not hope to suppress suffering, but rather he confiscated, in favour of the legislator with his knowledge of what is useful, the power of inflicting punishment in order to bring about an artificial identification of interests. It is left to the reason of the

[1] MSS. Univ. Coll. No. 98.
[2] See Bowring, vol. i. 411, ' All punishment is an infringement on liberty, etc.'

legislator to see to it, by despotically and methodically imposing suffering on individuals, heedless of their instinctive and sentimental protests, that finally and on the whole the sum of pleasures shall outweigh the sum of pains.

3. THE DOCTRINE AND THE AGE

The *Introduction to the Principles of Morals and Legislation* after many delays appeared in 1789. It did not, however, attract public attention to any great extent. It was in the year 1788 that Bentham met his future editor and reviser, Dumont of Geneva, and many years were to pass before the appearance of the *Traités de Législation Civile et Pénale*. In 1785, Lord Shelburne, first Marquis of Lansdowne, who had been Bentham's patron for the past three years, discovered Samuel Romilly, a young and still obscure barrister.[1] Romilly got to know Mirabeau through Brand Hollis, Benjamin Vaughan through Mirabeau, and finally Lord Lansdowne through Benjamin Vaughan. Lord Lansdowne asked him for information regarding a Swiss gentleman, formerly a pastor, Dumont by name, whom he thought of making tutor to one of his sons. Lord Lansdowne and Romilly became intimate. When Bentham returned from Russia in 1788, he went to spend some time at Bowood Castle ;[2] there he met Romilly, whom he had already known at Lincoln's Inn, and Dumont, to whom Romilly had shown some of Bentham's manuscripts. In the same year Dumont spent two months in Paris with Romilly ; through Wilson,[3] Mirabeau met Dumont at the hotel where he was staying with Romilly and charmed him.[4] In a few months, thanks to Romilly, Dumont of Geneva found his vocation,—on the one hand as Mirabeau's private secretary, on the other as the disciple, editor and reviser of Bentham. But this shows what an array of special circumstances was necessary for Bentham to find a reviser. Is not this a typical case revealing the influence on history of little causes and individual accidents ? Bentham being too lazy to edit his own works, a French writer had to come forward to publish them, in Paris, and in a foreign tongue ; and consequently it was only after many years and by a curious detour that Bentham was able to exercise any influence on his countrymen.

In point of fact, even here, in the preparation of this particular event, general causes were at work. It was not because he was temperamentally lazy that Bentham entrusted the publication of his works to another and to a foreigner : indeed he consented to

[1] A pamphlet entitled a *Fragment on the Constitutional Power and Duties of Juries* drew Lord Lansdowne's attention to Romilly (*Memoirs of . . . Sir Samuel Romilly . . . by himself*, vol. i. pp. 86-7).

[2] Bowring, vol. x. 183. [3] MSS. Univ. Coll. No. 52.

[4] Dumont, *Souvenirs sur Mirabeau*, pp. 5-10.

publish in English the *Introduction to the Principles of Morals and Legislation*, which contained his fundamental ideas on penal law. It was rather because he felt that he was destined to be misunderstood in his own country because of the theories which he was putting forward, that he showed little readiness to publish his works. Historical circumstances demanded that he should turn for his audience to the public on the Continent. The state of opinion in England at the end of the eighteenth century was unfavourable to the success of Bentham's programme of reform—the revision of all juridical ideas from the point of view of the principle of utility, and the systematic *codification* of civil and penal law. For Bentham did more than introduce into civil law the notion, borrowed from Hume's psychology, of the feeling of expectation ; he did more than introduce into penal law the idea, borrowed from Beccaria, that a quantitative proportion should be established between crime and punishment : he added to these borrowed ideas perfection of logical arrangement and precision of scientific thought and language. But the law could only have these qualities when it had been written and *codified*.

There is always the same conflict between the point of view of general utility and the point of view of the interests of a corporate body or a class. It is to the advantage of a corporate judicial body that the law should be known by it alone and unknown to the public, and therefore that it should not be written. This is why in England by far the greater part of the law consists of what jurists call common law, or in other words, unwritten law, the age-old jurisprudence of the law courts. The unwritten laws, said Blackstone,' receive their binding power, and the force of laws, by long and immemorial usage, and by their universal reception throughout the kingdom '.[1] Since the successive sentences, of which they are a digest, were spread over an indefinite period, starting ' from a time whereof ', according to the legal phrase, ' the memory of man runneth not to the contrary ', they have the appearance of *eternity*. As there are a great number of these decisions, adopted throughout the whole kingdom, they have the appearance of *universality*. English jurisconsults ended by talking of common law as they talked of natural law in Rome ; in the eyes of the jurisconsult Coke it is the ' perfection of reason '. But this is pure illusion. The very antiquity of common law makes it out of date, and unadapted to the fresh needs of the times : there is a Benthamite adage that ' the antiquity of a law is no reason '.[2] Since it consists of a collection of ancient decisions it is obscure and calls for the mediation of an interpreter, of a lawyer who alone is competent, through a study of past decisions, to predict the future decisions of the judges. Further it is in this

---

[1] Blackstone, I. Comm. 62-4.
[2] *Traités*, Principes de Législation, ch. xiii. p. 67. (see Bowring, vol. iii. 206).

very obscurity that the members of the judicial body find their own interest contrary to the public interest. It endows them with a monopoly of the knowledge of the law and with the power, in each fresh case, arbitrarily to define what is right and wrong—' to kill men for not having guessed their dreams ',—with no other control than their conscience and an unwritten tradition. Wherever there is an unwritten law ' lawyers will be its defenders, and, perhaps innocently, its admirers. They love the source of their power, of their reputation, of their fortune : they love unwritten law for the same reason that the Egyptian priest loved hieroglyphics, for the same reason that the priests of all religions have loved their peculiar dogmas and mysteries .'[1] Therefore if, in the words of Beccaria, we wish ' the laws, protectors of all the citizens, to be favourable rather to each individual in particular than to the various classes of men who compose the state ',[2] the laws must be written down.

But it is not enough that the laws be written. The written law must also constitute a complete and systematic body of laws. In England this condition is imperfectly satisfied by the collection of parliamentary ' statutes ' which to some extent completes the ' common law '—statutes voted without reflection and drawn up without method. Indeed, if it is necessary that laws should be known, this is so in order to produce in men's minds the expectation that they will be enforced ; for it is this expectation alone which makes them efficacious. Now, in spite of the illusions of the principle of sympathy and antipathy—in spite even of the ascetic principle, which sprang from the régime of corporate bodies—all men naturally expect law to conform to the principle of general utility. Laws arranged on a system in agreement with the principle of utility are grouped in an order which is at once accessible to common sense, since all men understand the nature of pleasure and pain, and also indestructible by reason. A code based on this principle will be simple both in its arrangement and in the expression of its contents. From this point of view to systematise is not to complicate but to simplify. ' The more complex the law, the greater the number of those who cannot understand it '. But ' the more conformable laws are to the principle of utility, the more simple will be their systematic arrangement. A system founded upon a single principle might be as simple in its form as in its foundation. It only is susceptible of a natural arrangement and a familiar nomenclature '.[3] It is true that simplicity and familiarity are not necessarily synonymous : the truths of mathematics are perhaps simple because they are abstract, yet the study of them is toilsome enough. Bentham warns us in the preface to his *Introduction* that familiarity is indeed a sign, but a very deceptive one, of the easiness of a subject, and that there is no royal road in the science of legislation any more than in the science

---

[1] Bowring, vol. iii. 206. [2] *Dei delitti e delle pene*, § xli.
[3] Bowring, vol. i. 322.

of mathematics.[1] In the last resort, however, Bentham shares the common view of his century, and tends to confound what is rationally simple with what is intelligible to everyone, immediately and without preliminary training. The code, the systematic collection of all the laws, is called upon to become the universal manual of the Utilitarian morality. This code ' would speak a language familiar to everybody : each one might consult it at his need. It would be distinguished from all other books by its greater simplicity and clearness. The father of a family, without assistance, might take it in his hand and teach it to his children, and give to the precepts of private morality the force and dignity of public morals '.[2]

Hume had given the first rank among the benefactors of humanity to legislators and founders of states. He blamed antiquity for deifying the inventors, Bacchus and Esculapius, while Romulus and Theseus were only ranked as demi-gods.[3] Helvetius, inspired by the same idea, had extended the action of the legislator almost without limits. He had not thought of the legislator as having fulfilled his function when he had promulgated laws and inflicted punishments ; above and beyond this he thought of the legislator as primarily an educator who should form the actual character of peoples by stirring in them the feeling of honour, and directing human passions towards the general utility. Legislation, understood in this way, is an art whose principles, ' as certain as those of geometry,' have been recognised by a few great men in war and in politics : but if victory, asks Helvetius, depends as much on the courage of the soldiers as on the formation of battle order, would not a treatise on the art of inspiring the passions be as useful to generals as a treatise on tactics or on strategy ?[4] Bentham makes certain reservations on this point, and treats as ' political romancers ' those writers who, while tolerating direct legislation as a necessary evil, show great enthusiasm when they speak of the means of avoiding crime, of improving mankind and perfecting moral behaviour, and even seem ready to discover a new philosopher's stone, and to remake the human race. The less familiar the object, the more splendid the terms in which we think of it, and the imagination can make more play with vague projects which have not yet been submitted to analysis.[5] Following Beccaria, then, Bentham confines himself to drawing up a scientific-ally established catalogue of the ' indirect means of preventing crime ', in order to reduce ' all these indefinite hopes within the true dimensions of the possible '. But these dimensions are still con-siderable, even ' immense ' ; and he remains always the disciple of Helvetius. The influence of government, he tells us, extends to everything ; ' in fact, it embraces everything except temperament, race, and climate ; for even health may depend upon it in many

---

[1] Bowring, vol. i. p. 5.   [2] *Ibid.* vol. iii. pp. 205-9.
[3] Hume, Essay VIII. ' Of Parties in General.'
[4] Helvetius, *De l'Esprit*, dis. iii. chap. xxv.   [5] Bowring, vol. i. 533.

respects, so far as relates to regulations of price, the abundance of provisions, and the removal of apparent causes of disease. The method of education, the plan followed in the disposal of offices, and the scheme of rewards and punishments, will determine in a great measure the physical and moral qualities of a nation '.[1]

Now it happened that at this time there was no demand, in England, for the supply of a systematised and codified law. In one of his manuscripts Bentham enumerates the rewards which had been offered, over the greater part of Europe, to encourage the reform of criminal law. In 1764 a medal worth twenty ducats was promised by the *Société Economique* of Berne to the anonymous author of the *Dei delitti e delle pene*, if he would disclose his identity. In 1777, a prize of fifty gold louis was offered by the same society for the best plan for a whole penal code: Voltaire and the Englishman Thomas Hollis added fifty louis for *accessits*, and Bentham considered competing. In 1773, a medal was offered by the Academy of Mantua for the solution of a problem relative to the principles of penal law.[2] Frederick II gave Prussia a code ; the King of Sweden announced his intention of lightening and correcting the criminal laws ; the Grand Duke of Tuscany simplified the procedure in his States ; even in Spain and in Poland we find codes in project. As a contemporary observed some years later, there was a general fermentation abroad : ' everything seemed to be pointing to an approaching revolution in the legislation of the whole of Europe ; the philosophers were pointing out its abuses ; the princes seemed to be seeking the means of doing away with them '.[3] But it was the judicial institutions of England which were continually being cited by the reformers of the whole of Europe as a model to be imitated. In a general way, England appeared as the country where, in contrast with despotic countries—' like France and Turkey '[4]—it was not the authority of the government but the liberty of the subject which was regarded as unlimited ; where the acts of the individual counted as legitimate until a law declaring them illegitimate could be named, and where, finally, after the accusation had been made, the law seemed to take every precaution not to assure but to retard and hinder a condemnation. England knew nothing of the ' question ', or of torture ; she possessed the institution of the jury. The very complication of the judicial system appeared as the safeguard of the liberty of the subject : Montesquieu and De Lolme settled the opinion of common sense on this point.[5] How then could Bentham, who wished a code to be drawn up in order to impose an arbitrary rule on the legal profession, make himself heard in a country where the legal profession, with the assistance of the juries, were traditionally

[1] *Traités*, Principes de Législation, ch. ix. sect. ii. (Hildreth's translation, p. 41).
[2] MSS. Univ. Coll. No. 143 (under the heading *Reward*).
[3] Brissot, *Mémoires*, vol. ii. p. 17.   [4] Blackstone, IV. Comm. 343.
[5] Montesquieu, *Esprit des Lois*, liv. vi. chs. 1 and 2.

considered as the defenders of English liberties against the royal power which was always suspected of usurpatory designs ?

Paley's book is characteristic in this respect : it is a work at once liberal and conservative, and through it the principle of public utility penetrated the teaching of morality at the universities, and was applied to matters of law and to questions of judicial organisation and of penal law. He examined the English system of judicial organisation, and concluded : ' A politician, who should sit down to delineate a plan for the dispensation of public justice, guarded against all access to influence and corruption, and bringing together the separate advantages of knowledge and impartiality, would find when he had done, that he had been transcribing the judicial constitution of England '.[1] He applied the principle of utility to penal law, and like Bentham, but also like Blackstone himself,[2] assigned as the aim of punishment ' not the satisfaction of justice, but the prevention of crimes '.[3] This is why crimes which are morally equal are often punished with unequal penalties : for ' crimes are not by any government punished in proportion to their guilt, nor in all cases ought to be so, but in proportion to the difficulty and the necessity of preventing them '.[4] This principle allows Paley to justify all the strange inconsistencies of English penal law :—the fact, for example, that theft was punished by death or not punished by death according to whether it was committed in a shop.[5] Bentham states that in any given punishment, the two elements of intensity and certainty must vary in inverse ratio the one to the other, so that the punishment shall remain the same ; from the same principle Beccaria concluded that punishments could be lightened if they were made more certain. In 1784, Madan, in a paradoxical work which made some stir, concluded, from the principle that a punishment is inefficacious when it is uncertain, that the death penalty must be applied in all the cases in which it is prescribed by law.[6] Finally, Paley, starting like Bentham from the principle of utility, considered the uncertainty of the English law, ' the glorious uncertainty of the law ', as being one of its excellences.[7] Besides, in spite of this uncertainty the number of executions remained very high. But this is the normal result of there being no other penalty capable of inspiring a great enough terror, of the development of the great cities, of the very liberties enjoyed by the English people, for the liberties of a free people, and still more the jealousy with which these liberties are watched, and by which they are preserved, permit not those precautions and restraints, that inspection, scrutiny, and control, which are exercised with success by arbitrary governments.[8] Bentham had promised that the principle of utility should be a

[1] *Moral and Political Philosophy*, bk. vi. ch. viii. *sub finem.*
[2] IV. Comm. ii.   [3] *Moral and Political Philosophy*, bk. vi. ch. viii. *sub finem.*
[4] *Ibid.* ch. ix.   [5] *Ibid.*   [6] *Thoughts on Executive Justice.*
[7] *Moral and Political Philosophy*, bk. vi. ch. ix.   [8] *Ibid.*

principle of reform, and that when it was introduced into affairs
of legislation and of morals, the reign of science should succeed the
reign of vague generalities. Yet here in Paley the principle of
utility shows itself competent, by the same authority that attaches
to any form of the arbitrary principle, to justify any given institution,
to found a new scholasticism in social theory.

It is not necessary here to inquire how far the real facts corresponded to the theory held by English liberalism as regards judicial
institutions ; how far a magistracy whose decisions created jurisprudence without effective parliamentary control, an undemocratic
parliament and juries which were also undemocratic in composition
squared with the symmetry of the doctrine ; and how far Disraeli
was right when, in another century, he denounced the ' political
mystification ' of an oligarchy, who for a hundred years had
exploited a people without political rights and without education
by making them believe themselves the freest and the most enlightened people in the world.[1] We are much more concerned here
with the reality of the prejudice than with the reality of the facts,
to which the prejudice possibly did not correspond. Englishmen
were proud of their judicial institutions, and against this pride
Bentham's zeal was likely to be pitted in vain. If, by means of
empiricism and routine, they had secured the monopoly in Europe
of these admirable institutions, why should they be concerned to
rationalise their law ? Roman law was codified, and the procedure
consecrated by Roman law was secret, inquisitorial, and accompanied
by torture—it was the procedure of the Star Chamber ; the politics
consecrated by it were the absolutist politics of *quod principi placuit*.[2]
When in 1791 Bentham embarked on the study of the problems
relative to the reform of judicial procedure and organisation, he
stated that, to the English, ' a system of local judicature, distributing
justice upon the spot, in all its branches, is new, not only in practice
but in imagination '. In England ' no man has yet been found bold
enough to insinuate that fifty pounds may be too high a price to pay
for five shillings, or four hundred miles too far to go for it '.[3] He
remarked the complete inertia of opinion on these matters ; and in
the following year when he wrote a pamphlet denouncing the
glorification of the judicial institutions of England, pronounced by
Sir William Ashurst, Puisne judge of the King's Bench, he no doubt
also remarked that the discourse of this official personage was a
faithful enough expression of the average state of opinion.[4]

Nevertheless at the same time a great movement of reform and
philanthropy was being formed round about Bentham : there was

[1] Disraeli, *Sybil*, ch. i.
[2] De Lolme, *Constitution de l'Angleterre*, vol. i. p. 93.
[3] Bowring, vol. ii. 309.
[4] *Truth versus Ashurst* (Bowring, vol. v. 233).

at least one question of penal law, the question of the prison system, which preoccupied philanthropists, jurists and legislators. A new form of Christianity was being manifested, which was practical, social and ' utilitarian ' as well as pietistic. Its typical representatives were the ' saints ', men of the ' evangelical party ', a kind of methodists who had remained within the Anglican Church. They demanded and in time secured the abolition of bloody games, the strict observation of Sunday rest, the abolition of slavery, and finally the reform of the prisons. A law of 1773 for the first time instituted regular chaplains for the prisons, and it was from 1773 on that John Howard, the great philanthropist and friend of Bentham— who ' died a martyr, after living an apostle of benevolence '—devoted himself entirely, for the remaining seventeen years of his life, to the one idea of prison reform—visiting the penitentiaries of the whole of Europe, denouncing abuses and seeking improvements. Further, historical events had rendered the reform of the penitentiary regime to some extent necessary. Before the American War, condemned prisoners had been hired out on bail to the planters in the colonies : since the revolution this kind of export had become impossible like all others.[1] Condemned prisoners crowded the gaols of the metropolis and then the hulks at Woolwich, Langston and Portsmouth which had been set up by a law of 1776. The overcrowding increased the scandals of the régime—the ventilation of the buildings was bad or absent altogether, the food almost non-existent, the jailors corrupt ; each prison was a school of vice and a centre of contagion where prison fever raged. The question was therefore of an urgent nature for moralists, hygienists, and politicians, and Bentham was here only following the trend of opinion when in 1778 he took part, by his pamphlet called a *View of the Hard Labour Bill*,[2] in the discussion of a bill in which William Eden demanded the erection of two prisons of a new type. He tells us that he was inspired by Howard's book on the *State of the Prisons*, which soon became a classic. Howard was appointed, in conjunction with two other ' overseers ', to carry out Eden's bill, which was passed in 1779. Finally, Bentham here found himself in agreement with his adversary, Blackstone, one of the promoters of the law : according to Bentham, Blackstone might have taken advantage of certain ideas set forth in his pamphlet in order to improve the bill.[3]

Then, when in 1784 Parliament inaugurated the expedient of administrative deportation to Australia, Bentham opposed system with system ; and in contrast with the idea of deportation, he traced the plan of the model prison which he called the *Panopticon*. This was a new application of the principle of the artificial identification of interests, the idea of which he had found in Helvetius. ' If it were possible to find a method of becoming master of everything which might happen to a certain number of men, to dispose of

---

[1] Bowring, vol. iv. 5.   [2] *Ibid*. 3.   [3] Bowring, vol. ix. 605.

BENTHAM'S PHILOSOPHY OF LAW 83

everything around them so as to produce on them the desired impression, to make certain of their actions, of their connections, and of all the circumstances of their lives, so that nothing could escape, nor could oppose the desired effect, it cannot be doubted that a method of this kind would be a very powerful and a very useful instrument which governments might apply to various objects of the utmost importance.' [1] The prison realises the ideal of a school in which the educator is to be absolute master to determine the external conditions in which the pupil is situated, or of a society in which the legislator is absolute master to create at will all the social relations of the citizens among themselves. The penitentiary problem is a double one. On the one hand the supervision of the prisoners must be carried to the highest point of perfection, and on the other hand the supervision must be exerted as much as possible in the interest of the prisoners. It is by virtue of a political sophism which is too much current that men are loath to reform the prisons, on the pretext that prisoners must suffer in prison. They must suffer as much as the law intended, and inasmuch as they are in prison, but every additional punishment is expensive and superfluous.

Bentham accomplished the first part of his programme by what he calls a ' simple idea in Architecture '. This idea was invented and first applied in Russia by his brother Samuel,[2] whom Bentham visited at Crichoff in 1786. It was the idea of the *Panopticon*, a prison in which the inspector has *the faculty of seeing at a glance everything that is going on* ; a circular prison where one inspector, or at most a very small number of inspectors, is in a position to supervise all the cells which are arranged concentrically round a central pavilion : a system of blinds makes invisible the inspector who sees everything. ' The fundamental advantage of the *Panopticon* is so evident that one is in danger of obscuring it in the desire to prove it. To be incessantly under the eyes of the inspector is to lose in effect the power to do evil and almost the thought of wanting to do it.' The same architectural arrangement will make possible the admittance without being seen of outside visitors to inspect the prisoners and the administration of the prison : thus Howard's ideas on the importance of publicity could be realised. Many problems thus become simplified and overcome. For example, should the prisoners be isolated ? From the point of view of moral reformation, Howard considered isolation as neither necessary nor useful, beyond a certain period. Nevertheless, isolation may be necessary in order to avoid the contagion of evil counsels, and to avoid plots of escape ; and, in the twenty-one letters which make up the original part of the *Panopticon*, Bentham decided in favour of cellular isolation. Later, however, he perceived that the ' universal inspection principle ' obviated all the dangers in question without needing to

[1] *Panopticon*, Bowring, vol. iv. 37-172.
[2] Bowring, vol. x. 250.

resort to isolation.[1] In fact, the architectural arrangement avoids all conceivable difficulties : in an access of enthusiasm Bentham compared the privileged position of the inspector at his place of observation to the divine omnipotence.[2] He recommended that the principle should be extended to factories, mad-houses, hospitals, and even to schools, for the supervision of children during class hours and hours of recreation.[3] This pedagogic idea raises many objections. Would not the spirit of liberty and the energy of a free citizen be changed into the mechanical discipline of a soldier, or the austerity of a monk ? Would not this ingenious contrivance have the result of constructing a set of *machines* under the similitude of *men* ? This, answered Bentham, is not the question ; the only question is whether happiness would be most likely to be increased or diminished by this discipline. ' Call them soldiers, call them monks, call them machines, so they were but happy ones, I should not care. Wars and storms are best to read of, but peace and calms are better to endure.' [4] Liberty is not, according to Bentham, an end of human activity ; the doctrine of utility is not, in origin and in essence, a philosophy of liberty.

But in order to ensure that the inspector uses conscientiously the power of universal inspection which has been conferred on him, the occasional control of visitors foreign to the establishment does not suffice. Bentham completes the architectural invention of the *Panopticon* by an administrative innovation—*contract-management* or administration by contract. Bentham lays down three rules to which the administration of the prisons must conform. Rule of lenity: the condition of a convict ought not to be attended with bodily sufferance which may be prejudicial and dangerous to health or life. Rule of severity: saving the regard due to life, health and bodily ease, the ordinary condition of the prisoner ought not to be made more eligible than that of the poorest class of subjects in a state of innocence and liberty. Rule of economy: with the same reservations economy ought, in every point of management, to be the prevalent consideration: no public expense ought to be incurred, or profit or saving rejected, for the sake either of severity or of indulgence.[5] There is little fear that the second rule will be violated; but what plan of administration will protect the convict against the harshness of warders, and society against the wastefulness of administrators? The choice lies between *contract-management* and *trust-management*. '*Contract-management* is management by a man who treats with the government, and takes charge of the convicts at so much a head and applies their time and industry to his personal profit, as does a master with his apprentices. *Trust-management* is management by a single individual or by a committee, who keep up the establishment at the public expense, and pay into the treasury the products of the convicts' work.' Of these two

---

[1] Bowring, vol. iv. 71 *sqq.*   [2] *Ibid.* 45.   [3] *Ibid.* 60.
[4] *Ibid.* 63-4.   [5] *Ibid.* 122-3.

methods of administration, recourse must be had to the first if it is desired that the duties of the *entrepreneur* towards the individuals entrusted to his care should be ' so bound up with his interest that he would be forced to do for his own advantage anything that he was not inclined to do for theirs'—or, in other words, if the principle of the artificial identification of interest (what Bentham calls the *interest-and-duty-junction-prescribing principle*) is to be applied.[1] The bill of 1778 had already instituted *contract-management*, of which Howard had pointed to various applications in the prisons of Ghent, Delft and Hamburg. In 1787, Bentham completed the idea by a new administrative arrangement : he thought that life insurances formed an excellent means of ' linking the interest of one man to the preservation of a number of men '. Given three hundred convicts, the statistics will show that on an average, and taking into account the special conditions of the prison, a fixed number must die every year. Let the *entrepreneur* be given a sum equal to ten pounds for instance, or even double that sum for every man due to die, on condition that, at the end of the year, he shall pay back the same sum for every individual who has died in prison : the difference will be profit for the director, who will therefore be pecuniarily interested in lowering, in his prison, the average toll of mortality.

Thus, by means of two principles, *central inspection* and *contract-management*, ' the actual good conduct and the future reformation of the convicts is assured, the public security is increased while making an economy for the state : a new instrument of government is formed by which one man alone finds himself endowed with a very great power of doing good, and none for doing harm.' Just as Bentham was responsible for the delay in publishing the *Introduction*, so, in this case, it appears to have been his friend George Wilson who delayed the appearance of the work from the time when Bentham sent him his manuscript in December, 1786.[2] The work appeared at last in 1791, increased by two ample postscripts. Henceforward Bentham devoted all his time and all his fortune to spreading his ideas for the reform of the penitentiary régime. He hoped to make the principles of the doctrine of Helvetius which were despotic, philanthropic, and Utilitarian, but not in the least liberal, triumph in his own country on a point of detail.

Why did Bentham make up his mind, in 1789, to publish his *Introduction* ? He did so because the Utilitarian doctrine was making rapid progress in the current official morality, and because his friends feared that Paley, by means of his book which was already becoming popular, would deprive him of the reputation he deserved as an innovator and inventor. Why did he devote himself to the solution of the special problem of penitentiary reform ? It was

[1] Bowring, vol. iv. 12-13.   [2] Bowring, vol. x. 165-6.

because this question was being discussed round about him all over England, because Howard had become famous by his philanthropic zeal, and because parliament was seeking remedies for the scandalous condition of the prisons. We do not think in solitude. For the average man intellectual isolation, like every other form of isolation, is hostile to thought : for him, to think alone is to dream. In a general way we feel the need of confirming the inner accord of our thought with itself by its accord with the thought of our fellow-men ; several people are necessary to make action and writing (which is the intellectual way of acting) possible. Why is it, then, that Bentham left in manuscript the most important and the most fundamental part of his work ? It was for this reason, that in his concern to endow law with the form of an integral system, that is, of a code, he felt that he was isolated in his own country. The idea of codifying the laws was a continental and not a British idea. This is why Bentham conceived the idea of addressing to the Continent the ideas which the study of European thinkers had inspired, ideas for which Europe and not England was then ripe. First, in 1779, at the time when he was dreaming of securing the prize offered by the *Société Economique* of Berne, he wanted to set out for Russia with his brother Samuel and, with him, place his talents at the service of Catherine.[1] Samuel went alone : at least Jeremy counted on him to transmit his legislative ideas to the Empress. ' Rather than miss her, you must spie on her in the road, you must bow down before her ; and when you have eaten as much dust as you feel inclined you must thrust my note under her nose, or else at her breast if she will allow your hand to get there. Come, do not let us lose heart. She is well worth a little trouble.'[2] If she knew English, the English edition of the *Introduction* was to be sent to her as to the Grand Duke of Tuscany and to the Prime Minister of the two Sicilies, for whom Bentham had already two letters, fully drawn up, in his desk.[3] If she did not know English, she was to be sent the German translation, which Bentham was intending to address to the King of Prussia and to the King of Sweden. But three German translators in succession either were not approved or got out of the task.[4] Samuel, however, ceaselessly demanded a French translation : this was the suitable language for Russia, and even the King of Prussia preferred French to German.[5] Bentham agreed, but did not see how a translator was to be found. Where was he to find the one hundred and fifty pounds necessary to tempt De Lolme ?[6] Samuel answered that Jeremy must be his own translator. At first Bentham declined, as he was disinclined to waste six months on this work.[7] Then, in

[1] Add. MSS. Brit. Mus. 33,538, f. 275, to his brother, Jan. 1, 1779.
[2] *Ibid.* f. 423, to his brother, Dec. 28, 1779—the original letter is in French.
[3] Add. MSS. Brit. Mus. 33,539, f. 71, to his brother, Aug. 6, 1780.
[4] See *Ibid.* ff. 28, 45 (back), 104 (back).   [5] *Ibid.* f. 81.
[6] *Ibid.* f. 105.   [7] *Ibid.* f. 117.

1783, he decided to take his brother's advice ; three years later, when at Crichoff with Samuel, he was still engaged on completing his French manuscripts. In 1787 he wrote to ask Wilson to find him a Frenchman who could look them through and correct them—not a cleric, for the work was too irreligious. After his return to England, he made arrangements to start for Paris to find a corrector and a printer, as soon as he had finished certain parts of his *Code*, without which the rest could not appear. It was at this moment that he met, at Bowood, Dumont of Geneva, who became his disciple, carried off his manuscripts, and saved Bentham the journey.[1]

[1] See Bowring, vol. x. 86.

CHAPTER III

ECONOMIC AND POLITICAL THEORIES

IN every social philosophy, and in particular in the Utilitarian doctrine, there is, over and above the juridical problem, a double problem, on the one hand economic and on the other constitutional or political.

In order to support the officials whose business it is to make the laws, to apply them, to see that they are carried out, and to defend the nation against foreign enemies, the State must impose pecuniary charges on the citizens and injure their economic interests, at least in a relative and temporary manner. Further the State can set itself to protect the economic interests of the citizens against competition from outside, and, within, to protect the economic interests of any particular class. In a word, the State assigns itself an economic function. It was in 1776, in his *Wealth of Nations*, that Adam Smith tried to solve the economic problem by taking his stand on the principle of utility. In 1787, in his first attempt at political economy, Bentham adopted the fundamental ideas of Adam Smith.

The legislating, policing, and tax-collecting State may be of many various types. It may be either monarchic, aristocratic or democratic, or again it may be mixed, containing a combination of monarchic, aristocratic or democratic elements. But every State has a constitution. In 1776, in his *Fragment on Government*, which was inspired by David Hume, Bentham founded a criticism of current constitutional doctrines on the principle of utility.

Thus, in economic and constitutional as in juridical affairs, Bentham, the disciple of David Hume and Adam Smith, was a typical representative of the dawning Utilitarian movement. We shall now inquire how the principle of utility was applied by the eighteenth century advocates of the Utilitarian thesis, and in particular by Bentham, the future head of the school, to the questions of political economy and constitutional law.

I. ADAM SMITH AND BENTHAM

' I forget ', writes Bentham in the letter to Adam Smith which forms the conclusion to his *Defence of Usury*, ' what son of controversy it was among the Greeks, who having put himself to school to a professor of eminence, to learn what, in those days, went by the name of wisdom, chose an attack upon his master for the first public specimen of his proficiency '. Bentham proceeds in the same way, but he does not wish to be ungrateful. When on the point of preparing to refute Adam Smith, instead of maintaining that he owes him nothing, he says that he owes him everything. ' Should it be my future to gain any advantage over you, it must be with weapons which you have taught me to wield, and with which you yourself have furnished me ; for, as all the great standards of truth which can be appealed to in this line, owe, as far as I can understand, their establishment to you, I can see scarce any other way of convicting you of any error or oversight, than by judging you out of your own mouth '.[1] The principle of freedom to lend for interest, which Bentham sets out to defend without reservations, is in effect the dominant idea of the *Wealth of Nations*, the thesis of industrial and commercial liberty. Since from this time onwards Bentham claims to be, in political economy, not an inventor but an intransigeant disciple of Adam Smith, and since moreover, after forty years' evolution, Adam Smith's doctrine was incorporated into the ' philosophical radicalism ', it is necessary to define this fundamental idea, and also the link which binds it to the general principle of utility.

We have already given the formula and defined the origin of the fundamental thesis, of which all the other theses, in Adam Smith, are corollaries : it is the thesis of the natural identity of interests, or, if you like, of the spontaneous harmony of egoisms. Sometimes, no doubt, Adam Smith has recourse to the artificial identification of interests : for example, he imposes on the State ' the duty of erecting and maintaining certain public works and certain public institutions which it can never be for the interest of any individual, or small number of individuals, to erect and maintain ; because the profit could never repay the expense (to them) . . . though it may frequently do much more than repay it to a great society '.[2] Beyond this, there is not, in Adam Smith, an explicit denial of the principle of the fusion of interests : for does not his whole moral theory rest on the notion of sympathy ? And it must not be supposed that he changed his views between the time when he wrote the *Theory of Moral Sentiments* and the time when he wrote the *Wealth of Nations*, since in his course at Glasgow in the year 1763,[3] he

[1] Bowring, vol. iii. 20.   [2] *Wealth of Nations*, bk. iv. ch. ix.
[3] *Lectures on Justice, Police, Revenue and Arms.*

alternatively had recourse, according to the subject in hand, to the hypothesis of universal egoism in order to explain the mechanism of exchange,[1] or to the hypothesis of sympathy in order to explain the origin of governments or the origin of the idea of legal punishment.[2]   It remains true that in so far as he is concerned with the study of what we should to-day call economic phenomena, Adam Smith considers man as exclusively, or at least fundamentally, egoistic.   ' The principle which prompts to save, is the desire of bettering our condition, a desire which, though calm and dispassionate, comes with us from the womb and never leaves us till we go into the grave.   In the whole interval which separates these two moments, there is scarce perhaps a single instant in which any man is so perfectly and completely satisfied with his situation, as to be without any wish of alteration or improvement of any kind ' ; and ' an augmentation of fortune is the means by which the greater part of men propose and wish to better their condition.'[3]   But Adam Smith does not merely lay it down as a principle that ' every individual is continually exerting himself to find out the most advantageous employment for whatever capital he can demand ' ; and that ' it is his own advantage, indeed, and not that of the society he has in view '.   He adds that ' the study of his own advantage naturally, or rather necessarily, leads him to prefer that employment which is most advantageous to society .'[4]   If you persist in wishing to call egoism a vice, you will have to say, with Mandeville, that the vices of individuals tend to the advantage of the public.   The economic doctrine of Adam Smith is the doctrine of Mandeville set out in a form which is no longer paradoxical and literary, but rational and scientific.   The principle of the identity of interests is not perhaps a principle which is true to the exclusion of all others, but it is a principle which can always be applied, in a general if not in a universal way, in the sphere of political economy.

Passages abound, in the *Wealth of Nations*, in which Adam Smith interprets historical events from this point of view—when he shows, for instance, how the egoistic passions, the love of lucre, the love of luxury, directed by an ' invisible hand ', necessarily unite to realise the general interest either of a society or of civilisation as a whole, without the wisdom of the legislator having any effect in the matter.[5] But all these explanations of detail rest on the fundamental theory, which Adam Smith sets forth in the first pages of his book—the theory, which has become classical, of the division of labour.

' The annual labour of every nation is the fund which originally supplies it with all the necessaries and conveniences of life which it annually consumes, and which consist always either in the immediate produce of that labour, or in what is purchased with that produce

[1] *Lectures*, p. 169.   [2] *Lectures*, p. 9 *sqq.*
[3] *W. of N.* bk. ii. ch. iii.   [4] *W. of N.* bk. iv. ch. ii.
[5] *W. of N.* bk. iii. ch. iv.

from other nations. According, therefore, as this produce, or what is purchased with it, bears a greater or smaller proportion to the number of those who are to consume it, the nation will be better or worse supplied with all the necessaries and conveniences for which it has occasion.'[1] Now it is the division of labour which increases the productivity of labour and differentiates barbarian from civilised society. The division of labour increases the dexterity of each workman taken individually, specialised as he is in a single occupation. It is the cause, much more than the result, of men's having different aptitudes ; it involves a saving of time which, without the division of labour, would be lost in passing from one occupation to another ; and lastly it has brought about the invention of ' machines which facilitate and abridge labour, and enable one man to do the work of many '.[2] Doubtless Hutcheson and Hume had already perceived the importance of this principle, but it was Adam Smith who saw in it a proof of the theorem of the natural identity of interests and exhibited its logical connection with the principle of utility. Unlike Hutcheson,[3] he considered the division of labour not as a cause but as an effect of exchange. This verifies the fundamental thesis that the general good is not the conscious object but a kind of automatic product of particular wills. For the division of labour and the general wealth which is derived from it is not the effect of a calculation on the part of human ' prudence ' or ' wisdom '. ' It is the necessary, though very slow and gradual consequence of a certain propensity in human nature which has in view no such extensive utility ; the propensity to truck, barter, and exchange one thing for another.' This propensity can itself be considered either as primitive, or more likely as ' the necessary consequence of the faculties of reason and speech ', or, as Adam Smith said in his lectures, of ' that principle to persuade which so much prevails in human nature '. It is a propensity unknown to all animals and common to all men : and it brings about the immediate reconciliation of the general interest and private interests. Adam Smith, then, unlike Hume,[4] did not consider the division of labour as a social link, analogous to the ' union of forces ', and therefore as important for the same reasons as other forms of social co-operation. For deliberate co-operation in one and the same task presupposes a constant disposition for sacrifice on the part of the collaborators ; but this is not the case with the co-operation which is due to exchange and the division of labour. The individual who proposes an exchange to his fellow does not appeal to his benevolence, nor even to the interest which might be, for society, the remote advantage accruing from the collaboration, and might make up for particular passing inconveniences from the mutual assistance they are rendering each

[1] *W. of N.* beginning of Introduction.
[2] *W. of N.* bk. i. ch. i.   [3] *A System of Moral Philosophy*, bk. ii. ch. iv. § 5.
[4] *Treatise*, bk. iii. part ii. sect. ii.

other. He persuades him by appealing to his egoism.[1] The
observation is none the less exact because of its paradoxical aspect.
In so far as men agree to accomplish the same acts in common,
there is a constant divergence between particular interests and the
general interest. In so far as men accomplish different acts, each
one individually for his own interest, the identity of particular
interests is absolute. Exchange is constantly differentiating the
tasks of all individuals considered as producers, and constantly
equalising the interests of all individuals considered as consumers.
This is the form which Utilitarian individualism takes in political
economy.

Exchange is the simplest and the most typical of all social phenomena : it is the original cause of the harmony of egoisms. In
accordance with what rule, then, is exchange carried out ? Obviously,
in the first place, the object exchanged must be *useful*. But its utility
though it is the necessary is not the sufficient condition of the value
it has in exchange. An object which is very useful but exists in an
almost unlimited quantity, and is such that it cannot be appropriated
by an individual—such, for example, as air or water—has no value
in exchange.[2] An individual, *A*, has a certain quantity of an object
which he does not need, and which perhaps an individual, *B*, does
need. *B* has a certain quantity of an object which he does not need,
and which perhaps *A* does need. They will get into relation with
one another in order to make sure what their respective needs are.
The bargain will spring out of the comparison of their needs, and
each one will try to persuade the other that he needs the products
which he has put on the market. But the comparison itself can only
come about indirectly. The quantity of products brought by *A* or
by *B* constitutes the *supply* on each side, and the quantity of products
brought by *B* or by *A* constitutes the *demand*. The relation between
the supply and the demand constitutes the exchangeable value of a
product. If the supply remains a fixed quantity and the demand
varies, the exchange value varies in the same way as the demand.
If the demand remains a fixed quantity and the supply varies, the
exchange value varies with the supply. In this way are determined
the variations of current or market value.

The analysis of value is, however, not yet complete. A certain
quantity of produce is assumed to be brought to the market, and
given. Value in exchange varies as the function of an independent
variable according as this given quantity is greater or less. Finally,
by hypothesis, supply or demand can either of them equally well
be considered as independent variable, or as fixed quantity. But
to present things under this aspect, supply and demand must be
considered as consisting of two quantities of material objects brought
to the market, or, if you like, as expressed by these two quantities.
But is it not permissible to inquire why such a given quantity and

[1] *W. of N*. bk. i. ch. iv   [2] *W. of N*. bk. i. ch. iv.

not another was brought from each side ? A psychological element is implied in the very idea of demand : a demand is a desire or a need. Must supply, then, which is an objective quantity, be set in opposition to demand, which is a psychical element and either is not measurable at all, or at any rate is not measurable by the same means as supply ? In reality, the notion of supply is implied in the notion of demand ; so that in the last resort we are concerned not with two supplies of one and the same quantity of products, but with two psychological needs, that is, with two demands. It is demand, then, which regulates supply according to which side in a bargain is held to constitute the demand. If I work and go on working in order to produce beyond my needs I do so because I know, or think I know, that there is a demand for this surplus, and the quantity of work which I have devoted to producing the object will serve to regulate my demands when face to face with the purchaser. Or again, though this is no more than the expression of the same idea in another form, we are instinctively inclined to consider exchange as consisting in the truck of one product for another. Such, in effect, is the aspect which things assume in the first place. Exchange, and consequently comparison, occurs more often between objects and objects than between an object and a quantity of work. ' It is more natural ', says Adam Smith, ' to estimate the value of an object by the quantity of some other commodity than by that of the labour which it can purchase. The greater part of people, too, understand better what is meant by a quantity of a particular commodity than by a quantity of labour.'[1] This is, however, a superficial and inexact view of things. All exchange is essentially exchange not of an object with an object, but of a pain with a pleasure, of the pain of parting with a useful object with the pleasure of acquiring a more useful object : economic *value* resides essentially in this *equivalent*.[2] But then cannot the labour which has gone to produce the object, and which consists in taking pains to obtain a pleasure, be considered as the very type of exchange, since the notion of exchange does not of its essence presuppose two individuals, but merely the comparison of a pain with a pleasure? ' The real price of everything, what everything really costs to the man who wishes to acquire it, is the toil and trouble of acquiring it. . . . Labour was the first price, the original purchase money that was payed for all things. It was not by gold or by silver, but by labour, that all the wealth of the world was originally purchased.'[3] To produce is to labour, to exchange a pain with a pleasure ; to exchange is to labour again, to produce a definite object with the view of obtaining another. Either then, after the exchange, in any particular case, my labour

---

[1] *W. of N.* bk. i. ch. v.
[2] *Value* and *equivalent* are synonymous words in Adam Smith's language (*W. of N.* bk. iv. ch. vii.).
[3] *W. of N.* bk. i. ch. iv.

will not receive the expected remuneration, in which case I shall henceforth give up producing the object in question : or else it will receive the expected remuneration, in which case the market price will be indistinguishable from what Adam Smith calls the natural price, which is in turn the same as the real price.   In other words, I shall have obtained, in the products of the labour of someone else, the same value that I should have obtained if I had myself laboured instead of him.   Thus, the labour I have spent in producing the object can in this case be considered as equal to the labour which this object can command or buy on the market.   This conforms to the nature of things.   ' It is natural that what is usually the produce of two days' or two hours' labour should be worth double of what is usually the produce of one day's or one hour's labour.' [1] The natural price of an object is the total value of the labour which must be expended in bringing it to the market.

Here, in Adam Smith's economic theory, we meet again the expression ' nature ' which we have already met in Bentham's juridical theory.   The ' natural ' measure of punishment results, according to Bentham, from a comparison between the amount of physical suffering inflicted by the judge and the amount of physical suffering which resulted from the act classed as a crime.   The ' natural ' measure of value results, according to Adam Smith, from the comparison made between the amount of pain suffered, or, if you like, of pleasure sacrificed, to produce the object, and the amount of pleasure which is expected to result from the acquisition of the object, whether this acquisition occurs directly through labour or indirectly through labour followed by exchange.   For punishment to be effective, the evil of the punishment must more than outweigh the evil of the crime.   For labour to be effective, the good of the remuneration must more than outweigh the pain of the labour.   But, further, in order to regulate the gravity of the legal punishment by the gravity of the crime, it is not enough to include the element of intensity only ; seven characteristics must be considered if the estimation is to be complete.   Similarly, when I want to estimate the wage or remuneration demanded by any given labour, it is not enough for me to consider whether the occupation, considered in itself, is more or less agreeable.   I must consider, in the second place, whether it has been more or less difficult or more or less expensive to learn ; what degree of perseverance it manifests ; whether it involves trust in him who devotes himself to it, and how much ; whether success in it is more or less probable.   Adam Smith, then, with a view to a thorough-going valuation of wages, has a moral arithmetic which bears some relation to Bentham's moral arithmetic.   But in Bentham's juridical theory the calculus of pleasures and pains is the deliberate work of the legislator and of the magistrate, so that the natural proportion of the legal punish-

[1] *W. of N.* bk. i. ch. vi. vol. i p. 49.

ment to the crime is artificially established, while in Adam Smith's economic theory the same calculus takes place spontaneously. Not only is it not necessary for the legislator to interfere—it is necessary that he should not interfere, if labour is to receive its due reward, and if wages are to be proportional to labour. 'The whole of the advantages and disadvantages of the different employments of labour . . . must, in the same neighbourhood, be either perfectly equal or continually tending to equality. If, in the same neighbourhood, there was any employment evidently either more or less advantageous than the rest, so many people would crowd into it in the one case, and so many would desert it in the other, that its advantages would soon return to the level of other employments. This at least would be the case in a society where things were left to follow their natural course, where there was perfect liberty, and where every man was perfectly free both to choose what occupation he thought proper, and to change it as often as he thought proper. Every man's interest would prompt him to seek the advantageous, and to shun the disadvantageous employment.'[1] In short, in Bentham's juridical theory, nature tells the legislator the method he should follow, but it is possible for him not to follow it. In Adam Smith's economic theory, nature works for justice or for the satisfaction of all the individual interests, without the interference of the legislator. But on what grounds is this assertion of Adam Smith's based ? Our view is that it is based on three principal conditions. First, the principle according to which objects exchange proportionately to the quantity of labour which has gone to produce them is true only of those objects whose quantity can be indefinitely increased by labour. Secondly, exchange is only approximately regulated by the amount of labour. Finally, the principle is only true of a society in which, unlike actual society, account need only be taken in fixing prices, of the wages of the labourer, and not of the rent of the landowner nor of the profit of the capitalist. Let us examine these three restrictions in turn, so as to understand why it was that the new economic doctrine tended to minimise their importance, and after all to attribute a universal value to the principle of the identity of interests.

Adam Smith himself distinguishes between three sorts of rude produce. 'The first comprehends those which it is scarce in the power of human industry to multiply at all. The second, those which it can multiply in proportion to the demand. The third, those in which the efficacy of industry is either limited or uncertain.'[2] Let us leave the third sort, which is of a mixed character and falls in between the first two. Retaining only the two extreme cases, it is clear that the principle according to which products exchange in proportion to the quantity of labour devoted to their production

[1] *W. of N.* bk. i. ch. x.   [2] *W. of N.* bk. i. ch. xi.

could only logically apply to the second case. In both cases, the general principle is that exchange value varies with the degree of facility in obtaining the object. But in the first case, the difficulty of obtaining an object is explained by a scarcity which is determined once for all by the nature of things ; in the second case the scarcity is only momentary and provisional, and it is possible for human labour to lower it constantly and indefinitely. Hence, it is a curious question why political economy, particularly since Adam Smith, emphasises the importance of the second kind of product, and tends to define value as a function not of scarcity but of the difficulty of obtaining the object by labour. For on this point Adam Smith had the choice between two perfectly distinct traditional doctrines.

On the one hand, Puffendorf takes as foundation of what he calls ' the proper and intrinsic price ', that is to say of value, ' the aptitude of things or actions to minister either mediately or immediately to the needs, the comforts or the pleasures of life ', that is to say their utility. But utility, though the cause, is not the measure of value ; consequently Puffendorf introduces the consideration of a second element into his theory of value : the *scarcity* of things.[1] Hutcheson, who follows Puffendorf very closely, considers that ' when some aptitude to human use is presupposed, we shall find that the prices of goods depend on these two jointly, the *demand* on account of some use or other which many desire, and the *difficulty* of acquiring or cultivating for human use '.[2] In other words, given the demand, the respective values of two objects are as the difficulty of obtaining those objects. This language is very similar to that of Adam Smith, and even more exact on two points. By ' use ', Hutcheson, differing from Adam Smith, means not only natural or reasonable utility, but also any aptitude to produce a pleasure which is founded on custom or fashion : and, above all, by ' difficulty of acquiring ', he means not only the amount of work necessary in order to produce or to obtain the object, but, in a more general way, the scarcity of which this difficulty is only a particular instance.

Locke, on the contrary, founded value on labour : ' It is labour indeed ', he says, ' that puts the difference of value on everything '; and he estimated at nine-tenths and even at ninety-nine hundredths the part due to labour in the value of an object.[3] As we have seen, he concluded from this that things are appropriated by labour, and that it is a ' law of reason ' which allots the deer to the Indian who has slain it ; in other words, his economic theory of value was, at the same time and indivisibly, a juridical theory of the right of property. If justice demands that every man should be rewarded according to his labour, then, in order for nature to conform to justice, the part of the exchange value of an object which is due to natural scarcity and cannot be reduced to human labour, ought to

---

[1] *Devoirs de l'homme et du citoyen.*   [2] *Moral Philosophy*, bk. ii. ch. xii. 1.
[3] *Civil Government*, bk. ii. ch. v. § 40.

be negligible. Then the primitive state of civilisation in which it is true that objects exchange according to values which are proportional to the amounts of labour which have produced them, would, in the last analysis, be merged into that 'state of nature' which, according to Locke's political theory, had to be replaced owing to the injustice of individuals by a civil society, in which the natural rights of individuals are limited by the intervention of a government.

If therefore Adam Smith follows the tradition of Locke in his definition of value, may it not be because he is, consciously or unconsciously, similarly preoccupied? He wants the natural price to be the just price, and postulates as much as proves the principle of the identity of interests; and at the same time he postulates that the interests of all will be equally safeguarded, if each man receives in proportion to his labour. ' The produce of labour constitutes the *natural recompense* or wages of labour '.[1] In fact there are many juristic expressions, which it is difficult to reduce to the philosophy of utility, in Adam Smith's definition of the natural state of things in which objects are exchanged proportionally to the labour which produced them, without legislative intervention. He occasionally opposes what is right to what is useful. Sometimes, no doubt, utility only signifies the particular, or as Bentham would say the ' sinister ', interests of the treasury. Adam Smith complains, for instance, that ' the sacred rights of private property are sacrificed to the supposed interests of public revenue '.[2] Or again, when he forbids the ' sacrifice of the ordinary laws of justice to an idea of public utility, to a sort of reason of state, an act of legislative authority, which ought to be exercised only, which can be pardoned only in cases of the most urgent necessity ' [3]—this expression can be interpreted if by ' the ordinary laws of justice ' is understood utility reduced to general rules as opposed to utility considered in regard to any particular and exceptional case. But the freedom of every individual to seek his own interest in his own way is always defined as a right. Two laws which hinder the progress of the division of labour are declared to be ' unjust ', since they constitute ' evident violations of natural liberty '.[4] Any attack on the economic freedom of the citizens of a nation was, according to Adam Smith, a manifest violation of the ' sacred rights of mankind ',[5] and the programme which he drew up he called ' the liberal plan of equality, liberty and justice '.[6] Although his theory was already worked out on this point in 1763, it may be that he was decisively influenced by his journey to France and his association with the physiocrats who regarded natural laws as final, and the order of things as providential and in conformity with divine justice, and upset only by the arbitrary and guilty interventions of mankind.

[1] *W. of N.* bk. i. ch. viii.   [2] *W. of N.* bk. i. ch. xi.
[3] *W. of N.* bk. iv. ch. v.   [4] *W. of N.* bk. iv. ch. v.
[5] *W. of N.* bk. iv. ch. vii.   [6] *W. of N.* bk. iv. ch. ix.

In the second place, even in the case of those objects the quantity
of which can be indefinitely increased by labour, the rule is only
true in a general and average way. This new modification, which
must be made in the supposed proof of the principle of the natural
identity of interests, is really implied in Adam Smith's own definition : ' It is natural that what is *usually* the produce of two days'
or two hours' labour, should be worth double of what is *usually*
the produce of one day's or one hour's labour '.[1] If two hunters
set out at the same time to hunt a deer, and return each with their
deer, it will not matter that one captured his deer after two hours'
and the other after four hours' hunting ; the natural price of a deer
will be determined by the average time which it takes to capture a
deer in the particular society under consideration. Further, since
the natural price is itself defined in this way, the current price and
the natural price do not always coincide. To be accurate, the
current price must be said to be determined, on an average, by the
average amount of work necessary to put the object on the market.
This is proved by an analysis of the play of supply and demand.
Given a certain supply, there is an *effectual* demand from those
people who are prepared to pay the natural price ; and the effectual
demand, defined in this way, is distinguished from the absolute
demand. In a sense one may say that some very poor man demands
a carriage, for it is possible that he may desire it. But his demand is
not effectual, for the object can never be brought on the market
to satisfy it. Either, then, the amount supplied will be insufficient
to satisfy the effectual demand, in which case the price will rise above
the natural price because of the competition of those who demand.
Or else it will be too great, and the price will fall below the natural
price.[2] May not these oscillations above and below the level set
by the natural price be very marked and very prolonged ? Adam
Smith doubts this, and is inclined to treat them as negligible. ' The
quantity of every commodity brought to market naturally suits
itself to the effectual demand. It is the interest of all those who
employ their land, labour or stock in bringing any commodity to
the market, that the quantity *never* should exceed the effectual
demand ; and it is to the interest of all other people that it *never*
should fall short of that demand '.[3] ' Without any intervention of
the law, therefore, the private interests and passions of men naturally
lead them to divide and distribute the stock of every society, among
all the different employments carried on in it, as nearly as possible
in the proportion which is most agreeable to the interest of the
whole society '.[4] The theorist who is seeking a rational explanation
of natural phenomena is entitled to see, in the universality of a
phenomenon, the sign of a necessary law : impatient to discover
the necessary laws, he naturally tends to identify the general with

[1] *W. of N.* bk. i. ch. vi.   [2] *W. of N.* bk. i. ch. vii.
[3] *W. of N.* bk. i. ch. vii.   [4] *W. of N.* bk. i. ch. vii.

the universal, to abstract what he calls the accidental, and almost to deny particular exceptions, which, however, in a more complete science, would be capable of being explained by the disturbing influence of other principles.

We are thus entitled to ask whether Adam Smith's theory of the division of labour and of exchange value, instead of affording a proof of the principle of the natural identity of interests, does not really postulate the truth of the principle in order to make it possible to neglect the exceptions to which, in fact, his theory of exchange is liable. At any rate, Adam Smith sets himself to exhibit all the conditions, both physical and psychological, on the fulfilment of which the truth of the principle of the natural identity of interests is dependent. First it would have to be possible for objects to be brought to the market, at all times, from all places, and in indefinite quantities : the better this condition is satisfied, the more the market price remains constant, near to the natural price.[1] But above all, individuals would have to be, all the time, kept perfectly cognisant of their real interests. Adam Smith seems inclined to admit that the nature of economic phenomena satisfies this last condition. No doubt sellers may sometimes be mistaken, to a greater or less degree, as to what amount of a product it is to their advantage to bring to the market ; but, in the last resort, particular mistakes cancel out.[2] No doubt ' the principles of common prudence do not always govern the conduct of every individual ' : there are a certain number who are disinterested and prodigal. Nevertheless, these principles ' always influence the conduct of the majority of every class or order ' : [3] even among borrowers, who are not as a rule considered economical, the number who are economical and industrious ' considerably exceeds ' those who are prodigal and lazy. Not only has every individual an interest, but each individual is the best judge of his own interest : this, perhaps, is the fundamental postulate of the method. This postulate may be held to confirm, in a sense, the rationalistic character of the new doctrine : it presupposes that individuals who are perfectly selfish are also, as a general rule, perfectly reasonable.

Besides, even if there were no foundation for the above observations, even if Adam Smith did not neglect too much the variations of the market price about the natural price, even if he did not insist too much on the natural intelligence of the selfish individual, to say that the principles of political economy are only approximately true is not to class them with simple empirical data, or to deny the rational character of the doctrine. Statistics form the inductive method in economic and social matters ; and Adam Smith neglects and disdains them : ' I have no great faith ', he tells us, ' in political arithmetic '.[4] *It is true, absolutely, that, in a general way, the current*

---

[1] *W. of N.* bk. iv. ch. i.   [2] *W. of N.* bk. ii. ch. v.
[3] *W. of N.* bk. ii. ch. ii.   [4] *W. of N.* bk. iv. ch. v.

price is determined by the natural price : these words could be said to
sum up the doctrine of Adam Smith, in a single formula which
takes into account both the principle and the exceptions to the
principle. His method is always the method of Newton, which we
have already seen applied to psychology and morals : to attain, by
generalisation, certain simple truths, from which it will be possible
to reconstruct, synthetically, the world of experience. A metaphor
taken from Newton found its application in the new political economy:
on two occasions Adam Smith defines the natural price as being, as
it were, the central price towards which the market prices of all
commodities are continually ' gravitating '.[1]

But at this point the principle must be submitted to a third
restriction, more serious than the preceding ones. No doubt
there exists a primitive state of society in which the whole produce
of labour belongs to the labourer ; but, in time, labour produces a
capital which is not consumed in the ordinary course, and the
possessor of capital is prepared to advance it to the labourer, on
consideration of *profit* ; with time also the whole of the land becomes
occupied, and then it becomes possible for the landlord to demand
a *rent* in exchange for the use of the land which belongs to him.[2]
Now, neither *profit* nor *rent* are the *wages* of labour. If, therefore,
they enter as elements into the price of some commodity, it is
because there is a division of gain without a corresponding division
of labour ; and since it is the division of labour based on exchange
which produces the identity of interests, the identity is no longer
necessary, and there may be divergence. Moreover, Adam Smith
accepts the development of profit of stock and rent of land as natural
phenomena. In the definition of *natural* price we have hitherto
included, for convenience in exposition, only the element of labour ;
but to complete the definition it must be stated that a commodity
sells at its natural price, ' when the price of any commodity is neither
more nor less than what is sufficient to pay the rent of the land, the
wages of the labour, and the profits of the stock employed in raising,
preparing, and bringing it to market, according to their natural
rates '.[3] It may be, then, that the divergence of economic interests
is the work not of human artifice, but of nature itself.

At times, Adam Smith appears to admit this. He actually says
that, in certain countries, ' rent and profit devour wages ', and consequently admits that the interests of what he calls the two upper
orders and the lower order are in necessary opposition.[4] He admits
that the complaints of the capitalists are well founded from the point
of view of their particular interests, though he says they are ill founded
from the point of view of the general interest, when directed against
the increase of real wages which goes hand in hand, in civilised
countries, with the lowering of profits.[5] Further, he admits that

[1] *W. of N.* bk. i. ch. vii.   [2] *W. of N.* bk. i. ch. vi.   [3] *W. of N.* bk. i. ch. vii.
[4] *W. of N.* bk. iv. ch. vii.   [5] *W. of N.* bk. i. ch. xi.

' the rent of land, therefore, considered as the price paid for the use of the land, is naturally a monopoly price '.[1] Thus, according to him, there are natural monopolies, which ought, it appears, to falsify the mechanism of exchange in the same way as artificial monopolies. Finally, Adam Smith shows a disregard for the principle on the strength of which all interests are identical on the one hand, and each individual is the best judge of his own interest on the other. In a passage in the *Wealth of Nations*,[2] after analysing the economic condition of those three classes which are in a way natural, he formally concludes that their interests are not all equally in harmony with the general interest, and that the individuals who belong to the one or to the other respectively are not equally good judges of their real interest.—Because rent necessarily rises with the natural progress of wealth, therefore the interest of the landed class is closely and inseparably bound up with the general interest of the society. Unfortunately, landowners are bad judges of their interests, because they are the only one of the three classes whose income costs them neither work nor anxiety, but comes to them as it were spontaneously and independently of all forethought, and so they become indolent, and incapable of mental application and foresight.—Because the wages of labour rise with the demand for labour, the interest of the labourer is as closely bound up with the interest of society as is that of the landowner. Unfortunately, the labourer is ignorant, incapable either of comprehending that interest, or of understanding its connection with his own, unless the government takes pains to instruct him.[3]—Finally, the economic position of the capitalists is quite different and to some extent opposite. They are the best informed and the most intelligent. But the rate of profits is naturally low in rich and high in poor countries ; the interest of this third order, therefore, has not the same connection with the general interest of the society as that of the other two. There is no case in which the principle according to which each man is the best judge of his own interest is better applicable : by way of compensation for this, the deception, or naïve error, of the capitalists consists in their believing in the principle of the identity of interests, when really there is a divergence between their interests and the interests of the public.

But then, if nature is unjust, and if the interests of the capitalists are not the same as those of the landowners and wage-earning labourers, while the capitalists have a superior understanding of their particular interests, might not the government authority intervene in order to re-establish justice and the identity of interests by means of legislative artifices ? First, cannot the State conceive laws to protect the labourer from the capitalist who employs him ? Adam Smith himself admits that the principle of liberty suffers an exception

---

[1] *W. of N.* bk. i. ch. xi. [2] *W. of N.* bk. i. ch. xi.
[3] *W. of N.* bk. v. ch. i.

where traffic in money is concerned.[1] He acknowledges that the violation of natural liberty is legitimate in certain definite cases in which it would endanger ' the security of the whole society '.[2] Now, in the particular case of contracts between masters and workmen, on the one hand the interests of the two parties are in no way the same; and, on the other hand, the masters, being richer and less numerous, are in a permanent and unjust coalition against the labourers.[3] Adam Smith states this; but he does not ask for any state intervention; he does not even ask that the men should be allowed the freedom to combine; he merely denounces, in general terms, the spirit of combination and of corporation, and criticises the complicated system of governmental socialism in England, which was inherited either from the Middle Ages or from the sixteenth century, and whose arrangements are a perpetual obstacle to the free circulation of labour.[4] Inevitably, and as if in his thought there were no contradiction as between the principle of the identity of interests and an opposite principle, Adam Smith again repeats that the only way of protecting the workman is to leave him free, and once more identifies, in a formal text, ' natural liberty ' and ' justice '.[5] Is not the State, at least, the fixer of taxes? Could it not therefore arrange taxation so as to correct fiscally existing economic inequalities? This idea was very clearly put forward, fifty years later, in the writings of the leaders of Philosophical Radicalism, and of James Mill in particular. It is present in embryo in Adam Smith, who borrowed a good deal from the physiocrats, and admitted that rent was perhaps the form of income best suited to support a special tax.[6] But Adam Smith merely mentions this idea by the way; nor is any preoccupation to correct the unequal distribution of the produce between the three economic classes implied in any of those four rules, soon to become classical, which, according to him, should determine the fixing of the tax. On the contrary, he starts by laying down, as a general rule and ' once for all ', that any tax which ends by falling on one only of the three kinds of income mentioned above is necessarily unequal to the extent to which it does not affect the other two,[7] and must, therefore, be rejected; so that in defiance of the real divergences between the interests of the classes, it is again on the postulate of the identity of interests that the four rules depend.

How then can we explain that the thesis of the natural identity of interests should tend once again to predominate over the thesis of the divergence of interests in the doctrine of Adam Smith? How explain, also, that Adam Smith, having stated the fact of the natural divergence of interests, should be able to conclude, with some appearance of logic, in favour of the thesis of liberalism and governmental non-intervention?

---

[1] *W. of N.* bk. ii. ch. iv.   [2] *W. of N.* bk. ii. ch. ii.   [3] *W. of N.* bk. i. ch. viii.
[4] *W. of N.* bk. i. ch. vii.   [5] *W. of N.* bk. i. ch. x.   [6] *W. of N.* bk. v. ch. ii.
[7] *W. of N.* bk. v. ch. ii.

First, it should be observed that the theories relative to the distribution of wealth between the three economic classes were introduced into Adam Smith's doctrine too late and, as it were, from outside. They are like a foreign body which the organism is constantly tending to eliminate. There is no trace of them either in Hume's economic essays, nor in the rudiments of economic teaching contained in Hutcheson's *Moral Philosophy*, nor in the lectures delivered by Adam Smith at the University of Glasgow. The contribution made to modern political economy by those who were called in England, since 1763, the ' Glasgow theorists ',[1] consisted of the theory of exchange and labour. Then Adam Smith visited Paris, and it was only then, in his intimacy with Quesnay and the physiocrats,[2] that he dimly saw the possibility of discovering, by means of analysis, a certain number of irreducible elements in the value of exchangeable commodities. But, for Adam Smith, this theory was always a borrowed theory, lacking any systematic exactness. Hence the contradictory nature of the theory of value as expounded in the *Wealth of Nations* : the value of a commodity is measured now by the amount of work it has cost to produce it,[3] now by the amount of work it can command on the market, once it is produced.[4] The contradiction [5] does not occur in the lectures of 1763 ; [6] but this is because Adam Smith had not yet made the distinction which rendered it impossible to measure value purely and simply by the amount of labour which the commodity had cost —the distinction, namely, between the three elements of value— wages, profits and rent. To this was due also the lack of precison in the relations set up between the variations in wages, profits and rent. There was no fixed relation between the variations in profits and those in the other elements of value. There was no rigid definition of rent. Is it because of its absolute fertility that the land provides the landowner with an income equal to the *difference* between the wages of the labourer and the total product ? Or is it because of its relative fertility, that is to say its real sterility and scarcity, that it provides the landowner with an income equal to the *difference* between the produce of labour on the least fertile portion of the land and the produce of labour on the other portions of the soil ? Adam Smith lacked the logical energy necessary to decide between the theory of the physiocrats and the future theory of the Radical Utilitarians, of Ricardo and of James Mill.

The criticism here offered of Adam Smith is thus reduced, in the last resort, to this : that he failed to put his theory of the formation of wages, profits and rent into a sufficiently systematic form. Perhaps, however, this objection would not have affected Adam

[1] Rae, *Life of Adam Smith*, p. 61.   [2] *Ibid.* 215-7.
[3] *W. of N.* bk. i. ch. v.   [4] *W. of N.* bk. i. ch. vi.
[5] See Ricardo's criticism, *Principles*, ch. i. sect. 1.
[6] *Lectures*, p. 176.

Smith ; for the fundamental objection that he, for his part, urged
against Quesnay and his disciples, was just that they were too
systematic. He reproached Quesnay, who was himself a doctor,
for being too much like those doctors who do not rely on the *vis
medicatrix naturae*, and hold that the health of the body depends
exclusively on the rigorous observance of a scientifically determined régime. Yet, if a nation could only prosper ' under the
exact régime of perfect liberty and perfect justice ',[1] there is not a
nation in the world which can ever have prospered. Adam Smith's
chief complaint against all the laws by which governments try to
intervene in the economic life of nations, is perhaps less of their evil
consequences than of their inherent infirmity. Have not the Dutch
establishments of the East and West Indies developed in spite of the
régime of monopolistic companies, because ' the plenty and cheapness
of good land are such powerful causes of prosperity, that the very worst
government is scarce capable of checking altogether the efficacy
of their operation '.[2] Is not smuggling, which is tolerated and
encouraged by public opinion, a practical refutation of ' all the
sanguinary laws ' of the customs ?[3] Historical conditions, round
about the year 1776, were favourable to scepticism as regards the
efficacy of law. Was there ever a time when the executive and
legislative power was weaker than in the England of the eighteenth
century ? Surrendering before popular disturbances and before
the permanent combination of masters, it put into practice the
policy of *laisser-faire* before it found a justification, or even an
apparent justification, in the new doctrine.[4] The liberal thesis
found a powerful auxiliary in this governmental inertia and weakness.
But though a weak political power may have the advantage, from the
new point of view adopted by the theorists of commercial and
industrial liberty, of letting things go and practising *laisser-faire*,
it has the serious disadvantage of being spendthrift, of spending
and of allowing spending : on this point the supporters of the
new doctrine urged the government to cope with itself. It was
well that it should not intervene to regulate commerce and industry ;
but the levying of taxes also is a kind of intervention. It is expedient
—the two conditions are reducible to one only—that the government
should govern and should spend as little as possible. The original
meaning, not yet obsolete by the year 1780, of the expression *political
economy*, was in accordance with this conception. Adam Smith,
when he wrote his *Wealth of Nations*, and Burke, when he produced
his famous speech on economic reform, understood by ' political
economy ' a ' branch of the science of a statesman or legislator ', a
theory of practice, the science of the prudent management of the
public finances.[5] The growth of the huge debts which weighed

[1] *W. of N.* bk. iv. ch. ix.   [2] *W. of N.* bk. iv. ch. vii.   [3] *W. of N.* bk. iv. ch. i.
[4] See Carlyle's interesting remarks, *Chartism*, chs. vi. and vii.
[5] *W. of N.* bk. iv. Introd.

on the great military nations would end by proving their ruin. This was especially true of England, which had become immensely in debt through the conquest of her colonial Empire. Further, if one of the provinces of this Empire were to rebel against the capital, it was surely time ' that Great Britain should free herself from the expense of defending those provinces in time of war, and of supporting any part of their civil or military establishments in time of peace, and endeavour to accommodate her future views and designs to the real mediocrity of her circumstances '.[1] The *Wealth of Nations* closes with this circumspect and timid advice.

We are not concerned, then, to deny the co-existence of two distinct principles in Adam Smith's thought. On the one hand, Adam Smith shows that the division of labour, which identifies interests as it were mechanically, implies the development of exchange, inasmuch as it is its necessary and sufficient condition ; and the development of exchange itself implies the extension of the market of exchanges. It appears from other passages, however, that the division of labour is not adequate to identify interests, and that, in certain cases, a divergence of interests occurs between the capitalists, the landed proprietors, and the labourers. But even when they start from contradictory premises, Adam Smith's arguments arrive at a common conclusion—economic liberalism, the almost indefinite reduction of the functions arrogated to themselves by governments in these matters. Adam Smith never admits that the government should intervene to protect one class against another, even when his principles seem to justify this conclusion : he upholds industrial as well as commercial liberty. Since human society exists and subsists, it must be that the principle which identifies individual interests is more powerful than the principle which severs them ; and reason, which criticises social injustices, has little strength to remedy them, as compared with the instinctive power of nature. Thus economic liberalism can still be considered as being an optimistic doctrine, but it certainly cannot still be considered as optimism based on reason. It has often been questioned whether the economic method of Adam Smith should be defined as an inductive or a deductive method, as an empiricism or as a rationalism. Clearly the future deductions of Ricardo and of James Mill are present in germ in the *Wealth of Nations*. Clearly, also, there is, in the liberalism of Adam Smith, a logical conflict between two tendencies, the one rationalistic and derived from Newton, the other almost sceptical, or, more accurately, naturalistic and derived from Hume. Nevertheless, at a time when reformers are on the lookout for a common doctrine, if only the practical conclusions have the appearance of unity, they will be able to arrive by induction at unity of principle from the unity of the consequences. Therefore, they naturally prefer the rationalistic to the naturalistic principle,

[1] *W. of N.* bk. v. ch. iii.

since they hope to systematise or, if you like, to rationalise their ideas. The task of the theorists of the new political economy was to disguise Anglo-Saxon naturalism as rationalism.

Further, let us consider historical conditions. If industrial freedom, the non-intervention of the State as between the classes, is not logically deducible from the principles of Adam Smith, this is certainly not the case with commercial freedom. It is this second problem which attracted attention round about the year 1776. No doubt the Law of Apprenticeship and all the old State Socialism was departing bit by bit, not because the interests of masters and workmen were identical, but because of the rapid progress of machinery and the insufficiency of the old legislative framework to contain the new industrial society.[1] But Adam Smith practically neglected the important historical fact constituted by the invention of machines, and only mentions it in brief allusions. The great historical fact, of which Adam Smith's doctrine is the theoretical equivalent, is the American Revolution. This, in a sense by force, converted the English public to the new doctrine of commercial liberalism, and showed the possibility of establishing commercial cosmopolitanism in the near future. The idea of free-trade spread first among isolated reformers, then among the most enlightened part of the public, then among an ever-increasing section of the population, whose immediate interests were suffering from a prolonged war. These liberal ideas implied a principle; they needed a doctrine, and a thinker to arrange them in a system. At the propitious moment, Adam Smith gave them a definite and classical form. No commercial regulation can increase the amount of industry beyond what can be employed by the social capital. ' It can only divert a part of it into a direction into which it might not otherwise have gone ', and ' it is by no means certain that this artificial direction is likely to be more advantageous to the society than that into which it would have gone of its own accord '. Every individual tends to employ his capital as near home as possible, and, consequently, in a way which is as favourable as possible to the progress of the national industry ; he also tends to employ it in the most advantageous way possible. Thus, ' if the produce of domestic can be brought there as cheap as that of foreign industry, the regulation is evidently useless. If it cannot, it must generally be hurtful. It is the maxim of every prudent master of a family never to attempt to make at home what it will cost him more to make than to buy ', and ' what is prudence in the conduct of every private family can scarce be folly in that of a great kingdom '. It is thanks to external commerce that the narrowness of the home market does not hinder the division of labour in any particular branch of art or manufacture being carried to the highest perfection '.[2] Any regulation limiting the freedom of commerce—between two provinces, between a

[1] Webb, *Hist. of Trade Unionism*, p. 42 *sqq.*   [2] *W. of N.* bk. iv. ch. ii.

mother-country and its colonies, between two colonies of the same mother-country, between any two nations whatever—when it is not useless is evil, because it contradicts the principle of the identity of interests.

In short, in spite of so many restrictions, the principle whose triumph is consecrated by Adam Smith's book, is the principle of the natural identity of interests. Further, the *Wealth of Nations* should be considered neither as an Utopian nor as a revolutionary book. Contemporaneous with the Declaration of American Independence, the book was hardly a few years in advance of the average opinions of any supporter of the reforms which were both necessary and possible in the England of the eighteenth century. Any thinking man would find in it the ideas which he himself was already beginning to form, under the pressure of historical events, and with the tacit and permanent collaboration of all enlightened people. Such an one, above all, was Bentham. In 1784, his friend Schwediaur wrote to him from Edinburgh : ' Doctor Smith, with whom I am intimately acquainted, is quite our man '.[1] Since 1780 Bentham had been the close friend and periodically the guest of Lord Shelburne. Now, Lord Shelburne, who had been the friend of Adam Smith and Morellet [2] for twenty years, was the first English statesman to outline the new policy of commercial liberalism.[3] This he did in his short ministry in 1782 ; and it was at about the same time that Bentham, who had hitherto been completely absorbed by the purely juridical problem, seems to have turned his attention to the economic problem. To make doubly clear what were the reasons which, at about this time, inclined the theorists of the new doctrine irresistibly to emphasise the principle of the identity of interests at the expense of the dim apprehension that there are natural divergences of interest, it is only necessary to read, side by side with the work written by the master, the economic pamphlets of his disciple Bentham.

Political economy, Bentham tells us, includes a *science* and an *art* ; and the science must be taken to be closely subordinated to the art.[4] In conformity with the principle of utility, the end to be pursued in all branches of the art of legislation should be to produce the maximum of happiness, during a given time, in the society in question. In other words, Bentham defines political economy as Adam Smith had defined it, as a ' branch of the art of legislation ', the knowledge of the best use to be made of the national wealth, and of the means necessary to produce ' that maximum of happiness, in so far as this more general end is promoted by the production of the

[1] Bowring, vol. x. 136.   [2] Rae, *Life of Adam Smith*, p. 153.
[3] See Disraeli's curious remarks on his policy in *Sybil*.
[4] Bowring, vol. iii. 33.

maximum of wealth and the maximum of population '.[1]   But Adam Smith had prefaced his researches in political economy by three books of purely theoretical research into the conditions of the production and distribution of wealth.   Bentham, on the contrary, completely neglects this preliminary part of the task of the economist.   His one anxiety is to find a useful application of the theories, and so it is the solution of a practical problem which he demands of Adam Smith. He adopts his liberalism.   But the liberal thesis seems to imply the principle of the natural identity of interests as its necessary principle, while the examination of the distribution of wealth in a society composed of labourers, capitalists and landowners reveals natural divergences of interest.   Bentham does not go into the question, but is content to refer to Adam Smith, ' who has not left much to do, except in the matter of method and precision ' ; [2] and he leaves to others the task of this logical revision of the first three books of the *Wealth of Nations*.   In the words of Dumont of Geneva, ' the aim of Bentham was to determine what the law ought to be on such and such a point—what must be done, and above all what must not be done, for the national prosperity to reach the highest possible point '.[3]

Bentham agrees that it is difficult to fix a distinctive characteristic to distinguish specifically economic laws from all other laws.[4] Nevertheless, since a distinction has been made, in the ends of civil law, between security and equality, and between subsistence and abundance, all dispositions which tend to increase the national wealth by means other than security and equality may be taken to belong to the class of economic laws.   What, then, can the law do as regards subsistence and abundance ?   Any intervention on the part of the government is costly ;   it is therefore a cause of diminishing the national capital ;   it is therefore evil in itself.   But this is not a reason for condemning radically all government intervention, as is done by so many writers and orators who are ignorant of the true ' logic of the laws '.   Here, the calculus must be brought in, losses and gains must be compared, and it must be said that all government intervention must be held to be bad, when it is not proved that it involves an excess of benefit.   It will be necessary in cases where individuals lack inclination, power or knowledge with regard to the end they are pursuing.[5]   Now the first of these three elements, inclination, is practically never lacking.   For the whole mass of the national wealth is the sum of the particular masses which belong to individuals, and the inclination which leads the individual to increase his capital is constant.   In this way economic liberalism

---

[1] Adam Smith's definition in *W. of N.* bk. iv. Introd. ;   Bentham's definition, Bowring, vol. iii. 1.

[2] Bowring, vol. iii. 35.

[3] *Théorie des Récompenses*, liv. i. p. 247.   Cf. Bowring, vol. iii. 33.

[4] Bowring, vol. iii. 203.   [5] Bowring, vol. iii. 35.

seems to be the necessary consequence of the individualism of the Utilitarians. Power is either legal or physical. Legal power depends on the government in so far as the government refrains from restraining it by laws. Physical power, which consists of wealth itself, cannot be conferred by the government on one person without involving at least an equivalent loss for someone else. There remains knowledge. ' There are cases in which, for the benefit of the public at large, it may be in the power of government to cause this or that portion of knowledge to be produced and diffused, which, without the demand for it produced by government, would either not have been produced, or would not have been diffused.' [1] What is the use, for example, of advancing capital to men in industry ? Is it to encourage them to turn their industry to the best advantage ? But what except their ignorance prevents them from doing this ? The government therefore should give them information, not capital ; its function is to instruct and not to lend. The activity of the government should be confined to encouraging the study of the useful sciences; it should start prizes for discoveries and experiments; it should see to the publication of the processes used in every branch of industry, and of the prices of the various products ; it should protect inventors against theft and imitation : this should be the limit of governmental activity.[2] Beyond this it should lie low, and practise what Bentham calls *quietism*.[3] At the outset, Bentham had professed that in political economy he was studying not the science but the art. Now, in terms which at least seem to contradict his original declaration, he affirms that, in political economy, the science is almost everything and the art almost nothing : for the art in such matters is to know how to do nothing.[4] It was in this way that in ancient science the universal order seemed to be inevitably compromised by the sacrilegious intervention of human art. Does not the principle of the natural identity of interests, interpreted in this way, seem to contradict the modern idea of an active and conquering science ? In point of fact, many of Bentham's contemporaries who were partisans of commercial liberalism—such as Josiah Tucker and Edmund Burke—did tend to speak of the state of nature as a providential and divine state of things.[5] In any case, Adam Smith had laid down the principle, and on two points of detail Bentham developed, with a more logical thoroughness than Adam Smith had done, the consequences of his Liberalism.

In making his scientific classification of crimes, Bentham had, a long time previously, recognised the impossibility of assigning a place on the list to the supposed crime of usury.[6] Then, when he

[1] Bowring, vol. iii. 34-5.   [2] *Ibid.* 71.   [3] *Ibid.* 33.
[4] *Ibid.* 35.
[5] Josiah Tucker, *The Case of Going to War*, p. 31 ; Burke, *Letters on a Regicide Peace*, Works, vol. viii. p. 337.
[6] Bowring, vol. i. 118.

was in Russia, the news reached him that Pitt had declared his intention of once more lowering the maximum rate of legal interest, from five to four per cent. ; [1] so he prepared to resume his idea and discuss Pitt's measure. ' You know it is an old maxim of mine, that interest, as love and religion, and so many other pretty things, should be free '.[2] But his London friends warned him that the news had been fabricated.[3] Bentham therefore made his attack not against Pitt for making worse the existing laws against usury, but against his master, Adam Smith himself, for having given those laws his approval, in defiance of his principles. In his *Wealth of Nations* Adam Smith discusses and criticises the prohibition of lending money at interest, since such prohibition results in raising instead of lowering the rate of interest, because the creditor is to some extent obliged to insure himself against the law, and he states that ' in countries where interest is permitted, the law, in order to prevent the extortion of usury, generally fixes the highest rate which can be taken without incurring a penalty '. Then, without even examining whether this fixation is useful, useless, or harmful, he merely lays down that, on principle, ' this rate ought always to be somewhat above the lowest market price, or the price which is commonly paid for the use of money by those who can give the most undoubted security '. If this legal rate should be fixed below the lowest market rate, the effects of the fixation must be nearly the same as those of a total prohibition of interest,—with the result that the law is violated. If the legal rate is precisely at the lowest market price, it ruins the credit of all those who cannot give the very best security and obliges them to have recourse to exorbitant usurers. If it is fixed much above the lowest market rate, at eight or ten per cent. for example, the law would favour borrowers, prodigals, projectors, inventors and floaters of companies, who alone would be willing to pay such a high interest, at the expense of wise and prudent men.[4]

Bentham aims at extending the principle of the freedom of commerce to trade in money, and at showing that ' no man of ripe years and of sound mind, acting freely, and with his eyes open, ought to be hindered, with a view to his advantage, from making such bargain, in the way of obtaining money, as he thinks fit : nor (what is a necessary consequence) anybody hindered from supplying him, upon any terms he thinks proper to accede to '.[5] Why, indeed, is the notion of free trade in money not accepted by public opinion ? It is because of two inveterate prejudices, one religious and ' ascetic ', the other philosophical. On the one hand, the ascetic morality condemns the acquisition of wealth ; trade in money is therefore reprehensible. This prejudice is strengthened by anti-Jewish prejudice. On the other hand, Aristotle laid it down as a principle that *all money is in its nature barren*. Now, if he meant to say that

[1] Bowring, vol. x. 163.   [2] Bowring, vol. x. 167.   [3] *Ibid.* 171.
[4] *W. of N.* bk. ii. ch. iv.   [5] Bowring, vol. iii. 3.

interest on money is theoretically impossible, what need is there of taking so much trouble to forbid it ?   But as a matter of fact money does bring interest, and Bentham suggests a kind of physiocratic explanation and justification of interest ; money, which is barren in itself, bears interest because it represents natural forces, fertile in themselves, which man presses into his service.[1]

There is a *legal* definition of usury : to practise usury is to lend money at interest higher than the legal rate.   There is also a *moral* definition : to practise usury is to lend at interest higher than the average current rate.   Now the first definition is reduced to the second, if the legal rate can only be determined by the current rate. ' Custom, therefore, is the sole basis, which either the moralist in his rules and precepts, or the legislator in his injunctions, can have to build upon.   But what basis can be more weak and unwarrantable, as a ground for coercive measures, than custom resulting from free choice ? '[2]   Laws against usury are harmful in proportion to the number of men whom they prevent from receiving the money which they need.   ' Think what a distress it would produce, were the liberty of borrowing denied to everybody : . . . Just that same sort of distress is produced, by denying that liberty to so many people whose security, though if they were permitted to add something to that rate it would be sufficient, is rendered insufficient by their being denied that liberty.'[3]   They are harmful : for, by the very fact that they prevent the individual from *borrowing* under conditions which are held to be disadvantageous, they force him to *sell* under conditions which certainly are disadvantageous.   In so far as they are eluded, because they are badly drawn up, they are partly inefficacious and partly mischievous.   The law is ' nugatory as to all such whose confidence of its being so is perfect : it is mischievous, as before, in regard to all such who fail of possessing that perfect confidence '.

Besides, is it not the supporter of the laws against usury who ought to be proving his thesis, since it is he who is asking for restrictions to be made on human liberty ?   Will he then invoke the necessity of protecting *indigence* against *extortion*,[4] and *simplicity of mind* against *imposture* ?[5]   Adam Smith gave the answer when he said that every individual is the best judge of his own interests. Will he, like Adam Smith, appeal to the necessity of discouraging *prodigality* ?[6]   Bentham thinks that it is not prodigals who exclusively or chiefly borrow at high interest.   They have many other and more natural ways of making money for themselves.   There remains then only the argument that legal fixation of the rate of interest is necessary in order to prevent ' usury ' and to repress the temerity of projectors : it is against these two points that Bentham throws the weight of his criticism.

---

[1] Bowring, vol. iii. 16.   [2] Bowring, vol. iii. 4 ; *Defence of Usury*, letter ii.
[3] Bowring, vol iii. 9.   [4] *Ibid*. 7.   [5] *Ibid*. 8   [6] *Ibid*. 5.

Bentham's work essentially consists in the work of criticism of current language. Human language is badly made : its formation was determined by the principle of sympathy and antipathy rather than by the principle of utility. Every word has a connotation, either favourable or unfavourable, which is not necessarily justified ; thus it is that ' in the sound of the word *usury* lies . . . the main strength of the argument '. ' Usury is a bad thing, and as such ought to be prevented : usurers are a bad sort of men, a very bad sort of men, and as such ought to be punished and suppressed. These are among the string of propositions which every man finds handed down to him from his progenitors—which most men are disposed to accede to without examination ; and indeed not un-naturally nor even unreasonably disposed, for it is impossible that the bulk of mankind should find leisure, had they the ability, to examine into the grounds of an hundredth part of the rules and maxims which they find themselves obliged to act upon.'[1] The unpopularity of the business of the money-lender can easily be explained. ' Those who have the resolution to sacrifice the present to the future, are natural objects of envy to those who have sacrificed the future to the present. The children who have eaten their cake are the natural enemies of the children who have theirs.'

But *jockeyship* is a term of reproach which sounds as bad as usury ; yet the law has never tried to fix a legal price for horses on the market. ' I have already hinted at the disrepute, the ignominy, the reproach, which prejudice, the cause and effect of these restrictive laws, has heaped upon that perfectly innocent and even meritorious class of men, who, not more for their own advantage than to the relief of the distresses of their neighbour, may have ventured to break through these restraints. It is certainly not a matter of indifference, that a class of persons, who, in every point of view in which their conduct can be placed, whether in relation to their own interest or in relation to that of the persons whom they have to deal with, as well on the score of prudence as on that of beneficence . . . deserve praise rather than censure, should be classed with the abandoned and profligate, and loaded with a degree of infamy which is due to those only whose conduct is in its tendency the most opposite to their own.'[2]

The same thing is true of projectors as of usurers. Opinion regards them with disfavour : hence an unfavourable meaning is inseparably associated with the word, and the prejudice against them is strengthened. The thirteenth letter is addressed to Adam Smith and reproaches him for having, on this point, made use of ' the poverty and perversity of the language '.[3] ' I have sometimes been tempted to think, that were it in the power of laws to put *words* under proscription, as it is to put *men*, the cause of inventive industry might perhaps derive scarcely less assistance from the bill of attainder

---

[1] Bowring, vol. iii. 3.   [2] *Ibid.* 10.   [3] *Ibid.* 21.

against the words *project* and *projectors*, than it has derived from the act authorising the grant of patents. I should add, however, for a time : for even then the envy, and vanity, and wounded pride, of the uningenuous herd, would sooner or later infuse their venom into some other word, and set it up as a new tyrant, to hover, like its predecessor, over the birth of infant genius, and crush it in its cradle.' [1] In pleading the cause of the projectors, Bentham, the inventor of the Panopticon, was to some extent pleading his own cause. He understood that the régime most favourable to the development of inventive faculties was one of absolute liberalism. Moreover, in his criticism of Adam Smith, he based his view on the very principles which Adam Smith had himself laid down. Had not Adam Smith originated the criticism of common language ? Had he not protested against the unfavourable meaning which men instinctively attached to the words *regrater*, *engrosser*, *forestaller*, and pointed out the beneficent role played in the mechanism of exchange by the middlemen who speculate in corn ? ' You have defended against unmerited obloquy two classes of men—the one innocent at least, the other highly useful : the spreaders of English arts in foreign climes, and those whose industry exerts itself in distributing that necessary commodity which is called by the way of eminence the staff of life. May I flatter myself with having succeeded at last in my endeavours to recommend to the same powerful protection, two other highly useful and equally persecuted sets of men—usurers and projectors ? ' [2]

The abolition of the legal rate of interest had been called for in France by the economists,[3] and even in England, in an otherwise insignificant book by Playfair.[4] But it was to Bentham that public opinion attributed the honour of being the first to draw, on this point, all the conclusions of the new economic doctrine. The *Monthly Review* declared that ' among the great number of works of value of this kind which had attracted its attention, none should be ranked higher, by reason of the penetration of its arguments, and perhaps also of the national importance of its conclusions, than this little volume.' [5] According to Bentham, it was due to the influence of his pamphlet that, the year after it came out, the legal rate of interest was reduced in England from six to five per cent. According to Bentham again, Adam Smith, after having read it, declared himself a convert. ' The work ', Adam Smith had said, ' is one of a superior man. He has given me some hard knocks, but in so handsome a manner that I cannot complain '.[6]

Thus it was as an economist that Bentham first really attracted public attention. How could it be otherwise when the form in

[1] Bowring, vol. iii. 28.　　　[2] *Ibid.* 29.
[3] Turgot, *Sur la formation et la distribution des richesses*, lxxv.
[4] *The Interest of Money Considered*, 1787.　　　[5] May, 1788, art. i.
[6] Bowring, vol. x. p. 176.

which the Utilitarian doctrine was already meeting with success in the opinion of the England of his time was that of economic liberalism ? Moreover, Bentham did not restrict his efforts to criticising the laws against usury : in the general plan of political economy which he outlined, he once more took his stand on the doctrine of Adam Smith in order to condemn, more definitely perhaps than Adam Smith had done, the supposed economic utility of colonial possessions. Bentham laid down, as Adam Smith had done, at the beginning of the practical part of his work, the principle that ' industry is limited by capital '. ' If I possess a capital of £10,000, and two species of trade, each yielding twenty per cent. profit, but each requiring a capital of £10,000 for carrying them on, are proposed to me, it is clear that I may carry on the one or the other with this profit, so long as I confine myself to one ; but that, in carrying on the one, it is not in my power to carry on the other ; and that if I seek to divide my capital between them both, I shall not make more than twenty per cent. ; but I may make less and even convert a profit into a loss. But if this proposition be true in the case of one individual, it is true for all the individuals in a whole nation. Production is therefore limited by capital.' [1] But Bentham claims to follow up, with more consistency than Adam Smith had done, the application of this principle to the whole field of political economy. This principle suffices, on his view, to prove in a few words, the uselessness of colonies. ' I have a capital of £10,000 employed in commerce. Suppose Spanish America were opened to me, could I, with my £10,000, carry on a greater trade than I do at present ? Suppose the West Indies were shut against me, would my £10,000 become useless in my hands ? Should I not be able to apply them to some other foreign trade, or to make them useful in the interior of the country, or to employ them in some enterprise of domestic agriculture ? It is thus that capital always preserves its value : the trade to which it gives birth may change its form or its direction, may flow in different channels, may be directed upon one manufacture or another, upon foreign or domestic undertakings ; but the final result is, that these productive capitals always produce ; and they produce the same quantity, the same value, or at least the difference does not deserve attention.' [2] On this point, as between Adam Smith and Bentham, if there was no progress, there was at least simplification.

It was doubtless on the principle which states that ' industry is limited by capital ' that Adam Smith had mainly founded his ' political economy ' in the fourth book of the *Wealth of Nations*.[3] But at the very beginning of the work another principle had been laid down—the principle of exchange and of the division of labour, and this alone must be held to be really fundamental. This principle Bentham neglected—hence the exaggerated simplicity of his proof.

[1] Bowring, vol. iii. p. 43.   [2] *Ibid.* 54.   [3] *W. of N.* bk. iv. ch. ii.

Adam Smith had not been satisfied with pointing out that the monopoly in colonial trade had continually removed capital from other trades in order to transfer it to the trade with the colonies. He had also shown that, by the restriction of the market of exchange, this monopoly had necessarily helped to keep the rate of profit in the various branches of British commerce higher than it would naturally have been if freedom of exchange with the British colonies had been granted to all nations : hence there was a divergence between the interests of the capitalists and those of the mass of consumers.[1] He did not stop even there. He considered the hypothesis that monopoly, by forcibly attracting a certain amount of the national capital into colonial trade, might perhaps have found the most advantageous use for that capital ; and he set himself to prove in detail that this could not be the case as far as concerned colonial trade.[2] Bentham did not even discuss the problem : he wrote, ' It is therefore the *quantity of capital* which determines the quantity of trade, and not *the extent of the market* as has been generally believed.' In other words, he set up against one another, as if they were in contradiction, the principle of the limitation of industry by capital and the principle of the division of labour. Adam Smith had already stated that there was a kind of contradiction between the principles since the division of labour was to some extent accelerated by the existence of capital, and, conversely, the formation of capital was to a certain extent accelerated by progress in the division of labour. But he rightly gave precedence to the principle of the division of labour. Bentham neglected this principle ; hence these declarations, inspired by a singularly optimistic fatalism :—' Open a new market,—the quantity of trade will not, unless by some accidental circumstance, be increased ; shut up an old market,—the quantity of trade will not be diminished, unless by accident, and only for a moment.'[3] Such is the rough form which the ideas of the master, Adam Smith, took in the disciple, Bentham, until finally, alongside of Bentham and in his own school, they assumed a rigorous and systematic character which Adam Smith and Bentham had not foreseen.

The simpler the doctrine, the easier it was for Bentham to conclude from arguments of expediency that colonies were useless. But whatever the present uselessness of colonial possessions, Adam Smith thought, none the less, that the colonisation of the new world had been eminently useful ; it had enriched humanity by enlarging the market of exchange.[4] According to Bentham, colonies are absolutely useless from the point of view of the economist. Sometimes, they may have the advantage of providing an outlet for surplus population. Situated as they are in far-off climes, with different fauna and flora from ours, they have the advantage of varying the nature of social

[1] *W. of N.* bk. iv. ch. vii.
[2] *Ibid.*
[3] Bowring, vol. iii. 54.
[4] *W. of N.* bk. iv. ch. vii.

wealth. But they cannot increase its quantity: their economic utility is ' equal to zero '.[1] Adam Smith did not think it possible to suppress at one blow the regulations protecting the trade of the mother-country with its colonies, without stirring up a dangerous crisis: certain traders and manufacturers had, under the artificial régime which was created for them, a real interest in preserving the monopoly.[2] He also held that it was vain to hope that a nation would ever voluntarily renounce its colonies; national pride and the interest of the governing classes would oppose it.[3] Bentham neglected all these factors: if the interest of the mother-country was the only thing at stake, if the colonists did not sometimes need to be defended, he concluded that there should always be immediate separation, in cases where the inhabitants of the colonies were of the same race as the inhabitants of the mother-country.[4] *Emancipate your Colonies!* was the advice he addressed to the French revolutionaries some years later.[5] Already, since the publication of the *Wealth of Nations*, had not the fact of the American Revolution settled the problem? England had lost the finest part of her colonial Empire, and, commercially, she had not suffered from that loss. But what we are here concerned to make clear is the simplification to which the new doctrine was submitted in passing from the book of the student and scientist, Adam Smith, to the writings of the philanthropist and propagandist, Bentham. A theory may be too simple, in that it omits certain important aspects of reality, and nevertheless remain true. But this time Bentham falsified the theory of Adam Smith in proportion as he simplified it: obviously it was the very simplicity of the principle he set forth which endowed it for Bentham with the prestige of a truth.

Thus, about the year 1785, Bentham found that he had succeeded in fusing the economic theories of Adam Smith with his own juridical theories. They were in agreement as to the definition of the functions of the State. ' Since liberty ', wrote Morellet to Lord Shelburne, ' is a natural state, and restrictions are, on the contrary, the state of compulsion, by giving back liberty everything reassumes its own place, and everything is in peace, provided only that thieves and murderers continue to be caught.'[6] This, in epigrammatic form, is the actual view of Adam Smith. In other words, it is not the function of the State directly to increase wealth and to create capital; its function is to guarantee security in the possession of wealth once it has been acquired. The State has a judicial function

[1] Bowring, vol. iii. 52.
[2] *W. of N.* bk. iv. ch. vii.
[3] *W. of N.* bk. iv. ch. vii.
[4] He seems to think, however, that European control is beneficial to the East Indies (see Bowring, vol. iv. 417).
[5] *Emancipate your Colonies!* (Bowring, vol. iv. 407 *sqq.*).
[6] *Lettres de l'Abbé Morellet à Lord Shelburne*, p. 102.

to fulfil, but its economic function must be reduced to a minimum. By adopting the theories of Adam Smith, Bentham brought about a first step in the formation of that system of ideas which constituted the Philosophical Radicalism of forty years later. His powers as a logician, as an ' arranger ', more even than his inventive powers, inclined him to assume the control of this movement of systematisation. For the power of logical arrangement has two distinct uses. When it applies to established institutions and sets out to justify them, it is a power for reform : whatever its efforts, intelligence cannot succeed in systematising absolutely in relation to a single principle institutions which are incoherent. Blackstone, the arranger, was led to suggest certain reforms, just because he was trying to systematise English law.[1] When it is applied to various new ideas which spring up on all hands at one and the same time in the minds of innovators and revolutionaries, the power of logical arrangement plays the opposite part of a power for moderation : it eliminates ideas which are extreme and often contradictory, and introduces into the revolutionary instinct an element of fixity and stability. Let us try to estimate the logical solidity of the social theory which, barring future modifications which are always possible, from this time on consisted of the combined doctrines of Adam Smith and Bentham.

The principle is the same. Pleasures, in so far as they are pleasures, are capable of being compared with each other as regards their quantity : a calculus of pleasures and pains is possible. The end pursued by morals and legislation is the greatest happiness of the greatest number, or again the identification of the interest of all with the interest of each.

In their pursuit of this end, Adam Smith and Bentham encountered the same obstacle—the spirit of corporation. A corporation is a particular society formed within the general society, whose interests clash with those of the general society. Corporations live their own life and remain unchangeable while society changes round them ; they prolong the prejudices of the past into the present. Thus the struggle against corporations has the appearance of a struggle for intellectual emancipation, and the economists found themselves led, by the necessity of things, to confound economic liberalism with moral liberalism. ' The laws concerning corn ', Adam Smith tells us in a passage of his book in which he also admits the necessity of compromising with error, ' may everywhere be compared to the laws concerning religion. The people feel themselves so much interested in what relates either to their subsistence in this life, or to their happiness in a life to come, that government must yield to their prejudices, and, in order to preserve the public tranquillity, establish that system which they approve of '.[2] Or again :—' The popular fear of engrossing and forestalling may be compared to the popular terrors and suspicions of witchcraft. . . .

[1] Blackstone, I. Comm. 301-302.   [2] *W. of N.* bk. iv. ch. v.

The law which put an end to all prosecutions against witchcraft, which put it out of any man's power to gratify his own malice by accusing his neighbour of that imaginary crime, seems effectually to have put an end to those fears and suspicions by taking away the great cause which encouraged and supported them. The law which should restore entire freedom to the inland trade of corn would probably prove as effectual to put an end to the popular fears of engrossing and forestalling.' [1]   The new era is the era of ' freedom of conscience in trade ',[2] according to the Abbé Morellet, and ' the era of Protestantism in trade ',[3] according to Lord Shelburne. The corporations were abusing their power in order to extract from the State, within which they constituted so many small distinct states, penal laws to protect their own ' sinister ' interests, which became more and more numerous and severe. Adam Smith denounced the severity of the revenue laws against crimes which were created by the law itself ; [4] all the reformers of law at the end of the eighteenth century protested, in the name of humanity, against a penal law which was out of date. Yet this liberalism and sentimentalism were not characteristics proper to the new doctrine which was being worked out. It was the idea of utility and not the idea of liberty or intellectual emancipation which was fundamental in Adam Smith, and above all in Bentham (as we have seen, Bentham protested on several occasions against sentimental liberalism). They endowed the Liberal movement which was carrying everything before it in Europe with a Utilitarian formula peculiar to the Anglo-Saxon world.

Further, although the principle of utility is the common principle of Bentham's juridical philosophy and Adam Smith's economic philosophy, it has not the same sort of application in both cases.—The object of society is the identity of interests ; but the identity of interests is not realised spontaneously : therefore in order to establish it the law must intervene. Bentham's juridical philosophy can thus be expressed in syllogistic form.—Quite the opposite is true of Adam Smith's economic philosophy, now adopted by Bentham. Adam Smith tells us that the object of society is the identity of interests ; but the identity of interests is realised spontaneously : therefore, if it is to be realised, it is necessary for the law not to intervene.—In the two syllogisms the major is the same and the minors are different. Why, then, is the first syllogism true in juridical and false in economic affairs ? And, why, on the other hand, is the second which is true in economic not true in juridical affairs ? Even in the work of Adam Smith, it is possible to find, as we have tried to show, reasons for asserting that the identity of the interests of the wage-earner, the landlord and the capitalist is not spontaneously realised, and consequently that it is useful and even necessary for

[1] *W. of N.* bk. iv. ch. v.   [2] *Lettres de l'abbé Morellet*, etc., p. 74.
[3] Quoted by Lecky, *Hist. of England*, vol. iv. p. 444.
[4] *W. of N.* bk. iv. ch. viii.

the State to intervene in the economic relations of the citizens, from the point of view of the supporter of the principle of utility. Exchange is the fundamental idea in political economy, and the postulate implied in the principle of the identity of interests is the idea that exchange is constantly giving labour its recompense, and that the mechanism of exchange is just. But in fact, the laws of exchange are only in conformity with justice in cases when the individuals affected by the exchange are both of them labourers, deriving an equal produce from an equal labour. If then this condition is not realised, does not the principle of utility prescribe that, when the two notions of *exchange* and *recompense* do not coincide, the notion of *recompense* should be put before the notion of *exchange*, and legislative artifices should be conceived such that all labour may be guaranteed its recompense, and every need its satisfaction ?—Or else if, on the contrary, the principle of the spontaneous identity of interests is true, why should it not be applied in its entirety ? And why, since all constraint is recognised as bad, should not the State be refused the right of intervening by means of penal restraints in the social relations of the citizens ? Why should the idea of criticising the notion of punishment be considered Utopian, when it logically rests on the same foundation as does the criticism of all intervention by the State in the economic relations of the citizens ?

It is not impossible, however, to explain how a thinker of Bentham's school was able to justify this combination of two different interpretations of the principle of utility. In Bentham's words, ' the function of government is to promote the happiness of society by rewards and punishments '. Now, while the fundamental principle of the doctrine is that pleasure is the natural end of human actions, it is another principle, and one that is almost as essential, that, in nature, every pleasure is exchanged for a pain, and is bought at the price of labour, of effort, and of pain. At bottom, it is the forgetfulness of this natural necessity, and the preference for the pleasure which is secured immediately as opposed to what is useful, which is the cause of crimes. It is for the State to correct this human tendency towards impatience by inflicting punishments, on condition that the infliction of punishments is always reduced to the strict minimum, and that it is always borne in mind that the utility of the punishment resides not in the actual infliction but in the threat of the chastisement. On the other hand, it is going against the nature of things to try to make men act by the promise of a reward—apart from the fact that it is impossible to give to one man without taking from another and consequently that the giving of a reward always implies the infliction of a pain somewhere else. It is making men act through the attraction of pleasure pure and simple, and this is contradictory : for to act is to work, and to work is to suffer.[1] No

[1] See Bowring, vol. i. pp. 18-19.

doubt, Adam Smith seemed to us to be giving way to the preoccupations of a rationalistic optimism when he neglected all the accidents which were introduced into the economic world by the natural difficulties of production, and when, to establish his theory of value, he considered those objects only ' which can be indefinitely increased by labour '.   But even this amounted to saying that labour must be considered as a necessary condition of human existence if an economic science is to be possible ; it was established that labour alone is the measure of our needs, and consequently that needs, or what comes to the same thing, utilities, can no longer be compared and measured once there is abundance.   So that, in the last resort, the economic liberalism of Adam Smith and Bentham appears to be less an absolute optimism than a doctrine which is perpetually insisting on the difficult and painful conditions to which, by reason of the very constitution of things, we must submit when we apply ourselves to the methodical and calculated realisation of our interests.

2.   DEMOCRATS AND UTILITARIANS

What were the historical causes of the movement of democratic opinion which was shaking the Anglo-Saxon world at the time when Bentham was beginning to write ?   On what philosophical principles, more or less explicit, did the agitators take up their stand ?   What were the signs which were foreshadowing the still distant fusion of the Utilitarian and the Democratic ideas ?   How, above all, explain that the attitude to the first democrats adopted by the chief supporters of the Utilitarian morality seems at first to have been, generally speaking, an attitude of defiance or hostility ?   Such are the delicate problems to be solved in the welter of political ideas and the confusion of parliamentary parties.

It was in 1776 that Bentham published his first work, the *Fragment on Government*, in which he examined the principles of public law in Blackstone.   Now it was also in the year 1776 that the American Colonies declared their independence after twelve or thirteen years of semi-rebellion.   The colonists first refused to pay taxes to which their local assemblies had not agreed.   The disciples of Locke claimed that ' no taxation without representation ' was one of the clauses of the original contract.   Hume went so far as to find in this assertion an argument against the doctrine of the contract : what value, indeed, can be attributed to opinions which are so far removed from the common practice of humanity everywhere except in England ? [1]   If we are to believe Lord Camden, it is a natural law, and a consequence of the right of property.   ' For whatever is a man's own is absolutely his own.   No man has a right to take it

[1] *Essay*, XII. Of the Original Contract.

from him without his consent, either expressed by himself or representative. Whoever attempts to do it attempts an injury. Whoever
does it commits a robbery.' [1] When the Americans refused to pay
a tax which their representatives had not voted, the minister replied
by drawing a distinction between internal and external taxes, and also
by the theory of virtual representation. Although the Americans
were not represented in Parliament actually and by law, they were
at least virtually represented on the same ground as the inhabitant
of Manchester or Birmingham who sent no representative to Parliament, and who nevertheless paid the taxes voted at Westminster.
The Americans, however, refused to accept the doctrine of virtual
representation, a juristic expedient conceived to justify the
electoral régime in England, which was incoherent, out of date,
and deformed by the effect of time. To this theory of *virtual*
representation they opposed the theory of *real* representation : no
one is represented unless he elects his representative. This theory is
logically inseparable from the theory of universal suffrage. The
doctrine was inscribed in the local constitutions of several of the
American colonies, all of which were more democratic than the
English constitution, and some of which were altogether democratic.
In this way, in their struggle with the mother country, the American
colonies found that, in order to defend the principles of the Revolution
of 1688, they were naturally driven to lay down more fundamental
principles. In 1774, for the first time, the colonists solemnly
'declared' the 'rights' which they possessed 'by the unchangeable
laws of nature, the principles of the English constitution and various
charters and contracts '; then, in 1776, they definitely broke with
the mother country, and, as the English had done in 1688, enumerated
the ways in which George III had usurped the rights of his subjects ;
but, unlike the English of 1688, they prefaced this catalogue with a
purely philosophical exposition of universal principles. The
American Revolution provided the solution of a theoretical debate,
which had long been going on, whether a republic was conceivable
for a large territory, or whether the republican form is only suited
to small States. In the seventeenth century, Sidney inclined to
support the second alternative, and held that democratic government
was only suited to ' the convenience of a small town ', and this was
the reason why he preferred a mixed government for a large State.[2]
His view was shared, in the eighteenth century, by the great majority
of constitutional writers : by a republic they meant the Greek city
of antiquity, the Italian city of the Middle Ages, or, perhaps the
Swiss canton or the Dutch State. Hume alone, who was always
inclined to question received ideas, made certain reservations which
were justified by the American Revolution.[3] If by democracy is
meant the direct government of the people by the people, then a

---

[1] Lecky, *Hist. of England*, vol. iii. p. 338.
[2] *Discourses concerning Government*, ch. ii. sect. xvi.   [3] Hume, *Essay*, XVI.

democratic régime is possible only in a town or in a territory of small extent. But the idea of *representation* allows the exigencies of the régime to be adapted to a large territory, and the idea of *federation* allows the application of democratic government to be extended to a still vaster territory. Why should not the idea which had appeared in America spread in Europe ? Price, one of the most ardent English advocates of the American cause, asked whether universal peace would not be established on the day when the nations of Europe should follow America's example and form themselves into United States ? [1]

In fact, at this very moment the democratic idea was passing from America to Great Britain through the mediation of Price, Priestley and many others. John Cartwright, born in 1740, was a political writer who had formerly been a naval officer ; in 1776 [2] he published his *Take your Choice*. In it he exhibited the right of suffrage as an inalienable natural right and advocated the establishment of universal suffrage in England—the last stage of an evolution of ten or twelve years of political agitation. A series of violent incidents, which made famous the names of Wilkes and Junius, had just humiliated the power of the King, and consecrated the freedom of the journalist, which was henceforth guaranteed against the arbitrary power of the policeman, the judge and the parliamentary oligarchy. The first public meetings were being held, the first political associations formed. The election of Wilkes, continually repeated and continually annulled, made it clear that the king was able to use his corrupting ' influence ' against Parliament, and to make Parliament, which was supposed to arise from the popular will, serve as his instrument against the people's liberties. ' Representatives of the people ', declared the Lord Mayor to the King, ' are essential to the making of laws ; and there is a time when it is morally demonstrable that men cease to be representatives. That time is now arrived. The present House of Commons do not represent the people '.[3] The English now made use of the three liberties which were henceforth held to be inseparable—freedom of the press,[4] freedom to hold public meetings, and freedom of association [5]—to uphold a liberty which was more precious, a right which was more essential— the freedom of elections, the right of representation.

One way of protecting the freedom of parliamentary elections would be to demand a place bill specifying that members of Parliament should be excluded from certain employments, civil and especially military, in order to lessen the seductive ' influence ' of the King, the distributor of appointments. This, in fact, was one of the reforms demanded by the Society for the defence of the Bill of Rights,

---

[1] Price, *Observations on the Nature of Civil Liberty* . . . sect. ii.
[2] In 1774 he had published his *Proposals for recovering America* . . .
[3] *Annual Register*, March 14, 1770 (p. 200).
[4] Bowring, vol. i. p. 288.   [5] *Ibid.*

which was formed in 1769 at the time of the Wilkes affair, to protect the principle of the freedom of elections. Further, in order to put the legislative assembly into more frequent contact with the electoral body, a demand might be made for shortening the length of Parliaments, for reducing it from seven years to three, or even, more radically still, to a year. This Alderman Sawbridge, one of the most active politicians of the City of London, and one of the best known members of the Society of the Bill of Rights, periodically demanded in the House of Commons, beginning in the year 1772. Above all, however, the question of the freedom of elections, once put, involved unexpected and most serious consequences : to save the principle, it became necessary to undertake not only the defence of the existing electoral régime against usurpation by the power of the crown, but also the transformation of the régime itself—the reform of parliamentary representation. There were on the one hand those who thought that the venality of the electoral body was directly proportionate to the poverty of the electors. They held that under the English régime the constitution of certain districts was too demagogic, and required that the number of electors should be diminished in order to guarantee the real freedom of the elections.[1] But side by side with them were others, and these were more numerous, who used a different argument. They insisted on the thesis that the more restricted the number of citizens who compose it, the more venal the electoral body. It may be easier to buy the conscience of a poor man than the conscience of a rich man ; but it is far easier to buy a hundred electors than a hundred thousand. Besides, if you admit, as do all Englishmen, the maxim of ' no taxation without representation ', how can you require the restriction of the right to vote in a country and under a régime where so many citizens who are not represented in the electorate pay taxes ? To make the freedom of elections effective, the necessary reform lay, therefore, not in restricting but in enlarging the electoral body. Lord Chatham, who had been thrown into opposition and had just taken up the cause of Wilkes, began in the year 1770 to make a campaign in this direction, and Junius supported his policy, calling it ' admirable '. On July 23, 1771, the Society of the Bill of Rights instructed its members to work with all their power to secure ' a complete and equal representation of the people in Parliament ' ; and the Constitutional Society, founded by Horne Tooke after his sensational quarrel with Wilkes, sought to realise the same programme.[2] Already many people saw in the formula ' a full and equal representation ' not only the giving of new seats to the counties, as Lord Chatham demanded, but also the abolition of a certain number of rotten boroughs. This was the proposition which Wilkes made to the Commons on March

[1] See Josiah Tucker, *A Brief Essay*, etc. ; Burke, *Observations on* . . . ' the State of the Nation '.
[2] *Junius*, 1812 edition, particularly vol. i. p. 277.

21, 1776.[1] But already Lord Chatham, Horne Tooke and Wilkes had been outstripped.

However great the alarm which the members of the Society of the Bill of Rights and of the Constitutional Society—men who were later called the democrats of the ' old school '—caused to Whigs with conservative and aristocratic tendencies like Burke, at heart they were still moderates. They admitted *virtual* representation : after as before the realisation of their programme, there would be a restricted number of individuals who would vote in the name of the whole community. They admitted *varied* representation ; and agreed that boroughs should be represented as boroughs, counties as counties, different interests under different heads. If, however, the formula ' a full and equal representation ' is to have its full meaning it must be admitted that representation will only be really ' full and equal ' when *all* men are *equally* electors. We have an absolute right of property over our goods ; if we consent that the State should remove a portion of them, it is on the strength of the original contract and inasmuch as we shall always be represented in the counsels of the government. But we have likewise an absolute right of property over our person ; if therefore we agree that our personal liberty should submit to certain legal restraints, it is on the strength of the original contract, and also on condition that we are represented in a legislative assembly, so that we can control the faithful carrying out, by the executive, of the clauses of the contract. Consequently, just in so far as it is legitimate to say ' no taxation without representation ', it is equally legitimate to say ' no legislation without representation ' : anyone who obeys the law, and not only anyone who pays taxes, has the right to be an elector. The title of John Cartwright's pamphlet was in itself a manifesto : ' *Take your Choice ! Representation and Respect : Imposition and Contempt. Annual Parliaments and Liberty : Long Parliaments and Slavery.*' In it he laid down, for the first time, the principle of personal representation : ' that *personality* is the sole foundation of the *right* of being *represented* : and that *property* has, in reality, nothing to do with the case '.[2] Civil servants and soldiers (with the exception of the militia) alone should be ineligible. He demanded universal suffrage : all citizens of eighteen or older to have one vote and one vote only ; secret voting ; annual Parliaments, and elections carried through in one day ; and electoral districts each containing an equal number of inhabitants.[3] Experience showed that this programme could be applied. Did not England possess an elected militia, in which Cartwright served with the rank of Major ? If therefore the difficulties involved in electing, by secret voting, thirty-six thousand military representatives had been overcome, would it be impossible to choose five hundred and thirteen civil repre-

---

[1] *Speeches of Mr. Wilkes* . . . (1786), pp. 545 *sqq.*

[2] *Legislative Rights*, § 41.   [3] *Ibid.* § 152 *sqq.*

sentatives, given the *will* to undertake the task ?[1] The American colonies supplied another example in support of this. The democrats were in sympathy with the Americans ; and part of the task which the Society of the Bill of Rights set itself was to restore to America ' the essential right to be taxed by representatives of their own free choice '. Priestley attacked the anti-liberal policy of the government ' in Great Britain and the colonies ' ;[2] Price published his *Observations on the Nature of Civil Liberty, the Principles of Government, and the Justice and Policy of the American War* ; and Cartwright himself published a pamphlet on American independence in the year 1775.[3] In 1777, in the second edition of his book, he pointed out that the new plan for the constitution of Pennsylvania satisfied all the conditions which he had laid down.[4]

It seems that Cartwright was preceded in his demand for universal suffrage by Lord Stanhope in the year 1774. In 1779, Jebb gave his adherence to ' Major Cartwright's system '.[5] In 1780 Cartwright, with Jebb's support, founded the Society for Constitutional Information, which spread abroad the outlines of a Declaration of Rights, which had been drawn up by Cartwright. He entered into relations with the politicians of the Whig Party ; and from the alliance concluded with Fox and Sheridan arose the Westminster Committee of Correspondence, which adopted for a moment but without much conviction the programme of Cartwright.[6] He, having addressed himself in vain to Lord Shelburne, had already found an ally in the House of Lords, in the person of the Duke of Richmond, who brought in a bill on June 2, 1780. This bill affirmed ' the natural, inalienable and equal right ' of all the *commoners* of the realm, with the exception of infants, aliens and criminals, ' to vote for the election of their representative in Parliament ' ; and it demanded that parliaments should be elected annually ; and, since the number of members of the House of Commons was five hundred and eight, that the total number of adult males should be divided into five hundred and eight groups, each of which should have the right to elect one member.[7]—With the exception of a very small group, the democrats of this time were not republicans. Price agreed to the existence of a *Hereditary Council*, and of a *Supreme Executive Magistrate*. ' This will form useful checks in a legislature ; and contribute to give it vigour, union and dispatch, without infringing liberty ; for, as long as that part of a government which represents the people is a *fair representation* ; and also has a negative on all public measures, together with the sole power of imposing taxes and originating

[1] *Legislative Rights*, § 135.
[2] *The Present State of Liberty*, . . . etc., by an Englishman, 1769.
[3] In the same year he refuted Burke's speech on American taxation in an open letter.
[4] *Ibid.* § 154.
[5] See his *Memoirs*.
[6] Moore, *Life of Sheridan*, pp. 219, 220.
[7] Bowring, vol. iii. p. 553.

supplies ; the essentials of Liberty will be preserved '.[1] We have
seen the historical changes following which the democratic idea, as
thus defined and limited, took shape between the years 1769 and 1780.
Locke, a century earlier, in 1688, and Adam Smith at this very
moment, were each able to consecrate the appearance of a new idea
by the publication of a book of classical importance. But the thesis
of universal suffrage in the year 1776 had not this good fortune.
Neither Priestley nor Price was a thinker of the first class. Neither
Cartwright nor Jebb was, strictly speaking, a philosopher. It was
in the street, from Westminster to Mansion House, it was round
the hustings of Middlesex, in journalists' articles, in pamphleteers'
tracts, and in politicians' speeches, that the future ' Radical ' programme was drawn up, round about the year 1776.

But a programme is not a doctrine. It is conceivable that the
same programme of reforms may be based on different philosophical
principles, according to the individuals who draw it up. Now the
democrats of 1776 learnt in America the ideas they were spreading ;
and a few years later a French witness, Condorcet, in his *Tableau
des progrès de l'esprit humain*, reproached the American constitutions
expressly because they had as their principle ' the identity of
interests even more than the equality of rights '.[2] Was the philosophy of the Anglo-Saxon democrats really the philosophy of
utility ?

Let us first consider the state of public feeling, and note that
towards the end of the eighteenth century it was not only thinkers,
but Englishmen as a whole, who were speaking the language of
utility. The parliamentarians and the cynical courtiers of George III
professed and practised Mandeville's philosophy. ' I give you so
much,' said the older Fox, the great corrupter of 1760, ' and you shall
give me so much in return, and so we'll defy the world, and sing
Tol de rol '. From the formula which he applied to the purchase
of consciences, Adam Smith derived his philosophy of universal
free trade. ' Every set of men are honest ', said Fox again, ' it's
only necessary to define their sense of it, to know where to look for
it ; every man is honest or dishonest, according to the sentiments
of the man who speaks of him. . . . Nor are honesty and art absolutely opposite qualities, but I can conceive a sensible man very
easily to do what is called honest, that is punctual in his dealing, and
meaning well to the man he deals with to the best of his abilities,
and very artful at the same time.'[3] This was the expression, at

[1] *Observations on . . . Civil Liberty*, sect. ii.
[2] *Esquisse d'un Tableau Historique des Progrès de l'Esprit Humain*, 9me époque.
[3] Fitzmaurice, *Life of Lord Shelburne*, vol. i. p. 169.

once familiar and cynical, of the egoistic system ; and have we not already seen that a simple matter of transposition sufficed to lend a scientific colour to these paradoxes ? Was not the operation of this transposition already noticeable in the current language of politics ? Did not an Englishman speak of an *interest* in cases when Frenchmen would prefer to speak of a *class* or of a *right* ? Did he not say ' landed interest ' or ' moneyed interest ' to designate the class of landlords or of moneyed men, and ' vested interest ' to designate an acquired right ? Therefore, if the democrats were anxious for their ideas to spread and to become intelligible to their compatriots, were they not, so to speak, doomed, sooner or later, to speak the language of utility, to translate their programme of political reforms into the common language, and to do for it what Bentham and Adam Smith were doing for the programme of juridical and economic reforms ?

Now, there are two possible interpretations of the principle of utility. Either the identification of interests, which is the aim of morals and of legislation, is against nature, in which case if it is realised it must be the work of the artifices of the legislator ; or else it is the spontaneous work of nature. Bentham applied the principle in its first form to the solution of juridical problems. Adam Smith and Bentham applied it in its second form to the solution of economic problems. Its application to constitutional matters may be attempted in both its forms.

It was the principle of the artificial identification of interests which Priestley adopted in his *Essay on the First Principles of Government* in 1768. This work is of interest for the study of the formation of Philosophical Radicalism, since it is here that Bentham may have discovered the formula of the greatest happiness of the greatest number, and also because it is here that Priestley, long before Bentham, consciously brought about the fusion of the principle of utility with democratic ideas. The criterium of everything which concerns a State is ' the good and the happiness of the members, that is, of the majority of the members of any state '.[1] The best form of government will therefore be that which is ' most conducive to the happiness of mankind at present, and most favourable to the increase of this happiness in futurity '.[2] Therefore the problem in forming a government is, as Hume had already pointed out, to identify the interest of the governors with the interest of the governed. ' Suppose the king of England, and the two houses of parliament, should make a law, in all the usual forms, to exempt the members of either house from paying taxes to the government, or to take to themselves the property of their fellow citizens. A law like this would open the eyes of the whole nation, and show them the true principles of government, and the power of governors. The nation would see that the most regular governments may become tyrannical,

[1] Priestley, *Essay on . . . Government*, sect. ii.   [2] *Ibid.* sect. i.

and their governors oppressive, *by separating their interest from that of the people whom they govern* '.[1]   It is therefore necessary to guard against these dangers of usurpation.   ' The boundaries of very great powers can never be so exactly defined, but that, when it becomes the interest of men to extend them, and when so flattering an object is kept a long time in view, opportunities will be found for the purpose.'   How then is it possible to ensure that identity of interests of governors and governed which is thus compromised ?   ' It is nothing but the continual fear of a revolt, in favour of some rival, that could keep such princes within bounds ; i.e. that could make it their interest to court the favour of the people.' [2]

It is interesting to remark, however, that Priestley himself, in 1768, was a very moderate democrat.   A few years later Price defined Civil Liberty as ' the power of a *Civil Society* or *State* to govern itself by its own discretion ; or by laws of its own making, without being subject to any foreign discretion, or to the impositions of any extraneous will or power '.[3]   Priestley, on the contrary, expressly distinguishes, in his *Essay*, between the two notions of ' political liberty ' and ' civil liberty '.   ' Political liberty consists in the power, which the members of the State reserve to themselves, of holding public offices, or, at least, of having votes in the nomination of those who fill them '.   Civil liberty is purely and simply ' that power over their own actions, which the members of the State reserve to themselves, and which their officers must not infringe '.[4]   Now according to Priestley political liberty is neither a necessary nor a sufficient condition of civil liberty.   A condition of perfect political liberty is conceivable in a republic with a very small territory, which will always have the disadvantage of very great military weakness. In a big State, however, restrictions must be put on political liberty ; everyone must not be declared eligible for all functions, everyone must not be endowed with the right to elect to all functions. Priestley recognised, for example, the usefulness of a hereditary monarchy as exemplified by experience.   The only advantage of the democratic régime is that all the members of the State can hope in turn to have their share of the power, that is, to be tyrants in their turn.   In the last resort, Priestley thought it relatively unimportant to know who were the governors, how many they were, and how long they held office, ' provided their power be the same while they are in office, and the administration be uniform and certain ' ; and quoted to his purpose Pope's couplet :

' For forms of government let fools contest ;
Whate'er is best administered is best.' [5]

Thus even Priestley's doctrine, in spite of the democratic element included in it, leaves it in doubt whether there exists any close link

---

[1] *An Essay . . .*, sect. ii.   [2] *Ibid.* 18.   [3] *Observations* . . ., ch. i.
[4] *An Essay . . .*, sect. i. p. 9.   [5] *Essay on Man*, Epistle III i. 304.

between the principle of the artificial identification of interests and the democratic idea. In fact, if the mere knowledge of their interests must incline men to act in opposition to the general interest, then it must be that, in view of the interest of the whole, the power to minister to their own must be removed from individuals, to a varying extent. *Nemo in sua causa testis.* But would it not perhaps be otherwise if the second interpretation of the principle of utility were adopted ? Would it not then be necessary, as Sidney observed as far back as the seventeenth century, to reject the maxim, on which Filmer took up his stand, ' no man ought to be judge of his own case ', and to maintain, on the contrary, that ' naturally and properly a man is the judge of his own concernments '.[1] Here, a century before Adam Smith, we have what is practically Adam Smith's formula. The idea of the new economic doctrine is that the two notions of *society* and *government* are separable : granted the absence of all constraint, a commercial society results from the spontaneous play of exchange and the division of labour. Consequently, why should the principle of identity of interests be confined to the domain of economics and not be extended to the affairs of politics ? Had not Hume, in his *Treatise*, already rejected the theory of certain philosophers that ' men are utterly incapable of *society without government* ' ?[2] It remained for Thomas Paine to push this idea to its revolutionary conclusions. An unimportant English official, who had been driven from his native land by domestic troubles and arrest for debt, he became, in America, a great journalist and a redoubtable revolutionary. In January 1776, his *Common Sense* appeared. In it he began by reproaching ' certain writers ' for having ' so confounded society with government, as to leave little or no distinction between them ; whereas they are not only different, but have different origins.' Society is the product of our wants, government of our wickedness ; society promotes our happiness positively by uniting our affections, government negatively by imposing restrictions on our vices. Society encourages intercourse, government creates distinctions. Society is a patron, government a punisher. ' Society, in every state, is a blessing ; but Government, even in its best state, is but a necessary evil.' Now of all political régimes, democracy is the nearest approach to a society without government. In his *Fragment*, Bentham considers the classical definition of democracy, which was offered by Blackstone —namely, ' government of all ' ; and he objects that this form of government amounts to a negation of all government. ' Let him (Blackstone) examine it a little, and it will turn out, I take it, to be precisely that sort of Government, and no other, which one can conceive to obtain where there is no government at all. Our Author, we may remember, had shrewd doubts about the *state of*

---

[1] *Discourses concerning Government*, chap. ii. sect. i.
[2] *Treatise*, bk. iii. part ii. sect. viii.

nature : grant him his Democracy, and it exists in his Democracy '.[1]
Thomas Paine would not have objected to this view that the democratic régime is the nearest approach to the state of nature. The
principle of the natural identity of interests, when applied to the
solution of the problem of politics, seems logically to lead to the
anarchistic thesis.

But these attempts to interpret, albeit in different ways, the
democratic thesis from the point of view of the principle of utility,
were, for the time being, merely attempts which came to nothing.
At this time, the idea on which English political liberalism, taken as
a whole, was based, was the idea of contract—the very idea against
which Hume and Bentham set the contrasting idea of utility. The
reformers who were demanding universal suffrage or annual parliaments took their stand, not so much on the supposed utility of the
reforms, as on their conformity with the original clauses of an historic
convention established between the governors and the governed.
When, in 1771, Sawbridge began his series of motions in favour of
the annual dissolution of Parliament, Granville Sharp published, in
reply to Blackstone, an historical discourse, intended to establish that
the laws of Edward III obliged the king to summon a fresh Parliament every year. It was a return to Saxon institutions which
Cartwright was demanding when he required that annual parliaments
should be established, that the electoral franchise should be uni-
versalised, and that the militia should be organised.[2] Thus
did the agitators adapt their democratic doctrine to the formulas
of the current liberalism. [3] Is it not true that, in 1688, a contract was made between the King and his subjects, a contract which
is and must remain the basis of all English public law ? And is
not Locke's theory the theoretical equivalent of the Revolution of
1688 ? According to Locke, political society was founded by a
contract which established the law of majorities ; and the consent of
the majority makes legitimate the different constitutions which are
established in different countries. As one generation follows
another, the sons, in accepting the paternal heritage, give their consent
to the government which their fathers had themselves accepted. In
this way the original contract is continually reappearing in an
innumerable series of new and tacit contracts. The governors are
responsible before the governed. But the original contract was
not able to provide in advance someone to arbitrate between them :
if, therefore, the governors violate the contract, the governed must
have recourse to insurrection, to ' resistance '.[4] The ' Declaration

---

[1] Bowring, vol. i. p. 276.   [2] *Legislative Rights*, § 27.
[3] So that the thesis of the original contract should be susceptible of a conservative
interpretation (Burke's *Reflections*, p. 75).
[4] Locke, *Government*, chs. viii.-xix.

of Rights ' proclaimed that James II, because he had violated the conditions of the pact which bound him to his subjects, must be held to have, in fact, abdicated ; and a new contract was made with a new dynasty. So that the English Government is the one legitimate government in the whole of Europe, the one government which is based on a contract whose date can be historically fixed, and which by its very existence makes sacred the ' right of resistance '. From this follows the paradoxical conclusion, that up to the year 1760 it was the opposition, the Jacobite party, which condemned the right of insurrection, and advocated the doctrine of ' non-resistance ', or passive obedience, while the doctrine of the right of resistance was held by the Whig party, and by the reigning dynasty. Fox grasped and wittily expressed the paradoxical nature of the attitude of a government party which took the right of insurrection as its fundamental dogma, when he said that ' the sacred principle of resistance must always appear to the government as of a possible, and to the people as of an impossible application.' None the less, the principle remained for him a sacred principle. It was to remain so for all the writers of the Whig party up to the first years of the nineteenth century.[1] Thus, Utilitarians and Tories found themselves in agreement in discussing the political ideas of the Whig party. It was Hume, the precursor of the Utilitarian philosophy, who took up, in one of his *Essays*,[2] the ideas he had previously outlined in his *Treatise*,[3] and gave to the criticism of the contract theory its classical form.

In one sense, Hume was prepared to uphold the truth of the theory of an original contract. Every society is of its essence paradoxical since it consists of the government of the greatest number by the smallest number. Now the greatest number are the stronger ; therefore all governments, the most despotic no less than the most free, are founded on opinion alone. Since men are nearly equal in their physical and mental aptitudes, it can only be consent, together with the recognition of the advantages resulting from the establishment of peace and order, that can, originally, have associated them and submitted them to a government. The external goods which our labour and good fortune have acquired for us are continually exposed to the violence of other men. In order to endow the possession of these with a stability which was not allotted to them by nature, men have recourse to a convention, from which arose the ideas of justice and of injustice, of *property*, *right* and *obligation*. There is no need for this convention to be an express *promise* : a general feeling of common interest suffices. ' Two men, who pull the oars of a boat, do it by an agreement or convention, though they have never given promises to each other '.[4] Such was the nature of

[1] See Burke, *Speech on Army Estimates*.
[2] *Essays*, part ii. Essay XII. Of the Original Contract.
[3] *Treatise*, bk. iii. part ii. sect. v., vi., vii.
[4] *Treatise*, bk. iii. part ii. sect. ii.

the conventions from which arose language, and money. Further, the invention of justice, like the invention of language, is so simple and impresses itself so strongly on the intelligence, that it is impossible to think that humanity can have done without it for any length of time, and justifiable to consider the primitive state of society as having been a social state.   Yet this will not prevent philosophers from speaking of a state of nature, prior to the formation of civil society.   This is permissible, however, provided it is acknowledged to be only a question of a convenient means of expounding the facts in a logical way.   Psychologists may be allowed the same freedom as physicians, who habitually adopt the method of thinking of every movement as composed of other movements which are simpler and can be isolated, while thinking also that every movement is in itself whole and inseparable.

But the theorists of an original contract demand more than this. They do not confine themselves to seeking the explanation of the historical origin of governments in a convention ; they seek also in this convention the foundation of the authority actually exercised by governments at the present time.   All men, if we accept this theory, are born equal and do not owe submission to any prince or to any government, unless they are bound by a conditional promise which imposes obligations on the subject in the exact measure in which the sovereign grants him justice and protection.

Now, in the first place, this thesis is in opposition to the general opinion, and the appeal to universal consent, though it may not be conclusive in metaphysics and in physics, is the only suitable method for settling moral discussions.   How many men realise that their obedience to the government rests on a contract and is bound up with the carrying out, by the government, of the clauses of the contract ?   It is a fact of experience that all nations are attached to their ancient governments, and to the very names which have received the sanction of antiquity.   Antiquity always engenders faith in the law.   The mere fact that a man can declare that a government has been established for a long time is enough to lead him to obey it.   ' Obedience and subjection become so familiar to men, that the greater number of them do not any more indulge in an enquiry concerning their origin and cause, than concerning the principles of gravity, resistance or the most universal laws of nature.' [1]   Are we to say that the original contract, though unknown to the present generation, was none the less made between men of a previous generation ?   This is to suppose, on the one hand, that promises made by the father are binding on the son ; and we cannot, without making a wrong use of words, suppose that there was a *tacit* renewal of the original contract by succeeding generations. But, on the other hand, if we suppose that all legitimate governments are founded on a voluntary contract, which was signed when

[1] *Treatise*, bk. iii. part ii. sect. viii. x.

they were set up, then there are very few governments which are legitimate. How many systems of government had as their origin usurpation and conquest ! What are we to say of the conditions under which the pact of 1688 was concluded ?

In the second place, not only is the theory which founds the duty of obedience to the government on the existence of an original contract an abstract theory which does not correspond with things as they are ; but also even as an abstract theory it is contradictory, or, more exactly speaking, it explains nothing. To be convinced of this it is only necessary to refer to the criticism of the idea of con-tractual obligation, which is the basis of the whole theory of justice in the *Treatise*. The duty of obeying the government is based on the obligation to keep a promise. But promises are nothing but ' human inventions, founded on the necessities and interests of society '.[1] Consequently, far from its being suitable to found the obligation to obey the government on the obligation to keep one's promise, one and the same foundation—the public interest—must be assigned for both obligations. My reply to the question why I should obey is this : because otherwise society could not subsist. The reply of the theorist of an original contract is this : because we must keep our word. But why must we keep our word ? Once again, because otherwise society could not subsist. If, therefore, the principle of the contract brings us back by a detour to the principle of utility, what is the use of this detour, and why not have recourse, immediately, to the principle of utility ?

Adam Smith[2] and Paley[3] adopted Hume's formulas, almost textually, in criticising the idea of an original contract. The same is true of Bentham, when, in his *Fragment on Government*, he attacked the principles of Blackstone's constitutional philosophy. Blackstone's doctrine was characteristic of the attitude of the Whig Party, which was conservative through the exigencies of circumstances at the same time that it was still by tradition Liberal and ' Lockian '. It would be difficult to say whether or no he accepted the theory of the original contract. Blackstone did not consider himself entitled, either by history or by revelation, to admit that there was a time when society did not exist, and when ' from the impulse of reason, and through a sense of their wants and weaknesses, individuals met together in a large plain, entered into an original contract, and chose the tallest man present to be their governor '. But if it be admitted, on the other hand, that ' the only true and natural foundations of society are the wants and fears of individuals ', and that ' it is the *sense* of their weakness and imperfection that *keeps* mankind together ', it is this which Blackstone understands by the social contract. A contract ' which, though perhaps in no instance it has ever been formally expressed at the first institution of a State, yet in nature

[1] *Treatise*, bk. iii. part ii. sect. v.   [2] *Lectures*, pp. 11-13.
[3] *Moral and Political Philosophy*, bk. iii. ch. iii.

and reason must always be understood and implied, in the very act of associating together '.[1]   Bentham hoped that this chimera of an original contract had been effectually demolished by Hume, in the third volume of his *Treatise of Human Nature* ; and, in fact, there was less talk than formerly of an original contract.   He had asked the jurists to point out to him the page, in history, which told of this important contract, and Blackstone had replied that the original contract was not an historical fact, but a convenient theory by which to explain social facts as a whole, a useful *fiction*.   This, he thought, ' looked ill '.   Recourse is had to a fiction so as to justify a fiction. The nature of truth is to admit of no proofs other than truths. There was once a time, perhaps, when fictions had their use.   ' But the season of *Fiction* is now over : insomuch, that what formerly might have been tolerated and countenanced under that name, would, if now attempted to be set on foot, be censured and stigmatised under the harsher appellations of *encroachment* or *imposture.*   To attempt to introduce any *new* one would be now a *crime.* . . .   In point of political discernment, the universal spread of learning has raised mankind in a manner to a level with each other, in comparison of what they have been in any former time : nor is any man now so far elevated above his fellows, as that he should be indulged in the dangerous licence of cheating them for their good.'[2]   The legal fiction is a convenient procedure for the corporation of men of law, as it perpetuates their monopoly, and the chief fiction of which they make use is exactly this notion of contractual obligation.   Bentham had already begun the discussion of this notion in regard to civil law, when, as early as 1776, he discussed its political application in the *Fragment*.[3]

In the first place it is a fact that men are disposed to accede to this proposition, ' that compacts *ought* to be kept ; that men are *bound* by compacts '.   But why is this so ?   At bottom, ' men were too obviously and too generally interested in the observance of these rules to entertain doubts concerning the force of any arguments they saw employed in their support.   It is an old observation how Interest smooths the road of Faith '.[4]   Should it be said, for example, that the People promised obedience to the King, and that the King promised always to govern his subjects in view of their happiness ? But what is gained by this detour ?   Instead of saying that the People owe obedience to the King because they ought to obey the contract in which the King undertook to govern for his subjects' happiness, why not say that the People obey the King because, and just in so far as, he governs for their happiness ?   Because, it is said, men deem themselves better qualified to judge of cases where there has been the breaking of a promise, than to decide directly whether the King has acted in opposition to the happiness of his

---

[1] Blackstone, I. Comm. 47.   [2] Bowring, vol. i. p. 268.
[3] See MSS. of 1774, Univ. Coll. No. 28.   [4] Bowring, vol. i. p. 269.

people. But, when the contract is defined as above, it is impossible to separate the two questions. It must be determined whether the King has or has not acted in opposition to the happiness of his people in order to determine whether the promise he was supposed to have made has or has not been broken.

Now should another formula for the original contract be suggested ? Should it be said that the King promised to govern in accordance with the law ? This rule is in appearance stricter and more precise than the first one ; by this means it is the letter of the *law* that forms the tenour of the contract. Now, governing in opposition to law is *one* way of governing in opposition to the happiness of the people, since respect for the law is a condition of public peace. But, in order to convince ourselves of the inadequacy of an initial promise formulated in this way, let us consider first, that the method of governing in opposition to the happiness of the people, which is at once the most dangerous and the most feasible, is to set the law in opposition to the general happiness ; secondly, that the King can easily govern against the happiness of his people by interpretations of the law which respect the letter ; thirdly, that extraordinary occasions may now and then occur, in which the violation of the law may be more advantageous than respect of it ; and, fourthly and finally, that if every violation of the law were to be deemed an entire dissolution of the contract, it would hardly be possible to find, under the sun, a single government which could subsist for twenty years.

In short, either the notion of happiness is included in the formula of the initial contract—and between the notion of happiness and the notion of obedience to the civil power the intermediary notion of contract is valueless : or else the notion of happiness is not included, —and in this case the notion of contract is without a logical foundation. It is always necessary to come back to the principle of utility. —Negative proof. Suppose the King to promise that he would *not* govern his subjects according to law, and *not* with a view to promoting their happiness :—would this be binding upon *him* ? Suppose the people to promise that they would obey him under all circumstances, let him govern as he will, let him even govern to their destruction : would this be binding upon *them* ?—Positive proof. For what reasons *ought* men, actually, to keep their promises ? Because it is to the advantage of society that they should keep them, and because, if they do not keep them, they must be made to keep them in so far as legal penalties are efficacious. This is why subjects ought to obey kings so long as they govern with a view to their happiness, *so long as the probable mischiefs of obedience are less than the probable mischiefs of resistance.* But what common sign is there, perceptible to all, by which it can be recognised, in any given case, that the evils of obedience outweigh the evils of resistance ? ' *Common* sign for such a purpose, I, for my part, know of none,' says Bentham ; ' he

must be more than a prophet, I think, that can show us one. For
that which serves as a particular sign to each particular person, I
have already given one—his own internal persuasion of a balance
of *utility* on the side of resistance '.[1]—Should a distinction be drawn
between promises which are valid and promises which are void ?
But both alike are promises : it is necessary therefore to find some
superior principle which makes some promises valid and others
void.—Further, how can it be admitted that a contract made between
an ancestor of the present king and my own ancestors should still
be binding on the present king and on my contemporaries ?   If the
promise continues to be binding, it is not because of its *intrinsic*
character as a promise, but because of some extrinsic consideration.
' Now this other principle that still recurs upon us, what other can
it be than the principle of utility ?   The principle which furnishes
us with that reason which alone depends not upon any higher reason,
but which is itself the sole and all-sufficient reason for every point
of practice whatsoever '.[2]

Is this criticism, however, to be held to be decisive ?   Could not
the theory of an original contract be interpreted in a less literal way,
so as not perhaps to be affected by Bentham's objections ?   Should
not the contract be looked upon as declaring the obligation to respect
certain pre-existing rights, which were natural to man and imprescriptible ?   According to Locke himself, all men in the state of
nature are free and equal, and if the right to liberty of any one man,
a right which belongs to all equally, be violated, then, in the state
of nature, every individual has the right to punish.   It is because
individuals are not sufficiently impartial to be safely entrusted with
this right, and because the state of nature tends too quickly to become
(what is not the same thing) a state of war, that men saw the wisdom
of alienating a part of their original rights by an original contract,
and of forming a civil society.   In the contract theory conceived
in this way the fundamental idea is the idea not of contract but of
right.   In the words of Burke, who, in 1782, spoke in Parliament
rejecting all idea of electoral reform, the democrats of 1776 were
not merely a *political party* seeking to maintain the original constitution, they were also a *juridical party* demanding the reform
of the electoral régime on considerations of right.   They demanded
that each person should be represented as such, they held that the
notions of political or collective personality were merely legal
fictions, and recognised no other natural rights than those of the
individual.   According to Burke, nine-tenths of the partisans of
parliamentary reform held this view.[3]   In 1776, it was the thesis
adopted in England by Cartwright, and in America by the authors
of the *Declaration of Independence*.

These men no longer spoke as Anglo-Saxons, jealous of national

---

[1] Bowring, vol. i. pp. 287-8.   [2] Bowring, vol. i. pp. 271-2.
[3] Burke, *Speech on the Reform of Parliament* (*Works*, vol. x. pp. 94-5).

and hereditary privileges ; they were defending rights founded on universal reason and on the nature of things. They solemnly declared : ' We hold these truths to be self-evident : that all men are created equal, that they are endowed by their Creator with certain unalienable rights ; that among these are life, liberty and the pursuit of happiness ; that to secure these rights governments are instituted among men, deriving their just powers from the consent of the governed.' Henceforward the American Revolution assumed a remarkable philosophical importance. For Thomas Paine, the cause of America was to a large extent the cause of the whole of humanity ; for Price, it seemed to foreshadow the fulfilment of the Biblical prophecies, the coming reign of reason and virtue in which the Gospel of Peace should be better understood and should be glorified.[1] Though men are unequal in their intellectual aptitudes and in their physical strength, they are, on the contrary, nearly equal when all the events of their lives are considered as so many incidents in a great moral drama, equal in their obligations and in their destiny. Protestantism applied this individualism, this moral equalitarianism, to the affairs of politics. The men who, in the seventeenth century, drew up the first democratic constitutions on the other side of the Atlantic, were members of religious sects driven from England by the intolerance of the early Stuarts—Baptists, Quakers, the ' Cynics ', as it were, of Christianity, who opposed all forms and rites and were equalitarian and cosmopolitan. Thomas Paine, one of the latest emigrants, who, in 1772, took with him to the colonies a combination of energy and talent, was himself a Quaker. Such also is the spirit of Cartwright's philosophy. Already, in his pamphlet of 1774, on *American Independence*, he had stated that ' it is a capital error in the reasonings of several writers on this subject, that they consider the liberty of mankind in the same light as an estate or a chattel, and go about to prove or disprove their right to it, by the letter of grants and charters, by custom and usage, and by municipal statutes '.[2] Liberty is the immediate gift of God ; it is not derived from any one ; it is original in the nature of everyone ; and it is inalienable.

Now this thesis is, in fact, distinct from the thesis of an original contract ; and here, once again, the ambiguous nature of the contract thesis must be pointed out. About the year 1776, Priestley on the one hand, and Price and Cartwright on the other, may perhaps have considered themselves Lockians, and supporters of the theory of the social contract. It is clear, however, that the notion of contract plays, as it were, no part in their respective doctrines. From one point of view it may be held that men were obeying considerations of utility when they formulated the contract by which they became associated. Locke uses many expressions which would justify this

[1] Paine, *Common Sense*, 1776 : Price, *Observations . . . on American Revolution*, 1784.
[2] See *Life and Correspondence of Major Cartwright*, vol. i. pp. 62 *sqq.*

interpretation of the original contract, and it is this meaning which Priestley tends to give the contractual theory. But, in this case, what is the use of having the contract as intermediary ? Why not value the laws directly by the extent of their social utility ? From another point of view, it may be held that men formed the original pact in order to guarantee a certain number of pre-existing natural rights. This is the sense in which Price and Cartwright tend to interpret Locke's theory. But, in this case, once again, what is the point of the mediation of the contract ? When men have adopted a position of legitimate insurrection, what is the point of saying that they are rising because the contract which should have guaranteed their rights has been violated, instead of saying, more simply, that they are rising because their rights have been violated ? These ' absolute rights ' are held by Cartwright to constitute the compact itself, a ' real, invariable and substantial ' *compact* between the governors and the governed in all countries—a contract which is not of human but of divine creation : ' it was formed for them by their *Creator*, when he endowed them with reason and a sense of moral obligation ; in order to make them Beings *accountable*, not only to himself but to one another '.[1]   This is to say that the expression of the contract becomes a figurative way of representing the idea of moral obligation.

But, above all, the thesis of natural rights is distinct from the Utilitarian thesis. We have seen indeed that the expression ' natural right ' was capable of finding an interpretation in the doctrine of utility. In fact, whatever the positive laws may be, there are certain laws which are necessary or useful, and others which are useless or harmful : can it not be said of the first laws, of those which *ought* to be instituted, or if you like of the actions which are in conformity with them and which *ought* to be executed, that they are *right*, or in conformity with a *right* independent of positive laws, and superior and previous to them ? [2]   Priestley used the expressions ' natural right ' and ' unalienable right ', while conforming to the rule of indicating by these names rights ' founded on a regard to the general good '.[3]   It is, however, obvious that Bentham was faithful to the tradition of Hobbes and preferred not to admit into his juridical system the ideas of *right* or of *natural right*, which for him continue to be realised abstractions and legal fictions. He held that obligations and crimes were creations of positive law. Governments were instituted not because man had rights but because he had none ; and it is possible to maintain that from time immemorial it has been desirable that rights should exist, but this in itself proves that the rights in question did not yet exist.[4]   Cartwright, for his part, in *Take your Choice*, does seem to be disputing Bentham's

[1] *Legislative Rights*, § 102.   [2] What Bentham calls ' the dictates of utility '.
[3] *An Essay on . . . Government*, sect. ii. 1771 ed. p. 41.
[4] Bowring, vol. iii. 219.

Fragment, in the passage where he denounces those who hold that every notion of right is not founded in nature and in the necessary relations of a great design of providence, and that ' the greatest attainable *happiness* to the greatest number, is the *grand end* of all the laws of *morality* and *prudence* ; so, what you term *positive rights* of the people, are probably to be considered no otherwise than as natural *means* to the *end* in view ; and therefore still only *general abstract ideas of expediency* '.[1] To this Cartwright replies first that what is just and what is expedient are in the last analysis identical, but that the only way of discovering what is expedient is to seek in which direction justice lies. But, secondly, if individuals, taken individually and collectively, ought to aim at making themselves as happy as possible during their mortal life, this is only a subordinate end of their actions, the first supreme end of their existence is, ' by the study of wisdom and practice of virtue, to be constantly approximating towards moral perfection ; in order to the attainment of that future exaltation and happiness '.[2] To make him capable of attaining this end, man has been made free, and all men have been made equal as well as free. All men are submitted to the same moral obligations : the government should therefore guarantee them equal conditions in which to accomplish their duties. All men are equally persons, and as such they must have an equal part, if not directly at least through representatives, in the government of society. To the divine right of kings Cartwright opposed the divine right of individuals, not the utility of the greatest number.

In a word, is the social contract, which we are expected to hold in veneration, an historical charter, the very fact of whose existence makes it sacred ? In this case the theory of the original contract is purely absurd. Or is it to be maintained that it was concluded on the strength of considerations of public utility ? In this case why drag in the contract ? Why not found a social philosophy directly on the consideration of the general interest ? Or, finally, is it to be maintained that it was concluded in order to gain respect for the sacred rights of man as man ? If by rights be meant anything other than the needs of individuals, their faculty of experiencing pleasures which are susceptible of a mathematical comparison, then a supporter of the doctrine of utility can only hold the notion of natural rights to be a legal fiction analogous to the fiction of the original pact. But at this period, democrats usually based their demands on the notions of original contract and natural rights. The repugnance which their doctrine was capable of inspiring in the founders of the Utilitarian doctrine can therefore be imagined. Hume, Adam Smith and Bentham were conservatives in political affairs, and a study of their writings makes it easy to see that the time was not far distant when the theory of the rights of men, having won over first America and then France, was to meet, in Burke, and in Bentham

[1] *Take your Choice*, § 94 *sqq.*   [2] *Take your Choice*, § 1.

himself, resolute adversaries, who would take up their stand on the principle of utility.

Whenever Hume, in his *Essays*, weighed the comparative advantages of a liberal and an authoritative régime, he inclined to favour the thesis of authority.[1] Doubtless, from the point of view of the principle of utility, there are cases in which it is *useful* and therefore *legitimate*, to resist the wishes of the king. But, on the other hand, the principle itself teaches us that these are exceptional cases, and that obedience is the rule.—In truth, the adage *fiat justitia et ruat caelum* is manifestly false ; it sacrifices the end to the means : what town-governor would hesitate to burn down the suburbs to make the enemy's advance more difficult ? It is the adage *salus populi suprema lex* which is true ; and this adage may sometimes justify recourse to insurrection. But the whole question for men who use their reason, is to know how much necessity is needed to justify it ; and Hume admitted that he placed himself with those who wish to make the bond of social obedience as close as possible.[2] The same is true of public as of private right, of the obligation to respect the government as of the obligation to respect individual property. It is for reasons of utility that property or stable possession was established from the beginning, but it is useful that once it is established it should be recognised as a general law and that the utility of such and such particular disposition should not be examined in every given case. In the same way, prescription, *de facto* possession, the right of conquest, succession by inheritance— all the positive laws in short, which established governments demand —are justified although they have no logical relation to the principle of utility, because, as a general rule, it is useful that an established government should last and should be respected. There is no time in which the popular will has more difficulty in expressing itself than in time of revolution : how can the nation's passive acquiescence, in 1688, in a revolution desired and brought about by a faction be confused with an explicit consent ? The attitude adopted by Hume was a singular one. The sworn enemy of prejudice, he was favourable to the conservative policy which was, as it were, by definition the policy of prejudice. But the apparent paradox can be explained. Hume acquired the conviction that all human opinions are prejudices, and consequently that the safest thing in morals is not to reason further but to follow instinct, to accept prejudices, knowing that they are prejudices. What he detested above all was the prejudice which proudly sets itself up as truth ; and he was particularly out of sympathy with the theory of the social contract, a revolutionary dogma which had become an official commonplace. He took pleasure in braving the prejudices

[1] *Essay* XII. Of Civil Liberty.   [2] *Essay* XIII. Of Passive Obedience.

of the Whig Party, and the superstition of the ' glorious Revolution ',
and in causing scandal by offering an apology, in his *History of
England*, for the execrated, immoral, anti-national dynasty of Stuart.
But he feared the revolutionaries properly so-called far more than
the Whigs, or government revolutionaries.   He dreaded disturbance.
Voltaire, at the same period, was not a democrat : in the reign of
the philosophy of reason, he came across an obstacle in popular
superstitions : at a time when the lower classes were religious, the
anti-clericals were aristocrats.   Hume was indifferent in religious
matters, but detested the enthusiasm of the Christian leveller.   He
had suffered too much from the denunciations, excommunications
and vexations of all kinds of fanatics and zealots.   Mackintosh
somewhere inquires why Montaigne, Bayle and Hume, the three
most eminent representatives of modern incredulity, were advocates
of absolute power.   Is it the result, he continues, of a scepticism
which is unwilling to believe in the superiority of one government
to another ?   Or is it rather, for Montaigne, the result of the civil
wars, for Bayle, the result of the hatred felt for him by the French
Calvinists ; and for Hume, the result of the fanaticism of the Scottish
Presbyterians ? [1]

The same is true of Adam Smith who was the friend, and in so
many respects the disciple, of Hume.   We are told, on the strength
of contemporary authority, that Adam Smith was in theory a republican and an admirer of Rousseau : [2] why, then, did he have such
avowed antipathy for the American democracies with ' their rancorous
and virulent factions ', which would become ' ten times more virulent
than ever ' if they were separated ? [3]   We are told that throughout
his life he remained a faithful Whig of Lord Rockingham's Party.[4]
If this is true, he must have been, to use one of Hume's expressions
again, the most sceptical of the Whigs.   The freedom of the press
is perhaps the fundamental point of the Whig doctrine.   Nevertheless, Adam Smith reproached the common people of England
for being ' so jealous of their liberty, but like the common people
of most other countries never rightly understanding wherein it
consists ', for wasting their time in idle demands ; and for spending
enthusiasm on the political question, when it was the economic
régime which was demanding reform.   Why so much fuss about
general warrants, which are an abuse, it is true, but which will not
lead to despotism, and so much indifference about the law of settlement, which paralyses the world of labour ? [5]   In the same way, also,
the democrats and the Whigs and even Blackstone himself, the

[1] At this time Bentham clearly held himself to be Hume's ally in irreligion.
See MSS. Univ. Coll. 35,538, f. 109 ; Letter to Samuel Bentham, March, 17, 1777.

[2] Rae, *Life of Adam Smith*, pp. 123, 188-9, 231.

[3] *W. of N.* bk. v. ch. iii.

[4] Rae, ... pp. 130, 162-3, 320, 378, 387.   [5] *W. of N.* bk. i. ch. x.

most conservative of the Whigs,[1] kept up the old habit of denouncing permanent armies, which, according to them, would put the country perpetually at the mercy of a Cromwell or a Stuart, and the system of barracks, which was made for slaves and not for free men.   As if to defy the prejudices dear to the party to which he was held to belong, Adam Smith praised the professional armies, which had arisen as a necessary consequence of the division of labour, and which were useful in the rapid civilisation of a new country, and even in the defence of liberty : since a sovereign who feels that he is protected by an army can allow, with impunity, a freedom of expression which would be dangerous in a country in which he lacked the protection of an armed force, and so was always at the mercy of a conspiracy.[2]   Above all, Adam Smith was a sceptic in political affairs.   *That Politics may be Reduced to a Science* is the title of one of Hume's *Essays* ; but this is not, it appears, Adam Smith's idea.   As far as concerns the economic and financial legislation of a country, it is possible to proceed scientifically, to lay down principles and draw conclusions, to conceive an organisation which is suited, not to ' certain conditions only, but all conditions ', which is adapted, ' not to those circumstances which are transitory, occasional, or accidental, but to those which are necessary and therefore always the same '.[3]   But it is impossible to proceed in the same way as regards the political organisation of a country. And it is this incapacity of our reason which forms an obstacle to the adoption of economic measures, which are desirable in themselves.   It is possible to struggle against the rapacity of traders and manufacturers, but the violence and injustice of the rulers of mankind is an ancient evil, Adam Smith tells us, and an evil for which, he fears, ' the nature of human affairs can scarce admit of a remedy '.[4] Adam Smith does not see the possibility of a compromise between ' the science of a legislator, whose deliberations ought to be governed by general principles which are always the same ', and ' the skill of that insidious and crafty animal, vulgarly called a statesman or politician, whose counsels are directed by the momentary fluctuations of affairs '.[5]   If his social philosophy is compared with that of Hume, in which we found two different tendencies, one rationalist and the other naturalist, it might be said that in political economy Adam Smith tends to turn Hume's ideas towards dogmatism and rationalism, while in politics he turns them rather towards naturalism and scepticism.

Once the attitude to politics adopted by Hume and Adam Smith is understood, it becomes easier to define the attitude of Bentham, the disciple of Hume and Adam Smith.   In matters of constitutional

---

[1] I. Comm. pp. 413-4.   [2] *W. of N.* bk. v. ch. i.
[3] *W. of N.* bk. v. ch. ii.   [4] *W. of N.* bk. iv. ch. iii.
[5] *W. of N.* bk. iv. ch. ii.

law, Bentham himself also was a sceptic. He had not yet discovered, and had hardly inquired, whether the principle of utility involved the justification of some particular form of government, to the exclusion of all others. ' The state of my mind ', he wrote at a later date, ' was that of self-conscious ignorance ', and this ignorance did not even produce in him ' an uneasy sensation '.[1] And Bentham never felt that his thought was betrayed by Dumont's expressions, when, in his preface to the *Treatises*, he wrote of his master in the following terms : ' He thinks that the best constitution for a people is the one to which it is accustomed. He thinks that happiness is the only *end*, the only thing with an intrinsic value, and that political liberty is only a *relative* good, one of the means of arriving at this end. He thinks that a people which has good laws can arrive at a high degree of happiness even without having any political power, and, on the contrary, that it may have the widest political powers and yet necessarily be unhappy, if it has bad laws '.[2] Let us try to follow Bentham's attitude from his early youth, through the variety of problems then before him, and the multiplicity of influences which he successively followed, up to the years immediately preceding 1789.

In 1776, his predominating preoccupation in the *Fragment on Government* was to refute the commonplaces of Whig doctrine. The original contract of Locke and his disciples is a fiction. But the theory of mixed government is likewise a fiction. According to Blackstone, mixed government, the reflection of the Holy Trinity, would bring about the reconciliation of the three divine perfections : power, which corresponds to the monarchic element ; wisdom, which corresponds to the aristocratic element ; goodness, which corresponds to the democratic element. It could be shown by the same logic, Bentham retorts, that a mixed constitution unites, not all the perfections, but all the imperfections and all the vices, belonging to the three simple constitutions. If, as Bentham holds, the English constitution possesses that pre-eminence over all other known constitutions of which it boasts, other ways of justifying it must be found.[3]—The theory of the division of powers is a fiction.[4] Where are the logical limits separating the legislative from the executive powers to be set ? And how can a constitution be conceived of such a kind that it will succeed in suppressing every kind of reciprocity of influence between these two terms ?—The constitutional notion of powers is itself a fiction.[5] It is desirable that the government should legally be either able or unable to do such and such a thing. But government power is an actual power, not infinite, but indefinite, and limited only, according to the diversity of cases, by the resistance of the subjects. That which defines a *political society* is the *habit*, on the part of a group of men

[1] MSS. Univ. Coll. No. 126. [2] Preliminary Discourse of the *Traités*, p. x.
[3] I. Comm. p. 48. [4] Bowring, vol. i. pp. 278-9.
[5] Bowring, vol. i. pp. 289-290.

termed *subjects*, *of obeying* a man, or a group of men, termed *governor* or *governors*. If therefore a contract limits the power of the government to make laws, this will never be the fictitious, ' metaphysico-legal ' power of which the jurists speak ; it will be the real power in the case where, the convention being definite and known to the subjects, these had a common sign by which they could tell when, in their opinion, they ought to resist. Legal fictions can never settle the dispute ' between those two jealous antagonists, liberty and government '. By the way in which he applies the principle of utility Bentham solves the problem in favour of authority. The idea of a ' political society ', a system of constraints imposed and suffered, is a positive idea ; but the idea of a ' state of nature ', in which is lacking the habit of obeying a fixed government,[1] as also the idea of liberty which consists, according to Bentham, in the absence of constraint,[2] are purely negative ideas. Borrowing Montesquieu's definition, he tells us that, if we are to have clear notions, we must mean by liberty a branch of security. But liberty is generally understood to consist in this, ' that constraints are not imposed on ourselves ' ; and security in this that ' constraints are imposed on others '. Speak of utility, and you convince the individual that he must submit to constraints in order that the interest of each should be artificially identified with the interest of all. Speak of natural right, of the law of nature, and you invite everyone, strong in his own conscience and given up to the promptings of the principle of sympathy and antipathy, to take up arms against every law which happens to displease him.[3]   The philosophy of utility is not essentially a liberal philosophy ; in his youth Bentham was a Tory.[4] His family had long been Jacobite. He took the part of the King against Wilkes,[5] and also against the revolted Americans, dissatisfied with the reasons by which the insurgents justified their disobedience —dissatisfied also, it should be added, with the arguments of the government. *Right* was the weapon used on both sides. ' We have the *right* to be what we want to be ', said the Americans. ' We have the *right* to continue to force you to be what we want you to be ', replied the ministers. ' We have the *right* to impose laws on them, but we have not the *right* to impose taxes ', said Lord Camden so as to conciliate everybody : as if irreconcilable interests could be reconciled by a distinction which does not correspond to any real difference. In 1775, Bentham collaborated in a pamphlet in which his friend James Lind discussed the question and brought the debate back to the true principles.[6]

---

[1] Bowring, vol. i. p. 263.
[2] See Add. MSS. Brit. Mus. 33,538, ff. 79-80, Letter to John Lind.
[3] Bowring, vol. i. p. 303.
[4] Bowring, vol. i. p. 287.   [5] MSS. Univ. Coll. No. 62.
[6] *Remarks on the Principal Acts of the Thirteenth Parliament of Great Britain* ... (1775).

In 1781, Bentham made the acquaintance of Lord Shelburne. He owed this patronage and friendship, so he tells us, to the success of his *Fragment on Government*.[1] Bentham's Tory friends grew anxious, and feared that he would go over to the Americans. For, during more than ten years, Lord Shelburne, Lord Chatham's lieutenant and spokesman, had been the constant ally of Edmund Burke and the Whigs against the policy of the King and Lord North. He had preached, in the first place, a policy of reconciliation with the rebels, and then, when conciliation had become clearly impossible, total separation : he it was who, in 1783, signed, as Prime Minister, the treaty of peace with the colonies, which were henceforward independent. Bentham reassured his friends : he laid down as the condition of his friendship with Lord Shelburne that he should respect the freedom of his political opinions.[2] May we not suppose, however, that at about this time he was influenced by the surroundings among which he lived ? It was in 1782 in his essay *On the Influence of Time and Place in Matters of Legislation* that he declared that the English constitution was perfect ' in its leading principles ' ;[3] in the same year he defined these leading principles in his treatise on *Indirect Legislation* [4]—that is, on the indirect means that the legislator should employ to prevent crime. They consist in the division of powers, which, Bentham tells us, offers three advantages : it lessens the danger of precipitate action, the danger of ignorance, and the danger of lack of probity. Having previously criticised the principle of the division of powers, Bentham now tries to find a Utilitarian formula for the principle. But need we attach extreme importance to this change of view ? In spite of so much avowed corruption, and so much civil trouble, the English constitution was unanimously considered throughout Europe as a model to be imitated : how could any Englishman, however dissatisfied and however anxious for reform he might be, resist such a universal prejudice in favour of the constitution of his own country ? At any rate, Bentham took up again, later on, his criticism of the principle of the division of powers : and some years later, when he was preparing a French translation of his *Indirect Legislation* for Dumont's use, he suppressed the whole passage on the division of powers.[5]

Besides, Lord Shelburne was not a Whig, and the alliance of Lord Chatham's faction with Lord Rockingham's faction was temporary and in many respects accidental. At this time, the philosopher of the Whig party was the great orator and writer, Edmund Burke. According to him England, like the Roman Republic of old, owed its greatness to the party spirit. For it is in

---

[1] Bowring, vol. i. pp. 248-9.   [2] *Ibid*. vol. x. p. 98.
[3] MSS. Univ. Coll. No. 88.
[4] The English MSS. from which Dumont extracted the study of ' indirect means ' is MSS. Univ. Coll. No. 87.
[5] MSS. Univ. Coll. No. 62.

parties, where certain ways of thinking are handed down from father to son that the education of statesmen is carried on, and political customs formed.[1] One might say that Burke was a sociologist, indifferent to questions of truth and principle. His social philosophy was the philosophy of an anti-doctrinaire. Indeed, doctrinaires cannot do otherwise than detest political parties. There is nothing more opposed to the spirit of party (you *must* think with your group, you *must* conform to the traditions of your family or of your race) than the philosophic spirit, the method of the *tabula rasa* (you *must* free yourself from group prejudices, you *must* withdraw yourself from the influence of tradition). There is nothing more unintelligible to the man who devotes his entire life to proving that a certain political conception is true, and therefore should be realised, than the doctrine which says that it is good that there should subsist, as permanent institutions, differences of opinion and doctrine. The democrats were doctrinaires, and this is why the Whigs were not democrats. The democrats advocated a simple government, as opposed to the mixed constitution, complex and divided against itself, which was advocated by the Whigs. Did not Rousseau require that every kind of ' particular society within the State ' should be abolished, in order that the expression of the general will should be a faithful one ? In the same way, democrats in England, before, during and after the crisis of the French Revolution, manifested a constant scorn for the two factions, which were both equally aristocratic, and which, coming into power in turn, always threatened each other because of their common interests which were opposed to the general interest.[2] The republican and feminist, Mrs. Macaulay, found ' poison ' in Burke's writings ; [3] Horne Tooke defined a party as ' the madness of many for the gain of a few ',[4] and declared, in 1780, that of the parties, the Tories were the more honest of the two. Be that as it may, Lord Shelburne advocated a reform of parliamentary representation, following Lord Chatham, and against the opinion of Burke. He was in relation with the City agitators, and especially with James Townshend, who was the brother of a neighbour of his in the country. For some time, Horne Tooke associated with him on intimate terms. Cartwright addressed himself to him before addressing himself to the Duke of Richmond when he was seeking an advocate of universal suffrage in the Lords. He knew Franklin. Priestley was for many years his librarian. At his instigation, Doctor Price gave up theological for political work.[5] His *protégé*, Romilly, a Swiss by origin, and a friend of the republican propagandist Brand Hollis, was a Utilitarian democrat.[6]

---

[1] *Thoughts on the Causes of the Present Discontent*, Works, vol. ii. p. 223.
[2] See, *e.g.* Cartwright, *The Legislative Rights*, Preface.
[3] Lecky, *Hist. of England*, vol. iii. pp. 206-7.
[4] Stephens, *Life of Tooke*, vol. ii. p. 437.
[5] Morellet, *Mémoires*.   [6] MSS. Univ. Coll. No. 132.

In sum, if Burke was a conservative Whig, Lord Shelburne was a democratic Tory.

Was it therefore under the influence of Lord Shelburne's group that Bentham, at the beginning of the French Revolution, seems to have caught a momentary glimpse of the possibility of founding a justification of a purely democratic régime on the principle of utility ? Towards the end of 1788, he seemed to have thought of bringing to France, which was preparing for the coming election of her *Etats généraux*, the assistance of his reflections.[1] In an essay, written in French, and entitled *Essai sur la Représentation*, we find him advising the French to look for a model in the electoral constitution of America. He demanded universal suffrage : if, as a concession, he allowed an electoral census, he wished it to be as low as possible. He condemned the plural vote ; wished all elections to be held the same day, and to be completed in a single day ; and demanded secret voting so as to abolish ' the coercing influence of will on will ', and to leave merely the salutary ' influence of spirit on spirit '. The propositions of mental pathology on which he based the good of equality in civil law, he now applied to solve the fundamental problem of constitutional law : from the individualistic principle of his doctrine, he deduced political equalitarianism. The happiness of any one individual has no more value than the equal happiness of another ; or again, what comes to the same thing, everyone has an equal right to all the happiness of which his nature is capable. On an average, every individual has an equal capacity for happiness. Finally, all individuals have an equal desire for happiness. If, therefore, with all individuals, the capacity of estimating the tendency of a thing to increase happiness were equal to the happiness, ' the question as to which was the best form of government would be a very simple one ; it would only be a matter of giving every individual in this society a vote '. Thus, when you have excluded minors, lunatics and (for slightly different and less powerful reasons) women, you must, in the absence of any suitable rule for determining the degree of intellectual capacity necessary in an elector, accord equal political rights to all. Thus is brought about a kind of transformation of the theory of the rights of man into the language of utility. The principle of utility, Bentham tells us, has qualities which put it within the grasp of all minds, and recommend it to all hearts. It is so easy to grasp : it agrees so well with the theory, or, if you will, with the manner of speaking, of imprescriptible rights, a theory which is none the less attractive for being obscure and grounded on the hollow foundation of a mere *ipse dixit*. But this phrase itself shows the character which Bentham attributed to his own speculations : since the equalitarianism of Rousseau was in fashion, he set himself and laboured to find its Utilitarian formula.[2]

---

[1] See Appendix III. (not included in this translation).
[2] Bowring, vol. i. p. 134.

Care should be taken, however, not to attach an exaggerated importance to this logical exercise. Two months later, in an additional
note to his *Introduction*, he denounced the dangerous fiction 'of
imprescriptible rights. He never published his *Essay on Representation*. Other and stronger preoccupations prevented him, for the
time being, from taking an interest in the constitutional problem.

Lord Shelburne himself, particularly at this period of his life,
does not seem really to have been a sincere democrat, any more
than he was a Whig. He was a believer in a strong power, situated
outside and above party distinctions. At the time when he had
just entered into relations with Bentham, and, when, in 1782, he
was made Prime Minister, his instinct for authority was pronounced.
He spoke the language of a ' King's friend ', of a defender of the
prerogative, and, strangely enough, appealed to Lord Chatham's
principles when he declared that England should not be governed
by a party or by a faction, and that the sovereign should not be a
do-nothing King, a mere puppet in the hands of a Mayor of the
Palace.[1] When, in 1789, Burke denounced Warren Hastings as
a ' nabob ' and a parvenu, who, after having practised a policy of
usurpation in the East Indies, violated all traditions, ruined secular
monarchies, and insulted venerated religions, now came to England
to practise, for the King's benefit, a policy equally tyrannical and
equally disdainful of traditions ; and when Pitt abandoned him to
Burke, Lord Shelburne took his part. ' The Foxites and the Pittites ',
he wrote to Bentham, ' . . . only joined in covering every villain, and
prosecuting the only man of merit ' ; and he had put up in his
London house a bust of Hastings with an inscription pouring scorn on
the ingratitude of his fellow-citizens.[2] His ideas had less in common
with democrats, such as Price and Priestley, than with thinkers like
Hume, with whom he had been acquainted, like Adam Smith, whose
disciple he claimed to be, and like Bentham, who was one of his most
intimate friends, and the most regular of his guests at Bowood
Castle.

Did Lord Shelburne think for a moment of making of him a client
who would be capable of doing him service ? " ' Mr. Bentham ', said
he (in a sort of hurried way he had with him), ' what is it you can do
for me ? ' ' Nothing at all, my Lord, that I know of '—was my
answer : ' I am like Balaam the son of Beor : the word which the
Lord sayeth unto me that do I always do ' ".[3] Lord Shelburne,
therefore, respected Bentham's independence ; and his disinterestedness and originality ' revived him ', he said, ' as the country air
revives a London doctor '.[4] What Bentham, for his part, liked in
Lord Shelburne was his taste for innovations and reforms combined

---

[1] Fitzmaurice, *Life of Lord Shelburne*, vol. iii. p. 238.
[2] Bowring, vol. x. pp. 181, 185, 196.
[3] Add. MSS. Brit. Mus. 33,553, ff. 323 (written Jan. 12, 1828).
[4] Bowring, vol. x. p. 225.

with his scorn of party prejudice.[1] Bentham had an entire programme of juridical and economic reforms, based on the principle
of public utility, and of the greatest happiness of the greatest number.
In juridical matters he adopted the despotic principle of the artificial
identification of interests ; in economics, the liberal principle of
the natural identity of interests. Later, and it was a great deal
later, in order to incorporate them in a complete theory of representative democracy, he was to take up again his reflections of 1782
on the division of powers, and his essay of 1788 on universal suffrage.
But, for the moment, he does not appear to have taken seriously the
application of the principle, under one or other of its forms, to the
solutions of constitutional law. The disciple of Helvetius, he
trusted too much in the government of science to be able to support
the anarchistic thesis ; he trusted it too much even to accept the
solution of a mixed government, suggested by Priestley, to which,
in the end, however, he did give his support. About this time, he
was constantly insisting on the essential difference between constitutional law and the other branches of law ; on the impossibility
of providing penal sanctions against the governors, when they failed
to meet their obligations.[2] But is not this equivalent to denying
that constitutional law can be constituted on the basis of the scientific
principle of the general interest ? The moral sanction appears to
be the only sanction on whose influence Bentham counted for
intimidating governors : he wished to see governors submitted to
the incessant jurisdiction of what he calls ' the tribunal of public
opinion ' ; he demanded the absolute liberty of the press. But, on
this point, his attitude was no different from that of Helvetius, or
of Voltaire, or of all the philosophers on the Continent who counted
on a king, who should be advised, criticised and ' enlightened ' by
political writers, to bring about the necessary reforms, and to overcome the interested obstinacy of privileged bodies. Bentham would
perhaps have been prepared to affirm, with the French physiocrats,
that the interest of the governors is identical with that of the governed,
and consequently to think that in order to convert the governors to
the cause of reform, it would suffice to enlighten them as to their
true interest.

He was possessed by one fixed idea : to secure the drawing up and
the promulgation of his entire Code, everywhere, somewhere, no
matter where. Now, at the end of the eighteenth century it was not
the English Parliament, but absolute sovereigns who, from the North
of Europe to the South, were giving codes to their peoples. Bentham
noted the fact that of all European countries England was perhaps
the best suited to produce a good Digest, and yet it was the country
in which it was least likely that it would ever be adopted. Philip
had congratulated himself that his son Alexander was born in the

[1] Bowring, vol. x. p. 187.
[2] MSS. Univ. Coll. No. 33, under the title *Projet Politique Plan*.

age of Aristotle : Bentham congratulated himself that it was given him to write in the age of Catherine, of Joseph, of Gustavus and of Leopold ; if he wrote well, what he had written would not have been written in vain. For although a king is perhaps necessary to promulgate a code, its composition is not the work for a king : ' Engaged in the labyrinth of jurisprudence, a Caesar, a Charlemagne, a Frederick, would appear no more than an ordinary man ', inferior to those who had grown grey in barren studies and in abstract meditations.[1] A legislator is needed at the side of the king ; the sovereign would give the philosopher a share in his authority, the philosopher would give the sovereign a share in his science. This was the alliance of which Bentham dreamed. Since the Empress Catherine had chosen his brother Samuel to practise experimental civilisation in a province of her Empire, why should not he himself become the adviser and the legislator of her whom he calls ' his dear Kitty ' ? Why should he not, one day, be the Cocceji of another Frederick ? Was it even impossible, now that he had become acquainted with Dumont and Mirabeau, that Louis XVI might one day invite him to make laws for France ?[2] Ten years' work would suffice for the task : and the *Pannomion* could be promulgated on the first day of the new century. *Felicitas temporum, principes boni.* But the French Revolution broke out : it overturned or struck terror into princes, disconcerted philosophers and changed the aspect of problems.

[1] Bowring, vol. i. 160.   [2] MSS. Univ. Coll. No. 100.

PART II
(1789-1815)

THE EVOLUTION OF
THE UTILITARIAN DOCTRINE
FROM 1789 TO 1815

FOREWORD

BENTHAM had just published his *Introduction to the Principles of Morals and Legislation* when the French Revolution broke out; in the universal upheaval the book passed unnoticed. In the preceding year he had entrusted Dumont with the publication of the French edition of his *Principes de Droit Civil et Pénal*; it was not until fourteen years later, at the end of the revolutionary period, that the *Traités de Législation* appeared in Paris. In political economy, Bentham was a disciple of Adam Smith, and his *Defence of Usury* met with some success; in the reaction which was then raging in England, years were to pass before Adam Smith's ideas recovered their popularity. Along with Howard, Bentham became known as the author of a project for reforming the penitentiary system; but the mind of the public was at this time disturbed by other preoccupations, and the *Panopticon* became, for Bentham, simply a cause of disappointment and of ruin. Thus it is not surprising that even when he was in the house of Lord Lansdowne, the Lord Shelburne of former years, one of the heads of the ' Jacobin ' faction, and even when in relations with the revolutionaries of France, Bentham, a victim of the French Revolution, maintained a position of systematic hostility to the equalitarian and democratic principle. From the year 1789, in fact, there was as it were a pause in the history of Bentham's thought.

But what is true of Bentham's thought is not true of the Utilitarian doctrine. Alongside of Bentham, and independently of him, it was developing, and was being transformed and continually enriched by new principles. The Revolution, and the European crisis which it brought about, urgently confronted public opinion with the question whether both the exercise of political power and the enjoyment of wealth should not be more equally divided among citizens. A lengthy controversy began, provoked by the events in France. Burke, Mackintosh, Paine, Godwin and Malthus contributed to it in works which have remained classical. Now all these men, to whatever party they might belong, Godwin no less than Burke, Malthus no less than Godwin, were supporters of the principle of utility. It is clear that the doctrine of utility was becoming the universal philosophy in England, and that reformers were forced to speak the language

153

of utility if they wanted to make their opinions accepted or even understood by the public to which they were addressed.

In politics, Burke took his stand on the principle of utility in order to develop a traditional philosophy which ultimately bordered on mysticism ; while Bentham, and with him his disciple Dumont, took it as the foundation of a point by point refutation of the Declaration of the Rights of Man. On the other hand, in Mackintosh, Paine and Godwin, the principle of the identity of interests constantly tended to gain the upper hand over the principle of the equality of rights. The Utilitarianism of these men foreshadows the future Philosophical Radicalism.

In economics, Godwin took his stand on the principle of utility in his hope for the advent of a state of society in which individual property should disappear, and so all individuals would be equally and abundantly provided with the subsistence which they needed. Malthus in his reply took his stand on the principle of utility, and drove it home by insisting on the law of labour, which was always fundamental in the political economy of Adam Smith. Unless men can suppress their natural instinct, the number of consumers tends constantly to increase more rapidly than the quantity of available subsistence : the conditions to which human happiness is submitted are painful. Now, of these two, it was the Utilitarianism of Malthus and not the Utilitarianism of Godwin that was destined to become the orthodox doctrine.

At this time, therefore, one general fact was alone necessary for the principle of utility to become the mould in which all ideas of reform were to take shape—namely that, with the beginning of the war in Spain, the English people should once more become the champion of European liberty against the Napoleonic despotism. Henceforth, when liberal ideas once more gained some credit in England, was it not inevitable that they should be expressed in Utilitarian language, since it was, to a greater or less degree, the language spoken by everybody ? A particular circumstance, on the other hand, was necessary to make Bentham take over the leadership of the movement :—the meeting, in 1808, of James Mill and Bentham. James Mill, who had for a long time been an advanced Whig, converted Bentham to the cause of liberalism and then to political radicalism. James Mill instructed Ricardo. It was under his direction, and, as it were, under his supervision, that Ricardo merged the two Malthusian laws of evolution with Adam Smith's political economy, so that the entire economic doctrine might be unified and systematised. Finally, by all available methods of publicity, James Mill made himself the enthusiastic propagandist of Benthamism. For a long time, as far back as the eighteenth century, isolated individuals had been spreading the scattered ideas which only now, thanks to James Mill and under the auspices of Bentham, became concentrated in the Utilitarian school.

CHAPTER I

THE POLITICAL PROBLEM

IN 1789, the French Revolution insistently recalled the attention of the English public to the political problem, which they had been neglecting for some years. The war between parties once more became active ; a brilliant and violent controversy was carried on between the writers of the aristocratic faction who were supported by the vast majority of the population, and those of the Jacobin faction who were pleading the unpopular cause of the foreigner. As in 1776, it seemed to some people, to Burke, and even to Bentham, that the principle of utility was hostile to revolutionary principles. But there was this difference, since 1776, that now the republican philosophy itself was being constantly more and more invaded by the Utilitarian spirit. Even those people who were still speaking the language of the ' rights of men ' did not seem any longer fully to understand the juridical and spiritualistic meaning of the expression : in the same way we still make our exchanges under a republican régime with coins bearing the effigy of fallen monarchs, without noticing it and without thinking it important. Finally, Godwin based a purely democratic political theory on a rigorous and systematic application of the principle of utility, excluding the principle of the equality of rights. Thus, side by side with Bentham and unknown to him, preparations were being made, in imperfect and Utopian forms, for the future identification of the Utilitarian with the democratic principle.

I. THE PRINCIPLE OF UTILITY AS AGAINST THE DECLARATION OF THE RIGHTS OF MAN : BURKE AND BENTHAM

On November 4, 1789, the anniversary of the Revolution of 1688, which the dissenting churches have kept up the custom of celebrating, Doctor Price, the friend of Lord Lansdowne, delivered, in the Old Jewry Meeting-house, a kind of sermon-speech, on the *Love of Our Country*, which might also have been called ' of true and false patriotism '.   True patriotism implies neither the conviction that the laws and the constitution of our own country are superior to the laws and to the constitution of neighbouring countries, nor the hatred of other nations.   It merely signifies ' that our affections are more drawn to some among mankind than to others, in proportion to their degree of nearness to us, and our power of being useful to them '; and requires us to endeavour to make our country richer from day to day in *truth, virtue* and *liberty*.   The Revolution of 1688 had been a first revolution of liberty, it consecrated the three fundamental rights.   ' The right to liberty of conscience in religious matters.   The right to resist power when abused.   And, the right to choose our own governors ; and to cashier them for misconduct ; and to frame a government for ourselves.'   The King of England is the only legal king in Europe, the only one who derives his authority from the consent of his people.   But England does not yet enjoy either a régime in which religious toleration is absolute, or a régime in which the right of suffrage is shared by all equally.   It was in America and in France that Price thought he saw the dawn of the new era ; and he concluded his sermon with a triumphant ' Nunc dimittis '. ' I have lived to see a diffusion of knowledge, which has undermined superstition and error—I have lived to see the rights of men better understood than ever ;   and nations panting for liberty, which seemed to have lost the idea of it.—I have lived to see *thirty millions* of people, indignant and resolute, spurning at slavery, and demanding liberty with an irresistible voice ; their king led in triumph, and an arbitrary monarch surrendering himself to his subjects.—After sharing in the benefits of one Revolution, I have been spared to be the witness of two other Revolutions, both glorious.—And now, methinks, I see the ardour of liberty catching and spreading; a general amendment beginning in human affairs ; the dominion of kings changed for the dominion of laws, and the dominion of priests giving way to the dominion of reason and conscience '.

In spite of the sacredness of the place, the audience burst into cheers ; the next day they met together and decided to despatch to the Constituent Assembly an address, which they did in fact despatch, and the Constituent Assembly replied to the Dissenters by an official document.   This correspondence between the revolutionaries of the two countries alarmed Burke and decided him to reply by a refutation of the principles of the French Revolution. After a year's work his resounding *Reflections on the French Revolution* appeared.   This may be taken as the first decisive step [1] in the

---

[1] Burke had already denounced the Revolution in a speech in Parliament, February 9, 1790, *Speech on Army Estimates* (Works, vol. v. pp. 3 *sqq*.). Statements of Burke's political philosophy may be found in Morley's *Burke*, Graham's *English Pol. Phil.*, and especially Lecky, *Hist. of England*. vol. v pp. 436 *sqq*.

campaign against the French Revolution which he continued to conduct for seven years, and which made him the acknowledged philosopher of the counter-revolution. From a historical point of view, he had no difficulty in proving, as against Price, that the Revolution of 1688 was neither a democratic nor a philosophic revolution, but a ' revolution of stability ', which became necessary at a particular moment to defend a threatened aristocratic tradition. Soon, however, he entered upon the discussion of the philosophical problem set by the Revolution. The philosophy, the ' metaphysic ' of the French Revolution, was the theory of the Rights of Man, set forth in a solemn declaration :—on entering a society, men bring with them a certain number of inalienable rights, for the defence of which political society was instituted. Among these rights must be included the right of citizens to govern themselves, or themselves to choose their governors, who, being merely their delegates, must carry out their will, on pain of being dismissed.—Now, against this theory, Burke did not attempt to revive Filmer's ancient theory, the ' metaphysic ' of the divine right of kings. This was an exploded theory, now held only by ' fanatics of slavery ' : ' kings, in one sense, are undoubtedly the servants of the people, because their power has no other rational end than that of the general advantage '.[1] Thus Burke, like Bentham, made use of the principle of utility. He had already taken up the same attitude in 1774 when he was the legal advocate in Parliament, the ' paid agent ', of the revolted American colonists. He did not allow himself to raise the question of right, and insisted on the fact that the only question at stake was a question of political expediency.[2] In 1782, by adopting the point of view of utility, he refuted the ' juridical ' theory of the ' rights of man as man '.[3] As he said later, it is by their practical conse- quences that political doctrines must be judged : ' Political problems do not primarily concern truth or falsehood. They relate to good or evil. What in the result is likely to produce evil, is politically false : that which is productive of good, politically true '.[4] Hence the interest of his political doctrine to anyone who wishes to follow the historical evolution of the notion of utility, up to the time when it was about to unite, but had not yet united, with the democratic idea.

Burke preferred to Price's definition, according to which civil government is an institution of human prudence to defend the equal rights of all men against all attack, this other definition : ' Govern- ment is a contrivance of human wisdom to provide for human wants '.[5] These wants can, if you like, be called rights ; or, more accurately, the free satisfaction of each of these wants may be considered a right.[6] But if ' the civil social man ' is in need of liberty, he is

[1] Works, vol. v. p. 67.
[2] Burke, Works, vol. ii. pp. 375-6.　　　[3] Ibid. vol. x. pp. 92-108.
[4] Ibid. vol. vi. p. 207.　　　[5] Ibid. vol. v. p. 122.
[6] Ibid. vol. v. pp. 119-120.

equally in need of restraint.[1] Burke adopted the theory of the social contract, suitably interpreted and with an emphasis on its authoritative side. Constraint must be imposed on our passions, if we do not want them to have harmful consequences, either for others or for ourselves. Now constraint necessarily pre-supposes a power which is external and superior to those who submit to the constraint. Thus, if constraint is the essential element of society, the act by which a man may be thought of as entering a society is an act of abdication, an act of renunciation of the exercise of his active faculties. Hume, Adam Smith and Bentham had criticised the notion of the social contract because they associated it with the notion of the right of resistance ; Burke adopted it because he found in it a ground for condemning recourse to insurrection. The social contract means that men are bound, and not that the majority is free to shake off at will the social bond. To anyone who takes up the point of view of general utility, the dogma of the sovereignty of the people is false : ' no man should be judge in his own cause '.[2] There is nothing to prove that the will of the majority coincides with its interest. The sovereignty of the people, that is, the absolute powers of the majority, is as arbitrary in law and can be as harmful in its consequences as the sovereignty of the monarch, that is, the absolute power of a single man.[3]

From a Utilitarian philosophy Burke deduced an anti-democratic political theory. On his view, the theory of the Rights of Man was an unreal ' metaphysic ', the work of men of letters and philosophers, who were really responsible for the French Revolution. Now, thirty or forty years later, it was the writers of the reactionary party who became, in many respects, the ' metaphysicians '. With Coleridge, who was imbued with German philosophy, they saw in society an entity distinct from the individuals who composed it, a kind of Platonic ' idea ' ; while the Utilitarians, on the other hand, were now the democrats. How can this change of position between the two rival philosophies be explained ? The explanation is this : even when political science is thought of as a science of utility, it can yet be understood in two very different ways—as a demonstrative and deductive science (as it was understood by the Utilitarian reformers of 1832), or as an experimental science (as it was understood by the conservative Utilitarian, Burke). ' Man ', said Burke in one of his speeches in Parliament, ' acts from adequate motives relative to his interest, and not on metaphysical speculations '. This might have been written by Bentham as well as by Burke, but Burke adds : ' Aristotle, the great master of reasoning, cautions us, and with great weight and propriety, against this species of delusive geometrical accuracy in moral arguments, as the most fallacious of all sophistry '.[4] Now this sophism, if sophism it be, is fundamental to all Bentham's

---

[1] Burke, Works, vol. v. pp. 122-3.   [2] *Ibid.* vol. v. p. 108.
[3] *Ibid.* vol. v. pp. 177-8.   [4] *Ibid.* vol. iii. p. 114.

philosophy, since he wanted to introduce the exactitude of geometry, or of ' arithmetic ' into the language of morality. ' Political science is an experimental science like medicine and physiology ', wrote Burke in his *Reflections*, and is, ' like every other experimental science, not to be taught *a priori* '.[1] The method the political philosopher must employ is the observation of existing societies. The fact that a society exists is in itself a presumption in its favour, the beginning of a proof that it satisfies needs and consequently fulfils the true purpose of the State. The fact that a nation or a form of government has survived a long time is a further proof of its activity ; it has resisted the action of hostile forces, and expresses the accumulated experience of generations. This essentially empirical and therefore conservative political philosophy is summed up in two theories : the theory of *prejudice* and the theory of *prescription*.

Prejudice, according to Burke, is a necessary ingredient of our moral constitution. Anyone who wishes to solve the problems of practical life without prejudice would be forced to go back to first principles and to reconstruct for himself a complete philosophy for each one of the decisions which he found himself required to make. Thus he would condemn himself to a complete incapacity to act. It is prejudice, preconceived opinion and ready-made ideas which give unity and continuity to the life of the honest man, and make of virtue a habit.[2] Prejudice plays the same part in morals as capital plays in political economy :[3] it is a sort of moral capital without which action has no basis. It is a capital which individual saving alone cannot accumulate in sufficient quantities : the collaboration of several generations is needed ; prejudices are the accumulated experience of the race. The virtuous man loves prejudices ' because they are prejudices ' ; the true philosopher, as opposed to the false philosopher of France who criticises prejudices in order to destroy them, studies them, on the contrary, so as to discover the deep wisdom which is hidden in them.[4]

Religion is ' the first of our prejudices, not a prejudice destitute of reason, but involving in it profound and extensive wisdom '.[5] This prejudice consists, in a general way, of moral optimism, of the conviction that the universe, and human society in it, issued from the will of a good God who aims at the happiness of man. Society is therefore justified by means of religion and sanctified.[6] Burke moreover denies that he is returning to the theory of religion as ' good for the people ' : to say that religion is a necessary prejudice is not to confuse it with a useful error. Religion is true to the extent to which it is ancient, to which it rests on a long experience and corresponds to what is deepest and most lasting in human nature. Religion, together with morality, which is not separable from it, is

---

[1] Burke, Works, vol. v. pp. 123-4.   [2] *Ibid.* vol. v. p. 167.
[3] *Ibid.* vol. v. p. 82.   [4] *Ibid.* vol. v. p. 167.
[5] *Ibid.* vol. v. p. 176.   [6] *Ibid.* pp. 174-5.

that in us which most clearly bears the mark of eternity.   The mistake
of the French has been to wish to innovate in religion and in morals.
There are innovations and revolutions in the mathematical and
physical sciences ; but there are no innovations in morality.[1]

The aristocratic prejudice is, in two respects, almost as essential
and fundamental as the religious prejudice.

In the first place, it introduces into the constitution of society an
element with which it could not dispense.   The theorists of the
Rights of Man make the mistake of thinking of society as consisting
solely in a collection of individuals, in a sum of individuals who are
actually alive ; of thinking that society exists only *by* and *for* the
present generation.   ' Individual interests ', writes Bentham, ' are the
only real interests.   Take care of individuals. . . . Can it be conceived that there are men so absurd as to love posterity better than
the present generation ; to prefer the man who is not, to him who is ;
to torment the living, under pretence of promoting the happiness
of those who are not born, and who may never be born ? '[2]   Burke
sets out from the same principle as Bentham, but reasons differently.
The present generation is bound up with past generations, whose
experience is precious, and with future generations whose interests are
as worthy of respect as its own ; and this integral relationship of the
present with the past and with the future is society itself.[3]   Aristocratic institutions endow a society with the character of a family :
and a nation is indeed the reflection of a family.   Such is the merit
of the English constitution.   ' We have an inheritable crown ; an
inheritable peerage ; and a house of commons and a people inheriting
privileges, franchises, and liberties from a long line of ancestors '.[4]
This political system seemed to Burke to be the result of profound
reflection ; or rather the happy result of following nature, which is
wisdom without reflection, or superior to reflection.   A spirit of
innovation pre-supposes an egoistic temperament and narrow views.
Those who never look back to their ancestors will never look forward
to posterity.   Again, a nation can be compared to a corporation
with its traditional rules, the legacy of past to future generations.
It is in vain that theorists refuse to corporations any personality
but a fictitious one, and declare that ' men as men are individuals
and nothing else ' ; the theorists are wrong.   In economics Burke
held the same views as Adam Smith ; thus he was an individualist,
an enemy of the spirit of coalition and corporation.   Did he realise
that the principle of utility, interpreted as he interpreted it, led
him to political doctrines which are diametrically opposed to the
economic doctrines which are generally held to follow logically from
the same principle ?   ' Nations ', he says, ' are corporations '.[5]

[1] These precautions did not succeed in reassuring Wilberforce about the theory
of prejudice.   See *Life of Wilberforce*, vol. iii. p. 11.
[2] Bentham, Bowring, vol. i. p. 321.   [3] Burke, Works, vol. x. p. 97.
[4] *Ibid*. vol. v. p. 78.   [5] *Ibid*. vol. v. p. 255.

Burke invoked other considerations to justify the aristocratic prejudice—the considerations not of a doctrinaire but of a social psychologist and a sociologist. When, in a society, distinctions of rank are sanctified by long custom, they no longer inspire the superior with pride, nor the inferior with the feeling of envy. For the superior enjoys without fear a distinction which no one contests, and the inferior does not even think of envying a position to which he does not dream of aspiring. In so far as the strength of the aristocratic prejudice makes such distinctions of rank unshakable, there comes about as between the classes a kind of union, a sentimental alliance which constitutes the spirit of chivalry. But, alas, with revolutionary equalitarianism, ' the age of chivalry is gone. That of sophisters, economists, and calculators has succeeded : and the glory of Europe is extinguished for ever '.[1] Thus the Utilitarian morality led Burke to social views which were profoundly different from those to which it led Bentham : it led no longer to the condemnation, but on the contrary to the glorification, of sentiment. What Burke regretted in the past was that ' mixed system of opinion and sentiment ' in which the feudal system consisted, and ' all those pleasing allusions, which made power gentle, and obedience liberal, which harmonised the different shades of life, and which, by bland assimilation, incorporated into politics the sentiments which beautify and soften private society '.[2] The difference between the morality of the doctrinaire and that of the sociologist can here be seen. The latter is always concerned to defend the social sentiments (whose actual existence is revealed to him by local experience)—*esprit de corps*, the family spirit, the spirit of tradition : besides, Burke was already an aristocrat at the time when, as the orator of the Whig party, he was pleading the cause of the Americans. The former, on the other hand, sees in society an object of exact. science, concerning which it is possible to fix universally valid laws, by abstraction from local traditions : there was already some spiritual affinity between Bentham and the French Jacobins, although Bentham was still at this time a Tory, and, as we shall see, was at this very moment engaged in refuting the principles of the Revolution of 1789.

Further, is it possible to abolish all inequalities ? Those which, being entirely conventional, can be condemned as superstitious prejudices can assuredly be abolished. But there are others which are natural, and these are the most brutal of all. First the inequality of fortune : level all conditions, money must still make a difference.[3] Burke remarked the almost universal sympathy of the ' nabobs ', adventurers who had grown rich in India, for the Jacobin cause in England : ' they cannot bear to find that their present importance does not bear a proportion to their wealth '.[4] The same phenomenon

[1] Burke, Works, vol. v. p. 149.   [2] *Ibid*. p. 151.
[3] *Ibid*. vol. vii. p. 19.   [4] *Ibid*. p. 20.

had occurred in France, where the tax-farmers, in alliance with the men of letters, had turned the anger of the people against the property of the clergy and the privileges of the nobles. Doubtless, after 1791, Burke would have been compelled to admit that the financial aristocracy in France was wrecked along with all the aristocracies. But there remains another inequality, against which the theory of the Rights of Man remains powerless : the inequality of strength. In the dissolution of all constituted powers in France, one power among them all retained its strength, because it was armed—namely, the military power.[1]

Translate the theory of prejudice into its juridical form, and it becomes the theory of *prescription*. ' Prescription is the most solid of all titles, not only to property, but, which is to secure that property, to Government.' [2]

In private law, in the first place, prescription is the foundation of the right of property. There is, in every man, a very lively sentiment—the sentiment of expectation. Now every man naturally expects to keep that which he possesses ; he is disappointed if he loses it. The longer he has enjoyed possession, the greater is his disappointment. He is disappointed to an infinite extent, if the possession is of such long standing that the memory of its origin is lost. Thus justice, understood in this way in a purely conservative sense, is no more than respect of acquired rights, and property is justified to the extent to which the right of property is founded on prescription of long standing. Here may be recognised the theory of Hume, which was also the theory of Bentham. Bentham, however, in his theory of property had tempered the principle of security with the principle of equality : this tempering was lacking in the purely conservative theory of Burke. He who receives a title to property should never ask whether it was formerly acquired by violence or by fraud : the point of view of legal prescription is the point of view of indifference to origins. See in the *Letter to a Noble Lord*, his apostrophe to the Duke of Bedford, one of the leaders of the Jacobin faction. The Duke of Bedford, instead of reproaching Burke with his pension honourably earned in the service of his King, should consider what is the origin of his own titles to nobility and property : the first Duke of Bedford had taken his share, under Henry VIII, of the spoils of the clergy. Let him beware the day when, with the triumph of the Jacobin philosophy in England, there would be a revision of titles to property, and the nation would arrogate to itself the right to confiscate properties which had originally been formed by confiscations. But, as for Burke, he would contest this policy of confiscation, to which the Duke of Bedford rashly gave his support, and would defend, to the advantage of the Duke

[1] Burke, Works, vol. v. pp. 375-399.
[2] *Ibid.* vol. x. p. 96.

of Bedford, the principle of legal prescription : time makes legitimate
what was illegitimate, just what was unjust.[1]

What is true of private law is true also of public law. The
excellence of the English constitution lies in its being a ' prescriptive
constitution ', ' a Constitution, whose sole authority is, that it has
existed time out of mind '.[2] English subjects do not dream of
wondering why the constitution of their country is mixed, is at once
monarchic, aristocratic and popular ; they have forgotten the time
when the constitution was made. They accept it as an individual accepts
his physical nature. This is why, since before the French Revolution, Burke had rejected all reform of the right of suffrage based on
the theory of the rights of man : and this is why he refused likewise
to adhere to that subtler theory, according to which the very respect
for tradition makes reform urgent. It is in appearance only, it is
argued, that the constitution remains unchangeable ; for since the
moral aspect of the country changes while the constitution remains
the same, the relation of the constitution to the state of the country
is not the same as it was originally : to anyone who examines things
closely, the constitution has changed. Burke replies, however, that
the mistake here made is still the same and proves that the true
meaning of the notion of legal prescription has not been understood.
It is assumed that at a given moment the constitution was produced
by a conscious will, in conformity with an abstract theory from which
the constitution only deviated in the sequel. This is a gratuitous
hypothesis : ' a prescriptive government . . . never was the work of
any Legislator, never was made upon any foregone theory '.[3]
Questions as to the origin and the end of an established law should
never be asked ; or else we find ourselves reopening arguments on
political affairs, instead of adopting that method, whose wisdom
nature teaches us, and which consists in accepting existing institutions, because they exist, and as they exist. The inferiority of the
revolutionary philosophy, that is, the philosophy of the Rights of
Man, in comparison with the conservative and traditionalist philosophy, might be said to be that the philosophy of the revolutionary
policy commands its system to be logical, while the logic of the
conservative political theory allows it to be illogical.

To sum up, Burke's political philosophy is an empiricism, a
philosophy of experience : the duration whether of an idea or of an
institution, its mere persistence through time, is a presumption in
favour of that idea or of that institution. The theory of prejudice
is this : between an ancient opinion which has not been shaken by
long experience through a long series of generations, and a new idea,
born in the brain of a solitary thinker, the presumption is in favour
of the ancient idea or prejudice. The theory of prescription is as
follows : between an ancient right sanctified by a prescription which

[1] Burke, Works, vol. vii. p. 375. [2] *Ibid.* vol. x. p. 96.
[3] *Ibid.* vol. x. p. 99.

has endured for an age or perhaps for many ages, and a new right based on supposedly rational principles, the presumption is in favour of the ancient right which claims its origin from prescription, that is to say from experience. It is in this way that Burke's argument is profound. Our reasons for justifying actual institutions and for finding in them a systematic character, are inexhaustible ; but these reasons are always bad reasons, and the juristic scholasticism of Puffendorf and Blackstone is, to Bentham, the subject for easy witticisms. If existing institutions were other than they are, we should easily find other reasons. The decisive argument in favour of the given system, as against all imaginable conceptions of a future which is no more than possible, is that *it exists*, and that it is the necessary consequence of the past.—Thus the principle of utility, which was formulated for the first time in Hume, while it resulted in Adam Smith and Bentham in a doctrine of reform in economic and juristic matters, and made ready for the radicalism of the doctrinaires of 1832, at the same time took, with Burke, another direction, and made ready for what may be called the theological empiricism of Joseph de Maistre and Haller, and even for the theological metaphysic of Coleridge. But during the revolutionary period, Bentham himself was not yet a ' radical '. Burke was famous ; he was the prophet of the clergy and the nobility all over Europe. Bentham was obscure, and the works of this unknown philanthropist were to a large extent unpublished. At the sight of the deeds of violence of which Paris was the stage Burke lost all calmness of mind : his speeches in Parliament and his polemical writings, from the *Reflections* and from the famous sitting in the Commons when he broke with Fox, to the *Thoughts on a Regicide Peace*, including *The Appeal from the New to the Old Whigs*, the *Thoughts on Affairs in France* and the *Letter to a Noble Lord*, show the increasingly obvious signs of real mental distraction. Bentham remained calm, kept silence and took no public part in the controversy which had been started by Price's sermon and Burke's book.[1] Nevertheless, the attitude he adopted is not altogether unlike the attitude adopted by Burke. It can be defined in two words : an attitude of hostile indifference.

The difficult problem is to understand how Bentham, the guest and the intimate friend of Lord Shelburne, now Lord Lansdowne, was able to resist the influence of his surroundings, and not to become a Jacobin. Lord Shelburne left office in 1783 ; and when, after the fall of the Fox and North Coalition, the King entrusted

---

[1] According to Bentham's conversations with Bowring (collected by the latter round about 1830), Bentham had a great admiration for Burke at the time of the American War (Bowring, vol. x. p. 564). But too much importance must not be attached to Bentham's recollections when an old man. For his opinion of Burke in 1810 see Bowring, vol. ii. 464.

William Pitt with the formation of a new ministry, Pitt had no wish
to have near him as notable a subordinate as Lord Shelburne, who
had been his father's friend and right-hand man, and his own Prime
Minister two years earlier. He thought he had sufficiently paid the
debt of gratitude he owed Lord Shelburne in making him Marquis
of Lansdowne. Hence it is easy to understand the mixed feelings
inspired in Lord Lansdowne by the policy pursued by Pitt in the
five years preceding 1789. It was at Shelburne House that Pitt
had borrowed from Doctor Price the idea of the sinking fund; it
was there also, in the company of the Abbé Morellet and Dean
Tucker, that he first became acquainted with the ideas of Adam
Smith. Lord Lansdowne could not condemn the application of
ideas which were his own ; on the other hand, he would hardly
rejoice to see them plagiarised, and annexed by someone else.
Although he went into Parliament to support the project of a commercial treaty with France, he led a retired and isolated life : Pitt's
triumph seemed to have exiled him for ever from the life of action.
He became a collector of books, manuscripts, and antique statues.
Nevertheless social questions still interested him ; he collected
documents bearing on commercial and industrial questions, and
kept up unbroken relations with Paris. In 1789 Abbé Morellet,
Benjamin Vaughan, his son Lord Wycombe, and Dumont of
Geneva were keeping him informed of events in France. For at
this stage the French Revolution came to upset the policy of
parties in England. Insensibly, against his conscious will, against
the tradition of the Tory party, Pitt found himself thrown back upon
the old policy of war with the hereditary enemy ; insensibly Lord
Lansdowne found himself steadily converging towards his constant
enemy, Charles Fox, until, in 1794, they found themselves together
at the head of the new Whig opposition, the democratic and
' jacobin ' party.[1]

It was an illusion shared in England by all friends of France that
the Revolution of 1789 was a revolution of the English kind, in
imitation of the Revolution of 1688, and inspired by English ideas.
In the House of Lords, in 1793, Lord Lansdowne declared that it
was the actual ideas of Tucker and Adam Smith, and their criticisms
of the feudal régime, which were so much detested under the misleading name of ' French principles '. France thus seemed to have
presented itself as an experimenting ground for all the English
reformers. Lord Lansdowne's two friends, Romilly and Bentham,
set themselves up as advisers of the Constituent Assembly.

Romilly first, in collaboration with Bentham and Trail and at the
request of the Comte de Sarsfield, drew up a summary of the rules
of procedure used in the English House of Commons, for use in
the *Etats généraux*. This work was sent to the Duc de la Roche-

[1] For all details on Lord Lansdowne and his circle see Fitzmaurice, *Life of
William, Earl of Shelburne.*

foucauld, the friend of Lord Lansdowne, and was published after the death of the Comte de Sarsfield by Dumont and Mirabeau.[1]

A short time afterwards, Bentham undertook a task very similar to this. He drew up what he called ' *An Essay on Political Tactics* ; or, inquiries concerning the discipline and mode of proceeding proper to be observed in political assemblies ; principally applied to the practice of the British Parliament, and to the constitution and situation of the National Assembly of France '.[2] Tactics, etymologically, is the art of setting in order. All *order* pre-supposes an *end* ; and Bentham here for the first time lays down what he later called the theory of ' adjective law '. ' In this branch of government, as in many others, the end is, so to speak, of a *negative character*. The object is to avoid the inconveniences, to prevent the difficulties, which must result from a large assembly of men being called to deliberate in common. The art of the legislator is limited to the prevention of everything which might prevent the development of their liberty and their intelligence.' It is necessary to make a fresh distinction. For the good or the evil which an assembly can do depends on two general causes. The most powerful and the most obvious is its *composition* (Bentham refrained from publishing his *Essay on Representation*, and from taking sides for or against democracy) ; the other is its *method of action*. Thus the problem of parliamentary procedure seems to be at once defined and differentiated and also attached to the general doctrine of utility. It is an important problem. ' In this bye-corner, an observing eye may trace the original seed-plot of English liberty : it is in this hitherto neglected spot that the seeds of that invaluable production have germinated and grown up to their present maturity, scarce noticed by the husbandman, and unsuspected by the destroyer.' Later, in 1791, he published separately Chapter VI. of his *Essay*, ' Of the mode of proceeding in a Political Assembly in the formation of its decisions ', giving first the *rules* prescribed by utility on every point, then the *reasons* which justify each rule, then the *English practice*, and finally the *French practice*, taken from the *Etats généraux* and the *Etats provinciaux*. He was thus treating of Utilitarian and comparative legislation at the same time. Further, like Romilly, he suggested English parliamentary institutions as a model for France, and asserted that on almost every point English practice conformed to the prescriptions of utility. It was precisely because of this that the two works had so little success in France. ' Not that I promise you a prompt success ', wrote Dumont to Bentham, ' for the French are yet but children stammering in their National Assembly '.[3] But these children scorned to follow the traditions of grown-up England.

---

[1] *Réglements observés dans la Chambre des Communes pour débattre les matières et pour voter*. Translated from the English and published by Count Mirabeau, 1789.

[2] Bowring, vol. ii. pp. 301-373.   [3] *Ibid.* vol. x. p. 219.

When Mirabeau laid Romilly's work on the table of the *Communes* at the opening of the *Etats généraux*, he received, in effect, this reply : ' We are not English, and we have no need of the English '. [1]

Bentham, however, did not confine to this very specialised question the attention which he, like the whole of the society at Lansdowne House, gave to French affairs. The Constituent Assembly was reforming the judicial organisation of France in a revolutionary manner ; and it was probably his study of the Assembly's project of reform which led Bentham, at about this period, to enlarge the sphere of his studies, and no longer merely to study the problems of civil and penal law, but also to consider the problems of judicial procedure and organisation.

On April 1, 1790, Lord Lansdowne pointed out to the Duc de la Rochefoucauld a new work by the man whom he already knew as the author of a paper on *Political Tactics* and of a *Defence of Usury*. This was a critical study of the draught of a new French code of judicial organisation, or, more exactly, of a ' Draught of a code for the organisation of the judicial establishment in France : with critical observations on the draught proposed by the National Assembly Committee, in the form of a running commentary '. Bentham had just sent a hundred copies of it to the president of the Assembly. ' What I would request of you, M. le Duc,' Lord Lansdowne concluded, ' would be, to have it understood that it is the work of no ordinary person, that his time is valuable, and that his work certainly deserves more than ordinary attention.' [2] In this work, in which Bentham takes up the French draught, article by article, commenting on, approving or modifying each article in turn, there can already be discerned those dominating ideas, which he was again to develop, and with more success, thirty or forty years later,— ideas on the supreme importance of the publicity of debates, on the system of a single judge, on a geographical rather than a logical division of jurisdiction, on the opposition of the natural and technical systems in affairs of procedure. But above all, the Constituent Assembly's reform had a political importance. It suppressed all privileges in jurisdiction : ' Happy France ! where aristocratical tyranny is laid low ; while in England it is striking fresh root every day '. . . .[3] The Assembly substituted an elected judge for the judge appointed by the executive power ; and Bentham was called upon to give his opinion on the value of the reform.

The committee of the Assembly proposed that the judge be elected ' by electors chosen by the *active* citizens of the territory over which he is to be judge in the same manner as a member of the administrative body of that territory '. But it added : ' The

[1] Dumont, *Souvenirs sur Mirabeau* (Paris, 1832), pp. 115-116.
[2] Bowring, vol. x. pp. 226-7 ; *Draught of a Code*, etc., Bowring, vol. iv. p. 306.
[3] Bowring, vol. iv. p. 321.

judges shall be appointed by the king upon a presentation made to him of two candidates chosen for each vacant office '. . . . Bentham suppressed the second part,[1] and made the judge depend upon the electoral body, without any control from the executive power. Further, the ' power of amotion ' which Bentham conferred on the electoral body,[2] over and above the ' power of election ' emphasises the democratic nature of his system ; the judge is ' amovable,' and ' amotion ' can be pronounced either by a majority of the whole number of members of the administrative body next in rank above that of the territory of which he is judge ', or ' by the suffrages of a majority of the whole number of the electors, entitled to vote at the last preceding election, general or particular, holden for the choice of a magistrate, or of a member of the administrative body of his territory '. This lessens the independence of the judge ; but the essential thing in a judge is *probity* not *independence*. Independence on the part of a judge is a good thing in a corrupt constitution, but disastrous in a good one. It is better that the one should suffer now and then through the fault of the many, than that the many should be continually suffering through the fault of the one. More-over, Bentham adds, ' I have not that horror of the people. I do not see in them that savage monster which their detractors dream of. The injustices of the Athenians, had they been ten times as frequent as they were, would not, in my view of things, be much to the present purpose. Had the Athenians representative bodies—had they the light of two thousand years of history to guide them ? or the art of printing to diffuse it ? When the Athenians were cruel and unjust, were the Dionysiuses and Artaxerxeses less so ? ' Popular justice must no longer be judged by acts performed by a few unknown individuals in time of revolution ; and, besides, if examples are needed, is not the example of America decisive and favourable to the thesis of the election of judges ? [3]

Bentham thus, at first sight, appears to have been converted to the democratic view by the example of France. At bottom, he was not, at the moment, a sincere democrat. He applied certain new restric-tions of his own invention to the elective system. The ' power of deputation ',[4] by which he endowed the magistrate, once elected, with the power of appointing an unremunerated, permanent deputy implies the ' principle of gradual promotion ' : [5] it was from among these deputy judges that the electoral body would have to choose the magistrates. The parties in a suit were to choose their own advocates : the safest method, on the strength of the principle that ' everyman is the best judge of his own interest ', was to impose no restrictive condition on this choice. But parties were not to choose their judges : in this case it was necessary to restrain, ' without compunction ', the principle of popular election. For ' public

---

[1] Bowring, vol. iv. p. 307.   [2] *Ibid*. pp. 358-363.
[3] *Ibid*. pp. 362-3.   [4] *Ibid*. p. 368.   [5] *Ibid*. p. 370.

fame will tell them who has proved the best judge, after trial : private acquaintance only can say, before trial, who, among young and untried men, is *likely* to prove a good one '. Apprenticeships have been instituted where they were useless, while they do not exist where they should have been considered necessary.—Above all, the principle of ' patriotic auction ', the formula of which Bentham seems indirectly to have borrowed from Burke's speech on economic reform,[1] acts as a restriction both on the equalitarian and on the elective principle. The system of patriotic auction, by which candidates are invited before the election to offer to pay, on their assuming office, a sum of money less than, equal to, or even greater than the value of the expected appointment, does in a sense leave the electoral body free to make its choice. Everything is calculated, however, so that it should be tempted to choose the candidate who is patriotic enough, it is true, but also rich enough to make the highest bid.—Finally, Bentham took care to give notice that though he retained the elective principle in the system of judicial organisa- tion, this was not a *thesis* invented by himself, but a *hypothesis* which he accepted, and demanded that at any rate all its logical consequences should be accepted. He recognised that to entrust to the people at large the choice of the judges was a ' bold experiment ' ; he himself would have hesitated between the king and the representative assemblies. But, since the committee had the courage to look the idea in the face, Bentham was fired with a kind of academic curiosity, and demanded that since the decision to make the experiment had somewhere been arrived at, it should be fairly tried, in its simplest form.[2] Some time afterwards, he said that he had only thought of the adoption of the elective principle as a concession made necessary by circumstances, and that the making of the concession had gone ' against the grain '.[3]

Meanwhile the Revolution swept on. First it discouraged those of its English adherents who confused the Revolution of 1789 with a second Revolution of 1688, and expected to see France endow herself with a mixed régime and a Whig monarchy. Before long it discouraged those who confused it with the Revolution of 1776, and expected to see set up in France a democratic constitution on the American pattern. In less than five years the cycle was com- pleted, and the military were threatening the Republic. What, during this crisis, was the attitude of the group of Lord Lansdowne's friends, of Lord Lansdowne himself, of Romilly and of Bentham ?

Lord Lansdowne was a politician : the leader of a parliamentary party, he preserved, in pleading the cause upheld by his party, the relative and professional good faith of the advocate. He was one of the first Englishmen who were perspicacious enough to foresee

[1] Burke, *Speech on Economical Reform* (Works, vol. iii. p. 322). ' The service of the public is a thing which cannot be put to auction.'
[2] Bowring, vol. iv. p. 309. [3] *Ibid.* vol. x. p. 399.

the military power of revolutionary France, one of the first men in Parliament to understand the universal character of the Revolution. He congratulated Bentham on ' taking up the cause of the people in France : nothing can contribute so much to general humanity and civilisation as for the individuals of one country to be interested for the prosperity of another '. And he continues, as if the new philosophy of the Rights of Man were indistinguishable from the philosophy of utility : ' I have long thought that the people have but one cause throughout the world ; it is sovereigns who have different interests. . . . If the people of different countries could once understand each other, and be brought to adopt half-a-dozen general principles, their servants would not venture to play such tricks '.[1] No doubt he was deceived, in the early days, as to the extent of the reforms which France would need. On July 10, 1789, he thought that it would suffice to secure the freedom of the press, the abolition of *lettres de cachet*, the institution of provincial assemblies, and to fix a limitation of public expenditure.[2] But later he accepted accomplished facts. ' The Church lands which are sold can never be restored. . . . The nonsense of feudality can never be revived. The people can never be taxed again without the consent of some representative body consisting of one or more Houses. The Bastille cannot be rebuilt. The administration of justice and feudality cannot again go together. These fundamental points I call the Revolution, and must insure the essence of freedom '.[3] Ceaselessly he advocated a policy of peace, denouncing the ' metaphysical ' [4] nature of the war, and rejecting as pharisaical the accusations brought against French immorality.[5] He remained faithful to the cause of parliamentary reform, and when, in 1792, Grey proposed in Parliament a motion in favour of reform, he protested when a royal proclamation was made against the publication and propagation of seditious writings—a proclamation aimed at the Society of Friends of the People, to which Grey belonged, and which spread the ideas in question. He deliberately shocked public opinion, when proposing that the Government should intercede in favour of the King of France, by referring to him as ' Louis XVI ' ; [6] he accused an *agent provocateur* of having thrown the stone which broke the window of the royal coach in the streets of London in October, 1795 ; [7] he resisted to the utmost the adoption of the exception laws, and it was thanks to his efforts that the clauses of the Traitorous Correspondence Bill, by which the accused was deprived of means of defence, were modified in the House of Lords.[8] He was depicted by caricaturists as presiding, with Fox, over an execution at the guillotine ; as dancing patriotic dances, crying *Vive Barrère* ; as dressed up as a newspaper-boy disseminating

[1] Bowring, vol. x. pp. 197-8.
[2] *Life of Lord Shelburne*, vol. iii. pp. 488-9. [3] *Ibid*. p. 497. [4] *Ibid*. p. 527.
[5] *Ibid*. p. 529. [6] *Ibid*. pp. 509-510. [7] *Ibid*. p. 530. [8] *Ibid*. p. 533.

in Berkeley Square ' Malagrida's latest lie from Paris ' ; and as firing a gun in at the windows of the royal carriage.[1] In 1801, after Pitt's dismissal, a ministry was very nearly made up with Lansdowne and Fox as its chiefs. Lord Lansdowne died too soon to take part in the Grenville-Fox ministry of 1806.

Romilly, who was at once more independent and more sentimental, passed from enthusiasm to disgust. In 1789 he published his *Thoughts on the Influence of the French Revolution*, where the direct influence of Bentham can be distinguished in many expressions and which are inspired by a complete optimism. He expected of the French Revolution the advent of cosmopolitanism and the end of war ; ' the true interests of a nation never yet stood in opposition to the general interests of mankind, and it never can happen that philanthropy and patriotism can impose on any man inconsistent duties '.[2] In what concerned English interests more particularly, the end of despotism in France meant for England the end of wars with France ; and moreover, the success of the Revolution in France might by the prestige of example lessen the hatred of novelty which characterised the English spirit ; ' the singular advantage of having a free constitution has accustomed us to look with disdain at institutions, which, however wise in themselves, could not, it was thought, deserve imitation, because they were established under despotic governments. . . . The comparative excellence of our constitution has prevented its real excellence '.[3] All abuses will be criticised and corrected ; and those only will have cause for alarm ' who have, or at least who persuade themselves they have, interests distinct and indeed opposite to those of the nation at large ', the haughty peer, the official who accumulates offices, the colonial extortioner, the man of law ' who has crowded his memory, and overwhelmed his understanding with all the rubbish of positive laws, . . . and trembles at the very thought of a reform of the law, which would render his vast erudition useless, and would supersede the necessity of having recourse to him as a guide to conduct men through the maze of ambiguous statutes and inconsistent decisions '.[4] But, in the peroration, the notions of liberty and of rights are substituted afresh for the notion of utility : ' happy, indeed, is the rising generation which is destined to live in times, when to stand forth in defence of the equal rights of mankind will no longer be deemed a fair subject of derision, and when to secure to mankind the full enjoyment of those rights will no longer be thought chimerical ; . . . and when genius shall exert itself not in amusing the imagination, or exciting the most dangerous passions, but in concerting the best and most effectual means of rendering every description of men, free, secure, and happy .'[5]

[1] *Life of Lord Shelburne*, vol. iii. pp. 549-550.
[2] Romilly, *Thoughts on Influence of the French Revolution*, p. 5.
[3] *Ibid*. p. 13.   [4] *Ibid*. pp. 20-22.   [5] *Ibid*. pp. 23-24.

In 1790, he pleaded the cause of the National Assembly with
one of his French correspondents: there has been no human
assembly since the creation of the world which has done half as
much for the happiness of the human species. ' I will admit
all the violence, and, if you will, even the interestedness of the
leaders in the National Assembly ; but that men should act from
the pure motive of procuring good to others, without any regard at
all to themselves, is, I am afraid, more than one is entitled to expect,
even under the most perfect government that human wisdom could
desire, much more under such a government as that under which
the characters of all the men who are now acting any public part in
France has been formed.' [1] In 1791, he rejoiced that the success of
Thomas Paine's famous book on the *Rights of Man* should have
annulled the success, which seemed to him deplorable, of Burke's
Reflections.[2] In May 1792, he still held firm. ' Even the conduct
of the present Assembly has not been able to shake my conviction
that it is the most glorious event, and the happiest for mankind, that
has ever taken place since human affairs have been recorded.' [3] But
the tenth of August and the September massacres disabused him
all of a sudden. ' One might as well think of establishing a republic
of tigers in some forest of Africa, as of maintaining a free government among such monsters.' [4]

Bentham himself also seemed for a moment to have leanings
towards republicanism ; but this crisis was extremely short and
extremely superficial. Already the ' delirium ', the ' passionate
eloquence ' of the orators of the Constituent Assembly was getting
on his nerves. He considered the confiscation of the goods of the
church, and the restoration of the goods of their ancestors to the
descendants of the Protestants persecuted under Louis XIV, to be
an attack on the principle of security. When an association was
formed in England to counteract the societies for republican propaganda, Bentham was on the point of joining it : it was Romilly,
whom he chanced to meet in the street, who dissuaded him. He was
soliciting ministers on behalf of his model prison: for this Lord
Lansdowne was annoyed with him, and from 1792, Bentham gave
up his visits to Bowood.[5] When, in 1793, he sent to the minister
Dundas the pamphlets he had had printed four years previously,
he wrote : ' Some of them might lead you to take me for a Republican
—if I were, I would not dissemble it. The fact is, that I am writing
against even *Parliamentary Reform*, and that without any change
of sentiment.' [6] He was no doubt aware that France, by reason

[1] Romilly, *Memoirs*, vol. i. p. 409.   [2] *Ibid*. pp. 415-6.
[3] *Ibid*. vol. ii. pp. 1-2.   [4] *Ibid*. vol. ii. pp. 4-5.
   [5] MSS. Univ. Coll. No. 43, Confiscation of Church goods, No. 160 ; Meeting
with Romilly, No. 132 ; Breach with Lord Lansdowne, Add. MSS. Brit. Mus.
33,553, pp. 32, 33.
   [6] Bowring, vol. x. p. 293.

THE POLITICAL PROBLEM

173

of its revolutionary condition, was a country which was open to all
innovating experiments. To France he addressed his essay on
Parliamentary Tactics, and his Draught of a Code of Judicial Organisation. His *Defence of Usury* had just been translated in Paris.[1] In
1791, he sent his *Panopticon* to the National Assembly and offered
himself to organise and direct in France a prison constructed on
the model which he had advocated : ' France, towards which every
eye is turned, and from which models are exported for the
various branches of administration . . . is the country, above all
others, in which any new idea—provided it be a useful one—is
most readily forgiven.' And the Assembly voted the printing of
an extract from the work, ready translated into French, which
Bentham had sent with the book. In 1793 he presented Talley-
rand before his departure with a copy of his pamphlet entitled
Emancipate your Colonies,[2] in which, starting from first principles,
he attempted to show that the possession of a colonial empire is not
only unjust, from the point of view of the doctrine of the Rights
of Man, but useless and harmful to the interests of the colonising
nation and to the colony.[3] Lord Lansdowne shared Bentham's view
on this point. Why, he asked in the Lords in 1797, this folly of
attacking the Spanish possessions in South America ? In three or
four years they will separate themselves from Spain of their own
accord. ' A greater good could not be done to Spain, than to
relieve them from the curse of these settlements, and make them an
industrious people like their neighbours. A greater evil could not
happen to England than to add them to our already overgrown
possessions.'[4] It even appears that Lord Lansdowne, if we are
to believe his own statement, owed this revolutionary opinion to
Bentham :[5] that, said Bentham, is the thesis of one of my jaco-
binisms.[6] But, apart from this economic jacobinism, Bentham
remained an anti-jacobin.

When, thanks to the intervention of his friend and admirer Brissot,
the president of the committee which selected the names, he was
made a French citizen by the Assembly, together with Paine,
Priestley, Wilberforce and Mackintosh, he received the news with
some irony.[7] In the letter in which he acknowledged the receipt
from the ambassador Chauvelin of the minister Roland's letter,
notifying him that he had been nominated, he explained that he was
quite willing to become a French citizen in Paris on condition that
he remained an English citizen in London, and to become a republican
in Paris, on condition that he remained a royalist in London. It
was at this precise moment that the little house where he lived in
London became a ' refuge for *émigrés* '; and Bentham added that if
anything could lessen the joy involved in the acquisition of so

[1] Bowring, vol. x. pp. 246, 256.   [2] *Ibid.* p. 268.   [3] *Ibid.* vol. iii. p. 54.
[4] *Annual Register*, 1797, p. 186.   [5] Bowring, vol. x. p. 196.
[6] *Ibid.* p. 296.   [7] *Ibid.* pp. 280 *seq.*, and *Mémoires de Brissot*, vol. v. p. 253.

honourable a title, it would be the sight of so many unfortunate
beings who had to deplore the loss of it : would it not be possible
' to draw up a declaration—even on oath—by which, without
wounding their conscience or their weakness, the Republic might
obtain every security in the nature of things obtainable '.¹   In 1796
he suggested to Wilberforce the idea of a mission which, on the
strength of their titles as French citizens, they might undertake in
France in order to bring about a *rapprochement* between the two
nations ; but in the same letter he spoke, in a humorous vein, of this
title of French citizen.   How did they come to let his name and
Wilberforce's stray among so many names of republicans ?   And
why were the names of Paine, Priestley and Bentham separated
by a semi-colon from the whole cohort which followed, ' the *Wilber-
forces*, the *Washingtons*, *fortemque Gyan*, *fortemque Cloanthum* '.
He refers to France as *Pandemonium*, to the French as *Pandemonians*.
' True it is, that were they to see an *analysis* I have by me of their
favourite Declaration of Rights, there is not, perhaps, a being upon
earth that would be less welcome to them than I could ever hope to
be ; but there it lies, with so many *other* papers that would be equally
obnoxious to them, very quietly upon my shelf.' ²

Even as early as 1789 the theory of the Rights of Man was repudiated
by Bentham.   At the beginning of this same year, he added to his
Introduction a final note, in which he criticised the American ' declarations of rights ', and in particular the ' declarations ' of Virginia
and Carolina.   These two declarations lay down in their first article,
' that there are certain natural rights of which men, when they form a
social compact, cannot deprive or divest their posterity, among
which are the enjoyment of life and liberty, with the means of
acquiring, possessing, and protecting property, and pursuing and
obtaining happiness and safety '.   This amounts to saying that
' every law, or other order, *divesting* a man *of the enjoyment of life or
liberty*, is void ' ; in other words, that all penal laws without exception
are void.   Who can help lamenting that the American insurgents
should rest so rational a cause upon such bad reasons ?   It is still
the same scholasticism characteristic of all parties : ' with men who
are unanimous and hearty about *measures*, nothing so weak but may
pass in the character of a *reason* : nor is this the first instance in
the world, where the conclusion has supported the premises, instead
of the premises the conclusion '.³
But now France was following America's example, and Bentham
deplored the fact.   ' I am sorry ', he wrote to Brissot, ' that you
have undertaken to publish a Declaration of Rights.   It is a metaphysical work—the *ne plus ultra* of metaphysics.   It may have
been a necessary evil,—but it is nevertheless an evil.   Political

¹ Bowring, vol. x. p. 279.   ² *Ibid.* pp. 316-7.
³ *Ibid* vol. i. p. 154.

science is not far enough advanced for such a declaration. Let
the articles be what they may, I will engage they must come under
three heads—1. Unintelligible ; 2. False ; 3. A mixture of both. . . .
You can never make a law against which it may not be averred, that
by it you have abrogated the Declaration of Rights ; and the argument will be unanswerable '.¹ In 1795, Bentham collected his
critical observations on this subject in some manuscripts which he
entitled '*Anarchical fallacies* ; being an examination of the Declaration
of Rights issued during the French Revolution '.² Had not Burke,
five years previously, called the Declaration of Rights the Digest of
Anarchy ? Any declaration of rights was useless ; for what was its
purpose ? To set limits to the power of the crown ? A constitutional code would fulfil this purpose. To set limits to the
power of the various constituted bodies ? When they were made
dependent on the electoral body and on public opinion, their power
was limited in the only way which could be effective. A people
could not bind itself. The people's good pleasure was the only check
to which no other check could add anything, and which no other
check could annul. After these preliminary observations Bentham
turned the force of his criticism against two points.

In the first place, the language of the Declaration of Rights is
faulty. We are told that men *are* equal, that the law *cannot* alienate
the liberty of the citizens. This is false, and the proof is that men
make revolutions in order to re-establish the equality which has
been suppressed, and to defend the liberty which has been threatened.
What is stated in the indicative in the Declaration should be put into
the imperative, and it should be said, if you like, that men *ought* to
be equal, and that the law *ought* not to violate liberty. Herein lies
the difference between the ' rational censor ' of the laws and the
anarchist, between the moderate man and the man of violence.
The rational censor admits the existence of the law of which he
disapproves, and demands its repeal ; the anarchist denies its
existence, and sets up his own desire and his own caprice as a law
before which the whole of humanity is required to bow down.
That which is, is, the maxim of the ontologist, is stupid and empty,
but at least it is inoffensive. *That which is, is not*, is the dangerous
maxim of the anarchist on every occasion when he comes across
something in the form of a law which he does not like. France
had just reformed the language of chemistry, but knew not how to
reform the language of public law ; the phraseology used by Grotius
and Puffendorf was preserved, and had become revolutionary and
dangerous. A constitution which claimed to be the considered
design of a whole nation, was less wise, and less productive of happiness, than the ' chance-medley ' of the British constitution.³

¹ Bowring, vol. x. pp. 214-5.
² Published from Bentham's MSS. in Bowring, vol. iv. pp. 491 *seq.*
³ Bentham here revives an insulting expression used by Paine in *The Rights of Man.*

In the second place, the Declaration of the Rights of Man admits the existence of four natural rights : liberty, property, security, and resistance to oppression. Now, these four ' natural rights ' do not coincide with the four ends assigned to civil law in Bentham's philosophy.[1] Liberty? Every law is a restriction of liberty, and consequently forms a restraint on this supposed inalienable right, unless liberty be arbitrarily defined as consisting in ' the power of doing every thing which does not hurt another.' . . . But is not the liberty of doing evil also liberty? Article 11 draws a distinction between the use and abuse of liberty of thought and opinion. But who is to make the distinction between them? The task of determining what must be considered an abuse of liberty is left to future legislators. ' What is the security worth which is thus given to the individual as against the encroachments of government ? ' What is the use of a protection dependent on good pleasure merely ?—Property ? But it is law which determines property. The clause would become clear if it were admitted that all the rights of property and all the property possessed by any individual, no matter how, were imprescriptible, and could not be removed from him by any law. But every tax and every fine is an attack on the right of property, and consequently justifies resistance and insurrection. Article 13 declares property to be inviolable, except in case of *necessity*. But is it necessity which orders the construction of new streets, new roads, new bridges, new canals ? A nation could be satisfied with the natural means of communication received from nature, and still continue to exist : progress is not a necessity. In every change, there are disadvantages to be considered on the one hand and advantages on the other ; but of what avail are all the advantages in the world when set against the rights of man, which are *sacred* and inviolable and derived from the laws of nature, which have never been promulgated and which cannot be annulled ?—Security ? Every law which imposes a constraint or threatens with punishment is an attack on security.—As to the fourth ' right ', the right of resistance to oppression, this is not a fundamental right on the same ground as the others : it is a means pointed out to citizens whereby they can defend their rights whenever they consider them violated. The French, indeed, enlightened by six years' experience, avoided mentioning this right in the ' Declaration of the Rights of Man and of the Citizen ' of 1795. Nevertheless, the definition of it shows, with especial accuracy, the insurrectionalist and anti-social nature of the theory. The selfish and unsocial passions, which are useful and even necessary to the existence and the security of the individual, are none the less fatal to the public peace, when they are encouraged to the exclusion of the other passions. Yet this is the effect brought about by the Declaration of Rights, this is the morality of that celebrated manifesto, which acquired its notoriety by the

[1] Bowring, vol. i. pp. 301-2.

same qualities which made the fame of the incendiary of the temple of Ephesus.

Consequently Bentham, who was hostile to the principles of the French Revolution, as he had been to the principles of the American Revolution, remained indifferent to the political problem, although at one time [1] he had hoped to secure a seat in Parliament through Lord Lansdowne's patronage. He was passionately interested in reforms of detail. He was still the practical inventor, the ' man of projects ' which he had always been.

In 1795, he published simultaneously *A Protest against Law Taxes* and a pamphlet entitled ' *Supply without Burden* ; or escheat *vice* taxation '. In the first pamphlet, he demanded the abolition of the *law taxes* which made it to the interest of the corporation of judges to prolong suits, and to make the administration of justice expensive, and refuted two arguments which he held to be sophisms. One of these had been developed by Adam Smith, and was to the effect that ' the expense of an institution should rest on those who receive the benefit '. Very well, replied Bentham, but not to the point at which the benefit is annulled. The other held that this kind of tax is a ' check on chicanery '. But the direct purpose of the administration of justice is to render justice accessible and not inaccessible to all. But, it may be asked, what tax can be imposed to replace the tax which has been suppressed ? The second pamphlet replies to this question. The problem is : what kind of revenue is there whose twentieth part would be a tax, and a weighty tax, while the whole would not be a tax and would be felt by nobody ? Answer : an extension of the *law of escheat*, inheritances to be returned to the State, when the heir is beyond the degree of relationship within which marriage is forbidden.

In 1800 and 1801, he was busy on a more important financial project.[2] He proposed that the State should issue, following the example of private banks, bills for small sums, but bills bearing interest. ' Were the proposal expressed in these words—" Make your exchequer bills for small sums ",—this, though not completely nor correctly expressive of the measure, would express all the *innovation* of it. . . . The realisation of the project would present great economic advantages. . . . Were the proposed annuity-note paper to be emitted, " *Every poor man might be his own banker* " : every poor man might, by throwing his little hoards into this shape, make bankers' profit of his *own* money. Every country cottage— every little town tenement—might, with this degree of profit, and with a degree of security till now unknown, be a *frugality bank* '. But the proposed plan had political advantages also. As the Revolu-

[1] Bowring, vol. x. pp. 214 and 299.
[2] *A Plan for Saving all Trouble and Expense in the Transfer of Stock*, etc. (Bowring, vol. iii. pp. 105 *seq.*).

tion of 1688 had attached to the Government the whole class of holders of stock, the great monied interest, by the formation of the national debt, so Bentham's *Annuity Note Scheme* would attach to the established régime the whole mass of the population, the little monied interest. The national debt saved the nation from the tyranny of the Stuarts ; the new measure, by giving conservative interests to the poor, would preserve England from revolutionary anarchy.[1] Further, in 1796, Bentham contributed to the *Morning Herald* some critical observations on the *Treason Bill* ;[2] in 1797, to Arthur Young's *Annals of Agriculture*, some observations on the Poor Law, the reform of which was at that time the subject of parliamentary discussions ;[3] in 1798 and 1799, he drew up, in collaboration with Colquhoun, plans for laws to reform the London police ;[4] in 1800, he became alarmed at the great number of condemnations and executions for forgery, and in order to avoid this profusion of punishment, he looked for suitable means of preventing crime ; he busied himself, with almost as much enthusiasm, with the invention of a *frigidarium*, a freezing apparatus for preserving fruit and vegetables[5] ; in November 1800 he wrote for Cobbett's *Peter Porcupine* some *Hints relative to the Population Bill*, in which he defined the best methods to use in drawing up a new census.[6] But it was the *Panopticon* which absorbed the greatest part of his time. His father had died in 1792, and had left him, besides the house in Queen Square Place, Westminster, an income of between £500 and £600, mainly consisting of farm-rents.[7] This personal income Bentham spent in the expenses of propaganda and on advances on funds, in the same way as he lavished his time on schemes. Bentham was a philanthropist, but he was neither a republican nor a democrat.

He was not only a philanthropist and a man of projects ; he was the author of an entirely new system of juridical philosophy. One part of the system had been published in 1789, in the *Introduction to the Principles of Morals and Legislation* ; but at that time other events were demanding public attention, and the work passed unnoticed. The whole collection of Bentham's manuscripts were in the hands of Dumont, but the whole revolutionary period had to elapse before he could find time to edit them. Thus the French Revolution injured Bentham's philosophical reputation. It was not that Bentham did not feel himself to have the genius and the vocation for legislation ; he aspired to exert a practical influence by his works. He welcomed joyfully a speech made by Fitzherbert in a diplomatic club in 1790, in which he was termed the ' Newton of legislation '.[8]

---

[1] *A Plan for Saving all Trouble and Expense in the Transfer of Stock*, etc. (Bowring, vol. iii. p. 145.)

[2] *Ibid.* vol. x. pp. 320-2. [3] *Ibid.* vol. viii. p. 361. [4] *Ibid.* vol. x. p. 329.
[5] Bowring, vol. x. p. 346. [6] *Ibid.* p. 351. [7] *Ibid.* p. 279.
[8] *Ibid.* p. 238.

When his work on judicial organisation appeared, he was glad to see it read with interest by the little society of Lansdowne House : ' it contributes, with other things, to the slow increase of my school '.[1] It was his ambition, then, to found a school ; but he was still obliged to agree [2] that, like the prophets, he was less known in his own land than in neighbouring lands.   In his town house at Westminster, and in his country house at Hendon, he passed an obscure existence, ' seeing nobody, reading nothing, and writing books which nobody reads '.[3]

Nevertheless, even in France, Dumont was not hurrying to bring out the promised edition of Bentham's works.   He had always been lazy, and Romilly never tired of reproaching him with his indolence.[4] It was Romilly who made him decide to publish, in 1792, under the pseudonym of Groenvelt, a collection of *Letters, containing an account of the late Revolution in France, and observations on the Constitution, Laws, Manners, and Institutions of the English ; written during the author's residence at Paris, Versailles and London, in the years 1789 and 1790* ; and this strange work may be taken to be the first Benthamite book to appear.   It was to the *Fragment on Government* that Dumont owed the subject matter of his XVIth letter and the criticism of the theory of the division of powers ; the subject matter of the XIVth and XXth letters, the criticism of Blackstone's juridical philosophy, of English criminal law, of English criminal procedure, and of common law, he owed to manuscripts of Bentham's which were still unknown to the public.   But the XIIth letter is the most interesting of them all ; dated from Versailles, on August 29, 1789, it contains a refutation, based on the principle of utility, of the Declaration of the Rights of Man.   According to Dumont, this document does not exhibit the homogeneity and the simplicity which are the signs of truth.   The Declaration of the Rights of Man is more sentimental than rational : in the course of the theological debates from which it arose, ' each individual, conceiving that the rights of man were founded upon sentiment rather than reason, was desirous that the sentiments of others should be strictly in conformity with his own, and suspected insincerity in all who did not think like himself '.   Rights only exist by virtue of law : they do not precede society, but are produced by it ; they are not anterior to the formation of the body politic, they are benefits which we derive from our life in common.   It will be time, therefore, to draw up a Declaration of Rights, when the legal constitution of the country is completed.   Until then the expressions *law of nature* and *natural right* are no more than a ' senseless jargon ', convenient for the teacher who would involve his ignorance in the cloud of a long and elaborate harangue.   ' The only true and immutable principle is *the general interest*.   Utility is the supreme object,

[1] Bowring, vol. x. p. 246.   [2] *Ibid.* p. 316.
[3] Romilly, *Memoirs*, vol. i. p. 417.   [4] *Ibid.* vol. ii. pp. 28-30.

which comprehends in itself law, virtue, truth, and justice '. It alone can be the basis of the knowledge of morals as an objective science. ' Men who reason upon the principle of utility, can always understand each other, and are seldom likely to differ long in opinion, because they can have immediate recourse to experience, and the rule which is to fix the judgment of each, being plain, simple, and capable of but one construction, they may readily discover wherein their difference consists, which is the great secret of deciding all controversies.' If then it is through the general interest that the rights of such are discovered, and not the general interest through the rights of man, the method adopted by those who framed the Declaration is a vicious one : they should have applied themselves directly to the grand principle of general utility, without any intervening medium, and would have been enabled thereby to reason in a language intelligible to all mankind and ' gladly annihilate some thousands of volumes upon metaphysics, jurisprudence, and morals '. Instead of a Declaration of the Rights of Man there should have been prefixed to the constitution ' a few *social maxims*, founded upon general utility, and pointing out precisely the object of society, and the duties of government '. These maxims would never have pretended to the honour of forming the *credo* of a political religion.[1]

Yet, if we are to believe his own evidence,[2] was it not this same Dumont of Geneva who was one of those who drew up the French Declaration of the Rights of Man ? A committee of five had been chosen to draw it up. One of the five, Mirabeau, undertook the task, and then himself entrusted the task of framing the document to his secretaries, Duroverai, Clavière and Dumont. Dumont may have felt from the outset ' the falsehood and absurdity of this work ', of this ' puerile fiction '. He may have opposed the intended Declaration so eloquently that he carried with him the opinion of his collaborators and persuaded Mirabeau himself. When the project came up again before the Assembly, Mirabeau made objections to it, warning his hearers that ' any declaration of rights which came before a Constitution would be no more than a yearly almanach '. But of what avail against the opinion of the age and of a party is the opinion of an individual, even though his name be Mirabeau ? The idea of the declaration ' was an American idea, and practically everybody regarded such a declaration as an indispensable preliminary '. ' The miserable chattering ran its course and the wretched Declaration of the Rights of Man saw the light '.[3] By a curious historical paradox the Declaration of the Rights of Man and of the Citizen thus counted among its authors the first, or nearly the first, of Bentham's disciples,—the first and for a long time the only member of the Benthamite school, a supporter

[1] *Groenvelt Letters*, p. 228.
[2] See *Souvenirs sur Mirabeau*, p. 139.   [3] *Ibid*. p. 138.

of the morality of utility, and as such hostile to the theory of the
Rights of Man.

Dumont resumed his work of editing Bentham's manuscripts.
' I thank you again ', he wrote to Bentham in October, ' for this
work, which drags me forth from my inertness, and saves me from
the torments of *ennui* '.[1]   But he soon fell a prey once again to his
habitual laziness, since a year later Romilly was led to ask him
whether he had not put Bentham's manuscripts altogether on one
side.   ' Indeed, Dumont, you must come to a resolution of doing
something that will be useful to posterity '.[2]   Yet the work was not
given up altogether, for in 1795 Bentham was complaining that
Dumont was tormenting him with endless requests for advice.[3]
Then fragments of the work appeared in the *Bibliothèque Britannique*.[4]   In 1800, Bentham sent Dumont some fresh manuscripts.
The time of publication drew near.   ' I am extremely rejoiced,
wrote Romilly to Dumont on September 9, 1802, ' to hear that you
and Bentham are about to make your appearance in public so soon.
It is very entertaining to hear Bentham speak of it.   He says that
he is very impatient to see the book, because he has a great curiosity
to know what his own opinions are on the subjects you treat of '.[5]
During February and March Dumont kept Bentham informed as
to how the printing was getting on.[6]   Finally there appeared in
Paris, in June 1802, the ' *Traités de Législation Civile et Pénale*, a
work extracted from the manuscripts of the English lawyer, Mr.
Jeremy Bentham, by Et. Dumont, member of the representative
council of Geneva '. . . .   Three months previously the peace of
Amiens had been made, thus putting an end to the first part of the
great war ; a short truce divided the two periods of the European
crisis, the revolutionary period and the imperial period ; and it was
when a seal had, so to speak, been put on the end of the revolutionary
period by the Peace of Amiens that, in the last months of 1802,
Bentham was able to make his journey to Paris.

2.   MACKINTOSH, PAINE AND GODWIN

In the name of a half-empiricist, half-mystical philosophy, based
on the principle of utility, Burke denounced the French Revolution
and gave the signal for the crusade of Europe against the country
of the Rights of Man.   In the name of the principle of utility,
Bentham and his disciple Dumont refuted the Declaration of the
Rights of Man and of the Citizen.   But there were found in the
democratic faction writers to oppose Burke.   The *Vindiciae Gallicae*,

---

[1] Bowring, vol. x. p. 286.   [2] Romilly, *Memoirs*, vol. ii. p. 29.
[3] Bowring, vol. x. p. 313.   [4] *Bibl. Brit.* vols. iii. v. and vi.
[5] Romilly, *Memoirs*, vol. ii. p. 75.   [6] Bowring, vol. x. pp. 382, 383.

in which the young Mackintosh set out to correct Burke's partizan and passionate history of the first year of the French Revolution, and to justify the work of the Constituent Assembly against his denunciations, may be taken to be the reply made to Edmund Burke by the Whig party, or, to be more exact, by that section of the party which remained faithful to Fox. Thomas Paine's *Rights of Man*, whose two parts were published with a few months' interval between them, expressed the opinion of those societies for democratic agitation which had first arisen at the time of the American Revolution, and had just been resuscitated, and had multiplied after 1789 : this work was a revolutionary manifesto, the work of the journalist who fought for the republican ideal, first in America, then in England, and then in France ; it was sold for the benefit of democratic propaganda, and more than two hundred thousand copies were sold in less than two years. Through the alarm raised by its prodigious success, it brought about the first prosecutions for crime connected with the press and with opinion, and the proscription of Thomas Paine, and gave the signal in England for political and religious reaction. Then, in 1793, William Godwin, the friend of Thomas Paine, published his *Enquiry concerning Political Justice, and its Influence on general virtue and happiness* : a work which was both too extensive and too abstract to secure a public anything like as extended as that to which Paine's book had appealed. But it exercised a profound influence on a group of men of letters, young university students, and political agitators ; for a brief moment the book caused a scandal, while it had a profound influence which was permanent. Thus went on, from year to year, the controversy which Burke had started on the pretext of Price's sermon, and which, in the space of four years, produced four classical works for English political literature.

The respective doctrines of Mackintosh, Paine and Godwin exhibit at first sight a common feature which is of interest because it connects them with Bentham. All three agree with him in criticism of the theory, which Burke had endowed with a new splendour, of mixed government founded on the division of powers.

In his *Reflections on the French Revolution*, Burke had just developed the view that, since human nature is essentially multiple and intricate, a good political constitution should be complex so as to model itself on the complexity of human nature. The complication of the constitutional machine makes precipitate revolutions impossible ; it makes a policy of compromise necessary, and puts a check on the excesses of the arbitrary power. Herein lies the advantage of time-worn constitutions, like the English constitution, that they are at the same time liberal and complicated. ' We compensate, we reconcile, we balance. We are enabled to unite into a consistent whole the various anomalies and contending principles that are found in the mind and affairs of men. From hence arises, not an excellence

in simplicity, but one far superior, an excellence in composition.' [1]
And in this lies the profound difference between the new constitution
of France and the other European constitutions.   The variety of
the old constitutions is the cause both of their weakness and of their
liberalism.   The sudden and systematic simplicity of the new
French constitution is the cause both of its military strength and of
its despotic nature.   ' The design is wicked, immoral, impious,
oppressive ; but it is spirited and daring ; it is systematic ; it is
simple in its principle ; it has unity and consistency in perfection. . . .
Individuality is left out of their scheme of government.   The state
is all in all.   Every thing is referred to the production of force ;
afterwards, every thing is trusted to the use of it.   It is military in
its principle, in its maxims, in its spirit, in all its movements.   The
state has dominion and conquest for its sole objects ; dominion over
minds by proselytism, over bodies by arms.' [2]   What struck Burke
was not the fact that error is varied while truth is one, but that for a
free and living being the conditions of existence are complex and
varied.   Had not Montesquieu, a writer who had become classical
in England, said that simple laws were suited to despotic states ? [3]

Thus, on one point at least, there is some analogy between the
despotic and the democratic theses.   For in order to criticise the
mixed constitution of England, Paine, as early as 1776, had only
to remark in his *Common Sense* that, ' the more simple anything is,
the less liable it is to be disordered, and the easier repaired when
disordered '.[4]   The same thing applies to Mackintosh and Godwin.
Granted the principle of representative government, rules to prevent
the carrying out of the national will should not be instituted ; for
although it may sometimes happen that the majority of the citizens
are mistaken as to their real interests, it is on the other hand certain
that the general interest will be systematically opposed by every
privileged body, and by every political corporation.   What is the
real reason which makes the apologists of the aristocratic régime
happen also to be the advocates of complex constitutions ?   As well
ask why industrial corporations treat the proceedings of their craft
as secrets, knowledge of which is inaccessible to the public ; and why
Churches represent to laymen that the truths of religion consist of
mysteries.   The explanation of the theory lies in a caste interest ;
the noble, industrial and ecclesiastical castes will be able to enjoy
the monopoly of knowledge of the truth from the day on which
they succeed in persuading the masses that the truth is in itself
complex and obscure.   So that, according to Mackintosh and
Godwin, the theory of complex government rests, for Burke, on the
same principle as the theory of prejudice.   It amounts to maintaining
that *political imposture* is useful.   ' To pronounce that men are

---

[1] Burke, Works, vol. v. p. 304 ; see also *Ibid.* pp. 124-5 and 81.
[2] *Ibid.* vol. viii. p. 182.   [3] *Esprit des Lois*, liv. vi. ch. i.
[4] Paine, *Common Sense*, ch. i.

only to be governed by delusion is to libel the human understanding, and to consecrate the frauds that have elevated Despots, Muftis, Pontiffs and Sultans, on the ruin of degraded and oppressed humanity. But the doctrine is as false as it is odious. Primary political truths are few and simple.'[1] On this point, Godwin took up the ideas and even the expressions used by Mackintosh. In opposition to Burke, Paine, Mackintosh and Godwin held views on constitutional law similar to the views already held by Bentham in regard to private law. They thought that the principles of morals were at once clear, simple, and accessible to common sense, and were a suitable basis for a science.

But what are these principles? It is at this point that the agreement between the three adversaries of Edmund Burke came to an end. The differences between them are particularly interesting from our point of view, if we are to understand how, with the advocates of the democratic régime, the theory of general utility gradually, towards the end of the eighteenth century, took the place of the spiritualistic theory of natural rights.

The *Vindiciae Gallicae* is primarily an historical book; it is impossible, however, for Mackintosh to refute Burke without going back to a discussion of principles. Now, is the principle which Mackintosh sets up against Burke the principle of utility or the 'metaphysical' principle of the Rights of Man? It is impossible to answer this question, for Mackintosh himself does not appear to be aware of a logical divergence between the two principles. He does indeed defend against Burke the idea which inspired in America and later in France the drawing up of the Declarations of the Rights of Man: he sees in it the effect of the youthful vigour of reason and freedom in the New World, where, unlike Europe, the human spirit is not encumbered by that vast mass of customs and prejudices, the rubbish of centuries of barbarism. He blames Burke for being unable, after condemning the principle of natural rights, to refrain from making constant use of the expression. But, on the other hand, he obviously associates the success of revolutionary ideas in France with the spread of the ideas of Adam Smith: the end of that feudal régime, whose praises were sung by Edmund Burke, means for him above all the advent of commercial and industrial liberty. What he is fighting in the political *ancien régime* was what Adam Smith and Quesnay were fighting in the economic *ancien régime*,—government by the rich, whose very riches formed them into a close corporation: it was necessary for them to syndicalise and to coalesce, necessary for them to form distinct bodies, necessary for them to govern.[2] But the principle at the basis of Adam Smith's speculations, the principle of the natural identity of interests, had, in spite of certain obscurities in its wording, no logical relation with

[1] *Vindiciae Gallicae*, sect. v.   [2] *Vind. Gall.* sect. i.

the principle of natural rights. This Mackintosh implicitly recognises when after affirming that the primary political truths are few and simple, he attempts to define them : ' It is easy ', he thinks, ' to make them understood, and to transfer to Government *the same enlightened self-interest that presides in the other concerns of life.* It may be made to be respected, not because it is ancient, or because it is sacred, not because it has been established by Barons, or applauded by Priests, but *because it is useful .*' [1]

Throughout Mackintosh's entire work there is the same ambiguity in the expression of the first principle. In almost the same terms as Bentham he denies that the individual abdicates his natural rights when he enters a society with other individuals ; he does not even admit that these rights are diminished. The Rights of Man presuppose the pre-existence of the social bond, and all theories which imply the real existence of a state prior to the social state are either futile or false. Nevertheless he immediately comes back to the theory of natural rights, and distinguishes between the virtuality and actuality of these rights. A society is necessary in order to establish in practice the naturally equal rights of all individuals. But here Mackintosh suddenly begins to speak the language of utility again. The great question in politics is a question not of origin but of end ; it is not a question of right but a consideration of utility. Political forms are no more than suitable methods for securing a certain amount of public happiness. If the end is attained, any discussion instituted to ascertain whether the means were theoretically suited to produce it, becomes puerile and superfluous. Why then use the roundabout language of the Rights of Man ? It is because this roundabout language is at the same time an abbreviated language. All moral agents are powerless to estimate the utility of their actions taken individually ; but it can be shown that all general principles of justice are useful ; and it is this utility alone which endows them with the character of moral obligation. ' Justice is expediency, but it is expediency, speaking by general maxims, into which reason has concentrated the experience of mankind. . . . When I assert that a man has a right to life, liberty, &c. I only mean to enunciate a *moral maxim* founded on *general interest*, which prohibits any attack on these possessions.' [2] Hence the simultaneous use of the two expressions. The new Government of France is reared on the immutable basis ' of natural right and general happiness '.[3] A Declaration of Rights is the only expedient that can be devised ' to keep alive the Public vigilance against the usurpation of partial interests, by perpetually presenting the general right and the general interest to the Public eye '.[4] Mackintosh's logical attitude is an attitude of unstable equilibrium ; the balance was bound soon to lean in one direction or the other ; in fact, it already looks as though

[1] *Vind. Gall.* sect. v.
[2] *Ibid.* sect. iv.
[3] *Ibid.* sect. i.
[4] *Ibid* sect. iv.

it was inevitable that the principle of utility should, in his view, prevail over the principle of natural rights.

The same contradiction, or, if you like, the same confusion between the two principles, is noticeable in Thomas Paine's more famous book ; and it may perhaps be possible to examine, as it is actually going on, the process of transition from the first to the second principle, and see how it came about. The *Rights of Man* came out in two successive parts with a year's interval between the two. The first part, which was dedicated to Washington and appeared in 1791, forms, as stated in the sub-title, ' an answer to Mr. Burke's attack on the French Revolution ', and a point by point defence of the policy of the Constituent Assembly. The aim of the second part, which was dedicated to La Fayette and was published in 1792, is to ' combine principle and practice ' : having reaffirmed the principles of the philosophy of the Revolution, he inquires by what means any European country could put them into practice,—how England, following the example given by America and by France, could give herself a democratic budget and institutions. But it may be that Paine, unknown to himself, was not laying down the same principles in the two parts ; and it may be, if our interpretation is justified, that it is the spiritualist principle of natural rights which still predominates in the first part, while in the second the principle of general utility has already begun to take its place.

It is hardly necessary to point out how the juridical or spiritualist terminology of natural rights predominates over the Utilitarian terminology in the first part of the *Rights of Man*. The very title which Paine chose for the book defines its character. The popular history of the first year of the Revolution, told by Paine in order to correct Burke's inaccuracies, is nothing but a history of the conditions under which the Declaration was laboriously worked out. A first draught, hasty and enthusiastic, had been adopted on La Fayette's suggestion, on the eve of the capture of the Bastille, so that, if the National Assembly were to perish, some traces of its principles might survive the shipwreck. It was because the King hesitated to sanction the Declaration, which had now been adopted in its complete form, that the people marched to Versailles in the early days of October, victorious from the moment when the King consented to append his signature. Moreover was there any historian better qualified to tell of the Revolution of the Rights of Man than Thomas Paine, who had witnessed the fall of the Bastille and had been commissioned to carry to Washington the keys of the prison which had been rased to the ground, who was living in Paris at the time of the flight to Varennes, and who was perhaps the first to propose that a Republic should be established, who subsequently became a member of the Convention, and drew up, in collaboration with Condorcet, a new Declaration of Rights ? Paine's book further includes a translation of the Declaration, followed by critical observations ; in many respects this first part may be regarded as an English edition of the Declaration of the Rights of Man, accompanied by a philosophical and historical commentary.

The individual, *qua* individual, possesses, by right of his existence, a certain number of natural rights : such are the intellectual rights, or rights of the mind, and the various rights possessed by every individual of acting with a view to his personal well-being and happiness, in so far as the exercise of these rights does not threaten the natural rights of other men. The first rights, such as those ' of thinking, of speaking, of forming and expressing opinions ', always remain in their integrity by virtue of their very essence, for they are those ' in which the *power* to execute is as perfect in the individual as the right itself '. But there are others which man has an interest in partially resigning when he enters society with his fellows ; these are those in regard to which the right of the individual is perfect, but his power of execution imperfect.[1] Such are the rights to protection of the person, and to the acquisition and possession of property. They are civil rights, or rights of contract ; although they are natural rights which have been transformed, or ' exchanged ', (that is to say, rights a part of which we consent to sacrifice in exchange for the free enjoyment of the rest), they are distinguishable from natural rights in that, in the exercise of civil rights, we are acting under the guarantee of society. For example, man has a natural right to judge in his own cause ; and so far as concerns the right of the mind, he never gives up this right. But of what use is this right to judge in cases in which he has no power to redress ? He then borrows the arm of the society of which he is a member, in preference to and over and above his own. He requires that the society should become a government and should employ constraint to impose on his neighbour the respect of his own rights, and at the same time authorises it, if necessary, to impose on himself the respect of his neighbours' rights. He has ' deposited in the common stock ' a certain part of his natural rights ; society therefore, *grants* nothing to him. Every individual is the owner of the social stock, and has the right to draw from it under certain specified conditions. Now it is interesting to notice, in the theory of natural rights as set forth by Paine, certain analogies with the fundamental ideas of Bentham.

There can be no legitimate government, according to Paine, without a written constitution. Although English parliamentarians use and abuse the word ' constitution ', England has no constitution. What in England takes the place of one is to a true constitution what ' common law ' is to a written law, which alone is legitimate : and consequently the analogy of the ideas of Paine with those of Bentham becomes manifest. ' A constitution is to a government, what the laws made afterwards by that government are to a court of judicature. The court of judicature does not make the laws, neither can it alter

---

[1] *Rights of Man*, part i.

them ; it only acts in conformity to the laws made : and the government is in like manner governed by the constitution.' The United
States of America, whether taken as a whole or individually, have
constitutions. The State of Pennsylvania, in particular, has its
constitution, born of the people, who not only give authority to,
but impose a check on, the government : ' It was the political bible
of the state. Scarcely a family was without it. Every member of
the government had a copy ; and nothing was more common, when
any debate arose on the principle of a bill, or on the extent of any
species of authority, than for the members to take the printed
constitution out of their pocket, and read the chapter with which such
matter in debate was connected '.[1] Bentham spoke in the same terms
of his ideal code : and why should not the principle laid down by
Bentham for civil and penal laws be extended to constitutional laws ?
But Paine adds that, in order to make the government legitimate,
the constitution must be preceded by a Declaration of the Rights of
Man : and in this he again takes a different view from Bentham.

Paine also is an individualist ; and his individualism is expressed
by the same formulae as is the individualism of the Utilitarians.
' Public good is not a term opposed to the good of individuals ;
on the contrary, it is the good of every individual collected.
It is the good of all, because it is the good of every one : for
as the public body is every individual collected, so the public
good is the collected good of those individuals.' [2] Bentham, in his
Introduction, expresses himself in just the same way. Paine ignores
that solidarity of the generations which Burke considered the fundamental fact about society. Those who have left the world, and those
who have not yet entered it are as far apart from each other as human
imagination can conceive ; how then is a relation of obligation
between them conceivable ? How can it be laid down as a principle
and as a rule that of two nonentities, of which one exists no longer
and the other does not yet exist, the one should dominate the other
to the end of time ? ' I am contending for the rights of the living, . . .
Mr. Burke is contending for the authority of the dead, over the rights
and freedom of the living.' [3] Almost in the same words, Bentham
treats Burke's system, although diametrically opposed to the system
of the democrats, as being ' absurd and mischievous for similar
reasons : it subjugates the well informed to the ill informed ages. Of
all tyranny the most relentless is that of the dead : for it cannot be
mollified. Of all Folly the most incurable is that of the dead : for
it cannot be instructed '.[4] But Paine's individualism is a spiritualistic
individualism, founded on a theology : all men are born equal when
they come from the Creator's hands, and the only inequality which

[1] Rights of Man, part i.
[2] Dissertations on Government, the Affairs of the Bank, and Paper Money (1786).
[3] Paine, Rights of Man, part i. p. 16.
[4] July 8, 1795, under the heading Constitutional (see MSS. Univ. Coll, No. 43).

is not artificial is the inequality which divides the good from the bad.[1]
In Paris, in 1792, as in New York in 1776, Paine consistently remains
a Quaker even when he renounces Christian orthodoxy; and
through him the revolutionary Christianity of the English Protestants
in America joins hands with the atheism of the French *sans-culottes*.[2]
The individualism of Bentham or of Adam Smith rested on a quite
different principle.

But the analogies existing between Paine's political philosophy and
the Utilitarian philosophy are deeper than this. They have a
bearing not only on certain identical consequences drawn from
different principles, but also on the principles themselves. In spite
of some allusions to the 'indefeasible, hereditary rights of man',
the philosophy of the second part of the *Rights of Man* is very different
from the spiritualistic and juridical philosophy whose principles
Paine had developed in the first part. Paine now distinguishes
between the two notions of *society* and *government*: the notion of
government implies the notion of society, but, conversely, the notion
of society does not imply the notion of government. There is a
natural society, which was prior to the formation of governments
and which would continue to exist if forms of government were
abolished. But this primitive society is the economists' and not
the jurists' state of nature: it is founded on the principle of exchange,
in other words, on the principle of the natural identity of interests—
that is to say, on one form of the principle of utility. Paine no doubt
admits that it rests in part on a system of social affections which,
though not necessary to the individual's existence, are essential
to his happiness. But it rests, above all, on the selfish interests of
man. Nature has given the individual more natural needs than
power with which to satisfy them. Without the help of his fellows,
no man is capable of supplying his needs; thus it is the needs
themselves, which are common to all, which impel men to form an
economic society, 'as naturally as gravitation acts to a centre'.[3]
This, together with the Newtonian metaphor, dear to all the writers
of the school, is just the theory of the division of labour, which
Adam Smith had put at the foundation of his doctrine. 'The
landlord, the farmer, the manufacturer, the merchant, the tradesman,
and every occupation prospers by the aid which each receives from
the other and from the whole.'[4] As soon as men, at once by instinct
and by reciprocity of interest, have become accustomed to social
and civilised life, social principles are active enough to take the
place of the absent government formalities. Man is so much by
nature a being made for society that it is almost impossible to detach
him from it. All the great social laws are natural laws, laws of mutual

[1] *Rights of Man*, part i.
[2] See Paine's letter to his Calais electors in 1792 (Conway, *Life of Paine*, vol. i. p. 356).
[3] Paine, *Rights of Man*, 2nd ed. part ii. ch. i. p. 17.   [4] *Ibid.*

and reciprocal interest. Men conform to them and obey them, because it is to their interest to do so, and not through respect for the laws which the governments lay down. In short, society is capable of performing for itself almost all the functions which are ordinarily assigned to the government, and experience is constantly teaching us to reduce further the number of government functions. Consider, for instance, what went on in America during the first years of the War of Independence : in the absence of any regular government, the identity of interests was sufficient to bring about common security.

But how then, is it possible not to perceive that there is a formal contradiction between the two points of view which Paine successively adopts ? Nature confers on the individual more natural rights than power with which to defend them : therefore it is necessary to institute governments in order to preserve artificially the harmony of rights. Nature gives the individual more natural needs than power with which to satisfy them ; but in exchange individuals find means to satisfy their natural needs without resorting to any constraint, without any sacrifice of interest. We were able to see in the first part of the *Rights of Man* a propagandist edition of the Declaration of the Rights of Man and of the Citizen ; in the second part, it would be more accurate to see a pamphlet written in order to propagate Adam Smith's fundamental ideas, which are in this case no longer applied to the solution of economic problems, but also and above all to political problems.[1]

Thus with Paine the democratic philosophy returns to the philosophical tradition of Hume and Adam Smith, that is to say of the philosophy of utility. ' Instances are not wanting ', wrote Paine, ' to show that everything which government can usefully add thereto, has been performed by the common consent of *society, without government.*' We have already come across this tendency to separate the two concepts in Hume, in Adam Smith, and in Priestley.[2] We have seen how Thomas Paine, from the time of the American Revolution, drew revolutionary consequences from it. He now developed this thesis with fresh energy : the abolition of all regular government, far from necessarily resulting in the dissolution of society, should, according to Paine, act in the opposite way and strengthen the social bond. For governments are military in their origin and in the spirit of their institutions. Founded by robbers and bandits, by conquerors and usurpers, born of war, they are organised for war, and live by war. Why is the origin of all existing governments wrapped in a deep obscurity ? It is because it is to the interest of governments to conceal the anti-social nature of their origin. They know it is to their direct interest to perpetuate national prejudices, and national hatreds, to prevent the people from understanding that their interests are in reality one : such is the philosophy of war as

---

[1] *Rights of Man*, part ii. ch. v.   [2] See above, part i. ch. iii. part 2.

opposed to the philosophy of commerce. 'War is the faro-table of governments, and nations the dupes of the game.'[1] Why are governments so costly ? It is because in order to justify their existence, they have to make war, and war is costly ; it is also because they transport even into the interior of the countries which they govern the system of rapine which they have become accustomed to practise against the enemy ; now they make war in order to find pretexts for increasing the mass of taxes : government 'is the art of *conquering at home*'.[2] With the progress of civilisation European societies ought to learn to make ever greater economies in public expenditure : democratic government, since it is a minimum of government, is a cheap government. Nevertheless, the governments of western Europe, are becoming ever more expensive, by reason of their military constitution. Paine probably should be considered the original author, before Buckle and before Spencer, of the distinction between the two régimes, the military or governmental and the commercial. But in western Europe these two régimes to some extent existed side by side ; and the miracle is that commercial society, which Paine had identified with civilisation itself, had been able not merely to subsist but also to progress, under the governmental and military régime to which it was submitted. Man has a plastic faculty which enables him to adapt himself, and to adjust himself to all situations. 'Instinct in animals does not act with stronger impulse than the principles of society and civilisation operate in man.'[3] The optimistic naturalism of Hume and Adam Smith is recognisable here. Yet towards the end of the eighteenth century, with the advance of enlightenment, the contradiction between the two principles became too obvious to everybody for a reconciliation still to be possible. In America and in France the time of revolutions had arrived ; it was through revolutions that societies founded on the natural harmony of interests were to be substituted for governments that had issued from violence, and that after 'the age of chivalry' should come, according to the wise expression to which Burke wrongly gave a satirical meaning, 'the age of the political economist'.

It is but a short step from the political philosophy which is set forth in the second part of the *Rights of Man* to that which William Godwin developed a year later in his *Political Justice*. In the first place there are in the *Rights of Man* passages, side by side with those quoted above, in which Paine's criticism seems to bear not on the actual idea of government, but only on governments as they are—'*such as have hitherto existed in the world*' :[4] Paine asserts that it is an obvious truth that '*civil government* is necessary ',[5] and the two concepts of society and of government will cease to conflict when

---

[1] *Rights of Man*, part ii. ch. ii. [2] *Ibid*. part i. [3] *Ibid*. part ii. ch. ii.
[4] *Ibid*. [5] *Ibid*. part i. Miscellaneous Chapter.

government is defined merely as ' a national association acting on the principles of society '.[1]   In other words, Paine seems afraid to go through with his own ideas, and does not conclude, as he perhaps ought to do, with the radical dissolution of all governments.   In the second place, and this is more fundamental with him, Paine develops one after the other, in the two parts of his work, the ideas of a society founded on the obligation to respect the inalienable rights of the human personality, and of a society ' without government ', founded on the spontaneous identity of selfish interests ; but nowhere does he appear to understand that it is impossible to adopt these two doctrines at once without contradiction.   Godwin, on the other hand, was more isolated and less directly mixed up with the party struggle : in consequence he was less the dupe of fashionable political formulae, and so understood the necessity of choosing between the doctrine of the equality of rights and the principle of the identity of interests.   At the time when Paine still appeared, alike to those who detested and to those who adored him, to those who burnt him in effigy and to those who propagated his book like a Bible, as the incarnation of the doctrine of natural rights, Godwin was the first among the philosophers of the democratic party to criticise the notion of *right*, and to found on this criticism the radical conception of a ' society without government ',—the conception itself borrowed, as Godwin acknowledges, from Thomas Paine.[2]

Godwin's moral theory is the moral theory of utility ; and the expressions which he uses to define it are so much akin to those used, a short time previously, by Bentham in his *Introduction* that one is tempted to believe that Bentham had a direct influence on him. Utility is the criterium of morality.   Every moral system which is not infected with monastic prejudices must admit that in what concerns ourselves we ought not to refuse any pleasure except in so far as it tends to exclude some greater pleasure.   Other elements, moreover, enter into the calculus of pleasures.   Not only must not a greater pleasure be bartered against a lesser, nor the certain or probable expectation of some considerable pleasure against a hazardous speculation, but the pleasures of a plurality of individuals must be considered ; and, if the end of virtue is to add to the sum of agreeable sensations, impartiality must regulate virtue : we ought not, in order to produce pleasure for one individual, although that individual may be ourself, to exert an effort which could have been used to produce the pleasure of several.   In short, morality is the system of conduct which is determined by the consideration of the greatest general good ; the man who deserves the highest moral approbation is he whose conduct, in the greatest number of cases, or in the most serious cases, is governed by benevolent purposes, or is put to the service of the public utility.   But

[1] *Rights of Man*, part ii. ch. i.
[2] Godwin, *Political Justice*, bk. ii. ch. i.

Godwin does not once mention Bentham's book,[1] which had made little stir, and it need not be assumed that he plagiarised it ; for the general movement of contemporary thought, the common influences they had undergone, are enough to explain all these analogies of expression.   Godwin may have come under the influence of Paley, who was universally read and known.   He certainly came under the influence of Hume, Hartley and Helvetius.   To Hume and Hartley he owed his determinism ; to Hartley he owed his theory of the association of ideas, abandoning, like Priestley, the theory of vibrations ; to Hartley again, he owed, as Priestley had done, the theory of necessary and indefinite progress, and, finally, to Helvetius what might be called his intellectualism.   Helvetius and Godwin, in fact, agreed that individual differences in the human race could all, or almost all (Godwin makes some concessions on this point in the second edition of his book),[2] be explained from moral or social causes, and not, as Montesquieu had thought, from physio-logical or physical causes.   To this is due the extreme importance, for both of them, of the political problem, which resolves itself into a problem of pedagogy ; as opposed to education, properly so-called, whose action ceases after childhood, and to books, which only reach the select few, political institutions exert their influence on everyone and throughout the whole of life.[3]   But to all of them, without distinction, Godwin owes his Utilitarianism.

The actual interpretation given to the principle of utility by Godwin remains very uncertain.   Does he give his support to the principle of the natural identity of interests ?   He would seem to do so, since he borrows from Adam Smith his economic liberalism, and from Hartley his theory of indefinite progress.   Besides, a whole chapter in his first edition is devoted to showing that the practice of virtue is the true method to be employed in order to attain individual happiness.[4]   It is in vain that Godwin suppresses the chapter in the second edition ; it is in vain that he admits that it is a very different thing to convince men that a certain kind of conduct in the individual would be most in conformity with the general interest, and to persuade them that all selfish satisfaction must be put after considera-tions of general utility ; for he immediately repeats, without any connecting link, that egoism and disinterestedness, though they are in themselves so different, happen, in the last analysis, to prescribe the same line of conduct.   Yet Godwin holds that the egoistic system is founded on an equivocation, and condemns it.[5]   Are we to say, like La Rochefoucauld, that we are guided in all our actions

[1] On the other hand I can only find one allusion to Godwin in Bentham's works (Bowring, vol. x. p. 59).
[2] *Political Justice*, bk. i. ch. 3 and 4 (1st ed.), ch. 4 (2nd ed.).
[3] *Ibid*. bk. i. ch. 8 (1st ed.), ch. 4 (2nd ed.).
[4] *Ibid*. bk. i. ch. 9 (suppressed in 2nd ed.).
[5] *Ibid*. bk. iv. ch. 10 (2nd ed.).

by a calculus of personal interest ? or should we rather hold that, since every conscious state involves an element of pleasure or pain, the immediate sensation, whether agreeable or painful, must be taken to be the sufficient and necessary cause of the action ? But, in the second case, the motive of the pleasurable action may as well be disinterested as egoistic. In the last analysis, the principle of the fusion of interests is seen to predominate, in Godwin, over the principle of the natural identity of interests. All men are reasonable ; all men are aware that man is a being with the same nature in all individuals, and feel that the treatment which they receive one from another should be measured in relation to a common unity. Every man wishes to help his neighbour. Even the criminal invents sophisms to justify his action. In short, there is a natural tendency in man impartially to apply the criterium of utility, in other words, there is a natural tendency towards justice. Thus justice coincides with utility : ' By justice ', says Godwin, ' I understand that impartial treatment of every man in matters that relate to his happiness, which is measured solely by a consideration of the properties of the receiver, and the capacity of him that bestows '.[1] It is this tendency towards justice that the moralist has to develop, by disengaging it from all opposing tendencies, not only from egoistic tendencies, but from those which imitate morality. Family affections, and the feeling of gratitude, may oppose the action of the principle of utility in us ; these are feelings which can falsify ' the moral arithmetic ' and which must be eliminated from the calculus.

But, if it is general utility which determines my duty, the notions of duty and right are thereby incompatible ; or again, as Godwin says, thinking of the title of Paine's book, the idea of man and the idea of right are incompatible : ' individuals have no rights '.[2] What, in fact, is a right unless it be the freedom ' to do as we list ' ? Now of these actions which we can perform, some are useful and ought to be performed, and others are harmful and ought not to be performed ; there are no intermediate actions which the consideration of general utility leaves us free to do or to leave undone. Right is the power to use or to abuse ; but it is absurd to say that abuse constitutes a right. Paine is right in saying that ' princes and magistrates have no rights ' : for there is not a situation in their lives without its corresponding obligations, there is no power entrusted to them which they are not obliged to use solely with a view to the public good. But it is remarkable that, when this principle had been once laid down, the necessity of applying it to subjects and to citizens taken individually or in groups should not have been recognised. It is ridiculous to say that a religious congregation, or a political association has the right to adopt ceremonials or statutes which are detestable or absurd.[3] Is it not legitimate, however, to speak of ' rights to mutual assistance ' ? But in affirming that

[1] *Pol. Justice*, bk. ii. ch. 2 (2nd ed.).   [2] *Ibid.* bk. ii. ch. 5.   [3] *Ibid.*

' men have a right to the assistance and co-operation of their fellows
for the accomplishment of every honest action ', we give the word
' right ' a very different meaning from its usual one. Right becomes
the correlative of obligation ; it no longer means something discretionary and essentially voluntary. It would therefore be better
to avoid the use of an ambiguous term. For the notion of right,
in the current meaning of the word, is the source of all erroneous
moral notions : it is this notion which allows the prodigal to spend
and the miser to pile up his fortune without utility, and to think that
he is not violating justice. The Utilitarian morality, just because it
imposes duties, cannot confer rights.

Should, then, the right to the exercise of private judgment and
to the freedom of the press be condemned along with the other
rights ? [1] No ; but criticism must be made of an improper use
of the expression ' right ' in certain cases where it is absolutely impossible to restrict liberty without there being an excess of harmful
consequences, and even more so, in certain cases, where, rightly
regarded, liberty is in reality restricted and not extended. If no
restrictions are put upon freedom of conscience and of the press, this
does not mean that men have the right to deviate from the line of
action prescribed by duty ; it means that society, the sum of the
individuals, has not the right to assume the prerogative of an infallible judge, and imperatively to lay down the law for its members
in matters of pure speculation. On the one hand, all men are
fallible : no man can assert that he is right and impose his judgment
on another. On the other hand, even if I did possess an infallible
criterium of truth, I should not, for that reason, have the right to
impose by force the respect of it on my fellow men. For it is of the
nature of truth that it cannot be imposed by external constraint, but
must be adhered to freely. A truth that is imposed is not a truth,
it is an error : such was the newly discovered principle of liberalism,
whose thorough application was to transform the whole sphere of
political institutions. It had been introduced into political economy
by Adam Smith, and everyone took it to be theoretically proved
that the liberal régime was the most favourable to commercial
prosperity. Now the political application of the principle needed to
be discovered. Godwin was a democrat and considered the form
and the acts of the government as derived from the freely expressed
will of the citizen, by the very fact that he respected the exercise of
' private judgment ' on the part of every individual.[2] How ought a
nation to be governed ? Should it be in conformity with or in
opposition to the opinion of its inhabitants ? Without any doubt, it
should be in conformity with their opinion. This is not because
their opinion is a criterium of truth, but because, however erroneous
this opinion may be, we cannot find no better criterium. There is
only one way of improving the institutions of a people, and that is to

[1] *Pol. Justice,* bk. ii. ch. 6.   [2] *Ibid.* bk. i. ch. 4, § 1.

improve their intelligence.   But this absolute respect for the human intelligence implies political consequences which are more radical than the establishment of a representative and democratic régime would be.   The eighteenth century philosophers blamed both the religious and the industrial corporations for surviving when they did not contain any principle of progress, and for perpetuating in one era the intellectual prejudices and the industrial processes of another, and thus of forming an obstacle to that progress of the human spirit which pre-supposes the free communication of ideas. Now what is true of the constitution of a corporation is equally true of every political constitution, even the most democratic.   All constitutions, all permanent political institutions, are bad ;   they must be abrogated on the strength of the principle of freedom of conscience and of respect for private judgment.   Even a democratised society, governed by a single national assembly,—a society of which Paine discussed the theory in his *Rights of Man*, and of which the French Constitution of 1793 afforded a practical application—still only marks one step towards the final goal to which the progress of human society is tending.

For a government constituted in this way must be thought of as being endowed with legislative power, the power of making laws. But the objection which is valid against the notion of a permanent political institution is valid against the notion of law.   By this objection, Godwin renews the criticism originated by Hume against the notion of contract, and of fidelity to promises.[1]   If, for example, on attaining my majority I express my agreement with a system of opinions, with a code of practical institutions, must this declaration be binding on me for ever ?   Am I forbidden to complete and to modify my estimation of things for the rest of my life, or for the following year, week, or hour ?   The respect for contracts is founded on the obligation to keep one's promises.   But our faculties and our possessions are the means which enable us to render services to others, and it is with time that these means can develop their useful effects :   there is therefore nothing the free disposal of which is more sacred than that of time.   Now we diminish our freedom in the use we make of our time, when we force ourselves, to-day, to act at a given time in some determinate way.   He who ties up the capital of his knowledge in this way is just as short-sighted as he who ties up the capital of his wealth.[2]   But what is true of contracts is true of laws.   The law is efficacious to the extent to which it defines arbitrarily selected crimes, and condemns acts which the principle of utility does not condemn, but becomes proportionally less necessary as its prescriptions coincide more with the prescriptions of the public utility :   the direct observation of social phenomena then suffices, without recourse to the study of any positive law.   The law is essentially indefinite :   it has to multiply its prescriptions in order

<hr>

[1] *Pol. Justice*, bk. v. ch. 21.   [2] *Ibid.* bk. iii. ch. 2 and 3.

to try to equal by its complexity the multiplicity of the particular cases. Consequently, it is uncertain : it involves innumerable suits. Finally, and above all, it aims at foretelling the future, at foretelling future human actions, and at laying down decisions about them. The government which makes a law, sets itself up as a master of wisdom, so wise that it thinks it has nothing to learn from the future ; or else it undertakes, if the future does teach it new lessons, to take no notice of them. The law is the bed of Procrustes for social phenomena : in defiance of the great principle that there are not in the universe two atoms which are indistinguishable from each other, it attempts to reduce human actions, which are made up of a thousand fugitive elements, to a small number of types. Laws, like catechisms, creeds, and promulgations of dogmas, tend to immobilise the human spirit in a state of stagnation : they are principles of permanence whose action stems that ceaseless perfectibility, which is spiritual health.[1]

Godwin, in short, like Hume or like Paley, criticises the contractual theory of morality ; but Hume and Paley, when they had proved the inability of the contractual theory to found moral rules and political laws, found a kind of Utilitarian substitute or equivalent of the original contract in the theory of general rules. Now what Godwin abominates in the idea of the contract and of the promise is just this element of permanence or generality. While for Bentham the Utilitarian morality is the basis of a philosophy of law and of universal social rule, it leads in Godwin to the very different assertion that every law is bad because every law is a general rule.

But even if, according to Godwin's scheme, the National Assembly is deprived of the power of making laws, it retains the exercise of the executive power, which apparently escapes the objections which are valid against the legislative power : for the decisions of the executive power apply to particular given circumstances, and are not, like legislative decisions, set forth in the form of general propositions which are binding on the future. Further, it appears that the executive power belongs to the very essence of government ; and, if government is an evil, is it not a necessary evil ? Even now, are there any more important questions of government than questions of peace and war, or of taxation and of the choice of suitable times for the meeting of the deliberating assemblies ? [2] Is it not possible to conceive that with the progress of civilisation the executive power may tend to become all-important, while the legislative power will be reduced to nothing ? Possibly this would be conceivable, if a new difficulty did not spring up.

In fact, in order for the decisions of the authority to be executed, there must further be a sanction to guarantee their execution, and

---

[1] From this arises one of the chief paradoxes in Godwin's moral theory : the criticism of the contract, law, and institution of marriage.

[2] *Pol. Justice*, bk. v. ch. 21.

the non-execution of the command must involve the infliction of punishment. Now Godwin criticises the notion of punishment,[1] just as he criticised the notion of law. Like Paley, like Bentham (and like Blackstone himself), he refuses to consider punishment as a rational retaliation. Punishment should not be inflicted ' because there is apprehended to be a certain fitness and propriety in the nature of things, that render suffering, abstractedly from the benefit to result, the suitable concomitant of vice.' To punish by thus taking one's stand on a notion of suitability, in memory of the past and not in forethought for the future, is to be as mad as Xerxes whipping the waves of the sea. Punishment ought to be inflicted ' because public interest demands it '; but even this is impossible, and here Godwin, though he set out from the same principle as Paley and Bentham, outstrips these two philosophers in the consequences he draws from it. On the one hand, it is impossible to make punishments proportionate to crimes ; for the determination of the proportion depends on the knowledge, which is impossible, of the motives of the act and of the reaction of the punishment on the whole future conduct of the criminal. But on the other hand, and above all, the nature of punishment is incompatible with the nature of human understanding. The purpose of punishment is to teach men what actions they must hold just, and what actions they must hold unjust. But to teach is to prove. Now to punish is not to prove. Therefore to punish is not to teach. The superior who chastises an inferior either claims to be right, or else merely claims to be the stronger. If he thinks he is right, let him prove it. If he claims to punish because of the superiority of his strength, then the legal punishment of modern times is only a more hypocritical form of the *ordeal* of the Middle Ages, when the strongest was held to be right because he was the strongest. In the sphere of religion it had already been recognised that the principle of punishment contradicted the principle of freedom of conscience. But, through an inexplicable perversion of reason, men have made a difference between religion and morality, making religion the sacred province of conscience, and handing over morality, without restriction, to the discretion of the magistrate. It is their moral tendency which constitutes the value of religious opinions as of all theoretical opinions. The application of the liberal principle, which had already been applied to religion, must be extended to morality. In moral as in religious matters, the direct tendency of penal constraint is to make our understanding and our fears, our obligations and our weakness contradict each other. On the criticism of the notion of merit, Bentham founds a positive theory of punishment, and Godwin a criticism, with strictly negative conclusions, of the notion of punishment.

If, then, the government can make use neither of the legislative

[1] *Pol. Justice,* bk. vii. ch. i *seq.*

nor of the executive power without threatening individual freedom of conscience, the only power which it remains free to exercise is a power of arbitration. Its functions are reduced to those of a mere arbitrating jury, giving considered advice, in cases of urgent need, and not deciding but merely suggesting. But, why, in this case, let the government retain the character of a permanent institution ? Why not substitute for it juries, elected by the citizens on all occasions when there is felt to be a need for arbitration between opposing interests, functioning for a given occasion only, and dissolved immediately afterwards ? This will become possible when big States, with which a liberal régime is incompatible, are replaced by small communities. But what, after all, is the use of setting up such juries ? Does not the reasoning of one wise man carry as much weight as that of twelve ? And would not the aptitude of an individual for instructing his neighbours be sufficiently well known, without the formality of a regular election ? ' This is one of the most memorable shapes of human improvement. With what delight must every well-informed friend of mankind look forward to the auspicious period, the dissolution of political government, of that brute engine, which has been the only perennial cause of the vices of mankind, and which, as has abundantly appeared in the progress of the present work, has mischiefs of various sorts incorporated with its substance, and no otherwise to be removed than by its utter annihilation ! ' [1]

According to Godwin, then, the end of the progress of civil society is, properly speaking, anarchy. As a matter of fact, Godwin repudiates this expression ; he expressly requires that a distinction be made between anarchy and what he calls ' a well conceived form of society without government ', or again, as opposed to the theory of complex government which Burke had made fashionable, ' a simple form of society without government '.[2] But this is because Godwin understands anarchy in its revolutionary sense of violent suppression of established forms of government. Now, according to the fundamental principles of his philosophy, violence is a form of action which is always to be condemned. The only way of converting men is to convince them ; violence, used in the service of truth, defeats its own end ; while truth, once expressed, cannot be destroyed. ' It is a dangerous attempt in any government ', said Paine in 1792, ' to say to a Nation, *Thou shalt not read.*—Thought, by some means or other, is got abroad in the world, and cannot be restrained, though reading may '.[3] The fact that, in 1793, the democrat Godwin preached the doctrine of non-resistance and gave up what was formerly the favourite thesis of the democratic party, the doctrine of the right of resistance, can be explained quite naturally by the state of political parties in England. The Republicans, in

[1] *Pol. Justice*, bk. v. ch. 24.   [2] *Ibid.* bk. vii. ch. 5 ; and bk. viii. ch. 1.
[3] Conway, *Life of Paine*, vol. i. p. 369.

the interest of their cause, were bound to disavow the excesses of the revolutionary terror, in order to protect themselves from the excesses of the counter-revolutionary terror in England. In Erskine's famous speech for the defence as counsel for Paine in December 1792, he told the story, taken from Lucian, of Jupiter and the countryman. ' The countryman listened with attention and acquiescence, while Jupiter strove only to convince him ; but happening to hint a doubt, Jupiter turned hastily around and threatened him with his thunder. " Ah, ha ! " says the countryman, " now, Jupiter, I know that you are wrong ; you are always wrong when you appeal to your thunder." This ', concluded Erskine, ' is the case with me. I can reason with the people of England, but I cannot fight against the thunder of authority '.[1] Godwin seems to be recalling these words of the agitator and lawyer, when he proclaims on so many occasions ' the omnipotence of truth ' : ' ten pages ', he says, ' that should contain an absolute demonstration of the true interests of mankind in society could no otherwise be prevented from changing the face of the globe, than by the literal destruction of the paper on which they were written ' . . . But if by ' anarchical society ', no more is meant than what Godwin calls a ' society without government ', the expression provides a denomination of his system which is perfectly justified. Godwin's political philosophy starts with the criticism of one of Thomas Paine's principal formulae—the formula, which according to him is contradictory, of the ' Rights of Man '—and ends with a complete adhesion to another of Paine's formulae, that of a ' society without government ' ; Paine's only mistake was that he did not see all the consequences involved by the separation of the two concepts of ' society ' and ' government '.[2]

Godwin's book caused a commotion. Pitt argued from the price of the two large quarto volumes that he need not prosecute a book that was accessible to a select few only ; nevertheless, Godwin had a profound influence, for two or three years, in intellectual and literary circles. The revolutionary poets, Wordsworth, Southey, and Coleridge, from being disciples of Rousseau, became disciples of Godwin. Students in London and at Cambridge became enthusiastic for what was called the ' new ' or ' modern philosophy '. Godwin was a prolific novelist as well as a political theorist ; and his novel, *Caleb Williams*, in which he set out to refute Burke's chivalrous morality, the morality of honour, met with the same success as his *Political Justice* had done. Then came the reaction : the time arrived when the cause of the French Revolution was deserted, even by its most ardent defenders. But the number of attacks made against Godwin further prove his popularity. He was ridiculed in verse by the satirists, by the author of the *Pursuits of Literature*,

[1] Conway, *Life of Paine*, vol. i. p. 375.   [2] *Pol. Justice*, bk. v. ch. 15.

and by the youthful Canning in the *Anti-Jacobin*. Preachers denounced from the pulpit both his levelling equalitarianism, and certain special theses in his book which had caused a scandal, namely, his criticism of domestic affection and of cohabitation in marriage. Charles Lloyd wrote his novel, *Edmund Oliver*, expressly to refute him. Mackintosh himself, who had become reconciled with Burke and had broken with the Revolution, expressly repudiated Godwin's philosophy in his famous law lectures, given at Lincoln's Inn in 1797, and declared that Godwin's abstract man was as chimerical as a mountain of gold. But the ideas survived even the popularity of the system of which they were originally a part. It is interesting, and at this stage easy, to mark the place which Godwin occupies in the history of utility.

On the one hand, he was the first of the theorists of the republican party to separate the democratic idea from the idea of natural right ; it is this that distinguishes his doctrine from the still confused doctrines of Priestley, Mackintosh and Paine. No doubt his criticism of the notions of original contract, obligation and natural right had been anticipated by the first theorists of the Utilitarian morality, that is, by Hume, Adam Smith and Bentham ; but these were still taken in by the current political language, and included the idea of democracy and the idea of natural right in the same reproach. Godwin thus laid himself open to the same reproaches from the clergy as Hume had formerly incurred ' It is not ', says one of them in the preface to a sermon in which he denounces Godwin's moral theory, ' with Mr. Godwin's System merely, but with the Principle from which that System is deduced, and which may briefly be defined " the resolving morality into expediency ", that I am really at issue in the following pages '.[1] He regretted to see this principle adopted both by the most sincere defenders of Christianity, Law, Brown and Paley, and at the same time by the most declared atheists, beginning with Hume and Helvetius. But Hume, at the time when the Presbyterians were persecuting him, was a Tory ; Godwin was a republican and an enemy of all governments. His work created at once utilitarians and democrats. Such was Francis Place, who was then a simple workman, but presently became a master tailor. He was an active member of the political associations of the period, and later became one of Bentham's most zealous and most intimate disciples ; but long before he knew Bentham, he had already become converted to a kind of Utilitarian radicalism by his consideration of Godwin's book ; according to him, it was Godwin who taught him to doubt the existence of ' abstract rights '.[2]—Many more features of likeness between Godwin's doctrine and the future Utilitarian

---

[1] Thomas Green, *An examination of the leading principles of the new system of morals, as that principle is stated and applied in Mr. Godwin's Enquiry*, 2nd. ed. 1799, p. ii.

[2] Graham Wallas, *Life of Place*, p. 29, note.

doctrine could be pointed out. But neither the criticism of the
domestic affections and of unconsidered feelings, and of all moral
tendencies which are not submitted to an exact and impartial calculus
of all possible consequences, nor feminism, of which Godwin's
wife, Mary Wollstonecraft, gave the first systematic exposition in
her *Vindication of the Rights of Woman*, can be held to have been subsequently borrowed from Godwin by the Utilitarians : it should not
be forgotten that Godwin and Bentham came under the common
influence of Helvetius independently. Godwin's true *rôle*, in the history of the formation of Philosophical Radicalism, is to have brought
about the fusion between the Utilitarian and the democratic ideas.

On the other hand, many doctrines that belong to Godwin are
incompatible with the spirit of Bentham's philosophy. Bentham
called for written and codified laws, and considered that the principle
of utility would permit the foundation of scientific and penal laws.
Godwin was working to hasten the formation of a society without
government, without either civil or penal laws. Now the difference
between the two systems does not depend on different interpretations
of the principle of utility which is common to both ; it depends on
the fact that Godwin is not a pure Utilitarian : for he does not found
his criticism of the ideas of law and punishment on the principle
of utility. For him, man is not essentially a ' sensitive being, capable
of pleasure and pain ; he is essentially a ' rational ' or ' intelligent '
being. Men who live in society are to him, by definition, beings
who exchange not products but ideas. Had Godwin noticed that
the intellectualist principle is distinct from the Utilitarian principle ?
Perhaps not. He considers his absolute political liberalism to be a
mere extension of Adam Smith's economic liberalism, but Adam
Smith preaches liberalism because, by very reason of the natural
egoism of human individuals, interests are naturally identical ; while
Godwin preaches it in political affairs because, by reason of the
nature of intelligence, truth cannot be imposed by constraint, and
can only be propagated freely. In opposition to Burke's political
system, which is founded on political imposture and on prejudice, Godwin proposes a moral and political system, which is
founded on absolute sincerity ; and sincerity is given the first place
on his list of virtues.[1] This shows the opposition that exists between
the intellectualistic and the Utilitarian principle. In cases where
lying is useful, why not lie, unless you hold truth sacred ? But if you
hold truth sacred, is there a great distance dividing the intellectualist
principle, on which Godwin bases the freedom of conscience, from
the spiritualistic principle of the Rights of Man ? or the obligation
to respect the individual intelligence from the obligation to respect
the personal conscience ? Does not Godwin implicitly recognise
this when, in the second edition of his book, he reintroduces the
expression *right*, which had been banished from the first.[2] No

---

[1] *Pol. Justice*, bk. iv. ch. 6.   [2] *Ibid*. bk. ii. ch. 5.

doubt, he persists in condemning the notion of right, understood in the sense of discretionary power, and distinguishes between negative and positive rights, rejecting the latter and retaining only the former, the right to the assistance or to the respect of one's neighbour. All the same, the concession is striking. Bentham's disciples, through their common inspiration, belong too much to the eighteenth century for the idea of intellectual emancipation to be absent from their doctrine ; but it is not the fundamental idea of their doctrine, since their fundamental thesis is the thesis of the mechanism of the egoistic passions. The idea of intellectual emancipation does seem, on the other hand, perhaps unknown to himself, to be the fundamental idea of Godwin's system. In this he is akin, no longer to Bentham or Helvetius, but to the ultra-Protestants of the American Revolution and the authors of the Declaration of 1789.

CHAPTER II

THE ECONOMIC PROBLEM

'WHEN the rich plunder the poor of his rights', wrote Thomas Paine, 'it becomes an example to the poor to plunder the rich of his property'.[1] Thus, apparently, if the rich were merely to allow equal political rights to all citizens, they would thereby secure respect for the right of property. Godwin's equalitarianism, on the other hand, contests all rights which are defined as powers to use and to abuse, and consequently among the rest the right of property. 'Republicanism is not a remedy that strikes at the root of the evil. Injustice, oppression and misery can find an abode in those seeming happy seats. But what shall stop the progress of wisdom and improvement, where the monopoly of property is unknown?'[2] According to Godwin, therefore, one should not hope for the whole social problem to be solved by the suppression of political inequalities, for the problem of poverty remains. This problem arose not only for the pure theorist, like Godwin, but for the observer of contemporary facts. It was a time when, owing to the war, which was absorbing the whole energy of the peoples of Europe, England presented a picture, which was characteristic of the new industrial era, of the progress, to some extent parallel, of wealth and poverty. In order to stamp out poverty, is it enough to regulate production and to distribute wealth more evenly? Actually, the philosophy of utility, as presented by Godwin, resolves itself into communism. Or should the excessive growth of population be checked? In 1801, in a pamphlet in which he defended his work against the numerous critics who had attacked it,[3] he kept a place apart among his adversaries for the anonymous author of *An Essay on Population*, in which his own views were discussed, because of its impartiality, and because in it was discovered a new principle in

[1] Conway, *Life of Paine*, vol. i. p. 369.   [2] *Pol. Justice*, bk. viii. ch. 6.
[3] *Thoughts occasioned by the Perusal of Dr. Parr's Spital Sermon.*

political economy, which he recognised to be true. The author was Malthus, who, like Godwin, took his stand on the principle of utility.

Thus, along with the controversy raised by the theory of the Rights of Man was let loose the controversy relative to the *principle of population*. Malthus' book was anti-jacobin, expressly written to refute the equalitarian Utopia ; the Radicals nevertheless took it to be the necessary complement of Adam Smith's book, the completion of the new economic science. Ricardo's system, which is an essential part of Utilitarianism as a whole, derives at least as much from Malthus as from Adam Smith. If we are thoroughly to understand the Utilitarian doctrine, we must understand how this new element became a part of it.

I. THE RIGHT TO ASSISTANCE.
WILLIAM GODWIN

Bentham, drawing his inspiration from Hume, founded the right of property on what he called the principle of security. Since everyone naturally expects to keep what he has, it is useful that the legislator should not injure the natural feeling of expectation : respect for acquired rights sums up, in the doctrine of utility, the theory of the right of property. To him who accepts the principle of utility, however, the aim of civil law which is logically most important, is not security but subsistence. Hence, why not say, in so far as the doctrine of utility gives a meaning to the expression ' right ', that every man has a right to existence, a right to subsistence ? Further, if it be objected that real needs cannot be determined, and if each man be required to furnish, by the amount of labour he is prepared to provide, objective proof of the needs whose satisfaction is necessary to his subsistence, then the right to subsistence takes a very different form, and becomes the right to work. Now the right to subsistence and the right to work were both inscribed in English law at the end of the eighteenth century.

Since the reign of Elizabeth there had been in England a kind of state socialism which recognised the magistrate's right to fix the rate of wages, defined by legal dispositions the conditions of apprentice-ship, and finally allowed to the indigent, who were carefully dis-tinguished from vagabonds, the protection of society. In the majority of the countries of continental Europe, charity was left to the discretion of individuals, and the clergy, a sort of State within the State, relieved, or were supposed to relieve, the State from assuming the expenses of public assistance. In England, on the other hand, ever since the time when the advent of Protestantism brought about the disappearance of the monasteries, the law had recognised the right of the indigent, the infirm, the unemployed, and the labourers whose wages did not keep them from want, to assistance offered by the nation. There was legislation on this point in 1562, in 1572, and in 1601. In every parish Justices of the Peace were empowered to levy a poor rate on the inhabitants. Similarly an official list of the needy poor, able to work, had to be drawn up, and overseers nominated to superintend their work. This was a recognition, in the case of all the indigent who were considered unable to work under normal conditions, of the right of assistance through work offered by the town or parish under legally specified conditions.

But the law was destined to be constantly relaxed : the list of assisted persons was continually growing, and the conditions under which assistance was granted became continually easier. Protests had arisen, since the middle of the seventeenth century, against the system of outdoor relief. The expedient of workhouses was thought of. In 1722 it received the seal of the law : the churchwardens and overseers were authorised, with the consent of the parishioners, to set up a workhouse in every parish, and at the same time authorised to refuse assistance to all those who did not accept it in the workhouse, and did not submit themselves to the rules of the establishment. That is to say, that once again the stricter formula of the right to work superseded the less exacting formula of the right to existence ; and the system of workhouses, farmed out to undertakers, succeeded, not in the sense that it was the foundation of prosperous industries, but in the sense that it diminished the expenses of the poor law.

Then another period of relaxation began, the process becoming more acute after the French Revolution and the opening of hostilities between England and France. The Justices of the Peace, into whose hands the whole administration of the Poor Law had been concentrated more and more, were obsessed by the fear that the contagion of Jacobin ideas might spread through the English countryside ; and, in order to insure themselves, so to speak, against the peril of a rising of the agricultural labourers, were prepared to spend the money of the ratepayers lavishly. A law of 1795 empowered two overseers, if approved either by the parishioners assembled in the vestry meeting, or by a Justice of the Peace, to give outdoor relief to the ' industrious poor persons ' in certain conditions of temporary illness or distress. Further, the law gave the Justices of the Peace discretionary power, urging them to use it with what was called a just and proper discretion, to grant assistance for a period not exceeding one month on a written and reasonable request. In the same year a new advance was accomplished. Society no longer restricted itself to granting the necessary minimum of subsistence in cases of extreme poverty to recognised indigents, it further held that there was a normal wage, and that if the actual wage did not equal the normal wage, it is its duty to supply the difference. The resolution taken in 1795, a famine year, by certain Berkshire

magistrates, who decided that in future allowances must be made
to relieve poor workmen and their families, and fixed a scale of
assistance in proportion to the price of the loaf of bread and to the
number of children, amounted to this.   This resolution very nearly
became law : the bill, suggested by Pitt in 1797, which, if it had
become law, would have made general the two systems of outdoor
relief and of wage allowances, may be taken to be the last stage in
this evolution.

The bill laid down that if an indigent person residing in a parish
had undertaken, with the preliminary consent of the person or persons
appointed to administer the Poor Law in the parish, to work for a
wage which was insufficient to support life either for himself alone or
for him and his family, the Poor Law officials should be permitted with
the approbation of one or more Justices of the Peace of the district,
to complete the worker's wage, without imposing on the workman
assisted any obligation to work, from funds raised for the purpose
of public assistance.   The proposed law granted help, under the
same conditions, to fathers of families with more than two children
under five, to widows with more than one child under five, and,
finally, in cases where a needy person owned land or else had the
right to the enjoyment of a portion of communal goods sufficient for
the upkeep of a cow or other animal yielding a profit, the law allowed
the man to be advanced enough money to purchase a cow or other
animal.   This is the *cow-system*, to which Arthur Young gave his
support three years later, when he demanded that every agricultural
labourer, who was the father of three children, should be guaranteed
half an acre for planting potatoes and enough grass to feed one or
two cows.[1]   In short, just when the legal determination of the
rate of wages was being abandoned, it reappeared, in a roundabout
way, in the Poor Law.   The law no longer merely gave assistance
to the poor without work, it gave it also to the *industrious poor*, to the
labouring poor, to the worker who was working, but the wages of
whose labour were inadequate to support life.   It was no longer the
right to work, but the direct right to subsistence, which was consecrated by the law.

It was natural that the democrats should support the thesis of the
right to subsistence.   Neither Paine nor Godwin avoided the
problem ; and neither held himself discharged from solving the
economic problem, when he had solved the political problem.

In his *Rights of Man*, Paine calculates the number of men in
England who, after fifty years of age, ' may feel it necessary or
comfortable to be better supported than they can support themselves,
and that not as a matter of grace and favour, but of right ', and tries
to determine this assistance which, he repeats, ' is not of the nature

[1] *The Question of Scarcity plainly stated and Remedies considered*, 1800.

of charity, but of a right '.[1]   He goes further in his *Agrarian Justice opposed to Agrarian Law and to Agrarian Monopoly*, published in 1796, the reply to a sermon in which Watson, the Bishop of Llandaff, had celebrated ' the wisdom and goodness of God in having made both rich and poor '.   But Paine denies that the distinction between rich and poor is of natural or divine origin.   Poverty is a creation of what is called civilised life, it did not exist in the natural state ; and as, on the other hand, the state of nature was deprived of the advantages which arise from agriculture, from the arts, the sciences, and from manufactures, the end to be pursued is to avoid the inconvenience of the first while retaining the advantages of the second.   Although landed property began from the day when work was incorporated in the soil, it is nevertheless true that it is the value of the social improvement, and not the land itself, which is individual property ; it is for this reason that all owners of cultivated soil owe the community a ground-rent.   Any accumulation of personal property, beyond what is produced by the actual hands of the individual, comes to him from the fact that he lives in society : therefore on the strength of every principle of justice, gratitude and civilisation, he owes the restitution of a part of this accumulation to the society from which it all came.   Further still, it will be noticed that the accumulation of personal property is in many cases due to the fact that the labour which produced it was too little remunerated.   Paine adds : ' It is, perhaps, impossible to proportion exactly the price of labour to the profits it produces ; and it will also be said, as an apology for injustice, that were a workman to receive an increase of wages daily, he would not save it against old age, nor be much the better for it in the interim.   Make, then, society the treasurer, to guard it for him in a common fund ; for it is no reason, that because he might not make a good use of it for himself, that another shall take it '.   Consequently, Paine proposed by imposing a graduated tax on inheritances to form a national fund which would allow the payment, not only of a pension of £10 a year to every person over fifty, but also a sum of £15 to every person reaching the age of twenty-one.   Individuals thus assisted ' could buy a cow and implements to cultivate a few acres of land ; and, instead of becoming burdens upon society, which is always the case, where children are produced faster than they can be fed, would be put in the way of becoming useful and profitable citizens ' . . .   Already, Paine concluded, the conviction was spreading that the theory of representative government was the true one ; but the French Revolution would find an advocate and an ally in the heart of every man when a social system, arising from this political system, should be organised under conditions such that all men and women would inherit the capital they needed to begin to earn their living, and would on the other hand be assured of escaping

[1] *Rights of Man*, part ii. ch. 5.

the miseries which under all other governments accompanied old age.

Now, three years earlier, Godwin, from whom Paine drew his inspiration, had, in his *Political Justice*, conceived the same hope of seeing the political revolution completed by a social revolution. In contrast to Paine, he had not suggested any practical expedient which would realise the idea ; but he had, on the other hand, submitted the idea of individual property to a more rigorous criticism, based not on the idea of abstract right, but on the principle of utility.—Here we have a remarkable vicissitude in the history of the doctrine we are studying. From the principle of the natural identity of interests it may be concluded that economic inequalities are justified, and that the interests of rich and poor are identical. From the same principle Godwin, who nevertheless claims to be a disciple of Adam Smith, draws unexpected conclusions, and arrives at a system of equalitarian communism.

The theory of property, which was the subject of the eighth book of the *Enquiry*,[1] did not suffer any modification in principle, between the first and second editions ; it was, however, much less developed in the first edition, where Godwin tried completely to suppress the expression *right* in the language of political philosophy, than in the second, where he recognised the existence if not of *positive rights*, which are absolute rights to the use or abuse of things, at least of *negative rights*, which are only the reciprocals of as many obligations. ' We have in reality nothing that is strictly speaking our own. We have nothing that has not a destination prescribed to it by the immutable voice of reason and justice.' But, on the other hand, if there is an obligation for each man to assist his neighbour, each one has in return a ' right to the assistance of his neighbour '. Hence a complete inversion of the vulgar notion of property. In the general problem of property, Godwin makes a distinction between two special problems, which have to be solved one after the other. First, who is the person designed for the use of a particular object ? In the second place, who is the person to whom the preservation and distribution of any given quantity of these articles can most justly and most usefully be entrusted ? It is this second problem which is the problem of property in the strict sense.

To the first problem, the principle of utility can give only one answer. It bids me act always in that way which will be most profitable to society as a whole : thus every member of this society has the right to exact that I shall act in the way which will be most useful to him, taking into account absolutely all interests concerned, his, my own, and those of the other members of the society. In more precise terms, ' every man has a right to that, the exclusive possession of which being awarded to him, a greater sum of benefit or pleasure will result, than could have arisen from its being otherwise appropriated '.[2]

[1] *Pol. Justice*, bk. viii.   [2] *Ibid.* bk. viii. ch. 1 (2nd ed.).

But between the time when an object has been made fit for consumption, by the application to it of human labour, and the time when it is consumed, an interval elapses, and during this interval it is necessary that the article should not be given up to chance, but that some care should be taken to preserve it until the time when it is to be consumed. Who should be the factor or warehouseman during this interval, the man entrusted to see to the preservation and distribution of the object ? This is the problem of property.[1] For I do not call the man who chances to sit at my table the proprietor of what he eats there : ' property implies some permanence of external possession, and includes in it the idea of a possible competitor '. Now, of property there are three degrees. The first degree or the first form of property is directly deduced from the principle of utility : it is ' that of my permanent right in those things, the use of which being attributed to me, a greater sum of benefit or pleasure will result, than could have arisen from their being otherwise appropriated '. The right of property thus understood may be stated in the adage : ' To everyone according to his needs '.

The second degree of property is ' the empire to which every man is entitled over the produce of his own industry, even that part of it the use of which ought not to be appropriated to himself ' : to everyone according to his labour. Such a right must be taken to be a negative right, a particular form of the right of individual liberty : it springs from the obligation which rests upon others never to force me by constraint to dispose in a certain way of the products of my industry. It cannot be considered a positive right : I have not the right to dispose at my own free will of the product of my labour. This second kind of property is therefore less fundamental than the first. It is in one point of view a sort of usurpation. It vests in me the preservation and dispensing of that which, in point of complete and absolute right, belongs not to me but to someone else.

Finally, the third degree of property is ' a system, in whatever manner established, by which one man enters into the faculty of disposing of the produce of another man's industry '. This is the system which is established in all civilized countries, the system of hereditary property. We say that our ancestors bequeathed their property to us : it is a gross imposition. ' The property is produced by the daily labour of men who are now in existence. All that their ancestors bequeathed to them, was a mouldy patent, which they show as a title to extort from their neighbours what the labour of those neighbours has produced '. This third kind of property is in direct contradiction with the second.

Such is the doctrine. It sets up a double distinction : on the one hand, it distinguishes between the degree of property in which property is given to everyone according to his needs, in conformity with the principle of utility, and that in which it is allotted to everyone

[1] *Pol. Justice*, bk. viii. ch. 2 (2nd ed.).

according to his labour, without taking needs into consideration ; and on the other hand it distinguishes between the degree of property in which it is given to everyone according to his labour, and that in which everyone is disposing of the labour of someone else.   Now this double distinction is in conformity with the traditional principles of the philosophy of utility.

The first distinction had already occurred in Locke ; and Godwin, like Locke, based the right of property on the direct consideration of utility.   But he was more logical than Locke, for Locke after having founded property on utility immediately proceeded to found it on labour, starting from the consideration that labour determines the value of things in exchange, and implicitly admitting the postulate that nature is just.

As to the second distinction, it occurs in Adam Smith, who treats the question from a strictly theoretical point of view, yet cannot avoid constantly introducing notions of justice.   He sets himself to show how the transition from the primitive social state, in which property was founded on labour, to the actual constitution of property has come about ; and Godwin may have drawn his inspiration not only from the thought but even from the expressions of Adam Smith. ' The real price of everything ', said Adam Smith, ' what everything really costs to the man who wants to acquire it, is the toil and trouble of acquiring it '. . . .   He further said that ' labour was the first price, the original purchase money that was payed for all things ', [1]—and that, in this primitive state of things, prior to the accumulation of capital and the occupation of the soil, ' *the whole produce of labour belongs to the labourer* '.[2]   But, ' as soon as stock has accumulated in the hands of particular persons, some of them will naturally employ it *in setting to work industrious people*, whom they will supply with materials and subsistence, in order to make a profit by the sale of their work, or by what their labour adds to the value of the materials '.[3]   This profit must not be confused with a particular kind of wages, the wages of the labour of inspection and direction.   Profits are ' *altogether different, are regulated by quite different principles, and bear no proportion to the quantity, the hardship, or the ingenuity of this supposed labour of inspection and direction.*[4] And in the same way, ' *as soon as the land of any country has become all private property, the landlords*, like all other men, *love to reap where they never sowed*, and demand a rent even for its natural produce '.[5]   The existing social system is, therefore, for Adam Smith, as it is for Godwin, ' a system by which one man enters into the faculty of disposing of the produce of another man's industry '. In the same way, again, when Godwin condemns the imposturing language, according to which ' property ' and ' wealth ' are things which the rich possess and which they transmit to each other from

[1] Adam Smith, *Wealth of Nations*, vol. i. p. 31.
[2] *Ibid*. p. 50.   [3] *Ibid*. p. 50.   [4] *Ibid*. p. 50.   [5] *Ibid*. p. 52.

father to son, and when he does not want to admit into the world any other wealth than the labour of man, he sees, in what is wrongly called wealth, nothing but ' a power vested in certain individuals by the institution of society, to compel others to labour for their advantage '.[1] In doing this, he is only taking up again, and giving a more dramatic form to, propositions of Adam Smith's.[2] Wealth is power. It is not political, civil or military power, although it may happen to serve to acquire these. ' The power which that possession immediately and directly conveys . . . is the power of purchasing ; a certain command over all the labour, or over all the produce of labour, which is then in the market. His fortune is greater or less, precisely in proportion to the extent of this power ; or to the quantity either of other men's labour, or, what is the same thing, of the produce of other men's labour, which it enables him to purchase or command '.[3] These were Adam Smith's words. Godwin now expresses himself in the same way.

But how then can the same ideas, expressed in almost the same words, lead to such different conclusions with different authors ? It is interesting to note the nature of the logical crisis through which the principle of the natural identification of interests passed twenty years after the publication of Adam Smith's classic, and twenty years before the appearance of Ricardo's book, likewise a classic. The problem can apparently be solved as follows. Godwin retains what may be called Adam Smith's naturalism,—the distinction between the natural and the artificial, joined with the conviction that nature is just, and that the artificial is in opposition at once to nature and to justice. But Godwin draws, in a different place from Adam Smith, the dividing-line which is so difficult to determine, between the natural and the artificial.

No doubt Adam Smith closely connects the two ideas of individual property and of civil government, and asserts the union of these two ideas in a language which could be interpreted in an almost revolutionary manner. ' Wherever there is great property there is great inequality. For one very rich man there must be at least five hundred poor, and the affluence of the few supposes the indigence of the many. The affluence of the rich excites the indignation of the poor, who are often both driven by want, and prompted by envy, to invade his possessions. It is only under the shelter of the civil magistrate that the owner of that valuable property, which is acquired by the labour of many years, or perhaps of many successive genera-tions, can sleep a single night in security. . . . The acquisition of valuable and extensive property, therefore, necessarily requires the establishment of civil government. Where there is no property, or at least none that exceeds the value of two or three days' labour,

---

[1] *Pol. Justice*, bk. viii. ch. 2 ; *The Enquirer*, part ii. essay 2, p. 177.
[2] Cf. Godwin, *Pol. Justice*, bk. vi. ch. 9.   [3] *Wealth of Nations*, vol. ii. p. 293.

civil government is not so necessary ' . . .[1] But for Adam Smith,
although civil government is necessary to protect the inequality of
wealth, government is not the origin of this inequality,[2] and consequently it is a natural phenomenon, inseparable from the very production of wealth.[3] Godwin, on the other hand, sees in capitalism
and in landed property the effect of inheritance, that is to say of a
positive institution, a government artifice. ' The idea of property,
or permanent empire, in those things which ought to be applied to
our personal use, and still more in the produce of our industry,
unavoidably suggests the idea of some species of law or practice by
which it is guaranteed. Without this, property could not exist.'
' Property, under every form it can assume, is upheld by the direct
interference of institutions.' [4] Things should therefore be made to
tend towards the primitive state of things, not only as it is defined
by Adam Smith—and here is a new difference—in which everyone
receives according to his labour, but in which everyone receives
according to his needs, in conformity with the principle of utility.
The objection is made to this equalitarian theory that the merits of
individuals are different, and that they ought to receive different
rewards. But of what rewards are we speaking ? Are we to say
to the individual : ' If you show yourself deserving, you shall have the
essence of a hundred times more food than you can eat, and a
hundred times more clothes than you can wear ' ? [5] Here we find
still the same conception of right understood as the power to use and
to abuse—a right which implies the power, to the detriment of the
general interest, of the miser to accumulate without purpose goods
which could have been distributed in such a way as to secure the
well-being of thousands of individuals, and of the prodigal to waste
his wealth without thinking whether or no he is making it serve a
useful purpose. But the notion of justice is based not on the notion
of merit, but on that of utility. Further, it is generally admitted
that the miser makes a bad use of his fortune ; but public opinion
is, as a whole, favourable to the rich and generous man, who spends
without reckoning and *lives up to his fortune* ; he is, in truth, as
popular as the miser is unpopular. Now Godwin's thesis is that
the rich man, in so far as he is a rich man, cannot be socially useful ;
the distinction between rich and poor is an artificial distinction which
destroys the natural identity of interests. Godwin draws all the
logical conclusions from this thesis, and ends by developing the paradox that, in the use he makes of his fortune, the miser comes nearer
to moral truth than the prodigal.[6] Luxury is inseparable from
inequality of fortune : a civilisation based on luxury can only be
justified on the ground that it is a necessary transition from a barbarous equalitarianism to a civilised equalitarianism ; [7] the separa-

---

[1] *W. of N.* vol. ii. p. 293.   [2] Adam Smith, *Lectures*, p. 129.
[3] *Ibid.* p. 295.   [4] *Pol. Justice*, bk. viii. ch. ii. (2nd ed.).
[5] *Ibid,* bk. viii. ch. i. (2nd ed.).   [6] *The Enquirer*—of Avarice and Profusion.   [7] *Ibid.*

tion between the two notions of luxury and civilisation must be established, and a criticism must be made of actual society which is founded on luxury.

Luxury is not useful in the first place to the rich man, who enjoys it or who is held to enjoy it. Godwin distinguishes between four classes of good things; ' subsistence, the means of intellectual and moral improvements, inexpensive gratifications, and such gratifications as are by no means essential to healthful and vigorous existence, and cannot be purchased but with considerable labour and industry '. This last class, which includes the pleasures of luxury, is the one which sets the most obstacles in the way of a fair distribution of wealth : the respective quantities of the objects which provide the first three kinds of satisfaction are very small indeed when compared with those which procure the fourth. It may be estimated that only a twentieth of the inhabitants of England are employed in agriculture. Further, agriculture is such that it absorbs the labourer's whole time during certain parts of the year and leaves the other parts of the year relatively free : we may take these free times as equivalent to a labour which, if directed with a sufficient skill, would suffice, in a simple social state, to make tools, to weave clothes, to fulfil the tasks of the butchers and bakers. Consequently, according to Godwin, it does not appear in any way ridiculous to admit that the work of one man in twenty in society would suffice to supply the rest with all the absolute necessaries of life. ' If then this labour, instead of being performed by so small a number, were amicably divided among the whole, it would occupy the twentieth part of every man's time. Let us compute that the industry of a labouring man engrosses ten hours in every day, which, when we have deducted his hours of rest, recreation and meals, seems an ample allowance. It follows that half an hour a day, employed in manual labour by every member of the community, would sufficiently supply the whole with necessaries.' If so many men work ten hours a day it is because, by reason of the unequal distribution of fortunes, the great mass of humanity works in order to supply the minority with pleasures of the fourth kind—vain pleasures, whose emptiness is demonstrable ; pleasures whose essence lies in the love of social renown and distinction. But this is a passion which could be diverted and turned into a useful channel. The miser, at least, understands the vanity of these goods for which the prodigal spends so much money, and sometimes, in a naive way, thinks that he is, in this, serving the social interest.

Is luxury, which is useless even to the rich man who enjoys it, at least useful to the labourer who gets work from the necessity of supplying the needs of the rich ? Up to this point the criticisms of luxury offered by William Godwin are not noticeably different from the declamations which have been current with moralists in all times, with Epicurus as with Rousseau. But at this point, Godwin's observations become more interesting ; they mark a definite advance on Adam Smith's economic theories, and show up clearly a lack of harmony of interests in actual society which Adam Smith had only noticed in a confused way. Given a state of society in which wealth is unequally distributed, the indigent can only find means of livelihood in as far as the rich offer them wages for labour ; thus it seems that the more the rich contrive to find new ways of spending their wealth, and invent new superfluities, the more the poor will benefit. But this is an illusion. ' All refinements of luxury, every invention that tends to give employment to a great number of labouring hands, are directly adverse to the propagation of happiness.' For every new object of luxury invented simply means so much addition to the quantity of labour imposed on the lowest classes of society, and that without any increase, other than momentary, of wages. ' If every labouring inhabitant of Great Britain were able and willing to-day to double the quantity of his industry, for a short time he would derive some advantage from the increased stock of commodities produced. But the rich would speedily discover the means of monopolising this produce, as they had done the former.' The poor would not be paid more for ten hours' labour, said Godwin in the *Enquirer*,[1] than they had been for eight ; they would not be paid more for twenty hours' labour, he had already said in the *Enquiry*, than they were for ten. For the rich are few, and the poor many ; that is why, when the rich offer labour and the poor ask for it, the rich are masters and able to fix the wages of the labour at will, that is to say very low (did not Adam Smith speak of their ' tacit but constant and uniform combination ' ?). ' Those who, by fraud or force, have usurped the power of buying and selling the labour of the great mass of the community, are sufficiently disposed to take care *that they should never do more than subsist.*'[2]

This conception of luxury Godwin may have borrowed from Helvetius. ' Luxury ', wrote Helvetius, ' is harmful not because it is luxury, but merely because it is the result of a great disproportion between the wealth of the citizens '. And he added : ' If the number of landlords is diminished, the number of day-labourers will be increased ; when these are so numerous that there are more workmen than there is work, then the day-labourer will go the way of all kinds of goods, whose value diminishes when it is known. Besides, the rich man, who has more luxury even than wealth, has an interest in lowering the price of a day's work, and in offering the day-labourer *only the pay which is absolutely necessary for his subsistence* ' . . .[3] Godwin, perhaps, likewise drew his inspiration from Burke, who, in a youthful work, a curious essay devoted

---

[1] *The Enquirer*—of Avarice and Profusion, p. 177.
[2] *Pol. Justice*, vol. ii. pp. 429-430 (2nd ed.).
[3] Helvetius, *De l'Esprit*, dis. i. ch. iii ; cf. *Pol. Justice* (2nd ed.), vol ii. pp. 477-478.

to the defence of natural society, had contrasted the state of nature in which ' it is an invariable law, that a man's acquisitions are in proportion to his labours ' with the state of ' artificial ' society in which ' it is a law as constant and as invariable, that those who labour most enjoy the fewest things ; and that those who labour not at all, have the greatest number of enjoyments ', and depicted, in moving terms, the state of slavery to which British industry reduces its labourers.[1]   But it is more interesting to notice that Godwin may here also have found in Adam Smith the origin of his theory.

According to Adam Smith, when once the land is occupied and capital has accumulated, the labourer ceases to enjoy the whole produce of his labour ; his wages are fixed as the result of a bargain concluded between himself and his employer, a bargain in which the master necessarily has the advantage : he makes wages fall until he is stopped by a lower impassable limit : ' A man must always live by his work, and his wages must at least be sufficient to maintain him.'   But how, then, did Adam Smith fail to perceive the consequence to be drawn from this definition of wages ?   For if, under the influence of a minority of rich men, wages tend to an inferior limit at which they allow labourers just to subsist, and nothing more, a new feudal system has, in this way, taken the place of the old.   Burke was wrong when he said that the age of chivalry was gone : ' The feudal spirit still survives, that reduced the great mass of mankind to the rank of slaves and cattle for the service of a few '.[2]   Moreover, it was characteristic of the feudal lord that he spent his wealth in the practice of charity and hospitality.   But the age of exchange had now succeeded the age of the free gift : it was in exchange for work that the rich now allowed the poor to subsist. Godwin was one of the first to show up this fact, which had only been dimly seen by Adam Smith, that the conditions in which exchange is carried on between members of one and the same society falsify its fairness and seem to compromise the identity of interests.   When once commerce has become a profession, ' The buying and selling price of a commodity will always be different. If we purchase it of the manufacturer, he must not only be paid for the raw material, but for his industry and skill.   If we buy it of the trader strictly so called, he must be paid for his time, for the rent of his house, and for the subsistence of himself and his family. This difference of price must be left to his deliberation to adjust, and there is thus vested in him a large discretionary power.   Will he always use this discretion with perfect integrity ? '[3]   Godwin does not pursue the analysis far enough, and does not show in what sense the fixing of the price of an object for sale depends on the seller's

[1] Burke, *Vindication of Natural Society*, Works vol. i. pp. 71 *seq*.
[2] *Pol. Justice*, bk. viii. ch. iii (2nd ed.).
[3] *The Enquirer*—Of Trades and Professions, pp. 217-218.

discretion, nor in what sense and to what extent he finds himself unfettered by the necessity of economic laws. But further, comparing domestic service with slavery he shows precisely what it is which is misleading in the theory of the so-called voluntary contract. While admitting that the servitude of an English servant is less severe, he asks whether, on the hypothesis that I could constrain a man by the pressure of a series of circumstances to sell himself as a slave and authorise him to spend the purchase money on decorating his person, he would any the less be a slave : for ' it is the condition under which he exists, not the way in which he came into it, that constitutes the difference between a freeman and a slave '.[1] In actual society, founded as it is on the institution of individual property, there is a conflict and not a harmony of interests between the capitalist and the wage-earning labourer ; nevertheless, the principle of the natural identity of interests is not violated, since individual property itself rests on an artificial state of civilisation, since it rests on positive governmental institutions.

The end to be pursued is a society at once civilised and equalitarian, in which no one would be the owner either of the product of someone else's labour or even of the product of his own labour, but in which everyone would enjoy the product of his own labour, in proportion to his needs. By what means should the realisation of this end be brought about ? Godwin is compelled, by his intransigeant liberalism, to condemn all legislative intervention, all revolutionary action, everything in fact in the nature of a constraint. Doubtless it is useful and consequently obligatory that I should distribute the produce of my labour among the various members of the society to which I belong, in proportion to their needs. But, on the other hand, it would be a bad thing if the members of the society to which I belong should claim to impose on me, otherwise than by persuasion, some one determinate use or other of the wealth which I have acquired by my labour. The economic system which permits a man to dispose of the produce of someone else's labour is a bad system in the view of anyone who supports the principle of utility ; but any system of legal constraint which sought to substitute for this system a more equitable one, would be a remedy worse than the evil. Godwin goes as far as to be unwilling for inheritance to be suppressed by law, for, in the actual existent state of opinions and customs, such a law would necessarily be evaded. He asks that respect should be paid, in affairs of inheritance, to ' such laws and practices as are common to all civilised communities, and which may therefore be perhaps interwoven with the existence of society ', and that only positive laws and established practices which are ' peculiar to certain ages and to countries ',[2] for instance, the whole body of feudal institutions, should be annulled. In this

[1] *The Enquirer*—Of Servants, p. 211.
[2] *Pol. Justice*, bk. viii. ch. ii.

Godwin's programme of reform comes to the same thing as the programme of the French Revolution, though he had claimed that he went beyond this. It may be objected that a society founded on the equality of rights and the community of goods, is not capable of permanence. This is true, if it is brought about by a violent and accidental revolution. It is necessary that the reform of the laws should not precede the reform of custom and of ways of thinking, and, ' if by positive institution the property of every man were equalised to-day, without a contemporary change in men's dispositions and sentiments, it would become unequal to-morrow '. It may be objected that it is incompatible with the fragility of the human spirit.[1] That is so, if the human spirit be considered at its present point of development. The change to be brought about consists in the disposition on the part of every member of the society voluntarily to give up what would produce more utility when possessed by his neighbour than when in his own possession ; and the time when this disposition will prevail is still far off. But this time will come, because the state of society in which this disposition prevails is in conformity with reason, and because, by the natural progress of things, human reason tends to grow constantly stronger. In short, Godwin lays down a new condition for the harmony of interests, that is to say, that men cease to be egoistic and become reasonable. But he holds that the human spirit naturally tends towards this final state : in other words, he adopts the theory of progress and the principle of the natural identity of interests in the attenuated form which we have called the principle of the progressive identification of interests. It is on this theory that he takes his stand in order to refute, in what is perhaps historically the most interesting passage of his book, what he calls the objection drawn from the principle of population.[2]

It had been calculated that the average cultivation of Europe could be improved to the point at which it would nourish five times the actual number of inhabitants. Now, ' there is a principle in human society by which population is perpetually kept down to the level of the means of subsistence '. The conclusion must therefore be drawn that the established system of property may be considered as strangling in their cradles a considerable number of our children ; consequently, also, whatever may be the value of the life of man, or rather whatever may be his *capability* of happiness in a free and equalitarian social state, the system which Godwin criticises may be taken to put an end to four-fifths of this happiness and value at the threshold of existence. In short, it is for Godwin an obvious consequence of the principle of utility that the quantity of happiness experienced in a society is in proportion to the number of individuals capable of happiness and consequently to the total number of the individuals. Had not Paley interpreted the principle of utility in

[1] *Pol. Justice*, bk. viii.   [2] *Ibid.* bk. viii. ch. ix.

more or less the same way ? [1] The end of all rational politics is to produce the greatest quantity of happiness in a given territory. But the happiness of a society is made up of the happiness of the isolated members of that society, and the quantity of happiness can only be increased by increasing either the number of beings who experience it or the pleasure of their experiences. Now, in the countries of Western Europe at least, where economic conditions come near to equality, the quantity may be taken to depend principally on the number of individuals ; in any case, it may be assumed in all political argument that a greater amount of happiness belongs to *ten* people living in comfort than could belong to *five* people living in luxury. Thus the aim of the politician should be the increase of the population ; and it is in relation to this practical rule that Paley sketches an entire system of political economy, examining in turn every economic or fiscal measure, and approving or condemning it in proportion as it tends or does not tend to an increase of population.

There is, however, a serious problem raised by the increase of population. In 1761, in his *Various Prospects of Mankind, Nature and Providence*, Wallace had begun by advocating the abolition of private property. By means of this revolution all social obstacles to an indefinite increase of human population would be suppressed. But not, added Wallace, natural obstacles : for the earth would be incapable of constantly nourishing a human race whose numbers were always increasing, unless its fertility could continually be increased, or unless, by some natural secret, like the philosopher's stone, a magician could invent some way of keeping humanity alive entirely different from anything at present known ; in the end the earth itself would be full, and to find room for such multitudes as these, its dimensions would have to be constantly increasing. ' What a miserable catastrophe of the most generous of all human systems of government ! ' Godwin thought he could solve the difficulty. The suppression of artificial needs on the one hand, and the progress of cultivation and industry on the other would make it possible for man to support a far larger number of men in a given space than was possible at the present time. Besides this was foreseeing a danger which was too far ahead. Three-quarters of the habitable world were not cultivated ; the parts which were already cultivated were capable of incalculable improvements : myriads of centuries might elapse with a continually increasing population, and the earth might still be found sufficient for the subsistence of its inhabitants. But above all, with the advance of intelligence, man could prolong his life, and might even attain immortality : the function of reproduction would thenceforward become useless. ' The whole (of humanity) will be a people of men, and not of children. Generation will not succeed generation, nor truth have in a certain degree to recommence

[1] Paley, *Moral and Political Philosophy*, bk. vi. ch. xi.

her career at the end of every thirty years'.[1] Godwin did not look for this transformation of the conditions of the human race merely to the advance of medicine properly so-called. Since, if Hartley is right, the reactions of the human body pass, according to a constant law, from the automatic to the conscious and to the voluntary, the day may be looked forward to when all man's actions will become conscious and voluntary, when the soul will become master of the body. Some theologians, Malebranche in particular, had submitted an analogous hypothesis on the subject of the relations of soul and body before the Fall : the philosophers of perfectibility returned to the same conjectures, with the difference that they put the terrestrial paradise at the end and not at the beginning of history.

A year after the publication of Godwin's book, Condorcet developed views which were analogous, though perhaps less Utopian in their optimism, in his *Esquisse d'un Tableau historique des progrès de l'esprit humain.*[2] He counted on the progress of science, and on the progress of the arts which is inseparable from it, to bring it about that a space of land which was growing constantly more crowded should produce a more useful or more valuable mass of consumable goods. But is this progress indefinite ? ' Must there come a stage . . . when the increase in the number of men will be greater than the increase in their means, and there will necessarily result if not a continuous diminution of well-being and of population, which would be a truly backward step, at least a kind of oscillation between good and evil ? Would not this oscillation in those societies which had reached this stage be an ever-present cause of poverty, which would be to some extent periodic ? Would it not mark the limit at which all improvement would become impossible, and mark the stage which the perfectibility of the human species could attain in the immensity of the centuries, but beyond which it could never go ? ' To this objection Condorcet answered, as Godwin had done, that the time in question was still far distant ; and although, like Godwin, he counted on the progress of science indefinitely to prolong the life of the individual, he did not draw from it the same conclusions as Godwin. He counted above all, and in this he differed from Paley and Godwin, on a progress in human morality to put a stop to the prejudice in favour of an irrational increase in population. ' Men will realise . . . that, if they have obligations with regard to creatures who are not yet in existence, they consist in giving them not existence but happiness. The purpose of these obligations is the general well-being of the human species or of the society in which they live, of the family to which they belong, and not the puerile idea of loading the earth with useless and unhappy creatures. There might therefore be a limit to the possible mass of subsistence, and consequently to the greatest possible population, without there

[1] Godwin, *Pol. Justice*, vol. ii. p. 885 (1st ed.).
[2] *Progrès de l'esprit humain*, 9ᵉ époque.

resulting from this that premature destruction, which is so contrary to nature and to social prosperity, of creatures who have received life.' Thus Condorcet abandoned the theory in which Paley and Godwin had seen a direct application of the principle of utility. But in spite of their differences, Godwin and Condorcet still had at least one idea in common : the idea of the indefinite perfectibility of the human species. ' All that in which the human mind differs from the intellectual principle in animals, is the growth of society. All that is excellent in man is the fruit of progressive improvement, of the circumstance of one age taking advantage of the discoveries of a preceding age, and setting out from the point at which they had arrived.'[1] Condorcet held that Turgot, Price and Priestley were ' the first and most illustrious apostles ' of the new doctrine.[2] But Priestley owed the doctrine to Hartley, that is to say to one of the precursors of the future associationalist Utilitarianism. It was fundamental in the eyes of all the ' jacobins ' of 1792 ; we shall see in what shape and after what vicissitudes it was to become an integral part of ' Philosophical Radicalism '.

Let us leave on one side Godwin's Utopia—in which reproduction becomes a useless physiological phenomenon as soon as man has conquered death, and the human race, remaining always equal in number, has no need to be renewed through reproduction ;—and let us likewise for the moment leave on one side Condorcet's idea— that men will understand that the happiness of humanity is not directly proportionate to the number of men who are capable of happiness, and will learn to counteract the normal operation of the sexual instinct ;—let us retain from both of them only the funda- mental idea of indefinite progress, of the domination, growing constantly more perfect, of man over nature. Was not this idea confirmed by the rapid progress made at the time by industrial machinery ? Adam Smith had paid only slight attention to this phenomenon ; the commercial problem attracted his whole attention ; almost his sole aim was to show, in free exchange and in the extension of commercial trade, the necessary condition of the division of labour and of the identification of egoisms. His theory formed a kind of abstract translation of the historical event of the American Revolution, to which may be attributed the original success in England of the ideas of commercial liberty. But now an industrial England was growing up, a new economic world which set fresh problems for the observer. The French Revolution accentuated this movement. While the continental powers were spending all their energy in revolutions and in wars, England was winning the monopoly of commerce and industry throughout the world. Ad- vancing from one mechanical invention to another, the manufacture

---

[1] *Pol. Justice*, bk. viii. ch. viii. (2nd ed.).
[2] Priestley develops the theory of indefinite progress at length at the beginning of the Essay of 1768.

of cotton was being perfected, and was producing a new society in
the North of England, with its own sufferings, its own joys and
crises, of which Adam Smith had not dreamt a few years previously.
It was here, in the world of big capitalists, that Robert Owen,
himself a big capitalist, worked out and formulated his theory of
overproduction, before giving an organisation and a name to
' socialism '. For with the progress of human industry poverty
continues and grows worse. Is there a causal relation between the
two phenomena ? Bentham and Paley, before Godwin, had asked
the same question.

Bentham recognised that the substitution of mechanical for human
labour had disadvantages by reason of the principle of the limitation
of industry by capital. If by making a more skilful use of natural
forces a manufacturer became able to perform with a thousand
workmen the same amount of labour which required two thousand
labourers before the improvement in question, the result would not
necessarily be to double the amount of the produce ; for unless there
happened to be an increase of pecuniary capital at the same time, it
would not be possible to keep the same number of workmen, because
the production and upkeep of the machines would also involve
expenses, and because it might also happen that the workmen would
not be paid at the same rate in different industries.[1]

Paley, for his part, considered the disadvantage temporary and
negligible. The question is whether, ultimately, the demand for
labour is diminished or increased ; it is increased, Paley replied :—
' Goods of a finer texture are worn in the place of coarser : this is the
change which the invention has produced, and which compensates
to the manufactory for every other inconveniency '.[2] And this
reasoning was enough to reassure Paley.

But it is by no means enough to reassure Godwin as to the socially
beneficent nature of machinery, to know that there will result from
the progress of machinery an ever-increasing demand for labour.
The thing for which he condemns civilisation as it stands, founded
on luxury and the inequality of conditions, is precisely this, that it
requires from man an ever-greater amount of labour for the same
wage. He does not, however, think that machinery is to be held
responsible for pauperism : the fault lies with the capitalists, with
the actual distribution of fortunes, and with the respective conditions
of the employer and the workman when the labour contract was
concluded. Once the existing régime of unnatural inequality is
abolished, the machines would have the result of enabling men
to do without industrial co-operation and the division of labour which
results from it, and which enslaves and represses the individual
intelligence.[3] To-day, the labour of several men is necessary in

[1] Bowring, vol. iii. pp. 38-39.
[2] *Moral and Political Philosophy*, bk. vi. ch. xi. § 6.
[3] *Pol. Justice*, bk. viii. ch. viii. (2nd ed.)

order to fell a tree, to cut a canal, to run a ship. But consider the complicated machines which man has invented, such as weaving machines and steam engines, and think of the economy of labour which they involve. Where will this progress stop ? ' At present such inventions alarm the labouring part of the community ; and they may be productive of temporary distress, though they conduce in the sequel to the most important interests of the multitude. But in a state of equal labour their utility will be open to no dispute. Hereafter it is by no means clear that the most extensive operations will not be within the reach of one man ; or, to make use of a familiar instance, that a plough may not be turned into a field, and perform its office without the need of superintendence. It was in this sense that the celebrated Franklin conjectured that mind would one day become omnipotent over matter '. This progress will end, then, by almost putting a stop to the necessity of manual labour. Lycurgus forbade it to the citizens of Sparta ; the legislator of the city of the future might forbid it likewise, but the obligation to labour would no longer have to be cast upon slaves. ' Matter, or, to speak more accurately, the certain and unintermitting laws of the universe, will be the Helots of the period we are contemplating.' Thus leisure will be increased and put within the reach of everyone.[1] In short, the conclusions of Godwin's analysis are contrary to those of Adam Smith's analysis. For Adam Smith, the progress of the division of labour and the progress of machinery go hand in hand. For Godwin they go in inverse ratio to each other, or, if you like, the division of labour insensibly passes from man to inert matter. In Adam Smith's philosophy, the division of labour allowed all individual egoisms to be satisfied without conflict. For Godwin, on the other hand, once the artificial, unnatural and rigid institutions which make man egoistical are abolished, he will no longer have need of egoism in order to live : the products of labour will be distributed in accordance with their utility, they will easily find their proper level, and will of their own accord flow from the place where they abound to the place where they are lacking. ' Egoism is the habit which springs from monopoly.'

We have emphasised Godwin's economic doctrine thus strongly for the same reason that we emphasised, above, Burke's political doctrine. Godwin deduced his theory of property from the principle of utility, from which Burke deduced his theory of government : a history of the principle of utility which did not take account of these two theories would therefore not be complete. With Godwin, who criticised the notion of private property in the name of the principle of utility, we come across a split in the doctrine, which has led, by a series of perfectly logical deductions, to modern socialism. Godwin drew inspiration from Adam Smith, just as William Thompson and Hodgskin, in some ways the precursors of Karl Marx,

[1] *Pol. Justice*, (2nd ed.) vol. ii. p. 481.

did later from Ricardo ; and it is easy to follow the natural development from Godwin's doctrine to socialism.   Robert Owen is known to have borrowed his ideas from Thomas Holcroft, the revolutionary agitator.   But Holcroft was himself an intimate friend and a disciple of Godwin ; [1] and the analogies between the doctrines of Godwin and Robert Owen are striking :—small societies, strictly equalitarian, without distinction made between the sexes, without individual property, without laws, where the only existing authority would be simply the authority of arbitration.   Why, however, were the intellectual radicals of 1832, who were no less than Godwin and Owen disciples of Helvetius, conservatives on the question of private rights, and hostile to the equalitarian and levelling system of Godwin and Owen ?   At this stage the paradoxical nature manifested by the march of ideas in history should be pointed out.   Godwin's claim was to have derived his entire system from the single principle of public utility.   Nevertheless, *almost without knowing it*, he based it to a great extent on the principle of freedom of conscience, which has logically nothing to do with the principle of utility.   But Godwin's intellectual liberalism tends to be confused, in its economic consequences, with the naturalist liberalism of Hume and Adam Smith ;   it shows the same antipathy to State interventions and to sudden revolutions.   In this way, where in good logic he is furthest from the principle of utility, Godwin is far less removed than one would think from economists such as Smith and Ricardo.   On the contrary, his theory of the right of property is a strict application of the principle of utility.   Nevertheless, it is in this that he differs most profoundly from all the authors whose works were preparing the way for the future Philosophical Radicalism.   With all of them, in fact, *almost without their knowing it*, the law of labour fills a place which is perhaps as important as the law of utility itself.   Every pleasure is won at the price of a pain ;   it costs labour, or the produce of labour.   But is it not to be feared that, if it is held just to allow the individual the free disposal of the produce of his labour, he will misuse this liberty and take advantage of it to set up kinds of property, which, when established in the form of positive institutions, will unjustly give to some the free disposal of the labour of others ?   To this question the reply came from Malthus.   It is not from this side, he said, that we should be apprehensive of danger ;   in the conditions which nature makes for man, the danger is not that the produce of human labour may be badly distributed, but rather that human labour may not produce enough.   In fact, in the same way that Burke's book called forth the answers of Mackintosh, Paine and Godwin, in which we saw the principle of utility insensibly replace the principle of the Rights of Man in the theory of the democratic régime, so Godwin's

[1] Holyoake, *Sixty Years of an Agitator's Life*, vol. i. p. 116.   For Holcroft's ideas see his philosophical novels and for his relations with Godwin see C. Kegan Paul, *William Godwin, His Life and Friends*.

book called forth Malthus' reply ; and it was Malthus, and not
Godwin, who was destined to become one of the fathers of the
Radical Church. But it was necessary to know Godwin in order to
understand Malthus.

2. THE PRINCIPLE OF POPULATION.
ROBERT MALTHUS

The economic condition of England at the end of the eighteenth
century was an anomalous one : there corresponded to the rapid
development of the great modern industry, a gradual disappearance
of the state socialism of the sixteenth century on one side (the statute
of apprenticeship disappeared bit by bit until in 1813 and 1814 it
was altogether repealed), and, on the other, an application of this
same state socialism in public charity, which became daily more
unrestricted and more expensive. Taking his stand on the principle
of utility, the reformer might have required that the principle of
governmental intervention should be extended, and everywhere
and in all matters maintained against the influences of the aristocracy
and the employers. But the current philosophy was Adam Smith's
liberal and anti-governmental naturalism : the reformers generally
demanded that an attempt should be made to re-establish the
harmony of the interests of all classes by extending all round the
principle of governmental non-intervention, and they criticised
the Poor Law and the right to assistance.

It would have been enough to make the disciples of Adam Smith
hostile to the principle of the Poor Law that they should favour, as
they in fact did, a policy of financial economy. For the application
of the Poor Law, which was becoming more and more relaxed, was
expensive, and became more expensive every day. The crushing
cost of the Poor Law was in a sense the price which the industrial
aristocracy agreed to pay for the suspension of the Act of Apprenticeship, and which the landed aristocracy agreed to pay for the setting
up of laws prohibiting the importation of corn. The result was
that the poor rates, which in 1770 had risen to a little over a million
pounds, rose, in 1800, to nearly four millions. But this was not
all : the very principle of public assistance, on which the Poor Law
rests, was in contradiction with the principles of Adam Smith's
economic theory. If the formula ' to everyone according to his needs '
is the true expression of justice, then the right to assistance is justified.
But Adam Smith's school seemed to prefer the other formula, according to which everyone has a claim ' according to his labour ' ; it
adopted this formula less, if you like, because it was the expression
of a moral truth, than because it fairly represented the primitive
reality of things, before the time when the appearance of rent on
land and profits of capital came to make the aspect of economic

phenomena more complicated. Thus if the State wishes to conform to the nature of things, it should only give help in return for labour provided by the individual receiving help. Another preliminary question arises. If the maxim ' to everyone according to his labour ' expresses the reality of things, it must be because nature metes out pleasures with a parsimonious hand. But will there not moreover necessarily be a kind of aggravation of the harshness of this law of labour, which we have found to be constantly involved in the law of utility, as understood by Adam Smith? Can it be laid down as a principle that the labour of man is, or always will be, capable of producing what is necessary? The number of men tends to grow without ceasing, and with them the amount of labour provided : but will the amount of available subsistence grow indefinitely, or will it grow in the same proportion?

In one of his *Essays*, Hume tried to define the causes of the movements of population. The increase in population which corresponds to the satisfaction of a natural instinct, is desirable in itself : ' For as there is in all men, both male and female, a desire and power of generation, more active than is ever universally excited, the restraints which they lie under must proceed from some difficulties in their situation, which it belongs to a wise legislature carefully to observe and remove '. Without these difficulties ' the human species . . . would more than double every generation '. But these difficulties are of two kinds. They are physical, and depend on the quality of available subsistence. They are also social : ' if everything else be equal, it seems natural to expect that, wherever there are most happiness and virtue, and the wisest institutions, there will also be most people '.[1] To give abundance and security to subjects is therefore to contribute to the increase of population. Hume, in his *Enquiry*, even goes so far as to hold that an equalitarian society is physically possible. ' It must, indeed, be confessed, that nature is so liberal to mankind, that, were all her presents equally divided among the species, and improved by art and industry, every individual would enjoy all the necessaries, and even most of the comforts of life ; nor would ever be liable to any ills, but such as might accidentally arise from the sickly frame and constitution of the body.'[2] Godwin never made use of a stronger expression than this. But a difficulty came in Hume's way. It is labour which gives things a value, and in an equalitarian society labour would not receive the necessary encouragement. ' Render possessions ever so equal, men's different degrees of art, care, and industry, will immediately break that equality. Or if you check these virtues, you reduce society to the most extreme indigence ; and instead of preventing want and beggary in a few, render it unavoidable to the whole community.' In reality, this objection

[1] *Essays*, part ii. essay xi.
[2] *An Enquiry concerning the Principles of Morals*, sect. iii. part ii.

contradicts Hume's observation as to the ' liberality ' of nature.
In the *Treatise* he went further still, and asserted not only that
man cannot live without labouring, but also that it is not in the
nature of things that his labour should be sufficient to enable him to
live. We possess, he said, three kinds of goods : the internal
satisfaction of our minds ; the external advantages of the body ;
and the enjoyment of the goods *which we have acquired by our labour*
and by our good fortune. In the enjoyment of goods of the first
kind, we are always perfectly secure. Those of the second kind
can be taken from us, but without any advantage accruing to him
who deprives us of them. ' The last only are both expos'd to the
violence of others, and may be transferr'd without suffering any
loss or alteration ; while at the same time, there is not a sufficient
quantity of them to supply everyone's desires and necessities. As the
improvement, therefore, of these goods is the chief advantage of
society, so the *instability* of their possession, along with their *scarcity*,
is the chief impediment.' [1] Hence the necessity of the two institutions of justice and property, which are inseparable from one another.
They both rest on the impossibility of dividing natural goods between
men in quantities which are equal and sufficient to enable them to live.

Adam Smith's language is, taken as a whole, more equivocal still.
He studies the movements of population in their relation to the
movements of wages. All species of animals naturally multiply in
proportion to the means of subsistence, and no species can multiply
more than this.[2] But in a civilised society it is only in the lower
classes of the people that the scarcity of subsistence can set limits
to the multiplication of the human species, by means of the premature death of a large number of children. It is therefore the duty
of the legislator to aim at once at an increase of population and at
a decrease of poverty, by using all methods suitable for securing a
liberal remuneration for labour ; but the methods to be used cannot
be other than indirect methods, consisting in increasing the productivity of labour, that is to say in increasing the amount of subsistence. Thus the argument is a circular one. ' What encourages
the progress of population and agricultural improvement encourages
that of real wealth and greatness.' [3] Now, to encourage economic
improvement of any kind whatever is precisely the same as to
encourage wealth : it could therefore be said just as well or perhaps
even better : ' what encourages wealth encourages population '.
There is here another ambiguity. Population, according to Adam
Smith, is limited by the means of subsistence. Are we to take it
that there is a kind of pre-established and permanent harmony
between the two terms ? This is the interpretation which Godwin
appears to have adopted when after reproducing Adam Smith's
formula and writing that ' there is a principle in human society by

[1] *Treatise*, bk. iii. part ii. sect. ii. [2] *W. of N.* bk. i. ch. viii.
[3] *W. of N.* bk. iv. ch. vii. part ii.

which population is perpetually kept down to the level of the means of subsistence ' he adds : ' Thus among the wandering tribes of America and Asia, we never find through the lapse of ages, that population has so increased, as to render necessary the cultivation of the earth '.[1]   Here we have at bottom the equivocal principle of supply and demand : here nature supplies subsistence and humanity provides the demand.   The general interest is assured, they maintain, by the fact that supply and demand are in equilibrium.   It would be more accurate to say that the equilibrium of supply and demand does not ever exist, but that it merely tends constantly to re-establish itself as the result of disturbances in equilibrium which are painful crises for humanity.   It should be added that Adam Smith was profoundly under the influence of the French physiocrats, who held that the cultivation of the soil naturally produced more than the amount necessary for the subsistence of the cultivator.   This also to some extent explains the uncertainty of the expressions used by Adam Smith on this matter : he actually wrote that, in civilised and laborious nations, although a great number of people do not labour at all and consume the produce of ten times or of a hundred times more labour than those who work ; ' yet the produce of the whole labour of the society is so great that all are often abundantly supplied.'[2]

There are noticeable, then, in Hume and in Adam Smith, certain formulae which foreshadow Malthus, [3] but, as we have seen, in a somewhat equivocal form.   Moreover, neither Hume nor Adam Smith applied their theory to the financial and practical problems raised by the Poor Law.   In 1786, however, an economist, Joseph Townshend by name, who knew Lord Shelburne and Bentham, devoted a ' dissertation ' to the question, and based his criticism of them on what might even at this stage be called the ' principle of population '.

Townshend started by laying down the principle that it is necessary to labour in order to live, and that any legal arrangement which imposes the obligation to work is weak and ineffective as compared with the natural sanction of hunger.   There must be some poor men, that is to say, men who are improvident and who are ready to perform the ' most servile, sordid, and ignoble ' of social functions ; by this, ' the stock of human happiness ' is in the last reckoning increased. Hunger, the desire to get bread, make the hardest work acceptable and sweet.   The Poor Laws, on the other hand, ' proceed from principles which border on absurdity, as professing to accomplish that which, in the very nature and constitution of the world, is impracticable '.[4]   For, ' in the progress of society ', it is necessary that some should come to suffer from want ; Townshend sets forth this

[1] *Pol. Justice*, bk. viii. ch. iii (2nd ed.).
[2] *W. of N.* Introduction.   [3] See *Principles of Population* (1st ed.), ch. i.
[4] *A Dissertation on the Poor Laws*, by a well-wisher to mankind, London (1786), sect. vii.

necessary law in the story of the island of Juan Fernandez.[1] A pair of
goats were put on the island. They were able to multiply without
difficulty or want until the time when the island was full : it was
then necessary for the weaker ones to disappear in order that abundance should be re-established. In this way the goats ' fluctuated
between happiness and misery, and either suffered want or rejoiced
in abundance, according as their numbers were diminished or
increased ; never at a stay, yet nearly balancing at all times their
quantity of food '.[2] In cases of excessive population, the disappearance of a few, which was a partial evil, became a general good
since it re-established abundance. The Spaniards wished to
destroy the goats, and for this purpose brought to the island a pair
of dogs. The dogs multiplied until the time when subsistence
became scarce. Then ' a new kind of balance was established. The
weakest of both species were among the first to pay the debt of
nature ; the most active and vigorous preserved their lives. It is
the quantity of food which regulates the numbers of the human
species '.[3]

Hence the impossibility, already pointed out by Wallace, of
instituting communism of goods while leaving everyone free to
marry : ' they would first increase their numbers, but not the sum
total of their happiness, till by degrees, all being equally reduced
to want and misery, the weakly would be the first to perish '. In
spite of the opinion expressed by Lord Kames that ' a nation can
scarce be too populous for husbandry, as agriculture has the
singular property of producing food in proportion to the number
of consumers ',[4] there is a point beyond which the fertility of the
soil in conjunction with human industry can yield nothing, and when
the human species has multiplied in proportion to this maximum
increase of food, it will not be able to go any further.[5] It is thus
absurd to cry out, as people do :—Population ! Population ! Population at any price ! ' When industry and frugality keep pace with
population, or rather when population is only the consequence of
these, the strength and riches of a nation will bear proportion to the
number of its citizens : but when the increase of people is unnatural
and forced, when it arises only from a community of goods, it tends
to poverty and weakness '.[6] Now the Poor Laws are a beginning
of communism : therefore Townshend condemns them one and all.
Perhaps Malthus, ten years later, came under the influence of
Townshend's ideas, unconsciously and in a roundabout way ; for it
seems to us uncontestable that Condorcet, in the passage in his
Tableau which Malthus discusses, is himself discussing Townshend.
In any case, Malthus had not read Townshend's little work ; and yet

[1] *A Dissertation on the Poor Laws*, by a well-wisher to mankind, London (1786),
sect. vii.
[2] *Ibid.* p. 38.   [3] *Ibid.* p. 40.   [4] Cited by Townshend, p. 56.
[5] *Ibid*, sect. viii.   [6] *Ibid.* sect. ix. p. 48.

the fable of the island of Juan Fernandez, by its striking form and by aphorisms which foreshadow not only Malthus but Darwin and Spencer, deserved to become a classic. But, for the principle of population to become popular, there was necessary on the one hand an economic crisis serious enough to show to everyone the pressing reality of the problem ; and there were perhaps also necessary the pseudo-scientific formulae which were to contribute powerfully to the prestige exerted by Malthus' doctrine.

The Revolution broke out in France ; at the end of three years, contrary to the principles which had up till then directed the Prime Minister's policy, England was brought to make war on the hereditary enemy. The expenses of the war, the difficulties of getting provisions from outside, and the very bad harvests of 1794 and 1795 caused an alarming scarcity, an economic crisis which occasioned popular troubles, led by the revolutionary societies. The government suppressed the troubles by force, and prevented future risings by the Exception Laws. But the economic crisis called for more decisive remedies than these. Hence the less rigorous application of the Poor Law. Hence Pitt's Poor Bill. The disciples of Adam Smith, chief among whom were Burke and Bentham, intervened in the debate and protested against measures which according to them made the evil worse instead of better.

Burke may be taken to be chronologically the first to interpret political economy as a pure conservative orthodoxy. In 1795, he paused in his counter-revolutionary campaign, to present his *Thoughts and Details on Scarcity* [1] to Pitt ; in 1796, in his third *Letter on a Regicide Peace*,[2] he drew an optimistic picture of the economic condition of England, and of the progress she had made since the declaration of war. In both these writings, he insisted on the thesis of the natural identity of interests,[3] the entirely negative obligation of the State not to intervene in the economic relations of individuals with one another ; he opposed all the schemes of public assistance, which the scarcity of 1794 and 1795 had called forth from theorists and politicians. He protested against any measure which would tend to establish a normal rate of wages. He did in fact contest that the rate of wages did not increase at the same time as the nominal price of provisions ; but he added that it was not in the nature of things that the two quantities should vary as the function of each other. In the fixing of wages a distinction should be made between the men who are able to perform the normal work of a man and those who are unable to work, or who are able to work, but not to perform the normal task of a day-labourer (women, children and the aged). The inflexibility of law cannot make this distinction ; whereas interest, habit, and the tacit convention that arise from a thousand obscure circumstances produce a *tact* that regulates without difficulty what

[1] Works, vol. vii. p. 325 *seq.*   [2] *Ibid.* vol. viii. p. 195 *seq.*
[3] *Ibid.* vol. vii. p. 334.

laws and magistrates cannot regulate at all. ' The first class of labour wants nothing to equalise it ; it equalises itself. The second and third are not capable of any equalisation.' [1]

Once this general principle is laid down, all proposed measures of economic regulation are easy to refute. To suggest levying a special tax on the farming interest is to fail to see that the interests of the farmer and the wage-earning labourer are the same. True, say the ' zealots of the sect of regulation ',[2] when the labourer is young and fit, and the farmer and the labourer can treat on an equal footing ; but in times of scarcity, illness or old age, when the labourer is burdened with a numerous family, and cannot live or feed his family on the natural remuneration of his labour, should not his remuneration be raised by authority ? Burke then asked the question whether the amount of subsistence in existence is sufficient to satisfy the demands of philanthropy. From the fact that the rich are few in proportion to the great number of the poor, Burke drew a conclusion diametrically opposite to that drawn by Godwin :—that it is impossible to suppress poverty by making an equal distribution of the superfluity of the rich.[3] The richer the capitalist, the more his private interest is identified with the general interest, because he can be satisfied to draw a small profit from his capital. Burke affirmed that there had been a rise in wages. Certainly men were working more ; but whether the increase in the amount of work supplied is, taken as a whole, a *good* or an *evil*, is a philosophical question which Burke would not follow Godwin in broaching. Without wishing to examine in all its aspects the policy of granting assistance to the poor, he stated that the English law assured a sufficient aid ' to decrepit age, to orphan infancy, and to accidental illness ', and that, by the application of the Poor Law, the lower classes received annually from the upper classes two millions sterling. But he protested against any lenient interpretation of the spirit of the law. To make a poor man believe that he had a right to the assistance of the State without working, was to make him a promise which it was impossible to keep. The current expression ' the labouring poor ' was got only from the *bon ton* of the day. Those who laboured must be recommended patience, labour, sobriety, frugality and religion ; the rest was downright fraud. It was a horrible aberration to call them ' the *once happy* labourers ' ; [4] ' when we affect to pity as poor, those who must labour or the world cannot exist, we are trifling with the condition of mankind '.[5] It is written that man shall eat bread by the sweat of his brow. ' The rules of commerce and the principles of justice ' require that everyone shall receive the price of his labour ; the man who cannot live on the

[1] Works, vol. vii. p. 342.   [2] *Ibid*. p. 337.   [3] *Ibid*. vol. vii. p. 328.
[4] *Ibid*. pp. 328-9, and vol. viii. pp. 299-300.   Cf. *W. of N.* vol. i. pp. 80, 82 and 85.
[5] Burke, Works, vol. viii. p. 300.

fruits of his labour does not take his stand on a right when he asks
to live, he makes an appeal to mercy ; here the sphere of public
justice ends, and that of private charity begins.[1]

In a fragment [2] which appeared at Geneva in 1798, through the
efforts of Dumont, in the *Bibliothèque Britannique*, but which had
been completed, says Dumont, ' many years earlier ', Bentham for
his part adopts without any alteration Adam Smith's principle that
' population is in relation to the means of subsistence and to needs '.
(' Montesquieu ', he writes, ' Condillac, Sir James Stewart, Adam
Smith, the Economists, have only one feeling on this point '.) Thus
the method of increasing population does not lie in encouraging
it directly by rewards and punishments, it lies in ' increasing the
national wealth, or rather in allowing it to increase '.   In 1795, he
discusses the article in the Declaration of Rights drawn up by Sieyès
in the terms of which ' every citizen who is unable to provide for
his own wants, has a right to the assistance of his fellow citizens ',
and in discussing it he is perhaps thinking as much of Godwin as
of Sieyès. To acknowledge the right of every citizen to the assistance
of his fellow citizens is to recognise his right to the assistance either
of individuals taken separately or of the community.   In the first
case, ' to give to every poor person a right to the assistance of every
individual who is not equally poor, is to overturn every idea of
property '.   In the second case the article of the declaration is very
vague ; for it is not enough to affirm a right, it must also be determined how the assistance is to be collected and distributed ; the
administration of assistance must be organised, inquiry officers
must be appointed, the steps which the poor must take in order to
avail themselves of their right must be regulated.   And the question
always arises : is the application of the right *possible* ?   It is possible
to imagine a state of scarcity in which it would not be possible to
provide bread for all those who needed it.   How then can we change
this, which is a duty of benevolence, into an absolute right ?   It
would be giving the indigent class the falsest and most dangerous
ideas.   It would not only mean the destruction of all gratitude on
the part of the poor towards their benefactors—it would mean
putting in their hands arms against all owners of property.[3] Now
this was to some extent the case in England during the years 1794
and 1795, and Bentham was led by the force of circumstances to
study directly the problems raised by the application of the Poor Law.

In February 1797, he addressed to Pitt some *Observations on the
Poor Bill*,[4] and his attitude is a curious one. He thinks that it is
enough to prove that the bill is an equalitarian measure in order to
condemn it : ' the *equalisation system*, as applied to *wages*, seems
hardly less threatening to *industry*, and thence to *property* (to say
nothing of the *expense*) than, as applied to *property*, it would be to

[1] Burke, Works, vol. vii. p. 343.   [2] See Bowring, vol. iii. p. 73.
[3] Bowring, vol. ii. pp. 533-4.   [4] *Ibid*. vol. viii. pp. 440-461.

property, and thence to *industry* '. He condemns any attempt to establish a normal wage, either by direct or indirect means, and particularly he condemns in Pitt's Bill what he calls the *Under-Ability, or Supplemental Wages Clause*. Taking up Burke's objection in more detail he asks whether this normal wage is to be the maximum or the minimum wage for a definite industry, or an average wage, taking all industries into consideration, or the maximum for the industry which employs the greatest number of workmen in the district. Add to this that the rate of wages, even valuing it at its lowest, varies considerably between one point and another : will a man in each district be free to choose at his own discretion between so many different valuations ? Besides, must one not choose, or can one, without contradiction, be favourable to the system of enclosures, which Bentham agrees with Burke in thinking equally favourable to the interests of rich and poor, and yet adopt the *cow-money* clause in Pitt's bill, which tends to restore the ancient patriarchal communism ? It is thought, no doubt, that ' when a man does his *utmost*, it is *hard* to leave him in a worse condition than his neighbours on account of an infirmity which is his *misfortune* merely, not his *fault* '. But this sentimentalism is destructive of all kinds of positive law. How draw the line between the idle and the industrious, when you no longer stop at signs which cannot be disputed such as old age and certain infirmities ? Finally, the clause of the bill which Bentham calls the *Relief-Extension* or *Opulence-Relief Clause*, specifies that anyone who has a house worth less than thirty pounds shall be allowed the benefits of the law. ' We commiserate *Darius*, we commiserate *Lear*, but it is not in the power of *parishes* to give kingdoms . . . to banish not only *misfortune* but *improvidence*.' Bentham did not treat the question merely as a theorist ; he treated it also as a practical reformer, as a man of projects ; in the *Outline of a Work to be called Pauper Management Improved*,[1] which appeared at the end of 1797 in Arthur Young's *Annals of Agriculture*, he applied to the solution of the problem the principles which he had laid down in the *Panopticon*—not only the architectural principle of universal inspection, but the principle of the artificial identification of interests, what he called the *duty and interest junction principle*. In regard to the administration of his system of assistance by labour, he set forth a system of centralisation and of administration by contract. The industry-houses were to be ruled by a central board set up in the capital and modelled on the India Company's board, elected by all the members of a society with shares worth five or ten pounds, which would exploit the labour of the assisted poor. The same principle as in the *Panopticon*, the *life assurance* or *life warranting principle* gave the administrators an interest in preserving the life of those assisted. The same principle of publicity (the *transparent management principle*) submitted them to the control of popular

[1] Bowring, vol. viii. pp. 369-439.

or moral sanction.   The same principle which defined the obligations
of the administrators also defined those of the persons assisted.   They
were only assisted to the extent to which they worked ;   and the
various principles which determine the conditions of their labour
which Bentham describes in picturesque terms, as the *self-liberation
principle* (no one will be liberated who has not paid the expenses of
his keep by the product of his labour), the *earn-first principle*, *the
piece-work*, or *proportionable-pay principle* ;   the *separate-work* or
performance distinguishing principle—all these are only particular
forms of the principle of the union of interest and duty.

Moreover, according to Bentham, the project offered certain
collateral advantages as well as the direct advantage ;   it would make
it possible to stamp out begging, to relieve temporary indigence by
a system of loans at interest, to substitute for friendly societies
a universal and complete system of insurances against old age,
of assistance in the event of marriage or unemployment, and of
help in the upkeep of a more than average number of children.
It would have, above all, a great pedagogic importance.[1]   The
education of the poor, which was much more socially useful than the
education of the rich because of the numbers of the poor, had been
neglected ;   now, the industry-houses would offer conditions under
which poor children would be submitted to the most effective
' plastic power ' which could be thought of.   ' The influence of the
schoolmaster on the conduct of the pupil in ordinary life, is as nothing
compared with the influence exercised by the Company over these
its wards.'   Bentham, like Godwin, had always accepted the principle
according to which individual characters are held to be the work
of social conditions ;   but Godwin, who was liberal to a fault, vaguely
looked forward to a state of civilised society without government,
in which the natural identity of interests would no longer be compromised by the survival of any positive institution, and so any
system of education would be useless ;   for Bentham, on the other
hand, the despotic principle of the artificial identification of interests
is the fundamental principle of his pedagogic as of his juridical
philosophy.   Bentham did indeed insist on the point that no
pauper should receive aid except in exchange for labour, and that
this labour should remunerate a private company : this company
would none the less be a monopolistic company, and would govern
the men whose interests were entrusted to it in accordance with
the principles of a pedagogic and philanthropic despotism, which
has few traits in common with the liberalism of Adam Smith and
his school.

The ideas which had been partially formed by Adam Smith's
school owed the definitive, classical form, which they were to assume
among Bentham's friends, not to Bentham but to Malthus.   In

---

[1] See Utilitarian formula of education suggested by Bentham (Bowring, vol. viii.
p. 395).

1796, when Pitt laid his bill on the table of the House, Malthus had not yet formed his theory. In an essay which he wrote at that time, under the name of *The Crisis*,[1] he discussed the view put forward by Paley, according to which the amount of happiness in a country is measured by the number of its inhabitants ; but he merely argued that the amount of happiness should be estimated by the increase in number, if not by the actual number of the inhabitants : for ' an increasing population is the most certain of all possible signs of the happiness and prosperity of a State ', whereas ' the present population can only be a sign of a happiness which is past '. He writes : ' But though it is by no means to be wished that any dependent situation should be made so agreeable, as to tempt those who might otherwise support themselves in independence ; yet as it is the duty of society to maintain such of its members as are absolutely unable to maintain themselves, it is certainly desirable that the assistance in this case should be given in the way that is most agreeable to the persons who are to receive it '.[2] Consequently, he advocated outdoor relief and commended the special relief to be accorded to fathers of more than three children, as proposed in Pitt's bill. It was Godwin who, in 1797, converted Malthus to ' Malthusianism ' through reaction. Malthus' father was a Jacobin, a disciple of Rousseau whose executor he had been, and, more recently, a disciple of Godwin. In discussing with his father the economic ideas set forth by Godwin in his *Enquiry*, and particularly in his *Essay on Avarice and Prodigality*,[3] Malthus became aware of the principle which justified his resistance to the Utopias of Godwin and Condorcet.[4] Better still, it could be proved that he borrowed from Godwin, and even more from Condorcet, all the elements of the theory which he urged as against the two equalitarians.

To Godwin he owed the actual term ' principle of population ' ; and to Condorcet he owed several of the expressions of which he made use in his definition of the principle. ' Must there not come a stage ', asks Condorcet, ' at which these two equally necessary laws (the law of the progress of human industry and the law of the progress of population) will come to contradict each other . . . the increase in the number of men exceeding the increase in their means ? '[5] Malthus takes up Condorcet's question, and answers it in the affirmative. He takes his stand on two postulates : the first, that food is necessary to man's existence ; and the second (this he cannot establish without having first refuted one of Godwin's Utopias), that the sexual passion is, and will always remain, more or

---

[1] *The Crisis*, a view of the Present Interesting State of Great Britain by a Friend to the Constitution.

[2] *Ibid.*   [3] *The Enquirer*, 1797, pp. 168 *seq.*

[4] *An Essay on the Principle of Population as it affects the Future Improvement of Society*, Preface, p. 1.

[5] *Progrès de l'esprit humain*, 10° époque.

less constant.[1] But the amount of available food does not grow at the same rate as the population. Thus there is a conflict between these two necessary laws; they contradict one another in the nature of things. In this way considerations drawn from the physical and physiological worlds come to modify the conclusions which could otherwise be legitimately drawn from the principle of utility.—Every man needs subsistence; now it is in the power of society to remedy the present inequality in the distribution of the means of subsistence; therefore every man has a right to subsistence, and, consequently, to the assistance of his fellow-men.—Every man has need of subsistence; but nature does not provide subsistence in sufficient quantities to supply the needs of an ever-increasing number of men; therefore the right to subsistence is an illusory right, which is not founded on the nature of things.

Condorcet, who was no doubt inspired by Townshend, foresaw that on the day when the conflict between the two necessary laws came about there would occur, ' if not a step which is actually *retrograde*, at least a kind of *oscillation* between good and evil ', which will be ' an ever-present cause of distress which is to some extent *periodic* '. Malthus uses the expression for his own purpose. There comes a time when the amount of food which had originally to be divided between seven million people, has to be divided between, let us say, seven and a half millions. Therefore there is a fall in the price of labour and a rise in the price of provisions. And hence, by an inverse movement, there results a decrease of births and a development in cultivation, with a consequent re-establishment of the proportion between population and means of subsistence. ' The situation of the labourer being then again tolerably comfortable, the restraints to population are in some degree loosened; and, after a short period, the same retrograde and progressive movements, with respect to happiness, are repeated.' ' This sort of oscillation will not probably be obvious to common view; and it may be difficult even for the most attentive observer to calculate its periods '.[2]

But the danger of such a retrograde movement in population and in human prosperity is, according to Godwin and Condorcet, extremely far off. ' Three-fourths of the habitable globe is now uncultivated. The parts already cultivated are capable of immeasurable improvement. Myriads of centuries of still increasing population may pass away, and the earth be still found sufficient for the subsistence of its inhabitants.' [3] ' It is equally impossible ', thinks Condorcet, ' to give one's verdict for or against the future reality of an event which will only come about at a time when the human species will necessarily have acquired enlightenment, of which we can hardly form an idea.' According to Malthus, on the other hand, the danger is a constant one. The amount of available

---

[1] *Principles of Population* (1st ed.), ch. i.   [2] *Princ. of Pop.* ch. ii. p. 31.
[3] *Pol. Justice*, vol. ii. p. 510.

subsistence is not a fixed amount which the increase in population is bound to reach at some future date ; neither is the amount of available subsistence an amount which is always growing until it attains a determined limit beyond which it cannot go. The means of subsistence, like the number of men, ' may increase for ever and be greater than any assignable quantity ' ; but these two quantities do not increase according to the same law. ' The power of population is indefinitely greater than the power in the earth to produce subsistence for man. Population, when unchecked, increases in a geometrical ratio. Subsistence only increases in an arithmetical ratio. A slight acquaintance with numbers will show the immensity of the first power in comparison with the second '. It was therefore a new development of that idea of indefinite progress which was fundamental to Condorcet, and to which Condorcet, a mathematician, liked to give a mathematical form which destroyed, in Malthus, the optimistic philosophy of indefinite progress.[1] The principle of natural identity found its application in Adam Smith only to those objects whose number can be indefinitely increased by human labour. It now appeared that a second restriction must be added to this one. The quantity of the products of labour may increase indefinitely ; but the demands for these products also increases indefinitely, and according to a yet swifter law. The idea which had been dimly seen by Condorcet, and which Malthus emphasised, could be formulated as follows : a law of evolution is not necessarily a law of progress. Thus, thanks to the new ideas which Malthus borrowed from Condorcet, the principle set forth by Adam Smith and Godwin, according to which population is constantly determined in relation to the amount of the means of subsistence, assumes a definite meaning.

The methods nature uses to reduce the race of plants and the race of animals to the desired proportions, are lack of seed, illness, and premature death. To restrict the human race it uses poverty and vice. Poverty is the necessary consequence of the operation of the law, and Condorcet had already alluded to this. Vice is a highly probable. consequence of it. Therefore the happiness of a given country is not measured by the number of inhabitants, but by the amount of subsistence, or to be more exact, according to the formula already suggested by Malthus in the *Crisis*, by the corresponding increase in population. Problems bearing on population had been disturbing inquirers for a long time already : but Richard Price and his critics adopted a method too exclusively statistical. Now statistics were not the method employed by the disciples of Adam Smith : the new economic science, based on the knowledge of certain primitive laws of human nature, adopted a synthetic method, and sought to discover derived laws which should partake of the certainty of the primitive laws. Population, Adam Smith tells us, is

[1] *Princ. of Pop.* ch. i.   Cf. Condorcet, *Progrès de l'esprit humain* 10° époque.

limited by the means of subsistence; but what must the word *limited* be taken to mean? Is it a question of an upper limit beyond which population cannot pass, but below which it can vary to an indeterminate extent? In this case we are unable to assert that the figure of population is rigorously determined for a given amount of subsistence; we have not yet found the law of population. But if the means of subsistence are a limit to population in the sense that population cannot, in any lasting way, either rise above or sink below this limit, then we can say, with a truly scientific exactness, that the amount of subsistence determines the number of consumers. By this the principle of the natural identity of interests seems to be seriously compromised: indeed, if the theory of population is to have the character of a scientific theory, it is necessary that the human race, taken as a whole, should be held to be distressed or needy.

But may we not go further, and ask whether the principle of the natural identity of interests, as stated by Adam Smith, would be applicable even to that future state of society, without property or government, which the optimism of Godwin and Condorcet had foreseen? Once the progress of human industry has brought about abundance, egoism will become useless, at the same time as the institution of property and the phenomenon of exchange disappear. Now the theory of the harmony of interests implies just these very notions of property, exchange and egoism. Malthus rejects the principle of the fusion of interests; he thinks that the feeling of benevolence is derived from egoism by a gradual evolution: to wish to substitute benevolence for egoism as the moving principle of society would only have the result of making the whole society feel the pinch of want, which is to-day only felt by the few. According to Malthus, we owe everything which distinguishes civilised from savage life to the established system of property, and to the principle of egoism, despite its apparent narrowness.[1] On this point Malthus appears as the faithful trustee of the tradition of Adam Smith. For a science of value to be possible, the Utilitarian economist, powerless to measure utility directly, measures it indirectly by means of labour. But men may give very different quantities of labour for an object of a given utility. The labour which measures the value must therefore be the maximum labour which a man is prepared to give in order to secure the enjoyment of the object. Thus, for the science of value to be possible, the maximum labour must be being constantly given somewhere, utility must appear as *necessity*, or again the economic man must appear as a *necessitous* being. Since Adam Smith's political economy would cease to be true when the limit of human progress foreseen by Godwin and Condorcet had been reached, the problem for Malthus was, at bottom, to find a law of progress which would ensure that the principles laid down by Adam Smith would be applicable for ever.

[1] 1798 ed., ch. xv. pp. 27 *seq.*

To apply the doctrine is to condemn the right to assistance and the Poor Laws in which it is sanctioned. The obvious tendency of these laws is to increase population without increasing subsistence ; the victuals consumed in the workhouses feed the least worthy members of the social body and reduce by the same amount the portions which, if there were no Poor Laws, would fall to others who are worthier and more industrious. The Poor Laws were costly : so costly that accusations of malversation were rife. They were tyrannical : the law of settlement was denounced by everyone, beginning with Adam Smith. But in truth the Poor Laws failed to solve the problem of pauperism, not because malversation might occur in the management of the funds collected, but because they went directly against the very nature of things. If they were applied in a tyrannical manner, it was because everyone tacitly recognised that it was impossible to apply them in their integrity. It is no more possible to stamp out poverty than to stamp out pain. The accusation might be brought against the rich that by unfair coalitions they prolonged a period of poverty for the poor ; ' yet no possible form of society could prevent the almost constant action of misery upon a great part of mankind, if in a state of inequality, and upon all, if all were equal '.[1] The truth is that the pressure of distress on the lower classes of society is an evil so deeply seated, that no human ingenuity could reach it. ' Were I to propose a palliative, and palliatives are all that the nature of the case will admit, it should be, in the first place, the total abolition of all the present parish laws '.[2] To this radical measure, Malthus added, as measures which were akin to it, encouragements favourable to agriculture at the expense of manufacturers. Chief among these encouragements to agricultural labour was the suppression of all corporative privileges. Everyone, at the end of the eighteenth century, was agreed as to this measure, but not for the same reasons. Adam Smith denounced the spirit of monopoly, the egoism of the industrialists ; Malthus the protection afforded to the industrial labourer at the expense of the agricultural labourer. Finally, for cases of extreme distress, workhouses might be opened in every county, and assistance might be granted in exchange for labour provided : but these would always be mere *palliatives*, for an evil which did not admit of a *remedy*. ' Hard as it may appear in individual instances, dependent poverty ought to be held disgraceful. Such a stimulus seems to be absolutely necessary to promote the happiness of the great mass of mankind ; and every general attempt to weaken this stimulus, however benevolent its apparent intention, will always defeat its own purpose.'[3]

The first edition of Malthus' book met with so great a success that a second edition was needed. It appeared in 1803, after Malthus had devoted five years to completing his theory by travelling

[1] *Princ. of Pop.* (1st ed.), ch. ii.   [2] *Ibid.* ch. v. p. 95.
[3] *Princ. of Pop.* (1st ed.), ch. v. pp. 85 *seq.*

for research, and to rearranging and developing the first edition.
The *Essay* of 1798 chiefly consisted of a criticism of the Utopias
of Godwin and Condorcet : in the 1803 edition this critical part
was reduced to its simplest expression, as was fitting at a period when
Godwin's philosophy had fallen into discredit.[1] In 1798, in the
preface,[2] Malthus had apologised for not having brought enough
statistical justifications to support his principle : in the second edition
the statistical part was greatly developed. But above all, the second
edition contained a modification of the thesis itself. Already in 1798,
Malthus had drawn a distinction between two checks to the increase
of population : the *positive* check which puts obstacles in the way of
an increase in population which has already begun ; and the *preventive*
check, consisting of a moral restraint which avoids an increase
in population which is only foreseen. Moreover, according to
Malthus, the second of these two, the preventive check, which
consists in foreseeing the difficulties involved by the education of a
large family, only operates in the upper classes of society, while the
first operates in the lower classes.[3] But, in the mind of Malthus,
the idea of the preventive obstacle was united by a kind of inseparable
association with the idea of vice ; and here, again, it is necessary to
know Condorcet in order to understand Malthus.

Condorcet had relied on a reasoned diminution in the increase of
the population for the solution at the moment of crisis of the problem
of the insufficiency of subsistence ; according to Malthus the gravity
of the problem is always actually present. Already in the first
edition he had taken up Condorcet's idea when, recognising that
' every obstacle in the way of marriage must undoubtedly be considered as a species of unhappiness ', he observed that ' as from
the laws of our nature some check to population must exist, it
is better that it should be checked from a foresight of the difficulties
attending a family, and the fear of dependent poverty, than that
it should be encouraged, only to be repressed afterwards by want
and sickness '.[4] But Condorcet joined to his observations an
attack, which clearly worried Malthus, against ' the ridiculous
prejudices of superstition ' and the morality of ' austerity '. Is
not the remedy advocated by Condorcet ' a kind of concubinage, or
mixing of the sexes, freed from all vexation, which would prevent
fecundity, or some other means of attaining the same end, which
would be no less contrary to all the prescriptions of nature '? This
is why Malthus, in the first edition, made the distinction between
vice and the preventive check a very slight one. ' Impelled to the
increase of his species by an equally powerful instinct, reason

[1] For a comparison of the two editions consult *Parallel Chapters from the First
and Second Editions of an Essay on the Principle of Population by T. R. Malthus*,
1803. New York and London 1895.
[2] 1st ed. Preface, p. 11.   [3] *Princ. of Pop.* (1st ed.), ch. iv.
[4] *Ibid.* ch. v. pp. 89-90.

interrupts his career, and asks him whether he may not bring beings into the world for whom he cannot provide the means of subsistence.' These considerations are calculated to prevent, and certainly do prevent, a very great number in all civilised nations from pursuing ' the dictate of nature in an early attachment to one woman . . . and this restraint almost necessarily though not absolutely produces vice '. He added that in old states such as England, the preventive check operated though with varied force through all the classes of the community. ' The effects indeed of these restraints upon marriage are but too conspicuous in the consequent vices that are produced in almost every part of the world.' [1] In the second edition, the association of the two ideas is broken, and Malthus developed without reservations the idea that the action of the preventive obstacle must be increased at the expense of the action of the positive obstacle. In the first edition he stated that it was impossible for the human race to escape from poverty, and demanded that humanity should refrain from resorting to so-called remedies which were absurd and costly : palliatives only were conceivable.[2] In the second edition he rejected certain suggested measures, emigration for example, precisely because he considered them to be not remedies but merely palliatives. Even more explicitly than in the first edition, he denied ' the *right* of the poor to support ', and proposed that a law be passed ' declaring that no child born from any marriage, taking place after the expiration of a year from the date of the law, and no illegitimate child born two years from the same date, should ever be entitled to parish assistance '.[3] The remedies to be used, apart from private charity, are institutions likely to increase the action of the preventive check—friendly societies which were already spreading in Great Britain, and above all institutions for public instruction. ' Till the language of nature and reason has been generally heard on the subject of population, instead of the language of error and prejudice, it cannot be said that any fair experiment has been made with the understandings of the common people ; and we cannot justly accuse them . . . till they act as they do now after it has been brought home to their comprehensions that they are themselves the cause of their own poverty.' [4]

Malthus, therefore, wished a pedagogic function to be assigned to the State : like Adam Smith before him, he advocated the system of parish schools where the children of the poor should receive an elementary education. Adam Smith had already demanded that the education given in these schools should be of a more practical nature than that which was given in the small ' charity schools ' already in existence, and that the elements of geometry and mechanics should be taught there. Malthus went further than this, and demanded a popular and practical teaching of political economy.

[1] *Princ. of Pop.* (1st ed.) ch. vi. pp. 63 *seq.*   [2] *Ibid.* bk. iii. ch. iv.
[3] *Ibid.* bk. iv. ch. viii.   [4] *Ibid.* bk. iv. ch. iii.

He was desirous that the current prejudices both as to the sale and hoarding of corn and as to the principle of population should be dissipated. It was objected that popular instruction made revolutionaries, and that the people only learnt to read in order to read Thomas Paine's pamphlets. Adam Smith had already refuted a statement of this kind ; but the additions to the programmes of popular teaching suggested by Malthus made it possible for him to refute it still more strongly.[1] Bentham's scheme for reform of the Poor Laws came in the end to a programme of popular education ; in Malthus also, in the last resort, it can be reduced to this. Popular education had already developed in England, through the efforts of the Nonconformists and especially of the Methodists. But Malthus brought a Utilitarian formula to the already existing movement. It is *just*, said the Protestants, that all men, since they are equal before God, should share as equally as possible in the knowledge of the sacred books, of the divine law and of the moral law. It is *useful*, said Malthus, that all men should know the physical laws which determine the development and the increase of the species, so that they will understand how to regulate the increase of their needs in accordance with the increase in the amount of pleasures which nature puts at their disposal.

We are now able to define Malthus' intellectual attitude. In a certain sense the *Essay* of 1798, the refutation of Godwin and of Condorcet, may indeed be taken to be a manifestation of the reactionary opinion which held sway in England round about 1800. For was it not Malthus' aim to point out the illusory nature of the theory of indefinite perfectibility ? He tells us that the conception of human life resulting from his doctrine is ' melancholy '. He did not intend, however, that a political theory of passive obedience or a moral theory of resignation should be derived from it, or that life should be concluded to be ' a state of trial, and school of virtue, preparatory to a superior state of happiness '.[2] God desires the good of man in this world ; and the purpose of the needs of the body is to rouse the spirit and make it capable of progress. It is to provide stimulants of this kind, to constrain man to put the whole earth under cultivation, that it has been ordained that population should increase faster than food : if it increased according to the same law man would never have emerged from the savage state.[3] Malthus therefore stood for the human idea of progress as against the supernatural idea of redemption. In fact he was, and always remained, a Whig.[4] In the very first pages of his book, he proclaimed his desire to hold the scales evenly between ' the advocate for the present order of things ', who regards political philosophers

---

[1] *W. of N.* bk. v. ch. i. vol. ii. p. 372 ; *Princ. of Pop.* (2nd ed.) bk. iv. ch. viii.
[2] *Princ. of Pop.* ch. xviii. (1st ed.).   [3] *Ibid.* p. 361.
[4] See Empson in *Edinburgh Review*, Jan. 1837, pp. 479 *seq.* for quotations from *The Crisis*.

indiscriminately as ambitious men or as seers, and ' the advocate for the perfectibility of man and of society ' who regards the defender of established institutions as a slave of prejudice or as a man who lives by abuses.[1] He did not reproach Paine for having laid down the ' rights of man ' : man has rights, and it is useful for him to know them. But there is nothing which counterbalances the evils occasioned by Paine's *Rights of Man* so effectively as the knowledge of the *real* rights of man. It was in America that Paine constructed his system ; and America differs from Europe in that its physical conditions allow the population to double itself every twenty-five years. Godwin said that man had the right to subsist prior to all social laws : you might as well say that he has the right to live a hundred years. But the important question, in both cases, is the question *not* of *right* but of *power*. Social laws increase the power, and so, if you like, the right of individuals to subsist. But neither before nor after the institution of social laws did an unlimited number of individuals enjoy the faculty of living ; thus, before as after, anyone who has been deprived of this faculty has been deprived also of the right of exercising it. Education and civil liberty alone will contribute to lessen poverty by giving the individual an enhanced feeling of his responsibility, a more developed power of reflection, and a greater prudence ; hence the appearance on the scene of the preventive check. A people which is ignorant and robbed of social rights justifies reaction and oppression by its violence and by its excesses : it is this which is fatal. ' Give to a state but liberty enough and it is impossible that vice should exist in it.'[2] And besides, is not the very idea of public instruction an equalitarian idea ? Does it not require that the State should rectify certain inequalities and diminish at the expense of the rich the distance which would otherwise separate the intelligence of the rich from that of the poor ?

Thus, the checks imposed by man's physiological nature and by the physical nature of the earth to the indefinite progress of the human species do not fundamentally contradict the idea of progress. Malthus rejects the Utopian part in the views of Condorcet and Godwin. He refuses to treat man as a pure intelligence, of which nothing can therefore stay the progress. But a distinction must be made between an unlimited progress and a progress whose limit cannot be determined. The first kind of progress is not applicable to man granted the actual laws of his nature. The second incontestably is applicable. Men will be gradually better and better instructed, and so will learn to regulate the increase in population by the increase in subsistence and will wait to found a family until they are assured that they can support it. But did not Condorcet say just the same thing ? Was Godwin mistaken when, in 1801, he declared in *Thoughts occasioned*

[1] *Princ. of Pop.* ch. i. (1st ed.).
[2] Quoted by C. K. Paul, *William Godwin* ... vol. i. p. 76, from an unpublished MS.

by . . . Dr. Parr's Spital Sermon, that Malthus' observations, far from destroying his theory, were a confirmation of it ? ' The more men are raised above poverty and a life of expedients, the more decency will prevail in their conduct, and sobriety in their sentiments. Where everyone has a character, no one will be willing to distinguish himself by headstrong imprudence. Where a man possesses every reasonable means of pleasure and happiness, he will not be in a hurry to destroy his own tranquillity or that of others by thoughtless excess.' [1] Condorcet had already expressed the same opinion. But Godwin and Condorcet were looking for the day when every distinction between rich and poor should be swept away ; Malthus was only aiming at the numerical increase of the middle class : [2] an important thesis, which later became fundamental for the economists, politicians and moralists of Philosophical Radicalism. It is necessary that there should be needy people, but the number of them could be constantly reduced. From this it can be seen how it was that Malthus' influence was first felt by the liberal section of opinion, since he only differed from the theorists of indefinite progress by adopting a more moderate interpretation of their own theory. In spite of Malthus' efforts to prove the providential nature of the law of population, Christians condemned a doctrine according to which Providence did not arrange the normal increase of subsistence in a harmonious manner. The *Edinburgh Review*, of Whig sympathies, was Malthusian from the start ; the Tory review, the *Quarterly*, never became converted. The influence exerted by the book will be better understood if a comparison be made between two speeches about the Poor Law, made by one member of Parliament, Samuel Whitbread, in 1796 and in 1807.[3] In 1796, he demanded that the justices of the peace should be authorised to fix the wages of labour at every three months' session ; and his motion, which had the support of Fox and of Jekyll, Lord Lansdowne's lieutenant, was opposed by Pitt who, a year before the introduction of his own philanthropic bill, protested against this policy of governmental intervention, reproached the Poor Laws for making no distinction between the unfortunate and the lazy, and authorised the development of societies for mutual aid. Eleven years later, Whitbread, applauded by Malthus,[4] proposed a bill whose principal features were a regularisation and democratisation of the right of suffrage in parochial assemblies, and a system of universal popular instruction. Between 1796 and 1807, the influence of Malthus had been felt by the Liberal party. It was a democratic influence. As concerns the education of the poor in particular, the radical theory of popular instruction is Malthusian in origin.

[1] *Thoughts occasioned by* . . . . *Dr. Parr's Spital Sermon*, pp. 73-74.
[2] *Essay*, ch. xviii. (1st ed.), p. 367.
[3] *Annual Register*, 1796 (pp. 47 *seq.*) and 1807 (pp. 128 *seq.*).
[4] *A Letter to Samuel Whitbread*, Esq., M.P., on his proposed bill for the amendment of the Poor Laws, London 1807.

Historical conditions in part explain the success achieved by Malthus' book. Between 1794 and 1800 there was a series of bad harvests in England at a time when the Continent was only able to supply very small quantities of corn, as against an ever-increasing number of inhabitants. The crisis reached its most serious point in 1800, when the price of corn rose to a hundred and twenty-seven shillings a quarter : it had already begun as early as 1795 when Burke wrote his *Thoughts and Details*. It is possible for the industrial production of a country to increase while its agricultural production remains stationary ; and consequently, because of the increase in population, it is possible for the wealth of a society to increase without a corresponding increase in the happiness of the labouring class.[1] ' I really cannot conceive anything much more detestable ', wrote Malthus,' than the idea of knowingly condemning the labourers of this country to the rags and wretched cabins of Ireland, for the purpose of selling a few more broadcloths and calicoes. The wealth and power of nations are, after all, only desirable as they contribute to happiness.' Godwin had drawn Malthus' attention to this economic phenomenon, which had been neglected by Adam Smith ; but Godwin explained it by an over-production which benefited only the rich, whereas Malthus, on the other hand, explains it by what may be termed ' over-consumption '. Men are too numerous, do not work enough and cannot work enough for all to be able to live in abundance.

Still, it might, no doubt, be possible to treat this phenomenon as a temporary one, and to impose empirical remedies for it, such as free-trade, which increases the number of objects to be consumed, and emigration, which diminishes the number of consumers. Malthus however, believed in protection, in order that the equilibrium between agriculture and industry might be maintained, and he considered emigration a ' partial expedient ', absolutely insufficient to make room for a population which grows without any limit. He was out to prove that the phenomenon with which he was concerned, the pressure exerted by the population on the means of subsistence, was a phenomenon which was not temporary but constant in virtue of a necessary law. And perhaps the absolute and mathematical nature with which Malthus endowed his doctrine, explains, apart from any historical conditions, the prodigious credit which it secured. The nature of Malthus' double law is indeed doubly approximative : population when it receives no check increases, according to Malthus himself, *at least* in a geometrical ratio ; under the same conditions food grows *at most* in an arithmetical ratio. Nevertheless, it is the pseudo-mathematical nature of the law, inspired by the vague analogy of certain physical laws, which conferred on the new doctrine a sovereign prestige. As Ricardo said twenty years later, ' surely in the minds of all reasonable men the principle for which Malthus

[1] *Princ. of Pop.* bk. iv. ch. x. p. 580 (2nd ed.).

contends is fully established '.[1] ' As to its mathematic basis ', said Hallam, ' there is no one who could question it that might not as well dispute the multiplication table '.[2] Now Malthus' main *idea* is possibly true : but it is common to him and to others, who, as we shall see, discovered the theory of differential rent at the same time and independently of him, and who were able to discover it without needing to know the law of the two progressions. Malthus' *law*, on the other hand, is certainly false : this law is peculiar to him, and constitutes his fame.

In sum, whatever may have been the historical causes of the success obtained by Malthus' book, we had to show how close were the links which bound the new theory to the Utilitarian tradition, incarnated in Adam Smith and Bentham. The philosophy of indefinite progress itself originated in Hartley and Priestley, the forerunners of the associationism of the Utilitarians : Malthus' achievement was to incorporate in a theory of progress the law of labour, which was fundamental to Adam Smith, and to give to that law itself the form of a law of progress. Moreover, Malthus was a conscious supporter of the philosophy of utility, whose formula he borrowed not from Bentham but from Paley.[3] ' I do not see how it is possible for any person who acknowledges the principle of utility as the great criterion of moral rules to escape the conclusion that moral restraint, or the abstaining from marriage till we are in a condition to support a family . . . is the strict line of duty.'[4] To be more precise, he is referring to the principle of the natural identity of interests. ' The happiness of the whole is to be the result of the happiness of individuals, and to begin first with them. No co-operation is required. Every step tells. He who performs his duty faithfully will reap the full fruits of it, whatever may be the number of others who fail. This duty is intelligible to the humblest capacity. It is merely that he is not to bring beings into the world for whom he cannot find the means of support.'[5] Besides there is a *vis medicatrix reipublicae*, ' the desire of bettering our condition, and the fear of making it worse ', the pursuit of personal interest, egoism, which ' is continually counteracting the disorders arising from narrow human institutions ', and acts, particularly in England, as a natural counter-check to all the artificial encouragements given by law to the marriage of the poor.[6]

But we must be clear on this point. If egoism, which is an instinct, commands the individual, in his own interest, to avoid an excessive increase in population, and first of all in our own family, ' egoism ' understood as obedience to all the impulses of instinct, commands us to obey among other impulses the impulse of the sexual

---

[1] Ricardo, *Letters to Trower*, p. 173.
[2] Miss Harriet Martineau, *Autobiography*, vol. i. pp. 209-210.
[3] *Princ. of Pop.* (1798 ed.), ch. xi, p. 213.   [4] *Ibid.* (1803 ed.), bk. iv. ch. iii.
[5] *Ibid.*   [6] *Ibid.* bk. iii. ch. vi. p. 307 ; bk. iv. ch. xiv. p. 477.

instinct, and of all the affectionate instincts which are bound up with it. ' In all societies, even the most vicious, the inclination to a virtuous attachment is so strong, that there is a constant tendency towards an increase of population.'[1] The result is poverty, which results not from defective social institutions but from the physiological nature of man set face to face with physical nature. Hence arises a modification of the principle of the natural identity of interests, a modification which will perhaps allow us once more to define the difference which divides Malthus from the philosophers of indefinite progress. For the latter, moral constraint is *in conformity with nature* ; for it consists in an act of reason ; now the law of progress, for Condorcet as for Hartley, is in its essence an intellectual law : and man is, in essence also, nothing but an intelligence. On the other hand, according to Malthus, man is by definition a physiological being who peoples nature : intelligence, which is in direct opposition to instinct, therefore works *against nature*. We are concerned less with two different conceptions of progress than with two different conceptions of what in progress is *natural* and what is *artificial*.

In other questions, at a later date, Malthus expressly referred to the principle of the artificial identification of interests. In the introduction to his *Political Economy*, he tried to show with what reservations the principle of Adam Smith may be accepted according to which ' governments should not interfere in the direction of capital and industry, but leave every person so long as he obeys the laws of justice, to pursue his own interest in his own way, as the best security for the constant and equable supply of the national wants '.[2] He was a protectionist, and his pamphlet of 1814 bearing on the problem of duties on the importation of corn, is a model of ' moral arithmetic ', since Malthus, after examining in detail the reaction of the abolition of the duties on the interests of various categories of citizens, concludes that this measure would be contrary to the happiness of the greatest number.[3] But as early as 1798, he contradicted Godwin, who had followed Priestley in condemning every kind of State teaching and compulsory instruction : Priestley and Godwin held intellectual progress to be a normal and spontaneous development of our nature. According to Malthus, on the other hand, egoism must be enlightened, the blind impulses of instinct must be artificially restrained, and for this purpose education must be developed. Adam Smith, it is true, had admitted that the State ought to take over popular education, at the same time that he accepted the principle of the natural identity of interests. But it is interesting to note that, in the two passages in his book in which he attributes a pedagogic

---

[1] *Princ. of Pop.* pp. 13-14 (1st ed.).
[2] *Principles of Pol. Econ.* etc. (1st ed. 1820), Introd. pp. 13-14.
[3] *The Grounds of an Opinion on the Policy of restricting the Importation of Foreign Corn*, etc., pp. 23-42.

function to the State, he is consciously violating the principle which he had originally laid down. For example, the principle of the equality of wages is a derivative form of the principle of the natural identity of interests. But it is contradicted, in certain cases, by the policy of the States of Europe, which increases the crowding in certain occupations beyond what it would naturally be : this is particularly true of the clergy and of men of letters, who are brought up at the expense of the State only to find themselves afterwards without employment, badly paid and losing caste. All the same, Adam Smith does not reproach the States concerned for being prodigal of education. ' This inequality is upon the whole, perhaps, rather advantageous than hurtful to the public. It may somewhat degrade the profession of a public teacher ; but the cheapness of literary education is surely an advantage which greatly overbalances this trifling inconveniency.' [1] Similarly, the principle of the division of labour is the actual expression of the principle of the natural identity of interests. The State's first obligation is to encourage it, or to speak more exactly, using a negative expression, not to impede it ; normally the division of occupations ought to place ' the greater part of individuals in such situations as naturally form in them and without any attention of government, almost all the abilities and virtues which that State requires '. But Adam Smith agrees that the progress of the division of labour, by confining every labourer to an occupation which is more and more both absorbing and specialised, tends to make him ' as stupid and ignorant as it is possible for a human creature to become '. The labourer becomes incapable of realising the great interests of his country, and incapable of defending his country in war. ' His dexterity in his own particular trade seems, in this manner, to be acquired at the expense of his intellectual, social, and martial virtues. But in every improved and civilised society this is the state into which the labouring poor, that is the great body of the people, must necessarily fall, unless government takes some pains to prevent it.' [2] It therefore becomes obligatory for the State, in the interest of the greatest number to correct, by means of education, the effects of the division of labour, which are fatal in at least one particular. In other words, it becomes necessary to restrict the bearing of the principle of the natural identity of interests, and to say :—the interests of all individuals are identical, provided that the individuals know what their interests are ; it is a function of the State to teach them to know what they are.

[1] *W. of N.* bk. i. ch. x. part i. (vol. i. pp. 137-138).
[2] *W. of N.* bk. v. ch. i. art. ii. (vol. ii. pp. 365-366).

CHAPTER III

BENTHAM, JAMES MILL AND THE BENTHAMITES

THE ten years preceding 1815 were marked in England by a general revival of liberal and democratic opinions, after the eclipse which William Godwin's Utopian, anti-governmental and communist Utilitarianism had suffered. In 1807, Cobbett, the famous journalist, who had been a demagogue all his life, though not always a democrat, deserted the camp of the anti-jacobins to go over to the party of peace and reform : he used his influence towards the triumphant election of Sir Francis Burdett at Westminster. In the same year, Romilly devoted himself to the study of the reforms which were required by the condition of English law, particularly penal law. After Wordsworth, Southey and Coleridge, who had all turned Tory, there arose a new generation of revolutionary poets —Byron, to begin with, and a little later Shelley and Keats—who scandalised and at the same time struck the imagination of their contemporaries. Moreover, in 1808, after the invasion of Spain by Napoleon, the whole Iberian peninsula rose against the French occupation, and England helped the Spaniards by military expeditions and financial aid. As in the time of Louis XIV, England, though under a Tory Government, once more began to play the part of the nation with liberal traditions, in the face of despotism ' à la turque ', the tradition of which was being renewed by Napoleon on the Continent.

In 1808, Bentham made the acquaintance of James Mill.[1] James Mill was one of those hard-headed Scotsmen whose energy achieved the intellectual conquest of England towards the end of the eighteenth century. He was born in 1773, at the time when Bentham was first beginning to write, in that part of Great Britain which prides itself

---

[1] For all biographical details of James Mill, see *James Mill : a Biography*, by Alexander Bain, 1882.

on possessing the monopoly of deductive and abstract metaphysical genius to the exclusion of England and Ireland, in the county of Montrose, where the birth-places of Beattie, Reid and Campbell were to be seen only a few miles distant.   The son of a village cobbler, he had received an education superior to his status, under the direction of an ambitious mother, and through the protection of the aristocratic family of Sir John Stuart, the future godfather of his son.   He was a tutor in important Scottish families, a student in theology at Edinburgh University, and even began to follow the profession of a preacher : as late as 1810 there was a satchel in his house containing a collection of the sermons he had delivered.   But he was drawn by ' the high road that leads to London '. In 1802, he came to the capital in the suite of Sir John Stuart, who had recently been elected a member of Parliament. ' I am extremely ambitious to remain here, which I feel to be so much the best scene for a man of letters, that you can have no notion of it till you be upon the spot ',[1] he wrote to Thomas Thomson, the friend of his early days.   There he was living, following the trade of a journalist, sometimes as editor, sometimes simply as a contributor to the *British Review*, the *Monthly Review*, the *Eclectic Review*, the *Annual Review*, and the *Edinburgh Review*, at the time when he got to know Bentham.[2]   Was he already Bentham's disciple ? He leads us to believe, in one place, that he was, and his testimony may be relied upon.[3]   In any case, Bentham appears to have noticed him for the first time in 1808 ; the following winter we see him passing on to Dumont the complimentary notice which had been given him in the *Annual Review*, by the man who was to become to him a kind of second Dumont. ' This is excellent ', Dumont exclaimed, ' I like the man—he expresses his feelings out loud and in an intelligible manner—he is not like some luke-warm, half-ashamed admirers, whom I know, who tell you twenty fine things in conversation, and who either dare not or will not express a single one of them in writing.' [4]   Mill began to make frequent visits to Bentham from Pentonville where he was living, going often to dine and pass the evening at his house.   In 1809, he lived with him for three or four months in the summer together with his wife and his son John at Bentham's country house at Barrow Green.   In 1810, Bentham gave him Milton's house, which was next door to his own in Queen Square Place and which belonged to him, to live in.   The house was unhealthy, and Mill soon left it ; but in 1814, in order to sub-let it to him at half price, Bentham rented another house, close to the first one, where Mill lived for sixteen years.   Since 1806, Mill had been working at his *History of British India*, the idea of which may

[1] Bain, p. 37.
[2] See Bain, p. 162, and Bowring, vol. x. p. 329 and *passim*.
[3] *Fragment on Mackintosh*, quoted by Bain, pp. 71-72.
[4] Add. MSS. Brit. Mus. 383,544, p. 426.

perhaps have been suggested to him by a passage in the *Treatises* ; [1]
he was poor, and the review articles he wrote provided barely enough
for him to live on, until the time when his *History* was completed,
and he was granted, in 1818, an important position in the offices of
the East India Company. Thus by helping him to live, Bentham
rendered James Mill an inestimable service. But the truth is that
Bentham could not do without this man at his side, who, with as much
zeal and more perseverance, took up the note of editor and expositor
which had hitherto been filled by Dumont alone. With his ' need
of someone to admire ', which made him the ideal disciple for
Bentham, with his energetic temperament and despotic character
which made him, to all except to Bentham, a dreaded master, with
his genius for logical deduction and exposition, which gives a kind
of originality to his works even when they are expressing some
one else's ideas, Mill rendered Bentham as much service as Bentham
rendered Mill. Bentham gave Mill a doctrine, and Mill gave
Bentham a school.

I. THE BIRTH OF RADICALISM

In 1808, when he became acquainted with James Mill, Bentham
was sixty years old ; nevertheless, strange though it may seem, it
must be realised that he was still very little known by the English
public as a theorist and reformer of the science of law. For the wider
public, he was principally and almost exclusively the man who wrote
the *Panopticon*.[2] He was one of the ' men of one idea ' who were
at that time so numerous in England :—Spence, who preached
agrarian communism ; Cartwright, who advocated universal suffrage ;
Robert Owen, the man who stood for the moral regeneration of
humanity by means of quadrangular villages. Or, to be more exact,
for Bentham had no universal panacea, he was a philanthropist of
the type of Howard, the prison reformer, or of Wilberforce, the
opponent of slavery, who were both of them his friends. But,
towards 1808, Bentham might well have considered his philanthropic
campaign a lost cause. He was growing old, and had every
reason to ask himself whether his life had not been a failure.[3] In his
case disappointed philanthropy changed into misanthropy : he was
dissatisfied and discouraged.

The beginnings of his campaign go back as far as 1790, when his
brother Samuel Bentham's return to England gave him a competent
collaborator for the architectural part of the project. Since 1791,
Bentham had been in negotiation with Pitt. In 1792, the death of
Jeremiah Bentham, the father, gave him possession of a considerable
capital. In March of the same year he addressed to Pitt, the First

---

[1] See *Treatise on the Influence of Time and Place in Legislation.* Bowring, vol. i.
[2] See Bowring, vol. x. p. 403.   [3] Bowring, vol. x. p. 548.

Lord of the Treasury, and to Dundas, the Secretary of State, ' a proposal for taking charge of convicts to the number of a thousand, according to the above-mentioned plan of construction and management upon the terms therein mentioned '. In 1793, Pitt and Dundas came in person to examine the models of the penitentiary establishment at Bentham's house. Finally, in 1794, a law was passed which authorised administration by contract, and fixed as site for the prison the place called Battersea Rise, which Blackstone and Eden had already thought of utilising for the same purpose. Bentham's negotiations with the owners of the land came to nothing ; and it was on the other bank of the Thames that he finally bought from the Marquis of Salisbury a site of the value of twelve to fourteen thousand pounds, instead of the two thousand which Parliament had originally allotted to Bentham.   But the matter still dragged on, though it was again introduced by Colquhoun, with the warmest recommendations, before the Finance Committee of 1798.   Bentham was ruined ;—' I . . . am reduced to shut up my house (the residence of the family for three-and-thirty years), fortunate in finding a brother's to take refuge in.' [1]   Round about 1790 his project attracted the attention, in Ireland, of Sir John Parnell ; it was at his request and in the hope that it would be printed at the expense of the Irish Parliament that Bentham wrote his work entitled *Panopticon* ; but matters remained at this stage, and Bentham printed the work at his own expense. At Edinburgh, the architect Adam had drawn his inspiration from Samuel Bentham for the construction of a semi-circular prison : but it was Adam who secured both the moral and the material profit from the enterprise.

At last Pitt fell from power ; but Bentham came up against the same indifference in his successor. ' Mr. Addington's hope *is* what Mr. Pitt's hope *was*—to see me die broken-hearted, like a rat in a hole.   I may die any day : but so long as perfidy, and treachery, and oppression, and corruption, and arbitrary power, and contempt of Parliament, and the persevering propagation of immorality and misery are the order of the day with him, so long as I live he will find me living to his annoyance. Living did I say ? Yes ; and even when I am dead, he will not be rid of me.' [2]   He was now engaged on the production of three pamphlets : the first, entitled *Panopticon versus New South Wales*,[3] in which, in a letter addressed to Lord Pelham, he set forth a parallel between the two systems of the Panopticon and of deportation ;—the second which was successively called the *True Bastille*, then the *Constitution Conquered*, and lastly *A Plea for the Constitution*, in which he drew his inspiration from documents which were furnished innocently and without polemical intent by a former judge-advocate of the colony, and pointed out abuses of power which had been committed—undue prolongations

---

[1] Bowring, vol. xi. pp. 116-117.   [2] *Ibid.* p. 139.
[3] *Ibid.* vol. iv. pp. 173 *seq.*

of punishment, roundabout forms of slavery, ' in breach of Magna Charta, the Petition of Right, the Habeas Corpus Act, and the Bill of Rights ' ; [1] and finally, some *Observations on a Late Exercise of Legislative Power by the Duke of Portland, in Declared Contempt of Parliament* ',[2] which was so violent an attack against the person of the Duke that Bentham's most zealous friends—Romilly, who was spreading his ideas among the Whig circle at Holland House, and Wilberforce, who acted as intermediary between Bentham and the ministry—were perturbed on receiving the manuscript. ' On affaiblit tout ce qu'on exagère ', Romilly wrote to Bentham ; but he naively added that the pamphlet was, ' in point of law, a libel, and the more a libel for being true '.[3] Wilberforce pleaded the cause of the ministers with Bentham. Pitt had been negligent, but he was absorbed by so much business. Lord Spencer had brought about the failure of the first negotiations about the land, but was he personally responsible ? And finally, why these attacks on Lord Belgrave ? ' You speak with levity at least, if not ridicule, of his religious character . . . And is it for Mr. B., the reformer of the vicious—(and in no character has he ever appeared to me in a more amiable or dignified light, than when exercising the resources of his ingenious mind for so laudable a purpose)—is it for *him* to laugh at any one as a *propagator of Christianity ? ' [4] The two philanthropies, the Christian philanthropy of Wilberforce, and the philanthropy of Bentham inspired by Helvetius, are seen beginning to diverge. Wilberforce was a conservative, a man with many friends, who would be very glad if none of these were in the wrong. None the less he had the deepest pity for Bentham's ' sickness at heart ', and was interceding actively for him even while he was revolting him by his apparent luke-warmness.[5] He came to his aid in difficult times. ' Never was any one worse used than Bentham. I have seen the tears run down the cheeks of that strong-minded man, through vexation at the pressing importunity of creditors and the insolence of official underlings, when day after day he was begging at the Treasury for what was indeed a mere matter of right. How indignant did I often feel, when I saw him thus treated by men infinitely his inferiors ! I could have extinguished them. He was quite soured by it ; and I have no doubt that many of his harsh opinions afterwards were the fruit of this ill-treatment.' [6]

The insulted philanthropist, the unrecognised inventor, the projector who is continually treated as a madman, may end by falling into a melancholy state. But Bentham was too thick-skinned for this : he only modified, or to be more exact, completed his philosophy under the pressure of circumstances. He threw the responsibility for his mortification on the King, who, he imagined,

---

[1] Bowring, vol. iv. pp. 249 *seq.*   [2] See in particular Bowring, vol. x. p. 134.
[3] Bowring, vol. x. pp. 399-400.   [4] *Ibid.* pp. 391 *seq.*
[5] *Ibid.* vol. x. p. 391.   [6] *Life of Wilberforce,* vol. ii. pp. 171-172.

had not forgotten the controversy of 1789.[1] He also threw the responsibility on the apathy and egoism of the entire aristocratic caste and of the interested factions into which it was split up, and which loudly disputed over the enjoyment of political power. He remembered with irony the days of his youth when, a great reformer, he thought that it would suffice to enlighten the aristocracy in order to convert it to ideas of reform. He was mistaken, as he admits in a marginal note added to the *Introduction*, and he now understood that the aristocracy was in its essence hostile to reforms.[2] Judicial reform pre-supposes political reform, since, in politics as everywhere else, the spirit of corporation is the worst enemy of the spirit of the principle of public utility ; and the aristocracy is a corporation, a particular society formed at the heart of society as a whole, with interests other than those of that society. This was the conclusion whose premisses were for Bentham, not so much abstract principles, as the actual events which marked the last twenty years of his life. The day came when he reproached James Mill with detesting oppression less through love of the many than through hatred of the few.[3] Would not the observation in some ways apply to Bentham just as well ? The disappointment and the distress which he suffered made him a democrat ; in hatred of the monarch and his ministers, he became a deliberate enemy of monarchic and of aristocratic institutions.

These were the remoter causes which made the evolution of Bentham's thought take a democratic direction ; it will be well to examine the proximate causes which hastened this evolution and which, in about the year 1808, gave to it the nature of a sudden revolution. Until this time, Bentham found himself by the force of circumstances in relations with the Whig party : his two most intimate friends, Romilly and Dumont, were welcomed as friends at Holland House, the social centre of the faction. It was in Spain, in Portugal and in South America that the work of Bentham and Dumont secured the largest sale : Bentham therefore quite naturally became an ' Iberophil ' as they were at Holland House. In order to denounce abuses, he could not do otherwise than speak the language of the Whigs, enter a ' Plea for the Constitution ', and denounce ' the True Bastille '. Nevertheless, from his Tory education, and from his instinctive antipathy to the politics of parties and coteries, he preserved a tenacious hostility to the Whig party.

As he himself confided to Dumont in a private letter, he despised those politicians who are sometimes so profligate that they would be glad to give over the world to blood and fire for the sake of doing more harm to the ministry.[4] He detested Fox, and avoided all the attempts which Doctor Parr had made, in the interests of his

---

[1] Bowring, vol. x. p. 201. [2] *Ibid.* vol. i. p. 5. [3] *Ibid.* vol. x. p. 482.
[4] Bowring, vol. x. pp. 428 and 624.

philanthropic designs, to get him into touch with the leader of the Opposition.[1] But the following is the most characteristic fact of all. Since 1792, Bentham had lived in Westminster, and towards 1810 Westminster was to assume the importance in the political history of England which the county of Middlesex had had round about 1770. The two historical parties lost some of their prestige by the deaths of Pitt and Fox ; and when, in the 1807 elections, the Tory party exploited patriotic and anti-Catholic passions against the Whig party, and the Whig party retorted by denouncing the Tory party as the party of ' King's friends ' and unprincipled and corrupt courtiers, a great many electors were tempted to treat both charges as justified and to grant success to neither party. The old spirit of hostility, directed equally against both factions of the aristocracy, who though rivals were also accomplices, the *ins* as well as the *outs*, was revived, principally in the big cities and particularly at Westminster.   'The city and liberty of Westminster ', under the incoherent electoral régime which persisted until 1832, was an area with a widely extended electorate, but one in which the seventeen thousand electors had for long years obeyed the councils of the aristocratic factions and regularly, at every election, given one seat to a Whig and one to a Tory representative. In 1807, the charm was broken : Sir Francis Burdett, who had grown rich by his marriage with the daughter of the banker, Coutts, but was disgusted by the unavailing and ruinous attempts he had made to get into Parliament, consented to stand as a popular candidate, on condition that it should not cost him a single penny ; thanks to the intervention in the struggle, with his *Letters to the electors of Westminster*, of the famous journalist Cobbett, who had recently become a democrat—thanks to the action of some influential electors, chief among whom was Francis Place, the merchant tailor of Charing Cross—thanks above all to the awakening of public opinion, he was elected.   It was a sensational event : henceforth it was demonstrated that the electoral *ancien régime* itself allowed elections which were favourable to the popular party. Now, it was at Westminster, under the influence of the same men who caused the election of Sir Francis Burdett, that the group of Bentham's friends was finally organised as a party for political action. It was the borough of Westminster, in whose electoral body ' pig's flesh ' predominated, with its host of tradesmen and shopkeepers, worthy heirs of the tradition of Hampden, that Bentham was shortly to set forth before everyone as the model, already in existence at the heart of a ridiculous constitution, of the ' representative democracy ' which he was advocating.[2] Yet there is nothing in Bentham's letters to indicate that the election of 1807 moved him in any way. It seems as though the intrusion into his life of James Mill was needed to make him a democrat.[3]

[1] Bowring, vol. xi. p. 131.   [2] *Ibid*. vol. ii. pp. 469, 478, 524.
[3] See Bowring, vol. iii. p. 438.

For some years James Mill had been a Whig and, perhaps, an advanced Whig.[1] He stood for the theory of indefinite perfectibility. He agreed with the publishers of the *Edinburgh Review* in demanding the emancipation of the Catholics. Freedom of opinion and of the press was the cause which he defended with the greatest ardour. Now from the time when he made James Mill's acquaintance, we find Bentham giving his attention to political questions, and to the question of the freedom of the press in particular. *The Times* of February 20, 1809, pointed out abuses in the application of the laws concerning the press ; and Bentham laid down the principle, in a study which he gave up to the question, that the libel law was ' incompatible with English liberties ', and need only be executed coherently and completely in order to reduce the government to a despotism ; that it was the business of Parliament alone, by a formal definition of libel to supply a ' radical ' remedy for the evil ; but that, in the meantime, juries could act as palliatives to the law, granted that they performed their function, and were not 'special juries ', ' packed ' so as to conform to the desires of the government instead of controlling them. Bentham devoted himself to the criticism of this fraudulent institution : hence the title which he gave to his book—*The Elements of the Art of Packing* ;[2] and James Mill urged Bentham to complete and then to publish a work which had perhaps been begun at his own instigation. ' As to the *Elements* ', he wrote in the first letter of his to Bentham which has been preserved, ' for the outcoming of which I appear to be far more impatient than you . . . I have told Baldwin, that it must be, through thick or through thin, *published* in six weeks '.[3] James Mill undertook the advertising of the book in the *Edinburgh Review*. He wrote again, on September 27, ' I offer up my devotions every morning for the prosperity of Libel Law '. He had just been present at the debate on the freedom of the press in the Commons, and the weakness and timidity of all concerned, even of Sir Francis Burdett, had revolted him. ' They were afraid they should commit some blunder in regard to the requisite provisions of law, and, therefore, eat in their words. Oh ! if they but knew what law is, and ought to be, as well as you can tell them, on this most interesting of all points, we should find the boldness, I trust, on the other side, equal to that of the lawyers.'[4] But Bentham had another intimate friend in Romilly, who was a lawyer, and for reasons of prudence adjured Bentham ' sincerely and anxiously ', not to publish the *Elements of Packing*.[5] Consequently the printed work was not put up for sale. However, a restricted number of copies were distributed to Mill, Brougham, Whishaw, and Burdett, all of whom were democrats. At about the same time Bentham had dealings with the family of Lord Cochrane, Sir Francis Burdett's colleague in the representation

---

[1] See his *Commerce Defended* (1808).   [2] Bowring, vol. v. pp. 61 *seq.*
[3] *Ibid*. vol. x. p. 451.   [4] *Ibid*. p. 450.   [5] *Ibid*. p. 450-451.

of Westminster.[1] Romilly himself took an active part in the defence
of Burdett in 1810, when he was imprisoned in the Tower for a
crime in connection with the press ; and in 1811 and 1812 we find
Bentham in a direct friendly relationship to Sir Francis Burdett.[2]

Now this politician, with whom Bentham became connected, was
a disciple of Horne Tooke,[3] a disciple that is to say of the patriarch
of the popular party and the survivor of the revolutionary societies
of 1776 : Sir Francis Burdett was thus connected with the ' old
school ' of English democrats. For Horne Tooke had always been a
moderate and had never shared Thomas Paine's convictions, even
in the times of their common persecution. He claimed before his
judges in 1794 to have been the constant upholder of the traditional
constitution of England. But, in fact, in Horne Tooke's works,
tradition and custom became in the end confused with natural
right, with the prescriptions of reason. *Right* is what is commanded
(*rectum*, from *regere*). Are there therefore as many rights as there
are contradictory commandments among various nations ? But the
right revered by Horne Tooke was not the *jus vagum*, the capricious
command of princes or ministers. The laws of human nature are
derived from the law of God : ' I revere the Constitution and the
constitutional *laws* of England because they are in conformity
with the *laws* of God and nature : and upon these are founded the
rational *rights* of Englishmen '.[4] In short, Horne Tooke seems to
advocate together and indivisibly the restoration of the inalienable
rights of man, as man, and the return to the origins of the constitution
of the English people : two conceptions which were both equally
empty of meaning for anyone taking the point of view of the Benthamite doctrine. Moreover, he did not become an advocate of universal
suffrage ; and Burdett was really taking up his ideas when, on
June 15, 1809, he demanded the vote for all those, but only those,
who paid rates.[5] It was at this first stage that Bentham, who had
started from Toryism, and from now onwards was on the road to
Radicalism, paused in 1809, in spite of the difference between the
two principles. For the moment, the Benthamites did not go further
than this.

Such, notably, was the case with James Mill, who was the first of
the rising group of Benthamites to try, in January, 1809, to base the
theory of representative government on the principle of utility, in an
article published by the *Edinburgh Review*,[6] dealing with the republican constitutions of South America. ' Whenever the interests of
two sets of people are combined together in one concern, if the
entire management be left to one, it is perfectly clear that this
managing set will draw, by degrees, all the advantages to their own

---

[1] Bowring, vol. x. pp. 449 and 455.   [2] *Ibid*. p. 460.   [3] *Ibid*. p. 404.
[4] *Diversions of Purley*, part ii. ch. i. ; *Rights of Man*, vol. ii. p. 1 ; see Bowring,
vol. x. p. 504.
[5] Hansard, vol. xiv. pp. 1541 *seq*.   [6] *Ed. Rev*. Jan. 1809, vol. xiii. p. 305.

side, and throw all the disadvantages to the other : and if the joint interest is so wide and unwieldy a concern as that of a nation, so far is this inequality sure to proceed, as to ruin the interest itself, and destroy all national prosperity.'   Clearly, it was no longer a question, as it was for Paine and Godwin, of introducing into politics the anti-governmental principle of the natural identity of interests. James Mill's thesis was akin to the traditional thesis of the Whig liberalism, and he based himself, as Priestley had done before him, on the principle of the artificial identification of interests in order to demand that, granted the necessity of governmental control, the government itself should be submitted to an organised control. Besides, James Mill was still rather timid.   He was prepared to grant the States of America a democratic constitution, but he refused to entrust to the people the task of *forming* the constitution at the outset ; and as to the composition of the electoral body, while he did not wish it to be too restricted—for this would be to expose it to the disadvantages of corruption—he required that care should be taken not to make it too wide—for this would be to give rein to the ignorant and headstrong passions of the common people.

It was in the same year that Bentham attacked the problem, and began to draw up a *Catechism of Parliamentary Reform*, in the form of questions and answers, which he suggested to Cobbett in 1810 should be published in his *Register*.   Cobbett refused to put it in ; and this is perhaps a reason for the antipathy which Bentham always felt for him.[1]   But is it necessary to have recourse to such petty reasons in order to explain the continual scorn with which Bentham regarded Burdett, ' the hero of the mob ',[2] no less than Cobbett,[3] that ' odious mixture of egoism, malignity, insincerity and mendacity ' ? They might be made use of on occasion, for the basest criminals have their uses.   But Bentham felt for them the antipathy which the political philosopher feels for the politician.   In effect his essay of 1810 was a purely philosophical essay, consisting entirely of the enumeration of the reasons to be given in favour of Burdett's pro- positions, by an adherent of the principle of utility.   Everything can be reduced, it argued, to a calculus of the profits to be obtained, and of the losses to be avoided or reduced.   Care must be taken to make sure that there are present in the highest degree in the members of the electoral body, or, to be more exact, in the greatest possible number of these members, those faculties which are needed to make them competent to accomplish their function exactly ; and the elements of such competence themselves consist, according to Bentham, in *probity*, in *intellectual aptitude*, and in *active talent*.   It is necessary also to avoid, or to reduce to the smallest possible extent, the inconveniences involved in *elections* ; and also to avoid, or to reduce to the smallest possible extent, the inconveniences involved in

---

[1] J. F. Colls. *Utilitarianism unmasked.*   [2] Bowring, vol. x. p. 471.
[3] *Ibid*. vol. xi. p. 68.

the discussion of the *validity of elections*. We now come to the remarkable part of Bentham's doctrine at this precise point in its evolution. He enumerates five measures necessary for the realisation of the positive ends :—the exclusion of placemen ; the introduction into Parliament of official persons without the right to vote, but with the right to make speeches and to propose motions ; frequent elections (Bentham wishes them to be annual) ; the complete, authentic, regular and quick publication of speeches ; and permanence, punctuality and universality of assistance. Now the extension of the right of suffrage is not included in these five fundamental measures.

To these demands for constitutional reform, Bentham does, it is true, add others concerning the organisation of the electorate. While maintaining, under new names, the traditional British distinction between boroughs (*population* electoral districts) and counties (*territory* electoral districts), he requires that the number of electors should be approximately equal in all the electoral districts. He demands secret instead of public voting, and wishes ' the title of every elector ' to be ' *payment* made to a certain amount to *certain taxes* '.[1] But these measures which seem essential to us, have no other advantage, in his theory, than that of suppressing, or, as he says in his geometrical language, of reducing to the least possible dimensions, the inconveniences involved in elections, that is to say, ' expense and annoyance ' for the candidates, and ' loss of time, idleness, drunkenness, quarrels and riots ', for the electors and for the public in general. The secret ballot, with the power of voting by post, would abolish the need for the candidates to convey the electors to the poll, would do away with the tumultuous nature of the elections, and would simplify the examination of their validity ; in the same way, the regularisation of the right to vote would simplify the task of the judges. And moreover the reform would have the collateral advantages of developing the ' appropriate intellectual aptitude ' in the electors, and of improving the condition of the lower classes, by identifying their interests with the interests of the wealthy classes. The reform has no direct advantages in its democratic aspect ; strictly speaking even, the regularisation of the right to vote does not imply its democratisation ; and, in the reform of the electoral régime, it is the institution of the secret ballot, rather than the extension of the right of suffrage, which appears essential to Bentham.

It was nevertheless fated that, under the influence of his surroundings, the democratic idea should be unceasingly developing in Bentham. From 1811, Bentham was in touch with Major Cartwright, the first English theorist of universal suffrage, who

---

[1] This is Burdett's proposition, see Hansard, vol. xviii. 123, and Bowring, vol. iii. p. 467, note.

had been a popular man round about 1780, before the reaction by which, for fifteen years and more, all idea of reform was discredited in England. There is nothing to prove, however, that Bentham had given his support to the thesis of universal suffrage by 1811. They began by exchanging letters on the question of the reform of penitentiaries. Cartwright notified Bentham of the presence in London of three free colonists from New South Wales who would be able to supply information on the scandals over there; and Bentham suggested that Burdett ought to bring the matter before the House of Commons.[1] But above all, Bentham made the acquaintance in 1812, through James Mill, of that remarkable person, Francis Place, who was at that time forty years old. He was only a manual worker and a member of revolutionary societies round about 1792; and then, after 1800, became a merchant tailor at Charing Cross, an influential elector, and before long the chief political wire-puller of the locality. He contributed to Bentham's group his powers as an agitator and organiser, and became the political agent of the sect for thirty consecutive years.[2]

He was living in retirement when James Mill, in 1811, and Bentham, in 1812, made his acquaintance. It was Francis Place who organised Sir Francis Burdett's election in 1807; but at the time, in 1810, when Sir Francis Burdett was barricaded in his house in Piccadilly and resisted the efforts of the entire London police, Place recommended him to capitulate. It so happened that at the same moment Place was a member of the jury which was charged with the inquiry into a tragic death, for which public opinion held a member of the royal family to be responsible. He had concluded, with the whole of the jury, that it was a case of suicide; and the advanced democrats, led by Henry Hunt, having thrown against him the accusation, so common in parties of popular agitation, that he was in the pay of the government, that he was a government spy, an *agent provocateur*, Sir Francis Burdett quarrelled with him and did not make it up until 1819. But from 1814 James Mill, Place and Bentham were in agreement in an attempt to get Brougham into Parliament in place of Lord Cochrane, who had just been turned out because of a financial scandal. Brougham was a compatriot of James Mill, had collaborated with him on the *Edinburgh Review*, and promised to support the programme of Parliamentary reform which Burdett had supported in 1809.[3] Place, moreover, knew Cartwright, who paid him frequent visits in his shop at Charing Cross; and Cartwright, who had become rich again, resumed after 1810 with a new enthusiasm his campaign of propaganda. In 1811, he founded the 'Society of the Friends of Parliamentary Reform'; in 1812, the 'Hampden Club'; in 1813 he applied to the propagation of political ideas a procedure, which had long been applied by the Methodists

[1] Bowring, vol. x. pp. 463-466.   [2] Graham Wallas, *Life of Place*, pp. 5 *seq.*
[3] Bain, p. 115 and p. 129.

to religious propaganda, and became a 'field preacher', holding meetings in the open air, through the length and breadth of England. It was after the peace, in particular, that the movement became important. Until this time political agitation had been confined to Westminster; economic troubles had not yet reached the manufacturing districts of the North-West. After 1815, when the resumption of industrial production on the Continent lessened the demand for English products, and while the supply of corn remained stationary, through the obstinacy of the landed proprietors in defending the system of prohibitive taxes on the importation of corn, the crisis became general. Town labourers broke up machinery. Country labourers fired hay-ricks. 'Radicalism' at last became a force in politics.

Already, some time before this, the expression 'radical reform' had become a part of ordinary language. It had first been in fashion for a time round about 1797 and 1798, when Fox and Horne Tooke, derided by the *Anti-Jacobin*, had come to an agreement in order to demand a 'radical reform'; and in the epithet is represented that idea of return to origins, or *roots*, which is so widespread in the philosophy of the English democrats of the eighteenth century. Then the expression seems completely to have disappeared and does not occur again before about 1810. In a private letter of 1811, Cartwright contrasts the *radical reformer*, who offers the nation the constitution itself 'in all its simplicity of excellence', with the *moderate reformer* who offers something of his own fabrication and of his own fancy, something which (as he himself admits) is complex and very imperfect.[1] The adjective *radical* and the substantive *reformer* are used henceforward with increasing frequency.[2] 'The Radical Reformers', declared Ward in Parliament, 'certainly constitute the great majority of the reformers out of doors; and the Moderate Reformers the greater part of the Opposition';—and by Radical Reformers he meant not merely the supporters of annual parliaments and universal suffrage, but all those who wished to alter the constitution in accordance with some grand general sweeping plan; while by Moderate Reformers he meant those who were content with partial alterations, applicable to what they deemed particular grievances.[3] But it appears that it was not until 1819 that the adjective Radical was used, by an abbreviation, as a substantive.[4] Now, this was precisely the time when a considerable event in the history of Radicalism had just come to pass.

In 1817, Bentham had at last published his *Plan of Parliamentary Reform, in the Form of a Catechism, with Reasons for Each Article*, made ten times more important by the addition of an introduction, in which he tried to show 'the necessity of Radical Reform and the

[1] Letter to the Rev. Christopher Wivyll, April 15, 1811.
[2] *Ed. Rev.* vol. xiv. p. 277, etc.   [3] Hansard, vol. xxxvi. p. 761.
[4] See Miss Harriet Martineau, *Hist. of the Thirty Years' Peace*, vol. i. p. 226.

insufficiency of Moderate Reform '. In February, 1818, Henry Bickersteth, a young disciple of Bentham's, opened negotiations with Bentham and Sir Francis Burdett, with a view to getting them to agree to a common action to be taken in Parliament in favour of the cause of reform : ' Now England possesses two distinguished friends of reform, who, by their joint labours, are able to give the most advantageous promulgation to the best possible plan. The characters of Mr. Bentham and Sir Francis Burdett are too well known to each other to make it necessary or proper to say anything on that subject. . . . Conceive a plan of reform drawn up by Mr. Bentham—the best possible because framed by the person best qualified ; and promulgated by Sir Francis Burdett '. Burdett added his persuasion to Bickersteth's : ' Bentham and Burdett ! the alliteration charms my ear '. Some difficulties arose. Bentham stood *above all* for the secret ballot. He considered that it was he who had initiated the idea ; and although Cartwright's biographer rightly points out that as early as 1776 the ballot was included in Cartwright's programme, it is none the less true that for him the ballot was only one of the five fundamental points of the programme, while to Bentham, and to the members of his group after him, the organisation of the secret ballot appeared to be the really essential part of electoral reform. Burdett, while he did not object to it, emphasised the inopportuneness of the demand ' because of the prejudice to be surmounted '. Finally, Bentham made up his mind to draw up twenty-six *Resolutions on Parliamentary Reform*, which Burdett accepted and which, on June 2, 1818, he made the subject of a motion in the Commons.

It was the principle of the artificial identification of interests which was here rigorously applied in conformity, so Bentham insisted, with the traditional spirit of the English constitution. Bentham asserted ' that no adequate security for good government can have place, but by means of, and in proportion to, a community of interest between governors and governed ' ; ' that under the government of this country, no such community of interest can have place, but in so far as the persons in whose hands the administration of public affairs is vested, are subject to the superintendence and control, or check, of the representatives of the people ; such representatives speaking and acting in conformity to the sense of the people '. Finally ' that it is only in so far as the members of this House are in fact *chosen*, and from time to time *removable* by the free suffrages of the great body of the people, that there can be any adequate assurance, that the acts done by them, are in conformity to the sense and wishes of the people ; and, therefore, that they can in truth, and without abuse of words, be styled, or declared to be, representatives of the people '. He therefore demanded that Parliament should affirm the expediency and necessity of a comprehensive, free and equal suffrage and that it should make ' one great sacrifice of all separate and particular interests ; ' and proposed to institute universal suffrage, in other words ' to admit to a participation in the election suffrage, all such persons as, being of the male sex, of mature age, and of sound mind, shall, during a determinate time antecedent to the day of election, have been resident either as householders or inmates, within the district or place in which they are called upon to vote ' ;—the secret ballot ;—a fresh election at least once a year ' for more effectually securing the unity of will and opinion, as between the people and their representatives ' ;—the division of the territory of Great Britain and Ireland into six hundred and fifty-eight districts as nearly as possible equal in population, each district to return one representative ;—elections begun and ended on the same day ' for the prevention of unnecessary delay, vexation, and expense, as well as of fraud, violence, disorder, and void elections ' ;—the subdivision of election districts into sub-districts for the reception of votes.[1] As early as March 23, 1818, a public meeting of the householders of Westminster instructed Cartwright to transmit to Bentham ' that profound reasoner and pre-eminent writer on Legislation ' their thanks for his ' philosophical and unanswerable ' vindication of universal suffrage and of the ballot.[2] *The Black Dwarf*, a Radical journal edited by a friend of Mill, named Wooler, announced the publication, by instalments, of a new edition of the *Catechism*, which was out of print. A few days after the proposal of Burdett's motion, Parliament was dissolved. In July, Mill and Place were united to support his popular candidateship at Westminster, and Bentham, for the first and last time in his life, intervened personally in an electoral struggle : to the surprise of everybody he drew up a poster to oppose the candidature of his old friend Romilly, who, he said, is ' *no better than a Whig* ', and ' what is most serious of all, is a lawyer '.[3]

Bentham had arrived at the last stage. For a long time he had been indifferent or even hostile to democratic ideas, but now he found himself, under the pressure of a number of circumstances, insensibly led to profess the same doctrine as Cartwright, though basing himself on different principles. The spirit of corporation was, by definition, hostile to the principle of general utility, and the political aristocracy was a closed corporation. For long years, Bentham had suffered from the indifference which this aristocracy had shown to his philanthropic projects. He was living at Westminster, that is to say, at the very centre of the democratic agitation. There he made the acquaintance of James Mill, and through James Mill, of Sir Francis Burdett, of Place and of Cartwright. These are the many reasons which explain how, in the interval of ten years—between Sir Francis Burdett's first speech in 1809, which preceded, and prepared the way for, Bentham's first pamphlet on reform, and Sir Francis Burdett's second speech, delivered in 1818, which was the

[1] Bowring, vol. x. pp. 495-7.   [2] *Ibid.* vol. x. p. 499.   [3] *Ibid.* vol. xi. p. 61.

result of his collaboration with the head of the Utilitarian school—
Bentham, along with Cartwright, 'the father of Reform', became
the philosopher of the party, 'the chief thinker of Radicalism'.[1]

But the very fact that Bentham had become a Radical was destined
to change the nature of the Radical party. At first the Radicals
were confused with the revolutionaries, robbers and incendiaries—
disciples of Spence who advocated that the ownership of land should
return to the community—who struck terror into aristocrats and
bourgeois in the famine years. Brougham who, in 1814, had been
a Radical Reformer, in 1818 broke with Bentham, as represented
by Burdett, and in 1819 cursed the proceedings of the Radicals, who
'by abusing popular privileges . . . establish precedents for abridging
them,' and declared them to be 'so odious that a number even of
our own way of thinking would be well enough pleased to see them
and their vile press put down at all hazards'.[2] Bentham, however,
repudiated the doctrines of the new 'levellers', and in 1820 wrote
his *Radicalism Not Dangerous*,[3] to separate the cause of Radicalism
from the cause of what would to-day be called Communism.
There was no longer any question of demanding that established
governments should be overthrown by means of violent revolution :
Bentham soon quarrelled with demagogues such as Cobbett and Hunt.
Nor was there any question of aspiring, with Godwin, to the day
when, by the natural progress of intelligences, all governments would
become useless and would be abolished : Bentham and Mill applied
to political affairs not the principle of the natural identity, but the
principle of the artificial identity of interests. By means of the
institution of universal suffrage, they counted on organising the
representative régime under conditions such that the general
interest, and the harmony of the interests of the governors with
those of the governed, would infallibly result from the legislative
decisions adopted. At bottom, the Radical theory of the representative régime, interpreted in this way, tended to be assimilated to
the thesis of traditional English Liberalism. The party tended to
lose its Utopian and revolutionary character, and to become a party
of bourgeois doctrinaires—the party that, fifteen years later, was
to be called the party of 'intellectual' or 'Philosophical Radicals'.

2.   FROM ADAM SMITH TO RICARDO

In October, 1808, in an article in the *Edinburgh Review*,[4] James
Mill noted, with curiosity and regret 'the great difficulty with
which the salutary doctrines of political economy are propagated in
this country '. Between 1776, the year in which Adam Smith

---

[1] Dumont, *Souvenirs sur Mirabeau*, etc. (1832), p. xvii. note.
[2] *Life and Times of Brougham*, vol. ii. pp. 342, 348.
[3] Bowring, vol. iii.   [4] Art. III. *Money and Exchange*.

published his *Wealth of Nations*, and 1817, the year in which Ricardo published his *Principles of Political Economy and of Taxation*, not a single complete treatise on political economy appeared in England. Adam Smith remained the only authority, and he was little heeded. ' The late Orders in Council . . . respecting the trade of neutrals ; the popularity of Mr. Spence's doctrines in regard to commerce ; our laws concerning the corn trade ; a great part of our laws, in fact, respecting trade in general ; the speeches which are commonly delivered, the books which are often published, and the conversations which are constantly held ', are the melancholy proofs, enumerated by James Mill, of the low esteem in which were held the principles which he held to be the true principles of political economy. Does this mean that economic thought made no progress at all during this long period of war, political reaction and protective duties ? In the first place, without the knowledge or the assistance of the legislature, a new industrial world had arisen, which raised new problems. William Godwin worked out socialism, while Malthus refuted Godwin and gave an unexpected prominence to certain ideas which had already been recognised by political economists before him. Further, the suspension by the Bank of England of payments in kind in 1797 raised a controversy which, carried on through a long series of years, did a good deal towards perfecting the service of finance : it was with the study of questions of banking that there opened, with Ricardo, the last historical period of the ' orthodox ' political economy, just as in its first stages, in the time of Locke, it had begun with these questions. Lastly, England was still a great agricultural country, while it was becoming a great industrial country also : it was constantly concerned with the search for means to make the production of the country sufficient for its consumption. Hence there were instructive parliamentary inquiries, which seem likely to have determined the actual formation of the theory of differential rent in Ricardo and his disciples. It is, moreover, enough to compare Ricardo's book with Adam Smith's in order to measure the progress that had been secured : we now propose to inquire into the part played by Benthamism in this evolution of Utilitarian political economy between Adam Smith and Ricardo.

This part is generally held to have been an important one. Bentham and James Mill were friends of Ricardo. Bentham never tired of giving his attention to political economy : not to mention his *Defence of Usury* and his *Emancipate your Colonies*, he wrote a *Manual of Political Economy*, which appeared in 1811, incorporated with the *Rationale of Punishment*. He took an interest in the problems of the science of finance, and only gave up his labours when he discovered on reading Thornton's *Enquiry* [1] how unoriginal his views were. [2]   As

---

[1] H. Thornton, *Enquiry into the Nature and Effects of the Paper Credit of Great Britain.* 1802.

[2] Bowring, vol. x. p. 413.

to James Mill, he had always been particularly interested in economic questions. He published, in 1804, an *Essay on the Impolitic Nature of a Bounty on the Export of Corn*. In 1808, at the time when he made the acquaintance of Bentham (and may we not conjecture that it was because he had read this work that Bentham wished to become acquainted with him ?) he published his *Commerce Defended*, in which he pleaded the cause of free-trade against Spence (a disciple of the physiocrats and an advocate of the policy of economic protection), drew the ultimate conclusions from the thesis of the natural identity of economic interests, and, denying the possibility of overproduction, that is, of excess of supply over demand, re-stated the ' theory of markets ', which had already been formulated by J.-B. Say. After 1807 Ricardo was in touch with James Mill, who, in 1811, introduced him to Bentham, at the moment when Ricardo's labours on the depreciation of the bank-note had just established his reputation as an economist and brought him into relation in another connection with Malthus. From this time, James Mill became his intimate friend and confidant.[1] Ricardo, who had not received the education of a man of letters, mistrusted his aptitude to express his thoughts clearly, wrote with difficulty and hesitated to publish. Mill was the man of action who served, so to speak, as the will to Ricardo, who was timid and circumspect. It was James Mill who, in 1816, decided Ricardo to complete and publish his *Proposals for an Economical and Secure Currency*,[2] and, in 1819, to make himself responsible for the article on the *Funding System*[3] in the sixth supplement to the *Encyclopaedia Britannica*. To James Mill is due the honour of having made Ricardo make up his mind to write his *Principles*,[4] between 1815 and 1817 ; and it was through Mill's persuasion again that Ricardo entered Parliament in 1819. All the actions in Ricardo's life, after 1811, were willed by James Mill. ' I was the spiritual father of Mill ', said Bentham, ' and Mill was the spiritual father of Ricardo : so that Ricardo was my spiritual grandson.'[5] Wherein, then, lie the fundamental differences between Adam Smith's book and that of Ricardo ? And how far should they be explained by the influence of Bentham and James Mill, of the one or of the other, or of both together ?

The first difference between Ricardo and Adam Smith is this : they do not both understand the expression ' political economy ' in the same sense. For Adam Smith, political economy means the sum of the practical applications of a certain number of observations bearing on the phenomena of the industrial and commercial world. In the theoretic part which is *preliminary* and no more than prelimin-

---

[1] MacCulloch, *Life and Writings of Mr. Ricardo*, p. xxi.
[2] Ricardo to Malthus, Oct. 17 and Dec. 25, 1815.
[3] Mill to Napier, Sept. 10, 1819 (Bain, p. 187).
[4] Stuart Mill, *Autobiography*, p. 27.   [5] Bowring, vol. x. p. 498, etc.

ary to the constitution of political economy understood in this sense, deductive reasoning is mingled with induction in proportions which are not easy to determine ; but certainly Adam Smith, the friend and disciple of Hume, wished to proceed as an observer and as a historian. What for Adam Smith had been a preliminary became, for Ricardo, the essence of political economy. Political economy was now a theory detached from practice, whatever might subsequently be its practical consequences. ' The produce of the earth—all that is derived from its surface by the united application of labour, machinery, and capital, is divided among three classes of the community, namely, the proprietor of the land, the owner of the stock or capital necessary for its cultivation, and the labourers by whose industry it is cultivated. . . . To determine the laws which regulate this distribution, is the principal problem in Political Economy.' [1] According to Ricardo, the object of political economy is *laws* ; and this expression is significant ; it does not occur in Adam Smith. Thus political economy, which was for Adam Smith a branch of politics and legislation, has become for Ricardo the theory of the laws of the natural distribution of wealth. Is this change in definition due to the action of Bentham and Mill ? [2]

Let us notice in the first place that this new conception of political economy, understood as a theoretic science and as a science of laws, did not even originate in England ; it was in France, in the physiocratic school, that it developed. Hume in one passage [3] reproaches Montesquieu with the fact that, at the beginning of his *Esprit des Lois*, he had borrowed from Malebranche the theory of morals which makes the essence of law consist in abstract connections or relations. Now, the physiocrats did in fact borrow their notion of economic law from Christian theology, and, more exactly, from Malebranche's theology, from which there are barely disguised quotations in Quesnay, and which is expressly quoted by La Rivière in his *Ordre Naturel des Sociétés*, and by Mirabeau in his *Philosophie Rurale*. Hence arose a rationalistic optimism which is different from Hume's naturalistic optimism. According to Hume we live on the idea of the regularity of natural laws. No doubt, the exercise of reason shows us that this regularity is not founded on the nature of things, but is an instinct. But to live we are obliged to trust to instinct. Let us therefore renounce reasoning and live. According to the physiocrats, on the contrary, reason itself teaches us of the existence of laws which are laws of finality at the same time as laws of harmony : positive laws are nothing but simple acts which state natural laws, the necessary consequences of the needs of man, of the diversity of men's talents and of the necessity of applying capital to the land. The existence of evil is undeniable, but Quesnay falls back on his theology to solve the difficulty. The immutable rules

---

[1] Ricardo, *Principles*, Preface, p. i.   [2] Toynbee, *Industrial Revolution*, p. 6.
[3] *An Inquiry concerning the Principles of Morals*, sect. iii. part ii. note.

instituted by God to form and to preserve his work are the causes
of physical evil at the same time as of physical good. But they
produce infinitely more good than evil, they are instituted for good,
and only produce evil by accident—' they are obligatory laws for
good only ; they impose on us the obligation to avoid, as far as we
can, the evil which we ought to foresee by our prudence '. Besides,
it is likely that the true cause of physical and moral evil is man's
transgression of natural laws, ' the bad use made of man's liberty '.[1]
' It is of the essence of order ', says Mercier de la Rivière, ' that the
particular interest of one man should never be able to be separated
from the common interest of all : we find a very convincing proof of
this in the results naturally and necessarily produced by the fulness
of freedom which must prevail in commerce, in order not to injure
property '.[2] Here is recognisable the principle of the natural
identity of interests, which has become, so to speak, the principle of
the rational identity of interests.

Should this conception of the law be condemned, as it was condemned by Hume, because it cannot serve as the basis of a positive
science ?—In principle, it may be remarked, finalism is a legitimate
method and one that is constantly used in the study of
nature : to admit that there exist relations of cause and effect is
to assume that there exist in nature successions of phenomena which
are similar to one another, and that consequently there exist classes
and kinds which are endowed with permanence and fixity, in which,
consequently, the principles of existence prevail over the principles
of destruction, in which good prevails over evil, and which may be
taken at will to be either the ends whose means we are seeking, or the
effects whose causes we are seeking.—In fact, it is sufficient to notice
that the physiocratic conception of law was immediately transmitted,
without its theological element, to thinkers who were not merely
indifferent in affairs of religion, but hostile to the religious idea, and
who were the first theorists of what in the nineteenth century was
known as the positivist spirit.

Perhaps it is not sufficiently recognised to-day that about the year
1800 it was France and not England that owned a school of economists : it was in France that there was being formed a political
economy, understood as the science of the laws of the distribution
of wealth. Quesnay's ' natural law ' became for Turgot [3] ' physical
necessity ', ' physical law of nature ' ; and Condorcet expressed
himself in his *Esquisse* with a precision which was unsurpassed even
by Ricardo. ' What are the laws according to which this wealth
is made or divided, preserved or consumed, increased or dissipated ?
Also, what are the laws of that equilibrium which ceaselessly tends
to establish itself between needs and resources, and from which there

---

[1] Quesnay, *Le Droit Naturel*, ch. iii.
[2] *L'ordre Naturel et Essentiel des Sociétés politiques*, ch. xviii.
[3] *Sur la formation et la distribution des richesses*, v. xxii.

results a greater facility in satisfying needs and consequently more well-being, when wealth increases, until they have reached the limit of its increase ; and on the contrary, when wealth is diminishing, there result more difficulties and consequently more suffering until depopulation and deprivations have established the level again ? How, in this astounding variety of labours and of products, of needs and of resources, in this terrifying complication of interests which bind the subsistence and the well-being of an isolated individual to the general system of societies, and make him dependent on all the accidents of nature and all the events of politics, and which in a sense extend his faculty of experiencing both enjoyments and sensations over the whole globe—how comes it, in this apparent chaos, that there is nevertheless apparent a general law of the moral world causing the efforts of everyone in his own behalf to serve the interest of all, and also that, in spite of the external shock of opposed interests, common interest demands that everyone should understand his own interest and be able to pursue it without opposition ? ' [1] After him, in 1796, Germain Garnier, Adam Smith's first French disciple and editor, already assigned as the first object of political economy ' the laws or principles in accordance with which wealth is formed in a society as a whole, and distributed among the different members of which it is composed '.[2] In 1801, Canard made a rough attempt to find the mathematical formulae for the laws which are the object of political economy.[3] But most important of all, in 1803, J.-B. Say published his *Traité d'Economie Politique* a ' simple exposition of the way in which wealth is formed, distributed and consumed '.

This is an important date, not perhaps in the history of economic doctrines, but in the history of the methods of exposition of political economy. For J.-B. Say, in this treatise which soon became popular, emphasised the theoretic and systematic character which should be manifested in the teaching of this science. Say does indeed praise Adam Smith for having substituted the ' spirit of analysis ' for the ' spirit of system ', for having ' applied to political economy the new method of treatment of the sciences, in not seeking for principles in the abstract, but in going back from the most constantly observed facts to their causes '. Nevertheless, he condemns Adam Smith's book for being no more ' than a confused assembly of the sanest principles of political economy, supported by luminous examples, and of the strangest notions of statistics, mingled with instructive reflections ; but it is a complete treatise neither of the one nor of the other ; his book is a vast chaos of sound ideas, jumbled up with positive knowledge '.[4] It is, as Ricardo maintained, the logical arrangement of the contents which constitutes the superiority of

---

[1] *Prog. de l'esp. humain*, 9ᵉ époque.
[2] Germain Garnier, *Abrégé élémentaire des principes de l'économie politique.* An iv. (1796), p. 3.
[3] *Ibid.* An x. (1801).   [4] J.-B. Say, *Traité d'Economie Politique*, vol. 1. p. vi.

Say's book.[1] Political economy, according to Say, shows how wealth arises, is distributed and destroyed : the causes which favour its development, or bring about its decline : its influence on the population, on the power of States and on the happiness or misery of peoples. It is an exposition of *general facts*, which are constantly the same under the same circumstances. Laws of the production, distribution and consumption of wealth—this is the order of treatment invented and made classical by J.-B. Say. In the subject under consideration, as in all subjects, there are *general* or *constant* facts, which are the subject of political economy, and *particular* or *variable* facts, which are the subject of statistics. The complexity of phenomena alone conceals the link between particular facts, and this does not prevent the link from existing : the principle of gravitation is a ' general fact ' which explains the rise of a jet of water no less than the fall of heavy bodies. ' In political economy, it is a general fact that the interest on money rises when the lender is exposed to greater risks : shall I conclude that the principle is false because I have known money to be lent at low interest under risky conditions ? The lender may have been ignorant of his risk, gratitude may have required sacrifices from him : and the *general law*, disturbed in a particular case, would resume all its sway once the disturbing cause ceased to act '.[2] Hume condemned the definition of natural law proposed by Malebranche. The physiocrats, on the other hand, took it as the starting point of their speculations. Now it is true that Hume was one of Adam Smith's masters in political economy ; but the physiocrats were his masters too. From this dual influence springs the uncertainty in Adam Smith's method : is it inductive or deductive, empirical or rational ? At this time it was this same French rationalism, which, transmitted from the physiocrats to the ideologues, was once again influencing English thought, and was giving the victory as between the same two tendencies, naturalistic and rationalistic, which were contending with one another in the thought of Hume and Adam Smith, to the rationalistic tendency.

The conclusion is that the systematic and deductive nature of Ricardo's political economy may have originated from a French influence, introduced through the mediation of Bentham and James Mill. As regards Bentham, in any case, the matter is very doubtful. No doubt, Bentham had intended, as Say and Ricardo later intended, to put order into the ' chaos ' of Adam Smith ; and the Russian statesman Speranski, on receiving from Dumont the manuscript of Bentham's *Political Economy* in 1804, commended it in terms that could be applied to Say's book without any alteration. He praised ' the extent of its views, the clearness and precision of its classifications and the systematic character of its arrangements '. At last the prayers of Necker had been fully answered. ' Adam Smith has furnished us

[1] Ricardo, *Principles*, Pref. p. 6.
[2] J.-B. Say, *Traité d'économie politique*, discours préliminaire.

with inestimable materials. But, as he was more occupied in proving and deducing from experience the truths he established, he did
not think of making a *corps de doctrine* out of them. The more closely
he is examined the more obvious is the want of method ; . . . I
believe that in following the plan of Mr. Bentham, Political Economy
would occupy a position much more natural, more easily to be
studied, and more scientific '.[1] But the point of view which Bentham
adopted in order to systematise political economy was diametrically
opposed to the point of view of J.-B. Say and Ricardo. For Bentham
the principle of utility had always been essentially a precept, the basis
of a system of obligations. *It is necessary* to work in the interests of
the general utility, *it is necessary* to secure the identity of private and
public interest. Such is the art of the legislator, of which political
economy constitutes one branch. Therefore, far from neglecting
that part of economics, to which Adam Smith gave the name of
political economy, in order to transfer this name to that other part of
Adam Smith's work which consists of really theoretic investigations,
Bentham in his pamphlet completely suppressed ' the inquiry into
the nature and the causes of the wealth of nations ', and, instead of
separating theory from practice, he on the contrary completely
absorbed the theory in the practice.

But perhaps, within the limits which we have defined, the influence
of James Mill was more real. He had a taste for abstract deduction,
and his son Stuart Mill, when he later set himself up to judge his
father and master, held his chief fault to be ' that of trusting too much
to the intelligibleness of the abstract, when not embodied in the
concrete '.[2] Nothing is so characteristic in this respect as his definition of history in the preface of the *History of British India*. History
for him is not a recital, but a methodical description of social phenomena and the laws which regulate them. The historian needs ' the
most profound knowledge of the laws of human nature, which is the
end, as well as the instrument of everything ', ' the most perfect
comprehension of the principles of human society, or the course
into which the laws of human nature impel the human being, in his
gregarious state, or when formed into a complex body along with
others of his kind '. Finally he requires ' a clear comprehension of
the practical play of the machinery of government ; for, in like
manner as the general laws of motion are counteracted and modified
by friction, the power of which may yet be accurately ascertained and
provided for, so it is necessary for the historian correctly to appreciate
the counteraction which the more general laws of human nature may
receive from individual or specific varieties, and that allowance for
it with which his anticipations and conclusions ought to be formed '.
In this programme, which was much admired by Ricardo,[3] can be
seen an attempt to apply to general history the method which is

[1] Bowring, vol. x. p. 416.   [2] Stuart Mill, *Autobiography*, pp. 23-24.
[3] Ricardo to Say, Dec. 18, 1817

proper to the new economic science ; and it must be admitted that Mill, during the long walks which he loved to take with Ricardo, was chiefly concerned to give him lessons in method.

It should also be noted that Mill was acquainted with French economic literature.   Since 1814, he had been personally acquainted with J.-B. Say.   Say had gone to Place, with a letter of introduction from Godwin ; and Mill told Place that he would like an interview with Say to be arranged for Ricardo and for himself. This was arranged in December, when Say returned from Edinburgh, where he had been visiting Dugald Stewart.   He went to see Ricardo at Gatcomb, and Ricardo went with him to Bentham's house at Ford Abbey : thus, through the mediation of Place and Mill, the three principal representatives of the new ideas were together for a day. Was not James Mill a disciple of J.-B. Say ?   Later on he borrowed from him, with some modifications, his arrangement of economic subjects.   He had already borrowed from him, in 1808, in his *Commerce defended*, the theory which J.-B. Say had called the ' theory of markets '.[1]   According to this theory the production of commodities is the only cause which creates a market for the commodities produced. If the number of commodities is very great, then the people is abundantly provided : if it is small, they are scantily provided ; in the first case, the country is rich, in the second case, poor ; but always, one half of the goods is exchangeable for the other half, and the demand is equal to the supply.   This is a new development of the fundamental thesis of the natural identity of interests ; and J.-B. Say is right to include among the consequences of his theory the following, ' that each is interested in the prosperity of all, and that the prosperity of one kind of industry is favourable to the prosperity of all the others '.   This is proved not by an appeal to experience, which might be deceptive, since economic phenomena are constantly being changed by the arbitrary intervention of governments, but deductively, on the basis of the laws of human nature, like a theorem of Euclid.   It was Mill who, about the same period,[2] introduced for the first time into the language of political economy the Euclidean metaphor, which is even more audacious than the Newtonian metaphor.

James Mill moreover had studied the Physiocrats ; he undertook the article on ' Economists ' in the supplement of the *Encyclopaedia Britannica*, and attempted to prove the fundamental identity of Quesnay's philosophy with that of Bentham, in spite of the difference of expression.   At the same time he emphasised the nobility of the ambitions conceived by the Physiocrats :—to transform society without a revolution by taking stand upon a small number of simple theoretic principles.   In one of the notes he had added to his· trans-

---

[1] James Mill in his turn taught Ricardo the theory, whose origin he does not seem to have known before J.-B. Say's visit.

[2] *Ed. Rev.* Jan. 1809 (vol. xiii. p. 310).

lation of Villers' work on the Reformation,[1] he had already pointed out how few authors there were in France whose writings sufficiently prepared the way for the Revolution in the eighteenth century. Obviously when working, with as much success as persistence, at making Ricardo and Bentham, both of them heads of schools and heads of parties, together the heads of the same school and of the same party, he was thinking of the ' philosophers', of the ' encyclopaedists ' and of the ' economists ' : he intended to make of Ricardo the Quesnay of nineteenth century England.[2] Thus James Mill exercised a profound influence on Ricardo's intellectual destiny. But he was less a master than a professor, teaching the application of a method which he had not himself invented, and which he had learnt less from Bentham than from J.-B. Say and his French predecessors at a time when he may perhaps have already adopted the Benthamite philosophy of civil and penal law, but had not yet become personally acquainted with Bentham.

To mark the difference, however, between the two economic philosophies, is it enough to say that Adam Smith's method is more inductive and more historical, and Ricardo's more demonstrative and more deductive ?   This seems to have been the opinion of Stuart Mill, at the time when he escaped from his father's yoke and began his series of pitiful and fruitless efforts to escape from the narrowmindedness of the Philosophical Radicals, and set out to search for a complete philosophy.   One of the first ideas he discovered on his journey of intellectual exploration was, so he tells us, the idea which was then in vogue among the thinkers of Germany and France, that the progress of the human spirit follows a certain necessary order, that all questions of political institutions are relative, not absolute, and that different institutions not only do in fact but *ought* to correspond to different degrees of human progress ;—in short, that any general theory or philosophy of politics presupposes a preliminary theory of human progress, in other words a philosophy of history.[3] Now this gives rise to yet another distinction between Bentham and James Mill.
It can indeed be said that the idea of a philosophy of history is totally foreign to Bentham's thought.   It is, on the other hand, fundamental to James Mill ; and, under his influence and also under other influences which were contemporary with his, Ricardo's political economy may be held to be more imbued with the idea of history or progress than Adam Smith's political economy had been. Certainly, the same difference always persists between the two thinkers : the elements of philosophy of history which occur in Adam Smith he owed to the empirical observation of facts, while in Ricardo

---

[1] This translation appeared in 1805.
[2] This was clearly seen by Malthus (*Quarterly Review*, Jan. 1824, pp. 333 *seq.*).
[3] Stuart Mill, *Autobiography*, pp. 161-162.

progress is held to be submitted to laws, the necessity of which can
be established by arguing from certain simple and constant data.
In 1809, in the *Edinburgh Review*, Mill lamented that philosophers
had not yet succeeded in agreeing on the rules suitable for determining
the principal degrees of civilisation,[1] and his *History of British India*,
which was begun as early as 1806, was perhaps, for the most part, an
attempt to define the notions of civilisation and progress, by reference
to a particular example.   James Mill laid down the principle that a
nation is civilised to the precise extent to which *utility* is the object
of all its efforts ; [2] and, far from using the empirical knowledge which
he obtained from the history of British India to determine inductively
the necessary movement of progress from the barbarous state to
civilisation, he rather writes conjectural history, and, in most cases,
he takes as point of departure a definition of progress based on the
constant facts of human nature, and deduces from that what, in fact,
the progress of Hindu society must have been.[3]   According to Stuart
Mill the idea of a theory of progress and of a philosophy of history
was due to a reaction against the ideas of the eighteenth century,
against the philosophy of enlightenment.   This estimate is false : the
Saint-Simonians and Auguste Comte owed their philosophy of progress to Turgot and Condorcet ; and it is perhaps to Condorcet at
least as much as to Hartley, Priestley and Godwin that James Mill
from the earliest years of his literary production, owed the doctrine
which he held to be fundamental—that is, the doctrine that the human
species is essentially perfectible, or capable of progress.[4]   Political
economy was still thought of as a knowledge of laws, but these laws
were no longer merely static laws, laws of equilibrium, but were also
dynamic laws, laws of evolution or of progress.   It was no longer a
study, as it had been for Adam Smith, of ' the nature and causes ',
but of ' the nature and progress ' of economic phenomena.   The two
new truths which Ricardo incorporated in political economy, and made
in a sense classical, were the invention of Malthus : that is to say, the
law of population and the law of rent on land.[5]   At the beginning of
1810, Ricardo had just made Malthus' acquaintance : the two
families were on friendly terms after 1811.[6]   At this time James
Mill and, it seems likely, Ricardo also were already Malthusians, in
the sense that they accepted the principle of population.   In 1815,
Ricardo used against Malthus the law of rent which Malthus himself
had just formulated.   Now these two laws are laws of progress.   In
this way the dominant idea of Condorcet was perpetuated through
his adversary Malthus till it reached James Mill and Ricardo.   Let
us try to work out the stages through which was brought about this

---

[1] *Ed. Rev.* July, 1809, (vol. xiv. p. 413).
[2] *Hist. of British India*, vol. ii. pp. 149-150.   [3] *Ibid.* vol. i. pp. 172 *seq.*
[4] Condorcet, *Prog. de l'esprit humain*, 1re époque.
[5] *Ed. Rev.* Jan. 1837.
[6] See Ricardo's letters to Malthus, 1810-1811.

introduction into the Utilitarian political economy of the idea of a law of progress, or, if you like, a law of evolution.

Condorcet had demanded that, in the study of man, the knowledge of the laws of his individual nature should be completed by the knowledge of the laws of his social nature ; above all he had demanded that a science be constituted which should study not the co-existence of individuals in one and the same society, but the succession of social phenomena in time. ' If there exists a science of foretelling the progress of the human species, and of directing and hastening it, the history of what it has achieved should be the primary basis of this science '. Even prejudices and errors would be justified at every stage of our progress, by the general laws of our faculties ; and the development of intellectual and moral faculties, if followed from generation to generation in the mass of individuals, would present a picture of the progress of the human spirit. ' This progress is sub-mitted to the same general laws which can be observed in the indi-vidual development of our faculties, since it is the result of this development considered at one and the same time in a large number of individuals united in society. But the result supplied by each moment depends on that supplied by the preceding moments and has its influence on those in the time to come '. Hence it is possible in the social sciences as in other sciences, to found on the experience of the past a prophecy regarding ' the future destinies of the human species, from the results of its history '. ' Since opinions formed from the experience of the past, on objects of the same class, are the only rule of the conduct of the wisest men, why should the philosopher be forbidden to rest his conjectures on this same basis, provided he does not attribute to them a certainty superior to that which can spring from the number, the consistency and the exactness of the observations ? ' [1] Malthus discussed the theory of indefinite progress and objected to the current formula as not being sufficiently complex to square with the facts. Human beings are not only creatures endowed with intellectual and moral faculties ; they are physiological organisms, submitted to physical conditions of existence. Popula-tion on the one hand and subsistence on the other do not increase according to the same ' law ' : and there is here at once a double ' law ' of progress, which is stated by Malthus. Further, man is able, by the free exercise of his intelligence, to put a ' moral restraint ' on his instincts, and so to re-establish the harmony between the two increases.

But is this different from what was maintained by Condorcet ? Does not the difference between the two apparently rival philosophies of Condorcet and Malthus tend to disappear ? It seems that this was indeed the opinion expressed by James Mill in 1805 in a note in his edition of Villers' book. No doubt he maintains that ' those circumstances in the constitution of this world, which have

[1] *Prog. de l'esp. humain*, ire époque ; 9e époque.

been so largely descanted upon, which seem opposed to the establishment of perfect happiness or virtue on the earth, prove nothing ';
that the causes which check the ' natural and fixed ' tendency of human
nature towards perfection can only be temporary and accidental.
He does, however, pay attention to Malthus' objections : he intends,
so he tells us, to free the doctrine of perfectibility ' from the erroneous
application which may be made of it ', and, in accord with
Malthus on this point, he confines himself to seeing in the idea of
perfection the great model on which wise men and politicians must
bring their attention to bear ' with wisdom and discretion ', when
they are sketching or carrying out plans for the administration of
public affairs.[1]   In short, the problem is to reconcile the law of perfectibility with the law of population, to see in the latter no more than
the simple statement of the conditions which must be considered in
order to bring man nearer to perfection.   Malthus had already
approached this problem in the second edition of his book ; and this
became James Mill's main preoccupation, especially from the time
when, about the year 1808, he frankly gave his support to Malthus'
principle.   In James Mill and in Ricardo we shall again come across
the conflict, always springing up again but always beneath the surface,
between the two conceptions of economic progress, the one optimistic
and the other pessimistic.

But the problem to be solved became still further complicated
when, in 1815, Malthus formulated a new law of evolution derived in
the main from the two first laws, (since it places face to face and in
conflict intelligent man on the one hand, and on the other hand,
land of limited quantity and fecundity).   This is the law of rent.
' It may be laid down . . . as an incontrovertible truth, that as a
nation reaches any considerable degree of wealth, and any considerable fullness of population (which cannot occur without a considerable fall at once in the profits of capital and in the wages of labour)
the separation of rents, as a kind of fixture upon lands of a certain
quality, is a law as invariable as the action of the principle of gravity '.[2]
Now the law of rent on land, like the law of population, became
an integral part of the economic doctrine professed by Ricardo and
James Mill.

To what extent should Malthus be taken to have discovered the
new law ?   It is possible, as Buckle claims, that Hume may have had
an inkling of it ;[3] as early as 1777, Anderson gave its precise formula.[4]
But isolated intuitions cannot be held to constitute the invention of a
fundamental theorem.   Does not Anderson himself appear not to have
realised that his observations contradicted Adam Smith's ideas on

---

[1] *Essay on the Spirit and Influence of the Reformation*, by Villers, p. 25, note.
[2] Malthus, *Pol. Econ.* (1836 ed.), p. 153.
[3] Letter from Hume to Adam Smith, Ap. 18, 1776.
[4] Anderson, James, *Observations on the Means of Exciting a Spirit of National Industry*, p. 45, note.

rent ? The new theory of rent on land is, from one point of view, the end of the logical development of economic thought ; it may be taken to be implied in the law of population of 1797, and its formula can be seen disentangling itself with a growing clearness, in the successive editions of Malthus' book.[1] But above all, historical circumstances should here be taken into consideration. The period of the great war set up against each other in Great Britain two distinct economic worlds, whose interests only coincided by accident. Agricultural produce and industrial commodities are not produced under the same conditions : from the earliest editions of his book Malthus made many observations on this subject, roused by the scarcity years of 1794 and 1795, and then of 1800 and 1801. Inferior land had been put under cultivation during the war, and the price of corn had gone up, but at the same time rent on land had risen. Parliamentary inquiries showed up the correlation of the two facts ; and when in 1814 and 1815 the re-establishment of peace looked like putting an end to the accidental isolation of the English people, the landed proprietors, in defiance of the general interest, demanded a new Corn Law which, by protecting English corn, would prevent the inferior land from going out of cultivation, and the rent on land from falling.[2]

In 1814, the state of the countryside, the bad harvests, and the increasing difficulty of finding agricultural labourers disturbed the economist Wakefield, and he communicated his anxieties to his friend Francis Place.[3] Place himself studied the question, and declared to James Mill that, after a certain amount of statistical research, he would be able ' to shew a clear and concise view of the operation of the Corn Laws on the mass of the community '.   It was the people who must be enlightened since nothing could be done with Parliament, which was given over to the influence of the large proprietors.[4] Mill encouraged Place to converse with him on these questions.[5] In return Place ventured to suggest to Mill that he should deal with the problem himself in writing. The truth which needed to be spread was still the doctrine of Malthus. ' When will the wholesome truth be acknowledged, that population is constantly pressing against the limits of production, when will governments cease their attempts to counteract the inimitable laws of nature, cease to sacrifice one part of the community, to gratify the pride, the ignorance, and the folly of another part, cease to promote the misery of the many, to increase the power but not the happiness of the few, when will they learn that a virtuous and happy population is more worth, than mere numbers, that a wise

[1] Bonar, *Malthus and His Work*, p. 222.

[2] Cannan, *A Hist. of the Theories of Production and Distribution*, etc., pp. 147 *seq.*

[3] Add. MSS. Brit. Mus. 33,152, f. 78-9, Wakefield to Place, Aug. 17, 1814.

[4] *Ibid.* f. 84, Place to Mill, Sept. 9, 1814.

[5] *Ibid.* f. 92, Mill to Place, Oct. 14, 1814. ' Write to me particularly about Corn Laws.'

and free people are infinitely more to be desired than a nominally
rich nation of Tyrants, Slaves, and Fools '?[1]   The Malthusian work,
which Place demanded from James Mill, was to be written by
Ricardo ; and Malthus preceded Ricardo.   Besides, though the
Benthamites were not called upon to discover the new theory, did
they not foresee it ?   In 1814, in an article published by the *Eclectic
Review*, James Mill stated that there was a divergence between the
interests of the landed proprietors and the general interest and
warned the landowners of the consciousness of itself which the
majority would inevitably gain in the advance of knowledge, and of the
power which it could use so as to make its interests prevail by force.
He pointed out a divergence between the interests of the landed
proprietor and the interests of the farmer : the farmer would not
suffer from the free importation of corn if he could escape paying the
exorbitant rents extorted from him by the landlord.   To escape
from this abnormal situation, he advocated measures which were
almost revolutionary : that all the leases should be annulled or bought
back.   To buy them back would cost less than the subsidy paid
annually by England to a single foreign sovereign ; and it was just
that the landowners, like the officers on land and sea and like the
military caterers, should lose, on the re-establishment of peace, the
exorbitant gains which were brought them by the war.[2]   These
class conflicts seriously compromised, as we shall see in the sequel,
the principle of the identity of interests ; but they attracted attention,
and the Benthamites, who were the defenders of the interest of the
greatest number, were waiting for a doctrine capable of accounting
for them.   Then the moment would have come for them to play, as
always, their role of assimilators and organisers.   On every side, the
new theory was in process of elaboration.

In 1814, Buchanan, commenting on Adam Smith, remarked that,
' rent being a surplus above wages and profit, whatever yields this
surplus may be said to pay a rent.   The inventor of a machine for
abridging labour, were he to keep his secret, might sell his goods for
such a price as would yield a rent or surplus above wages and profit ;
but when the secret is known, and others come to abridge labour in
the same way, the competition reduces the price and his advantage is
lost.   In this manner improvements in manufactures benefit society
by a fall of price on the goods manufactured ; but improvements in
agriculture, which occasion no fall of price, benefit only the landlord
by an increase of rent '.   Further, why do not improvements in
agriculture involve a fall in prices ?   It is because ' manufacturing
industry increases its produce in proportion to the demand, and the
price falls ; but the produce of land cannot be so increased ; and a
high price is still necessary to prevent consumption from exceeding

[1] Add. MSS. Brit. Mus. 33,152, f. 93, Place to Mill, Charing Cross, London,
Oct. 17, 1814.
[2] *Eclectic Review*, July, 1814, pp. 1 *seq.*

the supply '.[1] Does not this application of the principle of population include all that is essential in the theory of differential rent ?

Then West, in an anonymous treatise entitled *An Essay on the Application of Capital to Land*, in which he set out the reflections roused in him by the labours of the Parliamentary Committees, and attempted to point out the uselessness of increasing the duties on importation, and, defining the laws of diminishing returns more rigorously than Malthus had done, tried to prove that, ' in the progress of the improvement of cultivation the raising of rude produce becomes progressively more expensive, or, in other words, the ratio of the net produce of land to its gross produce is continually diminishing '. He rejected the explanation proposed by Adam Smith, according to whom the lesser increase in the product of agricultural labour is due to a lesser development in the division of labour : for in this case the slow progress in agricultural labour as compared with industrial labour would be *comparative* not *positive*, while, according to West, there is an absolute or positive diminution of return for every equal quantity of labour. The difference depends on the very nature of agricultural labour, which must be used either to take new land into cultivation or to submit to a more intense cultivation land which is already under cultivation. The gradual diminution of the produce is, according to the particular case, either more than compensated, just compensated, or less than compensated for by the progress of the division of labour and of machinery. But, in the last resort, the causes which *tend* to make agricultural labour less productive must outweigh those which *tend* to make it more productive.[2] If returns from land and from industry were to increase in the same proportion, the profits on capital ought to be constantly increasing ; if they fall, it is because of the law of diminishing returns.

At the same moment, Malthus made known to the public his notes on the *Nature and Progress of Rent*,[3] which he had compiled while teaching at the East India College. ' It has been my intention ', he said, ' at some time or other, to put them in a form for publication ; and the very near connection of the subject of the present inquiry with the topics immediately under discussion, has induced me to hasten its appearance at the present moment '.[3] In the cultivation of land man is constantly obliged to have recourse to land of inferior quality by reason first of the constant increase of population and of the demand for food, and secondly, of the limited amount of land which provides a given fertility. Necessarily, therefore, the price of the objects of primary necessity rises without ceasing ; and con-

[1] *Observations on the Subjects treated of in Dr. Smith's Inquiry into the Nature and Causes of the Wealth of Nations*, by David Buchanan, 4th vol. of the 1814 ed., pp. 33 *seq.*
[2] Cannan (*A History of the Theories of Production and Distribution*, 1894) observes (p. 159) that the verb *tend* is found employed here for the first time in its generally accepted scientific sense.
[3] Malthus, *Inquiry into the Nature and Progress of Rent*, 1815, Pref.

sequently the remuneration of the labour and of the capital applied
to the first lands under cultivation would rise, if it were not that, by
virtue of the principles laid down by Adam Smith, profits and wages,
like the price of food, tend to be the same everywhere ; hence, on
the more fertile lands, there is a residue, which is precisely rent, that
is ' that portion of the value of the whole produce which remains to
the owner of the land, after all the outgoings belonging to its cultivation, of whatever kind, have been paid, including the profits of the
capital employed, estimated according to the usual and ordinary rate
of the profits of agricultural capital at the time being '.

Finally, it was in reply to Malthus' book that Ricardo almost
immediately drew up and published an *Essay* in which he treated of
the influence of a low price of corn on the profits of stock.[1]   Ricardo
accepts the definition of rent given by Malthus.   But, in regard to
this definition, he devotes himself to a task of logical revision in which
may be distinguished the influence of the peculiar genius of James
Mill.   He simplifies the theory.   Malthus distinguished between
three causes of the phenomenon of rent : in the first place, the power
of the land to provide a greater quantity of necessaries than are
required for the subsistence of the people employed in cultivating it ;
in the second place, the tendency of the supply of food to create its
own demand and to increase the population ; and in the third place,
the relative scarcity of fertile lands, which is necessary if a portion of
the general surplus is to be separated off in the specific form of a rent
offered to a landlord.   Ricardo retains only the third cause.   He
also universalises the theory.   Apart from the necessity for agriculture to have recourse to less fertile land, Malthus admitted the
influence on variations in rent of other causes, such as accumulation
of capital which lowers the profits on capital, increase of population
which lowers wages, and progress in agricultural industry.   Ricardo
neglects the last cause, to which can be attributed only very temporary
effects ; and above all, he treats the theory of rent, understood as the
difference between the costs of production on lands of unequal
fertility, as the fundamental theory from which are derived the
theories of wages and profits.   Variations in wages have an influence
not on rent, which is given, but on profits ; and Malthus was wrong
still to retain partially, on the subject of profits, Adam Smith's
theory, according to which profits rise and fall for commercial reasons
which are independent of the supply of food.   ' Profits of stock fall
only, because land equally well adapted to produce food cannot be
procured ; and the degree of the fall of profits . . . depends wholly
on the increased expense of production '.   This, Ricardo tells us, is
a very important principle and one that has been almost entirely
neglected by the economists.   Finally, Malthus, like the advocates of
the Corn Bill, argued from his theory of rent to the necessity of a
policy of protection.   Ricardo sets out to prove, like West, the

[1] Ricardo, Works, p. 373, note.

necessity of tolerating the free importation of corn : the rise in profits and in real wages will compensate, and more than compensate, the loss suffered by the landowners. Now, between the members of any one group of theorists, agreement is reached as much on the programme of practical applications as on the principles, and perhaps even more so ; and it was by associating the theory of differential rent with the theory of free-trade, that Ricardo definitely incorporated it with the tradition of Adam Smith and the orthodox political economy.[1]

This little treatise was the sketch of the large work which Ricardo published two years later. ' I hear from Mr. Mill ', wrote Ricardo to J.-B. Say, on August 18, 1815, ' that a number of people in this country do not understand me because I have not developed my ideas enough ; and he exhorts me to resume the exposition from the beginning and in a lengthier manner '.[2] ' These principles (the principles of Rent, Profit, and Wages) ', he wrote to Trower on October 29, 1815, ' are so linked and connected with everything belonging to the science of Political Economy, that I consider the just view of them as of the first importance. It is on this subject, where my opinions differ from the great authority of Adam Smith, Malthus, etc., that I should wish to concentrate all the talent I possess, not only for the purpose of establishing what I think correct principles, but of drawing important deductions from them. For my own satisfaction I shall certainly make the attempt, and perhaps with repeated revisions during a year or two I shall at last produce something that may be understood '.[3] We can now see clearly enough the part played, in the formation of the new political economy, by the principle of population, as completed by the law of rent which was derived from it : it was a principle of unification. Henceforth, variations in rent, wages, and profits could not be studied separately as they could in the time of Adam Smith : they are derived from one and the same law. And political economy, in conformity with the dream of James Mill, now resumed, though in a new sense, the rigorously systematic character which it had presented in France in the eighteenth century with Quesnay and the Physiocrats : in 1817 appeared the *Principles of Political Economy and Taxation*.

To sum up, to what can the influence exerted on Ricardo by Bentham and James Mill be reduced ? James Mill's personal influence was considerable ; and it is perhaps to this that political economy owes the systematic and deductive character which it assumed in Ricardo. But the idea of political economy understood as a science of laws—laws of equilibrium and laws of progress—static laws and dynamic laws—does not come from Bentham. The new ideas which, with Ricardo, were incorporated with the classical political economy

[1] Oct. 20, 1816. Add. MSS. Brit. Mus. 33,152, f. 225.
[2] J.-B. Say, *Mélanges et Correspondance*, p. 95.
[3] Ricardo to Trower. Oct. 29, 1815.

came to him from Malthus. The theoretic and rational method came to him from the French economists : it was taught him by James Mill, who had the temperament of a logician but also the temperament of a disciple, and borrowed his doctrines from others, being content to give them a new rigour and nothing more. James Mill did not so much give Ricardo *his* doctrine as transmit to him *a* doctrine ; or rather, he did not so much give him a doctrine as develop in him the doctrinal leaning and make him a doctrinaire.

3. THE EDUCATION OF THE PEOPLE

The question of knowing to what extent the useful qualities of human nature do or do not come within the range of the power of education, is one of the most important ones, wrote James Mill in the article which, in 1818, he devoted to ' Education ', in the Supplement to the *Encyclopaedia Britannica*. According to Helvetius, leaving aside the relatively small number of individuals who are born incomplete and obviously below the average, the vast majority of men may be taken to be equally susceptible of mental excellence, and remediable causes of their inequalities are discoverable. Certainly, only Helvetius was of this opinion ; but, said James Mill, ' Helvetius, alone, is a host '.[1] Bentham himself had been a disciple of Helvetius ; and moreover he had already, in 1797, in his *Administration of the Poor*, touched on the pedagogic problem. He had sketched a programme of popular education, and advocated the method, invented by Dr. Bell, of teaching by monitors.[2] But it was after 1808 that this part of Bentham's doctrine received all its development : James Mill was a born propagandist, and if education, as Helvetius maintained, was all-powerful in the formation of character, then education was the instrument to use in order to convert the nation to the Utilitarian morality.

James Mill tried on the person of his eldest son, John Stuart, the first experimental verification of Helvetius' theory. Stuart Mill, born in May, 1806, was two years old when his father made Bentham's acquaintance ; and it was in the following year that he took up the education of his son on a systematic plan.[3] ' It is, then, a fact, that the early sequences to which we are accustomed form the primary habits ; and that the primary habits are the fundamental character of the man. The consequence is most important ; for it follows, that, as soon as the infant, or rather the embryo, begins to feel, the character begins to be formed ; and that the habits, which are then contracted, are the most pervading and operative of all. Education, then, or the care of forming the habits, ought to commence, as much as possible,

[1] *Education*, pp. 18-20. [2] Bowring, vol. viii. p. 427, note.
[3] On J. S. Mill's education, see *Autobiography* ; Graham Wallas, *Life of Place* ; Bain, *John Stuart Mill*.

with the period of sensation itself ; and at no period, is the utmost vigilance of greater importance, than the first '.[1] We see, therefore, that James Mill took charge of the intellectual guidance of his son as early as possible. Did not Mill hope in 1809 to make his son follow the example of Bentham, who had begun his classical studies at almost as precocious an age ? John attacked the study of the Greek language with Aesop's *Fables* and with the *Anabasis*, and of arithmetic, while reading, for his own amusement, historical books and works ' which exhibited men of energy and resource in unusual circumstances, struggling against difficulties and overcoming them '. Then opened the second cycle of his studies. At the age of eight he was learning Latin. Soon he was studying Aristotle's *Rhetoric*, ' the first expressly scientific treatise on any moral or psychological subject which I had read ' ; this his father made him study with particular care, and then sum up in the form of synoptic tables. At the same time, during the second cycle, he was learning elementary geometry and algebra, the differential calculus and other parts of transcendental mathematics, and finally manuals of experimental science, and of chemistry in particular. His father excused him Latin composition more or less and Greek composition entirely, but he made him practice writing in English verse—for two reasons : first, that certain things are better and more strongly expressed in verse than in prose, which is a real advantage ; and secondly that men as a general rule attach more value to verse than it deserves : for this reason it is worth while acquiring the power of writing it. Finally, at the age of twelve, Stuart Mill entered on the third and last stage of his instruction : it was now no longer a question of the auxiliary instruments of thought, but of the thoughts themselves. It is characteristic that Stuart Mill did not know Bentham's own works until later, after the completion of his education.[2] His father had not wished John Mill to accept Bentham's ideas without examination, simply because they came from the venerated friend of his father, or for Benthamism to become for him a kind of religious belief of ' ipsedixitism ' or of ' dogmatism ', in the disparaging sense which Bentham had given to the word. None the less, he strove with all his powers to make of Stuart Mill, by a more arduous way, a typical thinker, citizen and man, in accordance with the doctrine of Helvetius and Bentham.[3] Stuart Mill studied logic in Aristotle's *Organon*, in some of the Latin treatises on scholastic logic, and finally in Hobbes' *Computatio sive Logica*. In 1819, he passed to the study of political economy (Ricardo's book had already been out two years), and applied the art of reasoning to the study of the mechanism of interests, to what has been called the dogmatics of egoism. The method of instruction was as original as the plan of studies. James Mill was an admirer of the Greek philosophers and in particular of the Socratics, and he used the maieutic method with

---

[1] *Education*, p. 32.   [2] *Autobiography*, pp. 64-67.
[3] See Bowring, vol. x. p. 473, Letter from Mill to Bentham.

his son. Intending, to what was perhaps an exaggerated extent, to
awaken the activity of the faculties by leading the pupil to discover
everything for himself, he gave his explanations not before, but after,
his son had fully recognised the seriousness of the difficulties. He
' not only gave me an accurate knowledge of these two great subjects,
(logic and political economy) as far as they were then understood, but
made me a thinker on both '. Having pedagogic principles of his
own on all teachable subjects, even on the art of reading aloud, James
Mill tried them on his son. He experimented on him with the
method of teaching by monitors ; and John Mill, as he learnt Latin,
taught it to his brothers and sisters as a supplementary method of
learning it himself.

In 1820, John Mill, at the age of fourteen, closed the period of his
earliest instruction by a journey to Paris. On the eve of his departure,
his father took him for a last solemn walk in Hyde Park, and
revealed to him the fact that he had received such an education as
would single him out among men. The fact that he knew more than
others know was to be attributed not to his personal merit but to the
exceptional and accidental advantage of having had a father capable of
instructing him, and prepared to devote the necessary care and time
to it ; he was not to be proud that he knew more than others who had
been less favoured ; it would be disgraceful if he did not know more.[1]
It was a systematic education, of which even the artificial nature
was to some extent intended—one cannot make an experiment without
having recourse to artifices and without *isolating* the phenomenon
which is to be observed so as to avoid the intervention of any disturbing action—but also to some extent involuntary. For James
Mill wanted to make his son at once a man of thought and a man of
action : but to attain the second end, was it enough to make him read
accounts of energetic lives and of heroic actions ?[2]   John Mill's
education was a constant subject of conversation among Bentham's
friends : it was discussed in Francis Place's shop. ' Wakefield ',
wrote Place, ' is a believer in innate propensities . . . and so fully is
he satisfied of the truth of his theory, that he expects to see your
John's innate propensities break out presently and form his character.
. . . The position I take against him is that the generality of children
are organised so nearly alike that they may by proper management be
made pretty nearly equally wise and virtuous '.[3]

If we are to believe Stuart Mill's testimony,[4] the facts would have
justified the disciples of Helvetius as against the partisans of innate
tendencies ; and truly, no one gives the impression of a *manufactured*
personality more than he does. Stuart Mill was indeed the work of
James Mill, working on the model suggested by Bentham. Nevertheless, although James Mill succeeded in making of his son a citizen

[1] *Autobiography*, p. 34.
[2] See *Life of Roebuck* for a description of Stuart Mill in 1824.
[3] Graham Wallas, p. 7.   [4] *Autobiography*, p. 30.

and a thinker, who if not eminent was at least eminently *useful*, there
are hints in Stuart Mill of an original nature, which was sentimental
and almost religious, and which was not made for the purely intellectual and abstract system imposed on it since childhood, and which
was all the time trying to react against it.

But James Mill, who was the disciple of Bentham and who, as it
were, set himself up as his master's Prime Minister, did not confine
his efforts to this isolated experience of individual pedagogy. Bentham and he (and Bentham through him), entered into relations,
round about 1810, with the philanthropists, religious or irreligious,
who at this time were obsessed with the idea of reforming humanity
by pedagogy. They were numerous : Bentham, and more particularly James Mill, who put Bentham's ideas into action, were
only distinguished from the others by a more enlightened understanding of the principles on which they took their stand, together
with more good sense and tenacity in action.

The tradition of Helvetius was perpetuated alongside of Bentham,
in Robert Owen, to whom it had been transmitted by William
Godwin. Owen denied the ideas of liberty, responsibility, merit and
punishment, and wished to reform humanity, and to form human
character by placing individuals, from birth, under certain social
conditions which he himself realised artificially in his model factory
in New Lanark. In 1813, Bentham became a shareholder in this
famous establishment, which was at that time under the direction of
Robert Owen and William Allen.[1] Romilly urged him to be prudent,
warning him that Owen was a madman.[2] No, replied Bentham,
Owen was not mad *simpliciter*, he was only mad *secundum quid* ; and
had not he himself been treated as a madman, in the days of
the *Panopticon* ? Bentham, who was so often unlucky in his
loans of capital, was justified this time as against the too-circumspect
Romilly : he drew profits from this philanthropic investment. It
was probably James Mill, the friend of William Allen, who acted as
intermediary between Bentham and Owen : for in the same year we
find James Mill and Francis Place engaged on revising Owen's *Essays
on the principle of the Formation of the Human Character*.[3]

William Allen was a Quaker, and from 1811, James Mill collaborated
with him in his journal, *The Philanthropist*. In 1809, he had been
persuaded by him to take an interest in the scholastic enterprises of
another Quaker, Joseph Lancaster by name.[4] Copying the methods
applied by Dr. Bell at Madras, he had founded a school in London,
and dreamt of covering England with establishments in each of which
a thousand children should receive, in squads of ten, instruction from
a hundred monitors, at the cost of five shillings per head per year. He
was a pure madman, lacking both the austere morals and the financial

[1] Bowring, vol. x. pp. 476-477. [2] Romilly to Dumont, May 26, 1814.
[3] Holyoake, *Sixty Years of an Agitator's Life*, vol. i. p. 120.
[4] Bain, pp. 113 *seq* ; Graham Wallas, p. 93 *seq*.

prudence which usually characterise Quakers, and he only escaped bankruptcy on two occasions thanks to assistance received from rich Quakers, dissenting ministers and independent philanthropists. In 1809, when the Royal Lancasterian Institution patronised by the King, the Queen and the Prince of Wales, was being organised to direct the enterprise, William Allen was one of the trustees and James Mill a member of the Financial Committee. It was in this Society that he made the acquaintance of Francis Place, who had been Lancaster's collaborator since 1810. Lancaster started his extravagances again. In 1813, after many efforts to reconcile Lancaster and the Society, the decision was made to retain the Lancaster system and to get rid of Lancaster, on whom an honourable title was bestowed. While the Association was being reorganised under the name of the British and Foreign School Society, James Mill, Place, Wakefield and Brougham were sketching the plan of a complete system of primary and secondary education for the town of London : the school which Lancaster had directed in London in the Borough Road was to be transformed into a training college, and London was to be divided into districts which were to be governed by independent school committees. To begin with, the West London Lancasterian Association was organised with the motto *Schools for All*, which was also the title of a pamphlet published by James Mill in 1812 to act as manifesto for the group.[1]

The novelty, in the idea of James Mill and his associates, was the extension of the Lancasterian system to secondary education. The idea came from Place, who belonged to the class of artisans who had become masters, and who suffered personally from the absence of educational establishments in which he could give his nine children a suitable education—not a simple classical education, but rather broad notions of mathematics, of the living languages, and of political and moral theory. It is the middle class which ' contains, beyond all comparison, the greatest proportion of the intelligence, industry, and wealth of the state. In it are the heads that invent, and the hands that execute ; the enterprise that projects, and the capital by which these projects are carried into operation. . . . In this country at least, it is this class which gives to the nation its character. The proper education of this portion of the people is therefore of the greatest possible importance to the well-being of the State '.[2] First Wakefield and then Mill gave their adherence to it. ' Mill ', wrote Wakefield to Place, ' is always at work, but never shows himself '.[3]

James Mill submitted the idea to Bentham who made it his own. He offered his garden for the site of the school. Two magnificent cotton-trees stood there : they were to be felled. A tablet on the wall of the garden recalled the fact that the house had once belonged to Milton : the wall and the tablet were to be destroyed.[4] Bentham

---

[1] *Schools for All not Schools for Churchmen only* (1812).
[2] *West. Rev.* vol. i. art. iv.   [3] Wakefield to Place, Dec. 7, 1813.
[4] Bain, p. 87 ; Hazlitt, *Spirit of the Age*, p. 6.

was especially concerned with tracing the architectural, administrative and pedagogic plan of the institution ; the result of his labour
was the work entitled *Chrestomathia*, ' a collection of papers, explanatory of the design of an Institution proposed to be set on foot under
the name of the Chrestomathic day school, for the extension of the
new system of instruction to the higher branches of learning, for the
use of the middling and higher ranks in life '.[1] The work was in
essence composed of two tables of contents : the first containing the
detail and the reasoned order of the subjects taught ; the second,
the principles of the new pedagogic system which was advocated.
Both programme and method were justified, from the point of view of
the principle of utility, by a comparison of the advantages received
and the disadvantages suffered, of profits and of losses. It was the
instruction which cost least : six pounds a year, Bentham estimated,
forty-two pounds for seven years. It was the instruction which
brought in most to the pupil, by reason of the arrangement of the
subjects taught, in order of decreasing utility, in such a way that no
pupil who left the establishment at any age lost the benefit of the years
of schooling that he had already had. Now for the first time, the
programme of a Utilitarian education, of a *chrestomathia*, was outlined :
classical teaching was suppressed,[2] scientific teaching was justified by
its utility.[3] Another way of comparing profits and losses was to
compare the amount of instruction carried to its maximum on the
one hand, and on the other, the amount of pain used to produce this
effect, reduced to its minimum by the application of the methods
conceived by Bell for making work attractive.[4] The programme was
concluded by a series of appendices. The first of these, which was
drawn up by Mill and Place, bore the title : ' Chrestomathic Proposal :
being a proposal for erecting by Subscription, and carrying on by the
name of the Chrestomathic School, a Day-School for the extension
of the new system to the higher branches of instruction and ranks
in life '. The following two contain documents relative to similar
pedagogic enterprises, previously undertaken. There remains a
fourth appendix, of enormous proportions and of a purely theoretic
nature. The chrestomathic school reminded Bentham of one of his
earliest manuscripts. In 1769, when he was discovering the principle
of the greatest happiness, he had seen in it the basis of what seemed
to him to be the only correct and instructive encyclopaedic arrangement—a map or plan of the field of thought and action ; and he
relates how he experienced the feeling of Archimedes, on discovering
his famous principle, when he scribbled on a sheet of paper his first
rough and imperfect draught.[5] After the lapse of forty, or nearly
forty years, he took up this draught again. It was a question of a
remodelling of d'Alembert's classification of the sciences, which was
now resumed from the point of view of the principle of utility: the

---

[1] Bowring, vol. viii. p. 1 *seq.*   [2] *Ibid.* p. 18.   [3] *Ibid.* p. 24.
[4] *Ibid.* p. 25.   [5] Bowring, vol. x. pp. 54, 79-80.

sciences were classed in relation to each other not by reason of the
intrinsic character of their objects or of their methods, but by reason
of their greater or less utility.   Now, this was also the order in which
things should be taught in the Chrestomathic school.   Bentham had
long since given up the study of principles, to pass to the examination
of practical applications ;   the examination of the pedagogic problem
now brought him back to the study of principles.   The same was
true, at the same period of James Mill ;   and this new turn which
James Mill gave to his intellectual activity was to have the most
important consequences as regards the formation of Philosophical
Radicalism.

It was James Mill who composed the article on ' Education ' for
the supplement of the *Encyclopaedia Britannica* in 1818.   He took the
word in its wide sense as it was understood by Helvetius.   ' Our
inquiry is concerned with everything which, from the first germ of
existence up till the final extinction of life, operates in such a way as
to affect the qualities of the mind on which happiness depends in any
degree whatsoever '. [1]   There was therefore a physical education,
which was little developed so far but the elements of which were to be
found in Erasmus Darwin and in Cabanis—a moral education,
which comprised domestic education, technical or scholastic education
(the only kind which is usually thought of in connection with the
word education)—and finally, social education, in which James Mill
distinguished, in another part of his article, between social education
properly speaking and political education.   The end of education
is first the happiness of the individual who is being educated, and then
the happiness of his fellows ;   it is defined by James Mill as ' the best
employment of all the means which can be made use of, by man, for
rendering the human mind to the greatest possible degree the cause of
human happiness '.   Further, practice cannot be separated from
theory :   for theory is nothing but the ' *whole* of the knowledge, which
we possess upon any subject, put into that order and form in which
it is most easy to draw from it good practical rules '. [2]

Now, the solution of the practical problem of education presupposes the preliminary solution of two great theoretic problems.
First, in order to know in what way things act on the spirit, it is
necessary to know how the spirit is constructed.   The least evil
which can befall him who tries to act on the spirit in ways which are
not adapted to its nature, is to lose his labour.   In the second place,
since happiness is the end, and the means must be exactly adapted to
the end, it is necessary to know which qualities of the spirit are chiefly
conducive to the happiness, as much of the agent himself as of his
fellows.   The solution of the second problem lies in a theory of virtue
which James Mill outlines, drawing his inspiration from the Greek
theory of the four virtues.   The solution of the first problem constitutes a theory of the mental life :   and thus James Mill found himself

[1] *Education*, p. 4.   [2] *Education*, pp. 3, 5.

led, in a pedagogic essay, to sum up, in a historical form, the theory of the association of ideas. For the laws of the succession of mental phenomena are the ' laws of human nature ', on which the science of education is based. 'As the happiness, which is the end of education, depends upon the actions of the individual, and as all the actions of man are produced by his feelings or thoughts, the business of education is, to make certain feelings or thoughts take place instead of others. The business of education, then, is to work upon the mental successions '.[1] The article of 1818 was an outline of Mill's great work, the *Analysis of the Phenomena of the Human Mind*, which appeared eleven years later, and which determined the psychological doctrine of Philosophical Radicalism.

But at the very moment when Bentham and his friends were trying to superimpose onto a reformed primary education, a secondary education conceived on the same plan, serious difficulties were threatening the execution of the first part of the programme. For the pedagogic problem was complicated by a religious problem. In opposition to the Royal Lancasterian Institution for the Education of the poor, which was directed by dissenters, liberals and freethinkers, there was founded in 1811 the National Society for promoting the Education of the poor according to the principles of the Established Church. To the name of Lancaster, who was applying Bell's principles, was opposed the name of Bell himself, a member of the Anglican Church. A bitter controversy arose between the *Edinburgh Review* and the *Quarterly Review*. James Mill was the acknowledged polemicist of the Lancasterian Institution ; in 1812 he wrote the anonymous paper already mentioned, the full title of which was : *Schools for all not Schools for Churchmen only*, and in February 1813 he contributed to the *Edinburgh Review* a long article devoted to the question. Bentham's *Chrestomathia* in 1818 and James Mill's article *Education*, in 1818, were only the sequel to this controversy.

James Mill, in the essay in the *Edinburgh Review*, recalled the fact, as a Scotsman proud of his origin, that the idea of popular education was a Scottish idea.[2] On the question whether the instruction of the people should be made a public service he admitted [3] that it was in conformity with the lessons of experience and with the principles of Adam Smith, to be as chary as possible of governmental intervention. Nevertheless, when it unfortunately happened that the people were extremely ignorant and too poor to pay for their instruction, it was necessary for the State to intervene to give the enterprise a push. To prevent the State abusing the powers which were entrusted to it and establishing a sort of intellectual despotism, one guarantee is enough— the freedom of the press. ' Grant, in any quarter of the globe, a

[1] *Education*, p. 9.   [2] *Ed. Rev.* Feb. 1813, art. ix. vol. xxi. p. 208.
[3] *Ibid*. pp. 211 *seq*.

reading people and a free press—and the prejudices on which misrule supports itself will gradually and silently disappear '.[1] And he declares that he is disposed, though with some hesitation, to desire that the State should come to the help of this great work, at least as concerns the erection of school buildings, and payment of small salaries, sufficient and no more than sufficient to ensure the residence of a master, chosen by the heads of the families of the district, and mainly paid by the pupils.   One thing, in any case, is certain, and is demonstrated by the ' analysis of ideas ' : this is that the universalisation of education is good in itself.   If education consists in communicating the art of happiness, and if intelligence is composed of two parts, the knowledge of the order of the events of nature on which our pleasures and our pains depend, and the sagacity which discovers the best means of attaining ends, the question of knowing whether the people ought to receive an education comes back to the question whether they ought to be happy or miserable.[2]   It may be objected that, in order to produce food and other objects of primary necessity, a great part of the human race must be condemned to toil, and consequently, in the absence of leisure, to ignorance.   But ' it is now almost universally acknowledged that on all conceivable accounts it is desirable that the great body of the people should not be wretchedly poor ; that when the people are wretchedly poor, all classes are vicious, all are hateful, and all are unhappy.   If so far raised above wretched poverty as to be capable of being virtuous, though it is still necessary for them to earn their bread by the sweat of their brow, they are not bound down to such incessant toil as to have no time for the acquisition of knowledge and the exercise of intellect '.   This again is inspired by Malthus ; though Mill seems to rely on a decrease in poverty to increase the aptitude for instruction, whereas Malthus counted on progress in education to decrease poverty.   But, if education is to be universal, it must also be neutral.   It is thus that the Lancasterian school thought of it.   Now here was a group of individuals wishing to supplant these schools, because they were open to all, without making any distinction between creeds, without giving any religious instruction.   The Church, having so often reproached the sects with their intolerance, had become sectarian in its turn.   James Mill provided the partisans of the Lancasterian schools with their classical arguments.   The Anglican system was financially extravagant : ' exclusive ' and ' restrictive ', it necessitated the erection of two schools where one school would suffice.   To say that the Church was in danger if all the children of the working classes were brought up in establishments which were open to all, was rashly to admit that it was lost as soon as it found itself on a footing of equality with other creeds.   The doctrine of the alliance of Church and State stood condemned by public opinion, together with the notion which it

[1] *Ed. Rev.* Feb. 1813, art. ix. vol. xxi. p. 213.
[2] *Education*, p. 39 ; cp. *Government*, p. 29

involved of a clergy, a corporation of priests to whom political powers were entrusted.[1]

It was in the course of this controversy that the anti-clerical and irreligious nature of Bentham's school was manifested. Bentham, who had been a free-thinker in the eighteenth century at Lord Lansdowne's, in a circle whose incredulity scandalised Priestley, found himself a free-thinker once more, this time in alliance not with an aristocracy disdainful of plebeian superstitions, but with the popular party. Was James Mill already irreligious, in the sense in which he later became so, before he knew Bentham ? Although he voluntarily renounced the career of a presbyterian minister it is a doubtful point, in spite of an assertion of Stuart Mill's. A family tradition, related by Bain, has it that his irreligious views did not take definite shape until 1808 and 1809 ; Mill was apparently converted to irreligion not by Bentham, but by Miranda, a former general of the French Revolution, and a revolutionary general in South America.[2] The quarrel over ' schools for all ' definitely made Bentham, James Mill and the whole group break with the Church.

In 1818, Bentham published his *Church of Englandism, and its Catechism examined*, in which he outlined the programme of a moral Christianity simplified in the extreme ; and it was about the same time that he composed his *Not Paul but Jesus*, which was only published in 1823, in which he devoted himself to proving that Paul was an impostor and an ambitious man, that his doctrine was on almost all points different from the doctrine of Jesus, and that he was the true Anti-Christ.[3] But the most direct expression of his anti-religious philosophy is contained in the little work entitled *Analysis of the influence of the natural religion on the temporal happiness of mankind*,[4] which was published in 1822 : this time young George Grote, who, in 1818, had made the acquaintance of James Mill through Ricardo, and of Bentham through James Mill, established himself, under a pseudonym, editor of the papers of the master. Just as, at about the same time, Bentham was founding a classification of the sciences on the consideration of their relative utility, so likewise, in this little work, he estimated the value of the religious idea from the point of view of utility, as distinct from the point of view of truth. ' Should the following reasonings be deemed conclusive, a clear idea may be formed of the temporal gain or loss accruing from the agency of Natural Religion. Whether the doctrines which this term involves be true or false, is a point on which I do not intend to touch '.[5] If false, they might be useful : if true they might be dangerous. Besides ' the warmest partisans of natural religion cannot deny, that by the influence of it (occasionally at least) bad effects have been

[1] Bowring, vol. viii. pp. 40 *seq.*   [2] Stuart Mill, *Autobiography*, pp. 38-39.
[3] *Not Paul but Jesus*, by Gamaliel Smith, London, 1823.
[4] Published under the pseudonym G. Philip Beauchamp, 1822.
[5] *Analysis*, Preface, p. iv.

produced ; nor can anyone on the other hand venture to deny, that it has on other occasions brought about good effects. The question therefore is, throughout, only as to the comparative magnitude, number, and proportion of each'.[1] Thus, to estimate the efficacy of the idea of posthumous penalties and rewards, Bentham applies the rules of his moral arithmetic. ' All inducements are expectations either of pleasure or pain. The force with which all expectations act upon the human bosom varies according as they differ in : 1. Intensity, 2. Duration, 3. Certainty, 4. Propinquity. These are the four elements of value which constitute and measure the comparative strength of all human motives '.[2] Now it is true that we are told that posthumous pleasures and pains are endowed with an infinite *duration* and *intensity* : but this is an infiniteness which is conferred on them by a fiction in order to counterbalance their real lack of *propinquity* and *certainty*. Happily, for if ' the expectations actually created in the mind corresponded in appalling effect to the descriptions of the fancy —and if the defects of certainty and propinquity could be so far counteracted as to leave these expectations in full possession of the mind—the result must be, absolute privation of reason, and an entire sacrifice of all sublunary enjoyment '.[3]

Note that Bentham's dialectic has always the same nature : it borrows as few elements as possible from empirical observation. It is not from history that Bentham draws arguments against the various religions, examined in detail. He defines religion *a priori*, and looks for the necessary consequences of religion as so defined. The religion he is discussing is, he warns us, natural and not revealed religion ; and we are tempted to see in this a use of the tactics current among irreligious polemicists, when they are addressing a religious public. ' If our present inquiry ', Bentham does in fact write, ' should demonstrate that Natural Religion has produced a large balance of temporal evil above temporal good, this will evince still more forcibly the necessity of a revelation such as to purge and counteract its bad effects '.[4] But Bentham's method is more subtle than this. He is not content, in opposing natural to revealed religion, to represent it as a religion simplified and freed from particular beliefs and accidental historical proofs which various revelations have added to it from one side or another : rather he puts forward an original definition of natural religion. By the word ' religion ' he means ' the belief in the existence of an almighty Being, by whom pains and pleasures will be dispensed to mankind, during an infinite and future state of existence ' ;[5] and it is from this abstract notion of omnipotence that he seeks to deduce the consequences which logically follow, on the practical side. Bentham's thesis is that ' natural religion invariably leads its votaries to ascribe to their Deity a character of caprice and tyranny, while they apply

[1] *Analysis*, part i. ch. i.
[2] *Ibid*. part i. ch. vi. pp. 46-47.
[3] *Ibid*. p. 49.
[4] *Ibid*. Preface, p. v.
[5] *Ibid*. part i. ch. i. p. 3.

to him, at the same moment, all those epithets of eulogy and reverence which their language comprises '.[1] It is the revealed religions (here Bentham speaks sincerely and without any of the artifice of the polemicist) which, to avoid the scandal of a like conception, have laboured to represent God as a Providence proposing as his end the good of the whole, and as a beneficent judge not as a despot. But why is a human judge beneficent ? It is because he exercises a delegated power, because he is dependent and responsible. On the contrary, without a revelation, God cannot be considered as other than wicked, since his authority is absolute.

Henceforth we have the means of estimating the loss resulting from such a belief for the individual considered in himself, his *sufferings without profit* or *useless privations*. For ' you wish to give proof of your attachment to the Deity, in the eyes and for the conviction of your fellow-men ? There is but one species of testimony which will satisfy their minds. You must impose upon yourself pain for his sake ; and in order to silence all suspicion as to the nature of the motive, the pain must be such as not to present the remotest prospect of any independent reward '.[2] Need the fatal consequences of the religious idea be enumerated ? A censorship of pleasures by pre- cedent scruples and by subsequent remorse ; indefinite terrors which, as experience proves, may lead to madness ; a degradation of the intelligence from the moment when, by recognising ' extra-experi- mental beliefs ', we separate belief from experience, from the moment when belief is set up as a virtue, and incredulity as a crime, and we are thus given other motives for believing and for not believing than the consideration of the intrinsic proofs : ' So far, therefore, as the reward is at all effective, it entices him to believe upon inadequate proof—so far as the punishment acts, it deters him from disbelieving upon adequate disproof '.[3] Finally, there are dire social conse- quences : religion is harmful ' not only to the believer himself, but also to others through him '. It creates, in the heart of society, factitious antipathies between men who believe and men who do not believe, between men who practise religion and men who do not practise it, or again between men who practise it in one way and men who practise it in another. Its worst effect is what may be called by the one word ' clericalism '—what Bentham calls the creation of a class whose interest ' is irreconcilably at variance with that of society ',[4] composed of men who, on the religious hypothesis, are held to be capable of interpreting the supernatural interventions of the hand of God. For this reason, the priests are naturally led to ally themselves to the heads of the State, for the State and the Church are two bodies having ' an interest incurably at variance with that of the community, and all sinister interests have a natural tendency to

[1] *Analysis*, part i. ch. iii. sect. 2, p. 21.   [2] *Ibid.* part ii. Mischief, i. p. 64.
[3] *Ibid.* part ii. ch. ii. Mischief iv. p. 110.
[4] *Ibid.* part ii. ch. ii. Mischief vi. p. 116.

combine together and to co-operate, inasmuch as the object of each
is thereby most completely and easily secured. But between the
particular interest of a governing aristocracy and a sacerdotal class,
there seems a very peculiar affinity and co-incidence—each wielding
the precise engine which the other wants ',[1] the one physical force,
the other moral ascendancy.

James Mill adopted the same uncompromising attitude. He
brought up his son in ignorance of all religious ideas. He held that
it was logically impossible either to affirm or to deny the existence
of God ; and one of his intellectual peculiarities was his sympathy
for the Manichean heresy : for it seemed to him intolerable to
attribute to God the creation of a universe in which evil abounds.
' I have a hundred times heard him say, that all ages and nations have
represented their gods as wicked in a constantly increasing progression, that mankind have gone on adding trait after trait till they
reached the most perfect conception of wickedness which the human
mind can devise, and have called this God, and prostrated themselves
before it. This ne plus ultra of wickedness he considered to be
embodied in what is commonly presented to mankind as the creed of
Christianity '.[2] At bottom, in Bentham and James Mill anti-
clerical and democratic opinions were confused : they thought of the
relation of man to God as the relation of the oppressed to the oppressor,
and of religion as the servility of the weak towards the all-powerful,
of the slave towards the tyrant. In the jargon current among the
group, churchmen were termed ' juggical ', from the chariot of
Juggernaut beneath whose wheels the faithful in India allow themselves to be crushed.[3]

There were, moreover, at this time a number of publicists around
Bentham who were shocking public opinion by preaching atheism.
It was at this precise moment that the deistic propaganda spread by
Thomas Paine's book on the Age of Reason was succeeded by really
atheistic propaganda. Bentham made the acquaintance, probably
through Wooler, manager of the Black Dwarf and editor of the
Catechism of Parliamentary Reform, of Richard Carlile whose first
exploit was the clandestine hawking of the Black Dwarf, during the
period of anti-democratic persecution which followed the passing of
the ' Six Acts ' of 1819. Bentham likewise collaborated with Hone
over his Reformer's Register, and it was Hone who, in 1817, inaugurated the publication of his blasphemous and anti-Christian works
with his Political Litany, illustrated by Cruikshank and printed by
Carlile, in which he parodied the litany, the Athanasian creed and the
Anglican catechism. In 1818, Carlile published Paine's theological
works ; then began his seven years internment in the prison at Dor-
chester, where he was later joined, in 1821, first by his wife and then

[1] Analysis, part ii. ch. ii. Mischief, vi. p. 137.
[2] Autobiography, pp. 40-41 ; Bain, p. 368.
[3] See, e.g. Bentham's letter to Place, April 24, 1831 (Graham Wallas, p. 82).

by his daughter, and whence he nevertheless managed, thanks to co-operation from various sources, to carry on without interruption the publication of his periodical, the *Republican*. Carlile's imprisonment once more raised the question of freedom of opinion : Carlile entered his prison a deist and went out of it an atheist. Persecutions created ' a fanaticism of incredulity '. Bentham's friends took up Carlile's defence—Ricardo by a speech in Parliament, and Stuart Mill by five letters addressed to the *Morning Chronicle*, and then by an article in the *Westminster Review*.[1] It was by their rabid anti-clericalism that Bentham's disciples made themselves most unpopular. Romilly, who was always prudent but from whose control Bentham had definitely escaped since becoming acquainted with James Mill, made every effort to stop Bentham publishing his *Church of Englandism*. His *Natural Religion* and the *Not Paul but Jesus* appeared under pseudonyms. In the complete edition of Bentham's works published by Bowring there is no trace of the *Church of Englandism* nor of the *Not Paul but Jesus* ; and Mrs. Grote—men are ever betrayed by their own kin—carefully covered up, in the biography she devoted to her husband, the part Grote had played in the publication of the *Natural Religion*. The fact was only revealed sixty years later in a biographical notice by Alexander Bain.

But it was not only the resistance of the Anglican Church, from the outside, which threatened the prosperity of the British and Foreign Society ; it was torn internally by religious dissensions. Among the promoters of popular education between 1810 and 1820 there were at the same time dissenters with pietistic tendencies and political liberals with lay tendencies. William Allen, the friend both of James Mill and of Robert Owen, was not pleased to see the latter tending towards agressive irreligion for the same reasons and at the same time as the Benthamites. The members of the ' Clapham brotherhood ' were hostile from the start to the suspect ' liberalism ' of the society,[2] and their great man, Wilberforce, whom Allen and Fox would have liked to make vice-president of the Society, declined the honour. In the British and Foreign Society itself, Place and James Mill secured in the first place that the rule in the statutes of the West London Lancasterian Association, that reading lessons should be taken only from the Bible, should be modified, and that the rule that all children should be taken to places of worship every Sunday, should be suppressed. But in 1814, Lancaster, who had been turned out, revenged himself by denouncing Place's atheism ; and Sir Francis Burdett also revenged himself by accusing Place of being a government spy. Place left the West London Lancasterian Association. In 1815 the evangelicals definitely got the upper hand in the British and Foreign School Society, and Place withdrew from it also. The project of the

---

[1] This article gives all the details necessary for a knowledge of the movement. *West. Rev.* July, 1824, art. i.
[2] See *Life of Wilberforce*, vol. ii. p. 239.

Superior Chrestomathic School likewise came to nothing. Funds were
lacking : four thousand pounds were wanted, and in 1817, only two
thousand five hundred had been collected. Even Bentham's own
enthusiasm cooled : in the end, in 1820, he refused the site which he
had promised for the erection of the school.[1] But ten years of effort
had not been wholly wasted. The speech which Brougham, who
owed all his ideas to James Mill, pronounced in the Commons in
1820, in favour of the organisation by the State of a complete system
of primary education, was the direct result of the Benthamite propaganda. University College and the Mechanics' Institute, which were
founded in London, the one due to Mill and the other to Place, were
new forms of Chrestomathic institutions, modified and better adapted
to the circumstances.

4. BENTHAM'S GROWING REPUTATION

' The case is ', wrote Bentham in 1810, ' though I have neither time
nor room to give you particulars, that now at length, when I am just
ready to drop into the grave, my fame has spread itself all over the
civilised world ; and, by a selection only that was made A.D. 1802,
from my papers, by a friend, and published at Paris, I am considered
as having superseded everything that was written before me on the
subject of legislation '.[2]   Yet in France [3] and in Germany [4] Bentham's
influence was insignificant.[5] But in less civilised countries, which
lacked a philosophic tradition of their own, Bentham's reputation grew
without check. This was the case in Russia. ' Could you have believed,'
wrote Dumont to Romilly in 1803, ' that as many copies of my
Bentham would have been sold in Petersburg as in London ? A
hundred copies have been disposed of in a very short time, and the
booksellers are asking for a new supply '.[6]   Bentham and his brother
had kept up relations there ; Dumont himself stayed there from
1802 to 1803, and caused Speranski to read and admire the work.[7] ' I
long to settle in England ', wrote the Russian Admiral Mordvinoff to
General Bentham in 1806, ' and, settling there, to be acquainted with
your brother. He is, in my eyes, one of the four geniuses who have
done, and will do most for the happiness of the human race—Bacon,
Newton, Smith and Bentham : each the founder of a new science :
each a creator '.[8] A Panopticon was built at Saint Petersburg.[9] In
1814 the Emperor Alexander called for Bentham's co-operation in
drafting a code, although on conditions which did not suit him.[10] But

[1] On the failure of the movement see Graham Wallas, *Life of Place*, ch. iv.
pp. 105 *seq.*
[2] Bowring, vol. x. p. 458.   [3] *Ibid.* pp. 395 and 396.
[4] *Ibid.* vol. iv. pp. 456, 514, 544 ; vol. x. pp. 578, 581.   [5] *Ibid.* vol. x. p. 525.
[6] *Ibid.* p. 406.   [7] *Ibid.* pp. 405, 408.   [8] *Ibid.* 419 ; cf. p. 413.
[9] Burnt down in 1818. See Bowring, vol. x. p. 499.
[10] Bowring, vol. iv. pp. 514-528.

it was in Spain, above all, that Bentham became a kind of demi-god.
' What do you think of Spain taking off 300 copies ? ' wrote Bentham
to Eden in 1802. ' Thrice as many, I believe, as it was thought
worth while to send to England. This was the number which,
according to the calculations of the French bookseller, would find
customers before the Inquisition would have time to fasten upon
them '.[1]   But the French invasion suppressed the tribunal of the
Inquisition in Spain ; then liberal Spain rose against the invader, and
appealed to England for help ; and Bentham's books entered the
peninsula with the British troops.[2] The Spanish editions of Bentham's works multiplied : the Cortes of Spain and of Portugal voted
that they should be printed at the national expense.[3]   Bentham intervened in the political discussions which were dividing the Spaniards,
advocated the Single Chamber system, and wrote to Count
Toreno his *Letters on the Penal Code*.[4]

From Spain, Bentham's reputation spread to the Spanish-speaking
countries of America. First a disciple of Bentham's, Lieutenant-
Colonel Aaron Burr, a former vice-president of the United States
who had withdrawn to England on account of a scandal, entered
into direct negotiations with him, and suggested that he should set
out for Mexico : Burr was to be Emperor, and Bentham legislator.[5]
General Miranda, a native of Venezuela, set off to organise a
revolution over there ; and Bentham thought of following him to
Caracas. ' The temperature is delightful, summer temperature all the
year round. Within sight of the sea, though almost under the line,
you have a mountain topped with ice, so that you may absolutely
choose your temperature, and enjoy the vegetable luxuries of all
countries. If I go thither, it will be to do a little business in the way
of my trade—to draw up a body of laws for the people there '.[6]   At
Buenos Ayres and in Chili, Ridavavia was his disciple and propagandist.[7] In Guatemala, José del Vallé aimed at substituting
Bentham's codes for the Spanish codes.[8]   In Columbia, the *Traités
de Législation* were adopted or suppressed as text books according
to whether the liberal party or the reactionary party, the party of
Bolivar, was in power.[9] Bentham's doctrine spread also in the
Mediterranean, to Italy [10] and as far as Greece. Edward Blaquiere,[11]
an enthusiastic lieutenant of marines, made himself Bentham's
' wandering apostle ' in these regions, the new Saint Paul of the new
God. He was in Sicily,[12] then in Spain [13] and then in Greece, whither

[1] Bowring, vol. x. p. 395.   [2] *Ibid*. p. 433.
[3] *Ibid*. pp. 525, 539, and vol. xi. pp. 19-20.   [4] *Ibid*. vol. x. p. 516.
[5] *Ibid*. pp. 432, 439, 444, 445. See James Parton, *Life and Times of Aaron Burr* (1864).
[6] Bowring, vol. x. p. 457.   [7] *Ibid*. pp. 500 and 513.   [8] *Ibid*. pp. 558-9.
[9] *Ibid*.   [10] Colonel Leicester Stanhope, *Greece in 1823 and 1824*.
[11] Bowring, vol. x. pp. 474-476.
[12] *Letters from the Mediterranean*, by E. Blaquiere, vol. i. p. 318-9, note, pp. 382,
389, 498.
[13] *An Historical Review of the Spanish Revolution*, Bowring, vol. x. pp. 514 *seq*.

he was sent by the Greek Committee which had been organised to assist the Greek revolutionaries, and which was in the hands of the Benthamites. A curious dispute arose between Lord Byron and Colonel Leicester Stanhope, a fanatical disciple of Bentham's, and a delegate of the Greek Committee. Byron demanded arms and munitions ; Stanhope, out of about five hundred pounds which he spent for the cause, used about a hundred only for aiding and arming the Greeks, and spent the rest in buying printing presses, in printing newspapers, and in founding Lancasterian schools at Athens and at Missolonghi.[1] It was the eternal quarrel of the philosopher and the man of action, of the idealist and the realist. ' J. B.', wrote Bentham himself some years later, ' the most ambitious of the ambitious. His empire—the empire he aspires to—extending to, and comprehending, the whole human race, in all places—in all habitable places of the earth, at all future time '.[2] Drunk with the praise that had long been showered on him by the zeal of his English disciples, and by the panegyrics of his Spanish-American devotees, Bentham, who had never very clearly distinguished between the domains of jurisprudence and morals, felt that he was becoming the equal of the legislator of old, of Solon or of Moses. He offered his project of a *Pannomion*, a *Complete Body of Laws*, without distinction to the President of the United States and to the Emperor of Russia. He dreamed of setting out for Switzerland, for Spain, for Mexico, for Venezuela, and of landing among a people whose traditional and local prejudices he ignored, like Epimenides at Athens or Plato at Syracuse. ' A prophet has no honour, except out of his own country '; and was Bentham not on the way to becoming a prophet in far-off lands ? [3]

' In my own country, of course ', wrote Bentham in the same letter in which he boasted of the advance of his doctrine outside England, ' less said of me than in any other : but still my fame is spreading, frequent references and quotations in books, and every now and then a panegyric in Parliament '. The *Treatises* of 1802 received, in 1804, the anxiously awaited criticism of the *Edinburgh Review* ; [4] and the reviewer was good enough to say that ' so large a quantity of original reasoning has seldom, we believe, been produced by one man '. But the principle of utility was condemned,[5] and this was enough to make Dumont shocked at the ' scandalous irreverence ' of the article.[6] In 1806 and 1807 we find Bentham exchanging views on the reform of judicial institutions in Scotland with the ministry directly.[7] Finally, in 1808, Romilly entered Parliament and assumed the task of devoting himself to law reform, or, to be more exact, to the reform of the criminal law.[8] Already, in 1807, Romilly

---

[1] *Greece in 1823 and 1824.*
[2] Bowring, vol. xi. p. 72.
[3] Hazlitt, *Spirit of the Age*, 1824, p. 1.
[4] Romilly to Dumont, May 31, 1803.
[5] *Ed. Rev.* April, 1804, art. i.
[6] Bowring, vol. x. p. 415.
[7] *Ed. Rev.* Jan. 1807.
[8] *Memoirs*, vol. ii. pp. 244-245.

had introduced the draft of a law, which was quite in conformity with Bentham's ideas, to diminish the unequal conditions imposed by English law on the transference of movable goods and of land ; [1] and already, in proposing the draft, Romilly had defined his own conception, which was opposed to the Benthamite conception, of a policy of reform : it was wrong to take a simple principle as starting point and draw from it certain consequences which would be true independently of considerations of time and place ; it was enough constantly to adapt the laws to the changing conditions of customs and civilisation. Bentham's influence on Romilly was none the less direct and profound ; never has there been an affiliation of ideas that was easier to trace.

In fact, though Romilly appears previously to have taken an interest in the reforms that should be made in English penal law,[2] he took a continuous interest in this kind of question only after he made Bentham's acquaintance at Bowood. The friendship between Bentham and Romilly, which developed more slowly than the friendship between Bentham and Dumont, was constantly growing more intimate.[3] On Romilly's side it was a boundless devotion, the almost filial affection that a pupil feels for his tutor. It was Romilly who had formerly communicated to Dumont Bentham's manuscripts, and who untiringly pressed Dumont to publish them ; he even considered for a moment, after the publication in French, undertaking the English translation of the work.[4] Romilly, a celebrated barrister, was much better known than Bentham, and was his regular go-between with political circles, communicating to the Attorney-General in 1801 one of Bentham's works,[5] and again acting as go-between, in 1808, on the occasion of the reform of the Scottish courts of justice. In his conversations with Bowring, Bentham spoke with some disdain of Romilly's work, of what he called his ' reformatiuncules ' ' miniature ' reforms ; ' had they been considerable, they would have been resisted with all Lord Eldon's might '.[6] And no doubt it is true that Romilly was only demanding reforms of detail ; nevertheless when, at Cowes in 1807, he determined to present two bills tending, the one to give the criminal courts the power of indemnifying people who had been detained and who were afterwards acquitted, the second to modify the severity of the criminal code, it was indeed the friend and the disciple of Bentham who was moving into action. Dumont had just brought him the manuscript of the *Théorie des Peines*, and Romilly's private letters bear witness to the profound impression produced on him by reading this work.[7] Thus it was certainly from Bentham that Romilly drew his inspiration, when he declared that one principle is evident to all, namely, that it is the certainty much

---

[1] *Memoirs*, vol. ii. p. 183.
[2] *Ibid*. p. 235.
[3] Bowring, vol. i. pp. 248-9.
[4] Bowring, vol. x. p. 396.
[5] *Ibid*. p. 362.
[6] *Ibid*. p. 186.
[7] Add MSS. Brit. Mus. 33,544, f 327.

300 PHILOSOPHIC RADICALISM

more than the severity of punishment that makes it efficacious.[1]
All the same he seems systematically to have avoided naming Bentham,
preferring to invoke the authority of Blackstone, ' the great com-
mentator ',[2] or of Beccaria.[3] His complaint against the English
penal law was that it was no longer applied, and that consequently
it was in contradiction with current opinion ; now it was discrediting
law constantly to vindicate opinion against law : laws must be put in
harmony with opinion.   But we may ask whether all this opportunism
was at any rate crowned with success.   Almost all Romilly's attempts,
between 1808 and 1813, to abolish some few capital felonies, came to
nothing either in the Commons or in the Lords.

After this, it can be understood why Romilly did not fulfil the
conditions necessary for becoming Bentham's ideal disciple. He was
a moderate, a conservative, and an opportunist : when in relation
with government circles, he found himself unable, despite the respect
his friend inspired in him, to be in complete community of feeling
and ideas with Bentham, who was unknown, isolated, dissatisfied and
revolutionary. He was constantly using his influence with Bentham,
to urge him to moderate his violence. He prevented him from
publishing his *Truth versus Ashurst* in 1793, his *Letter to the Duke of
Portland* in 1802, and his *Elements of Packing* in 1809.   In 1818, he
was anxious to persuade Bentham to hang up first the printing and
then the sale of *Church of Englandism*.   ' The subject is treated with
so much levity and irreverence that it cannot fail to shock all persons
who have any sense of religion '.   But at this time James Mill's
influence was too strong and prevailed over Romilly's.[4] Besides,
Romilly was Bentham's contemporary : an ornament of the English
bar, he was more illustrious and more popular than Bentham.   James
Mill, in contrast with Romilly, had all the qualities requisite for
becoming the disciple, one might almost say the apostle of Bentham.
He was twenty-five years younger. He was indebted to Bentham.
A journalist and a man of letters, he as yet belonged to no established
body.   His was an aggressive and militant temperament, and it was
not his doing that the *Elements of Packing* were not published :
Romilly's opinion prevailed once again.   He set himself up, alongside
of Dumont, with a like zeal but with that systematic pigheadedness
which was peculiarly his, as the arranger and editor of the master's
manuscripts.   Since 1803, Bentham had been engaged on a new
task, the theory of evidence ; in 1804, in a letter to Dumont, he
regarded his work as almost completed.[5] But, as usual, he lacked
the spirit of continued effort necessary for completing things. He
was distracted by other occupations, and the question of the reform
of the Scottish tribunals diverted his attention.[6]   It was at this point

---

[1] *Observations on the criminal law of England, etc.*, by Sir S. Romilly.
[2] Speech of June 15, 1808.   [3] *Ibid.* of May 18, 1808.
[4] Romilly, *Mem.* vol. iii. p. 336.   [5] Bowring, vol. x. p. 413.
[6] *Ibid.* p. 428.

that James Mill stepped in ; and he possessed to the highest degree just this gift of tenacity. After 1808, we see Dumont and James Mill both engaged at the same time in extracting a legible work from Bentham's illegible manuscripts, Dumont for use on the continent, Mill for use in English-speaking countries.[1] Already, in December 1809, the terminology and the philosophy of the work supplied the material for an article which James Mill wrote for the *Edinburgh Review*.[2] The English work was completed in 1812, under the title *Introduction to the Rationale of Evidence* ; but its tone was so bitter that all the publishers thought it too dangerous to publish, despite Mill's efforts : only part of it was printed (most important of which was the part called *Swear not at all*, a criticism of the formality of the judicial oath), and even that was not published.[3] In 1814, James Mill revised the *Table of the Springs of Action*, which appeared in 1817.[4]

But James Mill was perhaps even more useful to Bentham in other ways. No doubt through its director, Jeffrey, whom he may have known formerly at the University of Edinburgh in the days when they were both students, James Mill had already become a collaborator in the great liberal review, the *Edinburgh Review*, when he made the acquaintance of Bentham in 1808. After 1808 he systematically made use of his critical essays for the propagation of Bentham's ideas. The emancipation of the Spanish colonies in South America,[5] a work in French on jurisprudence,[6] the Napoleonic Code,[7] everything was made a pretext for calling the attention of the public to the name, the works, and the doctrine of the master. His zeal did not fail to meet with obstacles. It happened that Jeffrey considered that James Mill was abusing his rights as a writer, and he suppressed Bentham's name in some article or other while retaining his ideas—this resulted in Mill's being treated at Holland House as an ' impudent plagiarist '. He pursued the same task in the *Philanthropist* of his friend William Allen,[8] and again in the fifth Supplement to the *Encyclopaedia Britannica*, in which all his articles were just so many attempts to fix the Benthamite doctrine on various points. In legal questions, he accepted his master's doctrines to the letter, following him in his definition of the subject-matter of *Jurisprudence*, the principles of the *Law of Nations* and the rules to be followed in the administration of *Prisons* : did he not even at the outset make excuses to Napier for having undertaken this article, so strongly did he feel that he could add nothing to the *Panopticon* ?[9] He again makes excuses at the end of the article. ' The only merit ', he writes, ' we have to claim is that (if our endeavour has been successful) of adding

---

[1] Bowring, vol. x. pp. 451 and 454 and Bain, pp. 99-100.
[2] Art. vi.   [3] Bain, p. 120.   Bowring, vol. v., pp. 187-230.
[4] See Bowring, vol. i. pp. 195-220.
[5] Jan. 1809.   [6] Oct. 1809.   [7] Nov. 1810.
[8] *The Philanthropist* (cp. Bain, p. 113 seq.).   [9] Bain, p 201.

perspicuity to compactness '.[1]   In his articles *Beggar* and *Benefit Societies*, he drew his inspiration from Bentham's treatise on the *Administration of the Poor*.   The ideas he set forth in the article on the *Freedom of the Press* alone were his own, long before he became acquainted with Bentham.   In the article *Colonies* he combined Malthus' ideas on the question of population with Bentham's ideas on penal deportation ; in the article *Education*, he drew his inspiration in defining Utilitarian pedagogy as much from Helvetius and from Hartley as from Bentham ; finally, in the article *Government* which rapidly became a classic, he enunciated, alongside of Bentham, the fundamental principles of the doctrine as applied to constitutional affairs.

In 1807 appeared the *History of British India*, which had been begun in 1806.   It was Mill's great work, on which his reputation was founded, and may itself be considered, in a certain sense, as an instrument of Benthamite propaganda.   In his analysis of the institutions of Hindustan, James Mill does not separate critical judgment from historical exposition ; and it is by confronting the institutions with Bentham's principles that he estimates their value and suggests possible reforms.   ' For these many years a grand object of his ambition ', says Bentham, ' has been to provide for British India, in the room of the abominable existing system, a good system of judicial procedure, with a judicial establishment adequate to the administration of it ; and for the composition of it his reliance has all along been, and continues to be, on me '.[2]   And also, proud of the work that had been accomplished by his disciple under his inspiration, he declared : ' Mill will be the living executive—I shall be the dead legislative of British India '.[3]   For Mill was now famous : he never even had the leisure to undertake the literary projects that he was making at this time—to write a history of English Law, and a complete system of jurisprudence.[4]   Through the efforts of his friends, and particularly of Ricardo, he got a place in the offices of the East India Company.[5]   Ought this powerful company to be congratulated for having been magnanimous enough to pardon a bitter critic ?   Or should it rather be congratulated for being cunning and silencing a dangerous adversary ?   Hazlitt ironically remarked some years later that the Utilitarian organ, the *Westminster Review*, showed respect for practically no established institution except the East India Company.

In 1813, occurred a considerable event in Bentham's life.   It was now two years since a Parliamentary Committee of twenty-one members (' except Abercrombie, and myself, and Wilberforce ', wrote

---

[1] *Ency. Brit.* Sup. " Prisons."
[2] Bowring, vol. x. p. 590.   [3] *Ibid.* p. 450.   [4] Bain, p. 173.
[5] Bain, p. 183 *seq.* On Mill's financial position before this time see Graham Wallas, p. 67 *seq.*

Romilly to Bentham, ' no person friendly to you was present ') had published its *Second Report . . . on the Laws relating to Penitentiary Houses*.[1] Bentham's long philanthropic campaign was now about to result in the erection on the bank of the Thames of Millbank prison, in which several of Bentham's ideas were to be carried out, though not the idea of contract management. Further, the Report of the Committee recognised that Bentham ' has . . . a just right to expect, not only that the money so laid out should be repaid, but that a liberal remuneration should be made for his trouble and ultimate disappointment (he on his part accounting for any advantage that shall have accrued to him from the lands) '. The question of the indemnity was decided by two arbiters, John Hullock named by the Treasury, and John Whishaw [2] named by Bentham; and finally, in 1813, Bentham received an indemnity of £23,000. He became a rich man once more, and began again to spend his money rashly, not only in reformatory and philanthropic experiments, but also for his personal pleasure. In 1814, he rented the castle of Ford Abbey in Devonshire. He went on renting it for four years until the time when his financial difficulties began again. The contrast between the old radical philosopher and his sumptuous feudal dwelling amused all his friends, who have left us many full descriptions of the building.[3] There Bentham enjoyed a pure happiness. ' It is the theatre of great felicity to a number of people, and that not very inconsiderable. Not an angry word is ever heard in it. Mrs. S. (the housekeeper) governs like an angel. Neighbours all highly cordial, even though not visited. Music and dancing, though I hate dancing. Gentle and simple mix. Crowds come and dance, and Mrs. S. at the head of them '.[4] The reality was more austere and hardly corresponded with this exalted description of a haunt of delights. During the months which Bentham spent there the castle was like a lay monastery, where the hours of study, of meals and of exercise were fixed for everyone, for Bentham and his secretaries, for James Mill and his wife and children, and in 1817 and 1818 for Francis Place. The master worked until dinner; he breakfasted alone, and during breakfast, listened to the reading of the *Morning Chronicle*. Meanwhile, James Mill, who had always been up since six o'clock, divided his time between his *History of British India* and the education of his children. Then, after dinner, came the time for walks and conversations, the guests taking turns day by day to accompany Bentham. James Mill was serious; Bentham played the fool and scandalised by his sacrilegious jests his secretary Colls who later betrayed him.[5] Francis Place was amazed, and wrote long letters giving his wife an

[1] Bowring, vol. xi. p. 148 *seq.*
[2] The Whishaws had been friends of Bentham's for several years.
[3] Bowring, p. 478 *seq.* See also Bain, and Romilly's *Memoirs*.
[4] Bowring, vol. x. p 487.
[5] See the curious work, *Utilitarianism Unmasked*, by Rev. John F. Colls.

account of this life of toil,—' All our days are alike, so an account of one may do for all '.[1]

Thus Bentham's life was still what it had always been, a lonely and regulated life. Bentham remained ' the Hermit of Queen Square Place ', ' a quiet, painstaking inoffensive recluse, in whom though no man has a companion, every man has a friend, and who, though an Englishman by birth, is a citizen of the world by naturalisation ',—' a recluse, who takes no part in society and whose person is as completely in the hands of destiny as if he had shut himself up in a solitary cell '.[2]   For a long time Romilly's had been the only house he had frequented, and it was the last.[3]   In his own house, he was difficult of access : when Madame de Staël and Benjamin Constant visited England he refused to exhibit himself.   James Mill [4] and later Dr. Bowring, who, after 1820, gradually came to fill for Bentham the position of trust that had previously been occupied by James Mill,[5] had the right of entry.   Various accounts tell how through their offices young men and strangers secured an audience with the master, and the honour of dining with him, or of accompanying him after dinner on his hygienic walk at a running pace.[6]   From writing, always in solitude, manuscripts which he knew the public would not read, at any rate until they had been revised and corrected by a disciple, he came to write in a language which grew more and more obscure, and he made for himself a new terminology which he might indeed call ' natural ' in contrast to the ' technical ' terminology which was in use in the courts, but which in reality constituted a new technical terminology, as unintelligible to the layman as was the jargon of Westminster Hall, and which discouraged both his readers and his editors.   Dumont, who was working at the French edition of the *Rationale of Evidence*, trembled at it ;   Brougham and Francis Place complained of it to James Mill.   The article devoted by the *Quarterly Review*, in 1818, to the *Plan of Parliamentary Reform* was one long satire of the Benthamite jargon.[7]   Romilly himself, in the *Edinburgh Review*, protested against the obscure style used by Bentham in his *Codification Papers*.[8]   This is not to say that Bentham's phraseology was not always rich, living and expressive, nor that the new words which he made from English analogies were not often picturesque, nor that those he made from Latin analogies were not often useful and destined to secure a successful reception.[9]   But it remains true that his syntax made faulty use of subordinate clauses, and his

---

[1] Graham Wallas, *Life of Place*, p. 73 *seq.* and Romilly, *Mem.* vol. iii. pp. 315-316.
[2] Bowring, vol. x. pp. 439-507.
[3] Bowring, vol. x. p. 505.   [4] *Ibid.* p. 467.
[5] It was in 1820 that Bowring entered into relations with Bentham.   Bowring, vol. x. p. 516.
[6] See especially *Historical Sketches and Personal Recollections of Manchester*, by A. Prentice.
[7] Oct. 1817, art. v.   [8] *Ed. Rev.*, Nov. 1817 (vol. xxix. p. 237).
[9] The words *international*, *codify*, *codification* are Benthamite neologisms.

vocabulary of neologisms. He became obscure by dint of wishing to be precise.

It was not only the obscurity, but also the violence of the language which Romilly deplored in the *Codification Papers* : he was grieved to see ' one of the first philosophers of the age ' speaking the language of ' that unhappy class of literary persons, whom necessity impels, or the capricious appetite of the public invites to exaggerate, and misrepresent, and calumniate, in pursuit of a subsistence at once discreditable and precarious '[1]—Bentham descending to the level of Cobbett. Long humiliated by the indifference of his fellow-citizens, by the insolence of the ministries, he turned satirist—he who, in his *Introduction*, had condemned the spirit of satire : his attacks on men and on institutions became more bitter every day. He spared neither the *fee-fed* magistrates nor the aristocrats—the scum of the population, for whether it is a question of a saucepan or of a kingdom, is not the top the scum ?[2]—nor yet the priests. Nothing could be more caustic than his criticism of the technical and corporative system, in the *Rationale of Judicial Evidence*. But above all, he reached the very paroxysm of satiric violence in his *Indications concerning Lord Eldon*, a work in regard to which his friends dreaded legal action in 1824, because of its long parallel between Jeffreys and the Lord Chancellor.[3] The death of the victims despatched by Lord Jeffreys was swift ; the death of Lord Eldon's victims was as slow as his own designs. The death of the victims of Lord Jeffreys was public and the sufferers were supported by the sympathy of the people who were present in thousands ; the victims of Lord Eldon perished far from the sight of everyone, in that sadness and isolation that vanished wealth leaves behind it. Lord Jeffreys was an assassin, not a thief ; Lord Eldon plundered his victims as well as killed them. Jeffreys' heart leapt with joy at the sufferings of his victims ; Lord Eldon's unalterable good humour remained unaffected by them. Jeffreys was a tiger ; Lord Eldon was a stone. . . . But maybe there was some system in this flow of rhetoric. Bentham did not agree with Romilly that ' on affaiblit tout ce qu'on exagère ' : he thought that men erred more through excess of moderation than through excess of violence and indignation. His aim was to strike and to shock the imagination of the public and make them dissatisfied with existing institutions ; his life's work was to expose ' that system of abomination under which I have had the misfortune to live . . . to that full and general abhorrence which must take place before any effectual reform can be accomplished '.[4]

The obscurity of Bentham's writings had the effect of enhancing the oracular and sibylline character of the words of the old master. The violence of his attacks may perhaps have gained him the approval

---

[1] *Ed. Rev.*, Nov. 1817 (vol. xxix. p. 237).   [2] Bowring, vol. ix. p. 157.
[3] *Ibid.* vol. v. pp. 348-382.   [4] Bowring, vol. xi. pp. 54-55.

of the malcontents ; for he had a genius for scurrilous wit. But above all, it was to James Mill that this hermit, this maniac, owed the fact that he became the popular chief of a party that was half philosophical and half political. 'The disciples of Mr. Bentham ', wrote Mackintosh some years later, when trying to define the characteristics of the group, ' are more like the hearers of an Athenian philosopher than the pupils of a modern professor, or the cool proselytes of a modern writer. They are in general men of competent age, of superior understanding, who voluntarily embrace the laborious study of useful and noble sciences ; who derive their opinions not so much from the cold perusal of his writings as from familiar converse with a master from whose lips these opinions are recommended by simplicity, disinterestedness, originality, and vivacity ; aided rather than impeded by foibles not unamiable, enforced of late by the growing authority of years and of fame, and at all times strengthened by that undoubting reliance on his own judgment which mightily increases the ascendant of such a man over those who approach him '.[1] Now, this judgment has been contested by Stuart Mill, who declared that this conception of the influence exerted by Bentham was ' simply ridiculous '. ' The influence which Bentham exercised was by his writings. Through them he has produced, and is producing, effects on the condition of mankind, wider and deeper, no doubt, than any which can be attributed to my father. He is a much greater name in history '. But it was James Mill who, in contrast to Bentham, exercised a personal ascendancy. ' He *was* sought for the vigour and instructiveness of his conversation, and did use it largely as an instrument for the diffusion of his opinions. . . . It was my father's opinions which gave the distinguishing character to the Benthamic or Utilitarian propagandism of that time. They fell singly, scattered from him, in many directions '.[2] Stuart Mill goes further and denies that James Mill was simply Bentham's disciple ; he shows him to have been an independent thinker whose philosophy is composed of parts borrowed from Hartley, from Malthus, from Ricardo, and not only from Bentham. We think that these remarks are well founded.

If a Philosophical Radicalism was in fact coming into being about the year 1832, the formation of this collective dogmatism is no doubt explicable on general grounds. Certain reforms in the political, economic and juridical orders had been demanded by certain distinct sections of public opinion since the end of the eighteenth century. In 1815, it may be said that a considerable and daily increasing section of opinion was demanding them all with equal intensity. From this time it was inevitable that man, who is an intellectual being, should feel the need of systematising all these particular needs for reform in relation to a single principle. It was even almost inevitable that this principle should be the principle of utility, because this principle was the very foundation of the English understanding of the term,

---

[1] Mackintosh, *Dissertation* (1828), p. 237.   [2] Stuart Mill, *Autob.*, pp. 101-102.

and because all English thinkers, whether conservatives or democrats, communists or partisans of individual and hereditary property,
referred back instinctively to this principle. And because of this, in
one sense, Bentham found himself chosen to be the head of the movement. But had he been left to his own genius, would Bentham ever
have realised what had long been his dream ? Bentham based the
science of morals and the science of law on the principle of utility, or,
to be more precise, on the principle of the artificial identification of
interests. He adopted the economic notions of Adam Smith, which
were derived from the principle of the natural identity of interests.
But in 1808, he was still neither a Radical nor a Malthusian. It was
James Mill who converted him to advanced political liberalism. It
was James Mill who, having become a Benthamite, perceived the
logical link which connected the ideas of Bentham and of Malthus,
became a Malthusian and made use of Ricardo to incorporate the
ideas of Malthus with the tradition of Adam Smith. James Mill was,
by the qualities of his mind, the logician and the scholastic who was
needed to complete the formation of the doctrine, at the same time as,
by his moral character, he was the ideal disciple, destined to determine
the existence of the group and of the school.

' An acquaintance with the general facts of modern history ',
wrote James Mill in the *Edinburgh Review* in 1810, ' is, after all, but
an introduction to that accurate knowledge of affairs which can only
be gained from the study of Biography. Into this all the details of
the annalist, and much of the speculation of those who write the
philosophy of history, resolve themselves. In very long periods of
time, or in certain critical conjunctures, the operation of general
causes may be traced with considerable certainty ; but, in the details
of particular events, the opinions and actions of a few eminent
individuals are generally quite decisive ; and, while the eyes of the
multitude are fixed on the great movements of politics or war, the
governing springs are generally concealed from their view '.[1] James
Mill believed in the influence of individuals on history, and it is this
conviction which explains his sectarian zeal at Bentham's side. For
if he was ambitious, it was for Bentham, not for himself : in Bentham
he had found a great man, *his* great man, and he set it before himself
as the purpose of his life to give Bentham an influence in his own
time and in his own country. In his relations with Bentham, he was
systematically docile,[2] and determined, without ever abdicating his
own personal dignity, never to allow any whim on Bentham's part to
cool or extinguish a friendship which he considered necessary to the
good of humanity. In 1814, it happened that Bentham reproached
James Mill, with an offensive asperity, for riding with Joseph Hume,
instead of accompanying the philosopher in his walks. James Mill
understood that he had let himself get into the way of living on a

---

[1] *Ed. Rev.* Nov. 1810, art. iii (vol. xvii, p. 39).
[2] Bowring, vol. x. p. 450.

footing of too great intimacy with Bentham, and that he had made a mistake in accepting money from him. In a long, serious and beautiful letter, he explained to him that he was going to reform his life in these two particulars. But he knew, and he explained in the same letter, that his presence was necessary at Bentham's side, because he had adhered to his principles more completely than anyone else, and had devoted more years than anyone else to training himself in the trade of a disciple, and because he, more than anyone, was in a position to devote his whole life to the propagation of the system. It was in the interest of their friendship that he wished it to be less intimate. ' I could not suddenly depart, without proclaiming to the world, that there was a quarrel between us ; and this, I think, for the sake of both of us, and more especially the cause which has been the great bond of connection between us, we should carefully endeavour to avoid. The number of those is not small who wait for our halting. The infirmities in the temper of philosophers have always been a handle to deny their principles ; and the infirmities we have will be represented as by no means small, if, in the relation in which we stand, we cannot avoid showing to the world we cannot agree '.[1] James Mill was rightly aware that he was the indispensable intermediary between Bentham and the external world. The voluntary servant of Bentham, he became a tyrant everywhere else than with Bentham—a domestic tyrant when he was concerned with the upbringing of his children ; a social tyrant when he was concerned to develop, to organise and to create the Benthamite group. There were some, like Roebuck, in whom he always inspired a profound aversion.[2] George Grote, after his first interview with the man whose influence he subsequently felt so profoundly, was aware of his faults. ' His mind has, indeed, all that cynicism and asperity which belong to the Benthamian school, and what I chiefly dislike in him is the readiness and seeming preference with which he dwells on the *faults and defects* of others—even of the greatest men '.[3] He made himself dreaded more than loved ; but the kind of antipathy which he inspired was perhaps itself responsible for a part of his prestige. Apart from Bentham, Ricardo was the only man whom he really loved ; but Ricardo was for him another great man, a master far more than a disciple, or an agent for spreading Bentham's ideas. All the others he appreciated according as they were of greater or less use from the point of view of the end, disinterested indeed, which he was pursuing.

His efforts were rewarded with success. Bentham's French works began to be translated into English ; and it was to his son John that James Mill entrusted the publication of the English edition of the *Rationale of Judicial Evidence*, after Dumont had published the *Théorie*

---

[1] Bowring, vol. x. pp. 481-2.
[2] *Life of Roebuck*, by R. E. Leader, pp. 28-9.
[3] *The Personal Life of George Grote*.

des Preuves Judiciaires. Thanks to James Mill, a whole sphere of influence was created around Bentham. Francis Place, whom Mill had converted to Benthamism, had a shop at Charing Cross which was a centre of political action :[1] it was there that preparations were made for Hobhouse's election to Westminster in 1818,[2] and also for the repeal of the Combination Laws in 1824. He had pushed Ricardo into Parliament. Joseph Hume, who had a heavy mind, but who later won a reputation for himself by his pigheadedness in discussing budgets and in obtaining the necessary economies, was, in a sense, the creation of James Mill.[3] In the press, the great radical organ, the *Morning Chronicle*, belonged from 1817, and more especially from 1823, to John Black, an intimate friend of Mill's : in it was waged an active campaign for judicial reform. In the *Scotsman*, at Edinburgh, MacCulloch, another friend of Mill's, propagated the principles of Adam Smith and Ricardo.[4] A new type of humanity, with its virtues and its failings, began to be sketched out around Bentham, thanks not to Bentham but to James Mill. Bentham, despite his fits of impatience, was jovial, amiable and pleasant. He liked the country, he liked music, and he liked good cooking.[5] He was neither solemn nor serious. He described himself as ' a comical old fellow '.[6] Francis Place, putting this definition right, said he was ' the most affable man in existence, perfectly good-humoured, bearing and forbearing, deeply read, deeply learned, eminently a reasoner, yet simple as a child '.[7] The childish and naive side of Bentham's character was absent in James Mill. He was nothing more than the man of abstract convictions, a living example of the Utilitarian morality and of the absolute identification of private interest with the good of humanity, the type of the religious man—if the religious man is he who does not separate his existence from his ideas—and of the party man—if it is by ideas that men are united—without eyes or ears for the beauties of nature and art, having systematically destroyed in himself the spontaneous impulses of feeling—in short, the Utilitarian whose caricature was soon to become popular.

Is the precise date important when the denomination became in some sense official with the Benthamites of the second generation, who were between fifteen and twenty years old in 1820, contemporaries and friends of Stuart Mill, and formed by James Mill ? As early as 1791 we see Bentham rejoicing to find in Joseph Townshend a man

[1] See a curious article in the *European Magazine*, March 7, 1826, quoted by Graham Wallas, p. 189.
[2] For the relations of Hobhouse with the Benthamites see Bowring, vol. x. pp. 519-523 ; Graham Wallas, p. 83.
[3] Bain, pp. 7, 126. Stuart Mill, *Autob.*, p. 54. Wallas, p. 183.
[4] Bain, pp. 165-196. Stuart Mill, *Autob.*, p. 89 *seq.*
[5] Bowring, vol. x. pp. 25, 32.
[6] Graham Wallas, p. 81. Bowring, vol. x. p. 5.
[7] Francis Place to Thomas Hodgskin, May 30, 1817 (Graham Wallas, *Francis Place*, p. 81).

whose studies ' have lain a great deal in the same track with mine ;
he is a *utilitarian*, a naturalist, a chemist, a physician '.[1]   Twenty
years later when Dumont was looking for a name for the new doctrine
and suggested *Benthamite*, Bentham protested :   ' Benthamite ?
What sort of animal is that ? . . . to be sure a new religion would be
an odd sort of thing without a name :   accordingly there ought to be
one for it. . . . *Utilitarian* (Angl.), *Utilitairien* (Gall.) would be the
mot propre '.[2]   But the word, whose use became general, acquired a
bad sense.   It is so in Miss Austen's *Sense and Sensibility*.   It
is so in the *Annals of the Parish*, a kind of historical novel in which
the author, Galt, in telling the story of an English parish during the
last thirty years, makes the priest of the place, in 1793, denounce the
revolutionaries by the name of Utilitarians.   It was from this source
that Stuart Mill, when in the winter of 1822 to 1823, he founded under
the direction of his father a society of young people for the discussion
of problems of morals and politics, took the unpopular word, and,
with a kind of philosophical *sans-culottism*, gave the Society the name
of the *Utilitarian Society*.   ' For some years I called myself and others
by it as a sectarian appellation ;   and it came to be occasionally used
by some others holding the opinions which it was intended to
designate '.[3]

[1] Bowring, vol. x. p. 92.   [2] *Ibid*, pp. 389-390.
[3] Stuart Mill, *Autob.*, pp. 79-80.   *Utilitarianism*, p. 9 note.

PART III

PHILOSOPHIC RADICALISM

FOREWORD

THE difference between *error* and *fallacy* is easy to grasp. *Error* designates merely a false opinion ; *fallacy* designates also a false opinion, but which is made the means to an end '.[1] Thus writes Bentham in his *Political Fallacies*. Now what, according to him, are the causes of fallacies ? Every public man is constantly submitted to the influence of two distinct interests : the public interest, ' constituted of the share he has in the happiness . . . of the whole community ', and private interest, ' constituted of the share which he has in the well-being of some portion of the community less than the major part '.[2] A public man will have recourse to fallacy to the extent to which, when his private interest conflicts with the general interest, he necessarily wishes to defend the interest of the particular corporation to which he belongs against the general interest. To show that there was no identity between the interests of the governors and the governed, and to work for the realisation of such an identity was the tendency of the efforts of the reformers. To make people believe that this identity of interests between the governors and the governed had already been brought about was the tendency of all the speeches of the members of the governing corporation. Grouped under the banner of Bentham and James Mill, and finding at last, on the re-establishment of peace, a public to listen to them, the Philosophical Radicals attacked, systematically and *en bloc*, all the fallacies of the conservative parties.

First, they attacked economic fallacies. Each group of producers demanded the protection of the State against foreign competition ; but the result of this policy of protection was that all the consumers, that is to say all the citizens without exception, suffered. There was a conflict between the private interest of the groups and the general interest of the nation. The Utilitarian economists, Ricardo and his disciples, demanded that this policy which was both absurd and complicated, should be abandoned, and that the interests of the

[1] Bowring, vol. ii. p. 379.   [2] *Ibid*. p. 475.

groups should be sacrificed to the general interest. The industrialists were already giving up demanding the protection of the State, so that the owners of land and their clients made up the whole of the protectionist party. Yet the new political economy proved, with a mathematical exactitude, that the operation of the laws of nature enriched them necessarily, and without any effort on their part, at the expense of all the other classes of society. The Utilitarian reformers did not demand the confiscation of land : for such a policy of confiscation would imply the increase of the functions of the State, and of all corporations the governmental corporation appeared to them the most detestable. But they did demand that the State should stop increasing, by an iniquitous protection, the naturally enormous advantages enjoyed by the landowners, and that it should reduce its economic functions to nothing, and promulgate the free exchange of all products between all individuals throughout the whole world.

Secondly, they attacked fallacies which may be called specifically political. The conservative parties had succeeded in securing credit, in England, for the idea that complex government and liberal government are synonymous expressions. The truth was that the complexity of the political and judicial institutions in Great Britain was the bulwark of aristocratic privileges and not of popular liberties. If the electoral régime were simplified by the institution of universal suffrage, and all holders of executive power were put in close dependence on Parliament, and Parliament itself in close dependence on the majority, it would then become unnecessary to protect the liberty of the individual against the usurpations of the administrative power, by complexity of institutions and procedure. Since the administrative power would emanate directly from the will of the greatest number, it must happen that its decisions were in general in conformity with the interests of the greatest number ; these should therefore be made as easy and as swift as possible, by means of the simplification of constitutional laws and formalities. While the Whigs opposed the complexity of the liberal régime to the simplicity of the despotic régime, the Radicals of Bentham's school opposed the energy of the democratic régime to the delays of complex and aristocratic governments.

Finally, they attacked philosophical fallacies. These were, in a sense, the basis of all the others. According to Bentham, ' sentimental ' and particularly ' ascetic ' morality was the product of an aristocratic régime. Those who taught the morality of sacrifice, who exhorted the individual to sacrifice his interest to a higher ideal, who illogically opposed the interest of the individual to the interest of society, as if society were anything other than the collection of all the individuals, were not, properly speaking, the victims of an error ; they had, more or less consciously, become guilty of a fallacy. Themselves members of the governing corporation, they had urged individuals to sacrifice themselves to the interests of this corporation.

But the Utilitarians preached to men neither obedience nor humility ; it was by the egoistic defence of their own rights and their own interests that they invited them to realise the general prosperity. In order to convince them, they set about destroying the dualism established by the traditional philosophy between reason and sensation, between duty and interest ; as reason is the natural product of the arrangement of sensations, moral order necessarily results from the equilibrium of interests. Thus, thanks to Bentham and James Mill, the sophistical obscurities of morals and logic melted away, and the simplification of philosophic thought prepared the way for the simplification of law.

CHAPTER I

THE NATURAL LAWS OF
ECONOMIC SOCIETY

I T is instructive to compare the state of philosophic and scientific
opinion in England and in Germany about the year 1820. In
Germany, the thinkers who were forming public opinion were
philosophers who believed that they had discovered a synthetic form
of speculation, more comprehensive than any special discipline, and
such that it would satisfy at once all the needs of the spirit, of the
sentimental and the rational, the poetic and the positive, the religious
and the scientific. In England, the thinkers who were in the public
eye adopted, on the contrary, a point of view which they systematically chose as being as narrow and as exclusive as possible : they
looked at man under one aspect only, as a member of economic
society, as a producer and consumer of wealth, and they devoted
themselves to the methodical definition of the economic categories.
In France, there were enthusiastic followers of both schools. To
Victor Cousin, the admirer of Germany, Germany was the home of
metaphysical speculation. To Jean-Baptiste Say, the admirer of
England, England was the home of political economy. In addition
to this, both German metaphysicians and English economists
quarrelled amongst themselves ; and these disputes dismayed
Victor Cousin and Jean-Baptiste Say ; they threatened to obscure
the points on which agreement was fundamental to all, and to compromise, in the world at large, the prestige of German metaphysics,
and of English political economy.

In England, it was the economists who opened the campaign
against the laws regarding the importation of corn, against the
navigation laws, and against the whole system of customs' protections
and prohibitions. Until the re-establishment of peace, discussions
on political economy had barely passed the bounds of a narrow circle
of philosophers. Now, at last, public opinion did justice to the great

discoveries of economic science : Malthus and Ricardo were held, on the same grounds as the great inventors, Arkwright and Stevenson, to be benefactors of humanity and initiators of a new era. In 1816, Mrs. Marcet published her *Conversations on Political Economy*, in which, says the sub-title, *the Elements of that Science are familiarly explained* ; and this popular work gained an immediate success. Political economy penetrated into the University of Cambridge with Prynn in 1816 ; into Parliament with Ricardo in 1818 ; and into the University of Oxford with Senior in 1825.[1] All the economists were optimists, and agreed in adhering, in words, to the principle of the natural identity of interests. But, on the one hand, what interpretation of this principle must be given—the naturalistic interpretation, which was more in conformity with the spirit of Hume, or the rationalistic interpretation, which was more in conformity with the new tendencies of the school ? And, on the other hand, how can the thesis of economic optimism be reconciled with the discoveries of Malthus, the law of population and the theory of rent on land, which imply an increasing divergence of interests ? It was in vain that the economists regarded political economy as an objective science which would sooner or later impose the acceptance of its principles on people as a whole ; in fact, they interpreted it, for the moment, in different ways. Ricardo published his *Principles of Political Economy and Taxation* in 1817 ; but he immediately found in Malthus [2] and in Torrens [3] adversaries and not friends as he might have expected. Then in 1821, James Mill published his *Elements of Political Economy*, and MacCulloch, in 1825, his *Principles of Political Economy* ; and these two works are alike in that they are two manuals of political economy, two expositions of a science which its authors held to be complete in its definitions, its laws and its practical applications. James Mill, Ricardo's interpreter, represented the economic doctrine of the Philosophical Radicals. MacCulloch, though he did not belong to the group, was Ricardo's avowed disciple in economic matters, the populariser and publicist of his ideas ; he stood for those ideas at the precise moment when they were becoming collective, popular, and commonplace : for this reason, after Ricardo and James Mill, we shall give some attention to MacCulloch.[4]

---

[1] *West. Rev.* vol. vi. July 1827, art. vi.

[2] On the *Principles of Political Economy, considered with a view to their practical application,* 1820.

[3] *An Essay on the Production of Wealth, with an Appendix, in which the principles of political economy are applied to the actual circumstances of this country,* 1821.

[4] See on the whole of this chapter Edwin Cannan, *A History of the Theories of Production and Distribution in English Political Economy from 1776-1848.* 1893 ; (2nd ed. 1903).

I. RICARDO.

Sismondi visited England in 1818, and returned to the continent shocked by the spectacle that had met his eyes. He had come across nothing but incoherence and anarchy, excess of industrial activity and excessive poverty. The manufacturers, taken unawares by the re-establishment of peace, went on producing for markets which were not sending them any more orders ; badly paid workmen were dying of hunger in the face of this pile of useless wealth. As against these realities he found in possession of public opinion a supposed economic science which suggested no other remedy for the crisis than the abstention of the government, and ' which was so speculative that it seemed divorced from all practice '.[1] Ricardo, with his *Principles of Political Economy*, symbolised for him the new economic school whose triumph he deplored : ' as a whole his system tends to the conclusion that nothing matters, and that nothing does any harm to anything ; this simplifies science to a remarkable extent : there is only one step from this doctrine to denying the existence of evil '.[2] Such was, indeed, the current opinion about Ricardo's book ; his doctrine, which became the orthodoxy of the Utilitarian group, was held to represent economic optimism and quietism in their most absolute form.

This way of thinking of Ricardo's economic philosophy will appear less justified if it be remembered that his researches set out from a double starting-point : to this is due the character of his speculations, which is less over-simplified than one is at first tempted to believe. It was by his labours on the phenomena of monetary circulation and on the depreciation of the banknote that, in 1809, he revealed to the public his capacity as a theorist ; but it was in these matters also that the demands of the deductive and optimistic political economy were best satisfied. The phenomena studied were so simple in form and so abstract, that their detail seemed able to be deduced ' theoretically '[3] from the general conditions of exchange. If the equilibrium of the monetary situation is sometimes compromised, it is the fault of governments with their excessive issues of paper money ; the interested activity of particularly shrewd merchants, particularly well-informed on the state of the world's market,[4] may be counted on to keep this equilibrium normally and safely established, and to ensure that from the free ' choice ' of the parties there shall result an appearance of natural ' necessity ',[5] and that in the ' free competition ' of all with all, ' the interests of the individual and that of the community are never at variance '.[6] Then, in 1815, he brought his research to bear on the Malthusian theory of rent on land. No doubt he main-

---

[1] Sismondi, *Nouveaux Principes*, 1819, t. i. pp. 57-58.   [2] *Ibid.* t. i. p. 395.
[3] *Reply to Mr. Bosanquet's Observations*, etc. p. 319.
[4] *Ibid.*   [5] *Ibid.* pp. 335-336.   [6] *High Price of Bullion*, p. 265

tained that this theory, which was unknown to Adam Smith, left intact the free-trade theory which he had defended ; nevertheless he arrived at a new definition of political economy, conceived no longer as an enquiry ' into the nature and causes of wealth,' but into the way in which wealth, once produced, is divided, outside of exchange, between the classes which combine to make it.[1] Now, will this distribution be harmonious ? Will it be accomplished according to laws which favour equally the interests of all the classes between which the division is made ? This does not appear to be the case. Further, the laws of the distribution of wealth, as conceived by Ricardo, beginning with the fundamental law of rent, are derived from the law of population which is at once a law of disharmony and a law of evolution. It seems to us therefore that a distinction must be made, in Ricardo's economic philosophy, between the static and the dynamic points of view. To anyone who confines himself to considering in Ricardo the static laws of exchange, his doctrine is optimistic ; though the law of value, which seems to confirm the principle of the natural identity of interests, is limited in its operation by many disturbing influences which Ricardo sets out to define methodically. To anyone who analyses in Ricardo the dynamic laws of population, rent, wages and profits, the doctrine is, on the contrary, relatively pessimistic ; and the principle on which it rests might better be called the principle of the natural divergence of interests.

Let us first adopt the static point of view. The equilibrium of economic interests is held to be established by exchange. The cause and the measure of objects in exchange is the amount of labour which has been used in producing them.[2] Hence, if it be recognised as just to reward every producer in proportion to the labour he has provided, it is only necessary to leave exchanges to conform freely to the law which determines them, to make equity reign in the economic world : the natural laws of economic society appear to be the laws of justice, and optimism seems to be the true philosophy. But the optimism authorised by the classical law of value, taken as unrestrictedly true, is by no means absolute. Does Ricardo hold the law of value even to be unreservedly true ? We shall see that it admits of many exceptions, and it is by a conscious artifice in his method that he neglects these exceptions for the convenience of his scientific demonstrations. Is it even simply in the interests of theoretic exposition that he decides to neglect them ? Actually, his whole theory is dominated by the practical pre-occupation of justifying freedom of commercial exchange. The proof of this, as we shall see, is that if the theory of value, stated strictly, results in compromising, in any one particular, the success of the free-trade argument, Ricardo

[1] Ricardo to Malthus, Oct. 10, 1820.
[2] For the first statement of the theory of value which occurs in Ricardo see *High Price of Bullion*, p. 263.

at once sacrifices the theory and the methodical rules of simplification which had made it possible for him to establish it.

In the first place, the law which determines the value of the product in proportion to the amount of labour which has produced it does not justify a purely optimistic conception of economic society. It would perhaps be better to have a world in which abundance reigned, and in which every pleasure was not bought at the price of some labour. Ricardo knew this, and reminded Malthus of it, when he was indignant at the laziness of Irish workmen. The same thing, Ricardo pointed out, was said of the Mexican negroes : ' the land there yields a great abundance of Bananas, Manioc, Potatoes, and Wheat, with very little labour, and the people, having no taste for luxuries and having abundance of food, have the privilege of being idle '. But should they be pitied for this ? ' Happiness is the object to be desired, and we cannot be quite sure that, provided he is equally well fed, a man may not be happier in the enjoyment of the luxury of idleness than in the enjoyment of the luxuries of a neat cottage and good clothes '.[1] Ricardo also recognised that it would be better to have a world built like the communist villages dreamed of by Robert Owen, in which it would never be to the interest of the producer to restrict production and diminish abundance in order to increase the total value of the amount produced.[2] But in an economic world constituted in this way, a man might indeed possess wealth, but he would not know the value of it ; he might perhaps possess happiness, but he would know of no instrument wherewith to measure this happiness. If political economy is to be, as on the principles laid down by Bentham it aspires to become, a rational science of happiness, it must define value not by utility but by labour. J.-B. Say,[3] and after him Destutt de Tracy, wished to derive the idea of value directly from the idea of utility. Whatever may be the variety between the tastes and the needs of men, there is among them, said J.-B. Say, a general estimate of the utility of every particular object and what this estimate is may be gathered from the amount of other objects which they are ready to give in exchange for it. I can, for example, judge, if J.-B. Say is right, that the utility of a coat is three times as great as the utility of a hat, when I find that men in general are ready to give three hats in exchange for a coat. But this is confusing value in use which may be called simply utility, with value in exchange, which may, in an absolute way, be called value. For a product to have value on the market, it must have utility, but this in itself is not enough : for, as J.-B. Say himself asks, ' how can utility be measured ? What seems necessary to one person seems most superfluous to another '.[4] The only conceivable objective measure of utility is the amount of labour which every individual is prepared to provide in order to acquire the

---

[1] Ricardo to Malthus, Sept. 4, 1817.   [2] *Protection to Agriculture*, p. 467.
[3] Ricardo to Malthus, Oct. 10, 1820.
[4] Say, *Traité*, liv. ii. ch. 1.   Ricardo *Principles*, p. 260.

object. It is the competition not of consumers but of producers which determines the price of things. A society of individuals for whom the difficulty of producing objects for consumption was continually increasing, would constantly tend to become less rich exactly in proportion as everything would assume for them an increasing value. In short, utility can only become an object of science in cases when it is bought at the price of a pain. Thus Ricardo's political economy is optimistic, but its optimism is limited by, as well as founded on, the rationalism of the doctrine.

But is the law which determines the value of the product in proportion to the amount of labour which produces it unrestrictedly true when taken by itself? Ricardo knows the restrictions to which the operation of the law is submitted by the nature of economic phenomena. The quantity of labour applied to the production of a commodity, he wrote in the *Principles*, is, under many circumstances, an invariable measure correctly indicating the variations of other commodities.[1] What are these circumstances? Within what limits is it true to say that commodities exchange in proportion to the amount of labour which has been needed to produce them? This amounts to asking within what limits the actual phenomena of exchange justify the economic optimism which is deduced from the abstract law of exchange.

In the first place, by equal quantities of labour Ricardo means labours of equal duration. Yet labour is not a homogeneous quantity, it includes a variety of qualities : the working day of the jeweller, for example, is of more value than the working day of the day labourer. Should it be said—as Adam Smith was tempted to say [2]—that the consideration of various distinct elements, such as the hardship of labour and the skill of the labourer, must be taken into account in the valuation of the quantity of labour? But these elements differ from duration in that they cannot be estimated objectively ; they cannot be calculated in a science of the measure of value. To escape from this difficulty, Ricardo borrowed from Adam Smith another observation according to which the scale of wages, once fixed, is held to be subject, during the course of centuries, to insignificant variations only ; in this case, the relative estimation in which various kinds of labour may be held matters little : if a piece of woollen material which used to be worth two pieces of linen material, is now worth four, this means either that more labour is required to make woollen cloth, or that less is required to make linen. There is, however, a difference to be maintained between Adam Smith's thesis and the thesis which was supported by Ricardo. Adam Smith believed that the scale of wages remains sensibly the same at all stages of civilisation ; that any variations it may suffer are temporary ' revolutions ' which cannot be prolonged ' over any considerable lapse of time '.[3] Ricardo was more

[1] See *Principles*, p. 11. [2] *W. of N.*, vol. i. pp. 49-50.
[3] *W. of N.* p. 151.

circumspect. He wrote at the time when the industrial revolution
was beginning to transform the aspect of the economic world, and,
with the spread of the use of machines, was changing the scale of
wages in various branches of industry. He conjectured that the
relative estimation of different amounts of labour remained almost the
same ' from one generation to another ' ; and, in the end, he confined
himself to maintaining that, if there was any variation, it was very
inconsiderable ' from year to year ' and had little effect ' for short
periods ' on the relative value of commodities.[1] Here, then, is a
first restriction on the general theory of value : it is true to say that
to variations in the amount of labour there correspond equal variations in the value of the product, but only in so far as the relative
estimation of different kinds of labour remains invariable from one
period to another.

But there is a second restriction, which is equally necessary :
the general theory of value is not true of all the objects which are
brought to the market of exchange. There are rare objects—works
of art, archaeological curios, wines of famous vintages—which are
absolutely limited in quantity. It cannot therefore be a question of
measuring the intensity of the need they satisfy by the intensity of
the effort devoted to producing them, since they are such that, *ex
hypothesi*, no amount of effort can increase their quantity. Their
price is said to be a monopoly price, fixed by the competition of the
consumers and not of the producers, and varying indefinitely with
the wealth and the tastes of the purchasers.[2] In short, the condition
which is necessary if value is to be measured by the amount of labour,
is that the objects of exchange should be produced by labour and
should be able to be increased at will by labour without any assignable
limit.

This second restriction is still insufficient. Not only is the general
theory of value not true of all objects, but also it is not true, absolutely,
of any of the objects which are brought to the market of exchange.
The natural value of an object, as defined by the amount of labour,
is only a limit towards which the current price is constantly tending,
and about which it is always oscillating. In the words of Ricardo,
' If we had . . . an invariable standard, by which we could measure
the variation in other commodities, we should find that the utmost
limit to which they could permanently rise, was proportioned to the
additional quantity of labour required for their production '.[3] As to
knowing what will be the extent and duration of the oscillations which
actually keep real value distinct from natural value, experience alone
can tell, and this for two reasons. In the first place it is impossible
to foresee the extent of the oscillation to which prices will be subject
on the basis of observation of the variations to which supply is
subject in relation to ordinary demand. All the calculations
attempted on this basis have been deceptive. Too many elements

<hr/>

[1] *Principles*, p. 15.　　[2] *Ibid*. pp. 9-10, 150.　　[3] *Ibid*. p. 20.

are involved ; the wealth or poverty of the country in question, its power of preserving the superfluous amount of the produce for the satisfaction of future needs, and more or less probable conjectures concerning the future state of supply and demand.[1]   In the second place, it is impossible to define once for all, and without having recourse to experience, what is likely to be the duration of the oscillations in each branch of the national economy.   The agreement between the natural price and the market price depends on the facility with which supply can be increased or diminished ; but this facility is variable.[2]

Consider, for instance, ' hats, shoes, corn and cloth ' ; these are goods ' which are consumed and reproduced from year to year ' : in this case, the interval which elapses between the contraction of demand and the contraction of supply is held by Ricardo to be a short one.[3]   But this is not the case with ' gold, houses and labour '. The diminution of the amount of gold in circulation, which would be necessary to increase its value, could only be produced slowly, by a diminution in production, and by the hoarding of money already coined : ' the quantity of gold . . . would be a little diminished in one year, a little more, in another, and finally its value would be raised ' to the desired extent.   Again, take the case of diminishing the supply of houses, in order to adapt it to a lesser demand.   This diminution can only be brought about by the slow collapse of existing houses.[4]   Take the case, finally, of labour, understood as Ricardo understands it, as a commodity which has its price in the market. In order for an increase in the supply of labour to bring back the price of labour to its natural level, which is assumed to have been exceeded, it would be necessary for children to be born and to grow up to be wage-earners : this likewise requires an interval of many years.[5]   For different objects to exchange in a natural proportion, according to the quantity of labour which they have cost, it is necessary, in principle, that the exchange should be free, and that the various individual egoisms should have every faculty of adapting themselves to one another.   But the abstention of the legislator is not enough to realise these conditions.   For these oscillations of value to be as slight and as short-lived as possible, it is necessary for individuals, the atoms of the economic world, to be absolutely mobile, and also capable of knowing immediately what their interest is, and of immediately acting in accordance with it.   Now Ricardo does not think that it is always possible for them to do this. Human egoism is profoundly modified by ' the desire which every man has to keep his station in life, and to maintain his wealth at the height which it has once attained ' ;[6] and the system of acquired habits, by diminishing the mobility of economic agents, prolongs

[1] *On Prot. to Agric.*, pp. 465-466.
[2] *Principles*, p. 116.
[3] *Ibid*. p. 116.
[4] *Ibid*. p. 120.
[5] *Ibid*. p. 51.
[6] *Ibid*. p. 88.

crises and postpones the moment when the needs of the community will find their satisfaction in a new state of equilibrium.   The fact that workmen will refuse to work for wages below a minimum fixed by their previous habits may diminish the supply of a given product for an indefinite time ; the fact that capitalists feel disinclined to transfer their stock may prevent the solution of an industrial crisis for a long time.[1] On the other hand some crises are due to the fact that, since all labour is dependent upon capital, it is definitely difficult, in so far as this capital is fixed, to pass from one economic occupation to another without making a sacrifice of capital which annuls the advantage of the operation : such was the crisis which followed the end of the war in 1815.[2] These crises are more serious in proportion as nations become more powerful and richer and, consequently, machines become more numerous and more costly.

The theory of value which seems to be the basis of Ricardo's economic optimism is therefore only true with a great many reservations.   In order to understand the extent to which Ricardo's doctrine is optimistic, however, it should be estimated to what extent the disturbing influences which have just been enumerated hide the operation of the law.   Now it is a fact that Ricardo constantly tends to minimise the influence of disturbing factors.   He holds to be negligible the variations which occur in the estimation of different qualities of labour.   While the principle is true only of those commodities whose quantity labour can increase indefinitely, these objects, according to him, form ' by far the greatest part of those goods which are the objects of desire '.[3]   Finally, while prices are always oscillating round natural value, and while the equilibrium of the economic world tends to establish itself at the cost of a perpetual disequilibrium, Ricardo clearly tends always to insist on the temporary and fugitive nature of these oscillations.[4]   A letter which he wrote to Malthus, in a year of industrial depression, betrays Ricardo's uncertainty on this point.   He deplored ' the prejudices and obstinacy with which men persevere in their old employments ; they daily expect a change for the better, and therefore continue to produce commodities for which there is no adequate demand.'   In defiance of his principles Ricardo dreamt of correcting these prejudices by means of an enlightened despotism, an industrial providence : ' if a superior genius had the arrangement of the capital of the country under his control, he might, in a very little time, make trade as active as ever '.   In short, he felt it difficult to understand the crisis, though he was obliged to state that it existed.   ' If I wanted cloth and you cotton goods, it would be great folly in us both, with a view to an exchange between us, for one to produce velvets and the other wine ; we are guilty of some such folly now, and I can scarcely account for the length of time that this delusion continues '.   Finally, he tried to

[1] *Principles*, p. 160.　　　　　　　[2] *Ibid*. p. 161.
[3] *Ibid*. p. 10.　　　　　　　　　　　[4] *Ibid*. see especially p. 66.

hope that he had deceived himself : ' after all, the mischief may not be so great as it appears '.[1] This is the instinct of the logician and the rationalist who, in order to work out the fundamental principles of science, has to isolate the principles and abstract the disturbing causes, and in order to understand the abstract better, has to persuade himself that the abstract is identical with the real. He was aware himself that he used this method of systematic abstraction, of elimination of the accidental. ' If I am too theoretical (which I really believe is the case), you I think are too practical ' . . . he wrote to Malthus. ' It appears to me that one great cause of our difference in opinion on the subjects which we have so often discussed is that you have always in your mind the immediate and temporary effects of particular charges, whereas I put these immediate and temporary effects quite aside, and fix my whole attention on the permanent state of things which will result from them. Perhaps you estimate these temporary effects too highly, whilst I am too much disposed to undervalue them '.[2] Thus, on this point, Ricardo's rationalism strengthens his optimism. For anyone who adopts the static point of view and neglects the temporary oscillations of supply and demand, the dominating principle of Ricardo's economic philosophy is indeed, in the last analysis, the principle of the natural identity of interests.

Because Ricardo was essentially a theorist, it does not, on the other hand, follow that he was not inspired by any practical preoccupation. The practical consequence of the principle of the natural identity of interests was the policy of free-trade. It was free-trade which assured to every nation the advantage of the commodities produced in all climates. It was free-trade which, by breaking down economic frontiers, compensated for the irregularity of the seasons in each part of the globe. ' Under a system of perfectly free commerce, each country naturally devotes its capital and labour to such employments as are most beneficial to each. The pursuit of individual advantage is admirably connected with the universal good of the whole. By stimulating industry, by rewarding ingenuity, and by using most efficaciously the peculiar powers bestowed by nature, it distributes labour most effectively and most economically ; while, by increasing the general mass of productions, it diffuses general benefit, and binds together, by one common tie of interest and intercourse, the universal society of nations throughout the civilised world '.[3] But is it certain that the theory of value adopted by Ricardo supplies an absolute justification of the thesis of the universal identity of national interests ? Ricardo was too exact a logician to believe this. According to him Adam Smith was wrong in thinking that ' freedom of commerce, which undoubtedly promotes the interest of the whole, promotes also that of each particular country '.[4] For instance, Adam Smith thought he could prove

[1] Ricardo to Malthus, Oct. 10, 1820.   [2] *Ibid.* Oct. 7, 1815, and Jan. 24, 1817.
[3] *Principles*, pp. 75-76.   [4] Ch. xxv.

that the policy of protection adopted by the countries of Europe in colonial affairs, which was obviously harmful to the colonies, was likewise harmful to the mother-countries.   Ricardo, who is less sure of the harmony of interests, shows, in contrast to Adam Smith, that the trade of the mother-country with the colony can be regulated in such a way that it will be at the same time less useful to the colony, and more useful to the mother-country than an absolutely free trade.[1] Does Ricardo therefore abandon, at least partially, the thesis of free-trade, since it appears not to be normally derivable from the principle of his economic philosophy ?   On the contrary ; we see here a remarkable reaction of conclusions on principles.   The imperative need felt by the industrial classes in England about the year 1817 for universal free-trade, is the historical fact which doubtless explains the success of the new doctrine.   Now the theory of exchange, defined as it is by Ricardo, justifies the policy of free-trade in many respects ; but on certain points it tells against it.   Does Ricardo therefore sacrifice the cause of free-trade in order to preserve intact his theory of value ?   It is the opposite which happens.   In order to strengthen the free-trade cause, and show that the policy of free-trade is really favourable to the interests of the English people, Ricardo modifies the law of value and the psychological theory on which it is based.   It is necessary first to analyse his theory of foreign trade, in which the law of value no longer applies, in order properly to understand what we have called the static part of his economic philosophy.

For economic optimism to be rigorously true, it must be granted that all individuals are naturally egoistic and intelligent, that they are constantly occupied in seeking, and are capable of immediately discovering, the means of satisfying the demands of their pecuniary interest ; and the obstacles which time and space put in their way must be held to be negligible.   But is not man's attachment for the soil on which he was born, and on which he has become accustomed to live and work— and is not the feeling of solidarity which unites individuals of the same nation, who are attached to their native land, a psychological reality, a datum of experience, which the economist must take into account on the same grounds as he takes account of the egoistic motive ?   Ricardo, far from underestimating the importance of this new motive, bases his whole theory of foreign exchange, or, as Stuart Mill later put it, of international value, on the consideration of it.[2]   So long as every individual is left free to use his capital as he likes, it seems that he must look for the most advantageous use for it : he will be dissatisfied with a profit of 10 per cent, if, by transferring his capital, he can secure a profit of 15 per cent.   It is the restless desire, common to all capitalists, to leave a less profitable for a more profitable concern which tends to equalise the rate of profit over the

---

[1] *Principles*, p. 204 *seq.*

[2] *Principles*, p. 172 *seq.*   This theory is held by Ricardo's disciples to have been one of his greatest discoveries.

whole market of exchange. Nevertheless this law of the equalisation of profits only applies, according to Ricardo, in the interior of any one country. Let us consider, on the other hand, the case of two different countries which exchange their respective products. If to produce a certain quantity of woollen material, the labour of a hundred men is necessary in England, and the labour of ninety men in Portugal ; while a hundred and twenty men are necessary in England to produce the quantity of wine which can be produced by eighty men in Portugal, it is not at first clear, how, on Ricardo's theory, any exchange can come about between the wool of England and the wine of Portugal. The product of the labour of a hundred men could never be exchanged for the product of the labour of eighty men as between two parts of the same country, for example, between London and Yorkshire. It does nevertheless happen that, under these conditions, it is to the interest of Portugal to exchange her wines for English wool : the exchange value of two products is determined, as between two countries, not by the respective amounts of labour which are necessary to produce the two objects, but by the respective amounts of labour which would be necessary to produce them in each of the two countries considered by itself. Why is there this difference ? It is because capital can be less easily transferred from one country to another than from one province to another. Why, again, is there this difference ? Here we come back to the fundamental reason of the phenomenon, that is to say ' the natural disinclination which every man has to quit the country of his birth and connections '.[1]

No doubt it would be to the interest of English capitalists to go and manufacture woollen material in Portugal ; but experience shows that the real or imaginary insecurity of capital when it escapes the direct supervision of its owner, combined with the natural aversion which every man feels to breaking with everything to which he is accustomed in order to go and submit himself to a strange government and to new laws, puts obstacles in the way of an exodus of capital. Capitalists will be satisfied with smaller profits in their own country rather than go to seek a more advantageous use for their wealth in foreign lands. As a result of the feelings we have been analysing nations are so many economic worlds, relatively isolated from one another. ' These feelings ', adds Ricardo, ' I should be sorry to see weakened '.[2] Thus, in Ricardo, the theory of value and the theory of foreign trade rest on two psychological principles which are distinct and almost contradictory. But why do Ricardo and his disciples attach an equal importance to the two theories, almost without noticing that they contradict each other ? It is because there are two ways in which logical propositions can agree, either by the identity of the principle from which they are derived (this is not the case here), or by the identity of the conclusions to which they lead. An ever-increasing section of the English people desired free-trade.

[1] *Principles*, p. 149 (cf. p. 77).   [2] *Ibid.* p. 77.

This need for free-trade was met, in the first place, by the theory that the interests of all men are identical, and that humanity is a single nation, and nations are its provinces. But when several provinces unite to form a nation, may it not happen that some of them find themselves sacrificed in spite of the general prosperity ? Is it not to be feared that the same thing will happen when the commercial barriers which divide nations are broken down ; and that the whole of industry will leave the nations where labour is dear and move to those where it is cheap ! Will it be possible to set at rest the anxieties which may be aroused by this displacement of industry merely by showing that one day (after how many years, or centuries ?) labour will grow more expensive in the places where it is cheap to-day, and the equilibrium of the economic world will be re-established to the advantage of the nations which were temporarily sacrificed ? These anxieties are answered, much more directly, by the new theory of foreign trade, which is in contradiction to the preceding one, and according to which international values are governed by a different law from the law which governs interprovincial values—according to which, in other words, humanity is not a great nation and the nations its provinces. There is a true logic, in which the principle justifies the consequences ; and there is a false logic, the logic of men of action and of party men in which the end justifies the means.

Thus the static part of Ricardo's political economy can be summed up in the following terms : that it is possible, in conformity with the principles of the science of wealth, to establish a commercial cosmo-politanism by means of universal free-trade, and that the principle of the spontaneous identity of the interests of all men is true. If, moreover, the theory of value on which this static economics is based, calls for reservations, either these reservations are so unimportant that they can be neglected by the economist, who considers production as a whole and brings his observations to bear over long lapses of time, or else they are of such a kind that they reinforce the arguments which are favourable, in England, to the policy of free-trade. But at this stage a fresh logical restriction should be made of the theory of value, and one which is more serious than any of the preceding ones. When a certain number of objects identical in their nature and in their utility are thrown on the market they are all sold for the same price. In order for the law of value to find its application here it would be necessary for the production of each one of these objects, whose market value is the same, to have cost the same amount of labour. But it is the opposite which does occur ; the truth is that the value of each one is regulated not by what it cost to produce, but ' by the real difficulties encountered by that producer who is least favoured ', or ' by its cost of production to those who were the least favoured '.[1] However, the restriction would still be negligible and the theory of

[1] *Principles*, pp. 220 and 221.

value would tend to be applicable with an increasing exactitude if it could be proved that with time the difference between the costs of production of each category of objects tend towards zero. But if it were the opposite which occurred, if, for some classes of objects, and those the most essential of all to human life, this difference were constantly increasing, what would be the effect of this law of evolution on the general interest, on the greatest happiness of the greatest number ? It is a law of this kind which, as we shall see, is the basis of the whole of the dynamic part of Ricardo's political economy. Thus there is a diametrical opposition in Ricardo between the fundamental principles of economic statics and dynamics.

Population tends constantly to increase. But on the other hand, land, from which the human population demands its food, is limited in quantity, or, to be more exact—for the moment has not yet come when the human species is about to encumber the whole surface of the earth—land is of varying quality ; and those lands which have a given degree of fertility are limited in quantity. It is because the land is neither unlimited in quantity nor uniform in quality, and because, with the increase of population, lands of inferior quality come into cultivation, that rent arises for the land of superior quality. For without prejudicing his farmers in their competition with other farmers, the owner of the land can obviously exact, under the name of rent, ' the difference between the produce obtained by equal portions of labour and capital employed on land of the same or different qualities '.[1] While the spread of new technical processes makes this difference constantly smaller in the case of manufactured products, the ' physical conditions ' to which the human race is subject make it constantly greater as regards the food produced by agriculture. Thus it is true to say, with Adam Smith, that the income raised by owners of land as such will rise with the natural progress of society and wealth. But Adam Smith did not see the reason of this phenomenon, and this was why he concluded wrongly that the interests of the landlord are identical with the general interests of society.[2] Actually, the rise in the natural price of corn is to the interest of the landlords alone in the whole of society : for the rise in rent is the inevitable result of difficulty of producing, without which the natural price could not suffer a rise. Not only then is the landlord's position improved with the increase of population on land which is scarce and unfertile because he obtains an increased quantity of the products of the soil ; it is improved also because the value in exchange of this quantity is increased. If rent rises from fourteen to twenty-eight quarters, it is more than doubled because the landlord can buy, in exchange for the twenty-eight quarters, more than double the amount of commodities he could formerly buy with the fourteen quarters. In short, it is a necessary law that the landlord grows richer by the very fact that life becomes more and more difficult for

[1] *Principles*, p. 91-92.　　　　[2] *Ibid.* p. 188-189.

the human species. ' The interest of the landlord ', we are quoting
word for word from Ricardo's pamphlet of 1815, ' is always opposed to
the interest of every other class in the community. His situation is
never so prosperous, as when food is scarce and dear : whereas, all
other persons are greatly benefited by procuring cheap food '.[1]

In order to establish the law of the increase of rent, no doubt, it is
requisite to make a certain number of preliminary logical abstractions.
Especially, it must be assumed that there has been no improvement
in the agricultural industry : for the progress of human industry
might be able to substitute for the diminishing fertility of the soil a
sort of increasing and artificial fertility, might equalise the natural
inequalities between landed properties, and hide the operation of the
law by making the price of the food necessary for life fall as quickly
or more quickly than the physical conditions tend to make it rise.
But then these improvements are fatal to landlords, at least temporarily,[2] until the population has once more become too great, because
they make rent fall. It is to the interest of the landlords that the cost
of production of corn should be increased. But this is not to the
interest of the consumer. He requires corn to be cheap in relation
to money and to all exchangeable commodities : for it is with these
commodities or with money that he buys corn. Nor is this to the
interest of the manufacturer. For the rise in the price of corn brings
about a rise in wages without bringing about a rise in the price of the
commodities which he manufactures and sells : therefore he has not
only to give a greater quantity of these commodities for the corn
which he himself consumes, but he has also to spend more in wages.
' All classes, therefore, except the landlords, will be injured by the
increase in the price of corn. The dealings between the landlord and
the public are not like the dealings in trade, whereby both the seller
and the buyer may equally be said to gain, but the loss is wholly on
one side, and the gain wholly on the other '.[3] It is at this stage that
the new aspect of Ricardo's political economy makes its appearance.
' Political economy ', he wrote to Malthus, ' you think is an enquiry
into the nature and causes of wealth ; I think it should rather be
called an enquiry into the laws which determine the division of the
produce of industry amongst the classes who concur in its formation '.[4] Now the evolutionary law of rent is the foundation of political
economy as thus defined, and it is so precisely in so far as it is the
principle of a divergence between certain ' class ' interests. For we
now have to consider in society not merely individuals freely exchanging the product of their labour one with another, but classes ; and
these classes are not the work of governments setting against each
other interests which are naturally identical, they are the work of

---

[1] *Influence of a Low Price*, etc., p. 378.
[2] On this point Ricardo seems to modify his 1815 thesis in 1817. See Ricardo
to Trower, July 21, 1820.
[3] *Principles*, pp. 202-203.   [4] Ricardo to Malthus, Oct. 10, 1820.

laws of nature. It is by basing himself on the dynamic law of differential rent, and by studying the way in which it contributes to the formation of the various economic ' classes ', that Ricardo works out the theory of the distribution of wealth and of the incidence of taxation which Adam Smith had merely outlined.

Ricardo accepts in a modified form the law of wages formulated by Adam Smith. What had been for Adam Smith the minimum below which the price of labour cannot fall, becomes for Ricardo the natural price of labour below which wages cannot fall for any length of time, but also above which they cannot rise, except temporarily : this ' natural price of labour is that price which is necessary to enable the labourers, one with another, to subsist and to perpetuate their race, without either increase or diminution '.[1] It may indeed occur that the workman may profit by a rise in wages to increase his own comfort instead of taking on responsibilities as head of a family. But, if we are to believe Ricardo, ' so great are the delights of domestic society, that, in practice, it is invariably found that an increase of population follows the amended condition of the labourer '.[2] Hence arises a greater demand for food which cannot be indefinitely satisfied from a soil which is limited in quantity and mediocre in quality ; in this way wages are, in the last resort, perpetually prevented from rising. Should wages then be treated as a constant quantity while rent is a variable, varying according to a known law ? Because it is the normal increase of population which constantly brings back the market price of labour to its natural price, and because the law of population is pre-eminently a law of evolution—the first to be introduced into English political economy—is it not to be presumed that there must be an evolutionary law of wages like the evolutionary law of rent ? Actually, the natural price of labour has always a tendency to rise with the natural progress of society. But it must be noticed that this rise in wages is caused by the rise in the price of corn and of objects of primary necessity due to the increase in population and the increasing difficulty of producing agricultural commodities. If wages, estimated in terms of money, were to suffer a fall while all the objects which they serve to buy were more expensive, the workman would be doubly affected and soon would not be able to live. It is obvious therefore what is the essential difference between the rise in wages and the rise in rent. Rent is increased not only when estimated in terms of money, but also when estimated in terms of corn. The landlord receives more corn, and each given portion of this corn is exchangeable for a greater quantity of all the goods whose value has not varied. The workman's lot is less fortunate : he receives wages which are higher if estimated in money and lower if estimated in corn. ' While the price of corn rises 10 per cent., wages will always rise less than 10 per cent., but rent will always rise more ; the condition of the labourer will generally decline, and that of the

[1] *Principles*, p. 50.　　　[2] *Ibid.* p. 248.

landlord will always be improved '.[1] There is a real fall in wages, and only an apparent and nominal rise. We thus have a law which defines the divergence of interest as between the class of wage-earners and the class of land-owners.

The law having been determined which regulates the evolution of rent and wages, the nature and the evolution of profit remain to be defined. For it is legitimate that the labourer should be able to make whatever use he wishes of the product of his labour, and especially should be able, if he wishes, to draw a profit or some interest from it. It is moreover useful to society as a whole, that instead of consuming the fruit of his labour unproductively he should use it to increase production in the form of wages or machinery : it is therefore fitting that the capitalist should be remunerated in direct proportion to the time during which he refrains from using his capital unproductively. But what is the law which is to define the rate of profit and interest, the amount of the annual product of labour which is destined to fall to the capitalist ? On that land and on that part of the produce of human industry which pays no rent the value produced can be split up entirely into profits and wages : thus, if wages rise, profits fall ; and conversely, if profits rise, wages fall.[2] Does there not follow from this law of the inverse variation of profits and wages a fresh divergence of economic interests, as between the class of capitalists and the class of labourers ?

It was in this direction that the theory of the distribution of wealth, made classical by Ricardo, was soon to be developed by more democratic and equalitarian economists. William Thompson and Thomas Hodgskin were both Utilitarians : Thompson was a correspondent of Bentham's ;[3] Hodgskin a friend and *protégé* of Francis Place.[4] These neglected the divergence of interest between the landlords and the other classes of society which Ricardo had pointed out ; but they both of them borrowed from Ricardo the definition of natural wages and the law of the inverse variation of profits and wages : from which they very logically concluded that the capitalist régime was incoherent.[5] In this same direction Robert Owen had tried to show, on the publication of Ricardo's great book, how the introduction of machinery falsified the mechanism of the distribution of wealth. Machines compete with the workmen and reduce the number of workmen necessary for the same production, and the rate of wages for an equal number of men employed. Manufacturers get into the way of producing for foreign markets, which they imagine can be indefinitely extended, produce which they know cannot be absorbed by their own workmen, who are badly paid and dying of hunger. This

---

[1] *Principles*, p. 55.   [2] *Ibid*. pp. 60 *seq*.
[3] On the relations of Thompson with the Benthamites, see Bowring, vol. x. p. 506-7, and Mill, *Autobiography*, p. 125.
[4] See the study on *Thomas Hodgskin* by the author, 1903.
[5] See William Thompson, *An Inquiry*, etc.

LAWS OF ECONOMIC SOCIETY 333

theory is diametrically opposed to the optimistic theory of ' markets ',
invented by J.-B. Say and popularised in England by James Mill,
according to which all production creates its demand and, consequently, the results of the progress of machinery must always be
universally and immediately beneficial. Yet, in the third edition of
his book, Ricardo [1] includes a theory which is recognisable as Robert
Owen's theory, very much modified. Suppose that a capitalist, who
is both a farmer and a manufacturer, with a capital of £20,000, pays
over to his labourers a circulating capital of £13,000, and draws from
his industry an income of £2,000 at the end of the year : his gross
income amounts to £15,000, and his net income to £2,000. Suppose
that the following year he uses £13,000, half for the production of the
same commodities as the first year and the other half for the production
of a machine. The total value of the product would still be £15,000 ;
the net income of the capitalist would still be £2,000 ; but the gross
income would have fallen from £15,000 to £7,500 ; and the third
year the capitalist would only have £5,500 for the employment of
labour. This matters little to the capitalist, but it is clear how much
it matters to the labourers. It is a truth ' as demonstrable as any of
the truths of geometry ' ; [2] and the hostility to machinery manifested
by the working classes is not founded on ' prejudice and error ', but
is ' conformable to the correct principles of political economy '.[3]
No doubt Ricardo is inclined to believe that the fall in the value of
the produce of the machines and the greater facility, resulting from
this fall in value, with which the manufacturer can transform his
income into capital would ultimately find labour for a greater number
of workmen.[4] Thus the momentary crisis would have a normal
solution ; it would be one of the accidents which the static economics
systematically ignores. But on the other hand Ricardo emphasises
the fact that it is an accident which tends to reproduce itself in a
permanent way, under the influence of the dynamic law of population.
In proportion as the population increases, foodstuffs are subject to a
rise, because they become more difficult to produce on the last
land taken into cultivation. Hence a corresponding rise in wages.
Hence, finally, a tendency for capital to take the shape of machines
and of fixed capital. ' Machinery and labour are in constant competition '.[5]

Thus the law according to which profits and wages vary in inverse
ratio seems to represent a natural divergence of interest between the
class of capitalists and the class of wage-earners ; Ricardo himself
recognised that the constant tendency of capital to take the form of
fixed capital brings about a rivalry between the master and the
workman and between machinery and labour. It is nevertheless
certain that Ricardo never considered the accumulation of profits
as the essential cause of the fall in wages ; and the reason for this

[1] *Principles*, p. 235.   [2] Ricardo to MacCulloch, June 18, 1821.
[3] *Principles*, p. 239.   [4] *Ibid*. pp. 237-238.   [5] *Ibid*. p. 241.

fact is to be found likewise in the dynamic part of his economic philosophy; for Ricardo considered profits as subject to a law of evolution, which is a law of constant diminution. The fall in profits in a progressive society had already long been asserted by the economists; but Adam Smith was wrong in wishing to explain it by the increase in the supply of capital, and by the very accumulation of profits. As capital increases, so the demand for capital increases in exactly the same proportions. As J.-B. Say and James Mill had proved, all supply constitutes a demand.[1] It is from the law of differential rent combined with the law of wages, that is to say, in the last resort, from the law of population, that, according to Ricardo, the evolutionary law of profits is derived. Because the levying of rent equalises for all portions of the land under cultivation the part of the value of the produce which is divided between the capitalist and the labourer, and because, on the other hand, when the population increases and recourse has to be had to less fertile lands, the price of food necessary for human subsistence ceaselessly increases, it is necessary for the natural price of labour to increase in the same proportion, and consequently for the share of the capitalist to diminish constantly. The share of the *value* of the produce is always decreasing; the *rate* of profit decreases according to a still more rapid progression; finally, the accumulation of capital cannot compensate, beyond a certain point, for this double diminution, and the *total quantity* of the profits received by the capitalist itself diminishes. It is conceivable ideally that the natural value of labour might end by absorbing all the annual produce of industry which is not levied by the landowner; but long before this ideal limit is reached, society would stop in its natural progress at a state of things at which the rate of profit was so low that it would prevent all accumulation and *almost all the produce of the country*, after the labourers were paid, would be the property of the owners of the soil and the collectors of tithes and taxes.[2] It is not therefore the manufacturer but the landlord who grows rich by the poverty of the labourer; and the manufacturer grows poor for the same reason that the landlord grows rich. The regular evolution, the 'permanent variation'[3] of profits is as necessary, so Ricardo tells us, as the gravitation of the heavenly bodies.[4] The metaphor is not perhaps perfectly appropriate: for the law of gravity is a static law which should be likened rather to the tendency of market price to confuse itself with natural price. The law of profits, on the other hand, is a dynamic law: if, to manifest its necessary or 'natural' character, one wished to borrow a metaphor from the domain of the physical sciences, it could more exactly be compared, to-day, with the law of entropy or of the diminution of energy.

Some months before completing his *Principles* Ricardo was stopped

[1] *Principles*, ch. xxi. pp. 174 *seq.*
[2] *Ibid.* p. 67.   [3] *Ibid.* p. 60.   [4] *Ibid.* p. 66.

by an unforeseen difficulty.[1] He observed that the theory of the distribution of wealth reacts on the theory of value in exchange ; he consequently made the necessary modifications in this latter theory. This particular point of Ricardo's doctrine is especially instructive, if we are to understand the way in which, on his view, the distribution of wealth between the landowner and the capitalist, after the labourer has received his wages, is brought about.

Commodities possess in exchange values which are proportional to the quantities of labour which they have respectively cost. But economic production presupposes, as a general rule, the co-operation of labour and capital ; and the capital engaged in the production may, according to the case, possess the qualities either of ' fixed ' or of ' circulating ' capital, it may be more or less rapidly degraded, and may need to be built up more or less often ; it may, in short, vary very much in ' durability '.[2] In all cases in which men do not use fixed capitals, and in all the cases also in which men use fixed capitals of the same value and durability, it is rigorously true to say that exchange-value is proportionate to the value of the labour expended. But this is no longer true when producers, in various branches of production, use different proportions of fixed capital, or, if you like, capitals of different durability. A farmer and a manufacturer employ a hundred men each, the farmer to produce corn, the manufacturer to make a machine : the corn and the machine, which are the products of the same amount of labour, will have the same value at the end of the year. The second year, the farmer again employs a hundred men to produce corn, the manufacturer employs a hundred men to manufacture woollen material with the machine. For the law of value to be true, the value of the woollen material, the produce of the labour of a hundred men for two years, would have to be double the value of the corn, the produce of the labour of a hundred men for one year. Actually, it will be a little greater : for the farmer has begun his second campaign with the same capital as the first year, while the manufacturer, on the other hand, has added to his capital the profit which he received at the end of the first year, and is now demanding profits proportionally equal to those of the farmer on a greater capital than his. In short, the labour of a hundred men employed during two years produces more value than the labour of two hundred men employed during one year. Thus the duration of the cycle of production is a fresh cause of the increase of value over and above the amount of labour expended. Thus the more the natural progress of human ingenuity multiplies machines and prolongs the cycle of production, the more industrial products grow dearer in relation to agricultural products, in the production of which a smaller proportion of fixed capital is involved. Will it not follow from this law of

---

[1] He had long felt the difficulty of the problem of Value. See Ricardo to Malthus Feb. 7 and Oct. 5, 1816.

[2] *Principles*, pp. 20 *seq.*

evolution that industrial producers are constantly benefited as compared with agricultural producers and tillers of the soil ?

But the conclusion which Ricardo draws is quite different. No sooner has he laid down the principle which we have just stated, than he raises a new problem and asks how the relative value of two commodities, produced with different quantities of fixed capital, is affected by a rise in the value of labour. We know that the necessary and constant rise in the price of corn brings about a corresponding rise in wages, and an inverse movement of fall in profits. Let us therefore take up once more our example of the farmer and of the manufacturer of woollens, and let us suppose that the normal movement of a fall in profits is felt in the course of the second year under consideration. The fall in profits will have no influence on the price of the corn which the farmer will bring to the market at the end of the year, for it is exactly equal to the simultaneous rise in wages. To compensate, it will cause a fall in the value of woollens as compared with the value of corn, for the woollen merchant pays, *ex hypothesi*, the same wages as the farmer, but the fall in his profits affects a capital which is larger than the farmer's. Thus ' all commodities which are produced by very valuable machinery, or in very valuable buildings, or which require a great length of time before they can be brought to market, would fall in relative value, while all those which were chiefly produced by labour, or which would be speedily brought to market, would rise in relative value '.[1] Thus Ricardo started by asserting that the greater the amount of fixed capital, the greater is the rise. He finished by asserting that the greater the amount of fixed capital, the greater the fall. It is easy to see, however, that this fall only partially compensates for the inverse movement of rise which has been defined and explained above. But Ricardo's whole attention is concentrated on the second proposition, because it is closely connected with his philosophy of economic evolution, based on the theory of the decreasing fertility of the soil, and because it implies that agricultural products must necessarily grow dearer as compared with manufactured products, and that landed proprietors must grow progressively richer at the expense of the rest of society.

It is in this way that the laws which govern the evolution of rent, profits and wages produce not a harmony but a conflict of interests between the three classes of the economic world ; and Ricardo's abstract formulae are but the faithful expression of the spectacle presented by the history of his own time. A duel was being fought out under his eyes between two societies, the one immovable, and attached by its interests and its feelings to the corner of the earth on which the individuals which made it up were born and died ; the other infinitely mobile, without local attachments and always ready to transfer its capital, at a moment's notice, from one part of the world to another. Is not the whole difference, in Ricardo's political

[1] *Principles*, p. 23.

economy, between capital and land at bottom reducible to the fact that capital is a mobile, and land an immobile auxiliary of labour ? As soon as capital becomes fixed and immobile in the land, it can be said, in the economic sense of the word, that it becomes land, and that profit, according to Ricardo himself, ' will appear in the form of rent '.[1] Before 1815, manufacturers and landowners had lived in peace. The landowners, who were masters in Parliament, granted to the manufacturers the suppression of all the obstacles which the legislation of the sixteenth century had imposed on masters in their relations with workmen. The manufacturers allowed the continuation of the system of prohibitive duties, thanks to which the large landowners artificially raised the price of corn and the rent of land, and that without much inconvenience to themselves ; to such an extent were they the uncontested masters of the commercial market of the whole world. The rupture occurred after 1815. With the end of the war, industry was resumed on the continent ; Europe had less need of the products of English industry ; English industry had less need of workmen ; and the workmen, on lower wages, could no longer tolerate the régime of dear bread. The question arose as to whether there would ultimately be a fusion between the old landed aristocracy and the new commercial, industrial and financial aristocracy. Actually, the fusion did eventually take place ; the new moneyed aristocracy acquired the same prestige in England that it had formerly acquired in Venice and in Holland ; and England became a primarily industrial and commercial nation, without in any way losing its aristocratic character as a nation. But in England, in contrast to what had taken place in Venice and in Holland, the merchant aristocracy found itself opposed to an aristocracy of landlords who were in possession of all the political privileges, and whose interests were not identical with its own. Hence arose a crisis which at times took on an almost revolutionary aspect. The alliance of the *bourgeoisie* and the people, of capitalists and labourers, against the landed aristocracy—this was the formula which led finally to the economic Reform of 1846, even more important perhaps in the social history of modern England than the political Reform of 1832. The theory of the distribution of wealth, as set forth by Ricardo, is the expression of this critical period in the economic history of England. In England, at the beginning of the century, rent had risen, the rise in wages had been insufficient to counterbalance the rise in the price of corn, and profits had fallen. There might perhaps be conflicts of interests between masters and workmen, but in the common poverty of both, these conflicts were unimportant ; the only really serious conflict of interest, and one which was made constantly worse by the natural progress of things, was the conflict between the owners of the land and all the rest of society. Ricardo defines and denounces it : how, then, can

[1] *Principles*, pp. 162-163 (note).

it be claimed that his system is reducible to a kind of absolute optimism ?

But nevertheless—and it is this which justifies his opponents in condemning his fatalism—Ricardo wished that the State should refrain from interfering in economic relations as much as possible : on this point, in spite of divergences in doctrine, he remained faithful to the tradition of Quesnay and Adam Smith.   It seems as though no logical reconciliation were possible between the principle of the natural identity of interests, which sums up Ricardo's theory of economic equilibrium, and the principle of the natural divergence of interests, which sums up his theory of the distribution of wealth. Indeed, Ricardo is satisfied with a practical reconciliation, a reconciliation through consequences : from both the law of differential rent and the law of value he draws conclusions in favour of commercial liberty.   If the high price of corn is really due to excessive taxes, which the landlords seek to escape at the expense of the consumer, it is legitimate that imported corn should pay a duty equal to the tax. But if the rise in price follows the rise of rent and the cultivation of less fertile lands, in the interest of the greatest number rent should be lowered by allowing foreign corn to be imported duty-free.   It is clear, however, that this is only a temporary remedy : Ricardo knows that, after a time, less and less fertile lands must necessarily be exploited and consequently that the rent of the landowner must rise. He does not accept the principle of the natural identity of interests, and yet he unreservedly adheres to the principle of commercial and industrial liberty ; does this mean that the two principles are up to a certain point independent of each other ?   Ricardo having defined ' the laws by which wages are regulated, and by which the happiness of far the greatest part of every community is governed ' added without any transition : ' like all other contracts, wages should be left to the fair and free competition of the market, and should never be controlled by the interference of the legislature '.[1]   Now these laws of wages are the laws which, according to Ricardo's definition, perpetuate the poverty of the labourer and of his family, by virtue of a natural necessity.   What then is the logical link between the two principles which Ricardo thus sets down one after the other ?   Why, for no given reason, forbid the legislative power to interfere to restore to the labourer a more justly proportioned share of the produce of his labour ?   Is it because the policy of *laisser faire* and *laisser passer* can stand by itself, when the principle of the identity of interests is no longer accepted ?   Does it necessarily imply optimism, or can it be reconciled, perhaps, with a relative pessimism ?

Let us consider the problem of taxation, with the discussion of which the second half of the *Principles* is concerned.   Ricardo retains Adam Smith's four rules, the first of which presupposes the principle

[1] *Principles*, p. 57.

of the natural identity of interests. Apart from this, he bases his
whole theory of taxation on a single principle, the statement of which
amounts to a fifth rule, to be added to the rules of Adam Smith ;
taxation should fall as much as possible on income and not on capital.[1]
Now this new rule again implies, in a way, the principle of the
identity of interests. According to Ricardo, capital should not be
taxed, because this would be to ' impair the funds for the maintenance
of labour, and thereby diminish the future production of the country '.
In other words, in formulating this fiscal principle, Ricardo is
implicitly accepting the optimistic theory of Say and Mill, according
to which all production constitutes a demand, and so a general overproduction is logically impossible. But, on the other hand, does not
the law of rent, with the radical opposition of interest between the
landlord and the capitalist which it establishes, imply that the income
of society can be distributed in different and more or less beneficial
ways as between the various classes of economic society, according
to whether it takes the shape of profits for the capitalists or is
annexed under the name of rent by the unproductive class of landlords ? Is it not then conceivable that the State, by seeing that taxes
fall in preference on such or such particular incomes, should artificially re-establish an equitable division of public wealth ? A tax on
rent, for example, would hit only the landlord, and could not be
passed on by him to the consumers.[2] It would, it is true, be a class
tax ; but since it would help to re-establish the equilibrium between
the interests of a class privileged by nature and other classes of society,
why, in the logic of Utilitarianism, should this tax be held to be unjust ?
Yet Ricardo hesitates to accept this solution. He repeats Adam
Smith's formula that ' it would surely be very unjust to tax exclusively the revenue of any particular class of a community '.[3] Yet
Adam Smith's rule is not applicable to a case in which there is no
natural harmony of the interests of all classes. Besides, Ricardo
makes other objections to the tax on rent. These objections, which
strike him as more serious, concern the question as to whether the
tax, which is in essence just, is at the same time practicable. It is very
difficult to draw the necessary distinction, within the tribute which
the farmer actually pays to the landlord, between differential rent,
whose abstract definition is provided by political economy, and the
profits of the capital advanced by the landlord to the tenant, which is
confused with economic rent. Ricardo fully recognises indeed that
by altering the form of their contracts, the landlords could easily find
a way of dividing the two elements. He ultimately concludes,
however, that if this distinction were not successfully made, the tax
would fall, after a short interval, not on the landlord but on the
consumer, in so far as it hit elements other than actual differential
rent : consequently he condemns the tax.[4] He also points out that,

[1] *Principles*, ch. viii. pp. 87 *seq.*   [2] *Ibid.* p. 102.   [3] *Ibid.* p. 121.
[4] *Ibid.* p. 103.

in many cases, the land is purchased by a man who has earned his fortune himself by his own labour ;[1] in this case it represents the reward of this labour ; could a general tax on rent make an exception for this man ? Would it not be at once more useful and simpler to facilitate the transmission of real property by suppressing the taxes which in fact make it impossible, than to make it more difficult still by imposing on the land a tax which can be indefinitely increased ?[2] In the last resort, Ricardo hesitates to advocate the tax on the income of the landlord chiefly because of considerations of a practical nature— not because interests are naturally identical, but because the State finds that it is powerless artificially to re-establish harmony as between interests which are naturally discordant. Looking at it from the dynamic point of view, the economic universe is necessarily tending, according to the expression used by Torrens in a very orthodox article in which he supports Ricardo's principles against Owen's communism, towards a ' stationary and melancholy state '.[3] The danger is always that the State, by intervening either by regulations or by taxes, may hasten an already fatal evolution. Even from the static point of view, Ricardo admits that in much industrialised countries there may occur economic crises which are both serious and prolonged. But attempts should not be made to prevent or to shorten them by governmental artifices—' this is an evil to which a rich nation must submit : and it would not be more reasonable to complain of it than it would be in a rich merchant to lament that his ship was exposed to the dangers of the sea, whilst his poor neighbour's cottage was safe from all such hazard '.[4] The theory of economic freedom, in Ricardo, is on occasions less like an act of faith in nature than a recognition of man's powerlessness to correct the calamities which assail him. It is a fatalism rather than an optimism. The government must not try to interfere in economic relations ; for possibly the remedies it tried would be worse than the evils to be cured. Is this an exceedingly simple optimism, or a redoubled pessimism ?

In 1819, Ricardo entered Parliament ; he remained there for the last four years of his life, as the acknowledged representative of the new science.[5] Now, it is undeniable that both in the speeches he delivered in Parliament and in the pamphlet on agricultural protection which he published in 1822, the language of optimism predominates. No doubt he reminded his hearers that if the price of the necessaries of life tends to rise, it is because of the inevitable rise in the cost of production, and not through the fault of the government which is making laws. No doubt he recalled, in opposition to the theories of Robert Owen, that the true explanation of the economic crisis should be sought in the insufficiency of capital in relation to population, and that the insufficiency of capital was itself explicable

[1] *Principles*, p. 121.
[2] *Ibid.* p. 121. Cp. pp. 89-90.
[3] *Ed. Rev.*, Oct. 1819. vol. lxiv. art. xi.
[4] *Principles*, p. 161.
[5] See Hansard, n.s. ix. p. 816.

by the limited quantity of available land. The legislator could therefore only supply palliatives for the evil : notably he could avoid letting artificial causes, such as customs barriers and a crushing debt, be added to the natural causes of the exodus of capital ; it might also restrain a superabundant supply of labour, by teaching the working classes prudence. But Ricardo preferred to insist on the fundamental identity of economic interests. More than once he defended himself against the charge of being a capitalist, who, by his class-interest, was hostile to the interests of the landlords. Was he not himself a landlord ? Did he not buy an estate in order to secure the right of sitting in the Commons ? But this did not prevent him— a financier and the son of a financier—from continuing to see economic phenomena from the point of view of the capitalist.[1] He did not seek to emphasise, in his speeches in Parliament, the divergence of the respective interests of landlord, capitalist, and wage-earner.[2] He liked to think of the landlord as an agriculturist, that is to say as a capitalist and a labourer like the manufacturer. The only opposition of interests on which he insisted was that between groups of producers, who are all concerned to sell their respective products as dear as possible, and the sum of consumers, in other words all the individuals put together who are all without exception concerned that all products should be sold at the lowest price.[3] Now it is absurd to wish to protect, at one and the same time, by a series of detailed laws which will almost infallibly contradict one another, the interests of all the groups of producers, taken one by one ; in order to assure ' the greatest happiness of the greatest number ', it is the interests of the consumers that must be aimed at, the interest of all the individuals, considered as individuals and not as members of such and such an economic caste. In this sense, the new school can be called individualist, because it tends to consider the general interest as consisting not in a sum of group interests, which are often in contradiction with one another, but in a sum of individual interests which happen all to be identical. The remedy for the crisis is to wipe out the Debt, however drastic the necessary measures, and above all to abolish the corn laws, which unduly favour a special category of citizens at the expense of the community as a whole.[4] Even the landlords would gain from this by receiving their farm-rents more regularly, because of the increased steadiness in the price of corn.[5] Once these two evils were abolished, all prices would become ' natural and just ' ; and England would attain a pitch of prosperity and happiness which human imagination can hardly conceive.[6] This is the language of optimism.

But why was Ricardo, the parliamentary orator, more favourable to the thesis of optimism than Ricardo, the theoretic writer ? It is

[1] Hansard, n.s. iv. 1156, and n.s. ix. 461.
[2] *Ibid.* n.s. l. p. 331. [3] *Ibid.* n.s. vii. p. 1214.
[4] Hansard, n.s. vii. p. 654-655. [5] *Prot. to Agric.*, pp. 476-477.
[6] Hansard, n.s. l. p. 676, and n.s. vii. p. 655.

because Ricardo, when in Parliament, ceased to think for himself :
he became the member of a party, for the sake of which, and, to a
certain extent, by which, he thought.   Once again we see collective
thought using the thought of the individual tyrannically and for its
own ends.   Ricardo only passed for the incarnation of economic
optimism because the practical notion of commercial liberty was quite
wrongly confused with the theoretic notion of the natural identity
of interests.   Actually, the impotence of laws to bring about good
does not prove the power of good to come about spontaneously ;
and, also, although the Utilitarian morality which Bentham and James
Mill taught Ricardo lays it down that the general interest and the
particular interest ought to tend to become identified, it in no way
implies that this identity comes about spontaneously : this is a question of fact, independent of the fundamental precept.   Ricardo
himself, in so far as he was an autonomous thinker, though he might
perhaps, by an instinct for logical simplification, tend to neglect the
importance of accidents and crises, did nevertheless state that evil
is present in economic society, and that its tendency is to grow
incessantly, by virtue of a law of necessary evolution.   But, by an
accident of history, he found that he had become at once the representative, the theorist and the orator of a class which was optimistic
by profession—the great English manufacturers, who dreamt of
making the economic conquest of the world.   They needed to be
freed from all regulations regarding labour : they needed, in the
historical conditions in which England found itself placed about the
year 1820, to see the customs barriers broken down ; they needed
to believe that overproduction was impossible, and that all production
immediately created a corresponding demand ; they took over a
doctrine which seemed to justify their claims as against the interests
of the class of landlords—claims, which were on some points identical
with those of their workmen ; and the temperament of the men of
action gave its tone to the doctrine of the thinker.

2. JAMES MILL AND MACCULLOCH

In the spring of 1818, the *Edinburgh Review* published an enthusiastic article on the *Principles*.[1]   Ricardo knew that James Mill was
not the author of it ; and without hesitation concluded that the
Scottish journalist MacCulloch was the author.   For he knew of only
two economists who could be so completely in agreement with him.
' I have not many converts of which to boast, but when I can number
amongst them yourself, and Mr. Mill, I think mine is no mean
triumph '.[2]   Ricardo recognised in MacCulloch many qualities which
he himself lacked—a clearness of language and a faculty for com-

[1] *Ed. Rev.*, vol. lix., June 1818, art. ii.
[2] Ricardo to MacCulloch, Aug. 22, 1818.

position. ' Those who do not understand me,' he wrote, ' understand you clearly,' and he advised him to draw up ' a complete system of Political Economy, written in so popular a way as to be easily understood by the generality of readers '.[1] Before carrying out his master's wish, MacCulloch in the meantime disseminated his doctrine in the *Scotsman*, in the *Edinburgh Review*, in the Lectures on political economy which he started at Edinburgh,[2] and in the *Supplement to the Encyclopaedia Britannica* in which he published, under ' Political Economy ', an article in conformity with the new orthodoxy.[3] James Mill, on his side, organised in London the Political Economy Club, in which, from the year 1821 on, Ricardo and Malthus, James Mill and Torrens, and others besides, tried to come to an agreement as to the fundamental propositions of their science : and in 1821, in his *Elements of Political Economy*, he summed up the lessons which he had given to his son Stuart Mill,[4] and which were in conformity with Ricardo's theories. James Mill and MacCulloch were two intransigeant disciples who brought to bear on their economic propaganda the zeal of the Scottish religious enthusiast. But their intransigeance had the result of making them go beyond the doctrine of their master. Ricardo admitted that there were limitations and exceptions to his principles : James Mill and MacCulloch systematically neglected all these restrictions, and became, so to speak, more Ricardian than Ricardo himself. Let us examine in turn the two parts of Ricardo's doctrine ; the static laws and the dynamic laws, the theory of value in exchange and the theory of the natural distribution of wealth, in order to see how they were transformed in passing from the master to the disciples, that is, in ceasing to be the opinion of an individual and becoming the common doctrine of a school, the faith of a sect.

Commodities exchange, after oscillations which ultimately balance each other, in proportion to the quantities of labour which have been expended to produce them : this is the law of value which Ricardo formulated, a law of equilibrium and of justice. But no sooner had the *Principles* appeared than an economist, Torrens, who was on many points in agreement with Ricardo, put forward some objections.[5] The principle might perhaps be true in primitive society, previous to the accumulation of capital, for which it had been formulated by Adam Smith ; but for a capitalist society, that is for society as it is, it was not enough to admit, with Ricardo, that the principle ceased to be true in all cases where capitals of unequal durability were engaged in production ; it must be added also that capitals of equal durability might put into action different amounts of

[1] Ricardo to MacCulloch, April 7, 1819.   [2] *Ibid.* Feb. 9 and March 19, 1822.
[3] Supplement to 4th, 5th and 6th editions of the *Encyclopaedia Brit.*, vol. vi. pp. 216-278.
[4] Stuart Mill, *Autobiography*, pp. 28, 62.
[5] *Scots Magazine and Edinburgh Literary Miscellany*, Oct. 1818, pp. 335-338.

labour and yet produce equal values. Take the case of two capitalists who both advance a capital of two thousand pounds. The first capitalist manufactures woollen and the second silk material. The value of the two products must be equal ; otherwise capital will leave the less remunerative industry and transfer itself to the other. But this does not mean that the quantities of labour are equal : for wages, in the manufacture of silk, may be double what they are in the manufacture of wool. Take the case of our two manufacturers each with a capital of two thousand pounds. The first advances five hundred pounds for machinery, five hundred for raw material and a thousand for wages. The second likewise advances five hundred for machinery and five hundred for raw material, but he uses steam for working some of his machines, and so advances five hundred pounds for coal and only five hundred for wages. Twice as much labour is expended in the first industry as in the second. Yet the value will be the same, because the capitals are the same. It might be said in answer to the first objection that Ricardo had recognised the existence of various qualities of labour, although he thought he could rest all his economic proofs on the principle of the equality of wages. It might be said in answer to the second that if the sum of a thousand pounds instead of being spent entirely on wages is spent half on raw material and half on wages, the raw material also cost labour and the price of purchasing this raw material is proportional to this labour. It was MacCulloch who took up the defence of Ricardo in the very review in which Torrens' article had appeared : [1] according to MacCulloch, it is not refuting Ricardo to measure the value of the product by the quantity of capital advanced, instead of by the labour expended ; for Ricardo had included in the amount of labour ' the labour expended in forming the capital .' ' What is capital ', asks MacCulloch, taking over an expression from Adam Smith and Ricardo,[2] ' if not accumulated labour ? ' Ricardo himself does not seem to have troubled himself about the objection made by Torrens ; but with the circumspectness which was characteristic of him he threw greater emphasis, in the second edition of his *Principles*, in 1819, than he had done in the first edition, on the particular case in which the capitals used are not of the same durability, and commodities do not exchange in proportion to the amount of labour which they have cost.[3]

Malthus was a more unexpected opponent. Had not Ricardo set himself the task of revising Adam Smith's political economy on the basis of the new principles discovered by Malthus ? But, ever since the appearance of his *Principles*, Malthus seems to have adopted towards Ricardo the role of a contradictor with a preconceived opinion. He was, however, and remained his intimate friend and assiduous

---

[1] *Scots Magazine*, Nov. 1818, pp. 429-431.
[2] *Principles* (1st ed.), p. 568. and *W. of N.*, vol. i. p. 332.
[3] Ricardo to MacCulloch, Dec. 18, 1819.

correspondent.   As early as the month of August 1817, when he had
read the *Principles* for a second time, he inquired of Ricardo whether
his theory of international exchanges did not constitute an exception
to his theory of value, and Ricardo agreed.[1]   The theory of the
measure of value, which in 1820, in his *Principles of Political Economy*,[2]
he opposed to Ricardo's theory, did not originate, if we are to take his
own word for it, in any polemical intention ; he had apparently
deduced it, at an earlier date, from his theory of differential rent ; [3]
and we shall in fact see that this theory is the logical consequence of
the principles of Malthusianism.   It is difficult, however, to avoid
the impression that the reading of the first chapter of Ricardo's book,
though it may not have given Malthus the original idea of his theory,
undoubtedly helped to strengthen his dawning conviction.

   Ricardo blames Adam Smith for having measured the value of
commodities sometimes by the quantity of labour ' bestowed on their
production ', sometimes by the quantity of labour ' which they can
command in the market '.   But for these two quantities to be
equal it would be necessary, he tells us, for ' the reward of the
labourer to be always in proportion to what he produced ',[4] and this
is not the case in an industrial and civilised society in which, not to
mention rent, the capitalist can levy the difference between these two
quantities under the name of profit.   It is recognised besides, and
Ricardo himself states it, that the quantity of productive labour is not
exactly commensurate with the value of the products, in a society in
which capital co-operates with labour in the production of commodities.   But if, as Ricardo acknowledges, the two ways of understanding
the expression ' quantity of labour ' cannot be used indiscriminately,
and if, as he also acknowledges, the first results in an inexact theory,
should not recourse be had to the second, and should not value be
measured by the amount of labour which the product can purchase
in exchange ?   Ricardo is unwilling to do so because this latter is,
in his view, a quantity subject to as many fluctuations as ' the commodities compared with it '.[5]   But to support this assertion he brings
forward two examples, and bad luck will have it that the tendency
of these two examples is to prove just what he is contesting, that is
to say the invariability of the value of labour.   Let us suppose that,
in a given country, twice as much labour as was previously expended
is now needed to produce a given quantity of food and commodities
of primary necessity : the wages of the labourer, which constitute
what, in the political economy of Ricardo and Malthus, is called ' the
value of labour ', could be very little lowered by this, for, if he had
a smaller quantity of food and objects of primary necessity, the
labourer might die of hunger and cold.   Let us suppose, conversely,
that the advance of industry permits of an economy of three-quarters

[1] See Ricardo to Trower, Aug. 23, 1817.   [2] 2nd ed. (posthumous), 1836.
[3] *Measure of Value stated and illustrated*, Introd. p. v.
[4] *Principles*, p. 11.   [5] *Ibid.* p. 11.

of the labour needed to produce the labourer's shoes and clothes ; this would not put the labourer in a position to buy four suits or four pairs of shoes instead of one ; his wages would adjust themselves to the new conditions of labour and fall until he could buy just the same number of clothes as previously. Thus, on the strength of Ricardo's own observations, a day's labour always produces, *for the labourer*, no matter what may be the productivity of his labour, approximately the same amount of food, clothes, and objects of primary necessity.[1] In fact, it is a fundamental proposition of Malthusianism that the value of labour is a constant quantity, and that there is a natural and invariable wage, the wage, that is, ' which is necessary to enable the labourers, one with another, to subsist and to perpetuate their race, without either increase or diminution ',[2] for, on Malthus' theory, this constant value of labour is the actual regulator of population.

' And first let us ', writes Malthus, ' suppose, for the sake of clearness, that the common agricultural labour of each period, which may be taken as the standard, is exactly of the same degree of strength, and is employed for the same number of hours, and further, that there are some commodities which, both at these periods and during the whole interval between them, are produced by this kind of labour alone, and brought to market immediately ';[3] and he tries to establish, on this hypothesis, a procedure for the comparison of values, whether they be contemporaneous or separated by an interval of time. The hypothesis is strictly in conformity with the Malthusian theory of population, and consequently with Ricardo's political economy : it is the very condition of the existence of the human species on this earth that there should be poor men, men who toil and provide a *maximum* quantity of labour in return for a *minimum* quantity of subsistence. But, Ricardo objects in his letters addressed to Malthus, if the number of labourers is increased or diminished by a sudden immigration or emigration, by an increase in the number of births or by an epidemic, will not the value of labour be changed ?[4] For a time doubtless ; however, from Ricardo's own point of view, these temporary fluctuations do not prevent a constant law from bringing wages back to their lower and normal level. But, Ricardo again objects, if there are two countries, which are both equally skilled and equally industrious, and the inhabitants of one live on potatoes while those of the other live on bread, and if someone sends a barrel of wine from the potato country where it costs a hundred pounds, to the bread country where it costs a hundred and ten pounds, are we to say that wine is dearer in the exporting than in the importing country on the ground that it would command more labour there ? Certainly not ; but the example chosen by Ricardo implies

[1] *Principles*, p. 12.　　　　[2] *Ibid.* p. 50.
[3] *Principles of Political Economy* (1836 ed.), p. 96.
[4] See Ricardo to Malthus, April 29, 1823.

that natural wages are permanently different in the two countries :
this contradicts the principle of the equality of wages. In short, if
it be admitted that the amount of simple labour of which an individual is capable is a fixed amount, of which the various kinds of
specialised labour are multiples, and if we admit further that this
fixed amount of labour is purchased with a *minimum* quantity of
food—a quantity which is also fixed—then it does indeed seem that
the unit chosen by Malthus may serve as a measure of values in a
capitalistic régime. Values are then no longer considered, abstractly,
as exchanging one with another according to the quantity of labour
which is incorporated in them, but in relation to the individuals
who, in the existing distribution of wealth, have the power to dispose
of them : the value of a thing is now measured by the number of
men which it enables its possessor to put to work for his own advantage. The Malthusian theory of value implies the separation of the
capitalist and the wage-earner, and the power of the first over the
second : on the strength of the dynamic laws of distribution on which,
at bottom, Ricardo and Malthus are agreed, is not the economic
world a world in which labour is a commodity, and the one of all
commodities whose value varies least ? The Malthusian theory of
value contains, in a latent form, the Marxian theory of labour power,
just as the law of wages, in Ricardo, is the almost explicit statement
of the ' brazen law ' of Lassalle. It sets in relief the inharmonious
nature of the economic world.

Already, before 1820, Thomas Hodgskin, in his private letters to
the Benthamite, Francis Place, had remarked the equivocal nature of
the theory which proportions value to the quantity of labour in two
distinct senses, and had noticed the conclusions which should be
drawn from it, from the point of view of the economic condition of
the labouring class. But Ricardo's disciples ignored these observations as they ignored the criticisms of Malthus ; for a kind of instinct
led them always to separate, in their expositions, the theory of
exchange and the theory of the distribution of wealth, in order to
preserve for the world of exchange the appearance of a static, equili-
brated and harmonious universe. It is doubtful, however, whether
Malthus had perceived these consequences of his theory : hence the
abstract and scholastic nature of the controversy which he kept up by
letter with Ricardo. This does not mean, moreover, that Ricardo
was pig-headed about his own theory. He recognised that the
theory of value was ' encompassed with difficulties ' ; he would be
only too glad if one of his disciples succeeded in establishing ' a
measure of value which shall not be liable to the objections which
have been brought against all those hitherto proposed '. If he were
writing his chapter on value over again, he would now assign to the
relative value of commodities two causes instead of one—quantity of
labour, and profit, varying with the durability of the capital ; though
he immediately adds : ' Perhaps I should find the difficulties nearly as

great in this view of the subject as in that which I have adopted '.[1] However, the third edition of his *Principles* bears hardly a trace of these anxieties ; he does, it is true, throw more emphasis than ever on the exception, important from the logical point of view, which the principle involves ; yet he still maintains that the influence exerted on the variation of prices by the variation of profits is relatively small, and that much the most important effects are those which are produced by variations in the quantity of labour required for production.[2] We have now come to the time when James Mill and MacCulloch were becoming the acknowledged advocates of Ricardo's system, and were bringing to its defence an enthusiasm of which Ricardo was no longer capable.   In 1821, Torrens incorporated his theory of value in a complete work on ' the production of wealth ',[3] and it was James Mill who undertook to reply in the name of the new school.

In actual society, says Torrens, the real agent of production is the capitalist ; he expends no labour but advances capital in the expectation that this capital will be restored to him entire, plus an increase termed profit.   This capital, which is a necessary condition of production, is further split up into machinery, raw material and wages ; but the producer demands the same rate of profit on all parts of his capital, a rate that is fixed at approximately the same amount in all branches of industry, by the competition of capital.   The capital originally advanced constitutes the cost of production, or what Torrens, in his terminology, calls the ' natural value ' of the product. The ' market value ' of the product is always higher than the ' natural value ', because it is equal to the natural value, plus the profit ; but the variations of the two values, the natural and the market values, are always more or less equal.[4]   Consequently, natural value is equal and market value is proportional not to the quantity of labour which has been expended, but to the quantity of capital.   Equal capitals produce equal values.[5]   But what are we to understand by the phrase ' equal capitals ' ?   Obviously capitals whose value is equal ; but this value must in its turn be measured.   Should capitals be said to be equal if they produce equal profits ?   This would involve a vicious circle ; and besides, how could the value of the profits, which are presumed to be equal, be measured ?   Should capitals be said to be equal when they suffice for the subsistence of an equal number of workmen, that is, when, according to an expression once used by Torrens, they are worth the same number of working days ?[6]   In this case they would be measured by the quantity of labour, understood as it is understood by Adam Smith and Malthus.[7]   Or should we follow Torrens (who borrows the expression from MacCulloch, his critic of 1818) and call capital ' accumulated labour ' ?[8]   This would be to

---

[1] Ricardo to MacCulloch, June 13, 1820.   [2] *Principles*, pp. 23-24.
[3] *An Essay on the Production of Wealth*, London, 1821.
[4] *Ibid.* pp. 50 seq.   [5] *Ibid.* p. 34.   [6] *Ibid.* p. 37.
[7] Ricardo to Trower, Oct. 4, 1821.   [8] *An Essay, etc.*, p. vii.

say that two capitals are equal when they have cost, at the moment of their original production, the same quantity of labour. Is this not to approximate by a roundabout way to the theory of Ricardo ?

This is the objection which James Mill urges against Torrens in his *Elements of Political Economy*.[1] The works of Torrens and James Mill appeared at practically the same time, but already several months previously, Torrens had opposed his theory to Ricardo's at the Political Economy Club : and it is clearly the errors of Torrens that James Mill sets out to put right.[2] He agrees to say, with Torrens, that the cost of production determines the relative value of commodities in exchange ; but he points out that the expression is obscure. Production presupposes the co-operation of capital and labour. Either, then, value comprises two irreducible elements, capital and labour— this, at bottom, was Ricardo's theory, although he considered labour as by far the most important factor ; or else, one of these elements is reducible to the other. Now, is it to be labour which is to be reduced to capital, as Torrens wishes ? James Mill does not think so. For the first capital was produced by pure labour without the assistance of capital : it is this quantity of labour which then determined its value, and which indirectly determines the value of the commodities which this capital has subsequently helped to produce : thus capital can be resolved into labour.

But the labour which produced the capital is labour which is past, or ' accumulated ', according to the formula of MacCulloch and Torrens, in actual capital, in machinery, in tools, in materials and in wages. Thus, while workmen were labouring to complete a product, the value of the product would in no way be determined by their labour, but only by the previous labour of other workmen, which was necessary to produce the capital which they were using ; and the theory of value, when interpreted in this way, would give expression to yet another disharmony of economic society, the power exerted by past labour over the present labourers. True, answers James Mill,[3] if wages are included under capital : but this cannot be done without absurdity ; if capital and labour are treated as two factors of production which are actually distinct, it is a contradiction to go on to treat wages as part of capital. According to James Mill, the idea of wages is by definition included in the idea of labour, for in order to labour, it is necessary to have the wherewithal to subsist for the duration of the labour. Consequently, the value of the product represents nothing but labour, not only past or accumulated labour, but, in distinct proportions, past labour and present labour, accumulated labour and immediate labour. James Mill thinks that in this way he has re-established Ricardo's theory in its entirety. But what becomes of the restriction which Ricardo himself had made on his own theory ? How explain that two commodities, containing an

---

[1] *Elements of Political Economy*, 1821.
[2] *Ibid*. ch. iii. sect. ii.　　　　[3] *Ibid*. ch. i. sect. ii.

equal amount of accumulated and immediate labour, can have different values ? Also that one man labouring for two years produces more value than two men labouring for one year ? It is impossible, without being equivocal, to speak James Mill's language, and be satisfied with saying that wages and profits both of them 'represent' labour. If wages represent labour, it is in the sense that they allow the capitalist to purchase labour, that is to say in the sense of Adam Smith and Malthus. If profits represent labour, it can only be that labour which originally produced the capital ; this original labour could only be commensurate with the value of the capital if profits were proportional to it ; but, on Ricardo's theory, profits vary out of all proportion to the quantity of labour in question. James Mill is right as against Torrens when he points out the vicious circle contained in his theory : how can the value of commodities be measured by capital, which is itself a commodity ? But it is not clear whether he thinks that his theory is the same as Ricardo's or that it constitutes an advance on the latter ; the fact is that in either case he is deceiving himself. Ricardo had counted on James Mill 'to steer clear of the difficult word value ' ; [1] we shall see that James Mill's manual did not succeed in giving Ricardo confidence in a theory of which he was the original author.

In 1823, Malthus published his reflections on ' the Measure of Value,' in which he resumed his thesis of 1820 and tried to confirm it by fresh arguments ; the discussion by letter between Malthus and Ricardo was resumed and proved as barren as it had been in 1821. But Ricardo now found himself placed in a more difficult position : for MacCulloch, after James Mill, had just made himself his champion, in terms which Ricardo felt obliged to disavow.

When discussing the theory which measures value by the amount of labour expended, Malthus, in 1820, had brought as an objection the case of ' fifty oak trees valued at £20 each ' which nevertheless ' do not contain as much labour as a stone wall . . . which costs £1,000 '. ' Did you ever believe ', answers Ricardo, ' that I thought fifty oak trees would cost as much labour as the stone wall ? I really do not want such propositions to be granted in order to support my system '.[2] For, in the first place, it would be necessary to be able to subtract from the price of the oak that part of the price which represents neither profits nor wages but only the rent of land ; and moreover Ricardo never believed that the law of profits establishes a relation between the rate of profits and the quantity of labour which produced the initial capital. In 1821, Torrens admitted that his theory did not apply, any more than Ricardo's, to products which were limited in amount by natural causes, and concluded, ' then this particular wine, the product of a hundred days' labour, or of a hundred days' subsistence, might exchange against, or, in other

---

[1] Ricardo to MacCulloch, Jan. 17, 1821.
[2] Ricardo to Malthus, Nov. 24, 1820.

words, be of equal value with, the products of a thousand days' labour, or of a capital of a thousand days' subsistence '.[1] In 1822, in Torrens' own paper, Stuart Mill, when making his *début* as a writer, and taking up his father's defence, came up against the same decisive objection on the part of Torrens.[2] Yet it is just these exceptional cases which MacCulloch, in the *Supplement to the Encyclopaedia Britannica*, expressly claims to reduce to the general law laid down by Ricardo. He holds that the capital employed in preserving the barrel of wine until the day when it will be drinkable is setting in motion the activity of nature, that is, the forces which nature develops in the barrel, instead of putting into action human activity. The agent is different, but there is always labour. Thus profits may be considered as ' the wages of accumulated labour ', and all value can be resolved into wages. But it is obvious that the word ' labour ' is here used in an unusual sense, and that MacCulloch is suggesting a new theory of profits, according to which they represent the fecundity of nature, and not human labour, and according to which they partake of the nature of rent, and no longer, as MacCulloch would have it, of the nature of wages. This is in conformity neither with the intentions of MacCulloch nor with the doctrine of Ricardo : both are agreed that the element constituting differential rent should be eliminated from the cost of production, and Ricardo always held that profit can be estimated at so much per cent per annum on the capital without reference to the variable productivity of the forces of nature.

At first, Ricardo rejoiced to see his doctrine adopted by so important a publication as the *Encyclopaedia Britannica*, and congratulated MacCulloch on having loyally formulated and victoriously refuted all the objections raised to his ideas.[3] But soon he began to ask himself whether MacCulloch's argument was really so loyal : ' I cannot get over the difficulty of the wine which is kept in a cellar for three or four years, or that of the oak-tree, which perhaps originally had not 2s. expended on it in the way of labour, and yet comes to be worth £100 '.[4] In a conversation with MacCulloch [5] he secured from him the admission that the ' quantity of labour ' of which he spoke was not ' the quantity of labour actually worked up ' in the commodity, and consequently was not the cause of the value of the commodity, but only a measure of this value, which convention has chosen for the convenience of the science :—' a pipe of wine kept for three years has no more labour worked up in it than a pipe of wine kept for a day, but he says the additional value on account of time must be estimated by the accumulations which a like amount of capital actively employed in the support of labour would make in the same time '. But had MacCulloch really meant only to suggest a

[1] *An Essay . . .* , pp. 43-44.
[2] See *Autobiography*, pp. 87 and 88 and *Traveller*, Dec. 2, 1822.
[3] Ricardo to MacCulloch, Mar. 25, 1823.   [4] *Ibid*. Aug. 8, 1823.
[5] Ricardo to Malthus, July 13, 1823.

conventional measure of value ?   And if this was really all that he
meant, why choose this measure of value rather than any other ?
Ricardo was not convinced on this point.   The barren discussions
which took place on this question at the Political Economy Club[1] in
1822 and 1823, ended by discouraging him.   ' I am, however, only
labouring in my vocation and trying to understand the most difficult
question in political economy. . . . As far as I have yet been able to
reflect upon MacCulloch's and Mill's suggestion, I am not satisfied
with it.   They make the best defence for my measure, but they do
not really get rid of all the objections '.[2]   And barely a month before
his death he wrote : ' my complaint against you is that you claim to
have given an accurate measure of value, and I object to your claim,
not that I have succeeded and you have failed, but that we have both
failed. . . . In answering you I am really using these weapons by
which alone you say you can be defeated, and which are I confess
equally applicable to your measure and to mine, I mean the argument of the non-existence of any measure of absolute value '.[3]

  Ricardo died : but his disciples remained to spread a theory in
which he himself had ceased to believe.   In the second edition of his
Elements,[4] James Mill enlarges on what he asserted in 1821, drawing
his inspiration from MacCulloch.   He makes to himself the common-
sense objection which, as we have seen, Malthus made to Ricardo,
and Ricardo made to MacCulloch, and which Malthus had just taken
up again in an article in the *Edinburgh Review*—the objection of the
oak tree and the old wine ; but he thinks that he is in a position to
prove ' by the most rigid analysis ', that ' profits are commensurate with
the quantity of labour '.   The producer of a machine who instead
of selling it, once it is finished, at a price commensurate with the
quantity of labour expended, chooses to sell it on credit terms,
obtains payment in annuities which are the profit on his capital ; it
matters little whether these annuities repay the producer for his
advances in ten or in twenty years ; they are fixed by the competition
of the market ; consequently, concludes James Mill, they are the
exact equivalent of the capital.   But what competition is it which is
here concerned ?   Is it the competition of the labourers who produce
the capital, or of those who employ it ?   If so, it is forgotten that
the labourers are wage-earners, that they do not possess the capital
which they create or which they employ, and that they are not
interested in the question of knowing at what rate this capital will
be remunerated.   Is it a question of the competition of the capitalists, who withdraw their capitals from all branches of industry in
which they perceive that the profit is less than elsewhere ?   But,
then, we have fallen back again into the equivocal theory of Torrens,
which James Mill of course wished to refute.   From the point of

---

[1] Dec. 2, 1822 ;   Feb. 3, 1823 ;   April 3, 1823.
[2] Ricardo to Malthus, Aug. 3, 1823.   [3] *Ibid*. Aug. 15, 1823.
[4] *Elements*, (2nd ed. 1824), ch. iii. sect. ii. pp. 94-99 are added in the 2nd edition.

view adopted by Ricardo, even if it is true to say that at any given moment of time equal capitals yield equal profits, yet equal capitals none the less yield unequal profits at different times, and there is no relation between the variation of these profits and the quantity of expenditure involved, either of capital or of labour. Always there is the same trick, whether it is conscious or unconscious : namely, to neglect the theory of distribution in Ricardo's political economy, because the landlord and the capitalist receive shares of the whole value of the product which are not proportionate to any quantity of labour, and to pretend that exchange takes place between labourers, who are masters of the product of their labour, and thus, in accordance with the Ricardian theory of value, receive equal values for equal quantities of labour.

But James Mill was too good a logician not to be aware that the limitations which Ricardo himself makes to his own theory are serious ; in order to save the theory, however, he has recourse to a distinction which had just been suggested by De Quincey, another enthusiastic disciple of Ricardo.[1] It is not the same thing, said De Quincey, to treat labour as the cause and to treat it as the measure of value. Labour, says James Mill in the same sense,[2] only measures value in a purely 'ideal' sense; it is the 'regulator' of value and cannot serve as the practical measure of it. In the first place, two kinds of labour are applied to production, and immediate labour and accumulated labour are not rewarded at the same rate ; hence arise variations in the value of objects of exchange, which depend on the variable division of the product as between the two factors of production. In the second place, we have no practical means of determining in advance the exact quantity of accumulated labour which contributes to the production, because our only possible way of measuring this quantity is by the price which it fetches. In short, the law of value in exchange, with the optimistic consequences which it involves, is deduced *a priori* from the 'laws of human nature', but it remains indeterminate as well as abstract, and is incapable of experimental verification. This is not the nature of the law of gravitation, from which the economists borrowed their favourite metaphor when they wished to demonstrate the necessity and the universality of the laws of economic nature.

But even the logical distinction suggested by De Quincey and James Mill is not enough to make Ricardo's theory safe from criticism. Ricardo himself had refused to resort to it.[3] In 1825, in *A Critical Dissertation on the Nature, Measures, and Causes of Value*,[4] an economist philosopher, Samuel Bailey, showed that the quantity of labour can be considered neither as the measure nor as the cause of value. As a matter of fact, all the elements of his criticism are

---

[1] *Collected Writings*, vol. ix. pp. 35-36. [2] *Elements*, ch. iii. sect. iii.
[3] Ricardo to MacCulloch, Aug. 21, 1823.
[4] *A Critical Dissertation*, etc., pp. xi-xii.

borrowed from Ricardo's book. He established the fact that the quantity of labour is not the cause of value in cases of monopoly, and that the value of labour is itself a monopoly value ; that it is not the cause of value in cases in which a certain commodity can be produced in indefinite quantities, but with a constantly increasing cost of production ; that value cannot be explained by the quantity of labour, because labour is not a homogeneous quantity, and can be of various qualitites. Ricardo had already said all this : Bailey confined himself to insisting on the importance of the cases which Ricardo persisted in treating as exceptional. On another point he made an innovation : he emphasised the analogy between the benefit of rent and ' the extraordinary remuneration which an artisan of more than common dexterity obtains beyond the wages given to workmen of ordinary skill ' : the owner of fertile soil and the possessor of unusual skill secure a monopoly price, a monopoly which is restricted in the first case by the existence of lands of inferior quality, and in the second case by the existence of inferior degrees of dexterity.[1] But the origin even of this idea that value contains differential elements is to be found in Ricardo. Bailey's work was discussed as soon as it appeared in the little group of young men who at this time gathered round Stuart Mill at George Grote's house ; [2] and twenty-five years later, in his *Political Economy*, Stuart Mill took up again [3] the theory of what came finally to be called ' rent of ability ', and passed it on to the socialists of the Fabian school. Once again, the Ricardian theory of the distribution of wealth serves to refute the Ricardian theory of value in exchange, which has done so much to conceal, under the appearance of a state of static equilibrium, the natural disharmonies and injustices which the system really involves.

But, for the moment, Ricardo's disciples were not disconcerted by Bailey's criticisms. In 1825, in his *Principles of Political Economy*, which was only a development of the article of 1823, MacCulloch once more defined capital as the ' accumulated produce of labour '. According to him ' there is no difference between the work of labourers and that of machines. . . . A labourer is himself a portion of the national capital and may . . . be considered in the light of a machine ; . . . the wages which he earns . . . yield him, at an average, only the common and ordinary rate of profit on his capital, exclusive of a sum to replace its wear and tear, or, which is the same thing, to supply the place of old and decayed labourers with new ones '.[4] Moreover, MacCulloch expressly admits that the rise in wages and the fall in profits causes the fall in the exchange value of certain objects in relation to others ; but he suggests a logical expedient for eliminating this difficulty. If several commodities are produced with

[1] *A Critical Dissertation*, ch. xi. pp. 196-197.   [2] *Autobiography*, p. 120.
[3] *Pol. Econ.*, bk. ii. ch. xiv. sect. ii.
[4] MacCulloch, *Pol. Econ.*, p. 319. See pp. 114-116 and 313.

different proportions of material and of wages, or again—what in
MacCulloch's language comes to the same thing—of fixed and
circulating capital, the sum of the values of all these commodities
taken together will be the same as if the value of each of them taken
separately were measured by the quantity of labour which it contains ; in this way the possessor of each commodity will receive a
share which varies according to the quantity of capital engaged.[1]
But, granting that this hypothesis is admissible, the fact remains that
each of these products under consideration does not exchange for
others in proportion to the quantity of labour which it has cost :
and this needs to be proved, if the law is to be saved.   In this way
Ricardo's doctrine, in proportion as it becomes popularised, degener-
ates into a verbal scholasticism.   In the following year, James Mill,
in the third edition of his book, added fresh developments to his
chapter on exchange-value.   Let us suppose, he wrote, that a hundred
people manufacture a machine in one day, and that a hundred other
people make use of it the day after and wear it out : the two groups
of individuals will divide the product equally between them ; once
this is granted, James Mill thinks he can prove that profit represents
labour.   But the question is to know precisely whether this initial
hypothesis can be granted him.   For, on the system of Ricardo and
James Mill, the hundred workmen of the first day become the owners
of the capital which they have created by their labour; whereas
the workmen of the second day are their employees : and the laws of
rent, of wages and of profits attribute to each of the two groups shares
in the final product which bear no relation to the respective productivity of the labour of each.   Also, the hypothetical case chosen
by James Mill is one of the cases in which those who own the capital
have also produced it, and in which the ' payment of capital ' happens
accidentally to be the ' payment of labour '.   But is this always the
case, and when it is not the case, how can profits be justified ?   James
Mill did however ask the question.   ' It is no solution to say, that
profits must be paid ', he wrote in his third edition, ' because this
only brings us to the question, why must profits be paid ?   To this
there is no answer but one, that they are the remuneration for labour ;
labour not applied immediately to the commodity in question, but
applied to it through the medium of other commodities, the produce
of labour '.[2]   The problem which here exercised the disciples of
Ricardo is clearly a juridical problem.   If the productivity of labour
is increased by the assistance of capital, they do not hold it just that
the labourer should benefit by an increase in value which his labour
alone would not have sufficed to create.   But on the other hand, how
is it possible to remunerate labourers who have perhaps long since
disappeared ?   Will the irreparable nature of past injustices be able
to be hidden, by justifying the present remuneration of the capitalist ?
It was their instinctive taste for theoretic simplification which enabled

[1] MacCulloch, *Pol. Econ.*, pp. 312-313.   [2] *Elements* (3rd ed.), pp. 102 *seq.*

James Mill and MacCulloch to escape the dilemma : they conformed
to the optimistic principle, which is at once moral and aesthetic, of
the simplicity of the laws of nature.   That in the exchange of products every equal value should remunerate an equal quantity of
labour—here is a law which has the aspect of a law at once simple and
just, and which seems to be the foundation at once of the intelligi-
bility and of the harmony of the economic universe.   Strengthened
by this principle the disciples pushed their dogmatism and optimism
to the point of denying the difficulties which had caused embarrassment to their master.

Ricardo consoled himself on seeing his theory justly contested,
with the reflection that it might not involve the ruin of the rest of his
system.   ' Perhaps ', he wrote to MacCulloch, ' I should find the
difficulties nearly as great in this view of the subject as in that which
I have adopted.   After all, the great questions of Rent, Wages and
Profits must be explained by the proportion in which the whole
produce is divided between the landlords, capitalists and labourers,
and *which are not essentially connected with the doctrine of value* '.[1]
Now the laws of rent, wages and profits depend on the dynamic law
of population, which is a permanent cause of disharmony and poverty
in economic society.   If we consider what becomes of this pessimistic element in Ricardo's doctrine in James Mill and MacCulloch,
we notice that they are not both under the influence of the same
preoccupations when reducing the system of the master to the
simplest possible terms.   James Mill primarily simplifies as a teacher,
with a view to the needs of doctrinal exposition ; MacCulloch as a
publicist with a view to the justification of industrial and commercial
society against the protectionist state.   When it is a question of
developing those among Ricardo's theories which explicitly affirm
divergences of interests between the various classes in the economic
society, we shall see that James Mill tends to accentuate them, in the
cynical language of the logician, precisely because he is reducing them
to their simplest form, and that MacCulloch, on the other hand, tends,
of his own accord, to lessen and almost to efface them, in the loose and
confused language of the journalist.

Ricardo, in a work which does not, it is true, claim to supply a
systematic arrangement of contents, had given an exposition of the
theory of value and of exchange before the theory of the distribution
of wealth.   James Mill reverses the order and explains first how the
distribution of products between landlords, capitalists and wage-
earners is brought about outside of exchange.[2]   The laws of exchange
are dominated by the three great laws which are derived from the
Malthusian law of differential rent : ' We shall begin with the
explanation of Rent, or the share received by Landlords ; as it is the

---

[1] Ricardo to MacCulloch, June 13, 1820.
[2] *Elements*, ch. ii. (2nd ed.), p. 27.

most simple, and will facilitate the explanation of the laws, upon which the shares, of the Labourers, and of the Capitalists, depend '.[1] He gives an exposition of the theory of Ricardo, that is of the theory of Malthus simplified, in all its rigour, setting himself to prove the perfect agreement of real phenomena with the abstract theory. The difference of fertility of the lands which the human race is forced progressively to put under cultivation is the ' accident '[2] which accounts for all the contradictions of the system of economic distribution, considered in its historical development, and in particular of the divergence which exists between the economic interests of the landlord and those of the rest of society. The landlord endeavours to represent his own case as perfectly similar to that of the manufacturer but their positions are entirely different. He also endeavours to mix up his own case with that of the farmer : ' and upon the success of this endeavour almost all the plausibility of his pretensions depends '. But these pretensions are unfounded. ' The case of the landlord is peculiar ; that a high price of corn is profitable to him, because, the higher the price, the smaller a portion of the produce will suffice to replace, with its profits, the capital of the farmer ; and all the rest belongs to himself. To the farmer, however, and to all the rest of the community, it is an evil, both as it tends to diminish profits, and as it enhances the charge to consumers '.[3]

But if the law of rent sets in opposition the interest of the landlord and that of the capitalist and the wage-earner, this is because of the reaction of this law on the laws which determine wages and profits : in the analysis which he gives of this reaction, James Mill shows up more clearly perhaps than Ricardo had done, the strictly Malthusian and pessimistic nature of the doctrine.

Leaving out of consideration rent, which is external to the price of each commodity, the distribution of the value of a given object between the capitalist and the labourer results from a bargain, the conditions of which are determined by competition, according to the state of supply and demand. In the case in question, there is, according to the point of view adopted, a supply of, or a demand for a certain quantity of capital, and a supply of, or a demand for a certain quantity of labour, or, if you like, of a certain number of labourers.

If population increases without there being a simultaneous increase in capital, wages fall ; if capital increases without a simultaneous increase in population, wages rise. If both increase, but at a different rate, the result will be the same as if the one had not increased at all, and the other had increased by an amount equal to the difference. Actually, capital increases less quickly than population.

This can be proved, according to James Mill, by an appeal to the facts. If capital were to increase faster than population, wages would necessarily be increased ; they would place the labourers in a

[1] *Elements*, ch. ii. beginning.   [2] *Ibid.* ch. ii. sect. iii.
[3] *Ibid.* ch. iii. sect. xvii.

state of abundance and would free them from want.   Now, it may be
affirmed that ' in almost all countries, the condition of the great mass
of the people is poor and miserable ' : that the ' general misery of the
human race ' is a fact.[1]   It seems that on this point James Mill
accentuates the thesis of Ricardo.   In the ordinary way according to
him, granting some exceptions, wages are subsistence wages.[2]   By
definition the condition of the wage-earning labourer is servile.   In
the language of James Mill, since wages are the equivalent of labour,
the capitalist who owns the wages owns the labour also, in the same
way as if he employed not wage-earners but slaves.   ' The only
difference is in the mode of purchasing ', since the slave-owner has
acquired the perpetual claim to the labour of his slaves, while the
capitalist only owns a month, or a week or some other limited duration of the labour of the labourer whom he pays.   ' In the state of
society in which we at present exist, it is in these circumstances that
almost all production is effected '.[3]   Now, according to James Mill,
this state of society is produced by the operations of the laws of
nature ; how then can it be said that according to James Mill, nature
spontaneously establishes the identity of all interests ?

James Mill does not confine himself to stating the divergence which
exists between the rates of increase of population and of capital, he
wishes to explain it by its causes.[4]   He does not repeat the demonstrations of Malthus, nor the mathematical formula of the two
progressions, the arithmetical and the geometrical.   Malthus based
his theory on statistical observations ; but James Mill was faithful to
the method of Adam Smith and condemned this method as too
empirical for his taste.   Statistics, supposing that they were ever
accurate, would inform us of the pure and simple fact of the rate of
increase of population ; they can tell us nothing of the causes which
explain this increase ; in order to know these causes, we must follow
a deductive method and take a small number of well-verified facts
as the sure basis of our argument.   James Mill took as his starting
point the properties of human nature and in particular the ' facts
respecting the physiological constitution of the human female '.
He estimated the normal fecundity of woman at ten births, and
reduced this figure by half so as to take account of cases of sterility
and of infant mortality ; thus there remain five children per couple.
Thus it is possible to show by a calculation that, at the normal rate
of increase, population would be doubled in a few years.   But the
tendency of capital to increase is not so strong, and this James Mill
also showed deductively by taking his stand on the knowledge of
certain laws of nature :—psychological laws which govern man's
inclination to save ; physical laws which make the cost of production
of the food necessary to life progressively higher on the surface of the
earth.   In the first instance, all increase in capital is due to saving ;

[1] *Elements*, ch. ii. sect. ii.   [2] Cf. Place.   Diary, Oct 12th, 1826.
[3] *Elements*, ch. i. sect. ii.   [4] *Ibid.* ch. ii. sect. ii.

but the ' principles of human nature ' prove that the inclination to save is very weak in almost all the economic situations in which human beings may be placed. The poor are unable, and the rich are indisposed, to save. There remain the men ' of easy but moderate fortunes ' : these may have the desire to save, with the view of one day putting their children in the same position as regards wealth in which they themselves are. Thus a certain increase of capital is possible ; but this increase can only be a moderate one, like the fortune possessed by the members of the class in question. Yet this is the case which is the most favourable to accumulation, if it be agreed to neglect the quite exceptional case when civilised men are transported into an uncultivated land and can cultivate to an unlimited extent land of the most fertile kind. The same truth can be proved more directly by pointing out that the tendency of population to increase is a tendency which is always the same ; on the other hand, in proportion as capital accumulates, the difficulty of increasing it becomes greater, up to the point when all increase becomes impracticable : this proposition, according to James Mill, ' is the evident consequence of the law which determines the return on capital, when applied in successive doses ' to land. In short, in the Malthusian theory of population James Mill substitutes for the law of arithmetical progression the law of diminishing returns—yet another law, that is, which, though Mill uses it in a form which is perhaps more akin to that given it by West, was first discovered by Malthus.

From the law of rent and the law of wages is derived the law of profits, which was defined by James Mill as it was by Ricardo. The diminution of the productivity of capital on less fertile land, and the rise of nominal wages, submit profits to a double downward movement. This is a necessary consequence of the two inseparable laws of population and of diminishing returns.

Such a philosophy of progress obviously cannot be considered to be an optimistic philosophy ; it seems that all that man can do in such unfavourable conditions is to counteract the normal course of things by artificial means ; James Mill had no preconceived hostility to the idea of an artificial organisation of economic society. He defined political economy by analogy with domestic economy : ' Political Economy is to the State, what domestic economy is to the family '. But he adds that ' the art of him, who manages a family, consists in regulating the supply and consumption ' ; it may be asked, therefore, to what power in the State, on the analogy of what occurs in the family, shall be assigned the essential function of regulating ' the supply and consumption '.[1] Should it be left to the natural play of exchange, to the spontaneous division of labour ? This is the classical thesis of all the economists since Adam Smith, whose disciple James Mill declared himself to be. But here James Mill condemns the division of labour for being performed badly, precisely because it was

[1] *Elements*, Introduction.

performed ' practically as they call it ; that is, in a great degree
accidentally, as the fortuitous discoveries of individuals, engaged in
particular branches, enabled them to perceive that in these branches
a particular advantage was to be gained ' ; and it is his wish that
philosophers should take up the question, and should succeed in
making a systematic and considered redistribution of tasks by means
of analysis and synthesis.[1]   It is therefore not surprising that he puts
the problem concisely. Man has the choice of two methods of
raising and keeping wages higher than the miserable figure to which
they almost always fall, through a ' dreadful consequence ' of the
increasing difficulty with which the human race subsists on this earth.
He can either accelerate artificially the natural rate of the increase of
capital, or he can slacken artificially the natural rate of increase of
population.   Once this practical problem is set, James Mill discusses
it with that logical minuteness on which Bentham's disciples prided
themselves.[2]

In the first place, James Mill does not think it possible to induce
an artificial increase in capital. For if the legislator tries to use
indirect means, if he attempts to influence the tastes of the community
and make economy fashionable, or else bring about the distribution
of wealth most favourable to saving by means of sumptuary laws,
these are means which, according to James Mill, will either be
inefficacious, or else will constitute an unbearable interference by
the legislator in private affairs. There remains the use of direct
means : the setting free of some portion or other of the net
produce of the year, and the conversion of this portion into capital.
But by what means is this portion to be got hold of, and by what
means is it to be converted into capital ?

It appears that the legislator can, by some fiscal method, get hold
of that portion of the annual produce of labour which he wishes to
have capitalised ; and James Mill perceives, more clearly than
Ricardo, the possibility of correcting by a tax on rent the divergence
which naturally exists between the interests of the landlord and those
of all the other members of the community. He was profoundly
influenced by the physiocrats, who were the apostles of a single
land-tax. Further, when studying the history of British India he
noted that this was the system generally in force over there. It is a
system which conforms to the nature of things : ' Previous to allot-
ment, the productive powers of the soil are the joint property of the
community ; and hence are a fund peculiarly adapted to the joint or
common purposes and demands '.[3] That a different system has
prevailed in Europe is due, according to James Mill, to the fact that
the landlords, who became masters of the government in feudal
times, were able to impose on others the charges which the sovereign
ought to have imposed on them. In actual fact, it matters little to

---

[1] *Elements*, ch. i. sect. i.   [2] *Ibid*. ch. ii. sect. ii. p. 4.
[3] *Hist. of Brit. India*, vol. i. pp. 299 *seq*.

the capitalist, once he has paid the wages of his workmen and secured a return for his initial capital at the usual rate, whether he pays the surplus in the form of rent to an individual landlord, or in the form of tax to a government collector. Consequently, in a new country, in which the land had not yet become private property, if the government levied the whole of the rent for its requirements it would not cause the slightest industrial depression, and would defray the expenses of the government without imposing a charge on anyone. However, James Mill is faithful to the principle of security as Bentham had formulated it, and recognises that the theory would be difficult to apply in countries ' where land has been converted into private property . . . where it has been bought and sold upon such terms, and the expectations of individuals have been adjusted to that order of things '.[1] But this is only a difficulty of a practical kind ; James Mill himself indicates that it might be removed, if it were possible to distinguish between two elements : on the one hand, that quantity of rent which should be regarded as conferred on the possessor by previous legislation—this it would be unjust to remove from him ; and on the other hand, all that could be held to be in excess of this benefit—this could be retained for the service of the State without injustice to the possessor. Does James Mill, then, advocate the solution of the single land-tax as it was advocated later by his son and disciple Stuart Mill and by the agrarian socialists of the school of Henry George ? Not at all.

James Mill, like Ricardo, remained faithful to the principle laid down by Adam Smith : ' the true principle of distribution ', in regard to the sums required for the service of the state is, in his view, that ' a tax, to operate fairly, ought to leave the relative condition of the different classes of contributors the same, after the tax, as before it '.[2] But this principle implies the thesis of the natural identity of interests, which is nevertheless contradicted by the law of differential rent. This inconsequence is in truth constant in James Mill, and is the more surprising the cruder its form of exposition. In the *Encyclopaedia Britannica* he condemns castes, taking his stand on the principle that ' everything is to be considered as beneficently important, in proportion as it favours his (*i.e.* man's) progression ; everything is to be considered as mischievously important, in proportion as it obstructs and impedes that progression '.[3] Now the landlords may be regarded as a sort of hereditary caste ; and if we stop at the definition of the laws of economic progress suggested by James Mill, the appearance of at least one caste is the natural product of progress. But the admission that there are castes or classes in nature was instinctively repugnant to James Mill. Elsewhere he differentiates a class by ' community of interest : in other words, some thing or things, to be obtained, secured, or augmented, by the common endeavours of the class, and

[1] *Elements*, ch. iv. sect. v.   [2] *Ibid*. ch. iv. sect. viii.
[3] *Ency. Brit.* sup. iii. p. 92.

operating as a cause of pleasure to all of them '.[1] Do not the landlords then constitute a class, since they are distinguished by the
differential rent which is allotted to them by the operation of the laws
of nature ? No, since James Mill adds immediately afterwards that
' there is no Love of Class but in a Privileged Order,' and the privileges which constitute a class and which consist ' of Wealth, Power,
Dignity, one, or all, conferred by legislative act ', are ' not the result
of natural acquisition, but of a sort of force, or compulsion, put
upon other people '.[2] According to James Mill, therefore, there is no
longer any social class which enjoys private interests in opposition to
the general interest, except through the fault of some government
intervention, which changes the natural identity of interests.

It remains to solve the second problem. How is income, once
confiscated by the State, to be used productively ? How is it to be
converted into capital ? At this point appears the real and conscious
reason of the distrust inspired in James Mill by the intervention of
the government in economic affairs. The State may be conceived
either as lending at interest to the manufacturers, or as making its
capital bear fruit itself. But both methods (Robert Owen [3] had
advocated the adoption of the second) are equally impracticable, if
we are to believe James Mill. If ever capital were to increase more
quickly than its normal rate, the increase in population would itself
at once be more rapid in the same degree ; it would thus be necessary
to have recourse to the cultivation of lands of inferior quality, or to
more costly methods of cultivation ; and the return on the capital
would itself decrease so much the more quickly. It is thus the
pessimistic element in Ricardo's doctrine which forbids the envisag-
ing of the hypothesis that the State might undertake to accelerate the
formation of capital ; the State must not interfere in the play of
economic laws, not because it would compromise by this a supposed
identity of interests, which does not exist in nature, but because its
intervention would only aggravate existing divergences of interests,
by hastening a progress whose march is no less disastrous because
it is necessary.

Since wages cannot be raised by using strictly economic methods,
there remains the use of an extra-economic method : limiting the
number of births. But how can this be brought about ? By direct
methods ? By rewards and penalties ? The crimes would be
singularly difficult to define, the punishment and the rewards
singularly difficult to apply. Colonisation is the only legislative
method which supplies some kind of solution of the problem ; and
James Mill, who devoted an article in the *Encyclopaedia Britannica* to
the question, thought that emigration to the colonies was, with
certain reservations, the best remedy which could be provisionally

[1] *Analysis of the Phenomena of the Human Mind*, vol. ii. pp. 187-188.
[2] *Ibid.* p. 228.
[3] The hostility of the orthodox economists to Owenism had as yet no hatred in it.

LAWS OF ECONOMIC SOCIETY 363

conceived for an excess of population : for ' it is highly desirable, on many accounts, that every portion of the earth, the physical circumstances of which are not inconsistent with human well-being, should be inhabited, as fully as the conditions of human happiness admit '.[1] But the surest methods, those whose use promises to be the most constantly efficacious are indirect and moral methods.   The legislator can put in action (is not James Mill, who is here using Bentham's terminology, mindful also of Helvetius ?) the powerful weapon of popular sanction.   He can bring it about that ' an intense degree of disapprobation ' be ' directed upon the men, who, by their folly, involved themselves, through a great family, in poverty and dependence ; of approbation upon those who, by their self-command, preserved themselves from this misery and degradation '.[2]   The Poor Laws are to be condemned because they are laws which in a way legalise and sanction the condition of beggary.   What the State ought to institute is a system of education to teach men about the conditions of existence, which are laid down for them on this earth by the combined laws of psychology, physiology and physics.   Moreover, Savings Banks and Benefit Societies, institutions whose theory is laid down from the Malthusian point of view by James Mill in the *Encyclopaedia Britannica*, are likewise of a kind to make a man prudent and look ahead, to give him the taste for accumulating capital, to postpone the time of marriage and to diminish the number of births.[3]

Thus, the moral which is immediately derivable from James Mill's political economy is the moral of prudence ; but prudence is not an optimistic virtue.   During an evolution of ideas of which the head of the Utilitarian school remained completely unaware, two conceptions of progress come to contradict themselves in James Mill, who was a disciple of Hartley, Priestley and Condorcet, as well as of Malthus. To the first group he owed his belief in the progressive character of intelligence, which he considered to be the ' grand and distinguishing attribute of our nature, its progressivity, the power of advancing continually from one degree of knowledge, one degree of command over the means of happiness, to another '.[4]   Ricardo likewise held that the ' retrograde condition ' was always ' an unnatural state of society '.   ' Man from youth grows to manhood, then decays, and dies ; but this is not the progress of nations.   When arrived to a state of the greatest vigour, then further advance may indeed be arrested, but their natural tendency is to continue for ages to sustain undiminished their wealth and their population '.[5]   But this proposition itself contradicts the optimistic philosophy of progress, as it was when James Mill borrowed it from Priestley and Condorcet.   It

[1] *Colony*, p. 13.
[2] *Elements*, ch. ii. sect. ii, p. 4.   See James Mill's article, ' Beggar ' in *Ency. Brit.*
[3] See denunciation of the poor-laws in Ricardo's *Principles*, p. 579.
[4] *Elements*, ch. ii. sect. ii, p. 4.   [5] *Principles*, p. 160.

implies a condition of wealth and of population which is simply stationary and not progressive ; and even this is not all.   For anyone who accepts the theory of Malthus, an increase of population, on land of varying quality and of limited quantity, cannot be reconciled with a corresponding increase of wealth, unless wealth and value be confused.   The problem then is—to realise all the progress that is possible (and our thinking nature is susceptible of infinite progression) under physical conditions which are unfavourable to progress.

James Mill and his friends, though disciples of Malthus, soon went further than he did and came nearer, in one particular, to Condorcet. When in 1820, in his article on Colonisation, James Mill demanded that, in order to solve the problem of pauperism, ' if the superstitions of the nursery were discarded, and the principle of utility kept steadily in view, a solution might not be very difficult to be found '.[1] When in 1821, in his *Elements of Political Economy*, he mentioned the case ' when a desire, which gratifies itself in a hurtful course of action, and cannot easily be counteracted by reward and punishment, is drawn to gratify itself in a less hurtful or an innocent direction ', and, in order to reconcile the institution of marriage with the limitation of the number of births, he counted on ' the progress of legislation, the improvement of the education of the people, and the decay of superstition '.[2]   Such expressions can hardly be said to be equivocal ; and Condorcet had not said much more in the phrase which scandalised Malthus.   But Francis Place, in his *Illustrations and Proofs of the Principle of Population* [3] in 1822, was still more explicit.   After defending Malthus' theory against the objections that had recently been made by Godwin, he thought he ought to reproach Malthus for using the phraseology of an aristocrat and a lawyer.   According to Malthus, the rich man has the right to enjoy his wealth without working, while the poor man on the other hand has not the right to live when he is out of work.   According to Place, it is impossible to explain to the people that they have not the ' right ' to eat ; they must be taught that they can have something to eat, if they use the right means.[4]   ' If, above all, it were once clearly understood, that it was not disreputable for married persons to avail themselves of such precautionary means as would, without being injurious to health or destructive of female delicacy, prevent conception, a sufficient check might at once be given to the increase of population beyond the means of subsistence '.[5]   Sooner or later, with the advance of knowledge, this remedy would be approved by opinion ; but already the moment had come when those who knew the means of preventing the redundancy of population ' should clearly, freely, openly, and fearlessly point out the means ' ; and Francis Place concluded in Benthamite terms, with that scorn manifested by all Benthamites for

---

[1] *Colony*, p. 13.   [2] *Elements*, ch. ii. sect. ii, p. 4.
[3] *Illustrations and Proofs of the Principles of Population*, pp. 135 seq.
[4] *Ibid.* p. 165.   [5] *Ibid.* p. 173.

the fallacies of vulgar morality :—' it is " childish " to shrink from
proposing or developing any means, however repugnant they may at
first appear to be ; our only care should be, that we do not in removing
one evil introduce another of a greater magnitude '. Neo-Malthus-
ianism had just been born ; it was enthusiastically adopted by the
young men of the group, by Stuart Mill and his friends. The
doctrine of Malthus which had originally been offered as an argument
against the possibility of indefinite progress by improving human
happiness—this doctrine ' we took up ', wrote Stuart Mill, ' with
ardent zeal in the contrary sense, as indicating the sole means of
realising that improvability by securing full employment at high
wages to the whole labouring population through a voluntary restriction of the increase of their numbers '.[1] It was by the intransigeance of their Malthusianism as of their anti-clericalism that the
Benthamites chiefly shocked public opinion.[2]

But it is a far cry from the Malthusianism of James Mill or Place
to the optimism of Condorcet. The systematic limitation imposed
on human fecundity was to Condorcet primarily a natural result of
the ' progress of the human spirit ' ; while to the disciples of Malthus
it was an artifice conceived by intelligence to combat conditions of
existence for man on the earth which are naturally growing ever more
difficult. Condorcet thought that he perceived in the history of the
human race a constant tendency, favoured by nature, towards
absolute equality of conditions. The Utilitarians insisted on the
unsurmountable difficulties, which the natural laws of political
economy set in opposition to absolute equalitarianism. Bentham
had always considered equality as a merely secondary aim of legislation ; this original opinion could not but be strengthened by the
introduction of the law of Malthus into the integral doctrine of the
party. To those who tried to identify the radicals with the levellers
of Spence's school, Bentham and his followers replied that the
Utilitarian doctrine precisely demonstrated the impossibility of an
equal division of goods : was it not this very impossibility which,
according to the Utilitarians, was the basis of the necessity of political
government ? A man must work in order to live : ' this is no
doubt,' wrote James Mill, ' the primary cause of Government ; for,
if nature had produced spontaneously all the objects which we desire,
and in sufficient abundance for the desires of all, there would have
been no source of dispute or of injury among men '.[3] Bentham held
the same view : ' if such were the condition of human beings, that
the happiness of no one being came in competition with that of any
other—that is to say, if the happiness of each, or of any one, could
receive increase to an unlimited amount, without having the effect of
producing decrease in the happiness of any other, then the above
expression (viz., the greatest happiness of all) might serve without

[1] *Autobiography*, p. 105.   [2] Graham Wallas, pp. 81-82.
[3] *Government*, p. 4.

limitation or explanation. But on every occasion, the happiness of every individual is liable to come into competition with the happiness of every other. If, for example, in a house containing two individuals for the space of a month, there be a supply of food barely sufficient to continue for that time ; not merely the happiness of each, but the existence of each, stands in competition with, and is incompatible with the existence of the other '.[1] Nature has instituted inequality of conditions—economists tell us the laws by whose operation this is brought about. If this inequality were destroyed by force, there could only be substituted for it either a worse inequality, or universal poverty. To protect the inequality of fortunes against violence is, according to the definition which Bentham borrowed from Adam Smith, the *raison d'être* and the justification of governments.

Equality is still, indeed, a good, but only in so far as nature allows this good to be realised : ' the plan of distribution applied to the matter of wealth which is most favourable to universality of subsistence, and thence, in other words, to the maximisation of happiness, is that in which, while the fortune of the richest . . . is greatest, the degrees between the fortune of the least rich and that of the most rich are most numerous—in other words, the graduation most regular and insensible '.[2] The aim should be to develop the middle class : to this can be reduced the equalitarianism of Bentham and James Mill. According to James Mill, it would be absurd, in order to draw a greater amount of nourishment from the soil, to employ for the purpose not only an ever-increasing number of individuals, but an ever-increasing proportion of the total population ; the result would be that finally all men would have food, and none would have anything else. No more learned men, no more inventors, nor doctors nor legislators. The ' leisured ' class which society needs in order to ensure the progress of useful knowledge, is the middle class, the most useful of all classes and at the same time the happiest, being free from the necessity of manual labour without being exposed to the vices and excesses of the very rich.[3] Already in 1810, James Mill had seen in the existence of a middle class the best guarantee of public liberties ; some years later, the Utilitarians destined their pedagogic establishments for the education of the middle class ; finally, their political economy is a bourgeois political economy. James Mill, a small journalist who had become the head of an office, and Francis Place, a small artisan who had become a master tailor, were no doubt more democratic than the rich financier Ricardo, and adequately represent the spirit of the doctrine. They were hardworking and prudent men, they knew at the cost of how many pains nature finally gave them a comfortable position ; they saw with anxiety their family growing while, according to a law whose necessity struck them as evident, the income on their capital, the fruit of their savings, was, constantly falling.

[1] Bowring, vol. ix. p. 6.   [2] *Ibid.* vol. iii. p. 230.   [3] *Colony*, p. 11.

But though these doctrinaires of prudence—James Mill and Francis Place—may have had the narrow and rigid virtues necessary in the founders of an orthodox faith and the organisers of a school, they obviously lacked the capacity for illusion and optimism which was necessary in order to endow Ricardo's system with the universal popularity which it was nevertheless destined to acquire. To understand how it acquired it, and the laws in accordance with which the logic of a system is deformed when it becomes the logic of a popular party, and even the opinion of a whole age, the deviations to which the theory of the distribution of wealth was submitted must be studied in the works of the publicist MacCulloch.

MacCulloch borrowed the laws of wages and profits from Ricardo ; but he either modified them or failed to understand their logical bearing. Take, for example, the case of wages. Ricardo's natural or necessary wage was for him no longer the central point around which occur oscillations in the price of labour, but only the lower limit below which the current price cannot fall.[1] Take again the law of profits. MacCulloch, as opposed to Ricardo, held that ' profits depend on the proportion which they bear to the capital by which they are produced, and not on the proportion which they bear to wages '.[2] He thought he could conclude from this that, although the proportion of profits to wages remains fixed, yet profits can, at the same time as wages, increase in absolute quantity : thus there is a way of raising profits without there being a proportional fall in wages, and in this way there is one less disharmony in the system of economic interests. Now these modifications of the law of wages and the law of profits imply a new conception of the final state towards which economic progress tends. The ' stationary ' state is no longer defined by him as a state towards which economic progress is necessarily tending, but as a purely possible state whose advent can be indefinitely put off by the accumulation of a sufficient quantity of capital. ' To continue stationary or to retrograde, is not natural to society. Man from youth grows to manhood, then decays and dies ; but such is not the destiny of nations. The arts, sciences, and capital of one generation are the patrimony of that which succeeds them, and in their hands are improved and augmented and rendered more powerful and efficient, so that if not counteracted by the want of security, or by other adventitious causes, the principle of improvement would always operate, and would secure the constant advancement of nations in wealth and population '.[3] This passage, which is almost copied from Ricardo, does nevertheless form a profound modification, in an optimistic direction, of the theory of progress, and these two opposite conceptions of economic progress, held by Ricardo and by MacCulloch perhaps rest on two different psychologies, that is, on two opposite ways of thinking of the fundamental economic motive. ' Ambition to rise ', writes MacCulloch, ' is the animating

[1] *Pol. Econ.*, p. 335.   [2] *Ibid.* pp. 373-374.   [3] *Ibid.* p. 112.

principle of society. Instead of remaining satisfied with the condition of their fathers, the great object of mankind in every age has been to rise above it—to elevate themselves in the scale of wealth '.[1] But Ricardo and James Mill allowed an important place in their psychology to a different motive, a motive which consists of the desire not to improve, but to preserve, the economic position acquired. According to James Mill, man, as an intelligent being, is capable of indefinite progress, he can accumulate intellectual capital indefinitely ; but man, as a producer, is only capable of saving and of accumulating to a slight extent. James Mill, as we have seen, tried to prove this by starting from the ' known laws of human nature ', and based a new proof of the principle of population on this assertion. According to MacCulloch, on the contrary, the accumulation of capital is easy and natural. Thus the philosophy of progress once more becomes almost unrestrictedly optimistic.

MacCulloch could not however treat himself as a disciple of Ricardo, if he did not accept the theory of differential rent which is the basis of the whole doctrine. Now rent, by its permanent variations, is an expression of the increasing difficulty of producing objects of primary necessity ; and while it thus represents the increasing poverty of the human species, it progressively enriches the class of landowners ; hence a divergence of interests whose natural or necessary character MacCulloch was obliged to recognise. MacCulloch was not prepared, however, to consider the possibility of a single land-tax :[2] his objections were discussed by James Mill in the *Elements*.[3] He was so much in favour of landed property on a large scale that he justified the custom of primogeniture,[4] in defiance of the principles laid down by Bentham : from this arose the first controversy between the *Edinburgh Review*, in which MacCulloch had just been defending this conservative thesis, and the *Westminster Review*,[5] recently founded for the propagation of orthodox Benthamism. Once again, in defiance of the logical connection of ideas, the principle of the natural identity of interests prevails over the thesis of disharmony in this representative of the orthodox political economy.

At first, MacCulloch tried to identify variations of rent, which are permanent according to Ricardo, with the temporary variations which make current value oscillate about natural value. He recognised that ' a rise in the price of raw produce, which is advantageous to the landlord, is prejudicial to farmers, capitalists, labourers, and every other class of society ', that ' every increase of rent is, therefore, a proof that the power to accumulate capital and population, or to increase that fund, by whose extent the extent of the productive industry of the country must ever be regulated, is diminished '. ' But ', he added, ' it is not possible, however, that in any society, rent

[1] *Pol. Econ.*, p. 112.
[2] Article ' Taxation ', *Ency. Brit.*   [3] *Elements*, ch. iv. sect. v. (end).
[4] *Ed. Rev.*, no. lxxx. July 1824.   [5] *West. Rev.*, Oct. 1824, article by Austin.

and wages can ever absorb the whole value of a commodity ; for, long ere this could happen, there would be no motive to accumulate ; capitalists would live, not on profit but on capital ; a want of employment would be universally experienced ; population would rapidly diminish ; and inferior lands being thrown out of cultivation, the price of raw produce would be reduced ; rent and wages would fall, and capital would again yield a profit on its employment '.[1] In short, the dynamic point of view was in this way reduced, by MacCulloch, to the static point of view ; and economic evil was no longer anything but an accident, in relation to the general good which results from the normal operation of the laws.

Some years later, he devoted a whole series of articles, in the *Edinburgh Review*, to a criticism of the duties which the great landlords had had put on the importation of corn : the greatest possible number of people must be converted to the cause of free-trade. Hence arose again a tendency to identify the interest of the landlord with that of the rest of the community. He pointed out, in the first place, that the benefit secured by the landlords from the tax on corn was far less than the destruction of wealth to which the nation as a whole was submitted by these taxes. Let us admit, said MacCulloch, that their income is equal to a quarter of the value of the whole produce of the soil, and that a régime of protection raises the value of agricultural supplies. The landlords would then benefit by a quarter of this increase in value, but by a quarter only. The other three-quarters of the increase would increase the value of the share of the farmers and of the wage-earners, without any advantage either for the farmers or for the wage-earners or for the landlord himself.[2] Besides, if free-trade were to involve a fall in rent, it would at least ensure in it a stability which it lacked under the régime of sliding scales. Moreover, the poor-rate was the price which the landlords were paying for customs protection : they would save on this from the day they accepted free-trade. Finally, MacCulloch brought to bear more trenchant arguments, and concluded : ' it is the extreme of folly to suppose, that a system, which is so essentially injurious to the other classes of the community, can be really beneficial to those who have so deep an interest in the public prosperity as the landlords. Whatever advantage they may derive from it, can only be fleeting and illusory : for it must of necessity be purchased at the expense of those with whom their own interests are inseparably and indissolubly connected '.[3] This amounts to postulating the natural identity of individual interests, whereas it had just been denied in the statement of the law of differential rent. It is really a betrayal of Ricardo to summarise his doctrine in the following terms : ' the relation between rent and profits, between profits and wages, and the various general laws which regulate and connect the *apparently*

---

[1] *Ed. Rev.*, no. lix., June 1818, art. ii.
[2] *Ed. Rev.*, no. lxxxviii., Sept. 1826, art. ii. pp. 341 *seq.*   [3] *Ibid.* p. 345.

conflicting, but really harmonious interests of different orders in society, may thus be discovered, and established with all the certainty that belongs to conclusions derived from experience and observation '.[1]

' If, in the long and honourable career which is still open to the adversaries of commercial restrictions, monopoly, and preference ', declared Lord Grenville in 1825, ' the same resolution uphold the country and the Legislature—if full and uncompromising effect be finally given to a system confirmed by experience, and sanctioned by public applause, not this age, nor this country alone, will have reason to bless our exertions. There is no period so remote, there is no nation so barbarous, in which we may not confidently anticipate that these successful researches of British philosophy; this auspicious example of British policy, will become, under the favour of Providence a pure and ample source of continually increasing human happiness'.[2] This philosophy and this policy which Lord Grenville held to be national, are the philosophy and the policy of industrial and commercial freedom. But one of two things must be true : either the thesis of commercial and industrial liberty is really derived from the principles of the new school of political economy, in which case it does not imply the natural identity of interests ; or else it does imply this spontaneous identity of the interest of each with the interest of all, in which case the thesis of economic liberalism is not derived from the principles on which Ricardo based his system. About 1825, all the economists were in agreement in a general way on the conclusions which they drew from their doctrines : should it be argued from this, as they liked to argue, that fundamentally, and despite certain superficial disagreements, they were agreed about the principles themselves ? Or, on the contrary, that their agreement in regard to conclusions dispensed them from thinking about principles ? Merchants needed the thesis of the identity of interests to be true, in order to secure the most extended market for their products. Manufacturers needed to believe in the theory of indefinite progress, in order to be able to speculate on the progressive exploitation of all the forces of nature. Consequently it mattered little that certain economic laws brought serious restrictions to bear on the harmony of interests, or set a limit to the progress of the human race : the theorists were not free to keep their attention on considerations of this kind. In spite of them, optimism tended to prevail in their doctrine over pessimism. The industrial revolution, like the political revolution in France thirty years earlier, was demanding its principles.

It was at this time that the Statute of Apprenticeship was repealed, that the prohibitions on importation and exportation were removed at many points, that a first attack was made upon the system of the

---

[1] *Pol. Econ.*, p. 60.   Cf. pp. 155-156.
[2] Speech delivered at the dissolution of the Company of the Levant, quoted by MacCulloch, *Pol. Econ.*, vol. iii. pp. 108, 9.

Navigation Acts, and freedom to combine was granted to workmen. Ricardo, in Parliament from 1818 to 1823, Francis Place at Westminster as organiser, and MacCulloch in Edinburgh as publicist, were taking the initiative in the movement which was to grow and spread for thirty years more. Already, however, contradictory tendencies were appearing. The Statute of Apprenticeship had not yet been repealed, when the new factory legislation began to be organised, and the suppression of the laws regarding workmen's coalitions marked the first year of the era of modern socialism in England. Among the theorists of the budding socialist movement there were even to be found Utilitarians, disciples and friends of Bentham's. These men, if they wished to remain faithful to the principle of the natural identity of interests, would have to reject in Ricardo's political economy the supposed natural laws of rent and profits, which contradict this principle. But otherwise there was nothing to prevent them, without renouncing the principle of utility, requiring that the State should intervene, in order to correct by its intervention any disharmony which could be found in the system of economic relations. That Ricardo and his disciples were repelled by the idea of such intervention, may have been less through excess of confidence in nature than through excess of mistrust of the physician : it were better to resign oneself to necessary evils than to make them worse by inappropriate remedies. Again, even if economic liberalism is to be considered as an optimism, must it indeed be a rational optimism, founded on the knowledge of the laws of the universe ? Is it not rather that naturalistic and sceptical optimism whose formula Hume provided ? To be still more exact, in Hume we made a distinction between two tendencies : the one to some extent rationalistic and aiming at founding the moral sciences— the science of psychological phenomena and the science of social phenomena—on the application of a method at once experimental and abstract, analogous to the method of Newton ; the other a naturalistic and sceptical tendency, which finally led to the abdication of the reasoning faculties, before the incomprehensible miracle of instinct. Now, in the orthodox political economy, as it was constituted between 1815 and 1832, if we consider what the doctrines really were, we see that the naturalistic tendency was prevailing. If economic science were like other sciences, it ought, as soon as it was framed, to make it possible for the legislator who has studied it to foresee economic crises by its means and to provide for them by rational intervention. But economic science in Ricardo, in James Mill and in MacCulloch recognises that, up to a certain point, it is incapable of foresight ; it counts on the free play of the forces present, to teach it what, from one moment to another, is the natural value of products, the natural price of labour, and the natural rate of profit. It recognises in fact that it is incapable of providing for the crises which it mentions, except by a policy of systematic abstention ; it counts, not on the power of knowledge, but on the *vis medicatrix naturae*. The philosophy of free trade is at bottom naturalism or empiricism. But, on the other hand, the new theorists would not have consented to call themselves naturalists ; on the contrary they held themselves to be rationalists ; they believed and wished to believe that they were on the way to proving the thesis of the natural identity of interests, like a geometrical theorem. The very principles on which they took their stand, and which they had borrowed from Malthus—the principle of population and the law of differential rent—refute their claim. It is none the less true that in the last resort, nature remained for them a synonym for harmony, justice and reason ; that, almost without knowing it, they conformed to certain philosophical principles which did not justify their doctrine, such as the principle of the simplicity of the laws of nature and the principle of order ; and further that from this illusion, which they shared with their public, was to a great extent derived their prestige and their influence.

CHAPTER II

THE ORGANISATION OF JUSTICE
AND OF THE STATE

IN 1789, in a final note to his *Introduction*, Bentham had proposed to distinguish, in a complete body of laws, three distinct codes: the civil code, the penal code and the constitutional code. But in the *Traités*, which were published by Dumont, he suggested a new division of laws, into ' substantive ' and ' adjective ' laws. This second class of laws Bentham called adjective because they can only exist in relation to substantive laws, as the adjective, in grammar, exists in relation to the substantive : they are the laws of procedure whose object is, or ought to be, to give effect to the commands the sum of which constitutes substantive law.[1] Now, as far as concerns the two fundamental parts of substantive law, civil law and penal law, Bentham's doctrine had long been definitely formed ; the period of propaganda and of influence now succeeded the period of invention and of organisation of ideas. At last, Bentham had become a prophet in his own country : his *Sophismes Politiques* which appeared at Geneva in 1816, were translated into English by Bingham two years later. In 1822 there appeared almost simultaneously a third edition of the *Fragment on Government* and a second edition of the *Introduction*. In 1825, Richard Smith supplied an English translation of the *Théorie des Récompenses*, which was completed in 1830 by a translation of the *Théorie des Peines*.[2] Meanwhile Mackintosh and Peel undertook one after the other the reform of penal law in Parliament. There remained adjective law on the one hand, and on the other constitutional law, the third branch of substantive law. The *Introductory View of the Rationale of Judicial Evidence*, which was drawn up by James Mill from Bentham's manu-

---

[1] Bowring, vol. iii. p. 158, vol. vi. p. 7 and p. 210, vol ii. p. 5.
[2] On the various English translations of Bentham's works see Bowring, vol. x. pp. 497, 548, and Stuart Mill, *Autobiography*, p. 115.

scripts, had not found a publisher in 1812 ; but the *Traité des Preuves Judiciaires* appeared in French in 1823. Two years later it was translated into English ; two years later again, the original *Rationale of Judicial Evidence* appeared, arranged by Stuart Mill in a more developed form, from the manuscripts of the master. Moreover, while the theory of evidence appears to have been the subject of Bentham's labours during the first ten years of the century, the last years of his existence and his labour were absorbed by the drawing up of a complete *Constitutional Code* : he died in 1832 without having had time to complete the printing of it.

In Bentham's theory, adjective and constitutional law may conveniently be studied together as a whole.

In the first place, if we consider the definitions put forward by Bentham, adjective and constitutional law present numerous points of resemblance. According to Bentham,[1] the purpose of constitutional law is to confer ' powers ' on certain classes of citizens and to prescribe corresponding ' duties ' for the people who are invested with the powers in question. Now the powers are conferred and the duties prescribed for the purpose of supervising the execution of civil and penal laws. Thus the definition of constitutional law is in part reducible to the definition of adjective law. James Mill, the orthodox disciple of Bentham, defined the code of procedure as constituting ' that subsidiary branch of law, by which an agency is constituted for the purpose of carrying those enactments into effect '.[2] What operations are necessary to put them into execution ? By what individuals is it more likely that they will be well carried out ? What are the best guarantees to ensure the good behaviour of these individuals ? The general problem of adjective law, when it is thus split up into three special problems, includes the problem of judicial organisation, which is however a problem of constitutional law. Bentham devotes a chapter of his *Principles of Judicial Procedure* to the question of judicial organisation ; he devotes a book of his *Constitutional Code* to the same question.

Secondly, the combined study of adjective and constitutional law makes it possible, just because of the similarity of the problems dealt with, to understand what was the logical evolution which led Bentham, who was originally a Tory, to end by becoming, after 1815, the philosopher of the Radical party. At all times and in all matters he was a simplifier : on this point his views were always those of Godwin, of Paine and of Cartwright.[3] Complication he denounced as ' the nursery of fraud ' ; as to simplicity he almost made it divine and worshipped it : ' O rare *simplicity* ! handmaid of beauty, wisdom, virtue—of everything that is excellent ! '[4] Now, the ' simplification ' of the Benthamites shocked the liberal, or supposedly liberal, pre-

---

[1] Bowring, vol. i. p. 113.   [2] *Jurisprudence*, p. 24.
[3] Cartwright to Wyvill, May 21, 1812.
[4] Bowring, vol. x. p. 531, and vol. iii. p. 464.

judices which were particularly dear to public opinion in England, but which had been sanctified throughout the whole civilised world by the testimony of Montesquieu. It is a commonplace to the liberal party that simple institutions are suitable to despotic states, and complex institutions to free states : judicial formalities, complicated constitutions in which the various organs of the state are arranged in some sort of equilibrium, would be so many guarantees offered to the individual liberty of the subject against the abuses of the executive and of the judicial powers. Burke, the theorist of liberalism and the partisan of complex government confused in one and the same hatred the simplification of absolute monarchy and the simplification of pure democracy : in the name of the same principles he opposed first the usurping policy of George III. and then the jacobinism of the French. What, in contrast to this, was to be the attitude of Bentham and his group ? In questions of procedure, Bentham had always demanded the abolition of all the rules which in the evaluation of witnesses and evidence are made to tie the opinion of the judge, and which appear to the disciples of Montesquieu as so many guarantees of the liberty of the accused. In regard to judicial organisation, Bentham condemned the system of a multiplicity of judges and wished the judge to sit alone in order fully to feel his responsibility ; he affected to disdain the institution of the jury, the pride of English liberalism, and was satisfied that the publicity of debates alone would make the responsibility of the judge real. The ' single judge ' of the Benthamite doctrine is the ' enlightened despot ', as he had been dreamt of by the eighteenth century reformers, the master who drew his inspiration from the opinion freely expressed by a public composed of philosophers. Such was the Bentham of the first period, a philosopher of the type of Beccaria and of Voltaire. In regard to constitutional law, the Utilitarians now opposed the doctrine of universal suffrage to the Whig theory of varied representation and of the representation of interests : the ' representative democracy ' of Bentham and James Mill is only the adaptation of pure democracy to the necessities of existence of a great nation. Furthermore, at a time when the English were taking pride in the local self-government which made them the prototype of the free peoples of Europe, the Utilitarians were advocating a system of administrative centralisation, inspired primarily by the French system. Any act whether of an individual or of a government implies two moments : the deliberation previous to the act, and the execution of the act itself. The authoritarians, by the simplification of parliamentary routine, aimed at making the execution of governmental measures as swift as possible. The liberals, by the multiplication of constitutional organisation, wished to prolong as much as possible the deliberation which precedes the act. Bentham had never been a liberal ; always impatient of philanthropic reforms, he merely passed from a monarchic authoritarianism to a democratic authoritarianism, without pausing at the intermediary position, which is the position of Anglo-Saxon liberalism.

I. JUDICIAL PROCEDURE AND ORGANISATION

The terms in which Bentham put the fundamental problem of adjective law still show the same desire to give to legislation the nature of science, exact and as far as possible mathematical. Legislation has in view two kinds of end : a direct end and collateral ends. The direct end is this : it is necessary for justice to be executed as accurately as possible, and that as much time and money as possible should be expended for this purpose. The collateral ends are as follows : since loss of time, loss of money, and vexations are so many sufferings undergone, that is, so many evils, these evils must, if it is possible, be abolished, and justice must be executed with as little expense, as few delays and as few vexations as possible. Here, then, between the direct end and the collateral ends of justice there is a contradiction whose solution is reducible, once again, to a calculus of pleasures experienced and of pains suffered. It is tempting to believe that Bentham borrowed his distinction of the three collateral ends of justice from the triple vow exacted from the English monarch by Magna Charta : ' we will not delay, we will not sell, we will not deny, justice to anyone '. However this may be, only the merest germ of this view can be recognised in the rule of economy, which Bentham laid down when developing his project of *Panopticon*. There is no trace of it in the confused and insignificant *Plan of Procedure*, contained in Dumont's *Treatises*.[1] It was by another route that Bentham at this time connected the theory of procedure with his moral arithmetic : to him, procedure was the sum of the means required to endow legal punishment with the element of ' certainty '.[2] The Benthamite theory of procedure is for the first time explicitly stated in its definitive form,[3] in the pamphlet entitled *Scotch Reform*, in 1808. The formula was accepted by James Mill, in his *Introductory View of the Rationale of Evidence*,[4] by Dumont in the *Traité des Preuves Judiciaires*, and by Stuart Mill in the *Rationale of Judicial Evidence* ;[5] whereas Bentham, that indefatigable analyst, modified it again and complicated it, without great profit, in his *Principles of Judicial Procedure*, which were drawn up by him between 1824 and 1828, and were only published in 1839, seven years after his death.[6]

But Bentham, as a reforming philosopher, was always obliged to destroy, before he could construct ; and, in adjective as in substantive law it was the régime of corporations which hindered the

---

[1] Bowring, vol. iii. pp. 204-205.   [2] MSS. U. C., Nos. 50 and 51
[3] Bowring, vol. v. pp. 1-54.   [4] *Ibid*. vol. vi. pp. 1-188.
[5] *Ibid*. vol. vi. pp. 189 *seq*.   [6] *Ibid*. vol. ii. p. 15.

application of the utilitarian system. The end to be desired from any body of laws is the greatest happiness of the greatest number of the members of the society concerned. The end actually secured in all bodies of laws has been chiefly, if not exclusively, the greatest happiness of those who made the laws. For man naturally obeys the promptings of interest, whether it be the individual interest which isolates him from all his fellow men, or the class interest which isolates the closed corporation to which he belongs from the rest of society. Bentham, who had been less categorical in 1780 when he wrote his *Introduction*, now developed the theory of Helvetius without any restrictions ; and it was at this time that James Mill, who was putting these manuscripts in order, himself became an uncompromising supporter of the psychology of Helvetius. As concerns the laws of procedure in particular, says Bentham, these are the work of the judges ; but the judges, in so far as they form a class which is separate from the rest of society, have not the same interests as their fellow-citizens ; and the laws of procedure, as made by them, must favour the interests of the judicial corporation at the expense of the interests of the public. Procedure, as it is in fact practised, pursues two ends : the one positive and direct, which is to increase profit, the other negative and collateral, which is to diminish pain. The fee-gathering system, combined with the increase in the cost of justice, allows the judges to secure the two ends at one blow. If the clients pay, their profit is increased ; if to avoid the cost they give up pleading, the pain is diminished. A minimum of expense, of delay and of vexations for the parties concerned—this is the end they claim to pursue : what is really pursued, on the ground that it is a means to the principal end, is the maximum of all these things.[1] The general procedure employed by the members of the judicial corporation, that is, the association of judges and barristers—what Bentham calls ' Judge and Co '[2]—with a view to making the operations of justice a lucrative and an easy matter, consists in increasing the number of judicial formalities, which make procedure obscure, long and costly for the parties, and automatic for the lawyers and the judges : this complicated and intentionally complicated system is what Bentham calls the ' technical system ' as opposed to the ' natural system '. The return to the natural system consists, not in the definition of new rules, which would be *ex hypothesi* in conformity with general utility, but in the abolition pure and simple of all existing rules and formalities. According to Bentham, the attempt to withdraw the estimation of the value of judicial proofs from instinct in order to submit it to rules, is a task which, if it really falls within the capacity of human faculties, should at least be kept for the increased powers of a riper century. In the meantime, the domain of pro-

---

[1] Bowring, vol. vi. pp. 8 *seq.* and vol. vii. pp. 199-201 ; and *Preuves Judiciaires*, vol. i. p. 7.
[2] Bowring, vol. v. p. 369.

cedure is encumbered with technical rules. If these rules cannot
claim to have a scientific value, on what principle can they be justified ?
On the principle of their antiquity ? But there is a method of
administering justice which is older even than technical rules : on this
point Bentham's doctrine assumed a definite form with the appearance of Dumont's *Traités*.[1] Before there were states there were
families. Nature has put before us a model of procedure. Let us
look at what happens in the domestic tribunal ; let us examine the
way in which a father of a family behaves to his children or to his
servants. There we shall find the original features of justice, which,
moreover, are no longer recognisable, since they have been disfigured
by men who are incapable of seeing what justice is, or are interested
to disguise it. A good judge is only a good father of a family working
on a larger scale. The means which are suitable to direct the father
of the family in his search for truth must be equally good for the
judges. It is the original model for procedure from which man
started, and it ought never to have been set aside.[2]

Can it be said that the technical system, which is newer than the
natural system, may perhaps be an advance on it ? To be convinced
of the contrary it is only necessary to apply the technical system to
the preservation of order in a family : there is no family, be it only
composed of half a dozen members, which could subsist for twelve
months under the government of such rules. Thus, flattering in this
way certain prejudices which were current in the democratic party,[3]
Bentham ended by assuming the strictly ' radical ' point of view—the
point of view of a return to origins. ' Men have often spoken of the
supposed necessity of submitting political constitutions, and especially popular constitutions, to some operation or other which would
have the effect of bringing them back to their ancient principles '—a
contestable theory. ' However ', continued Bentham, ' there is
one branch of legislation in which it seems to me that primitive times
had the advantage : this branch is procedure. Without going back to
Greece or to ancient Rome, in England itself, where it is so complicated to-day, it was originally simple '.[4] Already in the works
edited by the two Mills, and above all in his *Petition for Justice*, of
1829,[5] Bentham develops, in the matter of procedure, a theory which
is nothing else than Cartwright's political theory transposed. The
technical system was introduced with the Norman conquest ; the
natural system is the Saxon system. ' Then and there, people or
lawyers made no difference ; language was the same. From the
presence of the judge, in any one of these small and adequately
numerous tribunals, directly or indirectly, was suitor ever excluded ?

[1] Opposition of the natural and technical procedure already present in *Judicial
Establishment*.
[2] Bowring, vol. i. p. 558.
[3] *Rationale of Evidence*. Bowring, vols. vi. and vii.
[4] *Ibid*.   [5] Bowring, vol. v. pp. 448.

No more than in a private family contending children from the presence of their fathers '. Here, as everywhere, the rule of utility is the rule of simplicity ; the system of complication is a system of absurdity, of incoherence and of injustice in all its forms. But the simplicity is here less the simplicity of rational science than the simplicity of common sense. Indeed, had not the philosophers of the eighteenth century been often inclined to confuse them ? In fact, in his great work on judicial evidence, Bentham does not weary of opposing to the common law and the customs of the judicial corporation, what he calls ' common sense ', ' common sense and common probity ', ' common sense and common honesty ', and ' unsophisticated common sense '.[1]

This is the measure of the distance which separates the Utilitarianism of Bentham from what may be called the liberalism of Montesquieu. According to Montesquieu, laws are less simple in monarchic than in despotic States : ' it is not therefore surprising to find in the laws of these States so many rules, restrictions and exceptions, which multiply particular cases, *and seem to make an art of reason itself* '. In the formalities of what Bentham calls the technical system Montesquieu saw so many guarantees of liberty. ' If you examine the formalities of justice with relation to the pains with which a citizen is able to get his goods returned to him, or to get satisfaction for some outrage, you will doubtless find too many of them. If you look at them in relation to the liberty and the security of the citizens you will often find them too few ; and you will see that the pains, the expenses, the delays, even the dangers of justice are the price which every citizen pays for his liberty '.[2] And Blackstone, in his *Commentaries*, insisted at length on Montesquieu's thesis.[3] But Bentham attaches little value to this vague notion of liberty—a logical fiction which men of law make use of to hide their abuses as much as the revolutionaries do to excuse their excesses. ' The judicial forms are the shields of liberty . . . What judicial forms ? . . . What liberty ? Whose liberty ? What in his dictionary means liberty ? What ? unless it be liberty in rulers to oppress subjects, and to lawyers to plunder suitors ? . . . The judicial forms are the shields of liberty . . . if, instead of liberty, we may read despotism, oppression, degradation and corruption '. ' The screen for corruption ', adds Bentham, ' the screen made out of the panegyric on delay and forms, I have seen it in use these five and fifty years : the name of the manufactory is visible on it. Esprit des loix the manufactory : Montesquieu and Co. the name of the firm : a more convenient or fashionable article was never made '.[4] Montesquieu was a lawyer, and as such was instinctively attached to the traditional custom of his caste ; Bentham, since his youth, had broken with the judicial corporation by leaving the

---

[1] See *e.g.* Bowring, vol. vi. pp. 414-471, and vol. vii. pp. 14, 39, 171, 385, etc.
[2] *Esp. des Lois*, liv. vi. chs. i. and ii.   [3] *III. Comm.*, pp. 422, 423-424.
[4] Bowring, vol. viii. pp. 478, 481.

bar. Montesquieu lived under a despotic government, and criticised
it with his eyes on England, a monarchic country in which the royal
power was kept within just limits by the traditional resistance of the
aristocratic and judicial corporations ; Bentham, on the contrary,
lived in England and had suffered personally from the conservative
and routine pig-headedness of the corporative aristocracies, and he
saw in this very régime of traditional and formalistic corporations the
true source of the abuses he was denouncing.[1]

Let us first consider, with Bentham, procedure taken in itself ; and,
in order to understand how the natural system is here opposed to the
technical system, the ' simplification ' system to the ' formalist ' system,
let us confine ourselves to following the regular course of a suit.
The first consequence of the adoption of the technical system—since
this system at once makes the essence of law consist in the respecting
of certain traditional formalities, which are unintelligible to the layman who does not know the history of the judicial corporation—is to
complicate and to obscure the science of law, and to make necessary
the intervention, between the pleader and the judge, of a man entrusted
with the interpretation of the mystery of the law, that is, of an
advocate. Thus advocates come to swell the ranks of the judicial
corporation ; like the judges, they find it to their interest that the
suit should last as long as possible and should be as costly as possible
for the parties : for them, as for the judges, justice becomes a ' business proposition ', in which their interests are distinct from those of
the parties. The advocate finds it to be particularly to his interest to
avoid as far as possible the presence of his clients at the debates, to
arrange things so that the whole matter should take place between
barristers in front of a judge, that is to say between individuals
affiliated to the same corporation. In fact every suit opens, in
England, with a first act, which has been given the name of special
pleading, and which entirely consists ' of a sort of written correspondence between two attorneys '.[2] The special pleading opens by the
declaration of the counsel for the plaintiff, who affirms his client's
grievances ; the defendant replies by a plea in which he either denies
the facts put forward by the plaintiff, or else recognises them, while
maintaining that the conclusions drawn from them by the plaintiff
are unfounded. In the first case, the suit is reduced to a question of
fact, and is put before a jury ; in the second case it is reduced to a
question of law which it will be within the province of the judge to
settle, without the assistance of a jury. The plaintiff, as represented
by his attorney, may reply to the plea, then the attorney for the
defendant may reply to the attorney for the plaintiff, and so on, the
exchange of written matter going on and on. This first act of every
suit is extremely important ; it determines the manner and the matter
of the suit : the manner, because on it depends the question of

[1] *West. Rev.*, vol. v. pp. 388-90.   [2] Bowring, vol. vii. pp. 559.

knowing whether the case should be conducted with or without a jury ; the matter, because the plaintiff and the defendant will not be allowed to prove before the jury anything except what it has been agreed, in this preliminary phase of the suit, to treat as the point to be debated. Thus the interested parties do not play any part in the special pleading. The science of special pleading, as it is called, presupposes an initiation of which men of the trade are alone capable ; it constitutes a science not in the natural but in the technical sense of the word, a science of erudition, a learning.[1] De Lolme, in his general admiration for English institutions, made an exception in the case of the civil procedure whose complications and refinements he criticised ; and Bentham often seems to have drawn inspiration from his criticism.[2] In fact, the procedure of ' written pleas ' is the surest of all the procedures of the technical system to favour the interests of the corporation at the expense of the general interest, and to give up the parties uncontrolledly to the mercy of the advocates.[3]

That every man should be able to be his own advocate, and that anyone should be able to be the advocate of anyone else, was the wish always expressed by Bentham, from the time of his *Draught of Judicial Establishment* of 1791. ' Every man his own lawyer ', is a maxim which is constantly repeated in his *Rationale of Judicial Evidence*.[4] It is a formula which brings to mind the economic formula : ' each man the best judge of his own interest '. But it is a formula also which can be likened to the Lutheran formula : ' everyman is a priest '. In the same way as the first theorists of free-trade had seen in the demand for freedom of commerce a kind of commercial Protestantism, so Bentham and the anti-clerical group around him saw in their Utilitarianism the last stage of a movement of emancipation, which had been begun by Protestantism in the sixteenth century. Priestcraft and lawyercraft are all one ; the law manufactured by the judges is as good as the religion manufactured by the priests. But men noticed the artifices of the clerical caste first : ' Near 300 years has religion had her Luther. No Luther of Jurisprudence is yet come;—no penetrating eye and dauntless heart have as yet searched into the cells and conclave of jurisprudence '.[5] In order to bring about judicial reform, it is only necessary, however, to revert from the complications of the technical system to the simplicity of the natural and domestic system. When a father wishes to judge a question which is dividing his children or his servants, it does not occur to him first to drive out the children or servants from his presence, and to bid them delegate advocates. No doubt, the difference in setting may make necessary the presence of

[1] Bowring, vol. v. p. 5.
[2] De Lolme, *Constitution de l'Angleterre*, vol. i. pp. 111 *seq.*
[3] For the Criticism of *Special Pleading*, see *West. Rev.*, no. vii. July 1825, art. v., no. viii, July 1826, art. iv.
[4] Bowring, vol iv. p. 318, see *e.g.*, *Ibid*. vol. vii. p. 189.
[5] *Ibid*. vol. vii. p. 270 note.

advocates in suits properly so called ; but we must remove ourselves as little as possible from the model offered us by nature, and so arrange things that advocates should never be substituted for their clients, but should remain merely advisers to the parties, who should them-selves always be present at the debates.   Special pleading must be suppressed root and branch : Bentham had insisted on the necessity of this reform ever since 1791.[1]   In the natural system every process would open with an initiatory hearing, at which the judge would make an attempt at conciliation in the presence of the two parties.   If the attempt at conciliation failed, the two parties would have to present themselves in person again for an anticipative survey of the cause before the judge.   Each party would submit to the examination of the judge the ' budget ' of evidence and testimonies which it claimed to offer ; the judge would decide what part of this evidence deserved to be retained for a profounder examination, and what part should be excluded at the outset ; then the actual suit would begin.

Is an abolition, pure and simple, of special pleading possible ?   I do not know if it can be done, answered Bentham, but I know that it is done.   Without mentioning the Danish courts of conciliation which had always attracted Bentham's attention,[2] certain English statutes had set up courts, called courts of ' summary procedure ', which avoided the complicated procedure of the courts of common law and equity, and so were exactly what Bentham meant by ' courts of natural procedure ' or ' of natural procedure restored '.   Such were the ' courts of appeal and of conscience,' which were established by Henry VIII., modified by James I. and reorganised by act of Parlia-ment under the first two Georges.   Established in London and in other large commercial towns they judged suits regarding unimportant debts : they came to their decisions in accordance with the principles of conscience, without being bound by any law, or by any form.[3]   Such again were the courts of arbitration instituted under William III. Bentham demanded that the system should be extended ; when the congestion of cases on the Rolls imposed on Parliament the necessity of reforming the Chancellor's Court, he intervened and suggested the institution of a court of summary procedure, which he called the Equity Dispatch Court.[4]   What Bentham liked in these courts was precisely what shocked the jurists, and Blackstone above all : they were of statutory origin, their procedure had not been ' manufactured by the judges ', it was not born of usurpations by the judicial corpora-tion of the functions proper to the legislative assembly.   But here again, in this apology for courts of summary procedure, Bentham was striking a blow at the national prejudices which passed as liberal convictions.   In current language, summary procedure was opposed to regular procedure.   Now the term ' regular ' was here not a

---

[1] Bowring, vol. iv. p. 319.   [2] *Ibid*. vol. vii. p. 22 note, etc.
[3] *Ibid*. vol. vii. pp. 320 *seq*.   [4] *Ibid*. vol. iii. pp. 277-317.

neutral but a sentimental term ; it was taken here in a good sense, as a ' eulogistic ' term, according to Bentham's expression. Respect for rules was taken to constitute the guarantee of liberty ; and so the term ' summary ' was, by contrast, taken in a bad sense.[1] Further, the courts of summary procedure sat without a jury ; now the jury was taken to constitute the fundamental guarantee of the liberty of the accused before his judges ; thus the courts of summary procedure were despotically instituted. But the question is whether judgment by jury should be considered as an end or as a means, and whether, in the last resort, the ends of justice are secured better by the regular procedure, with the co-operation of a jury, than by the summary procedure without a jury. Here already is a definite point on which Bentham's juridical radicalism was opposed to the traditional and currant liberalism.

By the abolition of special pleadings, the suit can be opened without delay ; and, from the outset, it is the business of the judge to examine the testimonies, and to weigh the value of the evidence. Of all the questions relative to adjective law the theory of judicial evidence is the most important ; and of all Bentham's works the *Rationale of Judicial Evidence*, published in 1829 by Stuart Mill from his manuscripts, is the most voluminous and also without doubt the most important. Bentham treated the question as a philosopher, going back to first principles, and starting with a theory of belief : it was when putting straight Bentham's manuscripts which bore on the question of evidence that James Mill and Stuart Mill, one after the other at an interval of ten years, set themselves to study the Benthamite philosophy. On this particular point of adjective law, Bentham again contrasts the technical and the natural systems ; it is here that he defines in the most circumstantial manner the contrast between the two systems.

The fundamental principle of the technical system with regard to judicial evidence is what Bentham calls the principle of exclusion.[2] When a certain amount of evidence, in a given case, is at the disposal of the judge, he will necessarily hold some of it valid and some invalid. The first kind will moreover offer certain common characteristics. Hence the possibility, in course of time, of establishing general rules, and of deciding beforehand that such evidence can be accepted because it is of such and such a nature, and that such other evidence should, on the other hand, be excluded because of its intrinsic nature. Hence, the intimate conviction of the judge will matter little, in any given case ; legally speaking, the crime will or will not have been committed according to whether the rules of the corporation allow or forbid him to hold the testimony as valid. The exclusion of certain evidence, considered unworthy of credence, and considered in the current language of English law, as ' not

[1] Bowring, vol. vii. p. 198.   [2] *Ibid*. vol. vii. pp. 335 *seq*.

competent ', may, moreover, be either positive or negative : positive when the testimony is not allowed, even in cases where, if allowed, it would be produced or offered ; negative when, either by negligence or by design, the means needed to secure the testimony have been omitted and so the service is not rendered.   But according to Bentham, the means used to exclude testimony matter little.   Evidence is the very basis of justice, and all exclusion of evidence is a denial of justice.   The principle of exclusion encourages all criminal tendencies, because it increases the chances of success for all evil causes : to exclude a class of witnesses is to allow all imaginable transgressions in the presence of a witness of this class. The principle of natural procedure is, by antithesis to the principle of exclusion, the principle of universal admissibility.   Evidence may be held to be suspect either because the fact invoked does not involve the existence of the fact to be proved except by indirect inductive reasoning, or because the information is not received from the actual source of information, or because the evidence is not obtained by those methods which are the most suited to guarantee its exactness, or because the person who supplies the information is suspect by reason either of his moral worthlessness or of his intellectual incapacity.   But in no case is it permissible to set up a motive of suspicion as a rule of exclusion.

Should one, for example, exclude so-called inferior or makeshift evidence[1] (and notably, as is the case in English law, hearsay-evidence), evidence, that is to say, when the testimonial fact, the fact which is put forward as evidence, is such that neither one nor the other of the ' securities ' which serve to guarantee the exactness and the completeness of the testimony can be applied to it ?   But why exclude them unrestrictedly ?   Is it because it is believed to be necessary to check the tendency, innate in man, to put faith in testimony ?   But there are no innate tendencies : belief in human testimony has only become natural to the point of seeming innate because it has been confirmed by a constant experience.   If the disposition to believe is the habitual condition, and incredulity the exception, it is because true assertions do indeed far exceed false in number.   Not to mention the other sanctions, political, religious and moral, the natural sanction acts in favour of truth.   There is, Bentham tells us, a pain which appears on the side of mendacity, a pain which is not of human institution, which acts on the witness immediately and *disposes* him to tell the truth when there is no superior counter-motive ; for it is easier to relate than to invent, easier to tell the truth than to lie.[2]   The tendency to believe testimony is well-founded since it is general ; on principle, it is proper to put faith in testimony except for suspending judgment, when, by exception, a particular reason for not believing is present. And, on the other hand, the very existence of rules of exclusion shows the falseness of the hypothesis on which they rest.   The rules of

[1] Bowring, vol. vii. pp. 118 *seq*.   [2] *Ibid*. vol. vi. p. 262.

exclusion imply a resolution on the part of the judge to ignore everything in the man of suspected evidence and to consider its falsity
certain, instead of which it possesses in reality varying degrees of
probability.[1] Thus, since the judges are the authors of these rules,
they prove that, at least in the judges, there is a tendency to estimate
testimony not above but below its true value.

Or again, should circumstantial evidence be excluded, that is,
indirect evidence in which, from the existence of a fact or of a group
of facts is inferred by induction the existence of the principal fact ? [2]
Here again no line of absolute demarcation can be drawn among the
infinite number of degrees of probability. There are no rules for
distinguishing the improbable from the impossible. The risk run by
the judge who tries to lay down rules of this kind is that the rule must
either be obvious, in which case it is useless, or else must succeed in
modifying, in each particular case, the decision which the judge
would have arrived at spontaneously, in which case its application is a
dangerous matter. For instance, what rule should be established to
define what circumstance should be considered as sufficient evidence
of non-virginity ? The birth of a child ? But this is a rule of mere
common sense which it is superfluous to state, since it will in any case
be constantly applied. Then it must be some other physiological
circumstance involving special scientific knowledge. In this case a
complete system of physical science would have to be established by
authority, and introduced into the system of judicial procedure :
limits would thus be set by law to the progress of all the branches of
physical science, and particularly of the most important of all, the
medical branch.[3] There is here recognisable, in the Utilitarian theory
of law, the familiar argument of the Utilitarian economists against all
fixed regulations, which are in contradiction with the mobile and
progressive nature of the human intelligence. General rules about
evidence are condemned like commercial and industrial regulations,
because they are blind.

What, then, is their origin, and why are they so general ? In
support of the technical system and of the rules of exclusion which
bind the conscience of the judges, appeal is made to the necessity of
guaranteeing the parties against the power which judges could abuse if
this legal restraint did not exist. This is a mere pretext. For, in the
first place, the rules of exclusion are not a real guarantee against the
abuses of judicial power. The nature of judicial reasoning is so
bastard that the judge can at pleasure either exclude the evidence by
invoking the ' rule ', or admit it by taking his stand on the ' reason '
of the rule ; he can interpret the rule either in its narrow or in its
wide sense, and take his stand in the party of rigorists with Lord
Camden, or in the party of liberalists with Lord Mansfield. If you
adhere to the rule, you will be praised for your constancy and the

[1] Bowring, vol. vii. p. 159.   [2] *Ibid.* vol. vii. pp. 1 *seq.*
[3] *Ibid.* vol. vii. p. 65.

superiority of your probity ; if you depart from it you will be praised
for your liberality and for the superiority of your wisdom.[1] Thanks
to the power of interpretation, the judge always escapes the supposed
constraint which the rules of the technical system are believed to
exercise over the variations of his judgment : he decides arbitrarily
what is true and what false, as he decides what is just and what
unjust, by virtue of what Bentham, in his satire on the technical
system, called the 'double fountain principle'.[2] Again, and most important of all, it is false historically to say that the rules of exclusion are
a constraint imposed on the judges by the legislature—for the very
simple reason that they are the work not of the legislator but of the
judge : their origin is not statutory but jurisprudential ; like common
law, they are of exclusively judicial manufacture.   Now it is absurd,
on the strength of the laws of human nature, to suppose that in creating these rules, the aim of the judges was to set limits on their own
power ; granted the separation of interests existing between every
corporation and the public, it was inevitable that these rules should
aim, whether consciously or unconsciously, at favouring the sinister
interest of the judges and advocates at the expense of the general
interest.   It is not the fault of the judges, who are proud of their
honesty, proud of never having allowed themselves to be bought (the
honesty of English magistrates is proverbial), if by the normal
functioning of the laws of human nature and by the constitution of the
body to which they belong, they are constrained to grow rich at the
expense of the public, and to obey the promptings of professional
corruption and indolence.   Chiefly, perhaps, of indolence.   It is too
easy to make a distinction between two classes of evidence, evidence
which is clearly acceptable, and evidence which is clearly of no value.
Actually, these are the extreme terms between which there is a scale
with an infinite number of degrees.   But what, in the technical
system, will be done with merely probable evidence ?   Since no
limit can be set between that evidence which is probable enough and
that which is not probable enough to be admitted, the system of
excluding it will be adopted.   In one way, it will always be to
the judge's interest to collect the testimonies in an incomplete form,
for the less complete they are, the less are his pains, and the more
his love of ease is satisfied.[3] The judge's task is simplified in proportion as procedure becomes ' mechanical ' thanks to the multiplicity of legal rules.   There would be an increase of pains for the
judge, if he had to make a new effort of reflection in the examination
of all evidence, in order to gauge its value.   There is a diminution of
pains, if he has to do nothing but refer to simple rules, laid down once
for all, and which declare a certain kind of evidence to be absolutely
valueless, and a certain other kind to afford absolute proof.   There
would be a further increased diminution of pains, if the mechanical

---

[1] Bowring, vol. vi. p. 145.   [2] *Ibid.* vol vii. p. 308.
[3] *Ibid.* vol. vii. p. 246.

procedure were to result in the exclusion of as much evidence as possible, and to reduce to a minimum the amount of evidence worthy of the consideration of the judge.

In his critical examination of the principle of exclusion, Bentham does not confine himself to discussing the direct causes of the exclusion of evidence. Besides the direct causes he discovers certain indirect causes which are due, especially, to the persistence of religious prejudices : hence the need for important reforms. Bentham gives the name ' preappointed evidence ' to evidence ' whose creation and preservation was commanded by law prior to the existence of some right or obligation in such a way that it would be necessary to exhibit this evidence in order to preserve this right or obligation '.[1] It is in this way that it has been established in advance, preappointed, that a contract of marriage, an act of birth or of death, taking place according to certain forms and in the presence of certain witnesses, shall be taken in law as the sufficient and necessary evidence of marriage, birth and death. But in the majority of civilised states, and particularly in England, religious policy has changed the nature of preappointed evidence. For the registration of a death, it has substituted the registration of the funeral ceremony, and that only in cases when it is accompanied by certain so-called religious formalities ; for the registration of a birth it has substituted the registration of the baptism, that is to say ' a ceremony which consists in sprinkling the new-born child with water ; on the occasion of which operation, certain words are to be pronounced in the form of a dialogue, in which one of the interlocutors must have been a priest ', and for the registration of the contract of marriage, the registration of the fact that a certain ceremony has been accomplished. ' An awe-inspiring formulary composed of vague generalities and historical allusions, and (by the careful exclusion of all specific delineation of rights and obligations) rendered as barren of useful and applicable instruction as possible '.[2] In all cases where the ceremonies in question do not take place there can be no legal evidence of birth, death and marriage. In order to extend to all citizens the benefit of preappointed evidence, by abolishing the monopoly of the Church, Bentham demanded that the State should take over the registration of genealogical facts, and entrust it, for example, to the justices of the peace. The judicial oath also is a formality of religious origin, which acts as a cause of the exclusion of evidence. Ever since his childhood, Bentham had suffered bitterly from the perjury which he committed at Oxford, when he undertook to respect statutes and customs which he ignored, and adhered to the thirty-nine articles of the Anglican Church in which he did not believe ; now, fanatical for sincerity, he takes his revenge for the perjury formerly imposed on him by the violent and blasphemous campaign which he wages on the formality of the judicial oath, in a chapter of his *Introductory View of the Theory of*

[1] Bowring, vol. vi. p. 508. [2] *Ibid.* vol. vi. p. 573.

Evidence, which he published by itself in 1817 under the title *Swear not at all*, despite the remonstrances of the scandalised Romilly and Mackintosh, and also by a chapter in the *Rationale of Judicial Evidence*.[1] The historical justification for exacting the oath lies in the fact that the priests found it to have the advantage of softening the customs of a barbarous age, and of exerting some control over the conscience of the soldiery : it is possible, therefore, that in the middle ages this formality offered more advantages than disadvantages. But such was not the case at the moment. The judicial oath is contradictory, says Bentham, because a false oath is punished, while the very formula of the oath entrusts to the Almighty the task of punishing the perjurer ; it is contrary to a precept of the Gospel ; it perpetuates, in the case of the coronation oath, the customs and prejudices of the past ; it is favourable to perjury and lying by the admitted banality of ' customs' house oaths ' and of ' university oaths '; from whatever point of view it be considered, the judicial oath is a formality which stands condemned. It is easy to understand why the judicial corporation seeks to perpetuate it ; it makes it unnecessary for the judges to think, and diminishes their pains : ' the less skilful or industrious a judge is, the more does he make the oath a pillow for his laziness, the more valuable does he hold it to be. Having satisfied the forms and saved his legal responsibility, he neglects the essential, and takes little pains to examine the intrinsic characteristics of the veracity of the witness '. But the advantage of the judge is disadvantageous for the public. The purpose of exacting the oath is to add solemnity to the juristic ceremony ; the opposite result is achieved, the oath is lowered to the level of a simple formality which everyone performs mechanically and without scruples. The atheist who will swear on the Gospel without thinking anything of it, is admitted as a witness : the free-thinker and the Quaker, whose convictions do not allow them to swear, are not admitted ; so that the formality of the oath excludes the best and the most truthful of the witnesses, and retains the most suspect and the least conscientious.

No evidence should be excluded ; this is the single principle which Bentham develops in his whole theory of judicial evidence. It is a strictly negative rule, consisting in the abolition of all rules. The judge must admit all testimonies, and use all means needed for their forthcomingness.[2] No means of collecting evidence should be excluded ; but oral questioning is the best method of extracting testimony. If the written pleas which congest the opening of the procedure did not retard the beginning of the actual debates, English procedure would be superior to all other procedures in this respect. There is a word in English juristic language which has no equivalent in any other language, just as there is no equivalent in the institutions of any other country for the thing expressed by the word : it is the word ' cross-examination ' (an examination in the form of a cross, a

---

[1] Bowring, vol. vi. pp. 308 *seq.*   [2] *Ibid.* vol. vii. pp. 305-6.

contradictory examination). In an English suit the witnesses for the prosecution or for the defence are examined by the advocates of the two parties in turn : the witnesses for the prosecution are questioned first by the prosecutor (examination), and then by the defendant (cross-examination) ; the same proceeding is followed with the witnesses for the defence, but in the opposite order.[1] Now this freedom of asking questions orally in all directions, and without rules, is a feature of the natural system ; the fact that it has been preserved by the English procedure compensates for the many vices in it which are due to the inroads of the technical system. ' The best possible method of extracting evidence—the method which would be used by a wise head of a family if he had to judge the conduct of a servant or child—in short, the method of extracting evidence by examination and cross-examination is a product of English origin '. The complete realisation of the natural procedure implies the universalisation of this proceeding, not only by extending the examination to the first stage of the procedure, when special pleading has been suppressed, but also by abolishing certain restrictions on freedom of examination which are still maintained by English custom. The right to examine must be granted ' to every person who can exercise it for the ends of justice, that is to say, every person who has a natural interest in the cause, and who can provide information '.[2] That all the actors in the judicial drama should be free to ask all the questions they like, when they like, and of whom they like—this is the final form of the natural procedure.

There cannot, however, be so much liberty, without some anarchy ; and, by a roundabout way, Bentham sets a restriction to the principle of the universal admissibility of testimonies. With a view to the direct end of justice, no evidence whatever must be excluded, since no rule of exclusion could obviate an error in judgment : this is true unreservedly. But occasion may arise accidentally for excluding certain evidence in view of the collateral ends of justice—when this evidence is either not pertinent, that is to say, having no relation to the matter of the case, or else superfluous—so as to prevent the time lost and the money spent, together with the vexations suffered by the parties and by the witnesses, producing a sum of evil exceeding the sum of good which results from a just sentence.[3] Here again, however, it is impossible to lay down laws. The legislator should refrain from imposing rules on the judge ; he should confine himself to providing him with instructions teaching him how to estimate the relative value and importance of judicial evidence.[4] Too many elements come into play for it to be possible to make generalisations on this subject. The amount of time which may, without excess, be devoted to the examination of evidence will vary, for example, with the importance of the suit ; the importance of the suit will vary with

---

[1] Bowring, vol. vi. pp. 25, 33, 34, etc.   [2] *Ibid*. vol. vi. p. 25 and 335 *seq.*
[3] *Ibid*. vol. vii. p. 343.   [4] *Ibid*. pp. 563 *seq.*

390 PHILOSOPHIC RADICALISM

the importance of the sum in dispute ; and this in its turn will vary
with the extent of the respective fortunes of the litigants ; and so on,
in a way, *ad infinitum*. All these considerations must be entrusted to
the judge's discretion, and he will decide in each particular case, like
a father judging in his own house a quarrel which has arisen between
his children or his servants. ' I understand ', writes Bentham, ' the
objections to this whole doctrine. It is certainly arbitrary : and the
judges could abuse their power. I answer, what is to be feared from
the point of view of Justice are the powers which they usurp from the
law, rather than those which they hold from it and which they can
only use under the eye of the public which is looking at them with
mistrust. What is least to be feared is discretionary powers which
are only entrusted to them on the condition that they justify on every
occasion the use they make of them. This control is sufficient,
because it leaves to them the whole responsibility '.[1]
    The conclusion of the matter is that, on Bentham's doctrine, the
judge is free to put what restrictions he likes, for reasons of non-
pertinence or of superfluity, on the production of evidence with a
view to the collateral ends of justice, whereas, on the other hand, he is
free to demand the production of all evidence, without any rules of
exclusion, with a view to arriving at a knowledge of the truth : this is
what is required by the analogy of the natural or domestic procedure.
The apprehensions which the summary procedure inspired in the
liberals seem therefore justified by the definition which Bentham
gives of them ; and Bentham himself was very well aware that by his
theory he was wounding not only the conservative prejudice of the
magistracy, but also the liberal prejudices dear to the majority of his
fellow-citizens. Not only were the English jurists agreed in dis-
allowing that anyone should be a witness in his own cause, or should
be allowed to accuse himself, or that the testimony of a person
interested in the cause should be admissible, or simple hearsays be
admitted ; they were further convinced that these rules of exclusion,
which favour the defence at the expense of the prosecution, were signs
at once of the excellence and of the liberalism of English judicial institutions. But Utilitarianism is not a synonym for liberalism ; in the
doctrine of utility, liberty is not a good in itself : and Bentham asked
himself whether these rules ' are not the chief cause of that weakening
in the power of justice, from which are seen to result, in England, so
inefficacious an administration of law and such numerous crimes '.
Hearsay evidence must be admitted ; English procedure is wrong not
to admit the account of the last words of a dying man, an account
which evidently cannot be controlled in a direct manner, but which
can be discussed and held to be more or less probable. Character
evidence must be admitted : English procedure is wrong to forbid
mention to be made, during the proceedings, of the acts and gestures
of the accused, and even of his previous judicial condemnations.

[1] *Rationale of Evidence* (Bowring, vols. vi. and vii.)

The testimony of the husband against his wife should be admitted : what is the value of the sentimental argument according to which confidences between man and wife must be respected because they constitute a kind of confession ? And what is the value of the technical argument according to which husband and wife, being ' but a single person ' cannot bear witness against one another ? Bentham goes further still. According to him there is no reason for keeping a special place for the advocate among the characters in the judicial drama, no reason for not treating his plea as judicial evidence, and for not admitting his testimony against his client. Bentham allowed a restriction on this rule in one particular only : the secret of the confessional must be respected, in consideration of the fact that the confessor is the magistrate's auxiliary, and the confessional one method of preventing crime. But all these paradoxes disturbed liberal opinion. Ever since 1824, after the publication in French of the *Traité des Preuves Judiciaires*, the *Edinburgh Review* denounced Bentham's theory ; the radicals of the *Westminster Review* replied ; and Stuart Mill continued the battle in the notes which he added to his edition of the *Rationale of Judicial Evidence*.[1] Bentham mistrusted liberal sentimentalism for the same reason that he mistrusted all sentimentalism, and held to the opinion which he had expressed in the *Traités* of 1802. ' All precautions which are not absolutely necessary for the protection of innocence, offer a dangerous protection to crime. I know no maxim in procedure more dangerous than that which places justice in opposition to itself—which establishes a kind of incompatibility among its duties. When it is said, for example, that it is better to allow one hundred guilty persons to escape, than to condemn one that is innocent, this supposes a dilemma which does not exist. The security of the innocent may be complete, without favouring the impunity of crime : it can only be complete upon that condition ; for every offender who escapes, menaces the public safety ; and to allow of this escape is not to protect innocence, but to expose it to be the victim of a new crime '.[2]

Nemo tenetur seipsum accusare; testis unus, testis nullus. These were two characteristic maxims of adjective law in Europe and in England, and which passed universally as having been inspired by liberal principles : what, according to Bentham, is their value ?

Nemo tenetur seipsum accusare. Notice first the ambiguous form which this maxim takes : that no man should be held, that is to say, obliged, to accuse himself is incontestable ; but the maxim came to signify, with the consent of all, that no man should be authorised to bring an accusing judgment against himself, which is quite different, and is absurd. To neglect the testimony which the accused bears against himself is to exclude that which of all testimonies is

---

[1] *Ed. Rev.* No. lxxix. Mar. 1824, art. viii. *West. Rev.* No. xiii. Jan. 1827, art. iv. Stuart Mill's notes to the *Rationale.* Bowring, vol. vii. pp. 476 *et seq.*
[2] Bowring, vol. i. p. 558.

most certain to prevent mistaken judgments and to serve the direct
end of justice ; it is to condemn oneself to resort to a mass of
indirect and inferior forms of evidence, when the most direct and best
evidence is available ; it is to exclude the testimony which best
serves the collateral ends of justice, that is, economy of delays, of
vexations and of expense, because the witness is present in any case.
This maxim was conceived in the interest of the delinquents.   It is
explicable, according to Bentham, by the liberal institutions of England, and in particular by party government : since the members of
each party may any day become the opposition, it is to their interest
to protect themselves beforehand from any attacks, be they justified
or unjustified, to which they may become exposed : and the natural,
if not the necessary consequence of such a constitution is a procedure
abounding in rules of exclusion which encourage injustice without
protecting innocence.   But, it will be said, it is ' hard ' to lead the
accused to inculpate himself, and this objection is what Beccaria's
argument amounts to, beneath its juristic and technical form :   ' To
insist that a man should be his own accuser is ', he said, ' to confuse
all relationships.   It is to insist that he hate himself, and act as if he
were his own enemy '.   Now it is doubtless true that it is repugnant
to a man to inculpate himself, but it is equally repugnant to him to
be inculpated by others.   It is likewise repugnant to him to suffer
the punishment.   But his repugnance is valued at nothing once the
crime is proved ; why then should it be taken into account when it is
a question of proving the crime ?   To argue against a judicial proceeding because it is hard, is a sentimental argument, the argument
of an ' old woman ', who protests against a surgical operation while
knowing that it is necessary.   And what is the result of this invasion
of the juristic domain by sentimentality ?   It is because there are so
many rules of exclusion to safeguard the impunity of acknowledged
criminals, that the number of crimes grows in proportion, and that,
so as to proportion in some way the gravity of the punishments to
the increase in the number of offences, the men of law make
things even by increasing the gravity of the punishment in the small
number of cases in which they apprehend the crime.   This is why
English penal law is so prodigal of the death penalty : ' ill-advised
benevolence produces just the same results as cruelty forewarned '.
Again it is said that the proceeding is not loyal—' 'tis unfair '.   The
critic in the *Edinburgh Review* discussing the *Traité des Preuves
Judiciaires* said that human beings must not be tracked like beasts of
prey without regard to the laws of the chase.   If society has to
sacrifice some one of its members, let it at least conform to general
rules, to common principles.   This, answered Bentham, is the
argument of a fox-hunter, the argument of a professional.   There is
a certain perversion of the sensibility common to all ' professionals ',
and to all craftsmen.   The fly-fisherman is scandalised and hurt if the
fly has been badly fixed on to the hook ; but he is insensible to the

suffering of the fly and also of the fish who bites the hook. The butcher is indignant if the joints of beef or lamb have not been cut according to the rules : but the sight of the butchery does not touch his heart. If the rules of the craft are respected, the results of the actions matter little : this is technical prejudice *par excellence*. *Fiat justitia*, *ruat cœlum*, let the heavens fall provided the rules of the game, the judicial formalities, are respected : this is the maxim of the professional magistrate. But the authorisation to make the accused bear witness against himself had been the characteristic of the Court of the Star Chamber, of the Court of High Commission, courts of Roman and Catholic origin, which were of an inquisitorial nature and were justly unpopular. It is precisely in this association of ideas, answers Bentham, that the origin of the maxim lies. But comparison is not reasoning. The Roman inquisitors were men who ate and drank ; should Protestants as such abstain from eating and drinking ? When the end pursued is evil, the means are evil likewise ; but the fault lies with the end and not with the means. A sword to be perfect must be sharp ; now the sharper it is the more dangerous it is if used against friends. Is this a reason for not using swords, or for using blunted swords only ? Reason tells us to use as sharp swords as possible, but to take care not to wound our friends. There is no point in just supposing the existence of bad substantive laws and then organising adjective laws for the purpose of eluding those laws. Certainly, as long as the law treats as crimes acts which are not crimes, it is desirable that certain technical crimes should escape the application of the law ; but it would be better for the law to stop treating them as crimes. The object of adjective law is not to protect the subject against the execution of bad laws ; it is, by definition, to ensure the execution of laws which are supposed to be good.[1]

Testis unus, *testis nullus* : this is another rule admitted by English law in spite of many exceptions and contradictions. ' Laws ', said Montesquieu, ' which condemn a man to death on the evidence of a single witness are fatal to liberty. Reason demands two, because a witness who affirms and an accused who denies make an even vote ; and a third person is necessary to settle it '. In the same way Beccaria had said ' One witness alone is not enough, because when the accused denies and the accuser affirms, nothing is certain, and the supposition of innocence prevails '. Blackstone supported their opinion ; but he made some reservations on the subject of the judicial proof put forward, and Bentham borrowed one of his objections from him. .' The laws which condemn a man to death . . .', said Montesquieu ; it is here, therefore, only a question of penal laws, and laws which involve the death penalty ; yet Montesquieu concluded with a universal proposition, which seemed to be valid for civil as well as for penal laws. ' A witness who affirms and a witness

---

[1] Bowring, vol. vii. pp. 445 *seq*, and 488.

who denies make an even vote '. This proposition implies that two
opposite testimonies are necessarily equivalent. This is absurd :
for there are no two testimonies which are equal in the order of human
things. The true method of valuing evidence is not to count the
witnesses but to weigh the testimonies : *pondere non numero*. And
finally the argument confuses and puts on the same level the different
actors in the judicial drama : the witness, the accused and the judge.
The accused is not a witness ; yet the ' witness who denies ' of
Montesquieu's proposition is the accused, and his denials have very
little value beside the affirmations of the witness ; and to speak of an
equal vote to be settled by a third party, is to call up the idea of a
college of judges delivering a sentence by the majority of votes ;
but witnesses are not judges. All these technical reasons which are
invoked in favour of the rule have only the appearance of being
reasons ; and the same is true of the vulgar and sentimental reason.
' The laws which condemn a man to death on the evidence of a single
witness, are fatal to liberty '. What is meant by this vague term
' liberty ' ? Security is the political end which Bentham has in view :
security as against evildoers on the one hand, and security as against
the instruments of government, on the other. Care must be taken
not to sacrifice the first of these branches of security to the second.[1]

But to reform adjective law it is not enough to simplify procedure
and to abolish all rules of exclusion concerning evidence and testimonies. The problem of procedure is closely bound up with the
problem of judicial organisation, with which Bentham had already
been concerned in 1791,[2] and the solution of which takes up almost
a third of his *Constitutional Code*.[3] In fact, the technical system
replaced the natural system, and the regular procedure was substituted for the summary procedure through the fault not of the
judges who actually sat in the judges' seats, but of the judicial institutions which set their interests in opposition to the general interest.
The principle of the artificial identification of interests had been
violated in the organisation of tribunals, and the Utilitarian philosopher, a disciple of Helvetius, knew that the true method of social
reform consisted not in moral preaching addressed to individuals, but
in modification of the social conditions under which they live, and
which determine them of necessity to act in one way and not in
another.[4]

Bentham alternatively gave two names to the system which he
opposed in his *Rationale of Judicial Evidence* : sometimes he called
it the technical system—we have already seen what Bentham meant
by that—and sometimes the fee-gathering system. The first name is

---

[1] Montesquieu, *Esprit des Lois*, liv. xii. ch. iii.   Beccaria, *Dei delitti e delle pene*.
ch. xiii.   Blackstone, iv. *Comm.* pp. 350-380.   Bowring, vol. vii. p. 521.
[2] See Bowring, vol. iv. p. 319.   [3] *Ibid*. vol. ix. pp. 454 *seq*.
[4] *Ibid*. vol. vii. pp. 212-3.

proper to the regular procedure itself ; the second is more proper
to the judicial organisation which is the first cause of the vices of
procedure. The English judges were payed by fees, they took their
remuneration out of the expenses of justice disbursed by the parties :
this is a method of payment which directly violates the principle of
the identification of interest and duty, or the artificial identification of
interests.[1] The judge is directly interested in the case costing the
parties as much as possible ; moreover, as it is easier for him to
increase fees by adding to the number of occasions on which fees are
exacted than by adding to the fees themselves, he is directly interested that the process should involve the greatest possible amount of
vexations and delays for the parties. When at the bar, Bentham had
studied personally the mechanism of writs of error and of warrants,
the interested system of delays which the clients suffered before the
King's Bench or in Chancery.[2] To re-establish identity of interests
between the magistrates and the public, to enable the judges to be
honest, payment by salary must be substituted for payment by fee.
It may be objected that the public as a whole bears the expense of
the salary, whereas only the interested parties have to pay fees. But
the really equitable method of dividing the expenses involved in the
payment of judges would be to make the non-litigants bear it all, and
to exonerate the litigants. For the object of justice is not so much to
ensure reparation for crimes already committed as to prevent future
crimes ; and those who go to law are already paying by the expenses
which they suffer and by the vexations inflicted on them, for the
security which the tribunals are guaranteeing them, while it is those
who are not pleading who have unmixed enjoyment of this security.[3]

For the benefits of the judicial organisation to be really within
reach of everyone, says Bentham, it is further necessary that the
tribunals should sit without interruption and that they should be
spread over the whole face of the national territory, instead of being
concentrated in the capital, as they were in England. In the division
of jurisdictions, the local or geographical principle should be preferred
to the logical or metaphysical principle. As early as 1791, Bentham
had congratulated the reformers of the Constituent Assembly for
having applied the local principle, while reproaching them for not
having applied it in full rigour, and for having still partly respected
the logical principle : they had preserved the distinction between
tribunals which judged civil and tribunals which judged criminal
cases, and further, had made a distinction between different kinds of
tribunal according to the pecuniary importance of the cases. Now
the pecuniary principle is a form of the metaphysical principle of the
division of jurisdictions, and is a principle which is always arbitrary
or rather impossible, in its application—for clearly it is the wealth of

---

[1] Bowring, vol. vii. pp. 197 *seq.*
[2] *Ibid.* vol. vii. pp. 215, and vol v. pp. 348 *seq.*
[3] *Ibid.* vol. ix. pp. 524-525.

the interested parties which determines the true pecuniary importance
of the suit, and the real pecuniary importance is almost in inverse
ratio to the apparent importance.   Why not allow all judges to judge
all cases without distinction, since all advocates are allowed to plead
them all ?   The local principle is simple, ' clear ' and incontestable
in application ; the logical principle is complex, obscure and continually raises disputes in its application.   The apologists for the
existing system, such as Adam Smith and Paley, in order to justify
the plurality of courts at Westminster, were obliged to have recourse
to a principle which is the very negation of the logical distinction of
jurisdictions : that is the principle of emulation.   Given an area
which is too populous for a single court of justice to be sufficient for
it, there is a choice of two methods.   The area can be divided into
two smaller areas (from this would arise an immediate economy of
delays, of vexations and of expense).   Or again two courts can be
established at the centre of the area (from this would arise an economy
of delays, of vexations and of expense, by reason of the rivalry which
would arise between the two courts and of the efforts which they
would make to attract customers).   But, in the first place, the first
of these two systems offers much the most secure advantages.   The
local principle admits of no discussion, because the distance between
two places cannot change and no expedient can diminish it.   The
other advantage, which is based on psychological conjecture, on an
estimation of the power of the feeling of emulation in the mind of the
judge, is much more problematical ; and it is because of this that it
seduces the professionals, for whom the uncertainty of arguments is
the surest guarantee of the prolongation of their monopoly.   In the
second place, for the argument to be valid, it would be necessary for
the so-called rival courts to have the same competence and the same
procedure.   Now this is not the case in England, nor in any of the
countries in which the logical principle is applied.   ' Original shortsightedness had divided the business, upon the logical principle of
division, among three courts : mutual rapacity had by degrees broken
down here and there the fences : mutual lassitude and impotence had
left things in this state.   The former arrangement, though made by
the legislator, was made so long ago that it could not but have been a
wise one ; the latter, though made in the teeth of the former, being a
work of lawyers, was still wiser.   Required to prove it so.   No other
argument being found, the principal of emulation offered itself, and
was received with open arms '.[1]   But the courts of Westminster have
not the same procedure : there is one procedure in equity and another
in common law.   They have not the same competence : the fact that
with time the Court of King's Bench, the Court of Exchequer and the
Court of Common Pleas have encroached on each other's attributions,
is only another proof of the impossibility of applying with rigour and
fixity the logical principle of the division of jurisdictions.   Moreover,

[1] Bowring, vol. vii. pp. 288, and vol. iv. pp. 328 *seq.*

they have only been able to lead to this confusion of jurisdictions by a
series of juridical fictions, which are intelligible to judges and advocates alone. The logical principle is obscure ; that is why it is an
object of predilection for professional jurists. The local principle is
as clear as it is simple. Thus arose a sort of antithesis between the
notions of the logical and the simple, which Bentham, at least in his
theory of substantive law, had tended to confuse, therein following the
example of the eighteenth century philosophers.

But Bentham's fundamental doctrine regarding judicial organisation, the doctrine which is the most directly connected with the
theory of the natural or domestic system, is the doctrine of the single
judge.[1] The system of a plurality of judges is once more the system
of technical complication, as opposed to the opposite system, which is
evidently a system of simplification. Only the presence of a more
fatal evil, the ' law-taxes ' and the ' law-fees ' which are paid to the
State and to the judicial corporation, hides the detestable results
produced by the excessive number of judges—denial of justice,
aggravation of delays, vexations and pecuniary expense. Now, on
this point also, Bentham was consciously attacking a prejudice which
was dear to traditional liberalism, a prejudice of which Montesquieu
made himself the theorist. In the *Esprit des Lois*, Montesquieu
condemned the system of the single judge : ' such a magistrate can
only exist in a despotic government '. Bentham declares that this
assertion is erroneous ; all that can be said is that the system of the
single magistrate may become a despotic institution under a despotic
régime. When editing his *Constitutional Code*, during the reign of
Charles X., Bentham admits that the system of a plurality of judges
has its own peculiar advantages for a France submitted to the régime
of an absolute monarchy. Their individual responsibility being
sheltered by their very numbers, the judges, though they had lost
their ancient right of refusing to register laws, were at least competent,
to a certain extent, to paralyse the execution of them. The excuse
for the system of the plurality of judges consists, therefore, in the fact
that it weakens bad laws ; but, once again, the problem, in the case of
judicial organisation as in the case of procedure, is not to assume that
the substantive laws are bad and oppressive, and then to seek the
most suitable means of guaranteeing the liberty of the subject against
the execution of these laws ; it is to assume that these laws are good,
and then to bring about their execution by the surest, the most
economical and the most speedy methods. With a substantial code
drawn up with a view to the greatest happiness of the greatest number,
the advantages of a plurality of judges become so many disadvantages.
Montesquieu compared the system of the single judge to the jurisdiction of the Turkish Pashas : there ' the way in which disputes are
ended does not matter, provided they are ended. The Pasha, when
he has been told the nature of the suit, commands blows to be dis-

[1] Bowring, vol. iv. pp. 325 *seq*. etc.

tributed at his pleasure on the soles of the feet of the pleaders, and
sends them back home '.[1] But an historical example is not a reason.
In Turkey, the judge may be single ; but in Turkey, also, there is
neither any written law, nor public, nor press, nor national assembly,
nor municipal assemblies, nor reports of debates, nor possibility of
appeal from one tribunal to another : these are all conditions which
Montesquieu's epigram does not take into account. So Bentham
does not give himself much concern on this point, but declares that
' without being an admirer of the summary justice of the Cadis, it
may be said that it is more like the justice of a father '[2] than the
regular justice which is derived from the technical system. Montesquieu's dictum, however, probably had its effect on the reforms of the
Constituent Assembly, when in the new judicial organisation, they
increased the number of judges in direct ratio to the importance of
the jurisdictions : first Condorcet and then Sieyès gave their authority
in support of the thesis of the plurality of judges. Bentham was
already opposing this thesis, and it may be said that except for certain
changes in terminology, his arguments did not vary from this date
until 1832. The ' simple ' system of the single judge conforms to
the two types of end, the direct and the collateral, at which judicial
organisation, like procedure, should aim. There is a diminution in
expense. For the salary of one judge costs less than the salary of
several. There is a diminution in delays. For one judge dispatches
a case more quickly than several would dispatch it : a single judge has
only one opinion to give, one class of motives to bring forward ; he
has not to reckon with the opinion of others ; he has no one to
convert, no one with whom to dispute. At the same time, the direct
end of justice is secured. All unjustified sentences are avoided. By
sitting alone, the judge gains in probity, in professional activity and
in intelligence, inasmuch as effort and exercise develop our faculties,
and the most definite result of the system is to increase individual
responsibility. ' A board is a screen ' :[3] any board on which
several people sit together confuses the results of the individual
activity of the members ; and, if there are other departments—
finance, for example—in which, since emulation and publicity are
lacking, it is not possible to count on the feeling of responsibility to
ensure that the services should function well, it may be that the
judicial functions are those in which individual responsibility operates
with the most force. If you put several judges on the tribunal, the
responsibility of each in the sentence will be less the more it is
divided. Moreover, it will happen, as a general rule, that one of the
judges, the one who presides in the debates, will get an ascendancy
over his colleagues strong enough to make him in effect the only one
delivering sentence. Yet his colleagues will share the responsibility

[1] *Esp. des Lois*, liv. vi. ch. 11.
[2] *Influence of Time and Place in Matters of Legislation*, Bowring, vol. i.
[3] Bowring, vol. v. p. 17.

with him ; thus, the supposed disadvantages of the system of the single magistrate will be combined with those of the system of the plurality of judges—arbitrary power in a single man, and a diminution of the feeling of individual responsibility.

The system of the single judge is a necessary but not a sufficient condition to ensure in the magistrate a feeling of his responsibility. Now, despite the opinion of the defenders of the technical system, we have seen that the judicial formalities in no way constitute such a check as will limit the power of the judge. There are only three checks which can prevent the magistrate from usurping a sort of despotic power : the power of appeal, the assistance rendered to the tribunal by a jury, and finally the publicity of debates.[1]

It was no doubt a study of the new judicial system organised by the Constituent Assembly which attracted Bentham's attention to the chaotic state of the English organisation concerning appeals. While admitting that the establishment of an appeal jurisdiction makes a complication in the judicial organisation, aggravates expenses and delays, and consequently makes it more difficult to attain the collateral ends of justice, he thought that it would be possible to conceive processes which would obviate these disadvantages, and saw an excellent check on any abuse of judicial power in the liberty of appeal against a sentence delivered by the first tribunal.[2] The régime of publicity, the establishment of the magistrate's legal responsibility, may, by increasing in him the feeling of responsibility, diminish the chances of voluntary error. They do not diminish the possibility of involuntary error, which is due to a lack of intelligence ; or, to be more precise, they only diminish it to a limited extent, in so far as a feeling of responsibility, by increasing the judge's application, helps to develop his faculties. Moreover, the sinister motives which turn a judge away from the straight path may be strong enough to resist the control of publicity. ' How,' asked Montesquieu when discussing the system of the single judge, ' could Appius in his judgment seat do otherwise than despise laws, since he violated even the law he had himself made ? ' Yet, as Bentham himself agreed, it was not for lack of publicity to sustain it, that Appius' virtue failed when he fell in love with Virginia.[3] Bentham insisted then on the necessity of organising a jurisdiction of appeal ; but perhaps, in the last resort, he was more preoccupied with the desire to simplify the jurisdictions of appeal, which were actually in existence in England, than to create a new administrative routine.[4] Although he recognised, as early as 1790, that the virtues of publicity were not ' all-sufficient ', he yet held them to be transcendent, and expressly declared that ' Division and subordination of judicial powers are no otherwise a guard to

[1] Bowring, vol. vii. p. 324.
[2] See especially Bowring, vol. iv. p. 338, and vol. ix. pp. 585-588.
[3] Bowring, vol. iv. p. 340.
[4] For Bentham's variations on this point see Bowring, vol. iv. p. 348.

probity, than in so far as the chance of disagreement and altercation presents a faint chance of occasional publicity.   Appeals without publicity serve only to lengthen the dull and useless course of despotism, procrastination, precipitation, caprice, and negligence '.[1]

The institution of the jury, which according to Blackstone is the ' palladium ' of English liberties, is, of all the liberal institutions designed to check the abuses of the executive, administrative and judicial power, without doubt the one which inspires most pride in English hearts ; but in Bentham it inspired nothing but defiance and disdain.   Only once in his life, in 1809, in his pamphlet, *On the Art of Packing Special Juries*, did he take up the defence of the institution, and demand that it should return to the purity of its original form, so as to be guaranteed against the perversions to which it was submitted by the arbitrary intervention of the executive. But it should be noted that at this time Bentham was under the influence of James Mill, a democrat and a liberal ; and it was with him, and to some extent under his inspiration, that he defended so ardently the independence of the jury, as a necessary guarantee of the freedom of the press.   Also, he took care to warn the reader, in this very work, that ' if, in the situation of judge, a man were not liable to stand exposed to the action of any sinister interest, or delusive passion opposite to the interest of the public, in respect of the *ends of justice* . . . the exercise . . . of the functions of the jury would not, in the character of a check to the power of the judge, be of any use ', and that, on this hypothesis, ' juries ought to be *abolished* ',[2] granted that they are an inevitable cause of factitious delays, vexations and expense for the public.   As a general rule, he always spoke in an ironical manner of this institution—' indiscriminately cherished and never-enough-to-be idolised '[3]—that ' parcel of people you know nothing of, except that they are housekeeping tradesmen, or something of that sort, are got together by hap-hazard, or by what ought to be hap-hazard, to the number of twelve and shut up together in a place from which they cannot get out till the most obstinate among them has subdued the rest '[4].

' Political orthodoxy,' adds Bentham, ' commands them to be looked upon as infallible.   I have no great opinion of human infallibility ; and if it were necessary to believe in it I would go to work by degrees, and begin with the Pope '.   About the year 1789, he expressly refused to allow himself to be duped by the classical arguments in favour of the institution of juries invoked by the acknowledged champions of Anglo-Saxon liberalism, Paley, Blackstone and De Lolme.   He deplored the fact that the Constituent Assembly had adopted that superstition.   For juries, though they are admirably useful in a barbarous century, are not suited to an enlightened century.   Bentham repeated as against juries the objection of prin-

[1] Bowring, vol. iv. p. 317.   [2] *Ibid*. vol. v. p. 88.
[3] *Ibid*. vol. vi. p. 478.   [4] *Ibid*. vol. vii. p. 388.

ciple which he opposed to all the complications of the liberal system, which were expressly designed to make the execution of the laws long and difficult, and consequently were as harmful when the laws were in conformity with the principle of public utility, as they could be useful when the law was the expression of the particular and sinister interests of a despotic government.[1] There is only one quality, according to Bentham, which justifies the retention of the institution in England, and that is its popularity. Since it is popular, though it creates evils of the first order, it at least does not create evils of the second order ; now the number of individuals who suffer from the evils of the first order is restricted, while the number of those who are affected by the evils of the second order is indefinite.[2] The first thing that is necessary is to possess the confidence of the people ; to deserve it, only comes second. But Bentham denied that the institution deserved the popularity which it enjoyed. In connection with the reform of judicial organisation in Scotland in 1808, he intervened to suggest that if the English institution of the jury were to be introduced in Scotland, it should only be in second instance, for the use of people who might want to appeal against a first judgment given by a single judge in a court of summary and natural procedure.[3] For judgment by a single judge is the natural method, which must not be departed from without special reason ; and the addition of a jury constitutes, in fact, a harmful complication of the system, a multiplication in the number of judges, which is necessarily accompanied by a diminution of responsibility and by an aggravation of delays, vexation and expense.

Some years later, Dumont, who was anxious to publish, after Bentham's theories on evidence, his theories about judicial organisation, never ceased to protest, in his letter to his master, against that ' abominable heresy ', the omission of juries. It was probably in order to yield to Dumont's entreaties, and to reconcile his personal conviction with the demands of the surrounding liberalism, that Bentham conceived in 1823 the formula of the quasi-jury.[4] Since ' to undo what legislators and lawyers have done, is the great use of juries ', Bentham still maintains that ' in so far as what is done, by these highest constituted authorities, is right—conducive to the greatest happiness of the greatest number—the institution of a jury cannot but be prejudicial—detractive from the sum of that same greatest happiness '. Thus the powers of the quasi-jury were to be less extended than those of the jury. The quasi-jury was only to intervene after the ' initial audience ', in which the judge, sitting alone, would have questioned the parties. It was to be composed of three members only : two ' ordinary ' members, and one ' select ' member,

---

[1] Bowring, vol. iv. p. 324.   [2] *Ibid*. p. 359.
[3] *Ibid*. vol. v. pp. 29 *seq.*
[4] Bowring, vol. ii. pp. 141-158 and vol ix. pp. 554-568, and see Brit, Mus. Add, MSS. 33, 545, f. 495.

chosen by the judge. Its function would be to suggest alterations in the sentence, while the judge would remain free to take account of or to neglect the offered suggestions. It would allow the plaintiff to appeal to itself, if the defendant were acquitted or if the plaintiff held that the punishment was too light. Conversely it would allow the defendant to appeal to itself, if he held that he was being too severely punished. The real and permanent utility of the jury is to ensure a representation of public opinion in the court : and this is why Bentham suggests substituting for a jury of judges a jury which is in a sense consultative. The institution of the quasi-jury makes necessary the presence of a public at all judicial debates. It is therefore useful to the public, to whom those debates should be, in Bentham's view, like an ever-open school of morality. It is useful to the judges in the performance of their function of judge ; but, in the last analysis, it only constitutes a new way of establishing over them the control of publicity, to which we find ourselves once more brought back.[1]

De Lolme wrote : ' It is in this very publicity of everything that lies that power which we have declared to be so necessary for supplementing the imperfections of the laws, and which keeps within their proper limits those who have any authority '. Obviously on this point, as on so many other questions of judicial organisation and procedure, Bentham was directly inspired by De Lolme. ' Anyone ' wrote the same author, ' who reflects on what it is that forms the motive of what are termed *grandes affaires*, and on man's unconquerable sensitiveness to the way in which his fellows think, will not hesitate to affirm that if it were possible for the liberty of the press to exist in a despotic government, and, what would be no less difficult, to exist there without changing the constitution, this alone would form a check on the power of the prince. That if, for example, in some Eastern Empire, there were to be found a sanctuary, which was respected through the ancient religion of the people and which would ensure security to those who brought to it their observations of whatever kind ; and if printed matter should be issued from this which should gain a like respect through the affixing of a certain seal, and if in its daily publications it were to examine and qualify freely the conduct of the cadis, of the pashas, the visiers, the divan and of the Sultan himself, this would immediately introduce liberty into that empire '.[2] Is it not this passage from De Lolme that Bentham had in mind when he defended, as against Montesquieu, the procedure applied by the cadi provided it was published ? And might it not serve as an epigraph for the manuscript which he edited in 1822 under the title *Securities against Misrule, adapted to a Mohammedan State, and prepared with particular reference to Tripoli in Barbary*.[3] One single word, the word for bad government, ' misrule,' is enough, Bentham declared, to give a general idea of the disease to be cured ;

[1] Bowring, vol. ix. pp. 535, 569.   [2] De Lolme, liv. ii. ch. xii.
[3] Bowring, vol. viii. pp. 555 *seq*.

another word, the word ' publicity ' is enough to give the idea of a remedy, the only remedy which could cure the disease without changing the form of government. For actions of appeal serve chiefly to keep each case longer in the public eye ; and a jury is essentially a delegation of what Bentham calls the ' tribunal of public opinion ', composed of all the citizens.[1] The fear of public opinion constitutes the essence of the feeling of individual responsibility. This is a conviction which Bentham acquired early and of which he was never rid. ' Without publicity, all other checks are fruitless : in comparison of publicity, all other checks are of small account. It is to publicity, more than to everything else put together, that the English system of procedure owes its being the least bad system as yet extant, instead of being the worst. It is for want of this essential principle, more than anything else, that the well-meant labours of Frederick and Catherine in the field of justice, have fallen so far short of the mark at which they aimed '.[2] The motive on which he based his system of judicial organisation in his *Constitutional Code*, is the same as that on which he had based his system of prison administration forty years earlier, ' the one whose influence is the most powerful, the most continuous, the most uniform and the most general, personal interest corrected by the widest publicity '.[3]

In short, the judge, as conceived by Bentham's doctrine, is a kind of monarch isolated in his tribunal, delivering his sentences without legal forms, and without any really efficacious control to prevent eventual abuses of power, other than the purely moral control exercised on him by public opinion. But such a doctrine bears no relation to the so-called liberal doctrine : it was almost in the same terms as these that the Caesarists of the nineteenth century were to demand the establishment of a government which should be personal, and responsible just in so far as it was personal. Bentham invoked the analogy of the family and of domestic government ; but in the seventeenth century, Sir Robert Filmer, who was refuted by Locke, had founded the theory of a theocratic and monarchic régime on the same analogy. By a curious detour, as the *Edinburgh Review* [4] justly observed, Bentham's radicalism, in the sphere of judicial procedure and organisation, involved a restoration of the patriarchal system advocated by Sir Robert Filmer, the defender of absolute monarchy.

2. CONSTITUTIONAL LAW

Until 1808, Bentham had taken no interest in the problem of political reform ; we have seen the reasons of a philosophical order,

---

[1] Bowring, vol. ii. p. 141.
[2] *Ibid*. vol. iv. p. 317.   [3] *Panopticon* Part II.: Bowring, vol. iv.
[4] *Ed. Rev.*, No. lxxix, March 1824, art. viii, p. 172.

and also the historical, local and personal influences which caused him to take an ever keener interest in questions of constitutional law, until he became the acknowledged theorist of the radical movement, along-side of the pamphleteer William Cobbett, the parliamentary orator, Sir Francis Burdett, and the popular propagandist, Major Cartwright. The Westminster elections almost dragged him, for an instant, into the conflict. Then insurrections broke out all over England, followed by violent repression. Hobhouse and Burdett were thrown into prison ; Cartwright, who was committed for treason, barely escaped the same fate ; and Bentham himself feared for his freedom.[1] But, at least, even if his own country was ungrateful, he had found in Spain and in Portugal disciples who were asking him for a democratic code for their emancipated nations. Consequently, from 1820 onwards Bentham devoted himself to drawing up a *Constitutional Code*, which was addressed not only to the two States of the Iberian penin-sula, but to all the nations of the earth. As early as 1824, he con-sidered the work to be complete in outline.[2] He intended to divide it into three volumes, the first of which was printed in 1827. In 1830, we find him hurrying on the printing and publication of a chapter of the second volume, bearing on the constitution of the army, in order to communicate it to La Fayette, at the time when the Revolution of July has broken out in Paris. The rest of the work was not printed and published until nine years after Bentham's death, when it appeared with an introduction consisting of a series of general reflections regarding the philosophy of constitutional law, taken from Bentham's manuscripts and very indifferently arranged by the editor.[3] There is therefore no need to examine the influence, probably insignificant, which the *Constitutional Code* may have exerted at the time of its publication ; in it must be sought only documents regarding Ben-tham's thought in the period between 1820 and 1832, when he had become the leader and inspirer of the group of intellectual Radicals.

Three principles form the basis of Bentham's political philosophy. The first principle, which Bentham calls the greatest happiness principle, is a practical principle which proposes an end for the activity of the legislator : the end which government ought to pursue in every political society is, Bentham tells us, ' the greatest happiness of all the individuals of which it is composed '. But this is not an end which can be realised so long as it is enunciated in this universal form. By reason of the law of population and of the continual insuf-ficiency of the means of subsistence, it is impossible simultaneously to realise the happiness of all the individuals who compose the society without exception. Thus, instead of saying ' the greatest happiness

---

[1] Bowring, vol. viii, p. 470.   [2] *Ibid*. vol. x. p. 542.
[3] On the MSS. from which the *Constitutional Code* was drawn, see editor's note. Bowring vol. ix. pp. iii-iv.

of all ', one should say, to be more exact, ' the greatest happiness of the greatest number '.[1]

The second principle is a theoretic principle, as the first is practical : the first tells us ' what ought to be ', the second tells us ' what is '. The second principle Bentham calls the *self-preference principle*, and he enunciates it as follows : ' the love of self is universal '. All individuals are, essentially and naturally, egoists. All professions of disinterestedness and of purity of intentions must be taken as so many lies.[2] The only reason why Washington did not act in America as Bonaparte acted in France, must be sought not in a difference of motives, which were egoistic in both cases, but in the difference of political conditions.[3] Bentham further perceives in this principle of universal egoism a necessary condition of the subsistence of the human race ;[4] but then, if Bentham is right, and if in the great majority of cases, the interest of the species implies egoism in the individuals, the principle of the natural identity of interests is the true principle. Yet, according to Bentham, this identity must not be regarded as absolute. This is why, in contrast to the first Utilitarian theorists of the democratic régime, that is, in contrast to Paine and particularly to Godwin, he did not arrive at the conception of a ' society without government ', but held it necessary, if what is and what ought to be are to be reconciled, and if the interest of the individual is to be subordinated to the general interest, to introduce, in cases where this subordination does not occur of itself, a third and last principle to complete the philosophy of constitutional law.

Now this third principle, which concerns the definition of the means to be used to attain the end of political government, is nothing else than the principle of the artificial identification of interests. In the *Panopticon*, in the *Theory of Rewards*, and in the *Chrestomathia*, Bentham had named it ' the interest and duty junction prescribing principle ' ; here he calls it ' the principle of the union of interests '. The problem is to place each of the members of the political society in social conditions such that his own private interest shall coincide with the general interest ; and the very statement of the problem presupposes that, in constitutional affairs, men are divided into classes, the one governing, and the other governed. For we know, on the one hand, that the law of population formulated by Malthus necessarily creates conflicts between individual interests : hence the necessity for a government to give individual property the protection of the law. Evidently, moreover, by reason of the principle of the division of labour, the functions of government cannot be carried out at the same time by all the citizens. Governing is work which absorbs the whole activity of the governors ; meanwhile it is necessary that the great majority should be constantly occupied in ensuring the subsistence of all, by work of a productive nature. To say that

[1] Bowring, vol. ix. p. 5, and vol. iii. p. 211.   [2] *Ibid*. p. 60.
[3] *Ibid*. p. 100.   [4] *Ibid*. pp. 5-6.

the best government is that government in which political power is exercised by all the members of the whole, is to enunciate a contradictory proposition ; it is to maintain the existence and the non-existence of a government at the same time and for the same society.[1] It appears, therefore, that the philosophy of constitutional law begins by creating a contradiction of interests, in order to suppress it later. The actual end of all government is the greatest happiness of the person or persons, who hold the governmental power.[2] The legitimate end of government is the greatest happiness of the greatest number, before all distinction between governors and governed. Thus the principle of the artificial identification of interests assumes a more definite form in affairs of constitutional law, once the distinction between governors and governed has been brought about, and becomes the problem of the artificial identification of the interests of governors and of governed.

At the beginning of his *Constitutional Code* Bentham explains the method which allows him to attach his system of ' pure representative democracy ' to the principle of utility. According to Bentham, the condition of man is such that every pleasure is bought at the price of a pain : it is perhaps the fundamental maxim of the Utilitarian philosophy that ' of two evils the lesser must be chosen '. This granted, how are we to act so as ' to bring happiness to its maximum ', or, as Bentham also says, so as ' to maximise happiness ' ? Two methods, and two only, must be used : official aptitude must be maximised, and expense minimised.[3] This is the general rule of which Bentham attempted a practical application in his project of a Chrestomathic school, and of which there is already an approximate expression in the *Catechism of Parliamentary Reform* : here is recognisable, under a slightly modified form, the fundamental problem of adjective law. In order that the functions of government may be well performed, they must be paid as much as possible, and the idea of expense must be given its widest signification. But all expense, since it involves a pain or the deprivation of a pleasure, is an evil: it is therefore desirable that the government should cost as little as possible. The problem is thus reduced to the mathematical form of a calculus of profit and loss.

Moreover, the ' official aptitude ' itself is not a simple notion ; it can be resolved into still more elementary notions. The intelligence, the morality and the activity necessary to the exercise of his function must be demanded from the functionary.[4] As regards intellectual aptitude, it would be ascertained by a preliminary examination that the candidate possessed the necessary judgment and knowledge ; also the political instruction of the candidates would be made easier by making the statement of the laws clearer, and by developing the use of statistics. The obligation imposed on the legislative body of sitting

[1] Bowring, vol. ix. pp. 95-96.   [2] *Ibid.* p. 4.
[3] *Ibid.* p. 150.   [4] *Ibid.* p. 191.

uninterruptedly, and on the members of being present uninterruptedly at the sittings, would guarantee the necessary legislative activity on the part of the elected representatives.   But the essential thing is to take guarantees against the eventual abuse of the power in the hands of the governors, abuses which would perhaps be all the more dangerous, the more intelligent and the more active the governors : in other words, the aim must be to secure the ' maximisation of appropriate moral aptitude '.   Every member of the government finds himself as such invested with the double power to punish and to reward, to threaten and to promise, to distribute pleasure and pain.   He can use this power for good or for evil.   The problem is to arrange things in such a way that he can use it for good and cannot use it for evil ; and the solution of the problem depends, according to Bentham, on this single rule—minimise confidence '.[1]   Now this rule, which Bentham attached to the principle of the greatest happiness, is in reality familiar to all English liberals.   The same formula, expressed in practically the same terms, occurred repeatedly in the articles of the first years of the *Edinburgh Review* : that the governed should mistrust the governors is a faith common to the most timorous Whigs and to the most intransigent Radicals ; it is the very foundation of the theory of the right of resistance, of the theory of the right of representation (which is, in a sense, the organised form of the right of resistance), and even perhaps of the theory of the division of powers which affirms the autonomy of the legislative power as against the executive power.   Must it then be admitted that Bentham under the influence of his friends, but also under the profound influence of contemporary opinion, came to incorporate, almost without knowing it, in his authoritarian Utilitarianism, the formulae of Constitutional Liberalism ?   Was his radicalism no more than a much more accentuated form of the traditional Whiggism ?   Bentham did not think of it in this way.

In constitutional law as in procedure, Bentham formally rejected the commonplaces of the current liberalism.   The democratic State whose constitution he defines is a State in which the legislature, the representative organ of all adult citizens, is ' omnicompetent ' : for any limitation of the competence of the legislative body contradicts, according to Bentham, the greatest happiness principle.   There must be no Bill of Rights, or Declaration of Rights, supposed to be perpetually obligatory from the day when it was promulgated.   Although Bentham holds that the constitution should be registered in a code, so that it can always be known in its entirety by public opinion,[2] and consequently be always subject to criticism and to reform, he does not want this constitution to be preceded by any declaration of principles held to be immutable and above all criticism.   Suppose a project for a law is suggested, and receives the unanimous consent of the nation.   Meanwhile it is found that it violates one of the

[1] Bowring, p. 62.   [2] *Ibid.* vol. ix. p. 9.

articles of the Declaration of Rights. In this case the law will not be able to be adopted ; and why ? Because it is contrary to the general interest ? No, but because it is contrary to what was the opinion and the express will of the sovereign in the far-off time when the Declaration was worked out. Why not proceed in political science as in all the other sciences, where no result is ever taken as definitely assured, where no limit is set to the present and future competence of the human spirit ; the notion of an inviolable charter is a conservative notion, which will not submit to the reforming spirit. A public declaration of this kind is useful to the exact extent to which the constitution is bad. If the monarch has undertaken, by a solemn act, not to commit certain specified acts of despotism, by that very fact public attention is drawn to the acts in question. And here is an obstacle, which is not legal and fictitious but real and to some extent physical, to the sovereign's abuses of power. For the people have the numerical superiority over the monarch. All the power the monarch possesses, he owes to public opinion. If popular confidence should come to fail him, his real weakness will be clear in the sight of all men. But a constitutional disposition which is only good in relation to a supposedly bad government, cannot be held to be itself absolutely good.[1]

To the classical principle of the division of powers Bentham brings forward the same objections as to the principle of a Declaration of Rights. It is impossible to take one's stand on the Whig doctrine of ' constitutional counterchecks ' in order to give the executive and the judicial power autonomy as against the legislative power. The essential function of the executive and judicial powers is to give effect to the wishes of the legislative power : if they refuse to obey the legislature, they falsify the whole constitutional machine. In the case of a rebellion of the military and of the judges, the legislative power must reserve to itself in the general interest, the right of usurping their functions. But, Montesquieu objected, to absorb the executive and the judicial powers in the legislative power is to establish a despotic government. Once again Bentham pits himself against the authority of the name of Montesquieu. Montesquieu, he says, never thought clearly ; his work is deserving of no respect. ' Of happiness, he says nothing : instead of security for the people against their rulers, he talks of liberty, and assumes without directly saying so, that to establish the most perfect liberty is the proper object of all government : whereas government cannot operate but at the expense of liberty, and then and there only is liberty perfect, where no government has place '.[2] The real despotism which is to be feared is that despotism which consists in the interested alliance of all the officials for the exploitation of the people ; and there is no separation of powers which can prevent the occurrence of this union

---

[1] Bowring, vol. ix. pp. 122-123 (cf. vol. viii, p. 557).
[2] *Ibid*. vol. ix. p. 123.

between functionaries and magistrates, under the irresistible pressure of interest.

Thus the radical may speak the language of the Whigs and demand the introduction of ' counterchecks ' and ' counterforces '[1] in the constitutional mechanism, but it is with a very different meaning. Political liberalism rests on a moral pessimism. Since man's nature is fundamentally bad, and incapable of understanding either the true interest of the city or the true interest of the individual, all governments are bad ; and the least bad constitution will be the one which opposes the greatest number of obstacles to the execution of government measures. Hence arises the idea of a mixed or complex constitution, in which the democratic element forms a ' check ' on the aristocratic element, and vice versa, and in which the executive power and the judicial power, the judicial power and the legislative power, the executive power and the legislative power, are like so many equal weights which balance one another in the machine. The liberal State is a State of which it may be said indiscriminately that it is a State without a sovereign or that it embraces several sovereigns. On the other hand the Radical State as defined by Bentham's Utilitarianism is a State which confers sovereignty on the people ; after which the people finds itself constrained to delegate a certain number of political functions to a minority of individuals, elected either directly or indirectly, not so as itself to limit its own power, or to abdicate a part of its sovereignty, but so as to make the expression and then the execution of its will more effective and more concentrated. Then the problem is to prevent the representatives of the people from depriving those who have put them in power of all or part of their sovereignty. Hence the necessity of finding ' counterforces ' capable of ' holding in check ' the egoism of the functionaries. But there is no question of ' counterforces ' set up one against the other so as to form an equilibrium of the various and contradictory elements in a complex society ; in the radical machine all the ' counterforces ' are, broadly speaking, directed in the same direction, so as to preserve the energy of a purely democratic régime as much as possible intact, and to prevent anything which might violate the popular sovereignty.

Nevertheless, the sovereignty of the people encounters an invincible obstacle in Bentham's system. Strictly speaking, it means the sovereignty of all the citizens, and implies unanimity of suffrages. But it may happen, and is likely to happen, that the suffrages of the supreme constitutive authority are divided : this, Bentham admits, ' is an inconvenience the existence of which is in the very nature of the case '.[2] Now, the inconvenience is a serious one, and the problem of the right of majorities was already disturbing some of the supporters of the Utilitarian philosophy : it caused anguish to Joseph Hume, the representative of the group in Parliament, and Hume communicated to Francis Place a whole series of objections with which he had been

[1] Bowring, vol. ix. p. 41.   [2] *Ibid.* vol. ix. p. 121.

faced and which he had been unable to answer.[1] If it is really true that the will of the minority must bow before the will of the majority, and that the interest of the minority must be sacrificed to the interest of the majority, does it not appear legitimate that in a society composed of thirty individuals, twenty-nine should agree to roast and eat the thirtieth, if they find pleasure in so doing ? Does it not appear legitimate that the majority of the poorest should agree to appropriate the goods of the majority of the rich, and that they should divide them for the benefit of the greatest number ? To this Place gave two answers. In the first place, if the majority really thinks it is to its interest to eat or to despoil the minority, it is inevitable that it should carry out its design. The power of the majority over the minority is a necessity of nature ; the more numerous are the stronger. In actual fact, we do resign ourselves to seeing constantly exercised about us the unjust power of the majority : ' Our laws relating to property are by no means such as they ought to be, but in respect of them the principle of utility badly understood is recognised. Does a man invade this right in certain ways, we hang him, and thus the twenty-nine agree to destroy the thirtieth '. Here the theorists of constitutional liberalism asked whether it was not desirable to conceive legal processes to slow down the action of the majority and to rein in its unjust violences. Bentham and his disciples did not believe in the efficacy of such constitutional expedients as might be conceived : they are more efficacious in slowing down the advance of reason than in opposing the force of passion. This is the general sense of the second answer which Place gave to the objections of Joseph Hume. The question is to know whether the real interest of the majority does command it to destroy or to despoil the minority : the morals and the political economy of the Utilitarians answer that it is not so. But the principle of utility can be clearly understood and practised by enlightened men. The question is then whether men are really enlightened, and whether, when they are left free to formulate and to express all their opinions, they are more likely to reach the truth than to remain in error, to know their true interest than to pursue their apparent interest. Now James Mill, before Francis Place, had expressly stated that : ' every man, possessed of reason, is accustomed to weigh evidence, and to be guided and determined by its preponderance. When various conclusions are, with their evidence, presented with equal care and with equal skill, there is a moral certainty, though some few may be misguided, that the greater number will judge right, and that the greatest force of evidence, wherever it is, will produce the greatest impression '.[2] It is in this way that the Benthamites justified the sovereignty of majorities ; as to Bentham himself, he barely discussed the problem. If he thought of it as an evil, it was a necessary evil ; for nature confers sovereignty on the strongest.

[1] Brit. Mus. Add. MSS., 35,145 ff. pp. 101 seq.
[2] Liberty of the Press, pp. 22 seq.

But is it certain that he did ever think of the sovereignty of majorities as an evil ? Did it not perhaps appear to him as the immediately necessary consequence of the formula which sums up his moral philosophy ? If every individual is really the best judge of his interest, all individuals are the best judges of the general interest, and the greatest number of individuals are in the best position for knowing the greatest happiness of the greatest number.[1]

In short, if the moral aptitude of the governors is to be brought to its maximum, it is first necessary, according to Bentham, to give the sovereign power to those whose interest it is that the general happiness should be brought to its maximum point : the people must be sovereign. Next it is necessary to bring to its maximum the responsibility to the possessors of sovereign power of all those to whom is entrusted the exercise of subordinate power.[2] But the responsibility of the governors to the governed can itself assume two forms : moral responsibility, when it results from effective subjection to the power of the moral sanction, as inflicted by the ' tribunal of public opinion ' ; or legal responsibility, when it results from effective subjection to the power of the legal sanction as inflicted by the tribunals which are set up by law.[3] Now, in his theory of procedure, of evidence and of judicial organisation, which was worked out long before his conversion to Radicalism, Bentham tended to exaggerate the importance of moral responsibility : in the absence of any more regular institution, it seemed that the control of publicity sufficed to prevent all abuses of power. Even now, in his constitutional theories, he still attaches the greatest importance to the constant supervision which public opinion must exercise over the actions of the government. It is because the House of Commons, in spite of its corruption and its vices, does constitute a sort of permanent delegation of this tribunal, that the English government, which is always obliged to reckon with freely expressed criticisms and complaints, is still the best government in the world after the government of the United States.[4] The fear of unpopularity is a powerful motive in the mind of the governors, and the democratic constitution suggested by Bentham laid upon it the greatest emphasis. But moral responsibility is only an imperfect responsibility and a *pis aller* ; the identification of interests can only be attained methodically and certainly by the application of legal rewards and punishments. In truth, Bentham's whole juridical theory rests on this notion that the law produces social union by artifices. No doubt, there is no legal sanction against him who is supposed to be invested with the supreme power. Who is to reward and to punish him, since the power to reward and to punish is put into his hands ? All sovereignty is absolute, by the very nature of things ; to speak of a divided sovereignty is to speak the language of legal fiction. But this difficulty which formerly made Bentham

---

[1] Bowring, vol. ix. p. 10. [2] *Ibid.* p. 62. [3] *Ibid.* p. 501.
[4] *Ibid.* vol. ix. p. 153.

halt, and kept him from extending to constitutional law the application of his juristic theories, at this stage ceases to cause him embarrassment : for to escape from it, it is enough to attribute sovereignty to the people. In a monarchy the identification of interests cannot be brought about because the monarch is bound to pursue the robbery and oppression of his subjects, and, to secure his ends, he must make use of corruption and imposture with the help of his soldiers, his lawyers and his priests : the only community of interest which can subsist between him and his subjects is the community of interests which exists between the beast of prey and the animals on which he preys : ' it is to the interest of the wolf that the sheep should be fat and numerous '. In a pure monarchy, the positive end of constitutional law is the greatest happiness of a single individual ; in a constitutional monarchy it pursues a more complex end, the greatest happiness of the monarch, limited by the greatest happiness of the ruling aristocracy ; it is only in a pure representative democracy, that the positive end of constitutional law is the greatest happiness of the greatest number.[1]

What, then, are the devices which Bentham conceived in order to prevent the governors setting themselves up as sovereigns, and ceasing to be, as they should be, the servants of the governed ? The idea of the constitution, at once democratic and representative, which Bentham described in his Code, was inspired by the constitution of the Anglo-American United States.[2] But this does not mean that it was a question of slavish copying : in order to define the constitution which he himself proposed, let us note the chief points on which Bentham deliberately departed from the model he had himself chosen.

We are not speaking of the defence of the system of a single Chamber. In his constitution, Bentham does not want two co-existent Chambers, because the second Chamber will either constitute, as in England, an aristocratic corporation, and, by definition, have class interests opposed to the general interest, or else will be recruited, as in America, according to a procedure analogous to the procedure for recruiting the first Chamber. In the first case as in the second the institution of a second Chamber implies a superfluous waste of time and money. It allows a minority of members, in the two Chambers taken together, to make its will prevail over the will of the majority. Above all, it makes the constitution less simple : now the more difficult it is for the people to understand the mechanism of the constitution, by reason of its complexity, the easier it will be, for the same reason, for the governors to draw profit from the exercise of their functions, unknown to and at the expense of the governed. To condemn the system of a second Chamber amounts in sum to

[1] Bowring, vol. ix. p. 69.
[2] *Ibid.* vol. ix, pp. 49, 63 and 113, and vol. iii. p. 437.

drawing the logical conclusion of the principle of democratic simplification on which the American constitution rests.[1]

To bring it about that the State functionaries should possess the maximum official aptitude, Bentham enunciated the responsible location principle or the nomination of subordinates by an effectively responsible superior : this is again an American and democratic principle. The ' Prime Minister ' of his constitution, whose functions—nomination of ministers, and communication with the assembly by means of messages—are very much akin to those of an American president, is elected not by the constitutive assembly, but by the legislative assembly.[2] The ministers in their turn appoint the functionaries of lower rank. Why is this appointment entrusted to the ministers and not, except very indirectly,[3] to the electors ? Bentham, in dealing with the question of judicial organisation to which he devotes a disproportionately large space in his *Code*, gives reasons for this which are valid as regards functionaries of all kinds.[4] If judges were elected directly by the people, or as Bentham puts it, by the ' Supreme Constitutive ', the judicial elections would be party elections. Supposing that the same party were to carry off, under the same names, several successive elections, the injustices committed for the profit of this party would never be able to be corrected. If the two parties were to gain the victory alternately, the injustices, instead of being committed to the prejudice of one party, would be alternately to the detriment of each. For similar reasons, the task of choosing judges ought never to be entrusted to the ' Supreme Legislative '. Nevertheless, Bentham, in his constitution, suppresses one degree between the judge and the legislative assembly. The minister of justice, alone among the fourteen ministers, is not nominated by the chief of the executive, but is elected directly by the legislative assembly.[5] Too much power would be united in the hands of the Prime Minister if he nominated the minister of justice ; he could form a coalition with him to pursue some sinister interest. It is in this way that the Whig principle of the separation of powers— separation of the legislative and judicial powers, and separation of the judicial and executive powers—finds a place in Bentham's system. Yet Bentham, who was anxious to compromise the principle of popular sovereignty as little as possible, reserves to the electors the faculty of exercising what he calls the ' dislocative function.' The principle of the greatest happiness requires that there should be no irremovable functionaries ; if the electors do not directly nominate the functionaries, they can at least dismiss them. On a petition presented by a definite proportion, say by a quarter of the electors of a district, all the electors are called upon to vote on the question whether there is good ground for dismissing a

---

[1] See *Tactique des Assemblées Législatives*, ch. iv. and Bowring, vol. ii. p. 308.
[2] Bowring, vol. ix. pp. 204 *seq.*   [3] *Ibid.* vol. ix. p. 62.
[4] *Ibid.* vol. ix. p. 530.   [5] *Ibid.* vol. ix. p. 609.

functionary, or even for punishing a functionary who is judged unworthy.[1]

But in the choice of the functionaries of his representative republic, Bentham introduces a new principle which tends to make public functions the monopoly of the rich at the expense of the poor. This is the principle of ' pecuniary competition,' a new and less ' sentimental ' designation for the principle of ' patriotic auction ', which Bentham advocated as early as 1790, with a view to economy.[2] By this principle, all the candidates for office should be asked to promise if nominated to pay a sum which might be less than, equal to, or even greater than, the emoluments of the post ; for the minister entrusted with the nomination, there would be, if not an obligation, at least a temptation to choose the richest candidate ; and in this way the application of the principle would have the result of making offices unpaid, and it might even make them a source of profit to the State. Bentham thought that he saw in the principle of pecuniary competition a theory which was conformable to the logic of his system—a procedure which would make the ' minimisation of expense ' bring about the ' maximisation of aptitude '. He even thought that he perceived in this principle an application of the economic principle of free competition. The people who thought that the price of all objects of exchange, including labour, ought to be 'minimised ', and that the only way of securing this minimisation was to apply the principle of competition uniformly, were becoming daily more numerous even among the governing classes. Why not then extend it to the affairs of politics ? Why persist in ' maximising ' the price of the labour of functionaries when it might be minimised ? But it is more likely that Bentham felt the influence of the social atmosphere in which he grew up : there were in England a certain number of honourable and unpaid public functions, and it was clearly in these institutions that Bentham found the experimental justification of his idea. He expressly states that if the aristocratic body of Justices of the Peace fulfilled its functions badly, this was not because these functions were unpaid, but because the law which the judges were applying was a bad law, a class law ; and it was also because the system of recruiting them did not provide the necessary guarantees of moral aptitude. Supposing their functions were paid instead of unpaid, they would render justice quite as badly, with the added disadvantage that they would cost the State money.[3] By this process of pecuniary competition, Bentham sets up a sort of venality of offices, and made the exercise of the functions of State a sort of privilege, if not aristocratic, at least plutocratic.[4] He distributed the posts no longer, as in the English system, to the landlords, to the representatives of the landed aristocracy, but to those men whose interests the Utilitarian economists defended against the feudal caste, the

[1] Bowring, vol. ix. pp. 155-6.   [2] Ibid. p. 287.
[3] Ibid. vol. ix. p. 524.   [4] Ibid. p. 289.

creators of movable wealth, the new rich, manufacturers and traders.

The constitutional code drawn up by Bentham is a republican code ; and it sometimes looks as though Bentham was demanding the immediate establishment of a republic in England. If I am asked what society I have in mind in my description of the society in question, he writes, I answer that it is no particular society, which amounts to saying that it is all societies without exception, and condemns without distinction both projects of electoral reform, the Moderate Reform and the Radical Reform, because the Radical as well as the Liberal respected the existence of the monarchy and of the House of Lords.[1] Bentham was a solitary man, he thought alone and ' dreamed ', and did not need to bother about the possible application of his theories. He felt a personal rancour against the monarchy ; he always attributed to the hostility of George III his disappointment over the *Panopticon*. But, in actual practice, the question at issue was not between an aristocratic monarchy and a popular republic ; and Bentham himself eventually recognised that his Code, which was entirely practicable for a republican nation, was not completely and immediately applicable in England. ' For England ', he wrote, ' (independent of any such sudden revolution as, under the provocations given, will be always upon the cards) it may, in proportion as it is well adapted to its purpose, be of use in giving direction to the views of all such persons as may feel disposed to occupy themselves in the effecting of inclination by gradual changes, which . . . will be so many approaches towards republicanism '.[2] The political party which recognised him as its leader, and whose philosophical portion was composed of his friends and disciples, with James Mill at their head, devoted itself entirely to the reform of the second Chamber and to the extension of the suffrage ; it was silent on the question of the House of Lords and it accepted the monarchy [3] ; it was a Radical without being a Republican party.

Yet it was Bentham again who gave English Radicalism its theoretical formula. The same year in which he drew up Sir Francis Burdett's motion, he published his *Plan of Parliamentary Reform*, augmented by an introduction almost ten times as long as the work itself. In it he developed the ' radical ' programme of universal suffrage, and excused himself for having delayed so long before advocating it, and for having until then stopped at the ' householder system '. Bentham demands five ' guarantees ' from the parliamentary representative in his dealings with the elector. Two of these guarantees he held to be ' primary or principal ' : dependence in relation to the electors, and independence in relation to the King and the Court. Two guarantees were called ' secondary or instrumental ' ; these serve as means to obtaining the principal guarantees :

---

[1] Written May 2, 1821 (MSS. U. C., No. 37).
[2] Bowring, vol. ix. pp. 1-2. [3] Stuart Mill, *Autob.*, p. 107.

they are, the condition of being submitted to re-election every year on the one hand, and on the other hand the exclusion of functionaries. Finally, a fifth guarantee consists in what Bentham calls the ' universal constancy of assistance '. The parliamentary electors remain to be defined. Bentham sums up his programme in four points : virtual universality of suffrage, practical equality of suffrage, liberty or authenticity of suffrage, secrecy of suffrage. The principle of universal, or virtually universal suffrage, Bentham bases on three principles which he states as follows.

The first of these principles is the principle of the universal comprehension of interests, a new application of the greatest happiness principle. All human beings are equally susceptible of pleasure and pain : consequently, when once the right to vote is granted to some, there is no reason for not granting it to all.[1] This is the rule but it is subject to exceptions, which are defined by the second principle, the principle of legitimate disqualification. Disqualification of minors : this has the advantage that it is only temporary, and there is no compelling reason for prolonging the minority till the age of twenty-one, since the exercise of certain rights, for example, the right of choosing a tutor, begins before that age. Disqualification of soldiers and sailors : this will remain necessary until suitable means are found of preventing them from voting in a mass under the orders of their commanders, and of serving the sinister interests of the Court. Disqualification of the illiterate : not only is this temporary, but it can be reduced at the will of the excluded individual, since in the space of three months anyone who wants to learn to read can do so. As for the disqualification of women, is it necessary ? It is difficult indeed to find in Bentham's works a certain answer to this question. Bentham refuses to grant them eligibility, and hesitates to grant them the vote. Yet he recognises that there is no reason to forbid its being granted to them. Women have the same interests as men ; like men, and to the same extent as men they are capable of pleasure and pain ; they are their inferiors neither in moral nor in intellectual aptitude ; they are held capable of reigning ; they vote in the elections of the India Company Office. The subordination of woman to man in the matter of private rights is necessary ; but this very subordination, which is solely due to the inferiority of their physical strength, is a reason for conferring on them and not for removing from them equality of political rights.[2] Finally, it is above all, the third principle, or principle of simplification, which makes it possible to reduce the number of disqualifications to a minimum, so that virtually universal suffrage tends to come indefinitely nearer to universal suffrage. The same principle which condemned the rules of exclusion in judicial evidence, condemns them in electoral law. Every rule of exclusion, owing to difficulties in interpretation, implies a triple

[1] Bowring, vol. ix. p. 107.
[2] James Mill differs on this point, see Stuart Mill, *Autob.*, p. 104.

expenditure of time, money, and tranquillity: these are sensible and real evils. As to the evils which exclusion aims at avoiding, these, in the last analysis, are impalpable.[1] Any right, if considered in relation to the individual who possesses it in its entirety, may be extremely important, and yet may be no more ' than a fraction of a fraction ' in relation to its distant ends, the elaboration and the execution of the laws. The exclusion of foreigners, criminals, vagabonds, bankrupts and aliens may therefore be neglected. It is the application of the principle of simplification which determined Bentham to pass from the ' householder plan ' to the ' virtually universal plan,' of which he thenceforward became the recognised theorist. ' Universal Suffrage,' ' Annual Parliaments,' and 'Election by Ballot' was the current formula at Radical meetings. ' Secrecy, Universality, Equality and Annuality of Suffrage.' is the more abstract formula which Bentham preferred. Major Cartwright encouraged Bentham with his good wishes, and impatiently awaited the publication of his *Constitutional Code*; but though Bentham may have adopted Cartwright's programme, he based it on new principles. With the *Plan of Parliamentary Reform* and the *Constitutional Code* was consummated the evolution of the theory of universal suffrage, by which the principle of natural rights became absorbed in the principle of general utility.

Immediately after the appearance of the *Plan of Parliamentary Reform*, Bentham's work became the classical work of the Radical party ; it was the ideas expressed in this work which Ricardo adopted under the influence of James Mill,[2] and whose defence he several times took up in Parliament. He did indeed remain moderate even in his Radicalism. He did not let himself be converted to annual Parliaments, and was satisfied with triennial Parliaments. He did not, like Bentham and Sir Francis Burdett, demand universal suffrage : the householder suffrage was enough in his opinion.[3] But this did not prevent him from declaring in 1818 to his friend Trower that he held himself to be Bentham's political disciple ; if he were to enter Parliament, he would take his seat there neither as a Whig nor as a Tory, and without going as far as Bentham, he had been convinced by him that it was necessary to entrust the control of the government to the only class whose private interests were not opposed to the good execution of public affairs, that is to say, to the popular class.[4] In 1819, in the very speech in which he declared that he would be satisfied with a suffrage ' much less than universal ', at a time when the unpopularity of Radicalism was at its height, and when press actions and convictions for crimes of opinion were multiplying, he dared to defend the honourableness of the advocates of thorough-going Radicalism ;[5] on another occasion he denied that large

[1] Bowring, vol. iii. p. 464.
[2] Ricardo to Malthus, May 25, 1818. Ricardo to Trower, June 27, 1818.
[3] Bowring, vol. x. p. 498.   [4] Ricardo to Trower, Mar. 22, 1818.
[5] Hansard, xli. p. 770, Dec. 6, 1819.

electoral bodies necessarily elect demagogues, and when citing on this point Montesquieu's opinion as to what went on in Athens and in Rome, it was from Bentham's pamphlet that he borrowed the idea and the quotation[1]. Finally, there is one point of Bentham's political programme on which his orthodoxy was absolute ; he thought introduction of the secret ballot would be ' a far greater security for the full and fair representation of the people than any extension of the elective franchise '.[2] For this was perhaps the point of capital importance for the Benthamites.   James Mill, the disciple of Bentham and the adviser of Ricardo, and George Grote, the disciple of James Mill, for their part emphasised the singular importance of this part of the Radical doctrine.   The one by an article in the *Supplement to the Encyclopaedia Britannica*, and by an article in the *Westminster Review*, the other by two short pamphlets, helped to fix the political doctrine of the group to which they belonged in a form at once more limited and more popular than their common master wished to do.   The circumstances by which this came about were as follows.

In December 1818, in the *Edinburgh Review*, Mackintosh had submitted the *Plan of Parliamentary Reform* to severe treatment.   He had criticised the doctrine of the ballot.   On his view, the secrecy would be fictitious ; the exercise of the right to vote would lose its attraction in becoming secret ; publicity of votes is necessary to give its true educative value to the exercise of the right of suffrage in England ; the tumults which rage around the hustings keep a taste for public life alive in the parties.   Mackintosh had discussed the principle of short term elections, and opposed to Bentham's present opinion the contrary view which he had himself formerly expressed with regard to judicial organisation.[3]   He had criticised the too frequent recourse to the so-called examples provided by the United States of America, where in reality, universal suffrage was not the rule but the exception, since twelve out of its nineteen states practised slavery ; where there were few large towns, where a new aristocracy of wealth was developing in the Southern States, and where the secrecy of the vote was often made illusory by the manipulations of the caucuses.   Finally, he had put forward as against the doctrine of universal suffrage the doctrine of varied suffrage, and against the doctrine of personal representation the doctrine of class representation, by a sort of inverted application of the Benthamite principle of the ' comprehension of all interests '.   For Mackintosh was in agreement with Bentham on principles : ' the question between us and Mr. Bentham ', he said, ' is whether all interests will be best protected, where

[1] Hansard, n.s. viii. p. 1285, Ap. 24, 1823.
[2] April 18, 1821 (Hansard, n.s. v. p. 449).
[3] Apparently inexact.   Bentham had contested the utility of forced intervals of exclusion but had declared that short-term elections were the best guarantee of the perpetual re-election of the same representative.   Bowring, vol. iv. p. 363.

the representatives are chosen by all men—or where they are elected
by considerable portions only, of all classes of men ' ; and Mackintosh
decided in favour of the second alternative. For either a uniform
suffrage would not be universal : in which case it would deny any
representation to whole classes of society. Or else it would be universal, and would result in the oppression of minorities by majorities.
What would become of the Protestants in Ireland ? And in England,
what would become of the inhabitants of the country districts whose
representatives would be annihilated in Parliament by the representatives of the large towns ? The best of all electoral systems,
according to Mackintosh, is the English system of representation
which is at once ' virtual ' and ' varied ', a system in which all
individuals do not vote, but in which all classes are represented, the
towns as towns, the country districts as country districts, the universities as universities ; in which, moreover, in some towns it is a more
restricted and in others a more extended portion of the population
and sometimes the whole population, which is endowed with the right
of suffrage. Mackintosh resumed, in the name of Liberalism, the
defence of complex or varied government as against simple government. ' The founders of new commonwealths must, we confess,
act upon some uniform principle. A builder can seldom imitate,
with success, all the fantastic but picturesque and comfortable
irregularities of an old mansion, which through a course of ages has
been repaired, enlarged, and altered, according to the pleasure of
various owners.'

The article *Government* which was published in 1820 by James Mill
in the *Supplement to the Encyclopaedia Britannica*, should be taken as
the answer of the Benthamites to the objections of Mackintosh : it is
an article remarkable for the vigour of its reasoning and for its clearness of exposition, but also for the opportunist nature of the political
doctrine which is defended in it.

From the moment when he became converted to Benthamism,
James Mill had always rejected, for convincing reasons, the Whig
theory of the balance of powers ; as early as 1809, he was referring to
the *Traités de Legislation* those who took seriously a theory which
was ' at bottom so vague and inaccurate, that some of the most deep-
rooted errors and the greatest mistakes in politics have arisen from
it '.[1] Either the powers supposed to be in equilibrium are two in
number ; in which case their reciprocal equality could only be
temporary and precarious. Or else they are three in number : in
this case it would necessarily come about that two powers would
coalesce against the third, and, also necessarily, in a mixed constitution the monarchic and the aristocratic elements would coalesce against
the democratic element.[2] Besides although James Mill professed
Benthamism, was he not also an admirer of Hobbes, whose logical

[1] *Ed. Rev.*, No. xxvi. Jan. 1809, art. ii. (cf. Bowring, vol. iii. p. 198)
[2] *Government*, pp. 14-15.

turn of thought he appreciated, at a time when his philosophy had
fallen into discredit ? And was not Hobbes a theorist of absolute
government ? Mill had also been influenced by the physiocrats, and
he expressed regret that Quesnay and his disciples, who were known
in England only in connection with the economic part of their
doctrine, were not equally esteemed for the progress which they
had achieved in the ' science of politics ' : for they had the
merit of establishing definitely that ' the legislative and executive
power are essentially the same, and cannot be separated except in
appearance ', and that ' no security for good government can be
found in an organization of counterforces, or a *balance* in the
constitution '.[1]

The physiocrats' only mistake was that they forgot the existence of
democratic government, and saw in absolute monarchy the only conceivable form of government without ' counterforces '.[2] A review
article published by James Mill in 1836, only a short time before his
death, was more definite still. Dissatisfied at seeing the House of
Lords oppose perpetual obstacles to the House of Commons' desires
of reform, James Mill now tried to separate the interests of the
monarchy from those of the aristocracy. Only ' very shallow politicians ' and ' great enemies of the monarchy ', he said, sought to confuse them. Hobbes and the Economists were right in these matters,
' A first magistrate is necessary ;' that is a fixed and undisputed point.
The necessity of unity in matters of administration, the use of concentrated responsibility, and many other considerations, seem to
place the balance of advantage on the side of the individuality of the
first magistrate. He should be one, and not two, or more '.[3] The
Benthamite thesis of the single magistrate and functionary served, in
the writings of the Radical writer, to justify the monarchic authority,
on condition that it shook itself free from its aristocratic body-guard
and identified itself with the popular interests.

But the article of 1820 was anonymous ; the work in which it appeared was not a Benthamite publication. James Mill was obliged to
be careful concerning both the publisher who printed it, and the public
to whom it was addressed.[4] He explicitly adheres in it neither to the
principle of utility [5] nor to the democratic idea.[6] He accepts the
existence of a monarchy and of an aristocracy, and if he demands the
institution of a representative assembly which shall exactly represent
the whole of the subjects, this is only so that the monarchic and
aristocratic powers should be held in respect. It is sufficiently
conformable to the established and fashionable opinions, he says, to say
that the excellence of a government depends on the right constitution

---

[1] *Sup. to Ency. Brit.*, article ' Economist ', p. 723.
[2] *Sup. to the Ency. Brit.*, article ' Economist '.
[3] *London Review*, No. iv., Jan. 1836, art. vi. ' Aristocracy ', pp. 302-305.
[4] J. Mill to Napier, Sept. 10, 1819. Bain, p. 188.
[5] *Government*, p. 3.   [6] See *Government*, p. 6.

of its 'checks'; and he adds: 'To this proposition we fully subscribe'. But what is this which James Mill calls the doctrine of checks if not the balance of powers, which is expressly condemned by himself? What are these 'established and fashionable opinions' to which he adheres, if not the same prejudices of Whig Liberalism, criticised by Bentham and by himself? The phrase is certainly ironical; but it is none the less true that in James Mill's written propaganda, under the influence of what may be called the logic of parties, the Radical thesis tends to approximate to the Liberal thesis.[1]

Burke, in 1784, had made the objection to the partisans of universal suffrage, that they were illogical in allowing an hereditary monarchy and an hereditary aristocracy to subsist in the face of their elected assembly. Bentham replied to this objection by suppressing the monarchy and the aristocracy in his constitution. But James Mill, who was more mixed up in the active life of the Radical party than Bentham was, and was obliged to take account of the necessities of existence of the faction, avoided the difficulty in a roundabout way. *If it is true*, he tells us, that the best way of disposing of the administrative powers of the government is to entrust them to a great functionary who is not elected but hereditary, then a monarchy such as the English monarchy is an indispensable branch of good government. *Suppose it true*, that, for the perfect performance of the business of legislation, and of watching over the execution of the laws, a second deliberative assembly is necessary; *and suppose also* that an assembly such as the British House of Lords, composed of great landlords and great dignitaries, were the best adapted to play the part of an Upper Chamber, then a representative assembly, whose interests were identical with those of the nation, ought to establish a House of Lords, constituted in this way, if there were not one already in existence. Consequently, those who maintain that an assembly which was really representative of the nation would destroy the monarchy and the House of Lords, and are for this reason hostile to the extension of the right to vote, contradict themselves. 'They maintain that a King and a House of Lords, such as ours, are important and necessary branches of a good Government. It is demonstratively certain that a representative body, the interests of which were identified with those of the nation, would have no motive to abolish them, if they were not causes of bad government. Those persons, therefore, who affirm that it would certainly abolish them, affirm implicitly that they are causes of bad, and not necessary to good government'.[2] This is the argument of a lawyer rather than of a philosopher: nevertheless it made its mark. George Grote made it his own in 1822, in the *Morning Chronicle*; Ricardo in 1823, in a speech in Parliament; finally Macaulay, the Whig orator *par excellence*, within three years of choosing the essay *On Government* as the object of his most bitter

---

[1] He even quotes Montesquieu in support of his thesis. *Government*, p. 13 (note).
[2] James Mill, article on *Government*, pp. 27, 28.

criticisms, endowed James Mill's argument with an almost classical character in one of his great speeches in 1832.[1]

It was therefore no longer a question of demanding the exercise of absolute power for the popular majority, but only of securing some place for the expression of the popular will in a complex constitution, made up of monarchic, aristocratic and democratic elements. Once radicalism has been thus reduced to its essential elements, James Mill follows Bentham's doctrine very closely.

He begins by examining what Bentham called ' the position of the parliamentary representatives ' : in other words, he seeks to define what conditions a representative body ought to fulfil in order to be a guarantee of good government. According to Bentham, the representatives should unite independence in relation to the monarchic power with dependence in relation to the electoral body. James Mill writes, in the same sense, that ' the checking body ' should possess on the one hand the amount of power necessary to fulfil this function, and on the other hand should have identity of interests with the society : if it failed to satisfy this second condition, it would be more dangerous the more power it possessed. Now, if it is impossible to limit by means of a law the intensity of the power of the people's representatives, it is at least possible to limit the duration of this power.[2] It was for this that Rome made its consuls annual ; on principle, those to whom the control of the acts of government has been delegated must be granted ' whatsoever time is necessary to perform the periodical round of the stated operations of Government ', and no more.[3] The limitation of the duration of functions does not, moreover, exclude indefinite re-election.[4]

James Mill then passes to the examination of what Bentham called ' the situation of Parliamentary Electors ' : he asks what conditions are required of the electoral body in order that it may acquit itself of its elective functions in conformity with the public interest. The advantages of the representative system would be lost in all cases where the interests of the electoral body were not the same as those of the society ; but in order to ensure that the interests of the society and of the electoral body should be the same, it is sufficient that the electoral body be composed of the whole community. No doubt some exclusions are necessary : those and those only ' whose interests are indisputably included in those of other individuals ' will be excluded. Thus the principle of virtual representation reappears in the Radical doctrine despite the apparent identification of Radicalism with the principle of personal representation. Children, whose interests are included in those of their parents, will be excluded. Women, whose interests are included in those of their parents or of

---

[1] Grote, *Minor Works*, p. 10. Ricardo, Speech of April 24, 1823. Macaulay, Speech of March 2, 1831.

[2] *Government*, p. 18. Cf. Bowring, vol. ix. pp. 49-50.

[3] *Government*, p. 19.   [4] *Ibid.* pp. 19-20. Cf. Bowring, vol. iv. p. 366.

their husbands will be excluded.[1] Age also, according to James Mill, is a legitimate principle of exclusion. Supposing the age at which the enjoyment of the right of suffrage is to begin, were fixed at forty, it is difficult to think of laws, made by men more than forty years old, from which the rest of the community would not benefit. Moreover, should the importance of sympathetic feelings be neglected? Have not the vast majority of old men sons ' whose interest they regard as an essential part of their own '?[2] But property is a less legitimate principle of exclusion. The qualification would either be very high : in which case the government would be aristocratic. Or else it would be fixed very low : in this case the disadvantages of the qualification would be null, but the advantages would be null likewise : ' for if the whole mass of the people who have some property would make a good choice, it will hardly be pretended that, added to them, the comparatively small number of those who have none . . . would be able to make the choice a bad one '. Here we have ' the principle of simplification ' finding a new application. As to the intermediary cases, James Mill makes a curious attempt, in conformity with Bentham's method, to express with arithmetical exactitude the extent to which the interests of the community would suffer according as the qualification adopted excludes or does not exclude the majority of the citizens.[3]

But could not the distinction between professions be considered as a principle on which the organisation of an electoral system might be based? The idea of a representation of organised interests, the notion according to which ' the best elective body is that which consists of certain classes, professions, or fraternities ', and according to which ' when these fraternities or bodies are represented, the community itself is represented '—this was the theme of Mackintosh's article, and it is difficult not to believe that Mill is thinking of it here, although he chooses as the object of his criticism a speech formerly delivered by Lord Liverpool. The real result of this ' motley' representation would be, according to James Mill, to produce a ' motley aristocracy ' ; it would then involve all the evil consequences which result from any kind of aristocratic régime, whether it be an aristocracy composed of landlords, or a mixed aristocracy composed of landlords, traders and manufacturers, officers of the army and navy, and lawyers.[4] At bottom, the reasoning which James Mill uses to defend the theory of the representation of individuals against the theory of the representation of interests is very like the argument which he and Ricardo brought forward against economic protectionism. At first sight, the idea of a ' representation of interests ' seems to be in conformity with the spirit of the Utilitarian philosophy : the principle of general utility prescribes that all interests without distinction should be at

[1] Bowring, vol. x. p. 450 ; and Stuart Mill, *Autobiography*, pp. 104-5.
[2] See MSS. Univ. Coll., No. 34, a note of Bentham's dated April 23, 1824.
[3] *Government*, p. 23.　　　　[4] *Government*, pp. 23-26.

once represented in the legislative assembly and protected by it. But the question is whether, in considering the problem of the protection of social interests, individuals should be regarded as producers or as consumers. The interests of all classes of producers are perpetually coming into conflict : each producer seeks to obtain the greatest possible quantity of the produce of the labour of others in exchange for the smallest quantity of the produce of his own labour. On the other hand, the interests of all individuals, when considered as consumers and not as producers, are identical : each individual, taken in isolation, finds it to be to his interest that all objects of consumption, without exception, should be sold as cheap as possible. Moreover, despite the diversity of interests, certain coalitions are still possible between different classes of producers : the old system of industrial protectionism issued from a coalition of this kind ; but such coalitions are always, in essence, aristocratic coalitions, which favour particular and ' sinister ' interests at the expense of the general interest. The same principle finds its application in electoral law. To grant the right to vote to professionally distinct classes of citizens is deliberately to regard individuals from an angle from which their interests appear contradictory and not identical. The principle of the division of labour creates differentiated aptitudes, and distributes men into hostile classes ; but, whereas all men as producers become different, all men as consumers are still alike, retain identical interests, and are equal to one another. Nations and societies should not be considered as organisations of syndicated professions, but as collections of individual consumers ; and this is why, for quite different reasons from those formerly suggested by the theorists of natural right, individualism is the true theory in political economy and in politics.

Side by side with James Mill, and under his encouragement, Grote was fighting for the same doctrine. In 1821, in a paper on *Parliamentary Reform*, he refuted Mackintosh's article.[1] Ten years later, at the moment when the battle over electoral reform was being waged, he defined, in another paper on the *Essentials of Parliamentary Reform*, the minimum programme of the Radical party. He rejected any limitation of the right of suffrage founded on a consideration of wealth : the very wealthy, he urged, are not the only property owners, and the rich are not more interested in the defence of the social order than the poor. He criticised the idea of ' class representation '. All that a class can do is to coalesce with other classes, and to sacrifice its own particular interests, in so far as they are contradictory to the particular interests of the other classes, to the defence of the particular interests which are common to them both. In 1831, he again attacked, and more precisely perhaps than James Mill had done, the system of the *Edinburgh Review*, according to which ' we must divide the people into classes and examine *the*

[1] See *Minor Works*, pp. 1 *seq.*

variety of local and professional interests of which the general interest is composed ' ; and he continued : ' The interest of an individual by himself apart—the interest of the same man jointly with any given fraction of his fellow-citizens—and his interest jointly with the whole body of his fellow-citizens—all these are distinct objects, abhorrent and irreconcilable in general, coinciding occasionally by mere accident. . . . Individuals compose the class, but the interest of the class is not the sum total of the separate interests of all its members : classes compose the community, but the interest of the community is not the sum total of the separate interests of all the classes. And a governing body which would promote the universal interest, must discard all inclination to the separate interest of any class whatever '.[1]

There was, however, one reform on whose extreme importance George Grote insisted : this was the introduction of the secret vote or ballot. Grote thought that any numerical increase in the electoral body would be vain unless the vote of every elector were first emancipated and made independent : now, this was only possible if a system to ensure the secrecy of the vote was adopted. In the name of the ' Advocates of Reform ', he declared that they did not insist on the absolute necessity of making the vote universal : it was the ballot which they held to be a ' vital ' necessity. He protested against the association which Mackintosh had established between the education of the political spirit, and the tumult of elections. He took up the same thesis again in 1831, and preferred five hundred electors with the ballot to two millions without the ballot.[2] Those who wished to be convinced of the excellence of this process he referred to James Mill, who had doubtless inspired his 1821 observations, and who had just dealt in a detailed manner with the question of the ballot in the *Westminster Review*.[3]

The characteristic feature of this article is the effort which James Mill makes to prove that secret voting is a mechanical artifice, capable of infallibly producing the identity of interests of governors and governed : here the tradition of Helvetius and Bentham is recognisable. The process, doubtless, does not succeed in every case, but when it does not succeed, it is possible to explain scientifically why it fails.[4] There are circumstances in which, if the electors were free from all external influence, they would vote well ; there are other circumstances in which the absence of all external influence would on the contrary determine them to vote badly. The first case arises when the interest of the voter inclines him to vote well, but when other individuals are likely to create in him an interest which inclines him to vote badly : in this case secret voting should be established. The second case arises when the interest of the voter leads him to vote badly, and public opinion acts on him as an inducement to vote well :

[1] *Ibid.* p. 30. [2] *Ibid.* p. 8 and pp. 37-46.
[3] *West. Rev.*, No. xxvii., July 1830, art. i.
[4] Cf. *Hist. of Brit. India*, bk. iv. ch. ix., Wilson's ed. vol. iii. pp. 508-509.

in this case the public voting keeps its advantages. It is necessary, for example, that the vote of parliamentary representatives should be public ; but, by a converse application of the same reasons, it is necessary that the vote of the electors who nominate the Members of Parliament should be secret. Under a system of public voting, elections are expensive for the candidate, and corrupt the morals of the electors. Preserve the same electors. Distribute them into constituencies in the same way. Do not even change the duration of Parliaments. But establish secret voting : the ballot exerts an action ' so powerful and so beneficent ' that the vices of the electoral régime would, by the fact of its institution, be much less severely felt. Should James Mill's argument be repudiated as being too abstract and as consisting entirely of *a priori* reasoning ? James Mill puts this objection aside, as only suitable for idiots : the claim of the Benthamites is to establish politics as an exact science.[1] Should the secret ballot be repudiated as being contrary to national traditions, as ' not being English ' ? This is one of the ' political fallacies ' already refuted by Bentham ; it is a too convenient means of avoiding criticism of the abuses round about one. Yet it was perhaps the most to be feared of all the objections with which the new system came into conflict ; in spite of the reiterated efforts of Grote and of many others, the principle of secret voting still for many years met with obstinate resistance not only from the aristocracy, who were interested in maintaining the existing institution, but also of general opinion, which was in favour of the amusing uproar of the hustings, and of votes given openly, in a tumultuous procession. James Mill had acted the prudent politician when he omitted to deal with the question of the secret vote in his 1820 article, and thanks to this omission, thanks also to many other artifices in its exposition, his study, which was reprinted in 1828,[2] became a classical work by whose means Bentham's ideas were freed from a difficult terminology and from wearying digressions, and became accessible to the public. Macaulay made it the object of the attack which he directed against the logical pedanticism of the Utilitarian sect in 1829, when he undertook to avenge the *Edinburgh Review* for the attacks of the *Westminster Review*. Three years later the great Reform Bill was passed, a law which, by enlarging the electoral body and by distributing seats in a more equitable manner, achieved for England the end of the Tory régime. The Philosophical Radicals played, outside of Parliament, the part of intermediaries between the faction of the Whig aristocrats and the mass of the people, and actively co-operated in the success of the law ; and the influence exerted by James Mill's article can be estimated from a consideration of the obvious loans made from this article by Macaulay in the brilliant speeches in which he defended the cause of reform in Parliament.

[1] *West. Rev.*, No. xxvii., July 1830, art. i. ' The Ballot ', p. 15.
[2] James Mill to Napier, Nov. 20, 1820 (Bain, p. 191).

Macaulay did not however plead the cause of universal suffrage in
1831 and 1832 ; the moderate reform which he demanded consisted
in the extension of the right to vote to the middle class ;[1] this was a
reform which in some areas, thanks to the incoherence of the electoral
régime, which was oligarchic in some respects and demagogic in
others, restricted the electoral body to the disadvantage of the masses.
Macaulay considered that the battle was being fought not between
the poor and the rich, but between the bourgeoisie and an aristocracy
based on a purely local principle, ' an aristocracy of mere locality '.
He prided himself on belonging to a party the bulk of which was
made up of ' the middle class of England, with the flower of the
aristocracy at its head, and the flower of the working classes bringing
up its rear '.   Now, on this point, the distance is not so great as
might be supposed between the Whigs, properly so-called, of whom
Macaulay was the spokesman, and the Benthamite Radicals.   When
Bentham, at the first stage of the journey which eventually led him to
pure Radicalism, advocated, about the year 1810, the ' householder
plan ', he was by this measure making the electoral franchise the
privilege of the middle classes to the exclusion of manual labourers
and of the indigent ; and later, when he adhered to the former
political programme of Major Cartwright, the party around him
still appeared to everyone a faction of the lower middle classes.   Was
not Francis Place, the organiser of the party, a small workman who
had become a master, in effect the typical representative of the middle
classes ?   On the side of the Whigs, Romilly, when in the electoral
campaign of 1818 he was faced with opposition from the Radicals,
denounced the ' little committee of tradesmen, who persuade themselves that they are all-powerful at Westminster '.   On the side of
the ultra-radicals, Hunt attacked ' a considerable faction, composed
principally of *petty shop-keepers*, and *little tradesmen*, who, under the
denomination of *tax-paying housekeepers*, enlisted themselves under
the banners of Sir Francis Burdett, in order to set themselves up as a
sort of privileged class, above the *operative* manufacturer, the artizan,
the mechanic, and the labourer '.[2]   The same denunciations occurred
persistently in workmen's centres until 1831, when the Radical
doctrinaires were playing the difficult part of negotiators between the
Whigs and the people.   Nor were they entirely unjustified.

In political economy, the Utilitarians considered inequality of conditions as natural and necessary.   They also considered that the
establishment of a régime of equality of political rights not only would
not abolish the inequality of economic conditions, but would not
suppress the influence, which was as natural as it was necessary,
exerted by the rich over the poor.   To be more precise, the influence
which the rich exert over the poor may be either good or bad according
to whether it consists of an influence of intelligence over intelligence,

[1] Macaulay, Speech of Mar. 12, 1831.
[2] Romilly, *Memoirs*, vol. iii. p. 360.   Henry Hunt, *Memoirs*, vol. ii. p. 75.

or of will over will.   In the second case it is a corrupting and oppressive influence ; but it is enough to institute the ballot to make this impossible.   In the first case it is a beneficent influence ; but, if we are to believe Bentham and James Mill, the establishment of universal suffrage and of the ballot favours it more than it weakens it.   What the Utilitarians were demanding was free admission for all to the economic market and also to what may be called by analogy the political market, and liberty for all in exerting the influence, naturally unequal, which is conferred on everyone by his wealth, his talent and his reputation.   But this natural inequality must not be artificially aggravated by monopolies or privileges which would have the result of bringing forth a small number of enormous fortunes to the detriment of real social interests : for it is to the interest of society that a numerous middle class should be formed—a class which is more economical than either the rich class or the poor class, and is consequently more capable of that accumulation of capital which determines economic progress.[1]   It is from among the members of the middle class that the people has become accustomed, in health and in sickness, in infancy and in old age, to seek its advisers, its doctors and its advocates.[2]   It is in this class too that the people, feeling its beneficent intellectual influence, will seek for its representatives, when all have been given the right to vote freely.   In fact, Bentham and James Mill go further still.   Bentham does not confine himself to requiring that the influence of the rich over the poor should be allowed to be exerted without hindrance : his ' pecuniary competition ' is a positive institution, constructed to ensure to the rich the monopoly of administrative power.   James Mill does not confine himself to pointing out the beneficent nature of the social influence exerted by the middle class : he affirms that ' the business of government is properly the business of the rich,' on condition that the rich are designated by popular election.   He accepts for himself the denomination of Aristocrat : ' We think it best, that government should be placed in the hands of the $\"A\rho\iota\sigma\tau o\iota$; not only in the sense of the Greeks, who understood by that term the $B\acute{\epsilon}\lambda\tau\iota\sigma\tau o\iota$: . . . Whoever are the $\"A\rho\iota\sigma\tau o\iota$ and the $B\acute{\epsilon}\lambda\tau\iota\sigma\tau o\iota$, we desire to be governed by them ; and, with the suffrage upon a proper footing, we have no doubt but that they would be the Rich '.[3]

In short, a ' pure representative democracy ' does not necessarily tend to the levelling of fortunes ; such was the profound conviction of Bentham and of his disciples.   When, in 1824, Joseph Hume and the Benthamite Radicals were campaigning to secure in Parliament the freedom of workmen's combinations, it did not occur to them that the associations of workmen might become centres of communist propaganda : they thought, on the contrary, that the workmen, when freed from a humiliating supervision, would be converted on the spot

[1] *West. Rev.*, No. x., April 1826, art. i.   [2] *Government*, p. 31.
[3] *West. Rev.*, No. xxvii, July 1830, on ' Ballot '.

to the economic doctrines of Malthus and Ricardo. Neither did the
Benthamites, when directing and organising the Radical agitation,
doubt that in the equalitarian democracy to which they were tending
the rich must remain the natural representatives of the poor : was
this not the way in which things were happening at Westminster ?
Was not Francis Place a notable bourgeois, and Sir Francis Burdett
a millionaire ? But it was not only the parliamentary area of Westminster that provided Bentham with some sort of a picture of the
future English democracy. The ' parish ' of Westminster still
offered, round about 1815, in the incoherent electoral régime of
the old England, an interesting case of the direct government of the
people by the people, practised as in the cities of antiquity. Each
parish then elected, in the vestry, a sort of administrative council
entrusted with the administration of the parish finances, and principally with the execution of the laws of public assistance. Sometimes
the vestry, which was then called a select vestry, was a small local
oligarchy, composed of all the *entrepreneurs* of the locality, and perpetually recruited by means of co-optation without control by the
rate-payers. Sometimes the vestry, which in these cases was called
an open vestry, consisted of the general assembly of parishioners, who,
in the church itself, ratified every three months the parish accounts ;
this was the régime in the parish in which Bentham and Francis
Place lived. This anarchical régime had its disadvantages, and corruption quickly tended to make it degenerate into despotism. The
Radicals, and particularly the Westminster Philosophical Radicals,
were anxious to make the system of vestries uniform and regular, by
the general introduction of a régime at once democratic and representative. ' If they who have the power had the requisite knowledge,
they would at once pass an Act giving to every parish both the right
and the power to elect their own vestries annually, giving to each
vestry the power to originate and control all parish matters in every
department, compelling them, however, to proceed in one uniform
way all over the country and publishing their audited accounts every
three months '.[1] Already in 1818 and 1819 some advance had been
made in this direction[2] ; and it had been made possible to transform
open vestries into representative vestries, elected by the rate-payers :
plural voting was however established in favour of the more substantial among the rate-payers. In 1831, at the instigation of
Francis Place, Hobhouse secured the passing by Parliament of a bill
establishing the elective system, with no plural voting, in every parish
which so desired.[3] The question for the Benthamites was not merely
to secure the regularisation of an electoral régime that was incoherent
and everywhere vicious ; it was primarily a question of withdrawing
from the members of the ruling class, the Justices of the Peace, the

[1] Graham Wallas, p. 155. Place to Hobhouse, Mar. 22, 1830.
[2] 58 Geo. 3, c. 69 s. 3 (1818) and 59 Geo. 3, c. 12, s. 1. (1819).
[3] Hobhouse's Act, 1 and 2 Will. iv. c. 60 (1831).

privilege they had kept of administering the local government of England without recognising the control either of the central power or of the subordinates, and of restoring the direction of the administrative power to paid officials under the control of elected representatives. Edwin Chadwick,[1] who was a fanatic for administrative uniformity and centralisation, conducted a campaign in the *Westminster Review* and in the *London Review* [2] against the English system of aristocratic self-government. The *Westminster Review* derided a French panegyric [3] of the system. It denounced the financial scandals, the purchase of votes where the vestry was elective, the withdrawal of honest men, and the invasion of all parish assemblies by dishonest *entrepreneurs*, the lack of agreement between the parishes, and the incoherent manner in which public works were executed in England.

In the last analysis, thought the Benthamites, the French centralising system is better than this : ' In spite of our natural or acquired fears of government and jobs, we still think that the whole system of roads ought to be one ; and we would be content for ourselves, that they should be placed under [a] corps *des ponts et chaussées* '. Bentham, at the same time, in his *Constitutional Code*, strengthened the administrative system. He created a minister of ' *ponts et chaussées* ', or, as he said, of ' interior communications ', a minister of public assistance (indigence relief), a minister of education, a minister of health.[4] It was in the same order of ideas that Bentham demanded, in judicial organisation, the institution of a public prosecutor and of a service of judicial assistance.[5] Some Benthamites were not even repelled by the idea of a State Church : all they wanted was for religion itself to be to some extent secularised ; and James Mill described as ' truly Catholic ' and ' without dogmas or ceremonies ' this State religion, which would teach the elements of social morality, of political economy, and of constitutional and civil law, to the accompaniment of music and dancing.[6] But at the same time, there can be noticed in the *Constitutional Code* the influence exerted on Bentham's thought by the debates regarding the reorganisation of the vestries, in his institution of sublegislatures, elected by the district to vote laws of local interest, just as the legislature votes laws of general interest.[7] One of the functions of the ministers of interior communications, of indigence relief, of public instruction and of health, consists in entering into relations with the local assemblies, so as to inspect and to advise them. To each sublegislature is attached ' a set of

[1] See his biography by B. Richardson at the beginning of the *Health of Nations* by Edwin Chadwick (1887).

[2] *West. Rev.*, No. xviii., April 1828, art. v. *London Rev.*, 1829. *Preventive Police, Public Charities in France*.

[3] *West. Rev.*, No. viii., Oct. 1825, art. v.

[4] Bowring, vol. ix, p. 441.   [5] *Ibid.* pp. 570 *seq.* and vol. x. p. 522.

[6] *London Review*, No. 11, July 1835, art. i., *The Church and its Reform*.

[7] Bowring, vol. ix. pp. 640 *seq.*

administrative functionaries ', bearing the same names, and exerting, within that local field, the same functions as the ministers of the whole State. Thus was outlined a system which was half elective and half administrative, and which eventually tended, through the active intervention of Bentham's disciples, to become, after 1832, a reality. When the sovereign is a monarch, the administrative autonomy of the local aristocracy may be favourable to the general interest, because it curbs the administrative power identified with the monarchic power. But when popular sovereignty is recognised, all increase of the administrative power is favourable to the rights and to the interests of the people, precisely because it strengthens the power of the sovereign.

Thus is completed the organisation of the State according to Bentham and James Mill. It is a representative and an administrative régime : for, in order that the functions of government may be exercised with the desired continuity and competence, they should be delegated to specialists. It is a ' pure democracy ', and by this Bentham understood two things. He understood in the first place a government freed as much as possible from every constitutional complication, for complex constitutions are only contrivances devised by those who hold the power to mystify and to exploit the governed. He understood, in the second place, a government freed from every kind of judicial fiction, and in this way he remained faithful to the principles on which he had formerly founded his criticism of the theory of Natural Rights. For it is absurd to wish to impose on a nation an everlasting respect for certain abstract rights, defined in advance and solemnly proclaimed : in fact, the national will remains perpetually free to violate them. A right only ceases to be a mere fiction and becomes a real right when it is sanctioned by force ; the right of force is real : this, without doubt, is the essential thesis of the philosophy of right founded in the seventeenth century by Hobbes, and developed in the eighteenth by Bentham. Only, it happens that the majority are the strongest, and moreover that the will of the greatest number is the surest protector of the interest of the greatest number. So that the philosophy of Hobbes leads to conclusions which contradict the constitutional theories of Hobbes himself, and the philosophy of Bentham results in consequences which Bentham, when he was younger, had not foreseen. At the time when Bentham was a Tory, the first theorists of the democratic régime tried to justify it by taking their stand on the principle of the natural identity of interests ; and, in a certain sense, their observation remains true. Every individual, we are told by the economists of the new school, is the best judge of his interests ; and the interests of all individuals are, as a general rule, identical. But there is nothing to prevent this identity from manifesting itself in the régime advocated by Bentham, since in it governmental authority is considered as emanating directly from the people, and the executive power as ' constituted ' by the will of all the interested parties. Only it is the principle of the artificial identification of interests which is constantly applied in the *Constitutional Code* : for Bentham demanded on the one hand a governmental authority, an administrative power, systematically to organise the defence of individual interests, while on the other hand he prescribed a series of constitutional artifices, which, by rigorously subordinating the governors to the governed, might prevent them from ever separating their particular interests from the interests of the nation. The State, as conceived by Bentham, is a machine so well constructed that every individual, taken individually, cannot for one instant escape from the control of all the individuals taken collectively.

CHAPTER III

THE LAWS OF THOUGHT AND THE RULES OF ACTION

IN a note, bearing the date of June 29, 1827, which has been preserved for us by his biographer Bowring, Bentham gives an abridged definition of the two principles of his doctrine : ' *Association Principle.*—Hartley. The bond of connection between ideas and language : and between ideas and ideas. *Greatest Happiness Principle.*—Priestley. Applied to every branch of morals in detail, by Bentham : a part of the way previously by Helvetius '.[1] The linking up of the two principles that was thus brought about reveals with what matters Bentham and his friends were preoccupied at this period. They felt that their social system would be incomplete so long as it was not based on a psychology and was not completed by a system of ethics.

The Philosophical Radicals wished to make social science a rational science ; they held that all social phenomena are reducible to laws, and that all the laws of the social world are in their turn explicable by the ' laws of human nature '. But the laws of human nature are themselves of two kinds : physical laws, the definition of which the economist and the jurist borrow from the physician, from the geologist and from the biologist, and psychological laws, whose very existence is still open to question. For many people question even the possibility of a scientific psychology, constituted on the pattern of the sciences of nature. The procedure which James Mill used to show that a scientific psychology is possible consisted in showing that it either existed already, or had begun to exist. According to him, Hartley had been the founder of it in the eighteenth century. Then the theories of Hartley had been completed by new discoveries. The part played by James Mill in the history of the new psychology is analogous, at all points, to the part played by Ricardo in the history

[1] Bowring, vol. x. p. 561.

of the new political economy. Ricardo brought Adam Smith's political economy up to date, taking into account the innovations of Malthus. James Mill, by his *Analysis of the Phenomena of the Human Mind*, which appeared in 1829, restored Hartley's psychology, incorporating with it the theories of Erasmus Darwin, Horne Tooke and Thomas Brown.

Once the general theory of the social man was completed and based on principles, it remained to make use of it and to transform it into a practical science. In the first place, it might be imagined that the advice of the Utilitarian philosopher would be exclusively addressed to the legislator, whose task it is to bring about the identity of all interests by artifices based on an exact knowledge of human nature. But Bentham did not think that the juristic State could play the part of an omniscient Providence and be able of itself to harmonise all interests. It is also necessary to have the co-operation of the individual wills which have become capable of identifiying their interest with the general interest ; and how are they to become capable of this otherwise than by the influence of an art, that is of morals itself ? It might also be imagined that the universal harmony of interests comes about spontaneously, without injunctions from the moralists, as also without the intervention of the legislators : the political economy of which Adam Smith defined the principles does, in the last analysis, authorise this anarchic conception of the social world. But the Malthusians had pointed out that the harmony of interests is brought about only on this condition, that individuals know what is their interest ; and they thought that a popular education given by the State was the only possible way of teaching them how to know it. Now, since this art of being egoistical and of understanding one's own interest well is capable of being methodically taught, is it not also, in a sense, a moral theory ? Bentham's *Deontology* and James Mill's *Analysis of the Phenomena of the Human Mind*, and *Fragment on Mackintosh*, make it possible to define the moral theory of the Utilitarians, and to determine its logical relations with their political economy, with their jurisprudence and with their political theory.

I.   KNOWLEDGE

From the time of Hartley until the publication of James Mill's book, the normal development of English thought seems to have passed, as it were, through a period of standstill : in 1810, one of Paley's editors lamented that no one in England was doing for the principle of the association of ideas what Paley had done for the principle of utility.[1] At the very time when this regret was expressed the man who was to bring about the necessary fusion of the two principles was already included among the group of Utilitarians. But he was as yet busy with other tasks.

[1] Meadley, *Life of Paley*, p. 83.

It is on the continent, in France, that the destinies of that philosophy
of which Bacon, Hobbes and Locke are universally held to be the
founders, must for the time being be followed up. Bentham's first
works were written and published in French, and it was in France and
in the other Latin-speaking countries, that they first made his name
popular. We have seen that England had few or no economists
between Adam Smith and Ricardo ; it was in France that the physiocratic school was most active in the organisation of the classical
political economy. In Great Britain, a confusion had arisen between
the psychology of association and the sceptical conclusions which
Hume had drawn from it ; and, at a time when the whole intellectual
life of the island seemed to be concentrated in Scotland, the scepticism of Hume was being eloquently refuted by the great professors
at Glasgow and Edinburgh. It was in France that from Condillac
up to Destutt de Tracy ideology continued the tradition of Locke and
Hume. James Mill had been the pupil and was long to remain the
disciple of Dugald Stewart, and it is a characteristic fact that he never
seems to have had a high opinion of Hume's works.[1] A philosopher
of an essentially dogmatic temperament, he held his pyrrhonism
condemned ; and as regards the criticism of the notion of cause or of
substance, whenever he seeks in his book to refer to some authority, he
invokes the authority not of Hume but of Thomas Brown,[2] the doctor,
man of letters and philosopher who brought about a sort of semi-
restoration of the discredited ideas of Hume at Edinburgh, and later
in the very chair which had been occupied by Dugald Stewart.[3] But
Brown had felt the influence of the French ideologists quite as much if
not more than that of Hume ; he borrowed so much from Destutt de
Tracy and from Laromiguière, that he has been accused of plagiarism;[4]
and in his lectures as in the lectures of his master, Dugald Stewart,
the sensualist philosophy was held to be the characteristic doctrine of
the French thinkers. ' Slight, ... as the distance is which
separates the two countries, the philosophy of France, in its views of
the phenomena of mind, and the philosophy of Britain, particularly of
this part of Britain, have for more than half a century differed as
much as the philosophy of different ages ; certainly in a degree far
greater than, but for experience, it would have been easy for us
to suppose. In France all the phenomena of mind have been
during that period, regarded as *sensations* or *transformed* sensations,
that is to say, as sensations variously simplified or combined '.[5]
Hartley's few English disciples, and the Benthamites in particular,
were well aware of this close affinity by which they were connected with the French contemporary philosophers. ' When an

[1] *Education*, p.11.   [2] *Analysis*, vol. ii. p. 329.
[3] See biography of Brown by David Welsh at the beginning of the *Lectures on the
Philosophy of the Human Mind*.
[4] Sir W. Hamilton, *Discussions on Philosophy and Literature*, etc. (3rd ed.), 1866,
p. 44.
[5] Brown, *Lecture xxxii*, p. 207-8.

Englishman and a Frenchman agree upon any point ', . . . ' there is a strong presumption that they are right ' : these are the opening words of a eulogistic article devoted to the *Théorie des Peines et des Récompenses* which Edgeworth vainly tried to get accepted by the *Quarterly Review* in 1814.[1]

As the Benthamites knew and valued the French thinkers, so did they ignore German thought, or else only knew it to detest it. The division between the two countries was a deep one ; and it was through the intermediary of the Frenchman Villers that Thomas Brown at Edinburgh,[2] and then James Mill in London, discovered the philosophy of Kant without appreciating or understanding it. The sympathy of the Utilitarians for the French ideologists, and their antipathy for the German metaphysicians were due to exactly the same causes. Bentham and James Mill were rationalists in the sense that they held that all the social sciences, and, as we shall see, the science of the mind on which they are based, were deductive sciences analogous to rational mechanics and to celestial mechanics. But it was for this very reason that they were shocked by the German philosophy, with its mystical definition of reason, and its scorn for the discursive processes of abstract understanding : they would doubtless have been prepared to agree with Mackintosh that Germany was ' metaphysically mad '.[3] There was another reason also why German thought was repugnant to them, namely that it was indifferent to research for principles and laws, and cared for the researches of learning, and for the purely historical sciences. They, on their side, were reformers ; and if they inquired into the facts, it was in order to draw from them principles which would in their turn be capable of modifying the facts. Twenty-five years earlier, Burke had denounced the metaphysics of the Rights of Man, and had taken his stand on history to defend the cause of the traditional monarchy. Now Burke had a school of followers in Germany ; and Bentham was just sufficiently acquainted with Burke's German disciples to know that he owed it to his principles to condemn them. ' The Germans ', he wrote, ' can only inquire about things as they were. They are interdicted from inquiring into things as they ought to be ' and, in more epigrammatic form : ' If you wish to follow the method of Savigny and his school, to the army and the navy of a country, substitute, for example, a history of the wars waged by that same country . . . to an order on the cook for dinner, substitute a fair copy of the housekeeper's book, as kept for and during the appropriate series of years '.[4] Thus was expressed the perfectly conscious hatred felt by a reforming and reasoning philosopher for a school whose tendencies were always to a certain extent traditionalistic and mys-

[1] Romilly to Dumont, May 26, 1814. *Memoirs*, vol. iii. p. 135 notes.
[2] *Ed. Rev.*, No. 11, Jan. 1803, art. i.
[3] Mackintosh to Dugald Stewart, Dec. 14, 1802.
[4] Bowring, vol. x. p. 562.

tical : a French ' Encyclopaedist ' or a French ' Ideologue ' would not have thought otherwise.

But the fact that Hume's ideas were discredited in England and Scotland and met with success in the France of the Revolution and of the Empire must not warrant the conclusion that James Mill's associationism was exclusively or even principally formed under French influence. He read and admired Helvetius, Condillac and Cabanis ; but he put Hartley much above Condillac, and Erasmus Darwin much above Cabanis ; and it would be difficult to say on what special points his psychology was inspired by Condillac or Cabanis.[1] It must not be thought, moreover, that he was the first in England to rediscover Hume and Hartley, after long years of obscurity. Actually, when James Mill had finished attending Dugald Stewart's lectures at Edinburgh University, and left Scotland to come to London, he found the tradition of Hume and particularly of Hartley faithfully upheld by two or three little groups of disciples.[2] Stuart Mill tells us that ' at an early period of Mr. Mill's philosophical life ',[3] Hartley's work had taken a strong hold of his mind. Now, at what date should the ' philosophical life ' of James Mill be taken to begin ? Was it at the time when, in 1807, he joined himself to Bentham, who although he did not make philosophical problems the special object of his study, had long regarded himself as a disciple of Hartley ? But at Edinburgh, and during the first years of his life in London, he had already displayed a very definite taste for the questions of psychology and morals ; yet at this period he remained the faithful disciple of Dugald Stewart. What, then, was the story of his conversion, and by what series of influences should it be explained ? At what time did he become acquainted with and begin to appreciate the works of the disciples of Hartley ? This is the problem which is of interest to us. To analyse these influences will be the best way of determining what were the fundamental ideas and the controlling hypotheses in the logic of the new doctrine ; it will at the same time show up whatever is new in James Mill's book in relation to Hume and to Hartley. For James Mill was not an inventor in psychology any more than in political economy : the fact that he was held to be the ' second founder ' of the psychology of association was not due to the originality of his discoveries, but to the power of his faculties of assimilation and exposition, and also to the advantages of the position which he occupied, at Bentham's side, at the very heart of the Radical and innovating propaganda.

While James Mill was studying at Edinburgh, and was seeking a vocation, finally choosing the method of seeking his fortune in London, the members of the Unitarian sect were preserving intact the legacy of the Unitarian and associationist philosophy which had been left them by Priestley. For Cooper, for Cogan, for Belsham,

---

[1] *Education*, pp. 20-21.
[2] Brown, *Lecture* xliii. p. 279.   [3] *Analysis*, Preface, p. xvii.

and for Carpenter,[1] Hartley was still the infallible master, and Priestley his authorised interpreter, until the time, some years later, when the reaction of spiritual enthusiasm was brought about in the sect by Channing.   The religion which they advocated was something like the religion of Voltaire, the religion of common-sense and of natural light.   They were determinists : but is not the dogma of Providence favourable to the determinist thesis ?   They were materialists, and held that ' matter can think ' : but is it necessary to have a spiritual substance of a simple nature, to make a future existence possible ?   If you take particles of matter exactly similar in number, kind, situation and properties as those which made up a man at the moment of his decease, it will necessarily happen, so Cooper tells us, that the being formed of them will have the same knowledge, the same passions, as those which were enjoyed by the vanished being ; he will therefore be subject to the same motives of action, and capable to the same degree of reward and punishment.[2]   In the last analysis, is not the dogma of the resurrection of the body a materialistic dogma ?

Thomas Belsham published in 1801, under the title *Elements of the Philosophy of the Mind and of Moral Philosophy*, a brief manual of logic, psychology and morals.   He warns the reader in his preface that he had tried to study Kant in his commentators, but had not succeeded in understanding him, and so had chosen to make no mention of his work : he wishes to popularise ' the doctrine of Association, opened by Locke, improved by Gay, matured by Hartley, and illustrated by the luminous disquisitions of Dr. Priestley ' ; [3] and in his book, as in all the writings of the Unitarians, there is an equivocal mixture of positivism and religiosity.   He first insists on the social importance of the new psychology, which ' not only qualifies the well-informed and sagacious statesman to judge correctly of the true interest of the community at large, but teaches him how to guide the various passions and contending interests of parties, and of individuals, to the general good '.[4]   But he does not forget that the true end of his associationist, Utilitarian, determinist and materialist exposition, is to edify the reader : for ' just views of human nature, and of moral obligation, have a tendency to impress upon the mind a proper sense of the inestimable value of the Christian revelation, which places the doctrine of a future life upon the only foundation which true philosophy can approve, a resurrection of the dead ' ; [5] James Mill, in May 1802, in the *Anti-Jacobin Review*,[6] analysed Belsham's recently published book ; this was perhaps the first time

---

[1] Cooper, *Tracts*, Cogan (Thos.), *A Philosophical Treatise on the Passions*, 1800, *Ethical Questions*, 1817.   Belsham (Thos.), *Elements of the Philosophy of the Mind and Moral Philosophy*, 1801.   Carpenter (Lant), *Mental and Moral Philosophy, Systematic Education*.

[2] Cooper, *op. cit.* pp. 455-6.   [3] Belsham, *Elements*, p. iii.
[4] Belsham, *Elements*, p. 4.   [5] *Ibid.* p. vi.   [6] May 1802, pp. 1 *seq.*

that he had had an opportunity of studying Hartley's philosophy directly, and of no longer knowing it merely through academic refutations. He judged it severely, and to its hypotheses, which he considered simplifying and gratuitous, he opposed the method of observation applied by Reid and Dugald Stewart, which on his view was more prudent and more certain. Four years later he was still denouncing a materialism which, ' whether cast in the mould of Helvetius or Hartley, appears to us equally abhorrent from reason, and mischievous in tendency '.[1] Then he became intimate with Bentham, became a Hartleyan, and accused Priestley's school of having helped to discredit the philosophy of association : for Priestley, on his view, ' was neither sufficiently acquainted with the science, nor sufficiently capable of patient, close, and subtle thinking, to go to the bottom of the principles which he attacked ; nor could he avoid such displays of ignorance and self-delusion, as afforded a colour to Dr. Reid and his followers for treating the book with contempt, and holding themselves exempt from the obligation of answering its objections '.[2] From this, according to James Mill, resulted the stagnation of philosophical studies in England. But was it not from a disciple of Priestley that he had learnt the first elements of the new doctrine ? Did he not recognise later his debt to Belsham's book ? ' Even Mr. Belsham,' he wrote in his *Fragment on Mackintosh*, ' though not a metaphysician of much power, clearly understood the scope of Dr. Hartley's investigation, and added some useful reflections '.[3]

While the ministers of Unitarianism confined themselves to popularising Hartley's philosophy, other writers were attempting to develop it, to deepen it and to apply its principles to the solution of new problems. It is an inherent tendency of this philosophy in some sense to materialise thought in order to find for the invisible and intangible psychological phenomenon, some palpable equivalent which can get hold of the methodical observations of the enquirer. The nervous element, for example, may be considered as the sign, or as the cause, or even as the substance of the psychological phenomenon. The word, again, is the sign, and in certain cases may even be considered as the substance of the idea. Erasmus Darwin suggested a physiological, and Horne Tooke a philological theory of the phenomena of the mind ; and their two theories, which are discredited to-day, had much success in England during some twenty years. Belsham quoted Darwin and Tooke in his *Manual of Hartleyan Philosophy*.[4] James Mill had probably been acquainted with Darwin's theory at the time when, as a student at Edinburgh, he saw it refuted near at hand by the young Thomas Brown ; some years later, he analysed and discussed, in the *Literary Journal*, the second edition of Tooke's book. The two authors exerted an influence

---

[1] *Literary Journal*, Jan. 1806, art. i.   [2] *British Rev.*, No. xi. Aug. 1815, p. 175.
[3] *Fragment on Mackintosh*, p. 323.   [4] See especially pp. 48, 114, 190, 191.

on the development of his thought, and consequently, through him, on the restoration of the associationist psychology.

When editing Hartley, Priestley had tried to show that the physiological theory of vibrations and the psychological theory of association were two distinct theories, and that, though they might be able to confirm each other, the abandoning of the one did not necessarily imply the falsity of the other.[1]   But Hartley had too often spoken of sensations and of their combinations in physiological language for one not to be tempted to follow him and transform the psychology of the association of ideas into a psychophysiology.   In 1794, Dr. Erasmus Darwin, in *Zoonomia*, or treatise on *The Laws of Organic Life*,[2] while he did not deny the distinction between matter and mind, put aside mind,[3] and, in the study which he made of sensations, ideas and their combinations, considered only the biological side of these phenomena, and therefore held himself authorised to employ the language of the psychologists in a purely physiological sense. Further, he rejected the theory of vibrations, by which Hartley, basing himself on the analogy of the laws of optics, had sought to explain nervous phenomena, and lamented precisely this, that modern enquirers, instead of studying the phenomena of life as they were given them in nature, were wasting their time in trying to reduce the laws of life to those of mechanics or of chemistry.[4]   In order for the particles of muscular fibre to affect each other in the phenomena of contraction, the existence of an intermediary agent is no doubt necessary ; in fact ' *nothing can act, where it does not exist ; for to act includes to exist* ' ; but Darwin did not think that the scientist either could, or ought to, give an opinion on the question whether this ' spirit of animation ' is a material fluid, analogous to electricity, or a spiritual power.[5]   In any case, in the theory ' founded upon nature ' by means of which he proposed to ' bind together the scattered facts of medical knowledge, and converge into one point of view the laws of organic life ',[6] he considered the laws of life as special laws, vital movements being as distinguishable from chemical movements, as chemical movements are from movements of gravitation.   He restricted himself to defining the different kinds of movement of which organic phenomena are capable—*irritation, sensation, volition, association* ;[7] and he resumed, from a biological point of view, Hartley's psychological theories of intelligence and action. ' The sensorial power is produced in the brain and spinal marrow by the fibrous actions of those glands like other secretions '.[8]   The word *idea* is used for ' those notions of external things, which our organs of sense bring us acquainted with originally ; and is defined a con-

---

[1] See above part i. ch. i.
[2] *Zoonomia, or the Laws of Organic Life* ; 4 vols, 1794-6.
[3] *Ibid.* sect. i.   [4] *Ibid.* 1794 Preface, p. viii.   [5] *Ibid.* sect. xii. p. 1 §i.
[6] *Ibid.* 1794 Preface, p. viii.   [7] *Ibid.* sect. v   [8] *Ibid.* sect. xii., viii.

traction, or motion, or configuration, of the fibres, which constitute the immediate organ of sense '.[1]   And it is a purely material resemblance between the external object and the sensitive organ, as modified by the presence of the external object, which, for Darwin, explains perception.[2]   Moreover, the movements of the organism are associated one with another in conformity with the law of habit, which states that ' all animal motions which have occurred at the same time, or in immediate succession, become so connected, that when one of them is reproduced, the other has a tendency to accompany or to succeed it ' : and it is by means of this law that Darwin thought he could explain, in his capacity as a doctor, ' the more recondite phenomena of the production, growth, diseases, and decay of the animal system '.[3]   Thomas Brown won his first success as a writer by criticising in Darwin both his materialistic theory of perception, and the view that an intermediary fluid of unknown nature is necessary to explain the action of the cause on the effect.[4]   It is, however, through Darwin that Brown first came to learn all that his psychology owes to Hartley, just in the same way as James Mill, in his turn, borrowed from Darwin through Brown.   Darwin's book does indeed contain enough interesting observations—we may mention in particular his reflections on the phenomena of vision,[5] or again on the origin of instinct [6]—to justify the success which it secured, in spite of its many erroneous medical theories, and of the author's philosophical inexperience.

But Darwin's book strikes us as important chiefly in that it marks the point of bifurcation in the ideas which make up the school of Hartley. Supposing that we do in fact consider Hartley's theory as being essentially a physiological theory : then, on this theory, I am conceived first as a being who acts and is acted upon,[7] before gradually becoming a conscious being, capable of feeling, and of distinguishing and organising its perceptions.   Suppose, on the contrary, that we consider this theory under its psychological aspect : in this case, I appear to myself, first as experiencing separate and interrupted sensations, and then as progressively succeeding in forming out of these sensations, isolated from each other, a continuous image of a spatial universe.   The second of these was James Mill's interpretation : at times, however, the first tendency reappears in his writings.   He himself acknowledges [8] that he borrowed his theory of the genesis of the notion of space from Hartley, Darwin and Brown : but what was the problem which first inspired the inventors of this theory ?   They

[1] *Zoonomia, or the Laws of Organic Life*, sect. ii., 7.
[2] *Ibid*. sect. xiv. pp. ii. 4.   [3] *Ibid*. sect. iv., vii.
[4] *Observations on the Zoonomia of Erasmus Darwin*, by Thos. Brown, Preface, pp. xvi, xvii.
[5] *Ibid*. sect. iii.   [6] *Ibid*. sect. xvi.
[7] *Observations on the Zoonomia of Erasmus Darwin*, by Thos. Brown, sect. xv., 4.
[8] *Analysis*, ch. i, sect. vii.

wished to explain the notion of the continuous by the apparent fusion of a multitude of small discontinuous sensations into one unique sensation. It was for this reason that Berkeley, the first of this school, concentrated on proving that the sense of vision does not immediately provide us with the notion of a continuous extension, and that the visual sensations only appear immediately as sensations of extension by reason of their close association with tactual sensations. Should the same be said then of tactual sensations as was previously said of visual sensations, namely, that they provide us immediately with the notion of a continuous extension ? In this case the difficulty has only been put off one stage ; and it was to overcome it once again that first Brown and then James Mill, continuing the analysis begun by Berkeley, explained the formation of the notion of space by an association which is brought about between tactual sensations, properly so-called, and muscular sensations. But what are these same muscular sensations, the idea of which is borrowed by Brown and James Mill from the physiology of Hartley and Darwin ? When one of our muscles contracts, certain parts of our muscles rub against certain others : on this hypothesis, are muscular sensations anything else than internal sensations of touch, which we then have to experience in the different parts of the muscle—that is, sensations which are not specifically distinguishable from those which we experience when the external parts of our body come into contact with other bodies ? And does this not amount to repeating, in a roundabout way, that it is tactual sensations which give us the notion of extension ? Or else, we introduce into the notion of a muscular sense the notion either of an accomplished voluntary effort, or only of a movement of the organisms : we therefore attribute to muscular sense the particular character of feeling extension immediately. But in this case we have not solved the problem, which was set by Berkeley, of explaining the sensation of the continuous by an adding up of discontinuous sensations. We insist on the physiological and no longer on the psychological side of the theory, and conceive the conscious being as first capable of continuous movements, and subsequently becoming aware of these movements until he finally becomes capable of forming isolated and discontinuous sensations. We are explaining the formation of the notion of space only by introducing a special kind of sensation, termed muscular, whose hypothetical function would be immediately to perceive the continuity of the organic movements, and would thus amount to being literally a *sense of the continuous*.

In order to make this better understood, let us follow the history of the theory of muscular sense from Hartley to James Mill. To the senses of sight and hearing, of taste and smell, Hartley opposed what he called *feeling*, grouping under this heading all the sensations which are not seated in a definitely localised organ. In feeling itself, he distinguished between general feeling, which includes the sum of the organic sensations, and particular feeling, which is more particularly localised in the hands and fingers, by means of which we distinguish ' heat, cold, moisture, dryness, softness, hardness, smoothness, roughness, also their motion, rest, distance and figure '.[1] Now, according to Hartley, all these impressions are really sensations of pressure, which in their turn are really sensations of muscular contraction, which we experience when in the act of handling or of walking ', we overcome the *vis inertiæ* ... of matter '.[2] Thus, while Hartley discovered muscular sense, he did not distinguish it from the sense of touch ; it would be truer to say that he defined tactual sense as muscular sense. It was on this point that Darwin, in terms which are, however, confused and crude, added something to Hartley. He distinguished between the tactual sense and the muscular sense. To the tactual sense, defined as Hartley defined it as the sense of pressure, he attributed the perception of the figure and solidity of objects, whether we exert a pressure of the organ of touch against the solid body, or whether we make the organ move along the surface of the body.[3] But ' the sense of pressure is always attended with the ideas of the figure and solidity of the object, neither of which accompany our perception of extension '.[4] It was here that Darwin introduced a new sense. ' The whole set of muscles, whether they are hollow ones, as the heart, arteries, and intestines, or longitudinal ones . . . may be considered as one organ of sense, and the various attitudes of the body, as ideas belonging to this organ '.[5] This is the muscular sense which, according to Darwin, is the sense of extension.

We have here all the elements of Brown's much more subtle analysis. Before explaining how, out of discontinuous sensations, we make up the notion of a continuous space, he multiplied the number and varieties of elementary sensations. Like Darwin, he distinguished between the sense of pressure and the sense of extension ; but he went further than Darwin and held [6] that tactual sensations properly so-called could not be reduced either to sensations of pressure or to the sensation of extension. For if, he says, you gently apply the point of a needle to the surface of the skin, you will receive an impression, and you will not receive either the impression that this sensation occupies a place, or the impression that a pressure is exerted on the epidermis. What then is the origin of the notion of space ? In the first place, by the fact that we experience successively, and can recall our sensations, we have the idea of time, that is to say, we have, not metaphorically but absolutely, the notion of length or of space with one dimension. It remains to be seen how we pass from this simple idea to the more complex idea of a plurality of directions in space : and the problem is solved when we consider that in simultaneously contracting the muscles of several fingers, for example, we

[1] *On Man*, Prop. xxviii. [2] *On Man*, Prop. xxvii, xxx. [3] *Zoonomia*, sect. xiv, ii. 1.
[4] *Ibid.* sect. xiv., vii. [5] *Ibid.* sect. xiv., vii. [6] *Ibid.* xxii-xxiv.

at the same time experience several series of muscular sensations, or again, in other words, we feel at the same instant several lengths or several directions.   But why are muscular rather than tactual, or even visual or auditory, sensations necessary to provide us with the idea of a space of several dimensions out of the idea of several simultaneous series of sensations ?   The reason, according to Brown, is that muscular sense is necessary in order to provide us with the second essential notion of our idea of a material space : the idea of resistance, which is inseparable from the sensation of pressure, the idea of the resistance ' which impedes our continued effort, and impedes it *variously*, as the substances without are themselves various '.[1]   This is to say once more, after a detour, that the muscular sense is a sense which is essential to our acquisition of the notion of space, because, in contrast to the other senses, it is the sense of the continuous.

James Mill borrowed from Brown his analysis of the notion of extension.   More explicitly still, he proposed to reduce the appearance of continuity to a very rapid succession of discontinuous sensations.   On the other hand, he neglected the idea of time in his analysis of the idea of space : consequently he attached a still greater importance to muscular sensations, and found himself faced with the same difficulty.   No doubt he took care to separate the idea of muscular sensation from the idea of a sensation of voluntary effort ; [2] but the idea of the sensation of a continuous movement always remains.   No doubt he carefully dismembered the impression which we experience of the movement of our muscles into a series of distinct sensations.   I touch a point on a body : first ' state of feeling '.   I give my finger ' the smallest perceptible motion ' : second state of feeling.   And so on until at last ' the antecedent states are in each instance united with the present by memory, and by the amount of the states, thus united, the amount of the motion is computed '.[3] But it remains true that each one of these ' states of feeling ', taken in isolation, gives us the impression of a continuous movement, and in order to represent by an image the succession of states of the soul here described by James Mill, its symbol would have to be not a series of isolated points, but a line interrupted at intervals : in his theory, the idea of a perfect continuity is reconstructed from an imperfect continuity, and not from a perfect discontinuity.   The result is that, in the end, by the very fact that he attributes so great an importance to muscular sense in his analysis of mental phenomena, James Mill seems to contradict his own conception of the explanation in psychology.   ' Of course, the thing precedes the name ', he writes in his analysis of the idea of division.   ' Men divided, before they named the act, or the consequences of the act.   In the act of division, or in the results of it, no mystery has ever been understood to reside. . . . The act of dividing, like all the other acts of our body, consists

[1] *Lecture* xxii. p. 134.   [2] *Analysis*, ch. ii. vol. i. p. 57.
[3] *Ibid*. ch. xiv. sect. vi. vol. ii. p. 145.

in the contraction and relaxation of certain muscles '. It seems, on James Mill's own avowal, to be actions and tensions of our muscles which form the continuous foundation from which is detached the unravelled system of our sensations. But James Mill, after immediately adding that the muscular movements ' are known to us, like everything else, by the feelings ', finally concludes that ' the act, as act, is the feelings ; and only when confounded with its results, is it conceived to be anything else '.[1] Thus, once more, the whole mental life is reduced to a collection of discontinuous sensations ; even the notion of muscular action and of continuous movement, is now only an appearance, and consists in reality in the fusion of a very great number of discontinuous sensations.

Whereas Darwin, as it were, sinks the soul in the body, and transforms Hartley's psychology into a physiology, Horne Tooke absorbs the idea in the word, and transforms Hobbes' psychology into a philology. Hobbes was the founder of modern nominalism in England ; James Mill, who admired him profoundly,[2] reproduced almost word for word his reflections on language,[3] which have become classical.[4] When a name is used not as a proper name, but as a common name, says Hobbes, and serves to designate one or other of the objects of a group, we say that it is a ' universal ' name ; but this name ' universal ' does not correspond to any reality in nature, it is the property of a name, the name of a name, and ' nothing else ' : there exist only individual beings, individuals make up the whole reality of the general idea.[5] But meanwhile, in the new subjectivism which emerged from the Cartesian revolution, the general idea was conceived if not as an objective reality, at least as the product of an original operation of the mind, of an elaboration of things by thought ; moreover, there were also still to be found thinkers— such as the grammarian philosopher Harris in his *Hermes*—who defended the thesis of Platonic idealism, understood in the traditional manner. In order to re-establish the nominalistic thesis against these hostile tendencies, Horne Tooke found himself led to improve further on the nominalism of Hobbes.

In his *Diversions of Purley*,[6] he assigns to language a new function, which he holds essential, to which, however, Hobbes neglected to call attention : the function of abbreviation. We experience an almost unlimited number of sensible impressions ; we should never have done, if we tried to think of a distinct sign to designate each one of these impressions by itself ; but we use one word to designate several, and this is the great rôle played by language, the rôle of economy.

---

[1] *Analysis*, ch. xiv. sect. ii. vol. ii. p. 467.

[2] *Education*, pp. 9-10. *Fragment on Mackintosh*, pp. 19-20.

[3] Cf. Hobbes, *Computatio sive Logica*, pars i. cap. ii., and *Analysis*, ch. iv.

[4] Hobbes' theory is resumed by Dugald Stewart, Thos. Brown, etc.

[5] Cf. *Comp. sive Log.*, pars i. cap. i.

[6] ΕΠΕΑ ΠΤΕΡΟΕΝΤΑ ; *or the Diversions of Purley*, by John Horne Tooke (1st ed.), 1787.

It is no longer enough to say, with Hobbes, that there is no *general idea*, since all realities are individual ; it must be said also that there is no *complex idea*, since all realities are simple sense impressions. If Locke had understood the true function of language, says Tooke, he would not have spoken of the ' composition of ideas ' ; you might as well speak of a ' complex star ' to designate a constellation, as of a ' complex idea ' to designate a collection of simple ideas ; it is not the ideas, but the terms which are general and abstract.[1] Neither is it of any use to consider the different parts of speech as corresponding to so many original and distinct operations of the mind. There is a ' trifling ' or ' childish ' etymology, which confines itself to going back from an English word to a French word, and from a French word to a Latin word, and so on without ever throwing any light on the meaning of the word used ;[2] but there is another etymology whose philosophical importance is greater than this. It shows us words changing their meaning and their position in grammar as a whole. It shows us, at the origin of all words, substantives which, having first designated concrete and particular things, end by being used in the most varied meanings and playing the part of ' parts of speech ' which appear to be utterly irreducible to one another ; it is in this way that former substantives have become for us adjectives, prepositions, and conjunctions. Then it seems that, in the formation of language there occurs, according to Horne Tooke, a movement in the opposite direction. Certain words used adjectivally, that is to say, in association with substantives, have been detached afresh from their habitual context and thereafter, set up as substantives owing to the fact that the substantive which ought to have accompanied them was understood, they have created the illusion of being independents, of existing apart from the concrete realities : abstraction is an ellipse.[3]

In short, in its primitive state of simplicity and clarity, among savage peoples, language only consists of an aggregate of isolated signs, which designate so many sensible impressions. To-day, to anyone who studies it etymologically, and goes back to the original meaning of the words which we use without thinking, it is still the same, although it appears to us as an articulate system of general names and of signs designating abstract relations. Hence the purely verbal illusion which has produced faulty metaphysics.[4] Language ceases to be the faithful image of things, and becomes a map of them on a reduced scale, or, if you like, a stenography ; and, for this very reason, it ends by appearing to have an existence independent of the things which it reflects. There are thought to be mental syntheses where there are only verbal syntheses ; there is thought to be the

---

[1] ΕΠΕΑ ΠΤΕΡΟΕΝΤΑ ; *or the Diversions of Purley*, by John Horne Tooke (1st ed.), 1787, part i. ch. ii.

[2] *Ibid*. part ii. ch. iv.   [3] Subaudition, *Diversions of Purley*, part ii. ch. iv.

[4] *Ibid*. part i. ch. ix.

unity of a spiritual act where there is only the unity of a word ; and the critique of the faculties of the understanding is undertaken, where nothing but a critique of the forms of language is necessary.[1] In 1806, in his *Literary Journal*, James Mill analysed the second edition of Tooke's book : he was still a disciple of the Scottish philosophers, and was alarmed at seeing the philosophy of Tooke leading to the nefarious system of Helvetius and Hartley. But already, although he made reservations in regard to Horne Tooke's philosophy, he gave his adherence to his etymological system.[2] Two years later, when he had become Bentham's disciple and lieutenant, we find him insinuating that, as regards the nature of the abstract idea, Dugald Stewart and Horne Tooke in the end think very much alike, and that their theory must be applied to the criticism of economic terminology.[3] His philosophical conversion seems to date from this same year : it can thus be seen how great may have been the influence exerted on him by Tooke's work at this critical moment of his history.[4] Twenty years later, in his work on psychology, he borrowed from Tooke both his theory of the origin of the parts of speech,[5] and his theory of abstraction.[6]

Now it is a question whether the theory of abstraction, which James Mill borrowed from Horne Tooke, does not introduce into his psychology a kind of contradiction, which it is important to define if the difficulties inherent in his method are to be well understood. According to James Mill, certain terms, namely adjectives, are always used to ' note ' certain sensible impressions and to ' connote ' others ; the word ' black ' directly designates a certain colour, but it implies that this colour has always been perceived as the colour of a thing, of a horse, of a man, and so on. To form an abstract idea of black, taken substantivally, is to let go all the accessory ideas ' connoted ' by the adjective, and to retain only the idea directly designated by the adjective. What does this mean if not that we first perceive sensible impressions in close connection, in time and space, with other sensations whose number extends step by step to infinity ; and that we only detach simple impressions from this context subsequently, in a rather artificial and factitious manner ? But the theory of the complex idea as Horne Tooke rigorously develops it, taking his stand on the very postulates of the associationist psychology, leads to opposite results. In the terms of this theory, we begin by experiencing isolated sensible impressions, which we only afterwards learn to group, so as to compose of them so-called ' complex ideas ', whose artificial and fictitious existence corresponds in reality to nothing but the unity of a word. In other words what is the simple element in which his analysis results, that is, *this sensation of red or of blue?* is it this

---

[1] See conclusion of the letter to Dunning of 1788.
[2] *The Literary Journal*, Jan. 1806, art. i., pp. 3 *seq*-p. 11.
[3] *Ed. Rev.*, Oct. 1808, p. 44.   [4] Mill to Place, Sept. 6, 1815.
[5] *Analysis*, ch. iv.   [6] *Ibid*. ch. ix.

determinate sensation, inseparable from its antecedents and from its
consequences, localised in time and space, a particular thing, an
individual essence ? or is it this determinate sensation, irreducible,
by virtue of its own nature, to any other sensible qualities, even to the
shades closest to red and blue, a mode of existence of the mind, a
simple quality ? If the first interpretation be adopted, the associationist psychology constitutes a kind of realism, or latent materialism; if
the second be adopted, it constitutes a sort of sensationalist Platonism.
But James Mill does not choose between these two interpretations : [1]
he does not even seem to be aware that there are two such alternatives.
At bottom, the two interpretations correspond to two equally strong
tendencies in his thought.   He wants what is primitive to be simple :
failing this, there can, in his view, be no possible explanation.   He
also wants what is primitive to be concrete : failing this his philosophy
would cease to be a philosophy of experience.   What then could be
done, if it were to appear that the abstract were the simple ?

Still James Mill did not push the nominalist thesis to the paradoxical limits to which it had been pushed by Horne Tooke. Like
Locke and like Hartley, and without taking Horne Tooke's criticism
into account, he still used the term ' complex idea ' to designate a
multiplicity of associated ideas ; [2] he held that there exist true psychological combinations, in which several ideas, originally distinct, are
resolved into one single idea ; and on this point the individual
influence exerted by Horne Tooke's book may have been counter-
balanced by another influence, exerted in an opposite direction, and
both more general and more profound.   In the chronological interval
separating James Mill's book from those of Hume and Hartley, a new
science, with its own categories and its irreducible elements, had been
established ; and one of the men who had founded it in England had
been no other than Priestley, the propagator of Hartley's philosophy.
Chemistry confirmed the Newtonian conception of nature, as distinguished from the Cartesian physics : once again, it appeared that
causal connection was not an intelligible link between cause and
effect, and that it was not possible to guess at the effect in the cause—
at the properties of water, for example, in the qualities of oxygen and
hydrogen.   Even if Newtonian science had allowed the hope to
survive that all the laws of nature might be deduced from the single
law of attraction, it now appeared that it was necessary on the one
hand to multiply the number of elements and laws, and on the other
to admit the production, by means of combination, of new bodies, in
cases where simple mechanical processes are powerless to separate
the elements.   But, since the seventeenth century, the science of the
phenomena of mental life seems always to have taken for its model
the sciences of nature, as they were conceived by contemporary

[1] See *Analysis*, ch. xi.
[2] His expressions are ambiguous, see *Analysis*, ch. iii.

scholars. Is there not then a presumption that the advances of chemistry had reacted on those of psychology ? The hypothesis is confirmed by the facts.

In order to refute the simplifying psychologists of the French philosophical school, who took their cue from Hume and Condillac, the Scottish university professors liked to develop the thesis that the advance of the sciences is not necessarily an advance in simplification, that the ' chemistry ' of the Ionian philosophers, of the Aristotelians and of the alchemists had been much more satisfactory as regards our demand for unity than was the new chemistry, and yet that the latter was much more in conformity with natural reality.[1] Although Thomas Brown was more akin to the ideologists, he brought the same objection against them,[2] and defined psychology as a science analogous to chemistry, as an ' intellectual analysis ' analogous to ' the analysis of bodies '. Now James Mill had long been a disciple of Dugald Stewart ; he was living at Edinburgh and attending the university at the time when Brown, in the same town and at the same university, was first making himself known. In addition, he made a special study of chemistry under the direction of Thomson, who was his intimate friend as well as Brown's :[3] one of the first articles which he published after his arrival in London he devoted to Thomson's recently published treatise on that science whose object it is to en-quire what are the simple uncompounded ingredients of which bodies are constituted, how these simple bodies act upon one another, how by means of combination they form the diverse substances which make up our universe, and what new bodies they are capable of forming as the result of artificial combinations.[4] Much later, he boasted, almost as if it were a discovery, of having established the importance in the life of the mind of these ' inseparable ', ' indis-soluble ' associations,[5] in which the mind cannot even by the greatest efforts isolate the component ideas. This declaration is surprising : for this theory is explicitly formulated in Hartley.[6] But, in holding that the idea was a new one, was he not yielding to the prestige which was being exerted on the minds of all men, by the newly established chemical science, which was giving a new force and a new aspect to an old hypothesis ?

Such were the contemporary influences which may have had an effect on the formation of the philosophical thought of James Mill. Bentham's influence alone still remains to be mentioned ; and in defining the influence exerted by him on James Mill recourse must always be had to the same formula. No doubt, if Bentham had never

[1] Dugald Stewart, *Essays* (Works, vol. v. pp. 13-15).
[2] *Lecture* xxxii. pp. 20 *seq.*
[3] In 1803 we see James Mill making use of Thomson to secure Brown's collabora-tion in the *Literary Journal*.
[4] *Anti-Jacobin Review and Magazine*, June 1802, vol. xii. p. 164
[5] *Fragment on Mackintosh*, pp. 172-3.   [6] Cf. Hartley, Prop. xii.

become acquainted with James Mill, Benthamism would never have become aware of the philosophical principles on which it is based. But certainly, if James Mill had never known Bentham, he would never have become the doctrinaire of the philosophy of the association of ideas and general utility. It was in 1815, at the moment when the question of pedagogic reform was perhaps making a preliminary philosophical reform appear urgent to the Benthamites, that we find him for the first time devoting himself in a considered manner to the study of psychology. ' I was glad ', Francis Place writes to him, ' to hear what you said of Berkeley, Hume, Reid, Stewart, etc. Still more so in contemplating the possibility of your writing a book some day on this subject ; which, after all that has been said against it, and after all the contempt with which those to whom close thinking is irksome beyond endurance affect to treat it, is the master science ; without it no man I suspect ever was a good moral or political reasoner '.[1] A few days later, James Mill published his reflections on Locke, Berkeley, Hume, Reid and Stewart, in an article in the *British Review*. He definitely broke with his master in Edinburgh, and took up against him the defence of the principle of the association of ideas. What, he asked, are these ' laws of thought ', which, according to Dugald Stewart, are ' implied in every act of thought ' ? The only implication which is intelligible to the philosopher is the connection between ideas which are associated empirically. While avoiding compromising the publication in which his anonymous article appeared by a too clear-cut declaration of principle, he showed how it would be possible to plead the cause of Utilitarian morality, and blamed Stewart for not having mentioned Bentham among the doctrinaires of utility whom he judged worthy of refutation. He set out to justify the empiricist theory, and reproached Dugald Stewart for not having seen that this was the conclusion to which his own theory of abstraction and of general terms naturally led. ' Excepting sense and consciousness, however, which are occupied about particular truths, we have no intellectual faculties but those which are occupied about *general* truths. But we have already seen, that the only *real* truths with which we are acquainted are particular truths. General truths are merely fictions of the human mind, contrived to assist us in remembering and speaking about particular truths. According to Mr. Stewart's chapter on abstraction, it therefore appears, that matter and mind belong to the class of fictions '.[2]

Henceforward the idea of the psychological work which he meant to write continually obsessed his mind. ' His (Hartley's) doctrine of vibration is altogether gratuitous ', he wrote to Place in 1818,[3] ' but I think I shall one day be able to make it appear that the account

---

[1] Brit. Mus. Add MSS., 33,152 f. p. 141.   Place to Mill, July 20, 1815.
[2] *Brit. Rev.*, No. xi., Aug. 1815 (p. 190).
[3] Brit. Mus. Add MSS. 33,152 f. p. 161.   Mill to Place, Sept. 6, 1818.

he gives of the world of ideas is the true one. He himself is an obscure and a very dull writer ; and hitherto readers, such as he required, have been very few. But his doctrine might be put in a point of view so clear and striking, that metaphysics thereafter would not be very mysterious '. A year later he embarked on Kant, and read him without interest and without being shaken in his conviction : ' I see clearly enough what poor Kant is about—but it would require no little pains to give an account of him. I have given a hasty reading to Hartley since I came here. Hartley's is the true scent ; but his book is obscurely written ; and it will require no little prose-writing to render the application of his theory perfectly familiar to any mind in every part of the field of thought. This I shall be going on doing, doing—but how long it will take to be being done will depend upon many circumstances '.[1] Thirteen more years were required for the completion of this work which, according to James Mill, was destined to make ' *the human mind as plain as the road from Charing Cross to St Paul's* ',[2] Meanwhile James Mill was practising and getting under way, first by a semi-pedagogic and semi-philosophical article on *Education* which he published in 1818, and then by the lessons in logic and philosophy which he gave to his son Stuart Mill from 1818 to 1822. From 1822 to 1829, seven consecutive vacations were turned to account by him in order finally to bring his task to a satisfactory conclusion.[3]

The *Analysis of the Phenomena of the Human Mind* fixed for the Benthamites what James Mill called ' the exposition ' or again ' the theory ' of the mind. Further, James Mill warns us with regard to the meaning which he wished to be given to the word ' theory ' : he wished the theorist to confine himself to ' observing, and correctly recording the matters observed ' . . . ' Unhappily ', he added, ' the word Theory has been perverted to denote an operation very different from this, an operation by which *viewing—observing*—is superseded ; an operation which essentially consists in *supposing, and setting down matters supposed as matters observed*. Theory, in fact, has been confounded with Hypothesis '.[4] There is at present no use in summing up the theory of psychological phenomena as it is expounded by James Mill ; for it may be accepted that it does not include anything which is not to be found in Hartley, in Darwin, in Tooke or in Brown ; but the question may be asked whether it does really constitute a theory, in the purely empirical sense in which James Mill wished the word to be understood. In order to define the logical attitude adopted by the whole Utilitarian group, it is indispensable to understand the view of the accredited philosopher of Benthamism as

[1] Brit. Mus. Add MSS. 33,152 f. 220. Mill to Place, Oct. 8, 1816.
[2] Brit. Mus. Add MSS. 33,155. Mill to Place, Dec. 6, 1817.
[3] *Autobiography*, pp. 68-69.
[4] *Analysis*, ch. xxv.

regards the method to be employed in psychology, and, in a more general way, as regards scientific explanation as a whole.

What ought to be expected of an explanation of psychological phenomena ? And, at the outset, what ought we to understand in general, by explanation ? If recourse be had to the analogy of explanation as it is practised in the sciences of nature, and if the hypothesis of universal mechanism be accepted, to explain is to find as equivalents for certain sensible phenomena certain movements which bodies communicate to each other either by contact, or in accordance with other empirically determined laws. The notion of explanation understood in this way thus implies the distinction between appearance and reality, and the translation of the language of appearance into the language of reality. But from the point of view adopted here, the real is the mechanical, the appearance the psychical, that is to say, the totality of sensible. qualities in so far as they are irreducible to the mechanical. This method of explanation cannot therefore without absurdity be transferred into the order of psychological phenomena ; if it were the only legitimate method, the attempt to explain psychological phenomena would have to be abandoned, since, in the science of the mind, the real being identical with the appearance would be by definition ' inexplicable '.

Such is indeed the conclusion at which Thomas Brown, the immediate predecessor of James Mill in the line of Anglo-Saxon psychologists, seems to arrive. Matter, he tells us, being by definition extended has by definition parts : it is therefore a legitimate undertaking to seek to determine the composition of a material object. But this method cannot be applied to the analysis of mental phenomena, ' since every thought and feeling is as simple and indivisible as the mind itself, being, in truth, nothing more than the *mind itself existing at a certain moment in a certain state* '.[1] By what detour then does Brown embark on the theory of the phenomena of mind ? It should be noted, in the first place, that the sciences of nature have two objects : a study of regularities of succession, and a search for the elements which enter into the composition of bodies. Even if it be admitted that every instantaneous state of the soul is absolutely simple and rigorously indecomposable, it would be possible to state certain regularities in the succession of the states of the soul, and to draw from this statement certain general observations which would be called laws, and which would allow the prediction of the return of certain psychical phenomena, without this ' theory ' implying any ' hypothesis ' with regard to the nature of the elements which may constitute the phenomena in question.[2] Does this amount to saying that the notion of composition and the search for simple elements absolutely must not be introduced into psychology ? Brown was not so categorical as this. No doubt, it cannot be said that A and B are the elements of the

[1] *Lecture* vi. p. 31.   [2] *Lecture* xxxvii. p. 236.

judgment A is B or A = B ; for there is in the judgment something
else besides the simple mental contiguity of the two terms. It might
be said, however, by convention and by analogy with the language of
chemistry, that the judgment is the compound of which the terms
are the elements. Thanks to this useful metaphor, it will be possible
to bring it about that ' the Science of Mind is, in its most important
respects, a source of analysis, or of a process which I have said to be
virtually the same as analysis ' ; and to study ' the complex, or
seemingly complex phenomena of thought which result from the
constant operation of the *principle of the mind*', much as we study the
corpuscular elements co-existent in a mass which is in appearance
continuous.[1] It is in this way that the explanatory point of view of
Hume and Hartley, which had before been condemned, secured a
kind of relative justification in Brown's system.

James Mill had come under the influence of Brown : he was
ready to come under it, since the thought of both had had the same
point of departure in the teaching of Dugald Stewart. He borrowed
from him his definition of ' theory ' and of ' hypothesis '.[2] Yet he
was not stopped by the same scruple as Brown in regard to the notion
of psychological explanation, and he seemed to consider possible,
without any reservations, a decomposition of the phenomena of
mental life. But is this possible without bringing about the re-
appearance of the distinction between appearance and reality, and
without substituting the point of view of ' hypothesis ' for that of
' theory'? James Mill, having categorically affirmed that in the study
of the phenomena of consciousness the sensations of the individual
are the supreme test of truth for psychology, avoids the difficulty by
remarking that the attention has the faculty of disengaging, in a state
of consciousness, a certain number of elementary phenomena, which
in the end are felt separately after having been unperceived. He
gives a definition of the end he is pursuing at the beginning of his
analysis of sensations : his end, he says, is to lead such of his readers
as are new to this species of inquiry to conceive the feelings distinctly.
' All men are familiar with them ; but this very familiarity, as the mind
runs easily from one well-known object to another, is a reason why the
boundary between them and other feelings is not always observed.
It is necessary, therefore, that the learner should by practice acquire
the habit of reflecting upon his sensations, as a distinct class of
feelings '.[3] The reality is the sensible appearance ; but the appearance changes according to the degree of attention, and states of
consciousness after the analysis instituted by James Mill bear precisely the same relation to the same states of consciousness, as they
were before the analysis, as an object looked at through a magnifying
glass or through a microscope bears to the same object as seen with

[1] *Lecture* x.
[2] See Brown, *Observations on . . . Darwin.* Preface, p. ix. and *Lecture* viii.
[3] *Analysis*, ch. i.

454 PHILOSOPHIC RADICALISM

the naked eye. Its nature is not changed, only its detail is better perceived.

But, on the other hand, James Mill, who, by the way, is merely developing one of Hartley's ideas, insists on the undecomposable and indissoluble character of certain associations of ideas. He borrows Hartley's expressions to express this coalescence of several ideas into a single idea, in cases where no effort of attention can undo for sensible consciousness the original association. In order to understand how it is here again possible to bring about the decomposition of the mental phenomenon, it is no longer sufficient to fall back on the comparison with a magnifying instrument, which merely reinforces the action of our sensitive organs ; we must resort to the analogy of certain instruments of indirect experimentation, the retort in which the composite body is resolved into simple substances, or the prism which decomposes white light. To *expound* is the verb which Mill most frequently uses to designate psychological explanation, and this verb may mean simply to expose or express what appears to the senses ; but, in the language of James Mill it is also the opposite of the verb to *compound*, which means to compose, and particularly to bring about a chemical combination ; it is therefore a question of chemical decomposition, in which the appearance of the observed psychological phenomena is destroyed ; and this once again presupposes, in mental life, the opposition of appearance to reality.[1] In appearance, I have a visual or tactual intuition of space ; but this appearance must be destroyed in order that, in conformity with the exigences of explanatory Reason consciousness may appear as consisting in reality of a sum of ' points of consciousness '.[2] In appearance, two laws seem to rule all the successions of psychical phenomena : the law of contiguity and the law of similarity. But Hartley had only mentioned the first ; and cannot the second be reduced to it ? Every time I perceive similar objects, the trees of a forest, the sheep of a flock, do I not perceive them as contiguous to each other ? James Mill himself felt how hazardous was the hypothesis : but it was necessary for association by similarity to be reduced to association by contiguity, in order that the principle of the simplicity of the laws of nature may be satisfied as far as possible. It is verified in the world of matter ; is there not a presumption, asked James Mill, that it should also be verified in the world of the mind ?[3] It is in this way that James Mill seems to consider as equally incontestable the two principles that reality is identical with appearance, and that truth is simple. He believes in the evidence of the senses, but it is because he believes that the senses, if only we learn how to bring them to the required pitch of tension and refinement, will reveal to him a nature simple in the elements of which it is composed, and simple in the definition of the laws by

---

[1] *Analysis*, ch. ii.   [2] *Ibid*. ch. i. sect. i. vol. i. p. 11.
[3] *Ibid*. ch. xi. vol. i. pp. 376-377.

which it is ruled. He was, if we may so put it, equally absolute in the affirmation of his empiricism and in that of his rationalism.

2. ACTION

No doubt a ' theory ', as defined by James Mill, is distinguishable from a ' hypothesis ', in that it aims solely at observing phenomena, instead of wishing to impose on them the arbitrary requirements of thought ; but at least, it reserves to itself the task of arranging the phenomena observed, and of arranging them according to a plan calculated to make the knowledge of them as available and as utilisable as possible. There is nothing so absurd, says James Mill, as the commonplace which says that an opinion may be ' good in theory and bad in practice ', if it is true that the theory of any subject whatsoever is nothing else than ' the *whole* of the knowledge, which we possess upon any subject, put into that order and form in which it is most easy to draw from it good practical rules '.[1] The true aim which James Mill set before himself in working at the theory of the phenomena of the human mind was to arrive at the practical, and to make possible a new logic, a new morality and a new pedagogy.[2] It was only after his death that Stuart Mill, his son and pupil, wrote out the logic of associationism. But Bentham and James Mill had already laboured to establish the pedagogy and the morality of the Utilitarians : it even seems as though it was pedagogic preoccupations which recalled Bentham's attention to the fundamental problems of action. In 1794, at the moment when he was advocating a complete system of public assistance and instruction as a remedy for pauperism, he was already outlining the plan of a theory of virtue.[3] In 1814, at the time of the Chrestomathic propaganda, he returned to these questions and began to draw up his ' theory of the suitable ', his *Deontology*.[4] But he at once drew a distinction between two forms of the deontology, one ' private ' and the other ' public ' ; and as it was always legislative and social problems with whose solution he was concerned, he abandoned his researches into morality properly so-called, or into ' private deontology ', in order to work at a ' public deontology ', which, after much rehandling, eventually became his *Constitutional Code*. In 1829, Macaulay made his literary *début* in the *Edinburgh Review*[5] with a violent attack directed against the constitutional theories of James Mill in particular, and against the whole Utilitarian system and group in general. Bentham thought that it was of urgent importance to reply ; he sent to Bowring, the director of the *Westminster Review*, the main points of a defence of the Utilitarian morality, and resumed the writing of his *Deontology*, which

[1] *Education*, p. 5.   [2] *Analysis*, ch. xxv.
[3] See above, part ii. ch. ii. 2.
[4] On Bentham's reasons for adopting this term, see *Deontology*, vol. i. pp. 34-35
[5] *Ed. Rev.*, No. xcvii., March 1829, *Utilitarian Logic and Politics*.

finally appeared only after his death, arranged in order by Bowring.[1]
In the same year Mackintosh, the reformer of penal law, and the
collaborator and friend of Bentham, allotted him an important place
in his *Dissertation on Moral Philosophy* among the moralists whose
systems he was passing under review ;[2] but he did this in order to
draw a distinction between Bentham's philanthropy, which was
efficacious and admirable, and the philosophical system he professed,
which was detestable and sterile.   James Mill replied by a *Fragment*
in which he answered these objections, but which was only published
in 1835, three years after Mackintosh's death.   In this way the last
labours of master and disciple came to be devoted to the definition of
the principles of their moral system.   Is it not possible that the last
researches of James Mill, who based his morality on a psychology of
the will, and the last reflections of Bentham, which were the conclusion of forty years of social study and of philanthropic practice,
may lead the student of Benthamism to a completer and a more
precise knowledge of the Utilitarian doctrine ?

The law of the association of ideas rules without distinction over
the intellectual and over the active powers of the human mind : to
extend the application of Hartley's method to the domain of action,
that is, to the moral sentiments, is one of the objects which James
Mill set himself.[3]   But if phenomena of the intellectual order and
phenomena of the active order are alike in this, that an identical law
rules over them both, wherein do they differ ?   There is, so James
Mill tells us, an important difference between our sensations.   Some,
and these are probably the most numerous, are, to employ a current
expression, ' indifferent ' : they are neither agreeable nor painful.
But a great number of sensations are some of them agreeable and
others painful ; and the philosophy of action studies sensations
just in so far as they are agreeable and painful.   Given on the one
hand the agreeable or painful character of sensations, and on the
other hand the principle of association, James Mill proposes to
explain the most complex phenomena of human activity.[4]   It should
be borne in mind how extraordinary a value Bentham attributed to
the principle of utility.   Considered as a maxim of action, it signified
that the greatest happiness of the greatest number must be aimed at ;
considered as the statement of a general fact, it signified that all men
naturally incline towards pleasure and flee from pain.   Thus, it can
be held to be either a moral precept or a law of human nature, according to whether it is given the imperative or the indicative form : if it
is understood in the second sense, James Mill's analysis may be
defined as an attempt to develop the principle of utility in aid of the
principle of association.

It is here that the difference between the interests by which
Bentham and James Mill were animated makes itself felt ; it is here

that James Mill's superiority as a philosopher stands out, and that the rôle he played in the working out of the doctrine is defined. It is true that Bentham had read Hartley's book and had given his adherance to the doctrine of association. It is also true that there are in the *Introduction* attempts to found morals and legislation on considerations of theoretical psychology. But Bentham had not the patience to arrive at practical application by way of theory. The end at which he aimed was to proportion the gravity of punishments to the gravity of crimes, to classify punishments and to classify crimes in the order of their gravity; and consequently all his researches into juristic philosophy resulted in classifications pure and simple. James Mill proceeded differently. He did indeed take up again the dichotomic classifications made by his master, and the terminological innovations which are, in Bentham, inseparable from them. But he did this in order to simplify them, and he was able to simplify them because he was more of a philosopher than Bentham, and saw in classification only the beginning of explanation, and in the various classes which Bentham had put side by side on the same level he saw only successive complications of original elements, regulated by a simple law. For Bentham, who remained a jurist even when philosophising, to analyse is to enumerate and to distinguish ; for James Mill, in whom the desire for a practical application acted only as a stimulant to his philosophical faculties, to analyse is to decompose into elements and to reduce to principles, so as subsequently to make possible the synthesis of the phenomenon considered. Some examples will show up more clearly the difference in point of view between master and disciple.

Bentham, in his *Introduction*, and James Mill in his *Analysis*, each devote a chapter to the problem of intention.[1] The problem, for Bentham, is to know to what extent the intentional or non-intentional character of a criminal act constitutes or does not constitute an attenuating circumstance in the crime and, consequently, in the punishment. With a view to solving the problem, he analyses the idea of intention : but his analysis consists purely and simply in a classification of the various kinds of intention. Once the ' logical field ', the study of which he set himself, is exhausted by the application of the dichotomic method, it remains to be seen in what cases and in what senses it is possible to speak of a good or of an evil intention, when consequences alone are recognised as making the value, whether good or bad, of actions. For James Mill, the problem of intention is quite different ; in a way James Mill begins his investigations where Bentham stopped. Bentham sought to define the intention in order to establish a rational proportion between crimes and punishments. James Mill seeks to define it in order to find in this definition a justification of his general philosophy, and to resolve this

[1] Bowring, vol. i. pp. 40-43. J. Mill, *Analysis*, ch. xxv.

phenomenon, which appears to be undecomposable, into simple ideas, regulated by the law of association. It is, he tells us, an illusion of language, born of the use of the ' active ' verb ' to intend ', *intendere*, which attributes a mysterious efficacy to the phenomenon of intention, an influence on the act and its consequences. ' Intention ' only differs from ' willing ' in that it concerns a future and not an immediate act ; it consists in the anticipation of a future event, considered as a resultant of our acts, in the belief that a phenomenon will take place, and will have one of our actions for its cause. If the intention does exert an influence on the production of the act, it is only in an indirect way, and because the stronger belief in the future reality of the event tends to reinforce the motive : it is in the same way that an oath, which is the simple verbal declaration of an intention, tends to bind the agent in an indirect manner, because it reinforces the motive. In order to found legislation as a science, to reduce everything to the objective knowledge of the consequences of actions, this was the great concern of Bentham. In order to found legislation as a science, first to found psychology as a science, and for this purpose, to destroy the illusion of psychical activity, understood as an irreducible power endowed with a mysterious efficacy, to reduce everything to constant and in some sort mechanical relations between elements which should be as simple as possible, this was the great and altogether new concern of James Mill. He went further and deeper than Bentham had done.

The difference is still more striking if the theory of ' motive ' in Bentham and in James Mill be compared. James Mill adopts Bentham's terminology ; but for his master's interminable ' tables of contents ' he substitutes genuine attempts at analysis properly so-called. He reduces the complex to the simple, and so considers himself henceforth entitled to neglect many details which Bentham's minute mind thought should not be omitted, and whose insignificance is shown up by James Mill's analysis.

According to Bentham, the term ' motive ' is applied to ' anything that can contribute to give birth to, or even to prevent, any kind of action '. Motives may be speculative or practical, they may act on the intelligence or on the will. Considering practical motives only, Bentham understands by this ' anything whatsoever, which, by influencing the will of a sensitive being, is supposed to serve as a means of determining him to act, or voluntarily to forbear to act, upon any occasion '. The practical motive itself may be understood either in a literal or in a figurative sense. In a literal sense it is an event which has a real existence and gives birth to the act. In a figurative sense it is a ' fictitious entity ', a passion, an affection of the mind considered as acting on the mind and inclining it in a determinate direction : such are avarice, indolence, benevolence. If motives are to be considered in the literal sense, a distinction must still be drawn between the internal and the external motive. The internal motive is the event looked upon as consisting in ' the *internal* perception of any individual lot of pleasure or pain, the expectation of which is looked upon as calculated to determine you to act in such or such a manner '. The external motive is ' any *external* event, the happening whereof is regarded as having a tendency to bring about the perception of such pleasure or such pain '. The internal motive being by definition ' a pleasure or pain . . . calculated to determine you to act ' must be, in a sense, anterior to the action : it is what Bentham calls the motive ' in *esse* '. But because the individual, in order to act, must foresee the appearance of a pleasure or the suppression of a pain as a future event, consequent upon an act yet to come, this pleasure, which is posterior to the action, constitutes what Bentham calls the motive ' in prospect '.[1] Once these distinctions are made, Bentham passes to the moral and juristic question with which he is always concerned, and inquires whether the motive can confer value on the act which it inspires. Now, it is doubtless true that it is the consequences of the act which make it good or bad, and the consequences of one and the same motive may be good or bad according to the circumstances. It may be admitted, however, that, on an average, the consequences of some one determinate motive are better than the consequences of some other motive. An habitual motive, which may be qualified as good or bad in general, is what Bentham calls a ' disposition ' : ' a kind of fictitious entity, feigned for the convenience of discourse, in order to express what there is supposed to be *permanent* in a man's frame of mind, where, on such or such an occasion, he has been influenced by such or such a motive, to engage in an act, which, as it appeared to him, was of such or such a tendency '.[2]

In a work which he entitled a *Table of the Springs of Action*, by a figure borrowed from strict mechanics to express the phenomena of dynamic morality, and which James Mill revised and prepared for the printer in 1813, Bentham complicates his terminology still further by loans which seem to have been made from Locke's psychology. He makes a distinction between desires and aversions, needs, hopes and fears, and finally motives. But the definitions are uncertain. In cases where Bentham cannot find a means of defining ' by *genus* and *differentia* ', he has recourse to definition by ' paraphrase ', that is to say by a series of approximate synonyms ;[3] but he does not seem to have had the idea of genetic definition, or definition by way of construction, which might have been suggested to him by the psychology of association. Hence the confusion of his terminology. ' Between the ideas respectively denoted by the words interest, motive, hope, fear, good, evil, pleasure, and pain, the connection is inseparable. Without motive there is no interest : without hope or fear there is no motive ; without good or evil, there is no hope or fear ; without pleasure or pain there is no good or evil. To the several sorts of

---

[1] Bowring, vol. i. pp. 46-48.   [2] *Ibid*. vol. i. p. 60.
[3] *Ibid*. vol. iii. pp. 593-4.

interest, therefore, correspond so many sorts or modifications of motives, hopes and fears, good and evil, pleasure and pain'.[1] But Bentham does not define these connections whose reality he affirms. It is in James Mill that the names which Bentham distinguished serve to designate the successive degrees of complication of psychological phenomena, and that we find ourselves in possession, in place of a table of contents, of a genealogical picture of the facts we mean to study.

Bentham had lamented that the poverty of language had constrained him to give the name motive without distinction to two facts of a very different order : a real event, which *ex hypothesi* gave birth to the act, and a ' fictitious entity ', an ideal being, passion or affection, which *ex hypothesi* inclined the human mind to take such or such a determinate direction, under the influence of the real event. Among the real events, moreover, which are motives in the first sense of the word, all are not motives with the same degree of proximity : the only one which strictly deserves the name ' spring of action ', the only one which acts by immediate contact, is the internal motive which consists in the expectation of the future event which must result from the action : the pain or uneasiness, for instance, which I feel at the idea of being burnt.[2] This distinction between the literal and the figurative sense of the word motive may perhaps have been the starting-point of James Mill's reflections on this question. But he found two words to designate the two ideas. He discovered in the second distinctions which Bentham had not perceived. Finally, and above all, he defined these different forms of activity as so many forms derived from one original form, according to the law of the association of ideas.

The expectation of the future event, the ' feeling of pain or of uneasiness which I experience at the idea of being burnt ', James Mill calls not the motive, but the desire or aversion. In his *Table of the Springs of Action* Bentham had already taken up again these two terms, but it was only in a very confused manner that he had allowed it to be conjectured wherein desire might differ from motive. In the expression ' uneasiness ' which he had used in 1789, may be seen a reminiscence of Locke : ' The uneasiness a man finds in himself ', Locke had written, ' upon the absence of any thing, whose present enjoyment carries the idea of delight with it, is what we call desire '.[3] But this definition implies, on the one hand, that desire is considered as essentially painful, and, on the other hand, that there is included in the definition of desire, over and above the actual state of consciousness, the association of this state of consciousness with the idea of an exterior cause. On these two points James Mill separates himself from Locke, and simplifies the definition of desire still more, if that is possible.[4] What the idea is to the sensation in general, that

---

[1] Bowring, vol. vii. p. 567.   [2] *Ibid*. vol. i. p. 47.
[3] *An Essay*, etc., bk. ii. ch. xx. sect. vi.   See *Deontology*, part. i. ch. v.
[4] *Analysis*, ch. xix.

the desire or aversion is to the sensation considered as agreeable or painful. Every sensation is capable of being revived, independently of all external action. But the idea of a pain or of a pleasure is not a pain or a pleasure ; and yet there are agreeable ideas and disagreeable ideas. There must therefore be a distinction between ideas, analogous to that which exists between pleasant and painful sensations. An aversion is purely and simply the idea of a pain ; a desire the idea of a pleasure. No doubt an idea of the future is implied in the common meaning of the words desire and aversion : but it is an association of ideas which, according to James Mill, should be shaken off, in order to endow philosophical language with suitable rigour.[1] In his *Table of the Springs of Action*, Bentham had included hope and fear, but he did not define them, except by accumulations of synonyms. James Mill, on the other hand, defines hope and fear, joy and affliction, as the first complications of desire and aversion, through the operation of the principle of association. The idea of pleasure—or of pain—plus the idea of the future, plus the idea of uncertainty, is hope—or fear ; the idea of pleasure or of pain—plus the idea of the future, plus the idea of certainty, is joy—or affliction.[2]

What Bentham called motive in the literal sense of the word, is what James Mill calls desire. But motive is, by definition, a stimulant to movement and to action ; now, the idea of action is absent from the definition of desire proposed by James Mill. What then becomes, in James Mill's theory, of motive in the figurative sense of the word, the affection or the passion, the ' fictitious entity ' which is supposed to impel to action ? Bentham confined himself to stating the existence of two different meanings of a single word. James Mill did not think the two ideas were too far apart to be connected : according to him the only difference between the real event and the ' fictitious entity ' is the difference between the simple and the complex. The principle of association provides the transition from desire to affection, from affection to motive, from motive to disposition ; for James Mill, to define psychological phenomena is to engender or to construct them.[3] With the idea of the agreeable or painful sensation is associated the idea of the exterior cause which produces it. Hence arise agglomerations of ideas associated with each other, designated in a more or less confused manner by words in current language, and which are affections : love, for example, and hate. But even an affection is not a motive, since the idea of action is not contained in the association of ideas of which it is constituted. A motive is an affection, plus the idea of the self as the possible cause of the object of the affection. Why, moreover, when two men are tempted by the idea of one and the same action, is the first seen to execute the act, and the second not to execute it ? It is because the same motives do not act on all men with the same

[1] *Analysis*, p. 193. [2] Bowring, vol. i. p. 208. *Analysis*, ch. xx.
[3] *Analysis*, ch. xxii. vol. ii. p. 256 *sqq.*

intensity ; and this in itself is due to different habits of association. Once again, James Mill draws his inspiration from Bentham's terminology : the proneness, characteristic of every individual, to obey one motive rather than another, is disposition.   Thus a science of human activity is founded ; thus the phantom of will is dissipated. Will is a phenomenon of the same order as motive ; to be precise, it consists in the same associations of ideas as motive, but arranged in inverse order.   In motive, the idea which commands all the others is the idea of the end, after which are arranged, in an order inverse from the chronological order, the ideas of the means, ending with the idea of the initial action.   In will the idea of the action commands all the other ideas of the group, which come to a head in the idea of the end. But the will is not an intermediary between the motive and the act, such as to endow the motive with the mysterious privilege of efficacy. Causality signifies purely and simply a constant relation of succession. Now, this constant relation exists between the motive and the act. It is all that science needs.[1]

In his *Introduction*, Bentham had drawn up a table of motives, which corresponded, point by point, to his table of pleasures : he found just as many motives as kinds of pleasures.   But the distinction which James Mill establishes between desire, a primitive and simple phenomenon, and the phenomena of affection and motive, which presuppose complex associations of ideas, allowed him to reduce Bentham's table to its necessary elements.[2]   Desire is by definition the idea of a pleasure ; aversion, the idea of a pain ; an idea is by definition the copy of a sensation.   Thus, there are as many desires as there are pleasures, and as many aversions as there are pains.   In order for there to be an affection or motive, it is only necessary that there should be established an association between the idea of a pleasure or of a pain and the idea of an external cause.   Now, one and the same cause can explain a plurality of sensations : from one point of view, the cause of an agreeable sensation may be considered the more 'interesting' the more remote it is, and the more the idea of it is, by that very means, associated with the idea of a greater number of immediate pleasures.   Food, for example, the cause of the pleasures of nourishment, is a less important cause of our affections than is money.   And why ?   Because money, which is all the more general a cause of our pleasure in that it is a less immediate cause of them, serves indirectly to procure for us all pleasures and to avoid for us all pains.   The principle of association of ideas, by making it possible to retain, in the classification of motives, those only in which the idea of a pleasure is associated with the idea of a sufficiently general cause, makes it possible to simplify Bentham's enumeration.   At the same time it removes from it the character of a mere nomenclature, and gives it an explanatory character.   In his classification of motives, properly so-called, as in his analysis of the active powers of the mind,

[1] *Analysis*, ch. xxiv.   [2] *Ibid*. ch. xxi. sect. ii.

desire, affection and motive, James Mill always adopts the genetic point of view.

The vice of the method of analysis applied by Bentham is manifested in the idle complications which, as he grew older, came to muddle up his table of pleasures and motives. The ' pleasures of sense ', for example, formed one of the fourteen classes distinguished in the *Introduction*, and Bentham made a distinction, within this class itself, into seven subordinate classes.[1] Then, in the *Table of the Springs of Action*, three subordinate classes—the pleasure of taste, sexual pleasure, and the pleasure of novelty—were placed on the list of simple pleasures, side by side with the ' pleasures of sense ', which should in reality have included them.[2] Finally, in the *Rationale of Judicial Evidence*, not only are the three subordinate classes in question set up as principal classes, but also the other ' pleasures of sense ' are not included in the table.[3] A work of methodical simplification was needed : James Mill undertook it, but it looks as though he found the principles of it in Bentham. In the *Introductory View* which James Mill had put in order, Bentham had enumerated five ' interests ' which are capable of turning an official away from the performance of his duty ; and these were, together with the love of ease, which acts in a constant way, and with the love of vengeance, which acts in an occasional way, the love of money, the love of power, and the love of reputation.[4] In 1827, in a manuscript fragment, he distinguished four ' immediate sources of pleasure ', or ' objects of general desire ', or ' elements of prosperity ' : wealth, power, natural reputation and factitious reputation.[5] It is the very classification adopted with some simplifications by James Mill. Wealth, power and reputation are the mediate causes of agreeable sensations, the examination of which allows us to neglect the innumerable immediate causes. The ideas of wealth and of power do not need, it appears, to be defined ; the idea of dignity is a complex idea, which includes, besides the simple ideas of wealth and of power, the idea of a good use made of these two instruments of enjoyment, and the ideas of knowledge and of wisdom. There corresponds to each of these general causes an affection, a motive, and a disposition. In James Mill we can recognise the disciple of Bentham, concerned to give to the expression of the phenomena of the mental life the rigidity of a scientific terminology, when he laments that current language in no case provides the three distinct words which are necessary to designate the three distinct phenomena of affection, motive and disposition.[6]

Now these three great sources of pleasure have a common character ; they are so many means of procuring us the services of our fellows, and constitute the only, or more or less the only, means that our fellows are able to use in order to render us services. Wealth allows

---

[1] Bowring, vol. i. p. 17.
[2] *Ibid*. pp. 197-8.
[3] *Ibid*. vol. vii. p. 567.
[4] *Ibid*. vol. vi. pp. 10-11 and note.
[5] *Ibid*. vol. x. p. 561.
[6] *Analysis*, ch. xxii. sect. i.

us either to purchase the services of other men directly, or else to purchase the objects which are themselves the products of human labour, that is to say, to purchase services indirectly, or else, finally, to increase our power and our dignity. But the power of a man signifies the disposition of other men to obey him ; and the dignity of a man signifies the faculty he possesses of inspiring in other men the feeling of respect, and the desire to serve him. Thus it is the services of our fellows which are the principal source of our pleasures. Hence the most expeditious and the most direct way of obtaining their services, is to love them, and not to love gold, power and honours so as by that roundabout way to secure their obedience and respect. ' How few men ', exclaimed James Mill ', seem to be at all concerned about their fellow-creatures ! How completely are the lives of most men absorbed in the pursuit of wealth and ambition ! With how many men does the love of Family, of Friend, of Country, of Mankind, appear completely impotent when opposed to their love of Wealth or of Power ! ' [1] This is a remarkable example of that association which arises between the idea of the end and the idea of the means, and which, by concentrating all our attention on the means, leads us to neglect the end. The man who loves wealth, power and honour, and who does not love his fellow-men, is like the man who loves gold, and, through love of gold, deprives himself of all the pleasures which this gold could have procured him had it been judiciously employed. He makes a false calculation, he is the dupe of a sort of psychological illusion, which is in perfect conformity with the laws of the association of ideas, and which it will be the task of the moralist to teach him, in his own personal interest, either to avoid or to correct. Thus, we find that we have passed, insensibly, from the theoretic to the practical order, and from psychology to morals. Every man tends towards pleasure. The object of morals is to ensure the greatest happiness of all men. How can the moralist persuade every individual to work for the happiness of others in order to arrive at happiness for himself ? Are the interests of all men so closely bound up, that it is enough for every individual to understand his own interests in order for the interest of the species to be safe ? And does all morality come back to the teaching of this identity of interests ? It may be so. Still, James Mill's psychology does provide a glimpse of other possible interpretations of the Utilitarian morality, interpretations which ought to be first examined, even if only to be rejected.

It may be remembered that there is an original method of explaining the moral sense, as Hume and Adam Smith explained it, by the feeling of sympathy ; and it is not at first sight clear wherein the psychology of the association of ideas is repugnant to the principle of the fusion of interests. If analysis must absolutely reduce all the

[1] *Analysis*, ch. xxi. sect. ii.

feelings to simple elements, which are as homogeneous as possible, and regulated by a single law, it is still not proved that egoism must be the simple feeling from which all the others are derived : it implies the idea of a self, and, consequently, more or less complex associations of ideas. It is not proved that sympathy may not be a feeling which is, if not simpler than physical and organic needs in their instinctive form, at least simpler than reflective egoism. Desire is the idea of a pleasure ; but it does not follow that this pleasure, of which I have the idea when I experience a desire, must be a pleasure experienced by myself rather than by another. ' The sight of the beggar excites in me the idea of his distress ; that suggests the idea of relief to his distress : the idea of relief to distress is a pleasurable idea, that is, a desire.' [1] Here is, in James Mill, an excellent analysis of the feeling of sympathy, which does not at all imply either the idea of a self, or the idea of the personal interest of the agent. Bentham, moreover, precisely because he was always concerned less to analyse and to explain than to classify and to set in order, never seems to have given up treating extra-personal motives as being as ' simple ' and fundamental as egoistic motives, nor to have regretted that, in his *Introduction*, he had treated the ' pleasures of association ' as a special class of pleasure,[2] leaving to James Mill the task of explaining, by means of the law of association, the successive formation of all the various kinds of pleasures. Even the theory, in the *Table of the Springs of Action*,[3] of the ' substitution of motives ' and the criticism of the vulgar psychology, which explains all our actions by superficial and apparent motives, amounts to no more than an extremely timid attempt to analyse motives. In the *Rationale of Judicial Evidence* Bentham asks the question why sympathy, in the sphere of domestic relations, is stronger when it goes from the superior to the inferior than when it follows the opposite direction, and explains the phenomenon by egoistic considerations : the father satisfies his love of power at the same time as he satisfies his feelings of sympathy.[4] But, in the same work, he refuses to give the word ' interest ' the exclusive meaning of ' personal interest ' ; [5] in analysing the feeling of justice, he discovers in it as constituent elements, besides the desire of self-preservation, various feelings of sympathy and antipathy : his editor, Stuart Mill, completes Bentham on this point in a note in which he explains the genesis of the feeling of justice by an egoistic argument which innumerable associations have ceaselessly verified throughout the course of history.[6] Further, to the four sanctions, the political, the moral, the physical and the religious, which he had previously dis-

---

[1] *Fragment*, p. 334.
[2] Bowring, vol. i. p. 19.   [3] *Ibid* p. 218.
[4] Bowring, vol. vii. pp. 576-7.   Cf. *Analysis*, vol. ii. pp. 220-221.
[5] Bowring, vol. vi. pp. 257-8.   *Ibid*. p.105, *Ibid*. vol. i. p. 46, *Ibid*. vol. i p. 211-2, *Ibid*. vol. ix. p. 46, and *Deontology*, part i. ch. vi.
[6] Bowring, vol. vii. p. 570.

tinguished, Bentham now adds a fifth which he terms the sympathetic sanction.[1]

However, in spite of this accumulation of quotations, which seems to contradict our thesis in advance, we believe that the explanation of all the phenomena of all our mental life by egoism tends constantly to predominate in Bentham's system ; we believe that James Mill, in giving to the Utilitarian morality a rigorously egoistical definition, was merely continuing the bent which had been followed for many years by his master's thought.

Let us first bear in mind that Bentham was daily experiencing the egoism and the wickedness of men ; cheated, derided, ruined, he grew bitter, became more ' satirical ' as he grew older, and often neglected the rule which he himself had laid down, of always using ' neutral ' expression to designate the motives which direct human actions. He now saw in the corporative régime a ' sharp-sighted artifice,' an ' express plan to oppress and despoil the people ', a ' numerous and complicated system of devices, all tending to the same altogether natural, but not the less sinister end ' [2] Whether as robbers in whom egoistic motives are stronger than unsocial motives, or oppressors in whom unsocial motives outbalance egoistic motives, the governors are always, essentially, enemies of the people : social motives never inspire them. Bentham was even inclined to see a stratagem of the aristocracy in ' sentimentalism ', that is, in the attribution of an intrinsic moral value to motives. It was the governing classes who made the language of morality, and who defined the purity and impurity of motives in such a way that the rigours of the law might be enforced against the governed, while the governors escaped all control. [3] An absurd theory, since all men are normally egoistical, and since the question whether their egoism is turned to the detriment or to the advantage of the collectivity merely depends on the social circumstances in which they are placed. No doubt it is true that Bentham recognised elsewhere that social pleasures and motives did exist ; he nevertheless affirmed with an increasing insistence the predominance and even the universality of egoism. Egoism operates everywhere : this proposition now assumed, for Bentham, the importance of a principle. It is the self-preference principle, proofs for which he was seeking, and which he wished to apply to the whole system of morals. [4]

But deeper reasons than these were driving Bentham to adopt the egoistic system and would doubtless have made of him a conscious upholder of this system, if he had thought more as a philosopher and less as a philanthropist. In his Introduction he had already affirmed that egoistic motives outweigh extra-personal motives in number and in force : granted his anxiety to found a social science, and granted

---

[1] Bowring, vol. vii. p. 569. Cf. Dumont to Bentham, Jan 15, 1822. MSS. U. C., No. 10.

[2] Ibid. vol. v. p. 4.   [3] Ibid. vol. ix. p. 193.   [4] Ibid. p. 60 and vol. vi. p.11.

his conception of science, he was bound to end by neglecting, in practice, the motive of sympathy. What the Benthamites wanted was to found a social science on the model of the exact sciences, the sciences of measurement, geometry and mechanics ; but we have seen why it is that the egoistical pleasures and pains which concern the well-being of our physical individuality, are the only ones which admit of objective equivalents, the only ones which can be measured. Moreover the Benthamites, more or less consciously, conceived of every science as an explanation by reduction, by decomposition into simple elements. Where then, except in individuals, who are the subjects of the egoistic motive, were the jurist and the economist to find the simple elements which were necessary for the organisation of their knowledge ?[1] Supposing the sympathetic feelings were stronger than the egoistic feeling, the social group in which the feelings in question prevailed, would, in a way, assume more social reality than the individuals which comprised it. But the ideas of punishment and of exchange would become changed by this : for, within this group, the jurist would only be able to punish individuals in the person of their kin, by the application of the indeterminate principle of collective or reversible responsibility, and the notion of exchange could not be applied, since every individual would be found communicating to others, unconditionally, the product of his industry. This group would, moreover, be essentially variable, and if the theorist of law or of economics tried to confine his task to the examination of the relations which exist as between groups, he would not know in what group the really irreducible element of society should be taken to be : should it be the fatherland or the village or the family, or all these groups taken indiscriminately, each one of them being taken to be a unity up to a certain point, which it would be impossible to determine rigorously ? The result would be that social science would be condemned never to possess the character of an exact science, with which the Benthamites tried to endow it.

This is undoubtedly the secret and perhaps unconscious reason why James Mill's psychology is individualistic. When I remember a past state of consciousness, the idea of that state is not, according to James Mill, a simple idea but includes, besides the idea of the past sensation, ' that train of consciousness, which I call *myself*. This last is necessary to constitute it *my* idea '.[2] But this formula is ambiguous. An idea may be *my* idea, in fact, without my consciously bringing about the attribution of this idea to my *self*. Yet James Mill held that this attribution accompanies all our states of consciousness, necessarily and constantly ; in the actual state of consciousness, whether it consists in a sensation or in an idea, ' the idea of what I call *Myself* is always inseparably combined with it '.[3] In order for the theory of association to be true, however, it is not necessary that this determinate association of ideas should occur ; and Mackintosh

---

[1] Cf. *Analysis*, ch. xiv. sect. iii.　　[2] *Ibid*. ch. xx.　　[3] *Ibid*. ch. x.

quite rightly makes this objection to James Mill : if the idea of the
self is a complex idea, the product of a great number of states of
consciousness, it should not be said that I have the appetite or the
desire for a thing, but that there is in me an appetite for one thing,
a desire for another. But James Mill's individualism revolted
against this way of thinking of and of expressing psychological phenomena. ' Unless understood figuratively, to speak of a desire's
having an object is simply nonsense. When a man's desire is said
to have an object, the real meaning, and the whole meaning is, that
the man desires. . . . Could Sir James (Mackintosh) never understand, that it is the man only who acts ? Those acts of his which get
abstract names for convenience, his desires, his volitions, etc., are
not things that act, they are the man's acts '.[1] ˚In short, James Mill
himself, the restorer of the associationist psychology, the philosopher
of the Utilitarian morality, wished the problem to be put in the
terms which we originally stated, and wished the moralist, granted
individuals who are primitively and fundamentally egoistical, to aim
at a reconciliation of the individual with the collective interest.

In his reply to Mackintosh, James Mill suggests to us a first method
of solving the problem thus stated. When discussing Hobbes, the
founder of the ' egoistic system ', Mackintosh blamed him for always
making out that a reflective calculation of personal interest was the
only existing motive of human activity, and for not admitting that
the pleasures of morality were themselves part of the interest pursued
by rational beings. This, answered James Mill, is to have an improper
understanding of the rôle and of the effects of analysis. To have
decomposed a white ray into seven differently coloured rays, and to
know as a result of this that white light is not a simple colour, does
not prevent the colour white from still appearing, or, which comes to
the same thing, from being white. In the same way, to have shown
that human affections are reducible to simple states of pleasure and
pain, does not result in these affections being destroyed, and in the
one motive of personal interest alone remaining to act in their place.
Gratitude remains gratitude, resentment remains resentment, and
every one of these feelings retains its nature, and produces its normal
effects, after as before the analysis which has explained its formation.[2]
Will not analysis at least provide the means of bringing about,
when we wish it, the decomposition of these complex feelings ?
No doubt, to dry up the ocean, it is not enough to know that water is
chemically decomposable : but does not chemical analysis allow us to
transform at will a certain amount of water into certain fixed proportions of oxygen and hydrogen ? But it may be that, on this point,
intellectual analysis has less power than chemical analysis : it allows
us, in all cases of indissoluble association, to know that a certain
feeling is complex in spite of its apparent simplicity, although our

---

[1] *Fragment*, pp. 85, 105-6.   [2] *Ibid.* pp. 51-52.

mental faculties do not put it in our power to bring about this de-composition : patriotic feeling, for example, is, according to James Mill, a type of those feelings in which an almost infinite number of small impressions are lost, and submerged in the close unity of a complex feeling.[1] James Mill was surprised that Mackintosh had blamed ' the best writers of Mr. Bentham's school ' for having over-looked the indissolubility of the associations of moral ideas, when it was he, James Mill, who ' first made known the great importance of the principle of the indissoluble association ',[2] and first applied the principle of indissoluble association to the psychology of will and action. Moreover, and lastly, even if it were possible for us to bring about the decomposition in question, it has not been proved that it is desirable to bring it about. Complex pleasures have none the less a nature of their own for being composed of simple pleasures, they are new pleasures, and the most worthy of the appreciation of human nature. Our internal experience tells us that they are so. Are they less pleasures because they are complex ? Does he who shows them to be complex do anything to lessen their value, or to prevent their being, as Mackintosh says, ' a most important part of that interest which reasonable beings pursue '.[3] Simple pleasures, asso-ciated with each other and with the ideas of their causes, produce affections ; affections produce motives; motives produce disposi-tions. If an enrichment of our sensibility, and an increase in the number of our pleasures, corresponds to the exercise of these dis-positions and to the acquisition of these habits, why should the egoistic morality condemn in us, even in our own interest, the cultiva-tion of our disinterested feelings ? Conceived in this way, James Mill's analysis would not only not destroy the complex feelings, but would provide both the reasons and the methods for producing them methodically.

This was, in fact, the way in which Stuart Mill interpreted the Utilitarian morality ; [4] but it is clear enough that he could not inter-pret it in this way without seriously changing the nature of the doctrine, and without returning to that sentimentalism which the orthodox Benthamites had only defined in order to condemn. The only pleasures which the Utilitarian moralist wished in the last analysis to take into account, were the pleasures which had their source not in the exercise of our mental habits, but in external causes, such as gifts, wages or rewards, those pleasures, in a word, which are included under jurisprudence and political economy. In his theory of penal law, Bentham neglected the motives and considered merely the consequences of action. To show that a certain motive is a source of pleasure for the agent, does not prove that for this reason the motive should be esteemed and the corresponding disposition encouraged or cultivated. For all motives are good in themselves,

[1] *Analysis*, ch. xxi. sect. ii. [2] *Fragment*, pp. 172-3, 323. [3] *Ibid.* pp. 52-3.
[4] *Autobiography*, pp. 141-2. The revolution in his thought occurred in 1826-7.

since all lead us to seek a pleasure or to avoid a pain, and because
pleasure is the only suitable definition of the good, and pain the only
suitable definition of the bad.   The whole question is whether the
action which follows the motive is the cause of a greater sum of
pleasures or of pains for the agent and for his fellows ; and this is a
question to which it is impossible to give a general answer for each
kind of motive.   For any motive may result in useful actions in
certain cases.   The motive of sympathy, for example, allows the
poor man to participate in the superfluity of the rich, and even brings
it about that the rich man's luxury becomes an agreeable spectacle and
a source of enjoyment to the poor man ; the motive of interest
creates wealth ; the motive of hatred has its utility, since it impels men
to denounce criminals.[1]   Such was Bentham's juridical conception,
and James Mill transferred it as it stood to the Utilitarian morality.
Further, it would still have to be proved that the cultivation of
sympathy procures a surplus of pleasure for the individual, and that,
in all those cases in which it condemns us to the sight of irremediable
sufferings, it does not produce sufferings which are themselves also
irremediable.[2]   Above all, it would still have to be proved that it
can procure for the normal man pleasures which are comparable,
in number and in intensity, to the pleasures which have material
and external causes.   Exchange, according to the economics of
Benthamism, is the fundamental social relation ; and, if social life
essentially consists in an exchange of services, social happiness must
essentially consist in acquiring wealth together with the enjoyments
which it procures.   Mackintosh let it be understood that the true
condition of the happiness of the individual is the cultivation in him
of moral habits, that ' the fine feelings of the agent are of infinitely
more importance than his acts '.   ' Good God ! ' replies James Mill,
' What a doctrine is this ?   Good actions, and all their effects, all the
happiness which human beings derive from the actions of one
another ; in fact, almost all the happiness which it is given to them
to enjoy ; is insignificant, compared with certain pleasurable states
of mind antecedent to action '.[3]   In short, neither the juridical nor
the economic theories of the Benthamites entitled them to regard
happiness for the individual as consisting in the cultivation of superior
and disinterested feelings.   From their point of view, to be happy,
is to receive happiness from one's fellows ; but if this be so, is not
the moralist condemned, by profession, to solve this absurd problem :
to bring it about in a society in which every individual is egoistical,
and owes it to himself to be so, that nevertheless every individual
should be disinterested ?

But there is another way of solving the problem, the seed of which
may likewise be found in the philosophy of James Mill.   James Mill

[1] See above, part i. ch .ii. 2. See *Fragment*, p. 161.
[2] Cf. *Deontology*, vol. i. pp. 177-178.   [3] *Fragment*, pp. 229-230.

believed in the progress of the human race, considered as being brought about in conformity with necessary laws. We have seen that, according to Priestley, who was one of the first to formulate it, this law of progress by which the sum of pleasures tends constantly, in society, to outweigh the sum of pains, is derived from the very law of the association of ideas.[1] But James Mill, in his *Analysis*, tries to show how the various feelings of sympathy, from the simplest to the most complex, from the love of parents to the love of humanity, are born from each other according to a necessary processus :[2] might not the rôle of the moralist, turned psychologist, be thought of as amounting to this—to demonstrate the necessary progress of the moral feeling up to the day of its final triumph ? Bentham, at about the same time, and possibly under the influence of James Mill, came to understand the philosophical importance of the idea of progress, and formulated the law of what he called ' the progress of sympathy ', not only in the individual but also in the species. With the growth of experience, commodities multiply and become to a high degree capable of extension and increase. The individual finds himself enveloped in an ever-increasing number of social ' circles '. But the more society spreads and the more complicated it becomes, ' the more men live in public, the more amenable they are to the moral sanction '. Thus they become ' every day more virtuous than on the former day ', and ' they will continue to do so, till, if ever, their nature shall have arrived at its perfection. Shall they stop ? Shall they turn back ? The rivers shall as soon make a wall, or roll up the mountains to their source '.[3] In other words, as social relations increase and tighten, the individual will find himself more and more tightly bound, by the force of things, to the accomplishment of his social task, until the day when it will no longer be possible to draw a line between the egoistic and the sympathetic feelings, and he will no longer be able not to act morally. On this hypothesis, might we not take it that the rôle of the moralist should be restricted to warning the individual of the end to which the progress of the species is necessarily tending ; that he should cease to preach and restrict himself to predicting—that is, that he should stop speaking in the present imperative, and only speak in the future indicative ?

Or again, if the moralist is required to make use of preaching and commandment, what efficacy there is in his art might be understood if it were compared to the art of the educator. The ' spontaneous order of events ', James Mill tells us, favour the development of benevolence in the child. In the close relations which bind him to his parents, he soon notices that the pleasures of those near him are an habitual cause of his pleasures, their pains, an habitual cause of his pains ; and thus their happiness insensibly becomes for him an object of desire, their unhappiness an object of aversion.[4] According to

---

[1] See above, part i. ch. i. and part ii. ch. ii. 1.   [2] *Analysis*, ch. xxi. sect. ii.
[3] *Deontology*, vol. i. p. 101.   [4] *Education*, pp. 34-5.

James Mill, the aim of education is to encourage this natural progress, and so to combine circumstances that the share of accident and of individual caprice should be as much as possible eliminated from about the child, and that the sympathetic affections should be in conformity, in their very detail, with the general law of their development. But again, why does the educator wish to develop sympathetic affections in the child, and to strengthen the action of the causes which naturally help to form them ? Is it not, in the last resort, because the law of the moral progress of the individual is also the law of the moral progress of the species, and because the educator wishes to adapt the one to the other in the interest of the individual ? There might be said to be a double incommensurability between the individual and society. On the one hand, the interest which the individual has in his personal preservation is infinitely great if it be compared with his interest in the preservation of someone else. But on the other hand, the strength of which the individual can dispose for his own preservation is infinitely small, if it be compared with the strength of which all the other individuals united together can dispose against him. Will not the individual then act wisely in accepting the law of number, and in trying to adapt his personal needs to the conditions of his social existence ? Morals, interpreted in this way, would result in a sort of fatalistic optimism, into whose composition resignation and hope would enter in equal proportions.

It was in this way, in short, that the evolutionism of Herbert Spencer understood the function of the moralist ; but it was not understood in this way by the original Utilitarians. The Benthamite borrowed a certain conception of the useful from the observation of consciousness, and made use of this conception in order to judge— to approve or condemn according to the case—the external march of events. The morality of progress and of evolution such as we have described it, on the contrary, avoids defining the useful directly and tries to guess its nature indirectly, through the knowledge of the law of the development of the species and of the end towards which it is necessarily tending ; if it passes judgment on the particular facts of history, it is by comparing them with this general march of progress. This conception of morality tends to identify the moral sense with the supreme instinct of the species, with those habits of action in which the human will would find its definitive equilibrium. But this assimilation of the moral sense to an instinct is precisely what James Mill complains of in his adversaries. If a man can be moral without any consideration whatever of the utility offered by his actions, by simply obeying one of the blind impulses of his nature, why, James Mill inquired of Mackintosh, should not animals be considered as moral agents ? Do they not (on Mackintosh's theory), fulfil all the conditions requisite ? [1] ' The mere fondness a man has for his child, the delight which an idiot is capable of having in the highest

[1] *Fragment*, p. 319.

possible degree, which we are not sure that the lower animals have not in the highest degree ',—is this to be considered of greater value than ' the outward advantages of parental virtue, the man's hard and persevering labours to supply the wants of his child, his perpetual study of its future happiness, the care with which he watches its inward movements, and endeavours to impart to it those habits which are best calculated to render its life a source of happiness to itself and others '.[1]   If actions were to have the character of moral actions, it was not enough, according to the Benthamites, for them to have consequences which were useful to the individual and to the species ; over and above this, they must be accompanied by consciousness and by intention ; and the juristic and economic theories of the Utilitarians again provide us with the reason for this requirement.   It was one of Bentham's theories that the judge, in giving sentence, should neglect motives, but take into account the intentional character of the action and the consciousness of the agent : how else could the punishment be relied on to produce an intimidating effect ?   James Mill applied Bentham's juridical theory in his morals, and conceived that moral value could not be attributed to an action unless its author were liable to legal punishment and would be responsible before a magistrate, if the case arose.[2]   In political economy, on the other hand, Bentham and his disciples did no doubt state that the human species obeys laws whose regularity is singularly like the regularity of instinct.   But the mechanism which adapts supply to demand with an admirable certainty, is in reality, to them, the resultant of a host of little conscious actions : exchange, which the Ricardian economist chose as the type of social relationship, brings together, by definition, two individuals endowed with consciousness and reason.[3] So that, once again, the strict interpretation of the Utilitarian doctrine leaves us face to face with the initial problem : if individuals must act with a distinct consciousness of the consequences of their actions, why ought individuals, who are moreover aware that their sympathetic feelings are only transformations of egoism, to accomplish actions about which they only know that their consequences will be useful to others and perhaps harmful to themselves ?

The task of the Deontologist begins, so Bentham tells us, where the task of the legislator ends.   Where it becomes impossible to combine the laws which identify the general interest, his task ' is to bring forth, from the obscurity in which they have been buried, those points of duty, in which, by the hands of Nature, a man's interests have been associated with his enjoyments—in which his own well-being has been connected, combined and identified with the well-being of others ; to give, in a word, to the social all the influence of

---

[1] *Fragment*, pp. 212-3.   [2] *Ibid*. pp. 315 *seq.*
[3] See Mill's conclusion of his discussion of Mackintosh, *Fragment*, pp. 295-296 and 300.

the self-regarding motive '.[1] In this way the problem is finally solved. The mistake of the moralists of the Utilitarian school lies in this, that they too often let it be believed, in their polemics with their adversaries, that they were in agreement with them in their conception of morality and their definition of the virtues, and that they were merely proposing to establish the ancient morality on a new and a more solid basis. In point of fact, the Utilitarians were really trying to bring about a revolution in the conception of virtue. Their attempt to reconcile the individual and the collective interest cannot be understood unless it is recognised that there is in their philosophy, first and foremost, an attempt to discredit self-abnegation and to rehabilitate egoism. Be benevolent and do good, on condition that your goodness always serves your own interest indirectly : this formula seems to sum up the whole theory of the virtues in Bentham and in James Mill.

Who first began to work out this theory ? Without doubt it was James Mill, who had long had a profound knowledge of the philosophical literature of the Greeks, and who seems to have found the first idea of the new theory in a Utilitarian interpretation of the Socratic theory of the four virtues. Was it not perhaps he who made Bentham decide to reopen the scholastic manual in which he had learnt morals at Oxford University.[2] But from this time onwards, it was Bentham who took possession of the problem. ' In writing my *Deontology* ', he tells us, ' I took the virtues as referred to by Aristotle—traced such of them as would blend with mine, and let the rest evaporate '.[3] He adds that he has modified the traditional classification on an essential point. ' Since the time of Aristotle, four virtues, Prudence, Fortitude, Temperance, and Justice, have taken the names of the cardinal virtues '. But this is not really the truth of the matter, for ' in Aristotle's catalogue the virtue of benevolence — effective benevolence — is forgotten, and there is nothing in its stead but *justice*, which is but a portion of benevolence in disguise '.[4] The idea is resumed by James Mill when he attempts to classify, in his essay on *Education*, those ' qualities of mind which chiefly conduce to happiness—both the happiness of the individual himself, and the happiness of his fellow creatures '.[5] He names two qualities which tend to the happiness of the agent : intelligence, which includes within itself knowledge and sagacity ; and temperance, which includes the power of resisting pleasure, and the power of resisting pain, or fortitude. He names two qualities which tend to the happiness of others ; justice, which consists in abstaining from doing them harm ; and generosity which consists in doing them positive good. Does this mean that my intelligence and my temperance are harmful to my fellows, and that my justice and

---

[1] *Deontology*, vol. i. p. 23.
[2] *Ibid*. vol. i. pp. 38, 49 *seq*.   [3] Bowring, vol. x. p. 585.
[4] *Deon*. pp. 140-141.   [5] *Education*, pp. 4-5.

my benevolence are harmful to myself? No, for the happiness of
the individual and the happiness of the species are bound by ties
which are too close ; and, as James Mill says in his *Analysis*,[1] actions
of prudence and courage are only distinguishable from actions of
justice and benevolence in that the first are useful to us in the first
instance, and useful to others in the second instance ; while the second
are useful to others in the first instance, and useful to ourselves in the
second instance. But then does it not appear that all the species of
the genus virtue without exception are reducible to a single one?
This is the objection which Mackintosh made to James Mill ; [2] and
it seems to be justified. If courage consists in staying where you are
when you clearly know that it is more dangerous to fly than to stay
where you are, will not the duty of the courageous man, in the opposite
case, be to fly instead of staying where he is ? James Mill protests
that the objection is of no value. As if the whole question consisted
in weighing the chances which are unfavourable to the life of the
individual ! As if there were no case in which, in good morals,
courage might demand of the individual that he should face certain
death ! [3] But what are the cases to which James Mill is alluding?
Those cases in which the individual has to choose between death and a
life worse than death ? Then, indeed, the individual ought to face
death ; but then, also, to accept death will have become, for him, an
act of prudence.

The classification of the virtues, with which Bentham stops in his
Deontology, is no doubt preferable to James Mill's, for it guards
against this objection. Bentham does not at the outset make prudence
a species separate from the two virtues which tend directly to the
happiness of the agent ; but he distinguishes between two species of
the genus prudence : personal and extra-personal prudence. It is
the business of the Deontologist to show up the utility of extra-
personal prudence, and the necessity of doing services to others, if we
wish to deserve the esteem and the good offices of our neighbour.
There remains ' effective benevolence ' under its two aspects, the
negative and the positive ; and the objection made by Mackintosh
might be resumed here, and it might be asked wherein, in the
Utilitarian morality, are actions of benevolence distinguishable from
actions of extra-personal prudence. ' Over and above any present
pleasure with which an act of beneficence may be accompanied to the
actor, the inducement which a man has for its exercise ' is purely and
simply, so Bentham maintains, ' that which the husbandman has for
the sowing of his seed : as that which the frugal man has for
laying up money '.[4] But this is the profound reason which justifies
the distinction established by Bentham.

As a fact, and whatever may be the psychological origin of these
feelings, we do obey impulses which are not egoistical: we simul-

[1] *Analysis*. ch. xxiii.   [2] *Dissertation*, Whewell ed. pp. 293-4.
[3] *Fragment*, pp. 170 seq.   [4] *Deontology*, vol. ii. pp. 259-260.

taneously experience the influence of certain unsocial motives and of certain social motives. The problem for the Deontologist is to submit all non-personal motives to the close control of personal interest. He tells us to avoid giving ourselves up to our malevolent feelings : passions such as anger or envy are in themselves painful to whoever experiences them ; they are, moreover, feelings the satisfaction of which is not necessary to the person who gives himself up to them, whereas they necessarily cause sufferings to others, and consequently threaten to bring down future reprisals upon the angry or envious man. ' Of these evils, one division might be composed of those, by the infliction of which no advantage in any positive shape is produced . . . to himself, by the agent '.[1]   Hence this general rule ' Never do evil, in any shape or quantity, to any individual, but for the purpose of some determinate and specific greater good : good to yourself, to the other party in question, or to third persons '.[2]   We must not, on the other hand, we are told, give ourselves up without reflection to the impulses of benevolence. For beneficence may or may not be exercised without personal sacrifice, according to the case. In the first case, there is no limit to the exercise of this virtue. Thus ' whenever you have nothing else to do—in other words, whenever you have no particular object in view, of pleasure or profit, of immediate or remote good—set yourself to do good in some shape or other ; to men, to sensitive beings, rational or irrational ; to one or to many ; to some individual, or to the whole race '.[3]   In doing this, you exercise your intellectual and bodily faculties ; by exercising them, you gain in return both a profit for the future and an immediate pleasure. You lay up for yourself in the heart of your fellows a treasure of sympathy. You ' contribute to a sort of fund, a savings-bank, a depository of general good will ' and this contribution has not cost anything.[4]   But these cases, Bentham tells us, are pretty rare ; and on the much more frequent occasions when beneficence implies a sacrifice, there are necessarily very strict limits to the exercise of beneficence ; it is absurd to give oneself up to it. The *Deontology* is ' a budget of receipt and disbursement, out of every operation of which he is to draw a balance of good '.[5]   We do, no doubt, often have to give up our happiness to others : but for what reason ?   It is because, ' in the commerce of happiness, as in that of wealth, the prominent question is, how to make circulation assist production. Hence, it is no more fit to call disinterestedness a virtue in moral economy, than to call expenditure a merit in political economy '.[6] In short, ' benevolence and beneficence are maximised when, at the least expense to himself, a man produces the greatest quantity of happiness to others '.[7]   The morality of Bentham and James Mill is a morality of prudence in the first place, and after that, of benevolence

---

[1] *Deontology*, part ii. ch. iv.
[2] *Ibid*. vol. ii. p. 193.   [3] *Ibid*. vol. ii. p. 286.   [4] *Ibid*. p. 260.
[5] *Ibid*. vol. i. p. 192.   [6] *Ibid*. p. 165.   [7] *Ibid*. p. 190.

and charity within the limits of prudence. Morality, as they define it, is the art of being happy.

Thus was egoism installed at the very basis of morality. The whole effort of the associationist psychology was to prove that egoism is the primitive motive of which all the affections of the soul are the successive complications. In return, the whole effort of the Utilitarian moralist was to subordinate the sentimental impulses, whether egoistical or disinterested, to a reflective egoism. Since the sum total of happiness is made up of the individual units, is it consequently not enough, in order that all may be happy, for each one to be egoistical? This was the argument of the leaders of the new school; and, in truth, Bentham did not call upon any other argument than this in support of his *self-preference principle*, or principle of universal egoism. The proof, he tells us,[1] that all men are egoistical, is that the human race subsists: for on the prudence of the individuals depends the persistence of the race. If I considered your interests more than my own, and if you considered mine more than I yours, I should be the blind man leading the blind, and we should fall together into the abyss. If Adam had shown more anxiety for the happiness of Eve than for his own, if Eve had subordinated her happiness to Adam's, Satan might have spared himself the pains of tempting them to their destruction. James Mill went further than this in his development of the principles of the morality of happiness. ' Nature ', he wrote in his essay on *Education*, ' herself forbids, that you shall make a wise and virtuous people out of a starving one. Men must be happy themselves, before they can rejoice in the happiness of others; they must have a certain vigour of mind, before they can, in the midst of habitual suffering, resist a presented pleasure; their own lives, and means of well-being, must be worth something, before they can value, so as to respect, the life, or well-being, of any other person '.[2] In short, to be capable of beneficence, it is necessary to be happy. Now, to acquire the external goods which are the positive conditions of happiness, it is necessary to be endowed with sagacity, prudence and all the egoistic virtues. The consequence is that egoism appears as the necessary condition of all the social virtues. In sum, it is the moral code of a new era which Bentham and James Mill are promulgating. It is no longer the religious or aristocratic, ascetic or chivalrous morality which makes current antipathies and sympathies the sentimental rule of its practical judgments,[3] which exalts the rare and showy virtues, and recommends to the masses, in the interest of a governing class, humility or sacrifice. It is a plebeian or rather a bourgeois morality, devised for working artisans and shrewd tradesmen, teaching subjects to take up the defence of their interests; it is a reasoning, calculating and

---

[1] *Deontology*, vol. i. p. 19. See Bowring, vol. ix. pp. 5-6.
[2] *Education*, p. 29.   [3] *Deontology*, vol. ii. p. 193.

prosaic morality.[1]   The morality of the Utilitarians is their economic
psychology put into the imperative.   Two centuries earlier Hobbes
had based a complete system of social despotism on the doctrine of
utility ; and in fact, the principle of the artificial identity of interests,
on which Bentham's juridical theory rests, justified such an interpretation of Utilitarianism : it is the threat of punishment inflicted by the
sovereign which establishes for the individual the connection between
interest and duty.   But, insensibly, the progress and the triumph of
the new political economy had determined the preponderance within
the doctrine of another principle, the principle according to which
egoisms harmonise of themselves in a society which is in conformity
with nature.   From this new point of view, the fundamental moral
notion for the theorists of Utilitarianism is no longer that of obligation, but that of exchange ; the motive of moral action is no longer
fear but rather trust.   The Utilitarian moralist dispenses the legislator from intervening just in so far as, by his advice and by his
example, he tends, in conformity with the hypothesis of the political
economists, to realise in society the harmony of egoisms.

[1] See *Deontology*, vol. i. pp. 90 *seq.*

CHAPTER IV

CONCLUSION

BENTHAM died on June 6, 1832, two days after the third reading of the Reform Bill, and one day before it had received the Royal assent. He left his body to science; and before his corpse on the dissecting table, his friend, Southwood Smith, pronounced the funeral oration of the man whom all those present held to be the precursor of a new era.[1] Bentham, in fact, was no longer famous only in Paris, where his reputation had been consecrated in 1825 by a triumphal reception, in the whole of Europe and in the two Americas; in his own country he had finally collected round him the supporters of Utilitarianism. He himself, at the head of the group, was the patriarch, set apart from the others by age and glory. John Bowring, a city merchant, a great traveller, a preacher of English free trade on the continent, a polyglot and polygraph, an economist and a poet, the friend of everybody, had assumed the rôle of favourite at Bentham's side; he had not been sorry to see Bentham break with Dumont of Geneva;[2] he helped to loosen the ties of friendship which bound him to James Mill. James Mill was too exclusive and too personal, and became too much absorbed in the ever more important functions which he fulfilled at the India Company to be able to be the factotum whom Bentham required.[3] Bentham was less sectarian than many of his disciples, and it probably did not displease him to be honoured as a philanthropist by many who detested his doctrine; he accepted the homage of Daniel O'Connell, the Irish agitator, who though no doubt a Radical, was a fervent Catholic, and whose democratic opinions bore no more than a remote likeness to the theories which the Benthamites had borrowed from the secular philosophy of the eighteenth century;[4] he opened a correspondence with the Tory reformer, Robert

---

[1] *Examiner*, June 10th, 1832: The last Act of Jeremy Bentham. See article in *West. Rev.*, July 1832.
[2] Bowring, vol. x. p. 185. *Ed. Rev.* No. clviii, Oct. 1843, art. viii.
[3] Bain, pp. 13-4. [4] Bowring, vol. x. pp. 594-5.

Peel ;[1] he even wrote to the Duke of Wellington, who was the living symbol of orthodox Toryism.[2]

Others besides Bentham were organising the Benthamite sect, beneath his eyes but not always under his direction. Some among these were sexagenarians, and friends and contemporaries of James Mill. Ricardo died in 1823 ; and the despair into which James Mill was thrown by his death astonished all those who had taken him to be a man of stone.[3] But Joseph Hume and Francis Place survived Ricardo, and were even to survive James Mill ; Francis Place was still organising agitation in London political circles, in the interest of Radical ideas ; Joseph Hume, who was slightly younger, was destined for a long while yet to watch over the management of public finances, demanding the suppression of sinecures and the systematic reduction of military expenditure. The other disciples of Bentham belonged to another generation ; the friends of Stuart Mill, they were not yet thirty : these were the true founders of the sect.

It was at the beginning of 1823 that Stuart Mill organised the little society, which he called the ' Utilitarian Society '.[4] To belong to it, it was necessary to accept the principle of utility, and also certain fundamental corollaries which Bentham and James Mill had drawn from it, and to undertake to come to Bentham's house every fortnight to discuss, on the basis of these premises, certain questions of philosophy or of politics which were proposed in advance. The society never numbered ten members. Prescott, William Eyton Tooke, the son of the economist, William Ellis, and a son of Francis Place, belonged to it. Also George John Graham and John Arthur Roebuck who became intimate friends of John Stuart Mill and formed with him what they humorously termed the ' Union of the three Jacks ', or ' Trijackia '. It was in 1824 that Roebuck arrived in England from Canada. He was introduced to Stuart Mill, and from him learnt the principles, the philosophy and even the name of Bentham ; as a member of the Utilitarian Society, he penetrated into the sanctuary of Queen Square Place. Soon, by the force of circumstances, he found himself face to face with James Mill ; but his violent temperament agreed ill with the authoritarianism of the philosopher. A quarrel broke out : James Mill, if we are to believe the testimony of Roebuck, had always, in spite of his democratic declarations, been susceptible to distinctions of rank and fortune, and had apparently despised him because he was low-born and poor. ' I, on the other hand ', Roebuck tells us, ' let him know that I had no fear of him who was looked upon as a sort of *Jupiter Tonans* '.[5] James Mill complained to his son of Roebuck's disrespectful attitude.

---

[1] Bentham's letters to Peel, March, April and May, 1826 and see MSS. U. C., No. 11.

[2] Bowring, vol. xi. pp. 9-12.   [3] Bain, pp. 207 *seq.*

[4] *Autobiography*, pp. 79-81, 120.

[5] *Life and Letters of John Arthur Roebuck*, ed. by R. E. Leader, 1897, pp. 28-9.

CONCLUSION 481

Stuart Mill refused point blank to sacrifice his friend. This was his first declaration of independence against the man who up till then had never ceased to tyrannise over him. Henceforward Stuart Mill was to be, alongside of his father, an active but autonomous propagandist of the Benthamite doctrine.

It was in the heart of the city, in the banking house which George Grote was managing with his father, that the three members of the ' Trijackia ' met with their friends twice a week from half past eight till ten o'clock in the morning. There were a dozen of them. Together they discussed James Mill's *Elements*, Ricardo's *Principles*, Samuel Bailey's *Dissertation*, various manuals of logic, and Hartley's book ; a little later on they resumed their interrupted meetings to study in collaboration James Mill's work which had recently appeared. It was in these reunions that Stuart Mill completed his philosophical education, and first conceived the idea of his treatises of logic and of political economy.[1]

In 1825, Roebuck and his friends invaded a ' Co-operative Society,' composed of disciples of Robert Owen, against whom, for five or six consecutive weeks, the young Benthamites defended the Malthusian theory. The success of these discussions, combined with the success, by now of long standing, of the Edinburgh ' Speculative Society ', which MacCulloch suggested to them as an example, decided them to organise a society for bi-monthly discussions, in which orators, drawn from all parties, should plead their respective theses [2] against one another. Members streamed in : at last the young Utilitarians had come out into the limelight. By their dialectical energy they proved how great can be, in a numerous assembly, the power of a party founded on a doctrine. They made recruits ; some they secured from without, principally from Cambridge. Here it was not Stuart Mill who had acted as intermediary between James Mill and the younger generation ; for James Mill had resisted all advice, and adopting Bentham's prejudices against the aristocratic and clerical organisation of the universities, had sent his son straight to India House without first going through Oxford or Cambridge.[3] But Charles Austin, the brother of the jurist, had spread the principles of Benthamism about him at Cambridge ; thanks to him, James Mill's essays constituted a sort of manual of political science among a group of students.[4] It was the old phenomenon recurring once more. Mystical and religious tendencies predominated at Oxford, while Cambridge was scientific and positive.[5] In the eighteenth century, Oxford University had produced the Methodist heresy, while Cambridge was adopting the philosophical teaching of Locke and the moral teaching of Paley. In 1793 the undergraduates at Cambridge were

[1] *Autob.*, pp. 72-3, 119 ; *Personal Life of George Grote*, p. 60.
[2] *Autob.*, pp. 123 *seq.* Bain, p. 292.
[3] Bain, p. 205, and Bain, *John Stuart Mill*, pp. 28-9.
[4] *Autob.*, pp. 77, 103.　　　　[5] *West. Rev.*, No. 11, April, 1824, art. vii.

enthusiastic over Godwin ; now they were advancing from Paley to
Bentham.   During this time, the poet and metaphysician Coleridge
was inspiring the Oxford theologians, until the time was ripe for the
explosion of a new movement of religious enthusiasm, the agitation
of the Tractarians and the philosophy of the Neo-Catholics.

But the Utilitarians were not satisfied with this moral influence,
exercised by a few young men on a small circle of friends.   Some
workmen had tried to found a sort of centre of teaching for the use of
the lower classes, a ' Mechanics' Institute,' in order to bring about by
themselves their own political and economic emancipation ; but they
lacked funds and appealed to the Benthamites who took up the idea,
and transformed the working-class institution into a Radical institution which soon became prosperous.[1]   For the public of the ' Institute '
to whom they addressed their philosophical and technical teaching,
a library was needed for purposes of popularisation : and in order to
secure the funds for the publication of these books for popular
teaching, the Benthamites resumed one of Bentham's ideas and
formulas and formed the ' Society for the Diffusion of Useful Knowledge.' [2]   Finally, they wished to set up in opposition to the two
university coteries of Oxford and Cambridge, a new University,
installed in the capital, whose constitution should be secular ; they
wished at the same time to resume the ' chrestomathic ' idea, and to
give the children of the bourgeois class the means of instruction
without the expense of a stay at Oxford or Cambridge.[3]   The
original idea of this foundation belongs to the poet Campbell, who
brought it back from a journey to the Universities of Germany in
1825.   First Joseph Hume, then Brougham, then Francis Place, then
James Mill, who for a long time opposed it, rallied to Campbell's
scheme ; on April 30, 1827, the first stone of University College was
laid, and the inaugural meeting was held on October 2, 1828.[4]   The
promoters came up against all the difficulties with which the affairs of
the ' Chrestomathic School ' had made them familiar.   The Anglicans
founded a rival University, King's College, to which the older Grote
subscribed a hundred pounds, while George Grote was helping the
organisation of the Radical University.   Wilberforce, the great
man of the Low Church and of the evangelical party, accused the
leaders of the movement of excluding religious teaching from their
programmes in order to get money from the Jews.[5]   The enemies
within, the Protestant Dissenters, who dreamt of using the new
institution for the instruction of their ministers, were equally dangerous.   They succeeded in turning aside the candidature for the chair
of philosophy of Charles Hay Cameron, who was supported by James
Mill ; James Mill was more conciliatory than George Grote, who for

[1] Bain, p. 214, and Halévy, *Thomas Hodgskin*, pp. 82 *seq.*   [2] Bain, pp. 291-2.
[3] *West. Rev.*, No. xii. Oct. 1826, art. i.
[4] Bain, pp. 262 *seq.*-294.   *Personal Life of George Grote*, pp. 54 *seq.*
[5] *Life of W. Wilberforce*, vol. vi. p. 257.

reasons of principle, did not want an ecclesiastic, and gave way and accepted the nomination of a clergyman, on condition that he should teach Hartley's psychology.[1]   At least the Benthamites secured the chair of jurisprudence for one of themselves.   To anyone who has read Hobbes, Paley and Bentham, John Austin's [2] Lectures have little interest : but they were revolutionary indeed as compared with the traditional teaching of law.   Mackintosh, for the first time since the time of Blackstone, had tried in 1797 to introduce into his country the philosophical teaching of law : ' If anyone need to learn,' cried in triumph one of the editors of the *Westminster Review*, ' the immeasurable distance between a philosopher and an ordinary politician, let him read this puerile attempt (by Sir James Mackintosh), and the masterly sketch of the science by Mr. Austin, Professor of Jurisprudence for the London University '.[3]

The *Westminster Review* had been founded at the beginning of 1824 by Bentham and his friends.   Since the Whigs had the *Edinburgh Review* and the Tories the *Quarterly Review*, it was natural that the intellectual Radicals also should try to have their own quarterly review.   When, in 1823, Bentham made up his mind to advance the necessary funds, he first offered the editorship to James Mill ; but James Mill refused, pleading as an excuse his occupations at India House.   This was Bentham's first complaint against his lieutenant. Bentham then fell back on John Bowring, who had already been his friend for three years.[4]   Hence arose round Bentham the beginning of a struggle of influences between Bowring and James Mill.   For some time, the *Review* printed three thousand copies ; but in the spring of 1828 it began to wane.   James Mill and Bowring both intrigued separately to reorganise it without the co-operation of the other.   Bowring was successful, thanks to the support of Perronet Thompson ; James Mill, Stuart Mill and their friends declared themselves betrayed and broke with the *Westminster Review* ; but up to this date they had been the assiduous collaborators of Bowring's friends. From 1824 to 1828 this publication was the most significant expression of orthodox Radicalism.

The two Mills devoted two articles in the first two numbers to defining and discussing the attitude adopted by the two great existing *Reviews*.   The organ of the Whig public, like the organ of the Tory party, was addressed to an aristocratic party ; both reviews tolerated, only with different degrees of indulgence, the same abuses; they existed on a common basis of traditional prejudices.   It was on these abuses and on these prejudices that the new *Review* declared a pitiless warfare. The editors of the *Westminster Review* demanded law reform: writing at the time of the appearance of the *Théorie des Preuves Judiciaires*, they exerted themselves chiefly on questions of adjective law and of

---

[1] Bain, pp. 263-4.   [2] On John Austin, see *Autob.*, pp. 63, 73-4.
[3] *West. Rev.*, No. xxx., Oct. 1831, art. i.
[4] On the difficulty of founding the *West. Rev.*, see Bowring, vol. x. p. 540, etc.

judicial organisation.[1] Bentham himself supplied an article on Humphrey's *Property Code* : he took up again an idea which he had always held in common with Romilly and demanded that property in land should be put in the same position, as regards facilities of transfer, as movable property.[2] As regards pedagogy, the chresto-mathic programme was propagated,[3] the teaching of Greek and Latin was attacked,[4] and the *Library of Useful Knowledge* was recommended.[5] In political economy, the editors of the *Review* agreed with Ricardo in demanding the lowering of customs barriers, and pleaded the cause of machinery against the Owenites and even against Ricardo.[6] In history Grote took up the defence of the Athenian democracy [7] against Mitford ; Stuart Mill refuted the paradoxes by which Hume had claimed to justify the Stuart monarchy, and made a study of the French Revolution.[8] Before the publication of the *Analysis*, two philosophical articles taught the theory of Hartley.[9] In a general way, they all attacked the prejudices which were embedded in public opinion and were perpetuating abuses : religious prejudices and the spirit of intolerance towards Catholics as well as towards Deists,[10] national prejudices and the scorn for the culture of the Continent, conservative prejudices and the illusion of the morality of Chivalry.[11] They scandalised and set out to scandalise opinion by the affectation of their intransigeance, and by the ostentation of their orthodoxy. They made it their mission to denounce all the ' vague generalities ' which had led moralists and politicians astray before the appearance of the Utilitarian philosophy :—the phraseology of natural right, which was used by all privileged people to justify their acquired rights, and the liberal phraseology which can, at the orators' pleasure, authorise any pillage or paralyse any reform.[12] The illusions of ' sentimentalism ' were to be dissipated at last.[13] The choice must be made between poetry and logic. The mistake of the poets was that they did not understand that their sole function was to amuse the public, not to instruct them : if they tried to instruct them, the philosophy which they would teach would be a poetic and con-sequently an illogical and perverse philosophy. The *Westminster Review* created a new kind of literary criticism, and claimed to give contemporary poets lessons in politics and logic.[14]

---

[1] Adjective law and judicial organisation, see Nos. i. vii. viii. ix. xi. xvi. xvii. vi. v. xiii.

[2] *West. Rev.* vii. Oct. 1826, art. viii.   [3] i. Jan. 1824, art. iv.

[4] vii. July 1825, art. ix.   [5] xiv. April 1824, art. i.

[6] *Articles on Political Economy*, see Nos. i. ii. iii. v. vi. vii. viii. ix. xii. xiii. xv.

[7] ix. April 1826, art. i.

[8] iv. Oct. 1824 ; x. April 1826, art. v. ; xviii. art. i.

[9] ii. April 1824, art. viii. and xi. July 1826, art. i.

[10] iii. July 1825, art. i. See Bain, *J. S. Mill*, p. 33, etc.

[11] xi. July 1826, art. iv.   [12] See *e.g.* *West. Rev.*, ii. April 1824, art. v.

[13] See especially ii. April 1824, art. x.

[14] See *e.g.* *West. Rev.*, No. i. Jan. 1824, art. ii.

The Whigs and Liberals were beginning to find the radical pole-micists compromising ; the *Edinburgh Review* replied to the attacks of the *Westminster Review*.[1] As early as 1824 controversies had broken out. By 1827 bitter words had been exchanged. Finally, to refute the *Essays* of James Mill and openly to declare war on the new group, Napier chose the young Macaulay, who was personally acquainted with several of the intellectual Radicals, and particularly with the most provoking of all, his Cambridge friend, Charles Austin. Macaulay proclaimed his respect for Bentham's legal work ; he was wise enough to make the necessary distinction between the head of the school and his insupportable disciples. At the risk of being treated as an ' idiot ', or, what amounts to the same thing, as a ' senti-mentalist ', he ventured to ask whether these men, who were by some considered as the lights of the world, and by others as incarnate demons were not ' in general ordinary men, with narrow under-standings and little information,' and whether the contempt which they express for literature was not the contempt of ignorance ; ' some teacher assures them that the studies which they have neglected are of no value, puts five or six phrases into their mouths, lends them an odd number of the *Westminster Review*, and in a month transforms them into philosophers '. The teacher of whom Macaulay was speaking was not Bentham but James Mill, a schoolman, a fifteenth century Aristotelean who had strayed into modern times. Bentham had discovered truths. But what had James Mill and the others discovered ? All that they had done was to make these truths unpopular. Bentham had studied the philosophy of law : all that the others were able to do was to bark at lawyers. There had been the Byronians who played at being enemies of fashions, customs and laws : here were new eccentrics who, by new methods, were seeking, as the Byronians had done, scandal for scandal's sake.[2] A year later Mackintosh, who was also a Whig and who was an old friend of Bentham, expressed himself with almost as much severity as Macaulay.[3]

Was the result of Macaulay's attacks to discredit the new school for ever ? Did they not rather help to hallow its existence, and to fix once and for all—in a caricatured form no doubt, but no matter—the typical Utilitarian ? There is no doubt that the young Bentham-ites had their faults and made themselves hated because of these faults. But were not their very faults respectable, if their exclusive-ness and their pedantry can be explained by their fidelity to an idea which was the object of their considered allegiance ? It may further be admitted that this idea was a narrow one, that it did not take into account all the facts in the moral and social world which they thought to explain, and even that it systematically disregarded many aspects

---

[1] See especially 1824 Nos. of *West. Rev.*
[2] *Ed. Rev.*, No. xcvii., March 1829, art. vii. pp. 160, 161., and *passim*.
[3] *A Dissertation on the Progress of Ethical Philosophy*, pp. 285, 286.

of human nature.   If, in active life, it is the definition of courage to
defend to the last extremity, in spite of all its risks, a position which
was at first freely accepted, is it not likewise a sort of speculative
equivalent of courage to dare to take an idea as the principle of all
one's opinions and of all one's acts, and then to accept without flinching
all the consequences which this original idea involves ?   And was it
not because they did this that the Utilitarian Radicals came to be
treated as living syllogisms and thinking machines ?   Success soon
rewarded their daring :   some of them entered the first reformed
Parliament and were able to try to form there, for the first time in the
history of Parliamentary England, a group of doctrinaires.   We
know from how many different sources their doctrine had been
drawn.   But now that the period of the formation of the doctrine has
come to a close, we can attempt to sum up Utilitarianism as it
appeared to the disciples of Bentham and James Mill—a closed
system of truths logically connected together and a complete philosophy of human nature.

There is a science of the mind : this is the first proposition of this
philosophy.   The mind consists of a multitude of sensations which are
at first scattered; the operation of certain simple laws of attraction, laws
which may be reduced to the number perhaps of two, perhaps of one
only, is enough to explain how these phenomena end by grouping
themselves into a system.   If two elementary sensations have been previously perceived in contiguity with one another, or again are like one
another, they tend to reappear associated : the whole mechanism of the
mental life is explained by the successive complications of these cases
of simple association.   Among other characteristics which make them
alike, sensations present the characteristic of being either agreeable
or painful, or, to express the same idea in a different form, of being
the objects of our desires or of our aversions ; the sensations which
are associated according to the laws of the mental mechanism with
agreeable or painful sensations, then become objects of desire or
aversion in so far as they are means of procuring these last sensations :
from this results the whole mechanism of our moral life.   Among
the bundles of elementary sensations of which our mental life is
composed, certain associations which are founded on a more limited
experience, remain peculiar to the individual, whereas others, which
are common to a plurality of individuals, and sometimes to the whole
of humanity, are what is called truth : logic is the art which enables
us to distinguish the second from the first.   Similarly, certain associations of pleasures, or of sensations accompanied by a feeling of
pleasure, are peculiar to the individual ; other associations of the same
kind are, on the contrary, shared by him with a number of individuals
which may embrace the whole species : these associations which
identify the interest of the individual with the interest of the species
are what is called the good, and morals is the art which allows us to

distinguish the second from the first and to know the means proper to their realisation. Hume and Hartley had formulated the principles of this positive science of the soul, which was destined to be the basis of a new logic and a new moral theory ; and the influence of Hume and the perhaps stronger influence of Hartley were exercised on the leaders of the Utilitarian movement. These, however, had long neglected theoretic researches concerning psychology, logic and morals. Reformers, they did not relish speculation ; positive minded, they lacked interest in the religious conclusions in which Hartley's philosophy resulted ; doctrinaires, they were annoyed by Hume's sceptical paradoxes. At the end of his career Bentham at last became aware that it was necessary to define the moral theory on which his social system rested. Towards the same time James Mill likewise came to understand that the psychology on which Bentham's moral theory rested had to be scientifically constituted. But, as has been seen, it was after the event that they gave their attention to justifying the results to which they had been led by long labours in jurisprudence, political economy and constitutional law.

All men want to be happy ; but may it not, must it not happen that the means employed by various individuals to become happy are contradictory to each other ? While one man wishes to enjoy the product of his labour in peace, another may wish to deprive him of it by guile or by violence. Two individuals who both wish to live from the product of their labour may dispute the ownership of the same piece of land or of the same tool. If therefore it be admitted that it is useful that the product of labour should belong to the labourer, if it be admitted, moreover, that it is useful, in order to conform to the feeling of expectation and to avoid the pain of disappointment, that established property should be respected, how can the labourer and the landlord be protected against the individual whose usurpations they dread ? Since he yields to the attraction of a pleasure, he must be threatened with the infliction of a pain at least equal in intensity to the pleasure for which he hopes. By these threats, some acts are made into crimes. Legislation is the science of intimidation ; the general utility is its *raison d'être*, and punishment is the sanction of the obligations which it imposes. Granted that human nature, which is composed of similar elements and regulated by the same laws, is about the same in all men, classes of crimes and classes of punishments can be established : the whole of society seems to be constituted by rules which, in order to be efficacious, must assume the form of written laws, and, in order to include the sum total of social phenomena, must be systematised into a code. The legislator is the great dispenser of pleasures and pains in society. It is he who creates the moral order, the equilibrium of interests. Society is the work of his artifices. In this way is applied what we have called the principle of the artificial identification of interests. Hobbes, in the seventeenth century, had been the first in England to formulate it.

But, after the Revolution of 1688, philosophy had taken another direction. It was from the continental philosophers of the eighteenth century, from Helvetius and Beccaria, from the theorists of enlightened despotism, that Bentham borrowed the original idea of his philosophy of law. Despairing of making a name in England, he first addressed himself, and with success, to the European public. In his own country he wasted his time and spent his patrimony in trying to secure the adoption of a system of prisons which was calculated to suppress crime at the source, and mechanically to transform criminals into honest men.

Meanwhile a different aspect of things struck the attention of social philosophers in England. They noticed that the identification of interests did not necessarily imply the providential intervention of a legislator, but that universal order was at once surely and instinctively established by the spontaneous division of tasks and by the automatic mechanism of exchanges. While the needs of the individual multiply, the individual becomes less and less capable of satisfying them all himself; instead of isolated individuals each labouring to satisfy his own needs, economic society more and more presents us with the picture of individuals each labouring to satisfy a single want which is common to a number of individuals. This economic union, based on the very diversity of tasks, has not been the considered and systematic work of the laws. The division of labour, we are told, presupposes on the contrary that no governmental intervention takes place. In space, the unity of interests is all the more perfect the more towns, provinces and nations avoid splitting up the commercial universe into a series of little isolated worlds by means of legislative artifices and customs barriers : economic cosmopolitanism is based on the immediate identity of all interests. In time, the harmony of interests becomes ceaselessly more perfect through the multiplication of specialities which results from the multiplication of needs and from the progress of the sciences ; governments, by reason of their incapacity to calculate the future increase of supply and demand, prevent the principle of the progressive identification of interests from exerting its influence every time they intervene to direct the course of economic phenomena. This conception of social phenomena, if generalised, makes it possible to foresee the progressive elimination of all laws, and even to demand their immediate suppression. This was, in fact, the conclusion arrived at, in Thomas Paine, and especially in Godwin, by the principle of the new political economy of which Adam Smith was the recognised founder. Yet Bentham incorporated Adam Smith's economic philosophy with his Utilitarianism. Later, in the time of Ricardo and James Mill, under the double influence of the surroundings and of the moment, the political economy of Adam Smith and his successors played a preponderating part in Bentham's system. In fact, Benthamism was the work of a jurist who was by accident an economist. Yet

Auguste Comte was committing the most excusable of historical errors when, ten years after Bentham's death, he saw in his doctrine ' the most eminent derivative of what is termed political economy '.[1]

Now, the two principles on which the juristic and the economic philosophy of the Benthamites respectively rest are two contradictory principles : the contradiction was continually breaking out in the current formulae of Benthamism. The ' natural law,' Bentham tells us in the *Treatises*, is not a ' reason ', it is a ' figurative expression ', a ' metaphor ', a ' fiction ' : if there really were natural laws like those to which Blackstone and Montesquieu appeal, far from serving as the basis of positive laws, they would prove that these were useless. Yet, the search for the ' laws of nature ' was the object which the economists of Bentham's school assigned to political economy ; and by laws of nature they understood not merely the general facts of physical nature combined with the inclinations which are common to all men ; they clearly tended to understand by them principles of harmony, laws of justice and goodness, whose existence condemns all the positive laws which have been clumsily made by men. According to Bentham, the philosopher of law, the idea of ' liberty ' is a generalisation without scientific precision : social science is the science of restraints as it is the science of laws. The respect for liberty and the suppression of all restraints is, on the other hand, the first and last word of the wisdom of the economists. Should we therefore restrict ourselves to solving the contradiction by saying that the two principles each find their application in a distinct domain, and that the principle of the artificial identification of interests is the true principle of the science of law, while the principle of the natural identity of interests is the true principle of economic science ? It is obvious that Bentham owed his juristic and his economic ideas to two distinct sources : and this is an excellent historical justification of the presence of two contradictory principles in one and the same system. But is this historical explanation equivalent to a logical solution of the difficulty ? This does not seem to be so. Where should the line be drawn between two domains which are as close to each other as are the domain of law and the domain of political economy ? If, by chance, they should overflow into each other, how could the distinction be preserved ? Benthamism contains an attempt at a solution of this fundamental difficulty.

It was undoubtedly the principle of the natural identity of interests which was the basis of the optimism of the classical economists, and these have been recognised to be the masters of the Utilitarian Radicals. But theirs was not a pure optimism. Nature may perhaps grant happiness to all impartially ; but it grants it, in the terms of the new doctrine, as the price of a struggle. In order to live it is

[1] Comte to Stuart Mill, Nov. 20, 1841 (*Lettres de Stuart Mill à Auguste Comte* p.7). Cf. *Autob.*, p. 76.

necessary to work : and this is the meaning of the classical law of value, according to which products exchange with one another in proportion to the quantities of labour which they have cost. This law itself involves a new restriction : products which are identical in nature with each other, but which have cost their respective producers different quantities of labour, have nevertheless the same value. How is this value determined ? Is it by the *minimum* quantity of labour, or by the average quantity of labour necessary to complete these products ? It appeared that it was by the *maximum* quantity of labour necessary. But at least, will this *maximum* quantity tend constantly to decrease with the progress of industrial processes ? It appeared that, for the commodities most necessary to life, it tends constantly to increase. Round about 1800, Englishmen, whose numbers were ceaselessly increasing, and who felt themselves imprisoned within the narrow confines of an island, were struck by the disproportion existing between the unlimited increase in the number of men, and the less rapid increase of subsistence, on a land of restricted quantity and fertility. Hence the doctrine of Malthus ; hence the prodigious success of this doctrine in England. Ricardo and the Benthamites adopted it. They thus admitted, with Malthus, that even now the quantity of subsistence is insufficient to allow all men to live in abundance. Thus an equal division of goods would result in universal poverty. Thus, in the interest of all, the State should protect the property of the rich against the poor. In this way Bentham's proposition that the good of security must be rated higher than the good of equality was verified by Malthusianism ; and the political economy of the Utilitarians demanded the intervention of the State as the protector of security. The Benthamites admitted, also, that the only remedy for poverty consisted in the voluntary limitation of the numerical increase of the human species : but how can men resist the instinct of procreation which commands them to multiply ceaselessly, if they remain illiterate and uncivilised ? All must therefore receive the rudiments of instruction, and must learn the elements of social science : hence the political economy of the Utilitarians demanded the intervention of the State as a universal educator.

Hence though the political economy of Adam Smith and of his successors was in the first place based on the principle of the identity of interests, it admitted the partial necessity of having recourse to the converse principle. Conversely, all governmental intervention is justified by the principle of the artificial identification of interests ; yet we see that government may be organised in such a way that there is a place in its constitution for the principle of the spontaneous identity of interests.

During the whole of the first period of his existence Bentham does not seem to have been concerned with problems relative to the improving of the constitution of the State : he considered happy those countries who had a despot—a Frederick, a Catherine—to execute the wishes of the philosopher promptly, without deliberation and without obstacles. Then the upheaval brought about by the French Revolution embroiled the princes and the philosophers. Bentham became the great man of the liberals of the continent. In England, he suffered from the indifference and insolence of ministers and their agents. He joined the Westminster Radicals, became converted to their opinions, and provided them with a theory. Does not the thesis of democratic government indeed find its place in the Utilitarian philosophy ? We propose, as the end of the moralist or of the philosopher, the greatest happiness of the greatest number ; further, we suppose that all individuals are perfectly egoistical. This granted, a monarch is the least safe of all masters : for being, on this hypothesis, absolutely free to do what he wishes, he will follow his own interest and not the interest of the greatest number. He is at the same time the weakest of all masters : standing alone against all men, he is at the mercy of a revolt, a plot, or an attempt on his life. Let us suppose, on the contrary, that the majority of the individuals which make up a nation is provided, by means of representative government and of the secret ballot, with the faculty of executing its desires promptly and surely. The majority which thus becomes the sovereign power is the least fallible of masters : for since each individual is the best judge of his interests, it is the majority of individuals which will be able to estimate the interests of the greatest number. It is, at the same time, the most irresistible of masters : for the most numerous are the strongest. Thus applied, the principle of the artificial identification of interests tends to come near to the principle of the natural identity of interests in proportion as the majority becomes more numerous in relation to the minority. If ever this majority were transformed into an unanimity, the code would become nothing else than the systematic expression of the social truths on which could be built, thanks to the diffusion of scientific and moral knowledge, an agreement of intelligences and of wills : the laws would have the same authority as the geometry of Euclid and the astronomy of Newton. Until then, social constraint is reduced to its necessary dimensions : it is always a majority which exercises it, and a minority which submits to it.

This is a brief summary of the doctrine which was professed by the disciples of Bentham in 1832. This doctrine, we are aware, had diverse sources. In certain respects it seems contradictory. But perhaps these contradictions are in the last analysis merely apparent, and perhaps this appearance depends on the complexity of a system which, although all its parts are well connected, none the less presents diverse aspects. How much too simple are the current definitions of the Utilitarian system ! When the good has been defined as pleasure, and evil as pain, how far are we still from exhausting its content ! It appears that, in order to disentangle the essential features of the system, there must be added to this proposition two fundamental postulates which were practically implied in the whole doctrine, although they were never formally enunciated. First postulate : pleasure and pain are susceptible of becoming objects of a calculus, and a rational and mathematical science of pleasure is possible. This is what we will call the rationalistic postulate of the Utilitarian doctrine. Second postulate : All the individuals who together make up society have an approximately equal capacity for happiness, and are aware that they possess an equal capacity for happiness. This is what we will call the individualistic postulate of the Utilitarian doctrine. The value of Bentham's system is the value of these two postulates.

The Utilitarians were, in the first place, rationalists. Does this not clearly emerge from the history of their school and from the study of their doctrine ? But, if this is so, the expressions which are in current use to designate them, whether they are called sensationalists, or whether they are called empiricists, give a bad enough idea of them as a whole.

' Sensationalists ', it is said. In spite of the attacks which Bentham made against the moral theory of asceticism, there is no word which would give a falser idea of their doctrine. The Utilitarians were much less concerned to set instinct free, and to establish the right of everyone to every pleasure, than to define the conditions, which are often painful, which nature puts in the way of the satisfaction of needs, and, to use a Malthusian expression, the ' moral restraints ' which are the logical consequences of these conditions. Towards the end of his career, Bentham modified his terminology,[1] and instead of saying ' principle of utility ' like Hume and Helvetius, suggested saying henceforward ' principle of greatest happiness ' ; Lady Holland appears to have made the objection to him that the first expression, which seems to ' put a *veto* on pleasure ' was an unsuitable one. But this is just the question—whether the word ' utility ' does not express better than the word ' pleasure ' the true nature of a moral doctrine which is constantly making pleasure the object of calculation, of exchange, and of labour. Human life is arranged in such a way that man must always exchange a pleasure for a pleasure, and must sacrifice a pleasure or impose on himself a pain, in order to obtain a pleasure : it is the law of labour which is fundamental to the whole economic philosophy of the Utilitarians. ' Pain alone ', we read in *Natural Religion*, ' and want or uneasiness, which is a species of pain, are the standing provisions of nature. Even the mode of appeasing those wants is a discovery of human skill ; what is called *pleasure* is a secondary formation, something super-added to the satisfaction of our wants by a farther reach of artifice, and only enjoyable when that satisfaction is perfect for the present, as well as

[1] Bowring, vol. i. p. 3. *West. Rev.*, No. xxii., July 1829, art. xvi. pp. 267-8. *Deontology*, part. i. Bowring, vol. x. pp. 567-582.

prompt and certain for the future. Want and pain are, therefore, natural; satisfaction and pleasure artificial, and invented '.[1] It is necessary to work and to save in order to live happily. Also one must know how to accept inevitable suffering. ' It is a sad reflection withal, that the quantity of happiness which any, even the mightiest, can produce, is small compared with the amount of misery he may create by himself or others. Not that the proportion of misery in the human race exceeds that of happiness ; for the sum of misery being limited, to a great extent, by the will of the sufferer, he posseses, for the most part, some power of relief '.[2] There is something of the Stoic in the Utilitarian Radical. In 1790, Bentham defined himself to Lord Lansdowne as ' a sort of mongrel philosopher . . . something betwixt Epicurean and Cynic ' ; and Stuart Mill seems to have had these expressions of Bentham's in mind when he tells us that his father had in him something of the Stoic, of the Epicurean and of the Cynic, not in the modern but in the ancient sense of the word. ' He had scarcely any belief in pleasure. . . . He was not insensible to pleasures ; but he deemed very few of them worth the price which, at least in the present state of society, must be paid for them. The greater number of miscarriages in life, he considered to be attributable to the over-valuing of pleasures '.[3] Not to go back to the sages of Greece, it would even be possible to establish certain analogies between the moral temperament of the Utilitarians and that of all the Puritanical sects which modern England has produced. Bentham compared himself to the ' Saints ' of the Low Church, and to the Quakers. ' A methodist . . . is what I should have been ', he wrote, ' had I not been what I am ; as Alexander, if he had not been Alexander, would have been Diogenes '.[4]

In short, ethics, according to Bentham and his disciples, is a laborious art ; which is, moreover, based, if we are to believe them, on a rational science. No doubt the Utilitarians were ' empiricists ' : but this again is a way of designating them which is likely to mislead with regard to the fundamental features of their philosohpy. No doubt, they belonged to the school of Locke, did not admit the existence of innate principles, and considered the whole of truth as borrowed from experience ; but they none the less affirmed the legitimacy and the necessity of the deductive or synthetic method. The Newtonian law of universal attraction is extracted from experience : but, once the law is enunciated, it is legitimate and useful, even in order to verify the law, to take it as a starting point and ceaselessly to extend synthetically its application to new phenomena. In the same way, it is no doubt true that the primary truths of geometry appear to the Utilitarians as derived from experience ; geometry none the less proceeds deductively without ever having recourse to empirical measurement : it is a rational science. Now, the ambition of the Benthamites was to

[1] *Nat. Religion*, ch. i.
[2] *Deontology*, part i. ch. i.
[3] Bowring, vol. x. p. 245. *Autob.* p. 47 *seq.*
[4] Bowring, vol. x. pp. 92, 568.

establish all the sciences on the model of the deductive sciences. In political economy, Ricardo and James Mill compared the certainty of the propositions they were advancing to the certainty of the propositions of Euclid.[1] The principle of their proofs is the principle of universal egoism : Bentham called it an axiom and likened it to the axioms enunciated by Euclid.[2] James Mill discussed with disdain the economists who were unwilling that ' *experience* should be sacrificed to *speculation* ' ; which means, on his view, ' that a narrow and partial experience should always be preferred to a large and enlightened one '.[3] In Malthus' quarrel with Ricardo, it was Malthus who represented empiricism. In politics and in jurisprudence also Bentham and James Mill proceeded by process of deduction. They may, perhaps, have had Hobbes in mind : in the same way, said Hobbes, as man, the author of the geometrical definitions, can, by starting from these arbitrary definitions, construct the whole of geometry, so also, as author of the laws which rule the city, he can synthetically construct the whole social order, in the manner of the geometers. The Utilitarians merely make the part of human free will in the establishment of political science smaller than Hobbes had done : if they consider a deductive science of politics possible, it is simply because they consider the laws of human nature simple and uniform. Man is composed, we read in the first page of the first number of the *Westminster Review*, of a fixed quantity and of a moving quantity ; but ' the sameness is in all cases much greater than the diversity ; the essential characteristics of humanity are mightier than climate, education, habit, society, government and events ; they are untouched by these causes, in all their combinations, and continually limit their results '.[4] There was, no doubt, a link between the rationalism and the political Radicalism of the Utilitarians. They remained Conservatives as long as they were still empiricists. Such was Edmund Burke, to whom utility meant opportunity confusedly perceived ; such, until 1807, was Bentham himself, who had not yet found the means of withdrawing politics from empiricism. By the beginning of 1832, Bentham and James Mill had organised constitutional law as a sum of corollaries of the principle of greatest happiness and of the principle of universal egoism ; and it was Macaulay, a Whig, and a disciple of Bacon and Locke, a partisan of the principle of utility, but at the same time an upholder of the experimental method, who denounced their claim to solve political problems deductively. ' When men, in treating of things which cannot be circumscribed by precise definitions, adopt this mode of reasoning, when once they begin to talk of power, happiness, misery, pain, pleasure, motives, objects of desire, as they talk of lines and numbers,

---

[1] James Mill, *Colony*, p. 25.   [2] Bowring, vol. ix. p. 5.
[3] *Ed. Rev.* No. xl., Nov. 1812, art. xiii.
[4] *West. Rev.*, No. i., Jan. 1824, art. i. p. 1.   Cf. James Mill, *British India*, bk. ii. ch. iv. vol. i. p. 279.

CONCLUSION 495

there is no end to the contradictions and absurdities into which they fall '.[1] Thus was the empiricism of the Whigs opposed to the rationalism of the Radicals.

Now, was this rationalism justified ? Truth to tell, the Utilitarians rather postulated it than justified it. For a social science to be possible, they wanted happiness to be considered as a sum of pleasures, or, to be more exact, as the excess of a sum of pleasures over a sum of pains, and that a calculus of these pleasures and pains should be possible. But why is it necessary that a science of social man, based on a quantitative comparison of pleasures and pains, should be possible ? Bentham prescribes that we should reject those principles in morals which he calls ' anarchical ', that is to say, those principles on the strength of which there are ' as many standards of right and wrong as there are men ', and ' even to the same man, the same thing, which is right to-day, may (without the least change in its nature) be wrong to-morrow '.[2] But why does not the principle of utility enter, in the last analysis, into the class of ' anarchical ' principles ? Wherein does the notion of happiness, or of pleasure, necessarily imply, to use Bentham's expression, ' dimensions ' ? Can present pleasure be compared with past pleasure, which, by definition, no longer exists, or with future pleasure, which, by definition, does not yet exist ? Can the pleasure experienced by one individual be compared with the pleasure of another individual ? The reason why the Utilitarian jurists did not base the right of property directly on need, and the reason why the Utilitarian economists did not make value in use the object of their speculation, was that they both of them understood the incommensurable nature of pleasures and pains. Ricardo expressly recognised this : ' One set of necessaries and conveniences admits of no comparison with another set ; value in use cannot be measured by any known standard ; it is differently estimated by different persons '.[3] Bentham himself states the difficulty : ' 'Tis in vain to talk of adding quantities which after the addition will continue distinct as they were before, one man's happiness will never be another man's happiness : a gain to one man is no gain to another : you might as well pretend to add twenty apples to twenty pears, which after you had done that could not be forty of any one thing but twenty of each just as there was before '. And Bentham concludes : ' This addibility of the happiness of different subjects, however, when considered rigorously, it may appear fictitious, is a postulatum without the allowance of which all political reasoning is at a stand : nor is it more fictitious than that of the equality of chances to reality, on which the whole branch of the Mathematics which is called the doctrine of chances is established '.[4] There is a fiction in both cases ; but if the fiction is successful, it is better to

[1] *Ed. Rev.*, No. xcvii., March 1829, art. vii. p. 168.   Cf. *Autob.*, p. 160.
[2] Bowring, vol. i. p. 31.   [3] *Principles*, p. 260.
[4] Bentham, MSS. U. C., No. 14.   Title of sheet, ' Dimension of Happiness '.

treat it as a reality, and, in order to save time, not to call to mind every time that it is a fiction. The rationalist postulate of the Utilitarian doctrine is, according to Bentham, justified by its consequences, if it is really the foundation of a system of knowledge capable of explaining a great number of social facts and of resulting in the establishment of scientific politics.

But it is just this that is being contested, whether the Utilitarians did succeed in founding social science as a rational science; it is contested whether the initial fiction of their method did succeed. The Utilitarians had foreseen and had looked for the attacks made on them by the 'sentimental' moralists, and by all those who were scandalised by the application of weights and measures to the phenomena of moral sensibility. But they came up against more embarrassing adversaries in the shape of the 'positivists', who denounced their pretended rationalism as an unconscious sentimentalism, and reproached them with having systematically shut their eyes to the complexity of the real, in their desire to discover simple laws and absolute principles, and with having ended by presenting us with a picture of social phenomena which was so much simplified that it had thereby become deformed. They demanded that, if social science is to exist, it must abandon the deductive method for the statistical method, which was criticised by Adam Smith and ignored by Ricardo, and must be constituted on the pattern not of the abstract sciences but on the sciences of observation. Actually there was still a profound difference between the abstractions made use of by the Utilitarian philosophers and those of the mathematicians. Given the definition of the circle, I am immediately on the way to tracing real circles, with an exactitude sufficient for all practical needs ; and I can also say, approximately enough, to what extent any given figure differs from the perfect circle. Is the same thing true of the definition of punishments and crimes in the philosophy of law ? Is it possible to measure the gravity of a crime with an exactitude which can in any sense be termed geometrical, and to establish a mathematical equivalence between the gravity of a crime and the gravity of a punishment ? For the magistrate who, from his seat in the court, proposes to set a value on crimes and punishments, there is for this purpose neither rule nor compass nor reckoning machine. Bentham's doctrine can only provide him with very general propositions, which are suitable to direct his native intelligence, while, in a given case, he must have enough tact to determine the gravity of a crime, and to divine the gravity of the penalty which should be applied. Is not that which is true of the juridical philosophy of the Utilitarians true also of their economic philosophy ? If we admit that their political economy is free from internal contradictions, is this enough to make it applicable to the real ? Ricardo defined the rent of land as differential rent ; but what use are we to make of this definition ? Are we to use it in a particular case, to determine what rent the farmer ought to pay the landlord ? No, since we can only determine the value of differential rent on the basis of observation of the rent which is in fact paid to the landlord by the farmer. Conversely, are we to make use of real rent to determine the value of the scale of differential rent ? No, since rent on land is never exactly equal to differential rent ; and neither Ricardo's theory nor the observation of the facts tell us to what extent it differs from it. Political economy, then, can have no more than the appearance of an exact science, and the numbers on which it operates can never be other than arbitrarily chosen numbers, out of all relation with the real.

What is the value of these objections ? To answer this question, it is necessary to make a distinction between those which concern the juristic rationalism of the Utilitarians and those which concern their economic rationalism.

From the juristic point of view, the objections of empiricism do not in any way touch Bentham's doctrine. Bentham never claimed that it was possible, nor that it would ever become possible, to measure the evil of a crime like the height of a mountain or the weight of a barrel of wine. No one insisted more than he did on the necessity of leaving the judge free to appreciate, without submitting himself to rules of any kind, either the value of evidence, or the gravity of crimes. Nevertheless, if one must, in the last resort, rely on the judge's faculties of divination, the judge who is required to divine, must know what it is he is required to divine. Now for this it is necessary to have definitions, and definitions which are as rigorous as possible ; it must be shown how, for example, the gravity of a crime would be measured, supposing, *per impossibile*, there were at our disposal instruments which allowed it to be objectively measured. Other criticisms of Bentham may be made ; he may be accused, for example, of not having, in his theory of punishment, attached to the moral reformation of the criminal all the importance which it deserved. But one thing is certain. Had he been less of a logician, less of a calculator, less infected with the mania for quantifying the language of morals, he would not so thoroughly have infected public opinion with these truths, which were then little known and rather shocking, that ' all pain is an evil ', and that ' the happiness of the worst man of the species is as much an integrant part of the whole mass of human happiness as is that of the best man '.[1]

From the economic point of view the objection seems to have more weight ; it must be recognised that Ricardo's political economy has in many respects now been refuted for a century. The part played by Ricardo and his friends in the organisation of economic science was none the less immense. It may be that their theories have been criticised and then reformed : Ricardo himself doubted whether his theory of value was of a kind to secure the agreement of all minds.

---

[1] *Deontology*, part ii. ch. v.

But the new political economy does not differ in the method it pursues from the political economy of the first Utilitarians : it starts from abstract definitions, and then proceeds by way of successive complications and syntheses ; it completes rather than denies the theory of value formerly propounded by Ricardo, including it, as a particular case, in a more general theory.   It may be, moreover, that economists are more sceptical to-day than they were in the time of James Mill and MacCulloch as to the possibility of applying the simple forms of abstract political economy immediately to an extremely complex reality ; it may be that they have been wise in having multiplied their monographs and their statistical researches. But would their detailed labours be possible if the economists of the first period had not provided them with the necessary framework, with a scientific language, and with the very idea of what an explanation in political economy ought to be ?   By them, and by them alone, were marked the limits of the domain of political economy.   By them were defined the elementary notions of that science.   In so far as political economy becomes a science, it will come nearer to the form which it was given by its founders, the contemporaries and friends of Bentham.

There is another objection to the social rationalism of the Utilitarians which remains decisive, and this objection is derived from the double way in which they understood the identification of interests. Does this identification come about through the conscious artifices of the legislator ?   This is the conclusion of their juristic theories. Does it come about spontaneously, by the action of the laws of nature ?   This is the view to which their economic theories amount. Now, in spite of all the attempts at reconciliation, the contradiction between these two principles is so deep that each must necessarily tend to trespass on the other in the system.   The first principle sums up the modern conception of science as active and as permitting man, just in so far as he is acquainted with nature, to act upon it methodically so as to transform it according to his desires.   The second principle sums up the old conception of science as contemplative, and as assigning to itself the single rôle of discovering the harmonious simplicity of the laws which nature obeys when undisturbed by man.   According to the first principle, science foresees evil in order to provide for it ; according to the second, it denies evil and so saves itself from providing for it.   It is not for the State, so the Utilitarians tell us, to assure to each one his just share in the product of the labour of society : for this is spontaneously provided for by the mechanism of competition.   It is not for the State, they also tell us, to regulate exchanges in such a way that there will not be overproduction at any point : for economic science proves that phenomena of overproduction are mathematically impossible. This optimistic quietism is not however the natural conclusion of all the economic theories of the Utilitarians, and all the simple laws which they enunciate are not laws of harmony.   The law of differential rent is a simple law : now it favours some men at the expense of others, and aggravates the inequalities it creates according to a constant progression. The law of the variation of profits and wages is a simple law : now it is on the basis of this law that the economists prove the necessity and the perpetuity of poverty. But, once the laws of nature cease to be laws of harmony, why should not human science intervene to correct their disastrous effects ? If the State were to confiscate the whole of rent, not only would it not modify in any way the mechanism of production, but it would make the whole community benefit from a revenue which is in actual practice the unjust privilege of a class of idle landlords. In the same way, the law of wages is not a ' brazen law ' ; and custom fixes the minimum of wages which satisfy the workmen differently according to times and places : therefore, according to times and places, it makes the workman more or less miserable ; is it absurd to suggest that the State should, directly or indirectly, help to establish or to fix by law customs which raise wages ? There is, of course, a limit to these State interventions : this limit is our ignorance. We know that the laws of nature are unjust, but we do not know the details of these unjust laws ; and in trying to correct them without knowing them, we run the risk of making the evil we want to cure worse. The mistake of the Utilitarian economists was to found the abstention of governments not on an acknowledgment of our powerlessness to correct the imperfections of nature, but on an act of faith in the beneficence of natural laws : they travestied a naturalistic scepticism, which remains quite legitimate, into a rationalistic optimism which was certainly sophistical. In so far as the science of economics is not established, and in so far as we are not certain of knowing the true laws according to which wealth is produced and distributed, perhaps the most prudent course is to abandon the economic progress of the nations to the gropings of instinct, to the diversity of individual experiences ; but in so far as a rational science of political economy is possible, the intervention of governments in the production and exchange of wealth appears to be a necessity, and in so far as economic science continues to make regular progress, it seems natural to believe that governmental interventions will make corresponding advances. The principle of the artificial identification of interests will tend ceaselessly to assume a greater importance in relation to the principle of the natural identity of interests ; and it is in this way that one of the principles of the Utilitarian doctrine serves to refute the other.

But it is not enough to define Bentham's Utilitarianism as a rationalism, as a doctrine in which happiness is held to be susceptible of measurement. The complete formula of Bentham's moral theory is not ' the greatest happiness ', it is ' the greatest happiness of the greatest number ' ; in other words, in order to exhaust the logical content of the ' principle of utility ' there must be added to the ' principle of greatest happiness ' what Bentham calls ' the *happiness-*

enumeration principle '. And here is the statement of this new principle : ' in case of collision and contest, happiness of each party being equal, prefer the happiness of the greater to that of the lesser number '.[1] Henceforward the character of the calculus of pleasures and pains becomes modified. It is no longer a question of adding together particular states of pleasure and pain, taking no account of the distinction between the individuals who experience them ; what must be added together are the individual happinesses considered as so many irreducible unities. Bentham demands that all biological metaphors be excluded from the social sciences, and that the figurative expression, *body politic*, be avoided, and with it all the ' false and extravagant ' ideas which are derived from it. ' An analogy, founded solely on this metaphor, has furnished a foundation for pretended arguments, and poetry has invaded the dominion of reason '.[2] Does not the ascetic principle, Bentham asks, which requires individuals to sacrifice themselves to the ' public interest ' or to the ' interest of the community ', rest on this radical confusion ? ' The community is a fictitious *body*, composed of the individual persons who are considered as constituting as it were its members. The interest of the community then is, what ?—the sum of the interests of the several members who compose it '.[3] In short, a second postulate must be added to the rationalistic postulate of the doctrine : this may be called the individualistic postulate.

All the thinkers who joined the Utilitarian movement towards the beginning of the century were in agreement with Bentham on this point. Helvetius had said before Bentham that ' a nation is only the collection of the citizens which compose it ' ; [4] and likewise Paley : ' although we speak of communities as of sentient beings ; although we ascribe to them happiness and misery, desires, interests, and passions, nothing really exists or feels but *individuals*. The happiness of a people is made up of the happiness of single persons ' ; [5] Thomas Paine, who was half a Utilitarian, Godwin, Malthus and MacCulloch expressed themselves in the same terms. From this principle they drew various conclusions. From the fact that collective happiness consists in the sum of individual happinesses, Paley concluded that in order to increase the collective happiness, the number of individuals capable of happiness must be increased, and that the happiness of a people will increase more or less in direct relation to the number of its inhabitants : this is not the way, as is well known, that Malthus argued. Bentham concluded that the juristic State ought to watch over the identification of the greatest possible number of individual interests. MacCulloch drew the conclusion of the natural identity of interests : since society is nothing more than an *aggregate collection of individuals*, it is plain ' he tells us, ' that each in steadily pursuing

---

[1] Bowring, vol. v. p. 211.   [2] *Ibid.* vol. ii. p. 306.   [3] *Ibid.* vol. i. p. 2.
[4] Helvetius, *De l'Esprit*, dis. ii. ch. viii.
[5] Paley, *Moral and Political Philosophy*, bk. vi. ch. xi.

his own aggrandizement is following that precise line of conduct which is most for the public advantage '.[1] But the idea which logically results from the individualistic principle is equalitarianism ; and, although the Benthamite equalitarianism was extremely moderate, it may be asserted that all the Utilitarians had a tendency towards equalitarianism in so far as they were individualists. Note the way in which Bentham formulated his ' happiness-enumeration principle ' : ' in case of contest ', he says, ' happiness of each party being equal, prefer the happiness of the greater to that of the lesser number '. This hypothesis, which consists in first supposing the happiness of each party to be equal, is the necessary basis of Bentham's argument. ' Number of the majority suppose 2001, number of the minority, 2000. Suppose, in the first place, the stock of happiness in such sort divided, that by every one of the 4001 an equal portion of happiness shall be possessed. Take now from every one of the 2000 his share of happiness, and divide it anyhow among the 2001 : instead of augmentation, vast is the diminution you will find to be the result '. Bentham expresses himself in these words, or again, ' at the outset, place your 4001 in a state of perfect equality, in respect of the means, or say, instruments of happiness, and in particular, power and opulence : every one of them in a state of equal liberty : every one of them possessing an equal portion of money and money's worth. . . . Taking in hand now your 2000, reduce them to a state of slavery, and, no matter in what proportions of the slaves thus constituted, divide the whole number with such, their property, among your 2001 ; the operation performed, of what number will an augmentation be the result ? The question answers itself '.[2] It seems as though the transition between the rationalism and the equalitarianism of the Utilitarians can be traced. In order to achieve the calculus of pleasures and pains impartially and with the necessary objectivity, it is necessary for the moralist and the legislator to be no respector of persons ; in this sense, for the moralist and for the legislator, ' one man is worth just the same as another man '. This sentence does not yet imply equalitarianism : it merely signifies that the impartial judge must ask himself, in the case of all individuals, whether they are worthy, or capable of the same quantity of happiness, and to yield, in solving the problem, to no kind of individual bias ; but it does not yet imply that all individuals are in fact worthy or capable of the same quantity of happiness. Yet, it leads by insensible degrees to an equalitarian conception of society : ' the happiness and unhappiness of any one member of the community—high or low, rich or poor—what greater or less part is it of the universal happiness and unhappiness, than that of any other ? '[3] Now, in a

---

[1] Paine, *Dissertation on Govt.*, etc. Malthus, *Essay on Population*, bk. iv. ch. iii. MacCulloch, *Principles of Pol. Econ.* p. 129.

[2] *Deontology*, part i. *History of the Greatest Happiness Principle.*

[3] Bowring, vol. v. p. 458.

philosophy which proposes the maximisation of happiness as the end of morality, does not the conceiving of all individuals as capable of an equal quantity of happiness amount, by a detour, to restoring the principle of equality of rights under the name of the principle of utility ? If the Utilitarians rejected absolute equalitarianism, it was not because they considered society as naturally hierarchical, but because they thought the quantity of subsistence actually available was not sufficient to allow all the individuals actually existing to live in equal abundance. In constitutional law, they were equalitarian Radicals, and ended by returning to the conclusions of the spiritualist democrats of 1776.

The individualism of the Utilitarians has been contested no less than their rationalism : there has been seen in it the natural effect of a certain conception of scientific explanation, which was much in favour in the eighteenth century and in the first half of the nineteenth century, but which to-day seems to some extent out of fashion. To anyone who accepted atomism as a directing hypothesis and as a method of research, to explain was to decompose into simple elements—to count the number of irreducible parts of which the whole to be explained is composed ; for anyone who sees in nature only continuous movements, functions of each other, to explain is simply to formulate the constant law which regulates the changing relations of these movements. The psychologists of the eighteenth century argued in the same way as the physicists of the same period : according to Hartley and James Mill the immediate data of consciousness must be simple states of consciousness, atoms of the psychic world. To-day, the true immediate datum, of which a new psychology offers a description, is the continuous stream of consciousness. Social science, at any rate, proceeded in the same manner. ' For ascertaining and knowing amounts ', wrote James Mill, ' some contrivance is requisite. It is necessary to conceive some small amount by the addition or subtraction of which another becomes larger or smaller. This forms the instrument of ascertainment. Where one thing, taken separately, is of sufficient importance to form this instrument, it is taken. Thus, for ascertaining and knowing different amounts of men, one individual is of sufficient importance. Amounts of men are considered as increased or diminished by the addition or subtraction of individuals '.[1] In this way the individual came to appear to be not a conventional but a natural unity of measurement in social science. The individual became in some sort the atom of the Utilitarian economist and moralist. But have we not learnt, since then, to conceive of the possibility of a social science capable of providing positive results, although dispensing with the search for social atoms and without a unity of measurement ? The Utilitarian philosopher, because he was individualistic, considered the individual as elementally egoistic, and all the disinterested inclinations as so

---

[1] *Analysis*, vol. ii. p. 90.

many transformations of this primordial egoism. The new sociological method is distinguishable from the old Utilitarian method in
that it accepts sympathy, or altruism, as an irreducible datum of
experience, and considers as elemental not the individual but the
social fact as such.

The inadequacies of the Benthamite individualism seem effectively to justify, at first sight, the at least temporary credit secured by
the new method. The safest method of securing the services of
others, is, so Bentham tells us, to appear disinterested, and the safest
method of appearing disinterested, is to be so in fact. But does this
amount to saying that by egoism we learn to become disinterested?
Is it not much better to admit that sympathy cannot be deduced from
egoism, and that our social existence implies the presence in us not
only of personal feelings but of disinterested feelings also, which
cannot be reduced to the first and which are quite as fundamental as
they are? Bentham and his friends were bidden by the logic of their
system to consider the individual as a purely egoistical being; but,
by the evidence of the facts they were constrained to recognise the
impossibility of reducing the motive of sympathy to this supposed
elemental egoism: the result is that in the Utilitarian doctrine the
egoism of the individual is at once explicitly affirmed and implicitly
denied. Let us consider that part of the doctrine which puts
forward the artificial and governmental identification of interests.
' Law alone ', Bentham declares, ' has accomplished what all the
natural feelings were not able to do: Law alone has been able to
create a fixed and durable possession which deserves the name of
Property '.[1] Do there not, however, exist natural feelings which
at least prepare and direct the intervention of the legislator? ' If it
were possible ', answers Bentham, ' to suppose a new people, a
generation of children, in which the legislator would find no ready
formed expectations to contradict his views, he might fashion them
to his will, like the sculptor deals with a block of marble '. But this
is not the case. ' Man is not a solitary being. With few exceptions,
every man is surrounded by a larger or smaller circle of companions,
united to him by the ties of relationship, marriage, friendship, or
services—who *in fact* share with him the enjoyment of the property
which *by right* belongs exclusively to him '.[2] Does not this amount
to saying that there exists an institution which is *in fact* anterior to
all those which the law is able to create, that is to say, the family—
and a property *in fact* previous to all legislation, that is to say family
property? Is not the same thing true if that part of the Utilitarian
doctrine which affirms the natural identity of interests be considered?
All the demonstrations of political economy, as understood by
Ricardo and his disciples, presuppose thoughtful, laborious and
egoistic individuals who pursue exclusively the satisfaction of their
material needs and the acquisition of the greatest possible quantity

[1] Bowring, vol. i. p. 307.   [2] *Ibid*. vol. i. p. 334.

of wealth. But the theory of international exchange presupposes in the individual the love of his native soil as well as the economic motive ; and the theory of wages presupposes that the individual exacts as the price of his labour the amount of subsistence necessary for the upkeep not of himself alone, but of himself and his family : so that once again social motives, and family feelings in particular, reappear in the doctrine as elemental data. But cannot the family be considered as the type, or as the germ of all society ? If once the Utilitarian doctrine includes family feelings, will it not destroy the postulate on which it rests ? The express will of one or of several individuals, by the intermediary either of law or of exchange, is no longer necessary to create the social link. The individual now appears rather as an accident of the social substance or as a product of social evolution.

We have not attenuated the gravity of these objections. But it is well to beware of the illusion which they may create, and not to come to see in individualism a philosophical eccentricity, an opinion peculiar to a few theorists. In the whole of modern Europe it is a fact that individuals have assumed consciousness of their autonomy, and that every one demands the respect of all the others, whom he considers as his fellows, or equals : society appears, and perhaps appears more and more, as issuing from the considered will of the individuals which make it up. The very appearance and success of individualistic doctrines would alone be enough to prove, that, in western society, individualism is the true philosophy. Individualism is the common characteristic of Roman law and Christian morality. It is individualism which creates the likeness between the philosophies, in other respects so different, of Rousseau, Kant, and Bentham. Even to-day, it is permissible to plead the cause of individualism, whether it be considered as a method of explaining social facts, or as a practical doctrine, capable of determining the direction of the reformer's activity.

Our aim is to constitute a social science, defined as a science of collective representations, passions and institutions : but how could we propose any explanation of these phenomena which did not rest on the individualistic hypothesis ? Are we to restrict ourselves to explaining social facts by attaching them to other social facts which have merely preceded them in time, to seeing in each institution the transformation of a previous institution ? Social science then ceases to be explanatory, in the proper sense of the word, and again becomes purely narrative ; it ceases to be science to become history. If, on the contrary, we do wish social science to be truly explicative we must admit one of two things. Either collective representation has, since its first appearance, been common to several individuals : in this case it still has to be explained how this representation came about in each of these individuals taken in isolation. Or else collective representation was first individual representation before it spread to a plurality of individuals and became collective : in this case, to explain collective representation, is to describe how the individual became social, and how representation was communicated from individual to individual. Further, in order for this process of explanation to be legitimate, it is not necessary for the transmission to be brought about by means of an express convention : Bentham himself rejected the hypothesis of an original contract. The individual may be constrained by the violence to which he is submitted by another individual, or may submit to the influence of another individual by sympathetic imitation. In any case, the Philosophical Radicals were right in seeing in the individual the principle of explanation of the social sciences.

What is true from the point of view of theory is perhaps even truer from the point of view of practice ; what is true of social science is truer still of social legislation. It may be said of all laws that they are, in their essence, equalitarian and individualistic ; in so far as they are laws they tend to consider all individuals as equal and to equalise the conditions of all individuals. Even the law which constitutes class distinctions, and imposes different obligations on the master and on the slave, on the noble and on the commoner, on the orthodox and on the heretic, on man and on woman, proceeds by means of general propositions and treats as equal all the individuals within each class so constituted. Moreover, if the rights of individuals differ according to the legal condition to which they are attached, is it not suitable, if the law is to be respected, that these unequal rights should be equally protected by the law ? The content of law may differ according to the class to which the individual belongs, but the form of law must be the same for all individuals of all classes ; the law may differ according to classes, but can its legality differ without the law itself ceasing to exist ? The whole progress of law seems to have consisted in the development of this equalitarian principle. At first the law tends to neglect this fact that individuals are unequal : instead of consecrating it by law, it restricts itself to insisting on the fact that individuals have an equal right to the protection of their person and property. Individuals are henceforth looked upon as all having an equal right to rise one above another. The wage-earner is a slave who has the perpetual right to become a master ; the poor man is a commoner who has the perpetual right to become a noble. But does not this right to change one's economic and social position, which is equal for all, run the risk of remaining unused in cases in which the inequalities once created would naturally tend to get fixed in hereditary castes ? It thus seems that, in order that equality in law may be equality in fact also, the law ought to intervene to guarantee to all the satisfaction of certain needs which are considered to be the normal needs of man. What are these needs ? This is not the place to define them. It is enough to have pointed out the equalitarian tendencies of all legislation as such, and the normal development of these tendencies. Conservative parties know that law is a leveller, and that is why they plead the cause of tradition and custom as against legislative uniformity. In spite of their resistance, the reign of law tends ceaselessly to triumph over the reign of custom ; and consequently individualism triumphs in so far as the law tends to neglect individual differences in order to consider all individuals as equal, or as having an equal need of happiness.

An equal need of happiness, granted. But is it not also implied, by the individualistic hypothesis, that they have an equal need of liberty ; and that they are all, to the same extent, the responsible and conscious authors of their happiness ? To this question the Utilitarian doctrine gives an uncertain answer. According to the principle of the natural identity of interests, every individual is the infallible judge of his own interest, or is at least less fallible than anyone else, and can pursue it freely and without restraint. According to the principle of the artificial identification of interests, it is the benevolence and the competence of the legislator that is counted on to establish the harmony of interests, by means of limitations imposed on individual liberties. But this authoritarian Utilitarianism, if it is not contradictory in itself, presupposes an accident, almost a miracle, if it is to be realised. What guarantee have we, in fact, that the sovereign possesses the intellectual and moral aptitudes necessary to make all interests harmonious ? Hence the solution which after 1807 was adopted by Bentham and his friends. They attributed sovereignty to the whole people, or at least to the majority. Some liberties are sacrificed ; but, on the one hand, these will always be the liberties of a minority ; and, on the other hand, the majority which has the power and is enlightened by the teaching of the Utilitarian economists will know the limits which, in the universal interest, the State ought not to pass. Only modern democrats have not, in fact, respected the limits which the Utilitarians had fixed to limit the intervention of the State ; they have frequently attempted an application of the principles of the artificial identification of interests which Bentham and Ricardo condemned in advance. Contemporary socialism is certainly opposed to individualism as defined by the Utilitarian economists. There is only one solution to this difficulty that we can see. We think that the opposition would perhaps appear less fundamental, if we went deeper into the notion of liberty and considered the interventions of the State as necessary not only to make individuals more happy but also to make them more free.

Let us return to the formulae used by Bentham himself. If every individual is the best judge of his own interest, and if all interests are harmonious, all governmental intervention is condemned. If every individual is the best judge of his own interest and if interests are contradictory, it is necessary for the government to exercise a control over the manifestations of individual wills. But the Benthamites did not admit unreservedly the truth of the principle that every individual is the best judge of his own interest, and it is at this point that the problem becomes complex.

The juristic, economic and political philosophy of the Utilitarians presupposes that all individuals know their own interest ; if it happened that on any point this condition were not realised and that State intervention seemed necessary to its fulfilment, this would be an intervention in whose theoretical justification there would be no difficulty. This is the conclusion which was reached by the doctrine of Malthus. Since on the one hand a powerful instinct pushes men to multiply and to consume without limit on land of limited dimensions and fertility, it is necessary for a general system of national education to enlighten all individuals, from their childhood up, so as to make them more thoughtful, more prudent, and more economical. At this stage all the countries of Western Europe have, more or less promptly, and more or less radically, organised compulsory instruction by the State, as the Utilitarians wished. It is a communistic system, for all individuals pay to the State according to their abilities, so that all children may receive the elementary instruction which they all need equally. It is a system of emancipation, for it is a question of making all individuals capable of wisdom and foresight. But might not other interventions of the State, which the Utilitarians condemned, be justified on the basis of this same principle, which the Utilitarians laid down ? It will now be said that the State must intervene not in order that the liberty of individuals may be limited, but in order that individuals may become free.

Another difficulty then arises. How should this liberating State be constituted ? Who shall be set up as judge of the governmental interventions which are necessary for the emancipation of the individual ? It must certainly not be an aristocracy of birth, for their interests would not be identical with those of the majority. Yet it is no longer clear why power should be given to the majority, if it is true that individuals are not the best judges of their own interests. At bottom, the problem thus set is an insoluble one ; all that can be done is to show how it seems gradually to be solved in the course of history. If it be recognised that society was not constituted by a contract originally concluded between rational and free individuals ; that individuals first belonged to a crowd of little societies, and that these little societies were submitted to before they were willed ; that individuals became conscious of their powerlessness to defend their interests against these little societies—family, religious and professional—in which they did not wish to be absorbed, and looked for a support to sustain them in their struggle against a tyrannical influence—is it not then conceivable that individuals constituted the State as a society to some extent artificial and as superior to the little natural societies, over which it exercised a control ? The State, defined in this way, represents the general society in opposition to

the particular societies, or, if you like, all the individuals in opposition
to all the groups. It should not be said that men were born free and
founded the State to increase their security at the expense of their
liberty. It should be said that men wanted to be free, and that, in so
far as they wanted to be free, they constituted the State to increase
simultaneously their security and their liberty.

The doctrine of Bentham and his disciples now appears before us in
all its real complexity. It is undeniably a morality of pleasure, but a
morality of pleasure which, in order to establish itself, postulates
rationalism and individualism, defined as we have said. Founded on
these bases, it is incessantly appealing to two distinct principles, which
are in a sense in competition within the system : the one in virtue of
which the science of the legislator must intervene to identify interests
which are naturally divergent ; the other in virtue of which the
social order is realised spontaneously, by the harmony of egoisms.
The question is to what extent were the Utilitarians entitled, by the
logic of their system, to appeal to one or other of these two principles :
the Utilitarian philosophers should be blamed not for having been
rationalists and individualists, but rather for not having, perhaps,
drawn all the necessary consequences from their rationalism and their
individualism. But, true or false, beneficent or evil, the influence
which they had over their century and over their country seems to
have been immense ; and to bring the history of Philosophical
Radicalism up to 1832, it would be necessary to begin telling, after
the history of its growth, the history of the influence which it had
already been exerting for years. A few words on this subject would
not be without their uses as a conclusion, though the question falls
outside the real sphere of our study, and though, moreover, a distinction must be made at the outset. It has been convenient for us,
in order to study the philosophy of utility as a whole, to draw it from
the little group of people who devoted their lives to systematising it
and to spreading the knowledge of it : but on all sides of this Utilitarianism, which was as it were concentrated, there was among the
English contemporaries a diffused Utilitarianism, whose influence
was felt by the Philosophical Radicals themselves. As we have said
above, Bentham and his disciples were rationalists and individualists ;
but were they not infected with this through contact with the social
reformers of the eighteenth century, all of whom, both in France and
in England, appear to have been rationalists and individualists likewise ? In studying the growth of Bentham's doctrine we have
tried to omit none of the causes, and if the causes were to be classed
in the order of their respective importance, it would no doubt be
necessary first to distinguish the general movement from the collective
thought, which, in a given period, imposes on the great majority of
men a common way of thinking, and compels them all either to argue
starting from the same premises, or to think of premises which justify

their agreement on certain conclusions after the event ; then the geographical and historical conditions which turn aside, slacken or accelerate the march of human thought—England's insular position, the American Revolution, the French Revolution, twenty years of universal war, the discovery of important coal-fields ; finally, the influence of a small number of individuals who were intelligent and energetic, passionately philanthropical, endowed with the systematic spirit and with the taste for intellectual domination. Now at the actual time when these individuals were acting on the public mind and on the institutions of their century, the general causes which had acted on the formation of their thought, continued to act around them on the public mind and on these institutions. How, except in a conjectural and approximate fashion, can these two influences be distinguished ?

Were the Benthamites needed to make England, who had formerly been so proud of the liberalism of her judiciary institutions, recognise, after 1815, that, owing to the European revolution, she was now far behind the continental nations in this particular, and that her civil procedure was scandalously expensive, and her penal law scandalously sanguinary ? A too manifest contradiction between laws and customs made it essential that the laws should be readapted to fit the customs. Robert Peel was neither a Benthamite, nor a Radical, nor even a Whig. A member of a Tory Cabinet but a reformer of the party to which he belonged, it was he who made Parliament adopt four statutes which suppressed the death penalty in more than a hundred cases specified by the law. Robert Peel's laws are laws of ' consolidation ' ; and the procedure of ' consolidation ' which was expressly condemned by Bentham, bore only a very distant relation to his programme of ' codification '.[1] Yet at about this time Robert Peel was on several occasions in correspondence with Bentham ; when in 1823 he undertook the reform of English criminal law it was from Mackintosh, Bentham's disciple on this subject, that he stole the glory of having executed this great reform ;[2] and when in 1833 a Commission was nominated to complete the revision of the criminal laws, the first name on the list of members was that of John Austin, the Utilitarian jurist of University College.[3] When the question arose of modifying the laws regulating real property, Bentham was consulted by the members of the Commission which the Government appointed for this purpose in 1828.[4] Upon the reform of judicial organisation, Bentham's influence is still easier to determine. The great speech delivered by Henry Brougham in February 1828 developed all

[1] On the influence of Bentham's doctrine on law, see Sir James Fitzjames Stephens, *A History of the Criminal Law of England*, vols. ii and iii. See also for more general considerations, A. V. Dicey, *Law and Opinion* (1905), pp. 125 *seq.*
[2] Bowring, vol. x. p. 403. Mackintosh, *Life*, vol. i. p. 234, p. 300, etc.
[3] See *Ed. Rev.*, No. cxxxiii., July 1837, art. vii.
[4] Bowring, vol. xi. p. 216, etc.

Bentham's theories on the reform of adjective law, from the suppression of special pleading to the institution of local courts ; and in spite of the fact that Bentham disliked Brougham, who was too changeable and often too timorous for his taste, Brougham was none the less his disciple, his spiritual son. In Brougham it was almost a ' Philosophical Radical ' who in 1830 reached the Chancellorship. He was probably expressing the general opinion when, some years later, in the preface to his speech, he declared that ' the age of Law Reform and the age of Jeremy Bentham are one and the same '.[1]

It was not the writings of the economists which emancipated the colonies overseas. But the American Revolution, once consummated, found its justification in the work of Adam Smith, and the emancipation of the Spanish colonies which threw open the whole of South America to English commerce, came in England to bring, after the event, a new argument in support of Adam Smith's theories. Bentham was the disciple of Adam Smith and up to the end of his life stood as an adversary of the colonial system : when he became a Radical, his economic objections were reinforced by political objections against a system which handed over the colonists to the mercy of functionaries sent out by the metropolis.[2]   Yet England was preserving a part of her colonial empire and founding new colonies. Were Bentham and his disciples going to demand that all the colonies should be abandoned ?   Colonisation is a fact before which their logic capitulated ; and besides the logic of their system is double : in so far as their philosophy advocates the artificial and despotic identification of interests, might they not be tempted to consider the colonial empire as a vast field for experiments in philanthropy and reform ?[3]   Bentham had always dreamed of making laws for India : now that James Mill occupied an important post in the India Company, might not his dream become a reality ?   ' I shall be the dead legislative of British India.   Twenty years after I am dead, I shall be a despot '.[4]   Twenty-eight years after his death the Indian penal code came into force ; it had been drawn up by Macaulay under the influence of Bentham's and James Mill's ideas, so that Bentham, who had failed to give a legal code to England, did actually become the posthumous legislator of the vastest of her possessions.   Meanwhile a young adventurer, Edward Gibbon Wakefield, worked out a plan for the systematic colonisation of Australia.   The government was to sell lands at a high figure, and then, with the profit obtained, was to organise the immigration of the labourers needed to put them under cultivation : thus an economically paying colony would be founded, and at the same time the mother-country would be rid of her surplus

[1] Brougham, *Speeches*, 1838, vol. ii. p. 287.
[2] See MSS. U. C. No. 8, an appeal to the Spanish People entitled ' Rid yourselves of Ultramaria '.
[3] See in Bowring, vol. iv. p. 418, the remarkable postscript added on June 24, 1829, to his pamphlet on the emancipation of the colonies.
[4] Bowring, vol. x. p. 450.

population.   Edward Gibbon Wakefield was the son of an intimate
friend of Francis Place ; he sought out Bentham who drew up, for his
benefit, a scheme for the formation of a joint stock colonisation
society.[1] The society was formed.   The most zealous among the
young disciples of Bentham, Grote, Molesworth and Stuart Mill,
belonged to it : so that it happened that the Benthamites were the
founders of the English Australasian colonies.[2]   It is true that some
others, such as Bowring and Roebuck, protested, in the name of their
principles, against Wakefield's colonial enterprises.   But soon all Bentham's disciples without exception, emancipators and organisers, were
to find an opportunity for collaborating in the re-establishment of peace
in Canada.   The French Canadians revolted, and Roebuck was their
acknowledged advocate in the Commons.   The revolt was crushed ;
and the Liberal ministry sent out as governor of the colony the head
of the Radical party, Lord Durham, accompanied by Wakefield and
by the Benthamite Charles Buller.   A liberal and democratic constitution, chronologically the first of the colonial constitutions, solved all
the difficulties after a few years of crisis.[3]   It is paradoxical that the
Benthamites should have played such an immense part in the foundation of the new colonial Empire ; but it is natural that they should
have helped to make this Empire into a federation of autonomous
nations.

In politics, there was no need of the Utilitarian theories to make
everyone feel the scandal of the persistence of an electoral régime
which was out of date in an England in which everything had changed
—the distribution of wealth between classes, as well as the distribution of population between counties.   Not only did Bentham not
invent the Radical programme : it was on this point that he was the
most tardy to perceive the necessity of reform.   But the Philosophical
Radicals gave the Radical agitation, which was tumultuous and disordered, the doctrinal solidity which it lacked.   They considered
themselves the heirs of the tradition of the French Encyclopædists.
Fired with enthusiasm by the Revolution of July, they thought they
were the precursors of a coming revolution in England, analogous to
the Revolution of 1789.[4]   Bentham, in the *Parliamentary Candidates'
Society*,[5] took an active part in the 1831 elections, and a number of
Utilitarians were included in the reformed Parliament : Molesworth,
the future editor of Hobbes, George Grote, Roebuck, not to mention
Charles Villiers and Charles Buller.[6]   Already in 1830 Hobhouse
had secured the optional introduction of secret voting into vestry

[1] MSS. U. C., No. 8, Colonisation Society, etc. (Date of MS., Aug. 11, 1831).
[2] See *Edward Gibbon Wakefield, the Colonisation of South Australia and New
Zealand*, by R. Garnett, 1898.
[3] See *London and West. Rev.*, No. i. Dec. 1838, art. viii.
[4] *Autob.*, pp. 62-63, 131, 172.
[5] See his pamphlet, *Parliamentary candidates' proposed declaration of principle*,
1831 (not in Bowring).
[6] Bain, pp. 367-8, etc.

elections; year after year George Grote demanded in the House of
Commons, but without success, that the parliamentary elections
should be carried out by secret voting.[1] In 1836, the reform of the
parliamentary electorate was completed by a still more democratic
reform of the municipal electorate, and three out of the five Radicals
who composed the Commission which prepared the reform were
Benthamites—Bingham, who collaborated on the *Westminster Review*,
Charles Austin, the friend of Stuart Mill, and finally Joseph
Parkes, the secretary of the Commission, a democrat from Birmingham, and a friend and correspondent of Bentham. The Chartist
agitation was soon to begin, and the ' People's Charter ' was nothing
else than the political programme of Bentham as well as Cartwright:
it was Francis Place who drew it up.[2]

The agitation for electoral reform became complicated after 1832
by an agitation for administrative reform : once the aristocrats lost
the monopoly of political power, it was natural that the privileges and
the charges of the local administration should be removed from them
to be entrusted henceforward to functionaries nominated by the
elected representatives of the municipality and of the nation. It
was therefore necessary that a system of administrative centralisation
should be developed in democratised England : for this there was no
need of the propaganda of the Benthamites. None the less it remained
true that the disciples of Bentham were the almost indispensable
auxiliaries of the partisans of reform. The new administrative
system came up against many prejudices : it was condemned as being
contrary to national traditions, as unconstitutional, and as inspired
by French models. Thanks to Bentham, the reformers did not
appear as servile imitators of a foreign system : the disciples of an
English philosopher, they were in possession of a doctrine which
allowed them to show up and to denounce in a resounding manner the
interested ' fallacies ' of the Conservative party. Edwin Chadwick,
in the labours of the preparatory Commission, and George Grote, in
the debates in Parliament, were the zealous promoters of the ' New
Poor Law ', which, in order to prevent the ruin of the ratepayers,
grouped the parishes into administrative ' unions ', and submitted the
bodies elected by the areas to the permanent control of a central
board, sitting in London. A health administration was organised :
Edwin Chadwick and Southwood Smith were the promoters of the
new organisation.[3] The county police was reformed : Chadwick was
one of its reformers. As regards public education, Roebuck replaced
Brougham, who had become too moderate, as representative of
Bentham's ideas in Parliament. He suggested Prussia and France as

[1] Grote, *Minor Works*, pp. 19-37.
[2] Lovett, *Life and Struggles*. Wallas, *Life of Place*.
[3] On Chadwick's rôle, see Edwin Chadwick, *The Health of Nations*. A Review
of the Works, by——, with a biographical dissertation by B. W. Richardson.
2 vols. 1887.

models for England ; he protested against the anti-governmental prejudices which became absurd in proportion as the government became democratic, and demanded the establishment of a universal and secular system of primary and technical instruction :[1] the reform of 1840 was the result, still only a mediocre one, achieved by the efforts of Roebuck and his allies. As was justly observed by a Benthamite, those who thought to weaken and not to strengthen the government by the electoral reform of 1832, would do well to meditate on the words of Hobbes : ' Whoever, judging the sovereign power too great, wishes to make it smaller, must necessarily submit himself to a power capable of limiting it, that is to say, to a greater '.[2]

But were the Utilitarian Radicals prepared to be favourable without exception to all the extensions which might be made in the administrative system ? Opinion was demanding laws to protect the labour of women, children and even of adults against the tyranny of employers. The Benthamites collaborated in this reform also : for Benthamites were to be met with everywhere. Southwood Smith and Edwin Chadwick were members of the Commission of 1833 which organised a central board of factory inspectors on the model of the central board of Poor Law Commissioners. Yet the doctrine exposed by Ricardo, James Mill and MacCulloch is frankly contrary to these governmental interventions : such measures, by paralysing the source of the national industry would, according to them, do more harm than good to the workmen whose condition it was proposed to ameliorate. Thus the progress of socialism made the Radicals sick of administrative reform. On the other hand, the Chartists, although their programme was strictly political, counted on universal suffrage to ensure the advent of a social republic and to suppress the privileges enjoyed by the capitalists. The social democracy of the Chartists made the Utilitarian philosophers sick of political Radicalism. After 1840, their whole activity was concentrated on the economic part of their programme of reform. And no doubt the industrial crises which periodically troubled England after 1815 were enough to prove to public opinion the urgency of a reform of the tariff, conceived in a free trade spirit: the Utilitarians played no part in the petition of London merchants which was presented in 1821 by Baring, and Ricardo himself had been an economist before knowing James Mill and Bentham. But without James Mill would he have written his *Principles* ? Would he have entered Parliament ? The abolition of the duty on the importation of cereals in 1846 was the supreme triumph of the principles of Adam Smith and Ricardo :[3] now, Bentham's disciples had for ten years been a real force in the organisation of the free-trade agitation. It was the London Radicals, Grote, Molesworth, Joseph Hume, and Roebuck, who, in 1836, founded the

---

[1] Speech of July 30, 1833.   [2] MacCulloch, *Ed. Rev.*, No. cxxviii., July 1838, art. ix.
[3] Guizot, a friend of Peel, recognised, though he did not name Bentham, the influence on Peel of the new philosophy.

Anti-Corn-Law Association ; it was a Philosophical Radical, Charles
Villiers, the contemporary and friend of Stuart Mill, who, starting
from 1838, every year presented his motion for the abrogation of the
Corn Law ; [1] and when the movement was transferred from London,
the political capital of the nation, to Manchester, the industrial and
commercial centre of England, Bowring, the last of Bentham's
confidants, was one of the first organisers of the ' League ' which was
to make famous the name of Cobden.[2]

Thus was developed in England, twenty years after Bentham's
death, a new and simplified form of the Utilitarian philosophy.
Disciples of Adam Smith much more than of Bentham, the Utilitarians did not now include in their doctrine the principle of the
artificial identification of interests, that is, the governmental or administrative idea ; the idea of free-trade and of the spontaneous identification of interests summed up the social conceptions of these new
doctrinaires, who were hostile to any kind of regulation and law :
after the ' Westminster philosophy ', as the doctrine of the parliamentary Radicals and the agitators of Charing Cross had been
called, it was the 'Manchester philosophy' which triumphed. While
Darwin was extending Malthus' law to all living species, Buckle
reduced the whole philosophy of history to the principles of Adam
Smith's political economy. In his *Social Statics*, Herbert Spencer
expressly assimilated the natural laws of the economists with the
natural law of the jurists, and founded his philosophy on the refutation of Benthamism, which made judicial law emanate from positive
law and from the will of the government.[3] He regarded with the
same scorn both the meddling Conservatism of Lord Shaftesbury
and the meddling Radicalism of Edwin Chadwick : both demanded
the intervention of governmental authority in social relations, and
this was enough to make them both stand condemned.[4] Towards
the same time Stuart Mill, who was circumspect on principle and
very much concerned to escape the accusation of being either
exclusive or fanatical, was bringing forward simultaneously the
objections of Liberalism as against authoritarian Democracy, and the
objections of Socialism as against the philosophy of laisser faire.
The contradiction existing between the two principles on which
Utilitarianism was based was now apparent to all men. Philosophical
Radicalism had now spent its strength, in the history of English
thought and English legislation.

[1] On Villiers' relations with the Benthamites see *Autobiography*, pp. 77, 125,
126, 128.
[2] Bowring (*Howitt's Journal*, 1847, vol. ii. pp. 123-6), pays homage to Bentham.
[3] *Social Statics*, introduction (1st ed.), 1851, pp. i. *seq.*
[4] *Essays*, ed. 1868, vol. ii. pp. 364-5.

APPENDIX

'TRAITÉS DE LÉGISLATION CIVILE ET PÉNALE'

' My task, which was of a merely subordinate nature, has been concerned with details only. It was necessary to select from among a large number of variants, to do away with repetitions, to throw light on obscure passages, to put together all that pertained to one and the same subject, and to fill up the gaps which the author left in his anxiety not to delay the work. I have had rather to cut down than to supply, rather to shorten than to extend. The number of manuscripts which has passed through my hands and which I have had to decipher and compare has been considerable. I have had to do much to secure uniformity of style and much in the way of correction, nothing or very little as regards the substance of the ideas. The profusion of his wealth called only for the care of a steward.' It is in these words that Dumont defines the nature of the work on Bentham's papers to which he devoted himself. An examination of the manuscripts in University College makes it possible to verify and on certain points to complete these indications of Dumont's.

I. *Date of writing of the manuscripts used by Dumont.*—The manuscript was not completed when Dumont carried it off. ' I owe it to the author ', he writes, ' to state that he only yielded them up to the entreaties of friendship, and that he often reluctantly gave up to me works which were incomplete, and sometimes material which was quite unarranged '. The greater part, however, was completed, not only as a rough copy or outline (*matière* as Bentham called it) but also as a fair copy (*forme* in the language of Bentham), and we may add, had been written for some years, already—in 1783, according to our estimate. At the end of 1780 Bentham was still resisting the entreaties of his brother that he should write his work in French (Add. MSS. Brit. Mus. 33,539,

p. 117). In August 1781 in a letter to Samuel from Bowood, where he was staying with Lord Shelburne for the first time, he wrote that he was being 'thoroughly lazy, partly from inclination, and partly on principle' (33,539, p. 209). It was in 1782 that he wrote long essays, in English, on 'indirect legislation' and on the 'transplanting of laws': it is not likely that Bentham spent much time on his French work during this year. But in October 1783 Samuel expressed the 'wish that *Projet* should not be printed before they met' (33,539, p. 455). Now *Projet* is the title given by Bentham to all the French manuscripts which were to be taken off by Dumont. A month later, Samuel suggested an expurgated edition, in French, for which he would assume responsibility, for use in Russia (33,539, p. 466). 'I hope you have nearly finished', he wrote again on June 20, 1784 (Add. MSS. 33,540, p. 74). A certain number of the manuscripts in University College do, however, bear the date 1786 —the year, that is, when Bentham was staying with his brother in Russia. The manuscripts dated 1786 often refer to the theory of the four ends of civil law. See, for example, MSS. Univ. Coll. No. 29. *Proj. Mat. Droit Distrib. Privé Plan Sept.* 1786 : ... 3. *Bons Effets de l'Egalité. Comment elle sert à augmenter l'effet de l'Abondance sur le Bonheur.* 4. *Mauvais effets qu'aurait l'Egalité parfaite à cause de son incompatibilité avec la Sûreté.* 5. *Cas où l'Egalité peut être favorisée sans blesser la Sûreté.* 6. *Si elle pouvait n'avoir pas la Sûreté pour opposant elle devrait triompher. Cas où cela a lieu.*— No. 32 fragments on *la Sûreté, l'Egalité et les moyens de les concilier* are dated May, 1786 ; and a chapter entitled *Projet Matière Dr. Privé Propriété II.* 2 *Sept.* 1786, deals with the '*quatre buts du droit distributif privé*' (cf. No. 100).—A fragment entitled '*Proj. Mat. Contents*', which contains the succinct plan of a general theory of civil law, penal law, international law, of the '*moyens raffinés*' bears the pencilled note 'Projected, Sept. 1786'.—In the '*Vue générale d'un Corps de Législation*', the Introduction to the '*Rubriques générales*' of the Civil Code is dated July 1786 (No. 33) : should the rest of this part of the '*Traités*' be perhaps attributed to the same date? Finally, it may be that the manuscripts relating to the '*composition*' and to the '*style*' of the laws are a little later : some of them are included (No. 98) under a cover on which is written '1785 etc. *Code Pénal*', and, under the same number, a fragment entitled '*Projet Forme Amélioration*' contains an allusion to an English legal case of April 1788. A bundle (No. 100) bears on the cover the statement '*Législation.* 1. *Composition.* 2. *Démonstration.* 3. *Interprétation.* 4. *Amélioration.* 5. *Promulgation.* 6. *Invention.* 7. *Enseignement,* 1782-6' : but one of the manuscripts which treats of Louis XVI and the States General certainly belongs to the beginning of 1789.

Bentham went on writing. But, where the date is subsequent to 1789, it may be said, as a general rule, either that it was the date

of revision, not of composition, or else that the manuscripts are
mere tables of contents which had been previously dealt with. In
July 1794, Bentham drew up, under the title *Dr. Civil Contents*
a table of contents of his theory of equality, which is accompanied
by this note ' Memorandum. July 1794. This and the next sheet
contents of the general or metaphysical part. But since these
contents have been entered, this part has been much enlarged and
altered : nor is yet finished '. See also MSS. Univ. Coll. No. 99 :
' Civil Brouillon 3 July 1795. *Moral. Rousseau prêtre de la perte.
Ce qu'il a dit moi je ferai.*' The fourth column of the MS. runs like
this : Facienda (var. Inserenda) for Dumont. 1. *Progrès etc.* p. 13.
Selon Rousseau plus à gagner par profit illégitime que par profit légitime.
2. *Liberté politique*, chap. iii., iv. v., p. 3. But if Bentham really
did, at this period, emphasise the anti-equalitarian character of his
doctrine, it is only necessary to compare Dumont's text either with
the manuscripts dated 1786, or with this table of contents itself, to
see that the original text was respected. Or rather Dumont confined
himself to very unimportant modifications. Bentham wrote, for
example (No. 33. *Projet Forme Economie*) : ' *On a vu que les moyens
les plus puissants pour amener l'abondance sont ceux par lesquels on
pourvoit à la sûreté des propriétés et ceux par lesquels on favorise
l'égalité par rapport à ces mêmes propriétés*'. Dumont wrote : ' *qui
favorisent doucement leur égalisation* ' (*Vue générale*, etc. ch. xxviii.)
—In July 1795, tables of contents for the *Code Civil* (No. 100).
In 1795 (July 30 and Aug. 9), several fragments on *Contracts*, but
these were drawn up in English and Dumont appears to have made
little use of them (No. 100).—A fragment dated from Queen Square
Place, June 13, 1795, is entitled ' *Sur la Méthode par rapport au
raisonnement justificatif du Code* ' (No. 100).—Various fragments
on political economy (particularly an analysis of the *Wealth of
Nations*) were only ' reviewed ', ' analyzed ' and ' tabulated ' in
June and August, 1801 (No. 99).—Bentham sent some documents to
Dumont, on October 24, 1801, with this note ' Had you had these ? '
Alongside, in reply, Dumont wrote ' *Non* '. But there was nothing
but tables of contents and outlines of essays on ' *l'influence des temps
et des lieux* ' and on ' *législation indirecte* '.

2. *Fusion of several manuscripts into one.*—' The changes which
I have had to make ', writes Dumont, ' have varied according to
the nature of the manuscripts. In cases where I have found several
bearing on the same subject, but composed at different periods and
with different views, it has been necessary to reconcile them and to
incorporate them so as to make of them a single whole. Where the
author was rejecting some topical work which to-day would be
neither interesting nor even intelligible, I was unwilling that it
should be altogether lost, but I have, so to speak, moved out of the
deserted house everything which was capable of being preserved '.
Having examined the manuscripts we venture to say that Dumont

exaggerates the importance of this labour of fusion. The following, to be more precise, are the elements of which Dumont made use in the composition of the *Traités*.

A.—He makes use of a theory of civil law in three books, which do not correspond exactly to the three parts of the *Principes du Code Civil* contained in Dumont's book. The first book was devoted to general principles ; it was far from complete when Dumont carried off the manuscript : we can only find (MSS. Univ. Coll. No. 32) rough drafts (*Projet Matière*) of chapters i.-v., x., xiii., of the *Principes de Législation* which Dumont composed ' by making use ', as he says, in addition of ' several chapters ' of the *Introduction to the Principles of Morals and Legislation* (cf. Bowring, x. 309, and Add. MSS. Brit. Mus. 33,543, f. 13 : Dumont to Bentham, Dec. 1799. ' My dear Bentham, I do not ask of you any more morning conversation, but I do ask you for the papers concerned, and for other analogous ones, if, in the course of your research, you come upon anything which might be included in " the false ways of reasoning " in matters of legislation '). The second book seems to correspond to the two first parts of the *Principes du Code Civil*. We have practically the complete manuscript of this, and sometimes both in its rough sketch and its complete form (MSS. Univ. Coll. No. 29. First Part, chap. ii., vii. ; No. 32 : First Part, chap. ii., vi., vii., viii., xi., xiv. sect. 1, xv., xvii.—Second Part, chap. i., ii., iii., v., vi., vii.). The third book corresponds to the third part (see MSS. Univ. Coll. No. 32 : chap. i., ii., iv., v.) : Bentham, in No. 99, in a table of contents dated 1795, gives it the title of *États de la personne*.

B.—The manuscript of the *Principes du Code Pénal* was likewise practically completed when Dumont carried it off (see MSS. Univ. Coll. No. 62). The first part contains, in the manuscript, eighteen chapters : three chapters on *mauvaise foi* become Dumont's sixth chapter ; two chapters on *motifs* become chapter viii. ; two chapters on *caractère* become chapter xi.—The second contains twenty chapters : Dumont suppresses the chapters on the *moyens de prévention contre la récidive*, and on the *occasions de la satisfaction*. For the content of chapters xiv., xv., xvii. (*Satisfaction honoraire, Satisfaction vicarière*), see No. 100, cf. Add. MSS. Brit. Mus. 33,543, f. 13 : Dumont to Bentham, Dec. 1795 : ' But, in the name of all the gods of Paradise, you have got one of my note books, from Book II of the *Principes du Code Pénal* containing a part on honorary satisfaction and the whole of the treatment of vicarious satisfaction—you took the note book at my request in order to complete this second heading—you worked at it—you did not complete it and you never returned it to me. I have been reminding you of it for three years and more '. Cf. 33,542, f. 520 : Dumont to Bentham, Jan. 8th, 1798—and MSS. Univ. Coll. No. 98 : *Satisfaction collatérale. Contents*, July 27th, 1795.—The manuscript of the third part is missing ; it may be assumed that Dumont kept it, after the publication of the *Traités*, in order to make use of it again in editing the *Théorie des Peines*. As to the fourth part, Bentham had already drawn up the plan of this in French (MSS. Univ. Coll. No. 62) under the title *Moyens recherchés*. But Dumont's fourth part is nothing but the almost literal translation of a study, in English, entitled *Indirect Legislation*, which makes up almost the whole of No. 87 of the MSS. of University College (cf. Bowring, x. 383). This study, as the opening lines testify, should constitute a sequel to the *Introduction*. It seems probable that it was written in the second half of 1782. In it Bentham alludes to an improvement lately introduced in the method of recruiting in the army, and bases his statements on a decision of the Secretary of State for War, Townshend, which was announced in the *London Gazette* of May 25, 1782 ; further on, Bentham quotes, in favour of the institution of a public minister, a case which was brought before the Court of King's Bench on June 28, 1782.—Bentham's manuscript (No. 62) further contains the elements of a *livre V*, entitled *Pénal Délits Particuliers*, dealing with *délits accessoires*, *délits contre la souveraineté*, *délits publics*, *libelles* ; this has no equivalent in Dumont. Should a long fragment on *Délits Religieux* (No. 98), not used by Dumont, be included in the same book ?

C.—The manuscript of the *Vue générale d'un Corps complet de Lois* makes up No. 33. Thus we possess the manuscripts of chapters i., ii., iii., vii.-xiii., xxii., xxiv., xxv., xxx. In No. 29, are the rough drafts for chapters iii., xiv., xv. For chapters iv., xxxi., xxxii., xxxiii., see Nos. 98 and 100. It seems that this was the central portion of the work, for a time. On Jan. 8, 1798, Dumont wrote to Bentham (Add. MSS. Brit. Mus. 33,542, f. 520 *sqq.*) : ' I think that in order to make the *logic of the legislator* more interesting, it will be necessary to include in it the summary of the principles of the Civil Code, and that of the principles of the Penal Code, more or less in the same way and in the same style as the extracts which you have seen in the British Library.—The work would have two volumes instead of one, but this is not too much for so great a subject '.

D.—The *Panoptique*, Dumont tells us, is a ' memorandum in the form of a discourse . . . sent by Mr. Bentham to M. Garran de Coulon, member of the Legislative Assembly and of a committee for the reform of the criminal laws '.

E.—The *Promulgation des Lois* had been drawn up in French ; it may have been communicated to Dumont as late as 1801 (No. 100).

F.—The Essay entitled *De l'influence des temps et des lieux en matière de législation* is the translation of an essay written in English and entitled *Of the Influence of Time and Place in Matters of Legislation* (No. 100). This essay belongs to the year 1782. In it Bentham declares that ' the constitutional branch of the law of

England taking in its leading principles would probably be found by far the best beyond comparison that has hitherto made its appearance in the world '; and, on the manuscript there is a note, written in red ink by Bentham, now turned Radical, warning us that this was ' written in 1782 '.

G.—Nature of the modifications which Dumont makes to the French text.—We mention as information only the corrections made to the style (Bentham writes : *délits réfléchis* ; Dumont : *délits reflectifs*. Bentham writes : *satisfaction supprimatoire* ; Dumont : *satisfaction suppressive*. Bentham writes : *entierté*—Eng. entirety of a body of law ; Dumont : *integralité*) and the modifications made necessary by the fact that the work appeared fourteen years after it was written (historical allusions). On three points the modifications made by Dumont are interesting to note.

1st. Dumont modifies the irreligious passages. He respects and translates without too much alteration the chapter on *Indirect Legislation*, which became chapter xviii. of his *Moyens Indirects*, because this chapter, although it is precise, is fairly moderate. But he suppresses, in his tenth chapter, the passage in Bentham which deals with ' religious impostures '. ' Instructions apprising the people of the villainies that have been committed under favour of the apprehensions entertained of the power and malice of spiritual agents. Histories of this kind are unhappily too numerous, though not so much as of the instances in which equal or greater miseries have been inflicted under authority by process of law through the influence of similar delusions sincerely entertained.' In the same chapter, in the passage where Bentham establishes that of all forms of government despotism is both the simplest and the roughest, the most suitable to barbarous times, Dumont suppresses this anti-Christian epigram : ' It is the first that is likely to occur, and to uncultivated mind the only one. We know where it is that one man's serving two masters has been pronounced to be impossible '. Above all, he completely did away with Bentham's long and important reflections on *délits religieux*, the attack on what Bentham calls *cathothéisme*, the plea for atheism,—reflections which foreshadow the future *Analysis of Natural Religion*.

2nd. Dumont tones down Bentham's style ; in Bentham's manuscripts, we can immediately recognise the school at which he learned to write in French so easily ; it is easy to recognise the child who read *Candide* at the age of ten, and translated the *Taureau Blanc* at twenty-five ; the reader of the *Esprit des Lois* and the *Essai sur les Mœurs*. See the discussion of the question whether a father has the right to castrate his own children ; the digressions on polyandry and polygamy : all this is suppressed in Dumont. See also (No. 33) the kind of philosophical tale, with Adonaï, Adam and the Angel Gabriel as its characters, which Bentham pretends to have borrowed from a recently discovered fragment of the Talmud, and which he places under the *Rubrique générale* : *Droit* of his *Code Civil*. Dumont suppresses it ; this was not altogether unjustifiable, for the tale is pretty bad. But the page has a Voltairian flavour which dates the work, and makes one regret the suppression after all.

3rd. But Dumont explains very clearly the most important and also the most happy of the modifications which he made to Bentham's text when he writes : ' When he gave himself up to too profound abstractions, to a metaphysic which was, I will not say too subtle, but too arid, I have attempted to give the ideas further development, to make them intelligible by using facts and examples, and I have permitted myself to scatter here and there with discretion a few ornaments ' ; and better still—' In making use of several chapters of this work to make of them the *Principes généraux de Législation*, I have had to avoid what might have prejudiced his success : forms which were too scientific, subdivisions which were too numerous, and analyses which were too abstract '. Dumont does not appear to have made the decision to abridge Bentham's book immediately. See Add. MSS. Brit. Mus. 33,542, f. 39 : Dumont to Bentham, April, 3, 1795 : ' The more I think of the end of our conversation, the more I become reconciled to the idea that the French might be less complete, provided you really have the idea and the courage to produce an English Edition : there would then be something wherewith to satisfy readers of different powers '.

BIBLIOGRAPHY

By C. W. EVERETT

(Fellow of the Social Science Research Council of America)

A. GENERAL.

    I. HISTORY.

    II. BIOGRAPHY.

    III. SOME CRITICAL OPINIONS ON BENTHAM.

B. THE WORKS OF JEREMY BENTHAM.

    I. COLLECTED WORKS.

    II. BOOKS, PAMPHLETS, AND ARTICLES:

        1. PHILOSOPHY.
        2. CIVIL AND PENAL LAW:
            a. Civil and Penal Law in General.
            b. Penal Law.
            c. Civil Law.
        3. PROCEDURE AND EVIDENCE.
        4. CONSTITUTIONAL LAW.
        5. POLITICAL ECONOMY.
        6. RELIGION.
        7. MISCELLANEOUS.

    III. CHRONOLOGICAL LIST.

A. GENERAL

The following list of works has been selected with the aim of furnishing supplementary reading on the period covered.

I. HISTORY

GENERAL HISTORIES OF THE UTILITARIAN GROUP

ALBEE, ERNEST. A History of English Utilitarianism. 1902.
    The chapter on Bentham is intentionally brief.

STEPHEN, LESLIE. History of English Thought in the eighteenth century. 2 vols. 2nd ed. 1881.
—— The English Utilitarians. 3 vols. 1900.
The standard English works on the period and the movement.

GENERAL HISTORIES WITH DEFINITE REFERENCES TO THE UTILITARIAN GROUP

Cambridge History of English Literature. Vol. xi. 1914.
Good chapter on Bentham and the early Utilitarians, with bibliography.

CANNAN, EDWIN. A History of the Theories of Production and Distribution in English Political Economy from 1776 to 1848. 2nd ed. 1903.
For the evolution of economic theory.

DICEY, A. V. Lectures on the Relation between Law and Public Opinion in England during the nineteenth century. 1905.
Expert opinion on the influence of Bentham on English legal reform.

HALÉVY, ELIE. Histoire du Peuple anglais au XIXe siècle, Vol. I. L'Angleterre en 1815. 1912. (English translation: A History of the English People in 1815. 1924.)
Contains an extensive critical bibliography; very useful for the study of the social and political history of the period.

HAZLITT, WM. The Spirit of the Age. Works, vol. iv. 1902.
Interesting portraits of Hazlitt's contemporaries, particularly Bentham.

HELD, ADOLF. Zwei Bücher zur socialen Geschichte Englands. 1881.
Contains valuable social and economic materials.

II. BIOGRAPHY

'Beccaria, Cesare', in Coleman Phillipson, Three Criminal Law Reformers. 1923.
A translation of Beccaria's 'Dei delitti e delle pene' is to be found in J. A. Farrer's Crimes and Punishments. 1880.

Bentham, Jeremy.
The Life of Bentham contained in vols. x. and xi. of Bowring's edition of Bentham's Works, Edinburgh, 1838-43, is the source of all later biographies, but is somewhat misleading. Bowring probably took down the reminiscences of Bentham's old age correctly, but Bentham's memory was not very accurate after he passed the age of seventy.

Stephen, Leslie. The English Utilitarians. 1900.
Vol. i. is a biography of Bentham.

Bentham, Jeremy. Charles Milner Atkinson. 1905.

Phillipson, Coleman. Three Criminal Law Reformers. 1923.
Has a good short Life of Bentham.

Two excellent articles by Graham Wallas should also be mentioned :
'Jeremy Bentham', Pol. Science Quarterly, March, 1923 ; and
'Bentham as Political Inventor', Contemporary Review, March,
1926.

Bowring, Sir John. Autobiographical Recollections, with a brief
memoir by Lewis Bentham Bowring. 1877.
Largely personal, with little information on the period.

'Burdett, Sir Francis ', in Hazlitt's Spirit of the Age.

Burke, Edmund : An historical study. John Morley. 1867.

Burke. John Morley, Viscount Morley. 1879.
Morley's two works have helped to bring about the present appreciation of Burke.

Burke, Memoir of the Life and Character of the Right Hon. Edmund,
Sir James Prior. 5th ed. 1854.
Still the standard Life.

Cartwright, Major, Life and Correspondence of. Edited by his niece.
2 vol. 1826.
Valuable for information on the democratic agitators from 1776
onwards.

Cobbett, Wm., Life of. G. D. H. Cole. 1924.
An admirable biography of the great, though eccentric, journalist
and agitator.

Fonblanque, Life and Labours of Albany. By E. B. de Fonblanque,
1874.
An important Utilitarian journalist.

Fox, Caroline. Memories of Old Friends. 1882.
Valuable for life of J. S. Mill.

Godwin, Wm. : His Friends and Contemporaries. Charles Kegan Paul.
2 vol. 1876.

Grote, George, The Personal Life of. Mrs. Grote. 1873.
Interesting and sometimes indiscreet anecdotes about the Benthamites, probably somewhat inaccurate.

Horner, Francis, M.P., Memoirs and Correspondence of. L. Horner.
2 vol. 1843.
A member of the Utilitarian group in Parliament.

Hume, David, Life and Correspondence of. J. H. Burton. 2 vol. 1846.
Still the authoritative Life.

Mackintosh, Sir J., Memoirs of the Life of. Edited by R. J. Mackintosh.
1835.

Malthus and His Work. J. Bonar. 1885.

Mill, James. A biography. Alexander Bain. 1882.

Mill, John Stuart. A criticism : with Personal Recollections. Alex.
Bain. 1882.

Mill, John Stuart, Autobiography. 1867.
See also the second and third vols. of Leslie Stephen, The English Utilitarians, for studies of the two Mills.

Molesworth, Sir William, Life of. Mrs. H. Fawcett. 1901.
See also The Philosophical Radicals of 1832, Mrs. Grote, 1866, for information about the Radicals, particularly Molesworth.

Paine, Thomas, Life of. M. D. Conway. New ed., 2 vol. 1902.
Conway destroyed the early scandals about Paine.

Place, Francis, Life of. Graham Wallas. 2nd ed. 1918.
Wallas's researches in the Place Papers brought to light a great deal of information on the practical politics of the Radicals.

Priestley, Life and Correspondence of Dr. Joseph. J. T. Rutt. 1831-2.

Ricardo, David. Ricardo's Works, edited by J. R. M'Culloch, 1846, contain a biography of Ricardo.
See also Ricardo's Letters to Malthus, edited by Bonar. 1887.
Ricardo's Letters to J. R. M'Culloch, edited by Hollander. 1895.
Ricardo's Letters to Trower, edited by Bonar and Hollander. 1899.
The Letters contain important information on Ricardo and his ideas.

Roebuck, J. A., Life and Letters of. R. E. Leader. 1897.
Roebuck was an important member of the Utilitarian group in Parliament.

Romilly, Sir Samuel, Memoirs of the Life of. Edited by his sons. 3 vol. 1840.
Besides this autobiography, see the ' Life of Romilly ' in Three Criminal Law Reformers. Coleman Phillipson. 1923.

Shelburne, Life of William, Earl of. Lord Edmund Fitzmaurice. 2nd ed. 2 vol. 1912.
Interesting account of Shelburne's relations with Priestley and Bentham.

Smith, Adam, Life of. John Rae. 1895.
The authoritative biography.

Tooke, John Horne, Life of. Alexander Stephens. 2 vol. 1813.
Diffuse and probably inaccurate.

Wilberforce, Wm., Life of. By his sons. 5 vol. 1838.
Contains some details of the life of Bentham.

The Dictionary of National Biography has an excellent article on ' Blackstone ' by G. P. Macdonell ; on ' Bentham,' with list of his works, by Sir J. Macdonnel ; on ' Romilly ' by J. M. Rigg ; on ' Burke ' by the Rev. Wm. Hunt ; and articles by Leslie Stephen on the two Mills, Hume, Adam Smith, Ricardo, and Godwin.

III. SOME CRITICAL OPINIONS ON BENTHAM AND HIS WORK

JOHN STUART MILL. Dissertations and Discussions, vol. i. pp. 330-392 : ' Bentham ', extract from the London and Westminster Review, August, 1838.

SIR JAMES MACKINTOSH. A Dissertation on the Progress of Ethical Philosophy, chiefly during the seventeenth and eighteenth centuries (Introduction to the Encyclopaedia Britannica, 1830, edited by Whewell, 1836, pp. 284 ff.).

EDWARD LYTTON BULWER. England and the English, 1833, Appendix B : remarks on Bentham's philosophy ; Appendix C : a few remarks on Mr. Mill (the two appendices are by John Stuart Mill).

LORD BROUGHAM. Speeches, vol. ii. 1838, pp. 287 ff. : Introduction to the speech of February 7, 1828, ' On the present state of the law '. An appreciation of Bentham as law reformer.

Edinburgh Review, No. clviii., October, 1843, art. viii. : ' Jeremy Bentham ' (article by Empson ; see the reply by John Stuart Mill in the number of January, 1844).

Fortnightly Review, 1877 (New Series, vol. 21, pp. 647 ff.) : ' Bentham and Benthamism ' (article by H. Sidgwick).

F. C. MONTAGUE. Introduction to edition of A Fragment on Government. 1891.

SIR HENRY SUMNER MAINE. Lectures on the Early History of Institutions, 1895, Lecture xii., and Sir Frederick Pollock, An Introduction to the History of the Science of Politics, 1890, pp. 96 ff. (criticism of the method of Bentham from the point of view of the historical method).

JOHN MACCUNN. Six Radical Thinkers. 1907.

A. SETH PRINGLE-PATTISON. The Philosophical Radicals. 1907.

Law Quarterly Review. Vol. xi., Nos. 41 and 42. 1895. (Articles by C. S. Kenny.)

Political Science Quarterly. Vol. 33. 1918. ' Bentham's Felicific Calculus ' (article by W. P. Montague).

Juridical Review. Vol. 35. Pp. 248-284. 1923. ' Bentham and his School ' (A. A. Mitchell).

Opinions littéraires, philosophiques et industrielles, 1825, de la législation, pp. 199 sqq. (Saint-Simonianism defined in relation to Benthamic Utilitarianism).

CHARLES COMTE. Traité de la Législation. 1827. Livre I. chap. xiv.

P. ROSSI. Traité de Droit Pénal. 1829. Livre I. chap. iv.-vii. ; livre II, chap. i. ; livre III. chap. iv.

BIBLIOGRAPHY

TH. JOUFFROY. Cours de Droit Naturel. 1833. 13ᵉ leçon : Système égoïste, Bentham.

LOUIS REYBAUD. Études sur les Réformateurs ou Socialistes Modernes. Vol. II. 1843, chap. iv. : les Utilitaires et Jérémie Bentham.

PHILARÈTE CHASLES. Études sur les Hommes et les Mœurs au XIXᵉ siècle. 1849. Pp. 86 sqq. : Visite à Jérémie Bentham.

M. GUYAU. La Morale anglaise contemporaine : morale de l'utilité et de l'évolution. 1879. Pp. 1 sqq., 265 sqq.

E. NYS. Études de droit international. 1901.

ROBERT VON MOHL. Die Geschichte und Literatur der Staatswissenschaften in Monographien dargestellt. Erlangen, 1858. Verlag von F. Enke. Vol. iii. No. 18, pp. 610 ff.

B. THE WORKS OF JEREMY BENTHAM

As no complete bibliography of Bentham's writings exists except in A. Siegwart's *Bentham's Werke und ihre Publikation*, Bern, 1910, the titles of his books and pamphlets are here printed in full. The works are classified logically, and chronological order is followed in each of the subdivisions. The subdivisions are : 1. Philosophy ; 2. Civil and Penal Law ; 3. Procedure and Evidence ; 4. Constitutional Law ; 5. Political Economy ; 6. Religion ; 7. Miscellaneous.

Reference is made after each entry to Bowring's edition of the collected works, unless the work in question was omitted by Bowring. Most of the titles are taken from the title-pages of the works, and sometimes differ from those given by Siegwart.

I. COLLECTED WORKS

Œuvres de J. Bentham (translated by P. E. L. Dumont). 3 vol. Bruxelles, Hauman. 1829-30.

The Works of Jeremy Bentham, published under the superintendence of his executor, J. Bowring. 11 vol. 1838-43. Edinburgh, Tait.

Colección de obras del célebre Jeremias Bentham (compilados por E. Dumont) con comentarios por B. Anduaga y Espinosa. 14 vol. Madrid, 1841-43. 4°.

Benthamiana : or, select extracts from the works of Jeremy Bentham. With an outline of his opinions on the principal subjects discussed in his works. Edited by John Hill Burton, Advocate. Edinburgh, Tait. 1843.

II. BOOKS, PAMPHLETS AND ARTICLES
1. PHILOSOPHY

An Introduction to the Principles of Morals and Legislation, printed in the year 1780 and now first published. 1789. London, T. Payne. In 4°, ix. 335 pp. + 32 pp. corrections.

A new edition, corrected by the Author, in two volumes. London, printed for E. Wilson and W. Pickering. 1823. 2 vol.

Reprinted by Clarendon Press, Oxford. 1876.

Bowring, i. 1 ff. [with some additions from Dumont].

[Extracts and partial translations appeared in :]

Espiritu di Bentham : Sistema de la Ciencia Social, ideado por el jurisconsulto Inglés J. B. y puesto en ejecucion conforme a los principios del Autor original por el Dr. D. Toribio Nuñez. Salamanca, 1820.

Principios de la ciencia social ó de las ciencias morales y politicas. Por el jurisc. Inglés J. B. ordenados conforme al sistema del autor original y aplicados à la constitucion española por D. Nuñez. Salamanca, 1821.

A table of the springs of action : showing the several species of pleasures and pains, of which man's nature is susceptible : together with the several species of interests desires and motives, respectively corresponding to them : and the several sets of Appellatives Neutral, Eulogistic, and Dyslogistic, by which each species of motive is wont to be designated : to which are added explanatory notes and observations indicative of the application of which the matter of this table is susceptible, in the character of a basis or foundation, of and for the art and science of morals,—otherwise termed Ethics,—whether Private, or Public—alias Politics—(including legislation), theoretical or practical alias Deontology—exegetical alias expository, (which coincides mostly with the theoretical), or censorial, which coincides mostly with Deontology : also of and for Psychology, in so far as concerns Ethics, and history (including biography) in so far as considered in an ethical point of view. London, 1815. Taylor. [Really first published by R. Hunter, London, 1817.]

   Bowring, i. pp. 195-219.

Chrestomathia : being a collection of papers, explanatory of the design of an institution, proposed to be set on foot, under the name of the Chrestomathic Day School, or Chrestomathic School, for the extension of the new system of instruction to the higher branches of learning, for the use of the middling and higher ranks of life. London, 1815, Payne and Foss. [Not published until 1816.]

Part II, being an essay on nomenclature and classification including a critical examination of the encyclopedical table of Francis Bacon, as improved by d'Alembert and the first lines of a new one grounded on the application of the logical principle of exhaustively bifurcate analysis to the moral principle of general Utility. London, 1817.

   Bowring, viii. pp. 1-192.

[Extracted from Part II. for a French work :]

Essai sur la nomenclature et la classification des principales branches d'art-et-science : ouvrage extrait du Chrestomathia de J. B. par George Bentham. Paris, 1823, Bossange frères.

Œuvres, Bruxelles, vol. iii. pp. 307-366.

BIBLIOGRAPHY 529

Deontology ; or, the science of morality : in which the harmony and
coincidence of duty and self-interest, virtue and felicity, prudence
and benevolence, are explained and exemplified. From the MSS. of
Jeremy Bentham, arranged and edited by John Bowring. 2 vol.
London, Edinburgh, Tait. 1834.

[Translations :]

French : Déontologie ou science de la morale, ouvrage posthume de
J. B., revu, mis en ordre, et publié par J. Bowr., traduit sur les MSS.
par Benjamin Laroche. Paris, 1834, Charpentier. 2 vol.

German : Deontologie oder die Wissenschaft der Moral, aus den MSS.
von J. B., geordnet und herausgegeben von J. Bowr. aus dem englischen
übertragen. 2 vol. Leipzig, 1834, Allgem. Niederl. Buchhandlg.

Spanish : Deontologie, o ciencia de la moral, obra posthuma de J. B.,
revisada y ordenada por Mr. J. Bowr. y publicada en francés sobre
el manuscrito original, traducida al español por Don Pascual Perez.
Valencia, 2 vol. 1836. Paris, 1839, gonas. 3 vol.

A Fragment on Ontology. [Written 1813, 1814, and 1821 ; first published
Bowring, viii. pp. 192-211.]

Essay on Logic. [Written about 1816 ; first published Bowring, viii.
pp. 213-293.]

Nomography, or the art of inditing laws. Bowring, iii. pp. 231-283
[with an appendix]. Logical arrangements, or instruments of invention and discovery employed. Bowring, iii. pp. 285-295.

2. CIVIL AND PENAL LAW
a. Civil and Penal Law in general

Traités de Législation civile et pénale, Précédés de Principes généraux de
Legislation, et d'une Vue d'un Corps complet de Droit : terminés
par un Essai sur l'influence des Tems et des Lieux relativement aux
Lois. Par M. Jérémie Bentham, jurisconsulte anglois. Publiés
en François par Ét. Dumont, de Genève, d'après les Manuscrits
confiés par l'Auteur. 3 vol. Paris, an X, 1802, Bossange, Masson
et Besson.

[Second edition :] Traités de législation civile et pénale. 3 vol. Paris,
1820, Bossange, Rey, et Gravier.

[Third edition :] ' revue, corrigée et augmentée '. Paris, Rey et Gravier,
1830. 3 vol.

[Another :] London, Taylor & Francis. 1858. 2 vol.

[Translations :]

German : Grundsätze der Zivil- und Kriminalgesetzgebung aus den
Handschriften des englischen Rechtsgelehrten J. B., herausgegeben
von E. Dumont, nach der 2. Auflage für Deutschland bearbeitet und
mit Anmerkungen von Dr. F. E. Benecke. 2 vol. Berlin, 1830,
Amelang.

Prinzipien der Gesetzgebung, herausgegeben von E. Dumont, nach der neuesten Auflage übersetzt. Köln, 1833, Arend.

English : Theory of Legislation by J. Bentham, translated from the French of E. Dumont by R. Hildreth. London, 1864.
[Another English translation appeared in America.]
Bentham's Theory of Legislation. Translated and edited from the French of Étienne Dumont by Charles Milner Atkinson. 2 vol. London, 1914.

[Russian : Two translations, the first in 1805.]

Spanish : Obras, Espinosa. Vol. 1-8.

Tratados de legislación civil y penal, obra extractada de los manuscriptos del Señor J. B. por E. D., y traducida al castellano con comentarios por Ramon Salas con arreglo á la secundo edición revista, corregida y aumentada. Madrid, 1821, 1822.

[Second edition appeared in 1823 :] edición hecha bajo la dirección de J. R. Masson. 8 vol. Paris, Masson y Hijo.

[Third edition :] Paris, 1838, Lecomte y Lassere. 8 vol.

[Extracts and a partial translation appeared in:]
Compendio de los tratados de legislación civil etc. con notas por J. Esriche. Paris, 1828. 2 vol.

Hungarian : Bentham Jer. Munkai. Polgári s Büntetö Törvényhozási értekezések Bentham Jer. késizataibol kiadta Dumont Istvan Francziábol Récsi Emil, 2 vol. Kolozvárt. 1842-1844.
[Also Polish and Portuguese translations are said to exist.]

Truth versus Ashurst ; or Law as it is, contrasted with what it is said to be. Written in December, 1792. And now first published. London, 1823, T. Moses. Bowring, v. pp. 231-237.

b. Penal Law

A view of the Hard-Labour-Bill ; being an Abstract of a Pamphlet intituled, ' Draught of a Bill to punish, by imprisonment and hard labour, certain offenders, and to establish proper places for their reception '.—Interspersed with Observations relative to the subject of the above draught in particular, and to penal jurisprudence in general. London, 1778. Printed for T. Payne.

Panopticon ; or, the Inspection House : containing the idea of a new principle of construction applicable to any sort of establishment, in which persons of any description are to be kept under inspection : and in particular to Penitentiary-houses, Prisons, Houses of industry, Workhouses, Poor Houses, Manufactories, Madhouses, Lazarettos, Hospitals, and Schools ; with a plan of management adopted to the principle : in a series of letters, written in the year 1787, from Crecheff in White Russia, to a friend in England. Dublin, printed : London, reprinted ; 1791. 2 vol. T. Payne.

Panopticon : Postscript ; Part i. : containing further particulars and alterations relative to the plan of construction originally proposed ; principally adapted to the purpose of a Panopticon Penitentiary-House. London, T. Payne, 1791.

Panopticon : Postscript ; Part ii. containing a plan of management for a Panopticon Penitentiary-House. London, T. Payne, 1791.

Letters to Lord Pelham, giving a comparative view of the system of penal colonization in New South Wales, and the Home Penitentiary System, prescribed by two Acts of Parliament of the years 1794 and 1799. London, 1802. 80 pp. + 72 pp.

A plea for the Constitution : shewing the enormities committed to the oppression of British subjects, innocent as well as guilty, in breach of Magna Charta, the Petition of Right, the Habeas Corpus Act, and the Bill of Rights ; as likewise of the several transportation acts ; in and by the design, foundation and government of the penal colony of New South Wales : including an inquiry into the right of the crown to legislate without Parliament in Trinidad and other British Colonies. London, 1803, Mawman, Hatcher.

Panopticon versus New South Wales ; or, the Panopticon Penitentiary system, and the penal colonization system compared. Containing,

1. Two letters to Lord Pelham, Secretary of State, comparing the two Systems on the ground of *expediency*.

2. Plea for the Constitution : representing the *illegalities* involved in the Penal Colonization System (Anno 1803 printed : now first published). London, 1812.

Bowring, iv. pp. 173-284.

Lettres à Lord Pelham, renfermant un parallèle du système de colonization pénale, adopté pour la Nouvelle Galles du Sud, et de celui des maison de repentir érigées dans la métrople, dont l'exécution a été prescrite par deux actes du Parlement des années 1794 et 1799. Traduites de l'anglais de M. Jer. B. et publiées en français par Ad. Duquesnoy. Paris, An XII.—1804.

Théorie des peines et des récompenses. Par M. Jérémie Bentham, jurisconsulte anglois, rédigée en français d'après les MSS., par Et. Dumont. Londres, 1811. 2 vol.

[Second edition :] Paris, 1818, Bossange and Masson. 2 vol.

[Third edition :] Paris, 1825, Bossange. 2 vol.

Œuvres, Bruxelles. · Vol. 2, pp. 1-238.

[Translations :]

Spanish : Teoria de las penas legales, por J. B., 2 vol. Paris, J. Smith, 1825.

Teoria de las Recompensas. 2 vol. Paris, J. Smith, 1825.

Teoria de las penas y de las recompensas, obra sacada de los manuscritos de J. B. . . . por Es. Dumont, traducida al español de la tercera edición . . . por D. L. B. Paris, Masson, 1826. 4 vol.

English : The Rationale of Punishment, by Jeremy Bentham. London, 1830. Robert Heward. [Trans. by Richard Smith ; some use of MSS.]

Bowring published this as Part ii. of the Principles of Penal Law together with the pamphlet published by Bentham in 1831 under the title ' Jer. Bentham to his fellow citizens of France on death punishment. London, 1831, Robert Heward.'

Bowring, i. pp. 388-532.

The Rationale of Reward. London, 1825, John and H. L. Hunt [trans. by Richard Smith]. Bowring, ii. pp. 189-266. [Book 4, being only an extract from the Manual of Political Economy, was left in that work, *i.e.* Bowring, iii. pp. 31-84.]

Letters to count Toreno on the proposed Penal Code, delivered by the legislation committee of the Spanish Cortes, April 25th, 1821 : Written at the Count's request. London, 1822, E. Wilson.

Bowring, viii. pp. 487-554.

The King against Edmonds, and others : set down for trial, at Warwick, on the 29th of March, 1820. Brief remarks, tending to show the untenability of this indictment. London, John M'Creery, 1820.

Bowring, v. pp. 239-251.

The King against Sir Charles Wolseley, Baronet, and Joseph Harrison, Schoolmaster : set down for trial, at Chester, on the 4th of April, 1820. Brief remarks, tending to show the untenability of this indictment. London, 1820, John M'Creery.

Bowring, v. pp. 253-261.

c. Civil Law

A commentary on Mr. Humphreys' Real Property Code, Being a Review of ' Observations on the actual state of the English law of real property with the outline of a code '. By James Humphreys, Esq. of Lincoln's Inn, Barrister. Westminster Review, vol. 6, No. 12. October 1826.

Article Eight of the Westminster Review. No. xii. for October 1826, on Mr. Humphreys' Observations on the English Law of Real Property, with the outline of a code, &c. London, printed by T. C. Hansard. Jan. 1827. Bowring, v. pp. 387-416.

Outline of a plan of a general register of real property.

Bowring, v. pp. 417-435.

Principles of International Law. [Written 1786-1789.]

Bowring, ii. pp. 535-571.

3. PROCEDURE AND EVIDENCE

Draught of a New Plan for the Organization of the judicial establishment in France : proposed as a succedaneum to the draught presented, for the same purpose, by the Committee of Constitution, to the National Assembly, Dec. 21st, 1789, by Jeremy Bentham, March 1790.

Bowring, iv. pp. 285-406.

Draught of a new plan for the organization of the judicial establishment in France, accompanied with a translation of the draught presented, for the same purpose, by the committee of constitution to the national assembly December 21st 1789 ; and observations designed to exhibit the comparative eligibility of the two plans. By Jeremy Bentham. No. V. containing chap. v. tit. iii. on judges of the ordinary courts July 16th 1790, in 8°. [Printed cover serves as title.]

Organization du pouvoir judiciare, vue sommaire des différences les plus remarquables entre le projet du Comité et le projet anglois dont l'auteur, Mr. Bentham, a fait hommage à l'Assemblée nationale. . . . 2 pp.

Sur le nouvel ordre judiciare en France, ou extraits des dissertations de M. Bentham adressées par l'auteur à l'Assemblée nationale, traduit de l'anglais. Paris, imprimerie du Patriote françois. 20 pp. [Extract from Courrier de Provence.]

Scotch Reform ; considered with reference to the plan, proposed in the late Parliament, for the regulation of the courts, and the administration of justice in Scotland : with illustrations from English Non-Reform : in the course of which divers imperfections, abuses, and corruptions, in the administration of justice, with their causes, are now, for the first time, brought to light. In a series of letters addressed to The Right Hon. Lord Grenville, etc., etc., with tables, in which the principal causes of factitious complication, delay, vexation, and expense, are distinguished from such as are natural and inavoidable, by Jeremy Bentham. London, 1808, R. Taylor.

Bowring, v. pp. 1-53.

[Second edition :] Same title, except that ' In a series . . . Lord Grenville ' is omitted ; and ' The second edition, with four additional tables, shewing the abuses in cases of appeal. 1811. R. Taylor ' is added.

Summary view of a plan of a Judicatory, under the name of the Court of Lord Delegates, proposed for the exercise of those judicial functions, the adequate discharge of which by the whole House has, for these six or seven years, been rendered confessedly impracticable, by want of time. 1808. 4 pp. fol.

. . . with four additional tables showing the abuses in cases of appeal.

Letter on the bill called Lord Eldon's.

Bowring, v. pp. 55-60.

An Introductory view of the Rationale of Evidence for the use of Non-Lawyers as well as Lawyers. [Edited by James Mill. 1810 ?]

Bowring, vi. pp. 1-187.

' Swear not at all ' : containing an exposure of the inutility and mischievousness, as well as antichristianity, of the ceremony of an oath : A view of the Parliamentary recognition of its needlessness, implied

534 PHILOSOPHIC RADICALISM

in the practice of both houses : And an indication of the unexceptionable securities, by which whatsoever practical good purposes the ceremony has been employed to serve would be more effectually provided for. Together with proof of the open and persevering contempt of moral and religious principle, perpetuated by it, and rendered universal, in the two Church-of-England Universities ; more especially in the University of Oxford. Predetached from an introduction to the Rationale of Evidence. London, 1813, Taylor. [This was not published until 1817, by Hunter, with the title slightly changed to ' exposure of the needlessness ', instead of ' inutility '.]

> Bowring, v. pp. 187-229.

The elements of the art of packing, as applied to special juries, particularly in cases of libel law. London, E. Wilson, 1821. [Written 1809 ; printed 1810.]

> Bowring, v. pp. 61-186.

Traité des preuves judiciaires, Ouvrage extrait des MSS. de M. Jéremie Bentham, jurisconsulte anglais, par Et. Dumont. 2 vol. Paris, 1823, Bossange frères.

[Second edition :] revue et augmentée. Bossange, 1830.

Œuvres. Bruxelles, ii. pp. 239-481.

[Translations :]

English : A Treatise on Judicial Evidence, extracted from the MSS. of Jeremy Bentham by M. Dumont, translated into English. London, 1825. Baldwin.

Spanish : Tratado de las Pruebas Judiciales, obra extraida de los manuscritos de M. Jer. B. ... escrita en francés por Estevan Dum. y traducida al castellano por C. M. V. 1825, Paris, Bossange frères. 4 vol. [Reprinted in Espinosa, vol. 11-14.]

Tratado etc. traducida de la secunda edición por Don J. L. de Bustamente. Paris, 1838, H. Bossange. 4 vol.

German : Theorie des gerichtlichen Beweises aus dem Französischen von Et. Dumont. Berlin, 1838, Ende.

Rationale of Judicial Evidence, specially applied to English practice, from the MSS. of Jeremy Bentham, in five vol. London, 1827, Hunt and Clarke. [Edited by J. S. Mill.]

> Bowring, vi. 188 ff. and vii.

Equity Dispatch Court Proposal : containing a plan for the speedy and unexpensive termination of the suits now depending in Equity Courts. With the form of a petition, and some account of a proposed bill for that purpose. London, 1830, Heward.

> Bowring, iii. pp. 297-317. [Pp. 319-431 contains an enlargement of Section 3 (Dispatch Court Bill. Some account of it.) entitled :] Equity Dispatch Court bill : being a bill for the institution of an

experimental Judicatory under the name of the Court of Dispatch, for exemplifying in practice the manner in which the proposed *summary* may be substituted to the so called *regular* system of procedure ; and for clearing away by the experiment, the arrear of business in the Equity Courts. Now first published from the MSS.

Letter to Globe, May 25th, 1830.   [Contains first attack on Brougham.]

1831 Boa constrictor alias Helluo Curiarum ; observations on the ' Resolved on ' absorption of the vice chancellor's court and the Master of the Rolls Court into the Lord High Chancellor's Court.

1831 Observations on the Bankruptcy Court bill. [First as 8 page pamphlet, then as 24 page.]

[Finally combined as :]

Lord Brougham desplayed : including

    I. Boa constrictor, alias Helluo Curiarum ;

    II. Observations on the Bankruptcy Court Bill, now ripened into an act ;

    III. Extracts from proposed constitutional Code. London, Heward, 1832.

Principles of judicial procedure, with the outlines of a procedure code. [Edited from the MSS. in 1837 by Richard Doane, and published in Bowring, ii. pp. 1-188.]

4. CONSTITUTIONAL LAW

A Fragment on Government ; being an examination of what is delivered, on the subject of Government in General in the introduction to Sir William Blackstone's Commentaries : with a preface, in which is given a critique on the work at large [anonymous]. London, 1776, Payne.

. . . Second edition enlarged. London, 1823.

    Bowring, i. pp. 221-295.

Reprinted 1891 : Edited with an introduction by F. C. Montague. Oxford, Clarendon Press. [Historical preface omitted.]

Preface intended for the second edition of the Fragment on Government. [Printed by Bentham in 1828, but not published until the Works appeared, where it is put after the preface to the first edition.]

    Bowring, i. pp. 240-259.

A Comment on the Commentaries, by Jeremy Bentham, being a critical examination of the Introduction to Sir William Blackstone's Commentaries on the Laws of England. Now first published from the MSS. with an introduction by C. W. Everett. Oxford, 1928.

Essay on political tactics, containing six of the principal rules proper to be observed by a political assembly in the process of forming a decision : with the reasons on which they are grounded ; and a comparative application of them to British and French practice :

536 PHILOSOPHIC RADICALISM

being a fragment of a larger work ; a sketch of which is subjoined.
London, 1791, Payne. 4°.

[Translations :]

French : Tactique des Assemblées législatives, suivie d'un traité des
sophismes politiques : ouvrage extrait des MSS. de M. Jérémie
Bentham, jurisconsulte anglais ; par Ét. Dumont. Geneve, 1816.
2 vol. J. Paschoud.

[2nd edition :]—revue et augmentée. Paris, Bossange frères, 1822.
Œuvres, Bruxelles, vol. i. pp. 371-576.

German : Taktik oder Theorie des Geschaftsganges in deliberierenden
Volksständeversammlungungen, nach Benthams hinterlassenen
Papieren bearbeitet von Dumont. Erlangen, 1817. [Bentham died
in 1832.]

Spanish : Tactica de las Asambleas legislativas, por Jeremias Bentham.
Paris, 1824, J. Smith. 18°. 331 pp.

Secunda edición, Tactica de las Asambleas legislativas de J. B. Traducida
al Castellano por F. C. de C. Madrid, 1835, Jordan.

[Another ed.] Paris, 1838, printed by Pillet.

Italian : La tattica Parlementare ; traduzione di Lor. Serazzi. Torino,
editore A. Pavesio, 1848.

[Second ed.] Tattica delle assemblee legislat. Naples, 1863.

[Third ed.] La tattica Parlementare. Note di Bentham e Dumont.
Brunialti, Bibl. di Scienza politiche. Vol. 4, Part 2. Torino, 1888.

An Essay on political tactics, or inquiries into the discipline or mode of
proceeding proper to be observed in political assemblies : principally
applied to the practice of the British Parliament, and to the constitution and situation of the National Assembly of France.

Bowring, ii. pp. 299-373.

' Traité des sophismes politiques ' was published together with ' Sophismes
anarchiques : Examen critique de diverses déclarations des droits
de l'homme et du citoyen ' in the ' Tactique des Assemblées legisla-
tives.'

[Translations :]

Spanish : Tratado de los sofismas politicas. Paris, 1824, J. Smith.

[Second edition :] Pillet, Paris, 1837.

[Neither of these editions included the sophismes anarchiques,
though both the following editions did :]

Nueva edición, aumentada con el tratado de los sofismas anarchicas por
el mismo. Paris, 1838, Lecointe y Laserre.

Tratado de los sofismas, sacado de los manuscriptos de J. B. por Et.
Dumont. 2 pt. Madrid, 1834, Amarita.

[The sophismes anarchiques were translated into Portuguese :]

Sophismas anarchicos : exame critica das diversas declaraçôes dos direitos
do homem e do cidadâo por Mr. B., traduzido por R. P. B. Rio de
Janeiro. Typ. nacional. 1823. 4°.

The Book of Fallacies : from the unfinished papers of Jeremy Bentham. By a friend. London, 1824.
[This was edited by Bingham, with the help of James Mill and Place, from Bentham's MSS. The MSS. of the Anarchical Fallacies had been lost, and this part was consequently omitted.]
Bowring, ii. pp. 375-487.

[This English text was translated into French under the title :]
Sophismes parlementaires, par. J. B., traduction nouvelle, précédée d'une lettre a M. Garnier Pages sur l'esprit de nos assemblées délibérantes, par M. Elias Regnault. Paris, 1840, Paguerre.

[The lost MSS. on Anarchical Fallacies was found by Bowring in time to be included in the Works, under the title :]

Anarchical fallacies ; being an examination of the declarations of rights issued during the French Revolution. Bowring, ii. pp. 489-534.

[See the present work for an account of a work of Dumont's under the pseudonym of Groenvalt :]

Letters containing an account of the late revolution in France and observations on the constitution, laws, manners and institutions of the English, written during the author's residence at Paris, Versailles and London, in the years 1789 and 1790, translated from the German of H. F. Groenvalt. London, 1792, Johnson.

Plan of Parliamentary Reform, in the form of a catechism, with reasons for each article, with an introduction, showing the necessity of radical, and the inadequacy of moderate, reform. London, printed in the year 1817, Hunter.
[This was reprinted the next year, with the addition to the title-page :]
. . . reprinted and republished with notes and alterations by permission of the author by T. J. Wooler, 1818.
[At the end was included : A Sketch of the various proposals for constitutional reform in the representation of the people, introduced into the Parliament of Great Britain from 1770-1812. By G. W. Meadley.]
[Another title-page reads :]
Catechism of Parliamentary Reform ; or, Outline of a plan of Parliamentary Reform : in the form of question and answer ; with reasons to each article.
[Also the magazine The Black Dwarf reprinted the ' Plan ' in a series of fascicules for its subscribers, 1818.]

[Translation :]
French : Catéchisme de réforme électorale, par J. B., traduit de l'anglais par E. Regnault, précédé d'une lettre à Timon sur l'état actuel de la démocratie en Angleterre. Paris, 1839, Paguerre.

Bentham's Radical Reform Bill, with extracts from the Reasons. Bill intituled Parliamentary Reform Act ; being an Act for the more

adequate Representation of the People in the Commons House of
Parliament. London, 1819, E. Wilson.

Bowring, iii. pp. 558-597.

Radicalism not dangerous. Bowring, iii. pp. 599-622. [Written 1819-20.]

Three Tracts relative to Spanish and Portuguese affairs ; with a continual
eye to English ones.

1. Letter to the Spanish Nation, on a then proposed House of
Lords (anno 1820).

2. Observations on Judge Advocate Hermosa's Panegyric on
judicial delays ; on the occasion of the impunity as yet given by him
to the loyal authors of the Cadiz massacre, a counterpart to the
Manchester massacre : Explaining, moreover, the effects of secrecy
in Judicature.

3. Letter to the Portuguese nation, on antiquated constitutions :
on the Spanish Constitution, considered as a whole, and on certain
defects observable in it ; in particular, the immutability-enacting,
or infallibility-assuming, the non-reeligibility-enacting, the sleep-
compelling, and the bienniality-enacting clauses. London, 1821,
Hone. 54 pp.

Bowring, viii. pp. 468-485.

[Translations :]

Spanish : [Tract No. 1 only :]

Consejos que dirige a las Cortes y al pueblo español J. B., traducidos del
ingles por Jose Joaquin de Mora. Madrid, 1820, por Repulles.

French : Essais de J. B. sur la situation politique de l'Espagne, sur la
constitution et sur le nouveau code espagnol, sur la constitution du
Portugal, traduits de l'anglais, précédés d'observations sur la revolu-
tion de la peninsule et sur l'histoire du gouvernement représentatif en
Europe et suivis d'une traduction nouvelle de la constitution des
Cortes. Paris, 1823, Brissot. 2 parts in 1 vol. [Translated by
Philarète Chasles.]

Œuvres, Bruxelles, iii. pp. 127-237.

[Also a Portuguese translation ; see Bowring, iv. p. 576.]

On the liberty of the press, and public discussion. London, 1821, W.
Hone.

[Edited by Bowring. Mora began the Spanish translation, but
was imprisoned before he had been able to publish it.]

Bowring, ii. pp. 275-297.

[Morning Chronicle, 14th April, 1820, has a short article on the liberty
of the press in Spain, by Bentham.]

Codification proposal, addressed by J. B. to all nations professing liberal
opinions ; or Idea of a proposed all-comprehensive body of law, with
an accompaniment of reasons, applying all along to the several pro-

posed arrangements : these reasons being expressive of the considerations, by which the several arrangements have been presented,
as being, in a higher degree than any other, conducive to *the greatest
happiness of the greatest number*, of the individuals of whom the
community in question is composed : including observations respecting the *hands*, by which the original draught, of a work of the
sort in question, may, with most advantage, be composed : Also,
intimation, from the author, to the competent authorities in the
several nations and political states, expressive of his desire and readiness to draw up, for their use respectively, the *original draught* of a
body of law, such as above proposed. London, 1822, J. M'Creery.
78 pp. in 8°.

Supplement to Codification Proposal [pp. 79-106 missing ?]. 1827.

Second supplement to the Codification Proposal [paged 107-118]. 1830.

  Bowring, iv. pp. 535-594. [Second supplement not reprinted.]

[Translations :]

French : [Biographie Universelle, 1843, vol. 3. p. 670 says there was one.
Not in B. M.]

Spanish : Propuesta de Codigo dirigida por J. B. a todas las naciones que
profesan opiniones liberales. En Londres, 1822.

De l'organization judiciaire et de la codification, extraits de divers ouvrages
de J. B. . . . par Et. Dumont. Paris, 1828, Bossange.

Œuvres, Bruxelles, vol. iii. pp. 1-126.

[Translations :]

Spanish : De la Organizacion judicial y de la codificacion, extractos de
diversas obras de J. B., por E. Dumont . . . traducida al espagnol por
Don. J. L. de Bustamante. Paris, 1828, H. Bossange. 3 vol.

Tradatos sobre la Organización judicial y la codificación, escritos por J. B.
Obras, Espinosa. Vol. 9 and 10.

Justice and codification petitions : being forms proposed for signature
by all persons whose desire it is to see justice no longer sold, delayed
or denied : and to obtain a possibility of that knowledge of the law,
in proportion to the want of which they are subjected to unjust
punishments, and deprived of the benefit of their rights. Drafts for
the above proposed petitions by Jeremy Bentham. London, 1829,
R. Heward. Bowring, v. pp. 437-548.

Pannomial fragments. Bowring, iii. pp. 211-230.

Leading principles of a constitutional code, for any state, by Jeremy
Bentham. London, 1823. Pamphleteer, vol. xxii. No. 44, pp. 475-
486.

' Leading principles of a constitutional Code, for any state.' Extracted
from the Pamphleteer, No. 44. London, Printed by A. J. Valpy, 1823.
  Bowring, ii. pp. 267-274.

Spanish translation : Principios que deben servir de guia en la formación de un codigo constitucional para un estado, por J. B. Extractado del Pamphleteer, No. 44. Londres, 1824, impr. de Q. Taylor. 15 pp. London.

Extract from the proposed constitutional code, entitled ' Official aptitude maximized, expense minimized '. London, 1816.

Official aptitude maximized, expense minimized, as shewn in the several papers comprised in this volume. London, 1830, Heward.

Paper 1. Preface to the whole.
2. Introductory view. [First appeared in 1816.]
3. Extract from Constitutional Code.
4. Supplement to the Extract.
5. Defense of Economy against Burke.
6. Defense of Economy against Rose.
7. Observations on Mr. Sec. Peel's . . . bill.
8. Indications respecting Lord Eldon.
9. [Extract from Constitutional Code.] On the militia.
10. On public account keeping.
11. Constitutional Code. Table of contents.

[Bowring, v. pp. 263-386, contains all except Extracts from the Constitutional Code, which are to be found in their proper place in Bowring, ix.]

Constitutional Code ; for the use of all nations and all governments professing Liberal opinions. Vol. i. London, 1830, Heward.

[The whole work was first published in Bowring, ix. pp. 1-662. It was edited by Richard Doane.]

[Doane says that the first chapter of vol. ii. was published by Bentham in 1830, but if so, no copy is known to exist. See Bowring, ix. p. iii.]

[Chapter vii., Sections 2, 3, 5-10, and 13-14, were published separately under the title : Parliamentary candidates proposed declaration of principles, or say a text proposed for parliamentary candidates. London, 1831, Heward.] *See also* Lord Brougham displayed.

[A letter of Bentham's to Lafayette in the Journal des Economistes, 5ᵉ serie, vol. 2, p. 368, speaks of a French translation of the Constitutional Code having been made.]

Jeremy Bentham, an Englishman, to the citizens of the several American United States. 1817. folio.

Papers relative to Codification and Public Instruction : including correspondence with the Russian emperor, and divers constituted authorities in the American United States. London, 1817, Payne and Foss.

Jeremy Bentham to his fellow citizens of France, on Houses of Peers and Senates. London, 1830, Heward.

Bowring, iv. pp. 419-450.

French translation : Jérémie Bentham à ses concitoyens de France, sur les chambres de Pairs et les Sénats, traduit de l'anglais par Charles Lefebvre. Paris, 1831, Bossange ; publié par Félix Bodin.

Anti-Senatica. [Written (1822-24) and sent (1830) to President Jackson of the U.S.A. ; edited from the MSS. and published by Everett in Smith College Studies, 1926.]

Securities against misrule adapted to a Mahommedan State and prepared with particular reference to Tripoli in Barbary. Bowring, viii. pp. 553-600.

5. POLITICAL ECONOMY

Defence of Usury ; showing the impolicy of the present legal restraints on the terms of pecuniary bargains. In a series of letters to a friend. To which is added, a letter to Adam Smith, Esq., LL.D., on the Discouragements opposed by the above Restraints to the Progress of inventive industry. London, 1787, Payne.

[Second edition,] 1790, Payne.

[Third edition,] 1816, Payne and Foss.

. . . Philadelphia, 1796, Carey.

[Fourth edition :] ' to which is added, third edition, A protest against Law-Taxes '. London, Payne and Foss, 1818.

[Translations :]

French : Apologie de l'Usure, rédigée en forme de lettres, addresées à un ami . . . traduit de l'anglais de J. B. Paris, 1790, Lejay fils.

Lettres sur la liberté du taux de l'intérêt de l'argent par J. B., traduites de l'anglais par E. Delessert. Paris, 1790, Grégoire.

Défense de l'usure, ou Lettres sur les inconvénients de lois qui fixent le taux de l'intérêt de l'argent, par J. B. . . . Traduit de l'anglais sur le 4ᵉ édition (par Saint-Amant Bazard), suivi d'un mémoire sur les prêts d'argent, par Turgot, et précédé d'une introduction contenant une dissertation sur le prêt à intérêt. Paris, 1828, Malher.

Spanish : Defensa de la usura, ó Cartas sobre los inconvenientes de las leyes que fijan la tasa del interes del dinero, por J. B., con una memoria sobre los prestamos de dinero por Turgot. Traducidas del francés por Don J. Esriche. Paris, 1828.

J. B. to the National Convention of France. London, 1793, R. Heward. 48 pp. [Bound with Draught of a New Plan.]

[Not published till 1830 and then under the title :]

Emancipate your colonies ! addressed to the National Convention of France, Anno 1793. Shewing the uselessness and mischievousness of distant dependencies to an European State.

Bowring, iv. pp. 407-418.

Supply without Burthen ; or escheat vice taxation : being a proposal for a saving of taxes by an extension of the law of escheat : including strictures on the taxes on collateral succession, comprised in the Budget of 7th Dec. 1795. To which is prefixed, (printed 1793, and now first published), a protest against law taxes : shewing the peculiar mischievousness of all such impositions as add to the expense of an appeal to justice. 2 vol. London, 1795, J. Debrett. 64 pp. + 94 pp. [2d edition :] 1816. [3d edition :] 1853.

Bowring, ii. pp. 573-600.

Observations on the poor bill introduced by the Right Hon. William Pitt ; written Feb. 1797. Not for publication. London, 1838. [Edited by Edwin Chadwick.]

Bowring, viii. pp. 440-461.

Situation and relief of the poor. Young's Annals of Agriculture, vol. 29, No. 167, pp. 393 ff.

[Prospectus and request for statistical information from readers. The work itself followed in vol. 30, No. 169, pp. 89 ff., No. 171, pp. 241 ff., No. 172, pp. 293 ff., No. 173, pp. 457 ff. ; vol. 31, 1798, No. 174, pp. 33 ff., No. 175, pp. 169 ff., No. 176, pp. 273 ff. When put into book form it was entitled ' Outline of a work entitled Pauper management improved '. Printed but not published.]

[In 1812 it was published as :]

Pauper management improved : particularly by means of an application of the Panopticon principle of construction. Anno 1797, first published in Young's Annals of Agriculture : now first published separately. London, 1812. Sold by Baldwin.

Bowring, viii. 360-439.

[Translation :]

Esquisse d'un ouvrage en faveur des pauvres . . . adressée a l'editeur des Annales d'agriculture par J. B., publiée en français, par Ad. Duquesnoy. Paris, Agasse, an X. (1802).

A Plan for saving all trouble and expense in the transfer of stock, and for enabling the proprietors to receive their dividends without powers of attorney, or attendance at the Bank of England, by the conversion of stock into note annuities.

Bowring, vol. iii. pp. 105-153.

[A part of the Théorie des Récompenses, dealing with political economy was translated under the titles :]

Italian : Manuale d'Economia politica compilato ed annotato da Stefano Dumont. Biblioteca dell' Economista, Serie 1 ; vol. 5, 1854, Torino, p. 825 ff.

Dutch : Handboekje der Staatshuishoudkunde getrokken mit de Geschriften von Jer. B. Naar het Fransch met korte Aant von B. W. A. E. Sloet. Tot Old huis. Dev. J. de Lange, 1851.

Manual of Political Economy. Bowring, iii. pp. 31-84. [Taken from the MSS.]

'Defense of Economy against the late Mr. Burke.' Pamphleteer, vol. ix. No. 17, 1817, pp. 1 ff.

'Defense of Economy against the Right Honourable George Rose, M.P.' Pamphleteer, vol. x. No. 20, 1817, pp. 281 ff.

[Both these articles were written in 1810, and were published both separately and together in one volume, London, 1817, and again in Official Aptitude Maximized, 1830.]

Observations on the restrictive and prohibitory commercial system; especially with reference to the Decree of the Spanish Cortes of July 1820. From the MSS. of Jeremy Bentham by John Bowring. London, 1821, E. Wilson. Pp. xi + 44.

Bowring, iii. pp. 85-103.

Observations on Mr. Secretary Peel's House of Commons speech, 21st March, 1825, introducing his Police Magistrates' Salary-raising bill. Date of order for printing, 24th March, 1825. Also on the announced Judges' Salary-raising bill, and the pending county courts bill. London, 1825, J. and H. W. Hunt. [In the same year this work also appeared in the Pamphleteer, vol. xxv. No. 50, pp. 405 ff.]

Indications respecting Lord Eldon, including History of the pending Judges' Salary-raising measure. London, 1825, John and H. W. Hunt. [The next year this work appeared in the Pamphleteer, vol. xxvi. No. 51, 1826, p. 1 ff.]

6. RELIGION

Church of Englandism and its catechism examined: preceded by strictures on the exclusionary system, as pursued in the National Society's schools: interspersed with parallel views of the English and Scottish established and non-established Churches: and concluding with Remedies proposed for abuses indicated: and an examination of the Parliamentary system of Church Reform lately pursued, and still pursuing: including the proposed new Churches. London, E. Wilson, printed 1817, published 1818. 2 pt.

The Church, etc., examined. A new edition, London, 1824, John and H. Hunt. [Five appendices of 1st ed. omitted.]

The Church, etc., examined. New edition published by Thomas Scott, Ramsgate, 1868. [Five appendices of 1st ed. omitted.]

[Extracts:]

Mother Church relieved by bleeding or vices and remedies extracted from Bentham's Church of, etc., examined, being matter applying to existing circumstances and consisting of a summary recapitulation of the vices therein proved to have place in the Existing System and of the particulars of the remedial system therein proposed. London, 1823, Carlile. [Contains part ii. App. 4, ss. 9 and 10.]

[2d edition:] London, 1825, John and H. Hunt.

The Book of Church Reform, containing the most essential part of Mr. Bentham's Church of Englandism examined, edited by one of his disciples. London, 1831, R. Heward.

Summary view of a work, intituled Not Paul, but Jesus: as exhibited in introduction, Plan of the Work, and Titles of chapters and sections. London, 1821, E. Wilson. 15 pp.

Not Paul, but Jesus by Gamaliel Smith, Esq. London, 1823, John Hunt.
[Put together by Francis Place for Bentham, according to Place's statement on his copy in the British Museum.]

Analysis of the influence of natural religion on the temporal happiness of mankind. By Philip Beauchamp. London, 1822.
[Philip Beauchamp was a pseudonym for George Grote, who edited the MSS.]
[2d edition :] 1875.

French translation : La religion naturelle, son influence sur le bonheur du genre humain, d'après les papiers de Jer. B., par G. Grote. Traduit de l'anglais par M. E. Cazelles. Paris, 1875, G. Baillière. [In the Bibl. de philosophie contemporaine.]

7. MISCELLANEOUS

'Gazetteer.' Three letters, Dec. 3, 1770 ; March 1 and 18, 1771 ; signed *Irenius*.

Voltaire, The White Bull, an oriental history. 2 vol. J. Bew, London.
[Translated by Bentham, with a long introduction. 1774.]

Marmontel, Novels, vol. i. Elmsley, London, 1777. [Translated by Bentham.]

An Essay on the Usefulness of Chemistry and its applications to the various occasions of life, translated from the original of Sir Torbern Bergman, London, 1783.
[Bentham made his translation, however, from a French translation, and not from the German text.]

'Public Advertiser,' 1789. Two letters signed *Anti-Machiavel*.
Bowring, x. pp. 201-211.

'Morning Herald,' 1796. Article on the ' Treason Bill '.
Bowring, x. pp. 320-322.

Cobbett's ' Peter Porcupine ', Nov. 1800, ' Hints relative to the method of taking the census.' Bowring, x. pp. 351-356. Signed *Censor*.

'Westminster Review,' 1824-1828, Nos. 1, 5, 7, 8, 9, 11, 16, and 17, a series of letters on judicial reform, articles probably by James or John Stuart Mill, possibly with Bentham's collaboration.

Opuscules législatifs, contenant divers fragments inédits de Bentham, Dumont et autres, extraits de l'Utilitaire, journal de la doctrine de Bentham. Genève, 1831, A. Cherbuliez. 3 vol.

Essay on Language. [First published by Bowring, viii. pp. 295-338.]

Fragments on Universal Grammar. [First published by Bowring, viii. pp. 339-357.]

Auto Icon, or farther uses of the dead to the living. A fragment from the MSS. of J. B. Not published. London. [Appeared about 1842.]

Junctiana Proposal. Proposals for the junction of the two seas,—The Atlantic and the Pacific, by means of a Joint-Stock Company, to be styled The Junctiana Company. [First published by Bowring, ii. pp. 561-571.]

III. CHRONOLOGICAL LIST OF BENTHAM'S WORKS

DATE.
1770-71. Letters in ' Gazetteer.'

1772. Beginning of work on legal reform.

1774. Taureau Blanc, trans.

1775. Punishments, written.
Comment on the Comms. written.

1776. Fragment on Government.

1777. Marmontel's Novels, trans.

1778. View of Hard Labour Bill.

1780. Introduction to Prin. of Mor. and Legis. printed.
Usefulness of Chemistry, trans.

1782-89. Materials used by Dumont in Traités de Légis. written.

1783. Usefulness of chemistry, publ.

1786. Vue gener. code compl. written.

1786-89. Internat. Law, written.

1787. Defense of Usury.
English MSS. of Théorie des Récompenses, written.

1789. Int. to Prin. of Mor. and Legis., published.

1790. Draught of Plan. Jud. Estab. in France.

1791. Panopticon, printed.
Polit. Tactics fragment, printed.

DATE.
1792. Truth vs. Ashurst, written.

1793. Protest Law Taxes, printed.
Emancipate Colonies,printed.
Manual Pol. Economy, written.

1795. Supply without Burthen.
Protest Law Taxes, publ.

1796. Letter in ' Morning Herald.'

1797. Observ. Poor Bill, written.

1797-98 Pauper Manag. Improved.

1800. Letter in ' Peter Porcupine.'
Annuity Plan, written.

1802. Traités de Législation.
Letter to Lord Pelham.

1802-05.}
1820-28.} Procedure Code, written.

1802-27. Prin. Jud. Procedure, written.

1802-12. Rationale of Evidence, written.

1803. Plea for the Constitution.

1804-08. Scotch Reform, written.

1807. Court of Lords Delegates, written.

1808. Scotch Reform, publ.
Summary View Judicature.

1808-21. Book of Fallacies, written.

1809. Elements Art of Packing, written.

1810. Elements Art of Packing, printed.

1811-16. Essay on Logic, written.

DATE.

1811. Théorie des Peines et des Récompenses.

1811-31. Nomography, written.

1812. Introd. View of Evidence, printed.
Panopt. vs. New S. Wales.

1812-16. Church-of-Eng., written.

1813. Swear Not At All, printed.

1813-21. Ontology, written.

1814-31. Deontology, written.

1815. Table of Springs of Action, printed.

1815-17. Chrestomathia, printed.

1816. Tactique Assembl. Legis.
Extract Const. Code.
Fragment Grammar, written.

1817. Papers Relat. Codif.
Defense of Economy.
Plan of Parl. Ref. printed.
Church-of-England, printed.
Swear Not At All, publ.

1818. Church-of-England, publ.
Plan of Parl. Ref. publ.

1819. Radical Ref. Bill, publ.

1819-20. Radicalism Not Dangerous, written.

1820. King Against Edmonds.
King Against Wolseley.

1821. Elements Art of Packing, publ.
Three Tracts Spanish Affairs.
On Liberty of Press.
Observ. on Commercial System.

1822. Letter to Count Toreno.
Codification Proposal.
Analysis Natural Religion.
Junctiana Proposal, written.

1822-30. Const. Code, written.

DATE.

1822-23. Securities Against Misrule, written.

1823. Traité des Preuves Judic.
Leading Principles Const. Code.
Not Paul, but Jesus.
Truth vs. Ashurst, publ.

1824. Book of Fallacies.

1825. Rationale of Reward.
Indications Resp. Ld. Eldon.
Observations Peel's Speech.

1826. Comm.on Humphreys' Code.

1827. Rationale of Jud. Evidence.
Const. Code, vol. 1, printed.

1828. De l'organization judiciaire.

1829. Justice and Codif. Petition.

1830. Const. Code, vol. 1, publ.
Rationale of Punishment.
Official Aptitude Maximised.
On Peers and Senates.
Emancipate Colonies, publ.
On Death Punishments, written.

1831. Parl. Cand. Declaration.
Boa Constrictor.
Observ. Bankruptcy Bill.
Death Punishments, publ.
Pannomial Fragments, written.

1832. Lord Brougham Displayed.
Outline Register Real Property.

1834. Deontology.

1838. Observations on Poor Bill.

1838-43. Bowring's Works.

1842. Auto Icon.

1928. Comment on the Commentaries.

INDEX

ABERCROMBIE, JOHN, 302
Adam, Robert, 252
Addington, Henry, 252
' Adjective ' law, 36, 166, 373, 483
Alexander I, Emperor, applies to Bentham, 296
Allen, William, collaborates with J. Mill, 285, 286, 301
Anderson, James, on law of rent, 276, 277
Anti-clericalism, 291, 365
Anti-Corn-Law Association, 513, 514
Apprenticeship, Statute of, 370, 371
Armies, professional, 141, 142
Ashurst, Sir William, 81
Associationism, Brown, 452 ; Gay, 11 ; Hartley, 7, 8, 9, 16, 17 ; Hume, 9, 10, 11, 435 ; J. Mill, 437, 438, 448 ; J. S. Mill, 455 ; Priestley, 440 ; Stewart, 450 ; Tooke, 447, 448
Austin, Charles, 23, 485
Austin, John, *Lectures*, 483 ; 509

BAILEY, SAMUEL, on value of labour, 353, 354
Bayle, Peter, 141
Beccaria, Cesare, 3, 4, 33, 56, 67 ; influenced by Helvetius, 21 ; on Blackstone's science of law, 36 ; influence on Bentham, 52 ; on punishment of crimes, 57, 58, 59, 64, 70, 71, 392
Bedford, Duke of, 162, 163
Bell, Dr. Andrew, 282, 285
Belsham, Thomas, *Philosophy of the Mind*, 437, 438, 439
Bentham, Jeremiah, 18, 251
Bentham, Jeremy, childhood, 5 ff., 18, 19, 144, 387 ; influenced by Helvetius, 18, 19 ; refutation of Blackstone,

23 ; in Russia, 24, 86, 87 ; and Paley, 24 ; prison reform, 24 ; pleasures and pains, 30 ff. ; moral system, 34 ; philosophy of law, 35 ff. ; punishment and crimes, 55, 56 ; meets Dumont, 75, 87 ; economic and political theories, 88 ; the social contract, 135, 136 ; influenced by Shelburne, 145, 147 ; political problems, 155 ff. ; a democrat, 168 ; his republicanism, 172 ; hostility to French Revolution, 177 ; security, 205 ff. ; industrialism, 222 ; reputation increased, 296 ff. ; and Alexander of Russia, 296, 298 ; his debt to J. Mill, 309 ; character summarised, 309 ; last days and death, 479
Bentham, Jeremy, chief references to Works :
Anarchical Fallacies, 175
Catechism of Parliamentary Reform, 258
Chrestomathia, 19, 286, 287, 288
Church of Englandism, 291, 295
Defence of Usury, 24, 89, 153, 173
Draught for a Code . . . in France, 167
Deontology, 455
Elements of Packing, 300
Emancipate your Colonies, 116, 173
Essai sur la Représentation, 147, 148
Essay on the Influence of Time and Place in Matters of Legislation, 67
An Essay on Political Tactics, 166
Essay on Representation, 148
Fragment on Government, 23, 120, 129, 133, 134, 143, 145
Indirect Legislation, 145
Introduction to the Principles of Morals and Legislation, 26, 35, 64, 75, 76, 77, 85, 86, 153, 178.

547

INDEX

81
83
86
88